Disorder on the Border

Civil Warfare
in
Cabell and Wayne Counties, West Virginia
1856-1870

Joe Geiger, Jr.

35th Star Publishing
Charleston, West Virginia
www.35thstar.com

Copyright. © 2020 by Joe Geiger, Jr.
All Rights Reserved.
First edition, 2020.
Printed in the United States of America.

No part of this publication may be reproduced, distributed or transmitted in any form or by any means, including photocopying, recording, or other electronic or mechanical methods, without the prior written permission of the publisher, except in the case of brief quotations embodied in critical reviews and certain other noncommercial uses permitted by copyright law.

ISBN-13: 978-1-7350739-4-1
ISBN-10: 1-7350739-4-6
Library of Congress Control Number: 2020946299

35th Star Publishing
Charleston, West Virginia
www.35thstar.com

On the cover:
Historic Barboursville image, credit: author's collection
Milton J. Ferguson, credit: Mahlon Nichols, courtesy of Robert Thompson
Chaplain of the 5th West Virginia Infantry, credit: L.M. Strayer Collection
Margaret Rece, credit: Special Collections Dept., Marshall University
Kellian V. Whaley, credit: Library of Congress
Eli Thayer: credit: Library of Congress
Albert Gallatin Jenkins, credit: National Archives
Henry J. Samuels, credit: Special Collections Dept., Marshall University
William H. Powell, credit: Richard A. Wolfe
Sergeants of the 34th Ohio Infantry, credit: L.M. Strayer Collection

Cover design by Studio 6th Sense LLC
Interior design by 35th Star Publishing

Publisher's Cataloging-in-Publication Data

Names: Geiger Jr., Joe, author.
Title: Disorder on the border : civil warfare in Cabell and Wayne Counties, West Virginia, 1856-1870 / Joe Geiger, Jr.
Description: First edition. | Charleston, West Virginia : 35th Star Publishing, 2020. | Includes bibliographic references and index.
Identifiers: LCCN 2020946299 | ISBN 978-1-7350739-4-1
Subjects: BISAC: HISTORY / United States / Civil War Period (1850-1877) | HISTORY / United States / State & Local / South (AL, AR, FL, GA, KY, LA, MS, NC, SC, TN, VA, WV)

LC record available at https://lccn.loc.gov/2020946299.

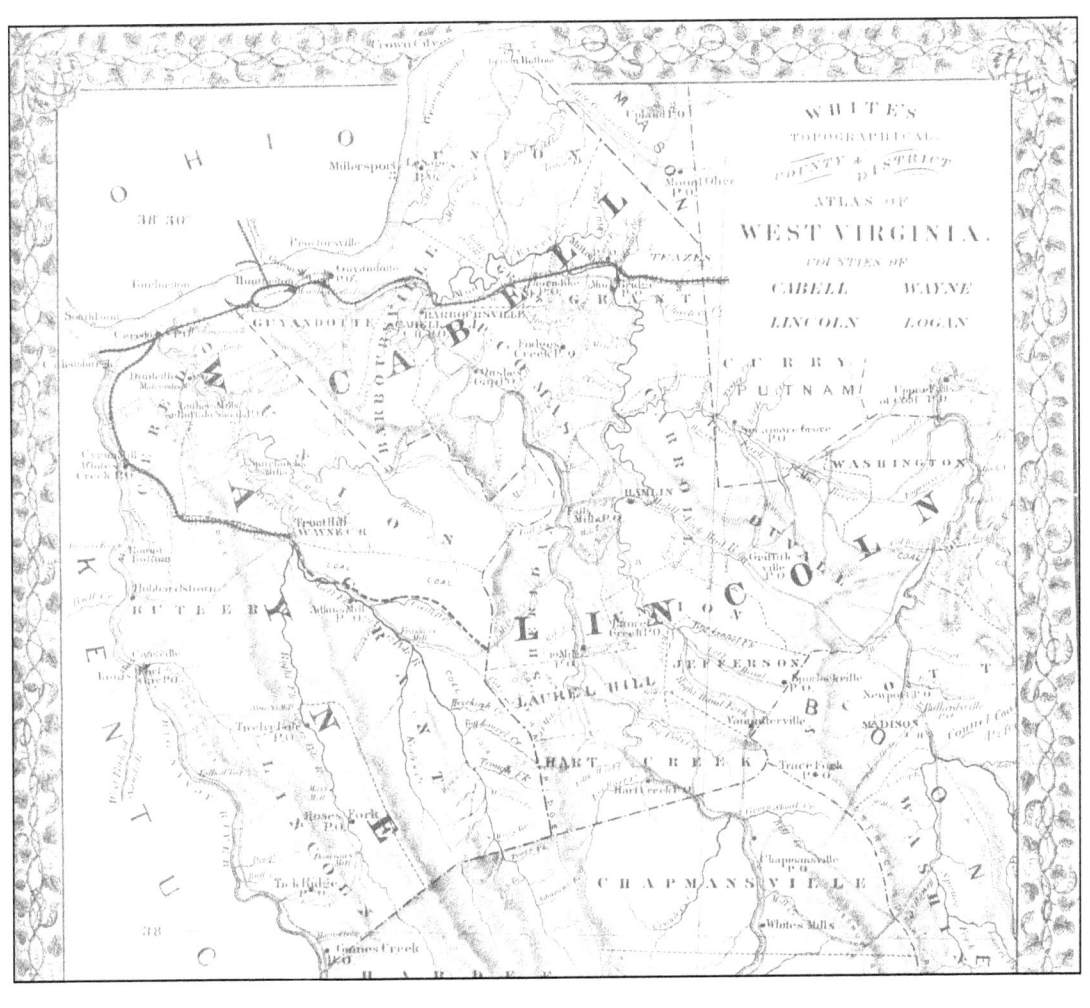

Table of Contents

Acknowledgments   xiii
Introduction   1
1 - The Antebellum Years in Cabell and Wayne Counties   3
2 - The Institution of Slavery on the Border   13
3 - The Road to Armed Conflict   33
4 - The Battle of Barboursville   55
5 - Lawlessness Abounds   73
6 - The Raid on Guyandotte   103
7 - Reaping the Whirlwind   119
8 - The Darkest Hour of our Perils   147
9 - Piatt's Zouaves   179
10 - Outrages and Fiendish Acts   207
11 - Welcome to Western Virginia   229
12 - The Plough Stands Still   247
13 - Depredations of the Most Shameful Character   275
14 - The War Ends?   307
15 - Federal Occupation   327
Epilogue   349
Notes   361
Bibliography   411
Index   421
About the Author   443

Illustrations and Photographs

Austin, George	66
Bailey, George	127
Bartram, William	280
Baumgardner, James	173
Bay, George	296
Beuhring, F. D.	60
Bing, Francis	143
Black (Adam) Home	14
Blundon, Edgar	315
Bolles, William	125
Border Rangers Reunion	356
Boreman, Arthur	331
Boyd, Samuel	230
Brown, Ethan	181
Brown, James	170
Brown, William	272
Buffington Mill, Remains of	123
Buffington, Peter	77
Cabell County Courthouse, Barboursville	5
Cabell County Jail, Barboursville	340
Carlile, John	83
Carroll, J. J. S. P.	328
Ceredo House	308
Corns, James	108
Cox, Jacob	56
Cox, Margaret Emily	311
Cranor, Jonathan	233
Cunningham, William	243
Dennison, William	19
Dove, David	255
Everett, H. C.	105
Everett, Henry Clay	353
Ferguson, James H.	312
Ferguson, Milton	76, 352
Floyd, John	103
Franklin, Freeman	202

Fuller (Achilles) Home	116
Gallup, George	278
Garrett, Morgan	269
Grand Army of the Republic Reunion	357
Griswold, Oliver	279
Guyandotte, Painting of	4
Guyandotte Suspension Bridge	107
Hall, James	273
Hambleton, Charles	220
Hartsuff, George	89
Hite, John	119
Hoard, Charles	351
Hoffman, John	281
Holderby (Susan) Home	201
Holderby, Susan	200
Howell's Mill	252
Jaynes, A. D.	291
Jenkins Home	6
Jenkins, Albert	35, 217
Jones, Junius	151
Laidley, John	18
Lamartine	159
Leete, Ralph	17
Lightburn, Joseph	212
Lunsford, Richard	58
Map of Cabell, Lincoln, and Wayne Counties	v
Map of Guyandotte	350
Map of Post Offices	8
Map, 34th Ohio Infantry	189
McClellan, George	161
McComas (William) Home	317
McComas, William	36
McGinnis, Ira	38
Merritt, Thomas	288
Mud River Covered Bridge	253
Neff, Andrew	242
Neff, George	62
Oley, John	87, 353
Orr, Samuel	242
Parker, Granville	34
Pate, Henry	110
Paxton, John	222
Piatt, Abram	197
Pierpont, Francis	168

Powell, William	177
Ramsdell, Z. D.	50, 261
Ratliff, William	15
Rece (Abia) Home	219
Rece, Margaret	111
Reilly, William	297
Ricketts, Lucien "Cooney"	42
Ricketts, Virginia	162
Roffe, Charles	138
Rosecrans, William	203
Rouse, James	113
Samuels, Henry J.	316
Savage, George	63
Shelton (Henry) Home	115
Smith, Bill	329
Spurlock, Burwell	37
Spurlock, Hurston	276
Spurlock, Stephen	59
Starr, William	163
Stewart, Milton	283
Strother, Stephen	81
Suiter, Doc	124
Thayer, Eli	25, 351
Toland, John	193
Trusler, Nelson	241
Turley, John	218
Vance, John	216
Washington Baptist Church	27
Whaley, Kellian	78
Wilson, Joel	16
Witcher, John	337, 354
Witcher, Vincent	232
Woodruff, William	57
Young, John V.	210
5th West Virginia Infantry, Chaplain of the	80
7th West Virginia Cavalry, Company G	310
34th Ohio Infantry, Marching through Barboursville	185
34th Ohio Infantry, Murder of Piatt's Zouaves	187
34th Ohio Infantry, Sergeants of Company A	180
34th Ohio Infantry, Skirmish at Devil's Elbow	184

Acknowledgments

My interest in the American Civil War began at a young age. My grandparents took me to Gettysburg when I was a boy, and I returned to that hallowed ground on our sixth-grade class trip. An elementary school teacher, Frances Terry, loaned me history books from her personal collection, helping to form the foundation of my fascination with the subject. More than thirty years ago, I began studying the Civil War in West Virginia, and learned that the parsonage at Barboursville where I had lived for three years was within sight of one of the first battlefields of the conflict. Books by Jack Dickinson and Terry Lowry detailed events in the area during those tumultuous years and sparked a desire to do further research on the war in Cabell County. When I contacted Jack, Terry, and Tim McKinney, another West Virginia Civil War author, all were kind enough to respond and encouraged my efforts. Jack and his wife Kay even invited me to their home and shared research materials. Stan Cohen – author, publisher, and the owner of Pictorial Histories Publishing Company – agreed to publish my manuscript, and the result was *Civil War in Cabell County, West Virginia: 1861-1865*. Without the encouragement of these individuals and the publication of this book, my own career in the field of history would not have been possible. I am grateful to each of them. Thoughts of updating the publication surfaced occasionally, and this project was initially aimed at doing only that. A vast amount of new research material was discovered, however, and it became apparent that starting from scratch and expanding the subject matter was the best approach.

I am thankful for everyone who has provided assistance with this project or who has been supportive of my work over the years. I am grateful to all of my public school teachers from Peterstown Elementary, Barboursville Junior High, and John Marshall High School and my professors and fellow students in the Graduate Studies program of the History Department at Marshall University. Karen Nance, a good friend for thirty years, furnished the articles on the 1856 brawl in Quaker Bottom that provided a logical starting point for this work. For additional research assistance and support, thanks to Patty Tyler, Steve Cunningham, John Proctor, Steven Cody Straley, Brandon Ray Kirk, Betsy Allen, Lisa Estes, Mary Johnson, Mike Adkins, Maryann Grannis, Larry Martin, Sydney Hanson of the Ceredo Historical Society Museum, Ceredo Mayor Paul Billups, Marta Ramey and Katie Fugett of the Phyllis Hamner Room, Briggs Lawrence County Public Library, Mary Kay Rader of the Lawrence County Historical Society, Director Lori Thompson, Jack Dickinson, Elizabeth James of the Special Collections Department at Marshall University, and Aaron Parsons and the entire staff at West Virginia Archives and History. Manuscript materials were furnished by the Filson Historical Society, and research assistance was provided by the Portsmouth

Public Library and the Sedalia Katy Depot (Missouri).

A large number of images used in this publication were obtained from the Special Collections Department, Marshall University. Others were procured from the Portsmouth Public Library and the West Virginia State Archives. Photographs from personal collections were generously provided by Cathy Callen, Jack Dickinson, Todd Godby, Jim Hale, Roger Hunt, Terry Lowry, Evelyn Booth Massie, the family of Bernard Nicholas, Maylon Nichols, Larry M. Strayer, Robert Thompson, Marilyn Brasher Wade, and Richard A. Wolfe.

Thanks to Steve Cunningham and 35th Star Publishing for reviewing the manuscript and getting it prepared for publication in quick fashion. I am extremely grateful to Jack Dickinson and Terry Lowry for their selfless assistance in reviewing the manuscript, offering suggestions, and providing primary source materials. Thanks to Phil Hatfield and Debra Basham for reviewing rough drafts and offering comments. My father, Dr. Joseph Geiger, and mother, June Geiger, were also enlisted to edit the work. I am extremely grateful to all for their time and expertise. Any errors in the publication, however, are solely the author's responsibility.

I wish to express appreciation to my family for their patience during this process. Thanks to my wife, Lois Geiger, our children, Matthew and Rachel, and my stepmother, Marsha Geiger. I am also grateful for the love and support of my grandparents, Lena Martin and John Quinn and Velma Geiger, and all other kin. I have been extremely blessed throughout my life and thank God for all I have received.

Introduction

Slavery and the Civil War years in Cabell and Wayne counties have been covered extensively by historians in recent years. Jack L. Dickinson penned two books on Albert Gallatin Jenkins, two on Confederate cavalry units from the area, a book on boy soldier "Cooney" Ricketts, and a history of Wayne County in the Civil War. Robert Thompson has published numerous books on Wayne County, including several biographies of Civil War figures and another on slavery in the county. Carrie Eldridge has written several books documenting the early history of Cabell County, one on the manumission of the slaves of Sampson Sanders, and another listing the men from Cabell County who served in the Confederate and Union armies. Publications by Kenneth R. Bailey, Cicero Fain, Brandon Ray Kirk, Karen Nance, Seth Nichols, Matthew Perry, Jeannette Rowsey, and others have shed light on various parts of the story. Still, there is even more work yet to be done. Original documents surface nearly every day providing fuel for new studies, and it is hoped that others will continue to expand our knowledge of individuals and events in this area during the most tumultuous period in American history.

It is important to note that the vast majority of sources utilized in this publication were written by individuals who supported the Union. This was certainly not a conscious choice, but one born of necessity, as most of the contemporary documentation relating to the Civil War years in this region was written by occupying Federal soldiers or by Union citizens who resided here and contacted state or federal officials with urgent pleas for assistance. Some correspondence was found from Confederate supporters who were arrested by Federal authorities, and more recently, numerous files on men from Cabell and Wayne counties have been added to on-line offerings, including testimony giving vivid details of the unrest in this area, particularly in the first year of the war.

This author does not claim to be a writer. As you will quickly note, the book relies heavily on the words of the participants. In most cases, this brings the story to life much better than my limited vocabulary could do. Brackets have been used to make clear that the misspelled word(s) were in the original quote, to add a word that was obviously mistakenly omitted by the writer, or to assist the reader in deciphering misspelled words. Periods have been added appropriately to make reading the quotes a little easier to comprehend, although the decision to leave the spelling unedited challenges the reader on occasion to decipher misspelled words. Still, reading the quotes is essential to getting a more complete picture of what was going on at that time in this place. That is the purpose of this book: to provide a detailed look at events occurring in Cabell and Wayne counties between 1856 and 1870. Many stories end with unanswered questions that hopefully will be resolved by future research. All along the long and winding highway, there were many side roads that the author chose not to explore. Again, I encourage those with an interest in those specific topics to delve deeper and to share their findings.

In the last half of the 1850s, the counties of Cabell and Wayne were a part of the national debate over slavery. Located only a stone's throw away from the free state of Ohio, some western Virginians practiced and defended slavery, and the contentiousness between supporters of slavery and those who opposed the institution increased dramatically as the nation moved closer to civil war. Blood was shed on the Ohio/Virginia border in 1856, and threats of violence accompanied the arrival of Eli Thayer and the establishment of Ceredo a year later. When the war erupted in 1861, disorder was the order of the day. Although the overwhelming majority of voters in Cabell and Wayne counties opposed the Ordinance of Secession, the most prominent and influential citizens in the area favored leaving the Union. When Virginia seceded, some who had opposed this step now cast their loyalty with their state rather than their country.

Although no large battles were fought in Cabell and Wayne counties, dozens of skirmishes, raids, and armed encounters occurred in the area during the Civil War. Union authorities struggled for the next ten years to exert authority over the residents, and peace only reigned in the land when Federal troops were present. This unrest continued after the surrender of the Confederate armies as officials of the new state struggled to retain political power. Even though disenfranchised, ex-Confederates worked with Democrats to regain their rights, and some continued to fight. Soldiers from the United States Army occupied the two counties from 1867 to 1869, and it was only with the statewide Democratic victory in 1870 that the lengthy struggle finally ended. Although those who created the new state of West Virginia and helped save the Union lost political control, they could take consolation that one victory would forever remain unchanged: slavery, the curse that led to the temporary division of the United States, was finally ended.

As we will see, voters in both counties overwhelming opposed secession from the Union, yet the civil unrest in this area of West Virginia was as deep and enduring as anywhere in the state. Federal supporters in Cabell and Wayne counties lived through years of terror, and their efforts to save the Union and create the new state of West Virginia are worthy of documentation. Their love of country and willingness to sacrifice even their own lives on its behalf ensured its survival from the greatest conflict in the history of the United States.

1
The Antebellum Years in Cabell and Wayne Counties

"The village of Guyandotte, at the mouth of the river whose name it bears, is situated at a point where a stranger from the east is struck with a fine view of the Ohio, descending through its broad rich valley with a gentle current. From the Guyandotte to the Sandy, a wide bottom on the Virginia side is distinguished for its pleasantness and fertility. To an agriculturalist it offers great advantages, and will probably become, ere long, one of the best cultivated and most densely peopled tracts on the Ohio."

Henry Ruffner, 1838

The area that became Cabell County was occupied hundreds of years prior to white settlement. When formed in 1809 from Kanawha County, Virginia, the county was named for William H. Cabell, who served as governor of Virginia from 1805 to 1808. An act creating the county was passed on January 2, 1809, noting the boundaries as follows:

> beginning at the corner of Mason county in Teases valley, thence a direct line to the mouth of the Spruce fork of Coal river, thence up the said fork to where the line of Giles county crosses it, thence with the said line to Tazewell county line, and with said line to the Tug fork of Sandy, and down the same to its conflux with Ohio river, thence up the same to the mouth of Little Guyandotte, in the county of Mason, and with the Mason line to the beginning, shall form one distinct county, and be called and known by the name of Cabell county.[1]

Cabell County at the time of its formation was much larger than it is today. The majority of the land included in the original boundaries was later broken away and used to form new counties.

John Shrewsbury, David Ruffner, John Reynolds, William Clendenin, and Jesse Bennett were selected as commissioners for the new county, and the governor was to appoint a sheriff. According to the legislation,

The justices to be named in the commission of the peace for the said county of Cabell, shall meet at the house of Thomas Ward, in the said county, upon the first court day after the said county takes place, and having administered the oaths of office to, and taken bond of the sheriff, proceed to appoint and qualify a clerk, and until the necessary public buildings are completed, at the place pointed out by the aforesaid commissioners, to appoint such place within the county for holding courts as they may think proper.[2]

In April of 1809, the government of the county was organized by Judge John Coalter in the home of William Merritt. A commission was named to determine a location for the county seat and public buildings, and on May 9, 1809, they decided on "the mouth of the Guyandotte, on the upper side, in the middle of a field occupied by William Holderby, as the most practicable place for said public buildings, etc." This location was "a square 100 feet on each side of what is now Bridge Street and extending back from the west line of Main Street to the alley between Main and Guyan streets and includes Bridge Street itself."[3]

While designated the county seat in 1809, the town of Guyandotte was not formally established until a year later. The seat of government remained there until 1814, when it was moved to Barboursville. Despite this, by the middle of the nineteenth century, Guyandotte was one of the largest shipping ports on the Ohio River.

Painting of Guyandotte, early 1820s.
Credit: West Virginia State Archives.

In 1845, Henry Howe described Guyandotte as "much the most important point of steamboat embarkation, as well as debarkation, in western Virginia, with the exception of Wheeling. It is a flourishing village, containing 1 church, 6 or 8 stores, a steam saw-mill, and a population of about 800." The Buffington Mill, which was located on Front Street, was reportedly the largest mill on the Ohio River between Pittsburgh and Cincinnati. The mill was a three-story building with an overhead runway which ran over Front Street and down to the Ohio River. Several profitable hotels operated near the town's busy wharf, which was located near the junction of the Guyandotte and Ohio rivers. A suspension bridge over the Guyandotte River was completed about 1852.[4]

The village of Barboursville was established on January 14, 1813. It became the county seat in 1814, and a courthouse was built later that same year. A brick building replaced the old structure in 1854. William C. Miller, who supervised the construction of the new courthouse, made a low bid of $4,500 to prevent it from being built in Guyandotte. Howe described Barboursville in 1845 as "on the Guyandotte river, 7 1-2 miles from its mouth, and 352 miles wsw of Richmond. The turnpike, leading from the eastern part of the state, by the great watering-place, to the Kentucky line, passes through this village, which contains about 30 dwellings."[5]

Cabell County Courthouse, Barboursville.
Credit: Jack L. Dickinson.

Other settlements existed throughout Cabell County. The present city of Huntington had not been established, although a few farms were scattered about the area. Marshall Academy was established in 1838, and a new four-room brick building was erected in 1839. The Virginia General Assembly changed the name to Marshall College in 1858. The town of Milton had not yet been founded, but a small community known as Mud Bridge was located on the left bank of the Mud River as early as 1830. Before 1834, a ferry was operated across the Mud River approximately two miles southeast of present-day Milton. A covered bridge was built at the ferry crossing by Charles Conner of Putnam County in 1834. A history of the community noted that the "timbers were felled and prepared at the site by broadaxe and adze and fitted with wooden nails and pegging."[6]

The Jenkins Home at Green Bottom.
Credit: Jack L. Dickinson.

In 1845 Henry Howe described Cabell County as "35 miles long, with a mean breadth of 20 miles. A considerable portion of the county is wild and uncultivated, and somewhat broken. The river bottoms are fertile, and settled upon." Howe noted that Thomas Hannan, one of the earliest settlers in Cabell County, came to Green Bottom, near the Mason County line, in 1796 from Botetourt County. These lands, initially granted to Joshua Fry, were later purchased by Wilson Cary Nicholas, governor of Virginia from 1814 to 1816. Nicholas established a slave plantation at Green Bottom, and by 1820, 53 slaves were working there. The property was later sold to county namesake William Cabell, whose agents sold the land to William Jenkins in 1825. Jenkins moved to Cabell County a short time later and constructed a substantial home on the Ohio River at Green Bottom. Jenkins and his wife Janetta had three sons: Thomas Jefferson, William Alexander, and Albert Gallatin. The plantation they owned spanned several miles along the river.[7]

Howe described the previous occupants of the property:

A portion of the beautiful flatland of what is called Green Bottom, lying partly in this [Cabell] and Mason county, a few years since, before the plough of civilization had disturbed the soil, presented one of those vestiges of a city which are met with in central America, and occasionally in the southern and western forests of the United States. The traces of a regular, compact, and populous city with streets running parallel with the Ohio River, and crossing and intersecting each other at right angles, covering a space of nearly half a mile, as well as the superficial dimensions of many of the houses, are apparent, and well defined. Axes and saws of an opaque form – the former of iron, the latter of copper – as well as other implements of the mechanic arts, have been found. These remains betoken a state of comparative civilization, attained by no race of the aborigines of this country now known to have existed. Who they were, or whence they sprung, tradition has lost in the long lapse of ages.[8]

In addition to Barboursville, Green Bottom, Guyandotte, and Mud Bridge, in 1857 post offices in Cabell County could be found at Bloomingdale, Falls Mill, Hamlin, Mud, Paw Paw Bottom, Ten Mile, and Thorndike.[9]

Over two decades, the majority of Cabell County was broken off to create several new counties. Logan County was formed in 1824 from parts of Cabell, Giles, Kanawha, and Tazewell counties. In 1847, Boone County was created from portions of Cabell, Kanawha, and Logan counties, and a year later, the new county of Putnam was carved from sections of Cabell, Kanawha, and Mason. Lincoln County would be formed after the war from parts of Boone, Cabell, Kanawha, and Logan counties.

On January 18, 1842, the Virginia General Assembly passed an act creating the new county of Wayne from the western part of Cabell County. The boundary lines were as follows:

Beginning at the mouth of Fourpole creek on the Ohio river, thence a straight line to the mouth of Long branch, (so as to include the house and farm of Asa Booton within the new county;) thence following the top of the dividing ridge between the said Long branch and the Beach fork of Twelvepole river, up to the mouth of Raccoon creek; thence crossing the Raccoon creek to the dividing ridge between the said Beach fork and Guyandotte river; thence along the said dividing ridge to the line dividing the counties of Logan and Cabell; thence with said line to the mouth of Marrowbone creek, a branch of the Tug fork of Big Sandy river; thence down said Big Sandy river, with the line dividing this state from the state of Kentucky, to the mouth of Big Sandy river; thence up the

Ohio river to the place of beginning, shall form one distinct and new county, and be called and known by the name of Wayne county, in memory and in honour of general Anthony Wayne.

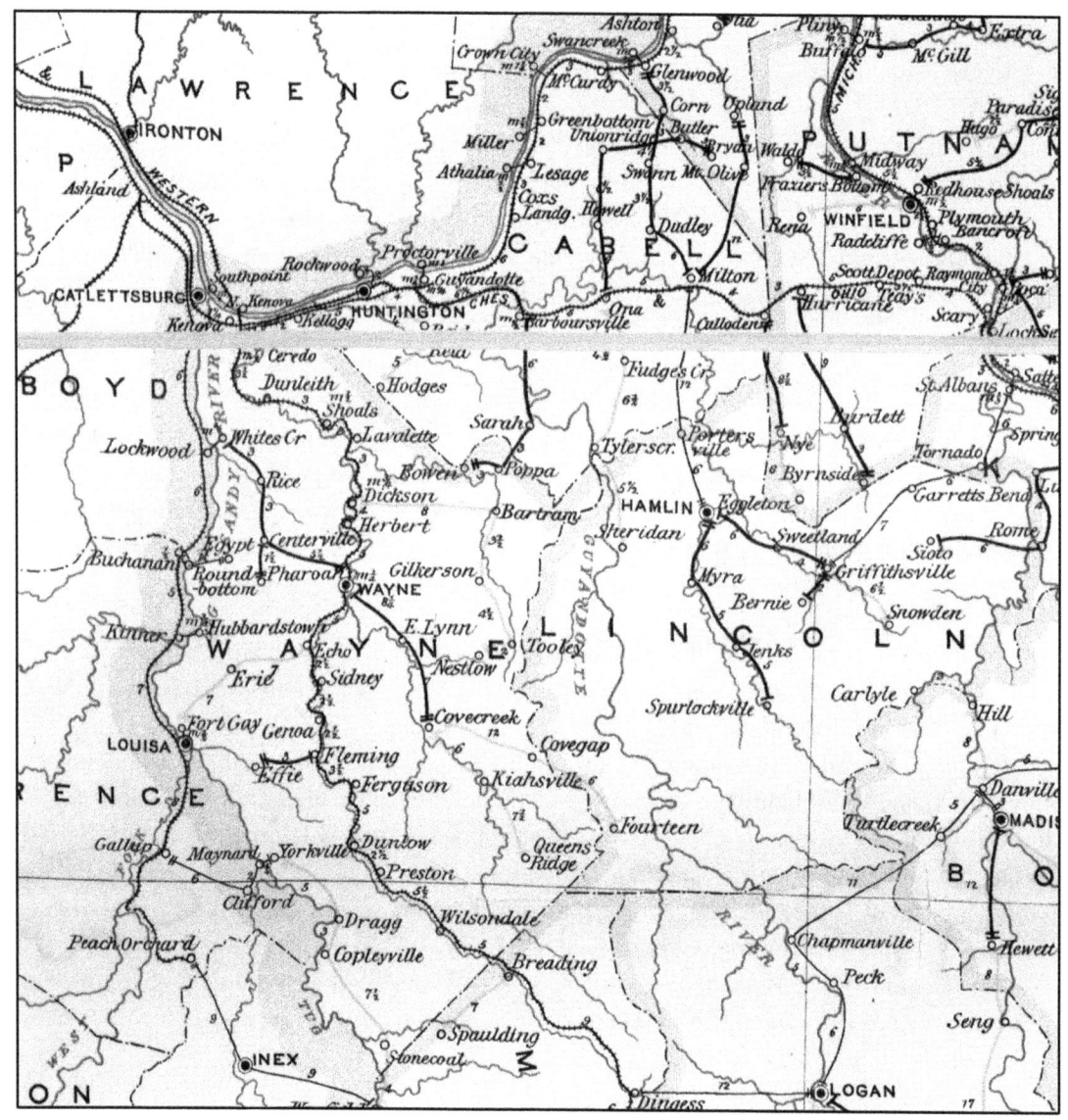

Section of Post Route Map of the States of Virginia and West Virginia, December 1896, showing post offices in Cabell, Lincoln, and Wayne counties.

The courts were to be held at or near the residence of Abraham Trout on Twelvepole Creek. The county surveyors of Cabell and Wayne, along with Joseph Nigley, John Wellman, and Burwell Spurlock, were appointed commissioners to run and mark the lines between the two counties. Henry Howe's book, published in 1845, notes that Wayne County was about thirty-five miles long and ten miles in mean breadth. Howe wrote, "The surface of the county is considerably broken, and it is sparsely inhabited." Cassville (present-day Fort Gay) became the first Wayne County community to be incorporated on Christmas Day, 1852. By 1857, post offices in Wayne County were located at Adkinsville, Amacetta (Lavalette), Falls of Tug, Falls of Twelve Pole (Dickson), Fort Gay, Hubbardstown, Round Bottom (Prichard), Savage Grant, and Trout's Hill, also known as Wayne Courthouse, which was incorporated in 1860. The rugged county was primarily farming country.[10]

In 1859, the *Sandy Valley Advocate* printed a description of the rich resources in Wayne County:

> This county lies on the Big Sandy River, in Virginia, and forms for some sixty miles up this river, the Western border of that State. It is a large county, and contains a large quantity of fine farming land; many farms handsomely improved, with a thriving, industrious and intelligent population.
>
> Its climate and soil is admirably adapted to the growth of Wheat, Rye, Corn and Grass, the latter should be much more extensively cultivated, as it would certainly make one of the best grazing portions of the country, and we know of no better investment than the purchase of lands in this county, and the raising of stock, sheep, &c.
>
> Considerable attention has been paid to fruit. The apple and peach are raised here to the greatest perfection, but the climate being so admirable for those valuable fruits, they should claim more generally the attention of the farmer, as nothing would be found more profitable, independent of the luxury of having them for home consumption. No portion of the West presents so many inducements to the Grape grower as the hills in this county. The Grape flourishes in this climate, and many of the hills, which are now useless, would, by cultivation in this valuable fruit, produce from two to three hundred dollars per acre. Its mineral resources are also very valuable and are now commanding the attention of capitalists. Twelve Pole River runs through, and Big Sandy bounds it on the West. Up the valleys of both, large deposits of Coal are found, and perhaps the largest deposits of Cannel Coal of any portion of this Coal region, which, from its location, must soon be appreciated by those who seek this kind of investment. Iron Ore abounds throughout the county; and perhaps no where is there to be found better timber of every description.
>
> Were its advantages made known in the East and North, we feel satisfied many now who are emigrating to the far West would find it to their interest to settle in this county. Lands are cheap, rich and fertile; and a climate healthy, with easy access to the best markets in the West, we hope at least this may call the attention of those who wish to better their condition in a new home, to its advantages, and induce them to examine for themselves before they go further West.[11]

Efforts were made in the first half of the nineteenth century to improve transportation in the area. The James River and Kanawha Turnpike, completed in 1830, was the primary east-west road in western Virginia, traversing through both counties and terminating at the Big Sandy River. Although Guyandotte was not on the turnpike route, a road was later constructed connecting the town with Barboursville, which was.

In addition to the economic advantages afforded by Guyandotte's location on the Ohio River, Cabell County leaders made additional efforts to expand the commercial possibilities of water transportation. The Guyandotte Navigation Company, chartered in 1849 by Peter Clarke and others, constructed six locks and dams on the Guyandotte River, opening up steamboat travel which carried both freight and passengers. On February 2, 1855, the *Guyandotte Herald* reported, "Once the Guyandotte is fairly opened, the increase of business will be beyond conception."[12]

The necessity for constructing railroads through western Virginia to extract the seemingly endless resources was recognized at an early date. The Board of Public Works of Virginia planned the construction of a railroad from Covington, Virginia, to the Ohio River, and land for the right-of-way was condemned as early as September 24, 1853. As the threat of civil war gripped the country in early 1860, citizens of Cabell County appealed to legislators in Richmond, urging them to complete this rail line. By 1861, some portions had been graded, and the piers over the Guyandotte River had been started, but completion of the railroad, later to become known as the Chesapeake & Ohio (C&O), would have to wait until the end of the war.[13]

On March 6, 1858, the Virginia General Assembly passed an act incorporating the Guyandotte River Railroad Company "for the purpose of constructing a rail road from a point at or near the mouth of Huff's creek, down Guyandotte river, by the nearest and most practicable route, to a point on the Covington and Ohio rail road, near the courthouse of Cabell county, where there may be a junction of the said roads, in such manner and under such regulations as the Board of public works may direct." The company was allowed ten years to complete its organization and begin work on the project. Among the directors were H. J. Samuels, John G. Miller, William C. Miller, Thomas Thornburg, Jerome Shelton and James McComas.[14]

Population naturally increased during the first fifty years of Cabell County's existence. In the 1810 census, taken the year after the county was created, its white population was 2,471. By 1840 this number had increased to 7,574, but ten years later population decreased to 5,902, due to the creation of Wayne County. In 1860, white population in Cabell County rose to 7,691, but the number would fall to 6,306 in 1870 with the creation of Lincoln County.

Free black population changed little in the fifty years of the county's existence prior to the Civil War. In 1810 there were twenty-five free blacks in the county; in 1860 there were twenty-four. There were 221 slaves in Cabell County in 1810, 392 in 1820, 561 in 1830, 567 in 1840, 389 in 1850, and 305 in 1860. In the first post-war census in 1870, only 123 African Americans lived in Cabell County.

The total population of Wayne County in 1850 was 4,760, with seven free blacks and 189 slaves. Ten years later, the population had increased to 6,747. The county still contained 143 slaves, but no free blacks were listed in the 1860 census. The population of Wayne County was 7,852 in 1870, 1,423 more residents than Cabell County. This figure includes 153 African Americans.[15]

Regardless of the numbers, the issue of slavery would become the center of debate in Cabell and Wayne counties in the years immediately preceding civil war due to several events that occurred in this area.

2
The Institution of Slavery on the Border

"But all this loud talk in Western Virginia about the 'Institutions' is only talk. The fact is, you have not negroes enough here to make an Institution. The negroes in Wayne and Cabell counties will not amount to one for every four square miles of Territory. You have no labor, either slave or free, at all adequate to your resources or your wants. You have the curse of the name of slavery, which sends emigration by you, without even a side glance towards your mighty resources, and on they go, to Minnesota, Nebraska, and Oregon. But as the number of slaves is diminishing, a few fanatics cry more loudly than ever, 'keep off!' 'do not meddle with our institutions!' So the six men who got up the late meeting in Guyandotte to misrepresent the position and sentiment of their fellow citizens, shout most lustily for the Institution, to let their masters at Richmond know that they are 'sound on the goose.'"

Eli Thayer, Washington Baptist Church, Wayne County, October 12, 1857

Although slavery was not as prominent in western Virginia as in the eastern portion of the state, its practice was carried into both Cabell and Wayne counties upon their creation. At a meeting of the Cabell County Court on July 5, 1814, court members William Buffington, Mark Russell, George Spurlock, and Jesse Spurlock,

> ordered that 'William' alias 'Isaac' a negro slave, supposed to belong to George Carter, now hired out by the county to Thomas Ward be rented out next Saturday to the highest bidder by the Sheriff of this county for the term of three months and that the sheriff admonish the person who hires the said negro that they will be obliged to furnish the said negro with one shirt and pantaloons or strong linen.[16]

In December 1836, more than seventy residents of Cabell County wrote to support a petition submitted by Lewis and Jack [Fullerton], "free coloured men of the county of Cabell praying permission to remain in the Commonwealth." These men had been manumitted by William Fullerton in his will due to their heroic efforts in saving his life

Adam Black Tavern. Jack Fullerton's wife and children were enslaved by Adam Black, and Jack and his brother Lewis leased a farm from him. Credit: Cabell County Annals and Families.

when he nearly drowned in the Mud River in March 1834. Lewis and Jack leased a one hundred-acre farm from Adam Black, and the results of their labor supplied "neighboring markets" and sustenance for themselves, their mother, brother, and sister. The latter two had been granted permission to remain in Virginia during the previous legislative session. Although both men were married, their wives and children remained in bondage.

The Cabell County residents who supported the request wrote,

> that previous to their manumission they were orderly, sober, obedient and industrious slaves, and that subsequent thereto they have maintained the same character in a high degree, as free men, that their daily avocation is a useful and peaceful one, and that their remaining in the Commonwealth will not only be free from danger to our slave population, but be in some degree a service to the neighborhood, that the county of Cabell is a border County, that there are but few blacks, licensed to remain therein, and that the effect of refusing permission to these boys to remain will be merely to drive them to the opposite

bank of the Ohio, where a refuge might be formed for our slaves. And lastly that these men Jack and Lewis have each a wife and several children, who are slaves owned by Citizens of this County and that driving Jack and Lewis from our territory will be but enticing their wives and children to follow.[17]

Sampson Sanders was one of the wealthiest men in Cabell County and owned a large number of slaves. When Sanders died in 1849, they were emancipated by his will and provided $15,000 to purchase homes. These former slaves resettled in Michigan and began their new lives. James Twyman, a wealthy landowner in Madison County, Virginia, died in February 1849. His will decreed the emancipation of his thirty-seven slaves and provided them with money, clothing, farming implements, and livestock. Most of them traveled four hundred miles to Lawrence County, Ohio, where they purchased land in Burlington, across the Ohio River from the mouth of Twelve Pole Creek.[18]

One of the most noted cases regarding slavery in western Virginia was the tragic story of the Polley family. Peyton Polley of Pike County, Kentucky, who had gained his freedom upon the death of his owner, was able to purchase his wife and eight children from David Campbell. The Polley family settled in Lawrence County, Ohio, in 1849. Campbell, however, owed several creditors, and one of them was given a bill of sale to the former slaves. This man, David Justice, a noted slave catcher, was determined to return the children to bondage. On June 6, 1850, four men employed by Justice crossed the Ohio River and kidnapped the seven children and a grandchild of Peyton Polley and took them to Kentucky, where they were sold back into slavery.[19]

Since the crime was committed in Ohio, the legislature of that state passed a resolution directing the governor to inquire into the matter and take measures to rescue the children from slavery. Four were in Kentucky; efforts to have them freed through the court system were successful in 1853, and they were returned to their family in Ohio. The remaining four Polley children had been purchased by William Ratliff, who owned a large plantation in the southern part of Wayne County.

Adjutant General Joel W. Wilson, who had been appointed by the Ohio governor to conduct the cases, went to Wayne County

William Ratliff of Wayne County. Ratliff (or Ratcliff/Ratcliffe) purchased four of the Polley children and successfully contested their return to freedom. He would later represent Wayne County at the Second Wheeling Convention and was a delegate in the Restored Government of Virginia. Credit: Jim Hale.

and "sued out a writ of Habeas Corpus & brought up the children on it." They were taken to the Cabell County Courthouse in Barboursville and brought in front of Judge Samuel McComas. Ratliff, who was not prepared for trial, requested that the habeas corpus be "abandoned as a mere matter of courtesy & a petition for freedom substituted." Ratliff's attorney raised the question of jurisdiction, but Judge George W. Samuels overruled the motion. The Polley children won their suit for freedom in Cabell County in 1855, but a year later the Virginia Court of Appeals reversed the verdict, ruling that because William Ratliff resided in Wayne County, the case should have been heard in that locale.

John Laidley, who had served as attorney in the Polley case in Cabell County, informed Ohio Governor Salmon P. Chase on March 26, 1856, that if he could admit the same testimony used in the former trial, he believed he would obtain their freedom in Wayne County. He wrote, "I believe I am entitled to the use of the depositions taken on the former cause between the same parties, yet as the deft Radcliffe will defend with all his energy I do not regard it precident, to submit to the hazards of delay." William McComas had served as counsel with Laidley in Cabell County but did not practice in Wayne, and Laidley asserted he did not need assistance with the upcoming case. He did seek funds to employ someone to take depositions, a task that had been filled by a young man named Henry Jefferson Samuels. Court in Wayne County was scheduled to begin the first week of April, and Laidley hoped the suit could be settled in the August term.[20]

Ohio Adjutant General Joel Wilson filed a writ of habeas corpus in Wayne County which moved the case and the children temporarily to Cabell County. Credit: Portraits of Eminent Americans Now Living.

On March 31, Ralph Leete of Ironton wrote to Governor Chase, pleading for his assistance with the case. He declared, "It is necessary that something efficient should be done for these in Va. or they will all go into hopeless slavery. The parents of these children reside only a few miles from this place." Leete wrote Chase again on July 26, observing,

> I suppose that now proceedings must be instituted in Wayne Co. Va. & the case all tried over again & the testimony retaken, so far as the witnesses can be found. The case has already cost the State a large sum, & has been five years, in progressing thus far. The negroes in the mean time are in slavery.

Yet it is wrong to let the case be abandoned now; if the Federal Government could spend $1,000,000 to reduce one man to slavery, certainly the state of Ohio should not withhold the necessary amount of means to restore three persons to freedom. One of the number has died since suit was brought.[21]

Governor Chase's private secretary wrote to John Laidley on April 3, 1857, asking for an update on the case. Laidley responded on April 8, informing Chase that the severe weather had prevented the taking of depositions from witnesses in Ohio and Kentucky. In September correspondence, Laidley noted that H. J. Samuels, who had taken depositions in three Kentucky counties, declined to continue the work. Laidley proposed to use Ralph Leete for the remaining depositions.

Laidley had been informed that William Ratliff had served a rule on him,

> to show by what authority I prosecute this suit & then it will be followed up by the appearance of eldest colored man who is 21 years of age, in open court who will direct the suit to be dismissed not deserving to have it prosecuted. This I learn from the opposite counsel.
>
> This is a new point in the defense but under the circumstances I do not apprehend will avail them. The fact is the colored people are very much attached to Ratcliffe & his family.[22]

Ralph Leete of Ironton. A friend of President Abraham Lincoln, Leete served as prosecuting attorney of Lawrence County and was employed to represent the state of Ohio in their quest for the return of the Polley children. Credit: Lawrence County Historical Society and Museum.

S. S. Rice, Chase's private secretary, informed the governor on February 16, 1859, that the case was stalled due to the inactivity of John Laidley. Rice complained "that the interests of the State and her enslaved freemen are in the hands of an old man who acknowledges himself superannuated who neither prosecutes the case to a termination, nor gives any explanation of the causes of the delay..." He also pointed out "that those freemen are spending their best years in slavery every year more endangering their permanent enslavement, apparently for want of adequate diligence in prosecuting their suit for freedom."[23]

On March 22, 1859, the case was dismissed from the docket of the Wayne County Circuit Court:

> This day came the parties by their attorneys, and the rule heretofore awarded

against John Laidley Esqr. to show cause why his assignment as counsel by this court should not be set aside, reversed and annulled, and why the proceedings had in this cause, should not be reversed and annulled; and why the petition filed in this cause should not be held for nought, and why the orders made in this cause should not be reversed, annulled and recinded; and why this cause should not be dismissed from the docket of this court.

Came on to be heard – upon consideration whereof and it appearing that the petition in this cause was presented to the court, and have granted the petitioners to sue for their freedom without their knowledge or desire; and for other reasons appearing to this court.

It is further ordered that the said rule be made absolute – And it is further ordered that the order assigning John Laidley Esqr. as counsel for the pliffs. be recinded and annulled.

And the proceedings had in this cause be also set aside, reversed and annulled; and that the orders heretofore made in this cause be recinded; and this cause dismissed from the docket of this court.

J. C. Wheeler deputy for Wash Adkins, clerk

John Laidley and Mary Hite Laidley of Cabell County. John Laidley represented the Polley children in their quest for freedom. Credit: Cabell County Annals and Families.

Ohio was not yet prepared to surrender. A. M. Gangewer, private secretary for the new Ohio governor, William Dennison, Jr., wrote to Ralph Leete on November 12, 1859, concerning the Polley case. The governor requested that Leete go to Virginia to investigate the situation and "ascertain the present position of the kidnapped negroes..." and promised to pay his expenses. Given that the state had expended thousands of dollars in the effort, the governor would not propose "doing anything more than this at present..."[24]

Leete informed Gangewer on November 25, 1859, that he would travel to Barboursville to ascertain the facts. According to Leete, "The case in Virginia has been bungled and shamefully missmanaged from the commencement." He had managed the cases heard in Kentucky and believed that additional attorneys should be employed in the Virginia case, particularly since the claimant had four attorneys. He suggested George Summers of Kanawha County, who "would probably do better than any one that could be sent from this locality." Leete added, "The frequent visits from the mother of these children to make inquiries about them and her anguish, are enough to move any person of correct feeling to energetic action."[25]

An article appeared in the *Ironton Register* on June 21, 1860, giving an update on the attempt to free the enslaved Polley children.

Ohio Governor William Dennison renewed efforts to free the Polley children in 1859. Credit: Library of Congress.

> Governor Dennison, in pursuance of the resolution passed by the Legislature, last winter, has made arrangements for the further prosecution of the suit of these negroes, (in Virginia) for their freedom. He has appointed Ralph Leete, Esq., of this place, as the agent on part of this State, to act in conjunction with counsel in Virginia. These persons (the Polly negroes) were kidnapped from this county, in 1850, and have been serving in slavery ever since. It is hoped that this litigation may now be speedily brought to a successful termination. Those of the same family, who were kidnapped at the same time, and taken to Kentucky, were set at liberty by the Court of Appeals of that State, six years ago.

Despite extensive efforts by the State of Ohio, the Polley children would remain in bondage for at least five more years, and the man who enslaved them, William Ratliff, would play a role in the creation of a new state during the coming war, a conflict that would finally ensure their permanent freedom.

In early 1856, a violent event occurred in present-day Proctorville, Ohio, that foreshadowed the increasing divide between free states and slave states and laid the foundation of animosity toward the Virginia town of Guyandotte. At this time, Proctorville was commonly called Quaker Bottom or Proctorsville. In December 1855, James Buffington, who lived in Quaker Bottom, encountered two African Americans on the road near his home and asked them for papers showing they were freedmen. When the two men admitted they were escaped slaves from Kentucky, Buffington had them transported across the river to Guyandotte and lodged in a hotel. The owner of the slaves came to town a short time later and retrieved them, and Buffington was reportedly paid a reward of $150.[26]

A neighbor, Alfred S. Proctor, was infuriated by Buffington's actions. In January 1856, Proctor, who was a school trustee, had an African American student enrolled in the local district school to the dismay of Buffington and others. In the latter part of the month, a public meeting was held in Quaker Bottom to "consider the relative character" of this action and Buffington's role in the return of the two slaves to bondage. A lively debate ensued both for and against Proctor's role in enrolling the black student, but there was no discussion regarding the Buffington affair.

Proctor, however, used the occasion to denounce James Buffington. Buffington was enraged and publicly stated on the following morning "that if the ice had not become too thin to cross, there would have been 150 persons over from the Virginia side, and A. S. Proctor would have been tarred and feathered." Buffington also said that "he had been three or four miles below Guyan, on the other side, and if any more meetings were held 300 persons would be over."[27]

Despite these threats, a large crowd gathered at another meeting held on February 14. Two questions were to be debated: "Is it morally right to seize a fugitive from oppression and force him back into bondage? What rights and privileges ought the colored people among us to enjoy?" The first question was discussed at length, but the second was "laid over for two weeks, at the request of the Slavery defenders."[28]

A large number of citizens from Union and Rome gathered at Quaker Bottom on February 21, 1856, "to consider the condition of the people of Kansas and our duties in relation thereto and to express our sympathies in their behalf." Resolutions were drafted by a committee appointed for that purpose, including one that declared "we deeply sympathize with our Free State friends in Kansas in their troubles; that if the President fails to afford them protection from lawless invasion and outrage, it is the duty of the people of the Union to furnish that protection; and that we will, individually, and according to our several abilities, contribute to their aid."[29]

About this time, Alfred Proctor filed a complaint against James Buffington with the Lawrence County prosecuting attorney "for a violation of the law of Ohio." On March 4, Judge William V. Peck ruled against Proctor. This decision "arrested all proceedings, and the capture of the negroes was spoken of at no meeting afterwards..." Other testimony noted that the "difficulty" between Buffington and Proctor "had been settled, and a degree of amity existed between them."[30]

It seems clear, however, that not only were the meetings anti-slavery in purpose, but that Proctor used them to assail the actions of James Buffington. At a meeting on

February 28, the gathered citizens were to address the question: "What rights and privileges ought the colored people among us to enjoy?", which had been "laid over" at the February 14 assembly. "The anti-negro party" was "in the ascendant," however, and "a resolution was adopted so abridging the freedom of discussion that no debate was had."[31]

Yet another public meeting was scheduled for March 14 in Quaker Bottom,

for the avowed purpose of vindicating the right of free discussion, and to consider the question formerly laid over. All parties were invited to attend and participate with the largest liberty and to the fullest extent. Those who now prate about the constitution and the law, then found it convenient to be absent. In their stead was a company of men from Virginia.[32]

William Buffington, the son of James, crossed the river to Guyandotte and convinced a number of the town's citizens, including his brother, Dr. Thomas Buffington, Percival Smith, James Sedinger, Lewis Peters, Henry Milstead, Isaac Ong, Joseph Gardner, and others to attend the forum so that "the Abolitionists would be answered." The gathering went off without a disturbance, despite Proctor's continued attacks on James Buffington. The Guyandotte men had "a fair understanding" that they would "do nothing to disturb the meeting in any way whatever." In fact, Proctor claimed he was unaware that citizens from Virginia were in attendance.[33]

As the meeting concluded, the attendees began making their way toward their homes. The men from Guyandotte were nearing the skiff that would carry them across the Ohio. Dr. Thomas Buffington called to his brother William to come along, but William Buffington was lingering near the meeting house with violent intent on his mind.

A. S. Proctor emerged from the building accompanied by Rev. Adams and Charles Hall. He recorded,

We crossed the fence without apprehension, and had proceeded a few paces up the street, when Isaac Miller called out, 'look out! Bill Buffington is going to knock you down with a club!' We turned round and saw him coming up behind with club in hand under the cover of darkness to do the dastardly deed. As he rushed upon me, I sprang and seized him, and succeeded in wresting the club from his hand. Having the club in my possession my first impulse was to serve him as he had attempted to serve me, but I restrained myself, and resolved to act simply on the defensive, and not to strike unless assailed again. Another rush was made by some of the party, I cannot tell whom, and I used my club, but without much effect, for it snapped off near my hand, and I was again without means of defense.[34]

Dr. T. C. Buffington was standing on the bank conversing with Henry Radford when the fight erupted. Buffington and Radford "walked together up to the crowd, and he joined in with it." The other Guyandotte citizens, about a dozen in number, rushed back to the scene of the fight, believing that the Ohioans were ganging up on William Buffington. They plunged into the fray, grabbing whatever was near at hand to aid their efforts.[35]

Meanwhile, the attack on Proctor was about to be renewed. He wrote,

> In a moment more I saw Buffington coming at me again with an axe drawn in both hands, and swearing he meant to kill me. Before he was quite within striking distance, I made a sudden spring and caught him, and as his axe was descending, Mr. Adams threw up his arm, receiving the helve upon it, injuring his thumb severely, and his arm somewhat. The axe balanced out of Buffington's hands and fell to the ground, doing me no injury. About the time the attack with the axe was made, I saw T. C. Buffington standing near by and heard him say 'G_d d__n him, kill him!' And from a part, if not all of the balance of his crowd, the cry went up 'kill him! kill him!' and so loud that it was heard on the opposite side of the river.[36]

Hearing the noise of the affray, Guyandotte citizens gathered along the Ohio and yelled at their friends, "Do you want any help? If you do, fetch over the skiff."[37]

Proctor was fighting for his life:

> It was clear now that their object was to murder me, and I set about defending myself as best I might. A struggle ensued in which I was tumbled over a pile of stove wood, he on my back, and seizing a stick of wood, he attempted to knock me on the head, but I succeeded in extricating myself, and in turn threw him upon the ground, and caught one of his hands in my right hand. In thrusting his other hand into my face, he accidently stuck his thumb in my mouth, which, however disagreeable, I could not decline holding for him. With my other hand I at once began to finger his wind instrument, and to modulate its tones as I thought the peculiarities of the occasion required.[38]

The brawl was occurring all around the two men. In addition to the injury to Rev. Adams, Henry Radford was struck in the head with a rock and cut severely, and a young man named Nathaniel Hall was knocked down several times. Judge Salmon Reckard was hurt, although one observer claimed a nephew of the judge threw a board that missed its target and was responsible for his injury. While Proctor sought to fight off William Buffington, his brother Dr. Thomas Buffington bashed his head with a chunk of wood.[39]

Despite the blow, Proctor hung on:

> With both of his hands fast, I had him completely in my power, and could have strangled him as easily as an infant; and amid the darkness and noise, no one could have discovered what was in progress until the work would have been done. But I thank God I was restrained. During the whole conflict, I had no desire to injure those who were seeking to kill me, nor to use more force than

was necessary for my own protection. And, as, under Providence, I owe my life to the faithfulness of friends, who suffered blows and wounds in my defence. For when I thought his breathing had been suspended as long as was prudent, and long enough to bring him to terms, I relaxed my hold upon his throat, and let him cry for deliverance. My own friends were first to demand his release.[40]

The melee finally came to a close, and the Guyandotte citizens headed toward their skiff. One "dared us to hold another meeting," Judge Reckard observed, "saying they would come over in numbers sufficient to whip the whole of us." Another yelled they would "whip your d___d one horse town into the river," while shouts of "hurrah for Guyan" rang out over the Ohio River.[41]

While citizens from Ohio claimed that the attack was pre-planned by the residents of Guyandotte, the latter blamed the former:

…the Virginians were returning home quietly, when the son of Major B who had come to Virginia and invited some of the citizens to hear the discussion, struck Proctor. The Abolitionists interfered; the Virginians returned and several engaged to help young Buffington out of the hands of an overpowering force of Abolitionists. Thus, it will be seen, that the whole affair originated with the Ohioans.[42]

Citizens from Guyandotte asserted that the fight was the result of a grudge between Proctor and the Buffington family. Proctor disputed the claim, writing, "Previous to the night of the mob, I had never had any difficulties with any of those parties – not even an unkind word, within my recollection. With Dr. T. C. Buffington I have had considerable business transactions during the past year – all of the most friendly character." His repeated inflammatory public statements about James Buffington, however, were undoubtedly the root cause of the incident.[43]

The *Ironton Register* believed the facts showed that the attack was "premeditated" by certain parties and stated that the incident was instigated by personal matters "combined with circumstances and feelings growing out of the accursed institution of slavery…" Alfred S. Proctor concurred with half of this assessment, writing, "I leave the people to judge how much of this tragedy was caused by merely personal considerations, and how much by the jealous and intolerant spirit of slavery."[44]

The editors of the *Ironton Register* wrote,

We have lived a neighbor to Guyandotte for about seven years, and have an acquaintance with many of its citizens, and so far as we have known or heard, they have ever borne the name of a quiet, orderly and highly respectable people; and the citizens of Cabell county, are not of the 'fire-eating,' 'agitating' kind, but have ever striven to maintain courteous and friendly relations with the people on this side of the river, and earnestly desire to continue such relations…

The people of Cabell are a just people, have no abiding interest in the institution of slavery; in fact, the Slavocracy of Eastern Virginia is their great curse, and they know it. Let us, then, cultivate a friendly spirit. There is no occasion for any differences between the people of Cabell and the people of Lawrence – not the least. Our interests are essentially the same, and, in a conciliatory spirit, we would have no trouble to agree even upon the 'peculiar institution,' the blight which rests like the pall of death upon Western Virginia, retarding its progress, and denying its people their due measure of rights.[45]

On March 28, another public meeting was held in Quaker Bottom, with a large crowd in attendance. The *Ironton Register* reported,

The threatened invasion by 'Border Ruffians' was not made. The 'sober second thought,' combined with the fact that the better class of citizens in Guyandotte utterly condemn the [we cannot decipher the word here] on the 14th, doubtless contribute to prevent a renewal of that disgraceful outrage. All passed off harmoniously, and the me[e]ting closed its session by resolving,

That we are utterly opposed to the extension of Slavery, and that we will demonstrate the truth of this declaration at the polls in October next, by voting for no man for the Chief Magistracy who is not unequivocally opposed thereto.[46]

Guyandotte had already developed a reputation as a rowdy town, one which the brawl at Quaker Bottom only enhanced. A resident of the community wrote on January 20, 1857,

Ther is the hardest times in Guyandotte that ever was and they are geting harder and harder. The times has got so hard that the people have stoped drinking and have turned out to fighting. We had one of the biggest fights last week that you ever witnessed. You could look in every direction an see the country people stretched on the ground and they served them just right. Go it Guyan for when you get old you cant.[47]

In 1857, the establishment of a new community in Wayne County would provide a glimpse into the civil warfare that would grip Cabell and Wayne counties for years to come. Eli Thayer, a United States congressman from Massachusetts, visited the area in July seeking support for a colony of Northern laborers. Thayer believed that organized emigration was the key to combatting slavery. Thayer and his "Emigrant Aid Society" intended to launch colonies in slave states, counting on the influx of Northern emigrants to eventually erode slavery's base of support.[48]

Eli Thayer purchased land from Thomas Jordan on the Ohio River between the Big Sandy River and Twelve Pole Creek in Wayne County and soon established the colony of Ceredo. Thayer attempted to drum up support for the endeavor by addressing a meeting in Guyandotte on July 21, 1857. Thayer told the crowd that he had no intention of disobeying any laws of the state, and that his goal was simply to make a profit. The citizens responded by passing resolutions welcoming the emigrants and encouraging development of the county's resources. Abolitionist newspapers in New York, Cincinnati, and St. Louis applauded the reception given to Thayer by the Guyandotte citizens.[49]

Many other observers, however, accused Thayer of attempting to abolish slavery in the state of Virginia and vowed to fight back. One wrote,

> We are surprised that the citizens of Guyandotte should suffer themselves to be so easily cajoled by the deceitful blandishments of the wily Abolitionist, and blinded to the real object of his free labor movement…We are extremely loth to interpret the proceeding at Guyandotte as a fair indication of public sentiment in Western Virginia. However disposed to foster and encourage the emigration to our state of 'good and law-abiding' citizens, the people of that section, will not countenance a movement set on foot with the avowed determination to make an insidious attack upon the institution of domestic slavery.[50]

The *Richmond Examiner* called the citizens of Cabell and Wayne counties "bubble-blowers, yankee speculators, anti-Virginians, &c." The *Examiner* also declared that should "Thayer ever appear in Guyandotte and the citizens don't apply tar and feather copiously and abundantly, it will be ample justification for Virginia to withhold all appropriations for a rail road connecting with the West in that direction."[51]

The *Guyandotte Unionist* responded sarcastically that the "codfish and oyster soup aristocracy…would run the C.&O.R.R. upon the reefs of Florida before it should pass through the valleys of Western Virginia." The *Kanawha Valley Star*, a Charleston newspaper, defended the citizens of Cabell and Wayne, stating,

Congressman Eli Thayer, who established the community of Ceredo in 1857. Credit: Library of Congress.

> we know that the bone and sinew of the Wayne and Cabell people are devotedly attached to all the cherished institutions and political principles of our State. We, therefore, hope that they will hold a public meeting and give utterance to the true loyalty and genuine Virginia feelings that pervade their section of the State, and thus stamp as false, the representations that have been made respecting them by the allies of the Homestead Aid Society.[52]

Some citizens of Guyandotte responded to this appeal by assembling at the town hall at 4:00 p.m. on August 26, 1857. On the motion of Colonel Isaac Ong, Colonel John Everett chaired the meeting, and A. J. Keenan served as secretary. Congressman Albert Gallatin Jenkins, who was in attendance, was asked to address the meeting. Jenkins had recently visited Ceredo and was opposed to the establishment of the colony. Jenkins took the floor and "explained the defamity of this abolition scheme, reviewed its origin and history, and traced its ultimate tendencies." The congressman "brought conviction to all who heard him." After Jenkins finished speaking, a committee, consisting of Jenkins, Owen Moore, Dr. Girard D. Ricketts, and Lewis Sedinger, was appointed to draft resolutions "expressive of the meeting." The resolutions were:

> 1st. That should Eli Thayer or his confederates, or any other person or persons, coming among us with the purpose either direct or contingent – immediate or eventual of raising any anti-slavery agitation – in any manner, shape, or form, whether in open or palpable violation of the Constitution and the laws, or should seek insiduously to disguise their object behind the forms of these, we shall take such decisive and positive correction of the evil into our own hands, as will prove a salutary lesson to such men for the future.
>
> 2d. That this correction, will not be delayed until the evil shall have taken root, but will be applied upon its first appearance, and we advise those whom it concerns to take heed accordingly.
>
> 3d. That the people of Cabell, acknowledge no superiors in their devotion to the time-honored institutions, of the 'Old Dominion.'
>
> 4th. That to no portion of her sons, could the 'Old Dominion' more safely entrust her rights – her interests – and her honor involved upon her border, than to the citizens both native and adopted of the county of Cabell.
>
> 5th. That though we are not expressly authorized so to do, yet our constant intercourse with the people of the other counties of 'Western Virginia,' warrant us in asserting, that they hold no less orthodox sentiments than those contained in the foregoing resolutions.[53]

The resolutions passed unanimously, and it was moved that the results of the meeting be published in the *Guyandotte Unionist* and sent to other Virginia papers for publication. The *Unionist* declared, "We claim for our citizens as much loyalty to our State, and as much devotion to our domestic institutions as belong to those of any other section of the State, and we will shed our blood as soon as our Eastern brethren to preserve the dignity and honor of the 'old Dominion'."[54]

Eli Thayer returned to western Virginia, and on Monday evening, October 12, 1857, he addressed a large crowd of citizens from Wayne and adjoining counties at

CHAPTER TWO   27

Washington Baptist Church, at its original location on the James River and Kanawha Turnpike in Wayne County. Credit: Ed Adkins Scrapbook, Ceredo Historical Society Museum.

Washington Baptist Church, located on Krout's Creek on the James River and Kanawha Turnpike a short distance from Ceredo. It was his first public engagement since the anti-Thayer meeting in Guyandotte a few weeks earlier, and Thayer sought to ease the growing tension caused by the new colony with his opening remarks:

> I have come before you this evening as a peace-maker between Wayne and Cabell counties. Wayne is the daughter of Cabell, and there should be no hostility between mother and daughter – no envy, no jealousy. To secure and preserve the friendship between them, let us without partiality commend the charms of both.
>
> Within the last few days I have heard several of your citizens charging the citizens of Cabell with hostility to your interests. They adduce as evidence of this the proceedings of a meeting recently held at Guyandotte, in which the position of the people at that town, deliberately taken at a former meeting, was reversed without any other reason than this; that Wayne county had been preferred to Cabell by Northern emigrants. Certain other acts of Cabell of earlier date are also adduced to strengthen the evidence of existing hostility.

> Now, ladies and gentlemen, the causes of disaffection which may have formerly existed, I am unable either to account or apologize for; but I will assure you, that the little meeting which was sprung upon the people of Guyandotte the other day, at thirty minutes' notice, did not reflect the sentiments of the people of that county. Let us therefore still cherish the most friendly feelings towards the great majority of the people of Cabell, whose hearts are with us and whose interests are identical with our own. A city of intelligent enterprising men, established in either county, will benefit both. The advantages and resources of both will be discovered and made available. The time has come for both to be understood and appreciated. The time has come for schools, and churches, and mechanic arts, to be planted here – and they *will be planted here*. Let us therefore still cherish the most friendly feelings with *Mother* Cabell, and not charge the follies of six of her sons, who got up the incendiary meeting which you judge prejudicial to the interests of Ceredo, upon six thousand who are innocent and friendly.[55]

Thayer reminded his listeners of the presentations he had made earlier in the year. Not only had he previously visited Washington Baptist Church, but he also addressed groups in Ashland, Catlettsburg, and Guyandotte and was greeted with overwhelming encouragement in each town. The report of the anti-Thayer meeting in Guyandotte, however, had a negative impact on the fledgling community. Thayer observed,

> It was made to appear by the proceedings of that incendiary gathering, that Western Virginia had reversed her former decisions and had been whipped into submission by the ultraists and extremists. The quiet and peaceful people of the North who were preparing to come and make their homes with you here, were to some extent intimidated. They did not know, and in fact, at the time had no means of knowing, how weak and insignificant that little meeting in Guyandotte was. And they have not found out to this day. So I have come to act the matter right, on the soil of the Old Dominion, not in a private way, but at a public meeting ample notice of which has been given everywhere within fifteen miles of this locality, and to show that no importance ought to be attached to the puerile threats made at the little meeting of little men in the little town of Guyandotte.[56]

Several prominent Cabell citizens had informed him that if their county had been selected for the site of Thayer's colony, "not one syllable of hostility would ever have been tolerated in Cabell county." Thayer declared that the assembly at Guyandotte had not intended to impede emigration to the area but wished to prove to the politicians in eastern Virginia that the town was a sound supporter of the institution of slavery. "It was urged that Eastern Virginia was opposed regarding any railroad facilities to infected districts," he stated, "and that if the Virginia Central Railroad should ever be completed, this fire-eating action might secure the western depot at Guyandotte. Well, if this is so, I have no fault to find," Thayer humorously noted, "for it is a very cheap way to buy a depot, by getting up an 'anti-Eli Thayer meeting.'" Thayer avowed that despite the recent public opposition to his colony, "Ceredo is a fixed fact – a manifest destiny." Those in attendance at this meeting, as at all the others save the latter gathering in Guyandotte, passed resolutions in support of Thayer's endeavor.[57]

Congressman A. G. Jenkins wrote to Governor Henry A. Wise on August 13 protesting the existence of the colony, but Wise refused to intervene. In December 1857, both Jenkins and Thayer traveled to Washington to be sworn in for the opening of the 35th Congress, where they would argue for and against the extension of slavery in the United States. Western Virginia remained deeply divided over the issue of slavery, and tension increased as the threat of war loomed over the country.

The editors of the *Ironton Register* paid a visit in October 1857 to the site of the new town of Ceredo. The drive was about twelve miles, and they recorded,

> As we approached, a busy scene presented itself on the opposite shore. Workmen and teams were engaged in digging down the high bank, and opening a highway from the river to the town that is to be. The grade will be carried far back, so as to be of the easiest and gentlest slope to be found perhaps anywhere on the Ohio. After reaching the top of the bank, some of the advantages of the location were apparent at a glance. One of the widest bottoms on the whole river, stretches away for miles above and below. The soil is sandy, eminently favorable to dry cellars and basements. There is a sufficient slope every where, to carry off all surface water. An excellent quality of building stone is close at hand, and in great abundance...
>
> The season was so far advanced when operations were commenced, that there can be little show of buildings this winter. However, quite a number of cellars are already dug, and foundation walls laid up. Forty thousand dollars' worth of steam engines, now lying at Parkersburg, will be floated down this week, and set in operation as soon as suitable shelter can be provided; and when Spring opens, the work will go vigorously forward. Ironton must share in the prosperity of Ceredo; the Iron City and the Bread-giving City join hands in friendly greeting across the beautiful Ohio.[58]

On January 11, 1858, a correspondent of the *Cincinnati Gazette* gave a detailed description of progress and sought to temper expectations:

> The situation of this town is on a beautiful plat of second bottom land, just below Twelve Pole Creek, and two miles from Big Sandy, the western boundary of Virginia. The land is a rich, alluvial bottom, gradually sloping from the adjacent hills toward the Ohio river, and furnishing as fine a site as could be desired for a town of almost any dimensions. Ceredo is the natural terminus of the Covington & Ohio Railroad, which is located to run through the town, and is a continuation of the Virginia Central Railroad, and upon which over a million of dollars has been expended, and to which Governor Wise recommends

an appropriation of a million and a half yearly until it is completed. There is also a railroad in process of construction through Kentucky to Ashland, seven miles below Ceredo, which must eventually form a continuous route from the East to the West, and become one of the most important railroads in the Union. Ceredo, from its location, must necessarily be the terminus of at least the Virginia road. And, besides, the Ohio, at this point furnishes much better facilities for navigation in low water than it does above the bar, at the mouth of Twelve Pole, which is just above the town.

The country back of the town is either rolling or hilly land, of medium productiveness for agricultural purposes, and is unexhaustible in timber, coal, and iron ore. These are the principal advantages which the situation possesses for the erection of a town. It is a mild, healthful climate, a tolerably productive soil, exceedingly rich in some localities, has an abundance of mineral wealth and timber, river navigation, and prospective railroad facilities.

Now, as to what has been accomplished. The Company have purchased about 3,000 acres of land, which they propose to divide up and sell in lots to sod purchasers. Almost any quantity of land can be bought in the vicinity at low rates. There are twelve dwelling houses, besides a building for stores and offices, completed, a large hotel nearly enclosed, a building for steam power to run saw and planning [sic] mills in process of erection, and receiving its machinery, a church and schoolhouse under way, to be done soon, and the foundations of a number of private dwellings laid. These, together with the shanties of a number of laborers, constitute the present town of Ceredo. Most of the trades and mechanic arts have here a representative. The enterprise has been hindered somewhat in consequence of unavoidable delays in getting steam machinery in operation, upon which dependence is made for lumber to construct buildings. These delays, it is expected, will soon be obviated by the employment of a large amount of steam power. A company of ship builders from New York are here getting out timber, and will soon have a vessel upon the stocks. Several are waiting in towns adjacent for dwellings to occupy, and a large number of lots have been sold to those who will undoubtedly build upon them the coming season.

So far as a week's careful observation and thorough inquiry furnish data, I can see no reason for disappointment at what has already been accomplished at Ceredo, or ground to test for its future. Sober expectations and practical knowledge of the delays and difficulties incident to building [t]owns will moderate the views of reasonable persons down to about what has been accomplished.

The fame of Ceredo may have outrun its progress. Some may have come here expecting to find a town already built, and had found but a few houses scattered around town what but a short time since was a wide field. True, streets are being graded and every thing is advancing. But the town is not built.

On the whole, Ceredo may be safely set down as destined to become an important town. How large, it may be safe to leave for the future to determine. The capital invested here, and the facilities possessed, in the hands of the men who control them, with the good wishes of the communities around, will not be likely to fail of important results – Ceredo is destined to be no small town, if its projectors are permitted to consummate their plans, which seem feasible, and as likely of success as any human enterprise.

The moral and social aspects of the place are yet undeveloped. In this respect it may possess important advantages, which shall make it exceedingly desirable as a residence.

C.M.[59]

On July 5, 1858, the town hosted a Fourth of July celebration, the first to be held in Wayne County. Attendees from Ohio, Kentucky, and Virginia enjoyed a day of food, speeches, and comradery. Although he was unable to be present, Joseph J. Mansfield, colonel of the Wayne militia and one of the county's most prominent citizens, wrote a letter from Wayne Courthouse that was read to the gathered crowd in Ceredo, and that reflected the area's general acceptance of the new community:

Gentlemen: I received yours of the 17th inst. inviting me to attend a festival at Ceredo on the 5th of July next given in honor of our national independence. It would afford me great pleasure to meet the people of Ceredo and vicinity around the festive board on that interesting occasion. To see citizens of this vast republic, from the North and the South – from the East and the West gathering together under the protection of one common flag, to commemorate the one great event in our national existence, is grateful to the heart of the patriot. It is an assurance that while this national spirit, and love of country exists, there still remains a common platform upon which we all can rally in fraternity and brotherhood, notwithstanding sectional jealousies and bitter sectional strife. While we can repose with pride beneath the ample folds of the stars and stripes, it is an assurance, that whatever bickerings we may have in relation to sectional prejudices and interests, we still regard the constitution of our country, as a great family compact, pledging amity among ourselves; and as a great treaty of alliance, both offensive and defensive, to protect each other from the aggressions of all others...

May the first celebration of the anniversary of American Independence at Ceredo, inaugurate a more fraternal sentiment between the North and the South upon the principles and compromises of the federal Constitution. In this spirit we welcome our northern breth[re]n 'to Old Virginia's shore.'

Your Ob't Serv't,
Joseph J. Mansfield[60]

The beautiful words written by Colonel Mansfield, and the unquestioned sincerity of their meaning would soon be swept away by the gathering winds of war.

3
The Road to Armed Conflict

"Let the decree go forth; yes let it go – go from every county, from every city and town, and hamlet; from cottage and mansion, and every rural district let the decree go, and let the hills and valleys reverb[e]rate the joyous fiat, – Virginia must and shall be divided – the West must and shall be a free and independent State, under the name and title of West Virginia."

Letter from Wayne County resident, *Wheeling Intelligencer*, January 28, 1861

On October 16, 1859, abolitionist John Brown and his followers launched a raid on Harpers Ferry designed to spark an armed slave revolt. On December 12, ten days after Brown was hanged for treason, a group of citizens from the Guyandotte area met to discuss the event. "The recent atrocities committed at Harper's Ferry," they recorded, "demand in our judgement, a calm, full, and earnest expression of the sentiments of our people." The inhabitants resolved that any outside interference with slavery would not be tolerated: "We know of but one course to pursue, and that is, to repel at all hazards…as Virginians, every inch of her soil is dear and sacred to us…we pledge our all to her defence."[61]

The last resolution passed by the residents stated, "We believe there is no natural, or necessary antagonism in our vast, and as yet but partially developed and sparsely settled country – between free and slave labor; but that the two systems, if let alone, will continue to adjust themselves to the wants of the country, with entire harmony…" The gathered citizens believed that the threat of war was being encouraged by "unpatriotic men, North and South, in order to excite and divide the people and serve their own selfish needs."[62]

The *Ironton Register* also believed sentiments were being inflamed:

'We Are In Arms!' So says Governor Wise, of Virginia, in his late Message; and it was not wholly an idle saying. We have it from good authority, that Governor Wise has sent 'munitions of war' to the several Virginia towns on the Ohio River – to Guyandotte, Point Pleasant, Parkersburg, and other points. We learn that two cannons and six hundred Sharp's rifles arrived at Point Pleasant, the other day.

For what is all this? whom to shoot? The people at Guyandotte and Point Pleasant don't know. The truth is, along all this part of the Ohio River – say, for fifty miles below this to a hundred above – the people are on friendly and intimate terms; the people of no two counties in Ohio are more so.[63]

Granville Parker, a Guyandotte lawyer, concurred with this sentiment and wrote of Cabell County's citizens: "The People are always on the very best of terms. They have a practical knowledge of the 'Peculiar Institution,' and a dissertation on its Barbarism, I have no idea, would be listened to by the people on either side of the River."[64]

In a letter to fellow congressman Gideon Camden, Albert Gallatin Jenkins of Cabell County observed, "Living as they [his constituents] do upon the border of a border state and having scarcely enough of the institution of slavery in their midst to justify the name; it is apparent that it will be an inviting point of attack on the part of northern fanaticism which is always vigilant & keen – sighted in its attempts to undermine the social system of the south."[65]

In April 1860, Jenkins, one of the largest slaveholders in western Virginia, defended slavery on the floor of the United States House of Representatives:

Granville Parker, originally from Massachusetts, moved to Guyandotte prior to the Civil War and wrote numerous articles on West Virginia statehood during the conflict. He represented Cabell County at the first constitutional convention and was the author of The Formation of the State of West Virginia. Credit: The Rending of Virginia.

A week or two ago, Farnsworth of Ill., in the U. S. House of Representatives mentioned the fact that John Wesley called slavery 'the sum of all villainies.' This brought up Hon. Albert Gallatin Jenkins, of our neighboring county of Cabell in Virginia, who wished to know if Farnsworth 'endorsed' the remark of Wesley. Farnsworth responded that he was 'pretty much' of Wesley's opinion, whereupon Hon. Mr. Jenkins said in polite language, 'Then you declare a lie!'

No blood flowed outside of the regular channels, in consequence.[66]

In the United States presidential election of 1860, the citizens of Cabell County split their vote among three candidates. Democrat Stephen Douglas received 407 votes, Union candidate John Bell received 316 votes, and Southern Democrat John Breckinridge of Kentucky received 161 votes. The winner of the national election, Abraham Lincoln, received only four votes in Cabell, and these men "were threatened

Congressman Albert G. Jenkins of Cabell County. Credit: Library of Congress.

to be sent across the river into Ohio for their Abolition principles." Guyandotte citizens cast 93 votes for Bell, 23 for Douglas, 9 for Breckinridge, and 3 for Lincoln. In Wayne County, Bell received 326 votes, Breckinridge 166, Douglas 82, and Lincoln 10. Bell received 55 votes in Ceredo, while Douglas received 23, and Breckinridge 17. Lincoln received all of his Wayne County votes in this abolitionist community.

Following the election, Virginia Governor John Letcher called for a special session of the General Assembly. This body passed an act which provided for a convention of the people of Virginia, to commence in Richmond on February 13, 1861, the delegates to be chosen in the same manner as the members of the General Assembly.[67]

Meanwhile, congressional leaders worked hard throughout the winter in Washington to mold a compromise which would prevent civil war. Senator John J. Crittenden of Kentucky headed a committee which constructed a possible solution. The citizens of Cabell County anxiously awaited news from Washington, hoping that the Crittenden Resolutions would be submitted to a vote of the people:

> We all saw the difficulty in the way of the Representative men of the Republican party making the concession, justice and the integrity of the Union imperatively demand; but we did not suppose for a moment, that any one would oppose the submission of them to their Constitutional masters, the People!
>
> Many of us in Western Virginia have had considerable experience of the practical working of both Free and Slave Institutions, and are therefore qualified to judge of the relative merits, and demerits, of the two sections, better than those who have seen but one side.

President Lincoln, however, refused to accept the compromise, stating that he was unable to budge regarding the extension of slavery.[68]

Correspondence from Amacetta in Wayne County on January 16, 1861, advocated secession for western Virginia, not from the Union, but from Virginia. This letter, which was published in the *Wheeling Intelligencer*, may have been written by Zophar D. Ramsdell, a native of Massachusetts who had moved to Ceredo in 1858 at the invitation of Eli Thayer.

In these times of adjustment, secession, nullification, treason and rebellion, permit me a brief article in your columns. The times demand brevity and decision. The rumor has reached us, and we doubt it not, that the Legislature has enacted the call for a Convention, to meet in February next – short notice. The first thing, then, on hand, should be the White Basis. Let the West with one united voice demand it. Yes, promptly and firmly demand it – and be satisfied with nothing less. Ninety-nine in every hundred will demand and maintain it. And the same with safety may be said of every other county in the State. This is no South Carolina flurry. It has been in contemplation years, and now is the occasion for carrying it into effect. Already the field is open, and many counties have expressed a willingness to turn in. Then, come, demand the white basis. It is now already demanded by us, and if we fail in this, let the people spring – spring into action, and all, as if with an electric bound, spring at once and take the only alternative. Let the decree go forth; yes let it go – go from every county, from every city and town, and hamlet; from cottage and mansion, and every rural district let the decree go, and let the hills and valleys reverb[e]rate the joyous fiat, – Virginia must and shall be divided – the West must and shall be a free and independent State, under the name and title of West Virginia. The people can then immediately form a Constitution according to the provisions in the Constitution of '87 and henceforth have a great and homogenious State – a peaceful union and brotherhood under the protection of the United States.

WAYNE[69]

William McComas of Barboursville, Cabell County's delegate to the Richmond Convention, voted against the Ordinance of Secession. Credit: Wikipedia.

The Richmond Convention, which was to determine Virginia's course in this crisis, began on February 13, 1861. Cabell County's delegate to the convention was William McComas of Barboursville, while Wayne County was represented by Burwell Spurlock.

William McComas was the son of Brigadier General Elisha McComas, one of the most prominent men in the region. McComas himself became a noted minister and attorney and was elected to the Virginia General Assembly and to the United States House of Representatives. He was serving as a judge at the time of the Richmond Convention. Reverend Burwell Spurlock, a retired Methodist circuit rider, was "noted for his conservatism, trusted for a high order of personal integrity, and honored for his great native intellectuality." He was selected to run against William Ratliff, a slaveholder who was an outspoken supporter of the Union, for Wayne County delegate to the Richmond Convention. Spurlock was elected and after a difficult journey on horseback, he arrived in the capital city after the convention had begun.[70]

For two months, the representatives debated, and the overall mood of the convention was somewhat moderate in nature. In April, however, events occurred outside the convention that determined Virginia's fate.

On April 12, Confederate forces in Charleston, South Carolina, fired on Fort Sumter, a Federal installation occupied by Union troops. At Marshall College in Cabell County, a group of young men were "having a ball game" when a mounted fellow student rode up and cried, "Fort Sumter has been fired on!" According to Thomas Ewing, later an officer in the 5th West Virginia Infantry, "The ball game was forgotten immediately and there was no more studying. The sympathies of the students were about evenly divided and the male students hurried away to take sides."[71]

Burwell Spurlock, who represented Wayne County at the Richmond Convention. Spurlock voted against leaving the Union on April 17, 1861, but he later signed the Ordinance of Secession. Credit: Special Collections Department, Marshall University.

Following the Federal surrender of Fort Sumter, President Abraham Lincoln issued a call for 75,000 troops to put down the rebellion. In response, the delegates in Richmond passed an Ordinance of Secession in a secret vote on April 17, 1861, with 88 delegates voting for its adoption and 55 against. The latter included William McComas of Cabell and Burwell Spurlock of Wayne, who both opposed secession from the Union. Spurlock, however, would later sign the Ordinance of Secession.

A militia group made up of Cabell County men had been organized in the winter of 1860 in Guyandotte, probably as a result of Lincoln's election. "Of the reasons and objects of this military organization," wrote one member of the unit, "I shall not now, if ever, speak, suffice this occasion to say that one half its members were then opposed to 'Secession'." The group was called the Border Rangers; their mission was to protect a Virginia state flag which was raised on a staff on the bank of the Ohio River. The locals "publicly drilled to music of fife and drum" and officers were elected. Ira J. McGinnis was chosen as the group's captain, Henry C. Everett, first lieutenant, and George W. Holderby, second lieutenant.[72]

These men gathered for a town meeting in Guyandotte on April 20, 1861. Also present at the event, which was held in front of the Planter's Hotel, were other militia companies and a large number of Cabell County citizens. A flag had been made for the occasion by the "secession ladies of Guyandotte, and Lewis Peters, esq., artist." The standard was raised by Elijah Ricketts and John W. Ong, two of the town's oldest citizens, as the crowd roared with approval.[73]

W. S. Laidley told of his first sighting of the new flag:

> We as country boys, went into the old town where we were wont to get the mail, and after attending to our duties, we strolled down towards the hotel on the bank of the Ohio river, and we met a young lady wearing an apron which to us was unusual and which we did not comprehend, yet we felt sure it was an indication of some sentiments and we dared not ask her to explain.
>
> We reached the hotel and in front of it on the river bank there had been erected a flag staff and thereon there had been hoisted a flag or banner, the like of which we had never seen before, and we noticed the resemblance of the flag to the apron. We were struck with the new emblems, but were slow to take in the significance of the same.[74]

Ira J. McGinnis, first captain of the Border Rangers. After the war, McGinnis was elected to the state senate and served as a circuit judge. Credit: Special Collections Department, Marshall University.

Reverend St. Mark Russell was called to address the crowd and did so, reviewing the causes of the present conflict. Soon, however, Russell was interrupted by the arrival of a steamboat which brought word that the Ordinance of Secession had passed. The crowd raised "deafening shouts" and salutes were fired for the Confederacy and for President Jefferson Davis. Russell was recalled to the stand and was followed by L. H. McGinnis of Logan, B. H. Thackston of Barboursville, and Dr. A. B. McGinnis. The meeting then adjourned to the Town Hall. G. D. Warren, who spoke next, "declared amid tremendous cheering, that the time for division in Guyandotte had passed; that those who were not for Virginia in her sovereign, independent position, were against her in toto; and would now be marked as her enemies; that if any such existed in Guyandotte they would be treated as traitors."[75]

Captain H. H. Miller of the Home Guard spoke next, followed by William H. Buffington. The following resolutions, introduced by Dr. A. B. McGinnis, were approved unanimously by those in attendance:

1st. That we approve the action of the Convention, if the ordinance has passed.

2d. That in our judgement the failure of the Convention to submit an ordinance of secession to the people, will inevitably involve the State in a double revolution, the like of which no parallel is found in history.

3rd. That we would deem it an act of political tyranny in the Convention to withhold from the people the priviledge of choosing whether their destiny shall be with the South or with the military despotism now being forced upon the people by the revolutionists of the so called Lincoln Government.

4th. That in our judgement the formal and legal withdrawal of Virginia from her connection with the late United States, and union with the Confederate States, is the surest, if not the only remedy for the troubles which now environ and disturb her social and political systems.

5th. That the secretary cause the proceedings of this meeting to be published in the Kanawha Valley Star, and that the Richmond papers be requested to copy.

P. C. Buffington, Pres't.
H. H. Miller, Sec'y.[76]

W. S. Laidley had taken a seat on the sidewalk in front of the hotel; he and his companions were reflecting on the day's events when

> we heard something strike the brick wall of the hotel just over my head. We soon took it in that it was from a gun from the opposite corner of the hotel. We became satisfied that the flag meant more than a man's joke, and once in our lives, perhaps, we were right.[77]

Albert Gallatin Jenkins rode into town and addressed the militia groups before the crowd dispersed. The Border Rangers returned with Jenkins to his home where they ate dinner and set up camp. One of the men later recalled,

> I expressed my views to this gentleman and one other person, as I was opposed to what was going on, or contemplated. The main argument for turning the Company over to Hon. Jenkins, was, that out of his private funds he was able and would arm, equip, and furnish the boys with horses, and the cavalry service was preferred by officers and privates. Particulars and minutiae are not necessary here, and I will only repeat as the general feeling, what the future 3d Lieut. said, 'Any thing if it is for the best.' This was the language of nature's warrior – the 'Marshal Ney' of Western Virginia – the brave, loved and lamented Capt. A. H. Samuels.[78]

Their weapons consisted mainly of shotguns, although "each man cut himself a piece of lead pipe of the Captain (Jenkins) for he had plenty." The troops camped at Jenkins's farm for a few weeks and then moved to the old Green Bottom Baptist Church. Here they were joined by some Mason County recruits. The men drilled at this location for about three weeks before being ordered to the Kanawha Valley. These novice soldiers, who "thought we could whip the world," would form the nucleus of Company E of the 8th Virginia Cavalry and would participate in many of the subsequent military actions in Cabell County.[79]

A writer for the *Kanawha Valley Star* issued a warning that reflected the general sentiment of Southern supporters in the area:

> The mountains of Trans-Alleghany Virginia are filled with able-bodied men – men accustomed from their youth to bear arms, every one of whom has one or more rifles in his cabin, and all of them are first-rate marksmen. These men number legions, and a little drilling would make them the best of soldiers. Should the abolitionists of Ohio send an invading army into Western Virginia, not a soldier of them will ever return alive. The mountain boys would shoot them down as dogs.[80]

The residents of Wayne County were divided on the war issue. Milton J. Ferguson and J. J. Mansfield advocated secession and were joined by many other citizens of the county on the side of the Confederacy while Union support was strong in Ceredo. In late April 1861, a large number of the county's citizens gathered at Wayne Court House. A secession flag was raised,

> amid the shouts of the people, the ringing of bells and the firing of guns. Being without cannon, our blacksmiths made one especially for the occasion. The secession feeling is gaining fast here. All regard those who appeal for the old Union as little better than Abolitionists. All the Union we want is a United South.[81]

However, throughout Cabell and Wayne counties, there were citizens opposed to secession who dared not speak out publicly for fear of retribution. Sallie P. Smith of Guyandotte wrote to her cousin on April 22 and described their agony:

> I don't know how or where to commence writing. My mind is so flusterated. Politics is high I can tell you! I don't know what the place or people are coming to. The Secessionists raised a flag last Saturday. They don't call it a Secessionist flag they call it a State flag. It has but fifteen stars and a coat of arms on it. Ed. Smith gave a half dollar towards it. His father and mother were in Cincinnati at the time. Things are in a desperate way here. I am afraid to open my mouth. I wish that I was some place else in the world; Oh I can't begin to tell you how bad Pa feels. He he [sic] is almost distracted. He scarcely eats or sleeps and as for Uncle Percival he looks like a dead person. I wish we were all away from

here. You can't imagine how badly we feel nor what we have to contend with, but please don't mention what I have written for some people have gotten themselves into trouble by not saying half as much as I have said to you. If we live through this trouble, I don't expect that we will live always in this place; but for God sake don't mention any thing that I have written for it would make against us a great deal.[82]

On the day Smith penned her letter, a large Union meeting was held across the river from Guyandotte at Rome Chapel for the purpose of organizing a military company. The Ohio citizens were undoubtedly aware of the event in Guyandotte two days earlier. One of the resolutions passed by those in attendance declared, "That in these times of treason and rebellion, when those who have been our neighbors have raised a flag of their own design, and repudiated the Stars and Stripes of our Union, and are arming themselves for purposes (as we think) other than the defense of our country's flag, it behooves us, as loyal citizens, to prepare for the defence of ourselves and families." The final resolution stated, "That our sympathies are with the friends of the Union, wherever found; and we detest traitors, and will not tolerate them in our midst."[83]

The Border Rangers moved to Camp Tompkins (near present-day St. Albans) in early May. Shortly after their arrival, Victoria Hansford and other female secession supporters made and presented the company with a flag. Hansford wrote, "It was a pretty one carefully made of the best material." One of the women delivered a speech to the Border Rangers, while Hansford's father held the flag "unfurled to the breezes as it was presented to the company." Hansford observed,

> They were all mounted and their horses were arranged in formation along the fence. They were under the shade of two locust trees that were in the yard of the old hotel near the covered bridge over Coal River. Captain Jenkins accepted it gracefully with a short and appropriate speech. We ladies stood on the lawn in front of the hotel with arms full of flowers in abundance which were showered over the officers and soldiers at the end of the ceremony.[84]

One of the women noticed a young man with the company and requested to present her bouquet to him. Jenkins called for the youngster, and "he rode forward on a little mule with a rope bridle and no saddle. He wore a little cap and a very plain suit of everyday clothing." Captain Jenkins introduced him and informed the crowd that Lucian "Cooney" Ricketts, who was thirteen years of age, had been drilling with the Border Rangers whenever he could borrow a horse. When the company was ordered to Camp Tompkins, Ricketts appropriated a "frisky little mule" and followed the men toward the Kanawha Valley. Captain Jenkins learned of his presence and sent word that Ricketts was to return home, but he continued to trail the column. Jenkins observed,

> Finding my orders disregarded, I rode to the rear and ordered him to go back home. I knew his mother, who was a widow and would surely be deranged

finding him gone. Another one of her sons, Albert Gallatin Ricketts, who is my namesake, is also in the company. When I began to reason with him he said 'Captain, the road is free, I will ride in sight of you by day and camp nearby at night.' When I told him he was too young for duty he said, 'I can carry water, I can wait on you and do about anything, but I am determined to go to war.' We could hold out no longer and that night we voted to adopt him as 'The Child of the Regiment.'[85]

Corporal James D. Sedinger recalled the support the Confederates received from home:

Our commissary department was looked after by the ladies of Cabell and Mason counties who kept us well supplied with boiled ham and roasted chicken, baked light bread and biscuit cake and pies. Everything that they could think of to tickle the p[a]late and we enjoyed ourselves better than we ever did afterwards. Our clothing the same way – whenever a wagon would come into camp the boys would make a break for it and he would be certain to find something for him from his sweetheart, sister or mother.[86]

Lucian Cincinnatus "Cooney" Ricketts served with the Border Rangers and was enrolled at VMI in 1863 by General Albert Gallatin Jenkins. A year later, he fought with his fellow cadets in the battle of New Market. Credit: Jack L. Dickinson.

On May 12 the polls opened in Cabell County for the election of a representative to the legislature. Edward D. Wright, the lone candidate, received the sixteen votes cast. Two days later, Confederate Lieutenant Colonel John McCausland, commanding the Department of the Kanawha Valley, issued an order for the "volunteer companies" of Cabell, Logan, and Wayne counties to rendezvous at Barboursville.[87]

Shortly following Virginia's secession from the Union, a mass meeting held at Clarksburg called for a convention to assemble in Wheeling. The delegates at this first Wheeling convention, held May 13-15, 1861, opposed secession but disagreed on how best to respond to the crisis. Although Cabell did not send representatives, the county was "represented" by the delegates from Harrison County. These men were acting under the authority of a convention which was said to have been held in Barboursville. Robert Hager of Boone County sought to justify the recognition of the alternates by saying,

I am informed by the delegate from Wayne, not-withstanding Ziegler had a regiment there, that all elections had to be guarded by his regiment. I do not know how many elections were held in Cabell County. However, they held one somewhere and the county is represented. If it requires a military force to hold an election, if Wayne County which borders on the Ohio River had to have a military force to hold an election at two points...with what difficulty are the counties represented.[88]

Despite efforts by John Carlile to create a state called New Virginia, on May 15 the delegates to the First Wheeling Convention were urged to return to their homes and encourage opposition to the Ordinance of Secession. If it passed, however, Union supporters would again convene in Wheeling.
On May 16, James A. Decker, a Union supporter living in Wayne County, wrote to friends in the Kanawha Valley. Decker reported,

All of the talk is about secession here. There is war in these United States now and I expect that it will be a tremendous war, but I hope that the Union will be saved. For if it goes smash, we will see hard times. We think that we see hard times now, but it is nothing now to what it will be if the war goes on. I hope that you and all of your neighbors are for the Union. Trouts Hill and Guyandotte is for secession. Trouts Hill is called [Sodom] and Guyandotte is called [Gomorrah] here among us Union men. We can't find a name that suits them better...[89]

On May 23, 1861, the voters of Virginia ratified the Ordinance of Secession. The citizens of Cabell and Wayne counties, however, voted overwhelmingly against the measure, as had their delegates to the Richmond Convention. Granville Parker maintained that the "arrogant assumption of the Secessionists has wounded the Virginia pride, and aroused a patriotism and heroism, hitherto dormant, in the humble, inexperienced masses."[90]
The *Wheeling Intelligencer*, a staunch Northern supporter, declared that the results were deceptive as Guyandotte was "a hot bed of secession and the southern folks do about as they please." Guyandotte voted for secession 69-31, the only town on the Ohio River to do so, and the "pomp and circumstance of glorious war" was everywhere. The *Ironton Register* added, "The secessionists rule there, supreme. The Secession flag has floated there, for nearly two months."[91]
A correspondent to the *Richmond Dispatch* wrote from Guyandotte on May 24, reflecting the secessionist perspective:

It may not be uninteresting to you in these perilous times to hear a word from your friends in some of the border counties, or those counties bordering on the Ohio river, and I believe the little town of Guyandotte is justly entitled to the name of the banner town on the Ohio river. You have heard before this that a few weeks since the loyal citizens to the proud Commonwealth of Virginia hoisted to the breeze the flag of the Southern Confederacy, coupled with and bearing the significant motto of the State, 'Sic Semper Tyrannis,' and she flutters to the great discomfiture of many a tyrant who views with (as they term it) 'holy horror,' 'the beginning of the end.' But Guyandotte still lives, and her vote on yesterday is one in comparison of which she may justly feel proud.[92]

A Wayne County resident made several observations about the Ohio River town, writing "Guyandotte, the river town of that county, has for weeks been a foul nest of hot-headed secessionists, and they have had things pretty much their own way. The wisest and most violent ones are Northern men by birth." Guyandotte, however, was the one bright spot for Confederate supporters, as a large majority of voters from Cabell and Wayne counties voted against the Ordinance of Secession. The writer noted that Cabell County "goes 650 majority for the Union," and observed that the county "usually polls eight to nine hundred votes."[93]

According to this observer, the election in Wayne County "was the most peaceable one we have had for years." Although the exact returns had not been reported as late as May 25, it appeared Wayne County had also opposed the ordinance of secession by a majority of more than five hundred out of less than eight hundred votes. In the eight voting precincts, the strongest sentiment in favor of the ordinance was at Wayne Courthouse, but according to this correspondent, no precinct gave a majority for secession. An observer wrote,

> The large majority for Union was rather unexpected, although, some work had been done. There were a great many uninformed on the matter in issue, who were inclined in their hearts to stick by the Stars and Stripes, but who have been made to believe that everything in the South was going for secession, and it would, therefore, be for their interest to vote for the ordinance. They got a little light, and voted Union, or not at all on the ordinance.[94]

A mass meeting was scheduled for May 28 at which delegates to the Second Wheeling Convention, scheduled to begin on June 11, would be nominated. "There is considerable enthusiasm," wrote a Wayne Countian, "on the subject of a division of the State. The honest and conscientious farming population are, some of them, deterred by the secession threat of vengeance for acting in such a treasonable scheme."[95]

On the following day, residents of Lawrence County, Ohio, were greatly alarmed by reports that a group of secessionists from Guyandotte were about to cross the Ohio River and attack Proctorville, also known as Quaker Bottom. Apparently a Guyandotte man had asked a friend from that community to purchase some goods for him in Cincinnati. When the goods arrived, the townspeople "encouraged" him to hold the goods as contraband. When this news reached Guyandotte, tempers flared, and some of the town's citizens threatened to cross the river and take the goods by force. Word quickly spread throughout Lawrence County and Ohio men began gathering to repel the "invasion." A correspondent reported:

10 o'clock, night, all quiet, 174 troops on duty in Proctorsville, and about 50 more stationed above and below, watching the movements of the enemy. We are just informed that a company of Virginia 'State troops' marched through Barboursville, today, for Guyandotte. An express was also dispatched from Guyandotte for the 'State troops' in Camp at Buffalo, on the Kanawha. And two rebels passed up river, supposed to be bound for 'Jenkinses,' (the seat of A. G. Jenkins, late Secession Congressman) for consultation, and for the company, it is said, Jenkins has organized.[96]

Toward the end of May, the steamer *Ben Franklin* passed Guyandotte as it moved along the Ohio River. One of those aboard observed, "The secession flag which has been flying for some time at Guyandotte, was no where to be seen. It is supposed that the close proximity of the Federal troops had something to do with its sudden disappearance."[97]

On June 1, Captain Willis's Home Guard company from Getaway, Ohio, advanced to the town of Burlington and disarmed African American citizens in Fayette Township. About forty rifles, shotguns, pistols, and knives were seized, causing some hard feelings among the residents. Apparently, the Home Guard company intended to borrow the weapons until they could procure their own, an agreement acceptable to most, but one which was apparently not communicated to some of the Burlington men. "Those who understood that the guns were wanted for the defense of the country, I believe, were satisfied," Isaac M. Ryan of Fayette Township observed, but in some cases, the Home Guard did not explain properly the reasons for seizing these private weapons and to the victims it seemed "like robbery."[98]

On June 6, the *Ironton Register* reported:

The Secession Flag, which for weeks insultingly floated at Guyandotte, was taken down some ten days ago, by citizens there – some say by the Union men; others, by the Secessionists. At any rate, there was terror in Guyandotte, after the formidable demonstrations of defense made at Proctorsville, on May 25; and we learn reliably that some twenty families left Guyandotte, the first of last week, for fear of an 'invasion' from Ohio. If the people of Guyandotte keep that traitor flag down, and attend to their own affairs, they need not be at all afraid of trouble from loyal citizens of the Government.[99]

A week later, the *Ironton Register* described the unsettled conditions in the county:

On Monday, 3d inst., the Virginia treason act was read at the Cabell Court House, Barboursville, by which it made treason to speak in favor of the Union; and we have been informed that some 75 Virginia Union men who attended a flag raising at Haskellville, in this county, on the 1st inst., were indicted for treason; whether true or not, great alarm was occasioned among these men. Also we are informed that a very onerous poll tax – reported at $10 per head – has been levied for the benefit of the Secession cause…At all events, there is a 'reign of terror' in that part of Western Virginia nearest us, and large numbers of individuals and families of Union sentiments, are being driven out.[100]

The same issue noted that "Secession is now rampant in the lower part of Western Virginia – at Charleston, and below the Kanawha. Many Union men have given in, and are now under the control of the Secessionists, while hundreds are fleeing – many crossing the Ohio into Gallia and Lawrence counties, and some going down the river on boats..."[101]

In response to Virginia's passage of the Ordinance of Secession, the Second Wheeling Convention began on June 11, 1861. Albert Laidley of Cabell County attended this convention but was not seated as a delegate. W. W. Brumfield and William Copley were delegates representing Wayne County. On June 14, an ordinance was adopted which provided for the organization of what became known as the Restored Government of Virginia, which was recognized by President Lincoln and Congress as the government for the entire state. At the first General Assembly of the Restored Government at Wheeling, Cabell County was represented in the Senate by Andrew Flesher and in the lower house by Edward Wright. William Ratliff of Wayne County served as a member of the Assembly. Francis H. Pierpont of Fairmont was elected to serve as governor of the Union government of Virginia.[102]

On June 21, George Walton of Quaker Bottom, Ohio, across the Ohio River from Guyandotte, informed John S. Carlile, soon to represent Virginia in the United States Senate, that

> the origin of terror paralys every effort for the redemtion as yet. Many have and are yet daily being driven to Ohio for protection and are ready to follow a leader to quash the rebels or sacrifise their lives. They can not meet on the 'Va soil' to organize or to drill. Arms would be taken from them as soon as the traitors knew of their having them, unless they could be organized under cover of the Stripes and then quietly cross, and so form a nucleus around which the Union men could rally. They could then soon oust the rebel officers and inaugurate law and order.[103]

Walton believed he could raise up to 500 men for the Union army "to be armed and equiped by the state and encamped at Guyandotte or vicinity to protect the Union men of Cabell Wayne, Logan, Boone, & Wyoming counties, oust the Rebel officers and inaugurate law & order compel Jenkins & Co to 'vamose' or to 'dance the sober jig' to the tune of Hail Columbia." Two men, including Nelson Cox, who was raised in Cabell County, were well versed in military tactics and anxious to raise companies. Walton noted, "It is with difficulty that the boys of the county (Lawrence, Ohio) especially of Virginia desent can be restrained from going over and executing summary venjince on the rebels who are driving their friends from their homes and destroying their property." The Ohio men wanted good rifles, "as the enemy are sharp shooters and our boys are rifle shots too so the game might be played both ways."[104]

A letter was sent to the delegates at the Second Wheeling Convention on June 24 from a committee of Union citizens in Cabell County:

> In consequence of the reign of terror which prevails here at present, it is deemed inexpedient for persons or families to hold or receive the office of Delegates to the Wheeling Convention lest some misfortune should befall either them or their property. We have therefore appointed B. D. McGinnis, of Wayne County, as alternate, to fill the vacancy occasioned by the absence of our proper Delegate, to represent us in your Convention, and earnestly desire and trust that you will receive him as such, and honor him with a seat among you.[105]

In Ceredo, a resident wrote, "The 'reign of terror' has not yet commenced in this county, but the traitors are trying it, and would, if they dared, begin to arrest and drive off Union men." Excitement had been at a fever pitch for three weeks, distracting citizens from conducting business and tending their crops. Union supporters were aware of the Confederate camp in the Kanawha Valley, as the secessionists were constantly recruiting in western Virginia. The residents of Ceredo held out hope that troops would be sent to Wayne County but recognized that Union men were on the defensive across the region. This meant that the Federal supporters in Ceredo would have to fend for themselves, and, according to one resident, "a good many will resist to the death."[106]

At a meeting held in Wayne County on June 26, with R. T. Luther serving as president and B. D. McGinnis as secretary, citizens petitioned Governor Pierpont for assistance:

> Honorable Sir Whereas, we, the Union citizens of Wayne County, for some time past, have been daily threatened by the Rebels in our midst, with the destruction of life, property, or subjugation to the rule of the so called Confederate States; by the instrumentality of an armed force. We, therefore, as loyal citizens professing allegiance both to Federal Constitution and the State of Virginia, under the Provisional Government now being established, do, most humbly, petition your Excellency that, an armed force of U. S. troops may be sent as speedily as possible among us, and stationed at Amacetta, 8 miles from Guyandotte, to protect us from the insults and outrages of Secessionists.[107]

In late June 1861, Captain Albert G. Jenkins and about fifty mounted Confederates left their camp in the Kanawha Valley and headed toward Point Pleasant. They seized two Union sympathizers on June 29 before returning to Camp Tompkins. Colonel Jesse S. Norton and about one hundred Federal troops left their post at Gallipolis, crossed the river, and pursued the Confederates as far as Thirteen Mile Creek. Colonel Norton then led the Union force to the Jenkins plantation at Green Bottom. One soldier noted, "Jenkins has turned his farm into a camp for the rebels, and as there was a lot of fine horses and cattle found there, they were declared contraband of war and are now at the disposition of the Governor." Eight men who were working on the plantation were detained but not arrested. The Union soldiers then destroyed crops and gathered horses and corn which were sent to Gallipolis.

Although Norton and his men were unable to overtake the Confederate raiders, they did arrest about thirty secessionists from the Mason County area. These men were sent to Camp Chase Prison in Columbus, Ohio, and were among the first of many western Virginians incarcerated there. The *Wheeling Intelligencer* observed, "They think it hard that they should be taken away from their families, and one or two of them are in real distress."[108]

Governor Dennison soon ordered that the men be returned to Colonel Norton.

> The reason assigned is, that the Confederate authorities have released and sent home the two members of the Virginia State Convention, and other Union men, they had taken as prisoners near Point Pleasant, Va., and as the men sent to Columbus were only held as hostages for the safety of the Union men taken there, they were, of course, released. They were sent to Gallipolis, consigned to Col. Norton, who will doubtless order their release.[109]

Kellian V. Whaley wrote Governor Francis Pierpont on June 29 to offer a general recommendation for J. C. Wheeler, whose "desire is to serve his country." For more than twelve years Wheeler had lived in Cabell and Wayne counties, and for a time he had published a newspaper, the *Guyandotte Unionist*, which had "done much at that time to desseminate Union sentiments in our corner of Virginia." Whaley noted that Wheeler had served for about three years as acting clerk of the circuit and county courts of Wayne County, and "while he held that position the Union men were safe from frauds & tricks in election."[110]

Wheeler "has been a persistent & consistent Union man," Whaley wrote, "and aided the party much in the late struggle..." While many Union men had given in to the wishes of the secessionists in the area, Wheeler

> withstood an insiduous unprincipled & cowardly sneaking warfare from the secessionists who were the office holders and politicians & their tools around the Court House and who were anxious to get him out of the way and not seeing that he could do any thing further for the cause there he moved to this his native town (Portsmouth), but with a promise to the Union men of Wayne that as soon as he could get his family comfortably located he would do whatever he could to aid them should they be threatened with imminent danger.[111]

Wheeler had "procured the promise of assistance" from Home Guards in the Ironton and Portsmouth areas in the event they were needed but sought legal authority from Washington and Wheeling. Like others in the region at this time, Whaley asked Pierpont to direct correspondence to an address in Ohio, as the mail in western Virginia had ceased.

Kellian V. Whaley had lived in Point Pleasant prior to the war, working in the lumber industry. He was elected to Congress in 1860 to represent Virginia's 12th congressional district and began his term on March 4, 1861. He soon became deeply involved in organizing Union resistance in western Virginia.

On June 29, B. D. McGinnis wrote to the Central Committee of the Reorganized Government of Virginia, which had met from June 11-25 and adjourned until August. McGinnis was selected by Unionists in Cabell County to fill the vacancy in the restored state government "occasioned by the reign of terror in that county." McGinnis had started to Wheeling but encountering low water and learning that the convention had adjourned, he returned to Cabell County. He did send the certificate from the county committee appointing both he and Edward D. Wright as delegates. McGinnis had been informed that the Wheeling Convention would meet again in August and asked that their appointments be approved by the proper committee.[112]

McGinnis informed the Union leaders in Wheeling,

> The people of Cabell wish me to represent to you and also to Governor Pierpont, the deplorable condition into which they are thrown by the depredations and brutal outrages committed by the armed bands that are ravaging the entire country days and nights, while their condition became more and more lamentable. Can they get help from the General Government. There are several Companies, at no great distance in Ohio, that are willing to assist them when authorized by the proper authorities. I have been especially cited to a Regmen at Oak Hill, Lawrence County Ohio ready drilled, armed and equiped, and desirous to enter Virginia at any time. Why can not they be ordered to Guyandotte? They only want orders till they will be on the march and in one days time can be at their destination.[113]

B. D. McGinnis wrote a note to Governor Pierpont on July 1 which accompanied a petition by Union citizens of Wayne County, "praying your Excellency to send Federal troops to protect them against the outrages of armed bands now roving among them." McGinnis also noted the anxious condition of the populace of Cabell County and stated his belief that if Federal soldiers were stationed at Guyandotte, "it will, I think, answer the purpose of both counties." Union troops were stationed in Oak Hill, Ohio, a day's march from western Virginia, and there were "many Home guards along the Ohio River willing to pass over at any notice to assist Virginians, but lack propper authority."[114]

On this same day, Governor Pierpont received a desperate entreaty from Hiram Welch of the Supreme Order of the Star Spangled Banner. Welch had learned of Pierpont's election and informed him of "the miserable codishion of the union men in Cabel and Boone Cos. We are driven from hour homes in Va a great many of us for owning sentiments independently." He complained about "the rebleous renogades scotin throw our countrys steeling" and requested that Pierpont "forward us ade as quick as practible both men and arms."[115]

Z. D. Ramsdell, one of the early settlers of Ceredo, wrote Governor Pierpont on July 2 regarding circumstances in Cabell and Wayne counties. According to Ramsdell, Confederate forces in the Kanawha Valley had been reinforced, were arresting Union men within ten miles of Ceredo, and "are determined to take posesion of this & Cabel

Ceredo businessman Zophar D. Ramsdell. Credit: Jack L. Dickinson.

Co in a few days..." The Confederates were scouting in Wayne County and had been prevented from arresting Union men only by the presence of local militia armed with the few rifles and muskets they had collected. Ramsdell had received reliable information "that they intend to come upon us now with a force that we can not resist & then establish a camp either here or at Guyandott." He requested that a regiment of Federal troops be sent immediately, believing it would not only lend protection to Wayne and Cabell counties, but also cut off communication between the Confederates in the Kanawha Valley and those still lingering in the westernmost part of Virginia. Ramsdell asserted that a strong Union force would give the protection necessary to enable the formation of loyal regiments from Virginia and Kentucky. He avowed that with this safeguard and sufficient arms, "we will show you that we will not onely defend ourselves but you may safely count on Wayne Co to assist in puting down the most acursed plot ever invented by man."[116]

On the same day, John Adams of Amacetta in Wayne County informed Governor Pierpont that Wayne "is emphatically a union county but now we are tyranized over by Letcher's minions I mean his military officers who all happen to be rebels. They threaten all kinds of indignities." Adams, who lived on Twelve Pole Creek about seven miles from Ceredo, had moved to the area from Vermont three years earlier as part of Eli Thayer's emigration efforts. A farmer and trader, he had remained in western Virginia despite the fact that "most of the N. E. men who came out here 3 yrs ago when I did, left Ceredo, through fear & threats."[117]

The precinct in which he lived was overwhelmingly Union, and "the rebels," Adams noted, "say I am the one that made it so." Adams faced constant threats from Confederates, and a guard stationed at his home each night observed mounted horsemen and wagons continually traveling along the road in the darkness. A Home Guard unit had been organized, but they were for the most part unarmed and unable to defend themselves. Still, a United States flag flew at Amacetta, while secessionist flags which had "hung to the breeze" at Trout's Hill and at Guyandotte had been taken down. Adams believed the county justices would take the oath of allegiance, but the Union men of Wayne County wanted those who had voted in favor of secession to be removed from office. They also wished to see the Confederate leaders of Wayne hanged for committing treason and requested Federal troops to offer protection and arms to help defend themselves.[118]

A number of citizens were forced to flee Cabell County to avoid apprehension by Confederate cavalry. On July 3, 1861, Guyandotte resident Granville Parker left the area half an hour before some of the Border Rangers arrived to take him prisoner. Other Union men in Cabell County, including future General John S. Witcher, were also compelled to cross the river into Ohio during the early part of the month.[119]

Governor Francis H. Pierpont wrote to B. D. McGinnis on Independence Day regarding the recent proceedings by citizens of Wayne County: "I exceedingly regret to hear of the cruelty practised by the rebels upon our Union and loyal men in that quarter. You and your friends are authorized to enter the territory of Virginia at such times and places as may be deemed advisable, and suitably chastise the rebels and give peace or and protection to our loyal and good people of Wayne, or any other county in the state." Pierpont closed by thanking McGinnis "most cordially for the solicitude you and your friends of Ohio manifest for our success in suppressing the vile insurrection gotten up by the hot heads of the Southern States." He also informed him that if Federal troops held Point Pleasant, McGinnis was to report to the Union commander there.[120]

On July 9, B. D. McGinnis again contacted Governor Pierpont:

This is to say that the citizens of Cabell & Wayne Counties have petitioned every authority known in the Government praying for protection against the marauding bands plundering the counties west of Kanawha River, but there is still no relief – their petitions have been spurned while they are left the prey of the ravagers.

Confidence is lost, to many, of the efficiency of the General Government. Many of our best citizens have either been captured by the Rebels or forced to flee the county. We can depend no more upon the officers of the Gen. Government for protection. They have kept us hoping for help till nothing but ruin stares us in the face.

The people of Ohio have looked with sympathy upon our constitution, till they too have become impatient, and now offer their service to relieve us. Can their cares be legalised. If so attend to it. Give the authority, we shall ask no more. We can route the camp at Kanha while the officers of the Government, are consulting upon the best combination for a morning drink, before making ready to advance upon the enemy. Legalise the course & we will trouble you no more.

The Ohio boys are organised in home guards – Can't go to Virginia without permission.

They will act only temporarily with an understanding to return home, when the route is made.

McGinnis closed with a pointed barb against the Virginia governor, writing, "Would to God we were under [Ohio] Govenor Dennison's care – then the ravages would cease."[121]

On the morning of July 11, 1861, Captain Albert G. Jenkins and the Border Rangers were near his home above Green Bottom when they discovered the steamer *Fannie McBurnie* moving up the Ohio River. The Border Rangers dismounted, slipped down a ravine, and hid in a pawpaw thicket. With his men concealed, Jenkins hailed the steamboat, which then moved toward the Virginia shore near his plantation. As the *Fannie McBurnie* approached the riverbank, Jenkins whistled, and, as James D. Sedinger, a member of the unit, recalled,

> When she made the bank we charged her. Old Capt. Blagg turned to Mr. Holloway the pilot and told him to back her out after hiding behind the smoke stack of the boat. The pilot told him to come up and take the wheel if he wanted her backed out. We went aboard and searched the boat and took everything we could find that would do a soldier service.[122]

According to another account, Jenkins swore "terribly" at the captain and pilot for the slowness of their movements and threatened their lives. The soldiers took four revolvers and a case of swords, and Captain Jenkins seized pistols from two acquaintances, C. G. Hawley of Ironton and George Willard of the Iron Bank. He told Hawley to call on H. S. Neal, his former agent who lived in Ironton, and he would reimburse him for the pistol. The boat was then permitted to go on its way.[123]

James D. Sedinger, a member of the Border Rangers, recalled, "We mounted our horses and rode down to the Captain's house. When we were about one hundred yards Mrs. Jenkins met us and the Capt. proposed three cheers for his little wife. The boys responded right nobly to the call and made the welkin ring."[124]

After the raid on the *Fannie McBurnie*, the *Wheeling Intelligencer* commented,

> If we are not mistaken Jenkins is a man of great wealth. He grazes a great number of cattle, which can be seen by the hundreds in abundant pastures along the Ohio, belonging to the Jenkins estate. These Fannie McBurnie folks can get their money if they want it.[125]

A day after the action at Green Bottom, General Jacob D. Cox received a telegraph from Captain John H. Dickerson in Cincinnati: "A boat was seized near Gyandotte by Virginians within the last two days. Yesterday I sent Cricket No. 2 & The Collier both loaded with supplies for you. Send the Hero or some other steamer down to meet them with a guard if possible."[126]

The *Ironton Register* recorded:

> It is well known that Guyandotte, Va., has been the meanest 'Secession Hole' on the Ohio river, that the Secessionists there, under the lead of A. G. Jenkins, late member of Congress from that district, have for a long time been carrying

things with a high hand, committing diverse outrages on Union men in that vicinity, and driving from their homes many old and respectable citizens of that portion of Virginia for no other crime than that they did not wish to destroy their Government. Appeal has often been made by Virginians themselves to the U. S. and Ohio military authorities for the protection of Union men in that quarter, but to no purpose.[127]

Help, however, was finally on the way.

4
The Battle of Barboursville

"We were exposed to a galling fire for the space of about half a mile. I saw there was no means by which I could obtain possession of the place except by storming at the point of the bayonet. I therefore ordered the charge to be made...After scaling the heights the bat[tal]ion rallied and formed in line on the summit, where we flaunted our flag the day being won by us."

Lieutenant Colonel George W. Neff, 2nd Kentucky Infantry
Report on the battle of Barboursville

In early July 1861 at Gallipolis, Ohio, four infantry regiments, a troop of cavalry, and a battery of artillery under the command of General Jacob D. Cox prepared to invade western Virginia. Their mission was to drive the Confederates under General Henry A. Wise from the Kanawha Valley. General George B. McClellan, who was in command of the Department of the Ohio, ordered Cox to "beat up Barboursville, Guyandotte, etc., so that the entire course of the Ohio may be secured to us." Cox began his advance on July 11, 1861, and upon learning of the Confederate raid on the *Fannie McBurnie*, he ordered the 2nd Kentucky Infantry to Guyandotte with orders to "suppress any insurgents in that neighborhood."[128]

Stating his reasons for detaching the regiment in a dispatch to McClellan dated July 14, Cox wrote:

> Knowing that we had considerable shipments of U.S. stores on the river, and that the river commerce would be secure, I was unwilling to leave that part of the country exposed, and thought it my duty to protect it, even at the expense of a temporary scattering of forces. I find that it has had no bad effect thus far. The rebels believe, as I am well informed, that my force in this valley is as great as the whole will be when concentrated, and suppose the Guyandotte force to be an additional column advancing, and I am confident of effecting the concentration in time for any necessity I may have, with the additional advantage of having produced a good moral effect upon the lower counties by the march of troops that way.[129]

General Jacob D. Cox commanded the Kanawha Brigade of the Department of Ohio and led the second prong of the Federal invasion into western Virginia. Credit: Massachusetts Commandery Military Order of the Loyal Legion and the US Army Military History Institute.

Colonel William E. Woodruff of Louisville, Kentucky, a Mexican War veteran and an ardent Union supporter, recruited the 2nd Kentucky Infantry at Camp Clay near Cincinnati. This unit was mustered into service on June 13, 1861, and would receive its baptism of fire exactly one month later. On the day the regiment departed from Cincinnati, a business owner assaulted one of the soldiers with a tumbler. When Woodruff learned of the attack, he marched to the coffee house, confronted the man with drawn sword, and "nearly severed his left hand from his arm."[130]

Six steamboats departed from Cincinnati on July 9 carrying the 1st and 2nd Kentucky Infantry regiments up the Ohio toward the Kanawha Valley. On the following day they passed Ironton, Ohio, where a "large concourse of people assembled on the bank to greet them and the thunder of our artillery was not light."[131]

As they neared Guyandotte on July 11, Colonel Woodruff ordered the 2nd Kentucky Infantry to prepare to march. The entire regiment was under arms in five minutes and the boat landed five miles below the town. Captain Albert Gallatin Jenkins and the Border Rangers were rumored to be in Guyandotte, so three of the companies were detailed to seize the suspension bridge, while Woodruff led the balance at "double quick" time.

Although no Confederate troops remained in Guyandotte, about forty "notorious Secessionists" were reportedly taken prisoner and a number of weapons were seized. The bridge was turned into a guard house, and the prisoners were driven onto it with a Federal company stationed on each end. When asked how he would prevent the secessionists from escaping the open bridge, Woodruff remarked "that if they wanted to jump off they could go down 70 feet without hurting his feelings." The officers were directed to quarter themselves in the ladies' parlor of a hotel, where the proprietor was reportedly happy to take the oath of allegiance.[132]

Shortly after taking possession of Guyandotte, six companies with a brass six-pounder "borrowed from Ohio" were ordered to set up a camp, named Camp Crittenden, about one mile outside the town in a wheat field owned by a Confederate supporter. Four companies remained in Guyandotte, and pickets occupied all approaches to the town. The colonel administered the oath of allegiance to several secessionists, although most had left the area. Woodruff also began organizing the Home Guard, exhorting the remaining citizens to join and support this military unit for the county's safety. Company A captured a "rebel markers flag," which was sent to Cincinnati. A critical correspondent for the *Cincinnati Commercial* wrote, "The secseshers must have been hard up for silk when it was manufactured. Its material is the cast off bonnet ribbon of some Southern belle, whose skill with the needle was about on a par with her patriotism."[133]

"As soon as it became known that our soldiers were in the town in force," this same writer observed, "the Stars and Stripes which, under the reign of terror, inaugurated by Jenkins, had been hid away, were brought out, and in a few hours they floated from nearly every house in town." Several small boats crossed the Ohio from Proctorville. In one of them was a uniformed Home Guard, their color-bearer a 52-year-old woman by the name of Caroline White. White was a milliner from Guyandotte who had been driven from her home, "her only crime an unconcealed devotion to the Union." When the boat landed, White presented an American flag to the Woodward Guards (Company D) and stated, "I thought I would live to see the time when I could again carry the Stars and Stripes in Guyandotte." White was loudly cheered by the Union soldiers, and "each one shook hands with the old lady, and received her blessing."[134]

Colonel William Woodruff, 2nd Kentucky Infantry. Credit: Massachusetts Commandery Military Order of the Loyal Legion and the US Army Military History Institute.

A newspaper correspondent penned his observations of the citizens of Cabell County:

> There is a class, I have encountered every step here, whom I can describe in no other way than as being opinionless, and resigned to the success of either party. They grant any request from either side, with cold and suspicious passiveness, that shows plainly how well their minds have been disabused of being freemen in a Republican country. They treat us kindly, though with suspicion, while it is evident they have a hatred for the rebels.

He also noted that the Union men in the county were "as violent as the secessionists profess to be, great numbers of them flocking to camp every day, and others, driven

Richard Lunsford, who lived on Tom's Creek, commanded a militia company at Barboursville. Credit: Special Collections Department, Marshall University.

from their homes, following the regiment, rifle in hand."[135]

Meanwhile, word spread throughout the area that Union troops had invaded Cabell County. Although the 120th Virginia Militia had apparently ceased to exist by this time, a number of residents began gathering in the village of Barboursville and prepared to contest the advance of the Federal invaders. These men were untrained and unprepared for the experience they were soon to confront. Some were equipped with "flintlock, muzzle-loading rifles loaded with one ball and three buckshot." Others carried shotguns, blunderbuses, squirrel rifles, and double-barrel pistols. Their only objectives were to defend their homes and families and prevent the occupation of the county seat. Rumors spread that the Union troops at Guyandotte "were stripping women and children and whipping them in presence of their defenseless husbands and fathers, and committing other atrocities upon them."[136]

The men served under various leaders. Richard Lunsford commanded some men from the area around Poore's Hill, while "Mexico" Smith, who lived on Long Branch, organized some of his neighbors and led them to Barboursville. Dr. A. B. McGinnis of Guyandotte claimed to be the ranking militia officer and tried to take charge, but it was clear that this small, disorganized band of Cabell Countians would not be enough.

A Guyandotte citizen wrote a message to Colonel Milton J. Ferguson, urging him to assemble the Wayne County militia (167th Virginia Militia) at Barboursville. Jamison Spurlock, a resident of Guyandotte, was chosen to carry the message through Union lines to Wayne Court House. Spurlock slipped out of Guyandotte on the night of July 11 and rode to the home of his father, Reverend Stephen Spurlock, on Beech Fork, arriving about midnight. Fisher Bowen rode the remaining ten miles to Wayne Court House where word of the invasion quickly spread.

Reverend Spurlock addressed a gathering at Keyser's Store on Beech Fork. He told the men, "Boys, all go. If you can't get guns, use hickory clubs; for one Southern man is worth six Yankees." The Wayne militia assembled early the next day and began the march to Barboursville, led by Colonel Milton J. Ferguson. Colonel Joseph J. Mansfield accompanied the militia, riding a gray horse furnished by his neighbor, Hugh Bowen. Mansfield had reportedly made a speech at Trout's Hill in which he said "he would die and go to h___, before he would live under Lincoln's Administration."[137]

Men began gathering throughout Cabell and Wayne counties to repel the invasion, but the uncertainty of the situation led to some strange encounters. Thomas Thompson and Rodrick Noel were at the home of Fredrick D. Beuhring on Four Pole

Creek. The men left Beuhring's home and walked about four miles to the Mount Union meeting house where they met a party of seven others, including Frank Eves and John Jarrell. Thompson, Noel, and Beuhring began walking away but were followed by Jarrell and his companions, who ordered them to halt. They ignored the demand and continued their journey for about five hundred yards

> when we were again ordered by the same company (they having followed us) to halt when F. D. Buhring, who was carrying a rifle gun turned about and replied 'halt, it is' at the same time drawing his ram rod from his gun when there was two shots fired by some of the party following us. Buhring then immediately leveled his gun & napped it at them, and at the same time two more of the same party leveled their guns at Thos Thompson when he drew up and simul[t]aneously fired both the barrels of his gun at them – not knowing at the time that either shot took effect. The party then retired, and we continued on our journey without any further molestation.[138]

At a gathering on Beech Fork, Reverend Stephen Spurlock urged Wayne County men to oppose the Federals at Barboursville, telling them, "Boys, all go. If you can't get guns, use hickory clubs; for one Southern man is worth six Yankees" Credit: Special Collections Department, Marshall University.

On the night of July 11, the Kentucky regiment at Camp Crittenden was uneasy about the militia camp outside of Barboursville. A correspondent for the *Cincinnati Commercial* described the troops' nervousness:

> Our position there was not a strong one, and much apprehension was felt the first night concerning an attack from the rebels encamped some six miles distant, at Cabell C. H. (or Barboursville, as the town is called.) Our men were aroused by the long roll half a dozen times before daylight, and formed in line of battle on the parade ground and the pickets alarmed by stragglers through the adjoining wooded hills, fired their guns and withdrew to camp. No enemy appeared, however, and the next day our position was made comparatively secure, by the arrival of the balance of the regiment, which evacuated Guyandotte, leaving a small detachment to hold the place.[139]

Colonel Woodruff was apprehensive that the rebels would immediately attack his force. He urgently requested that the 1st Kentucky Infantry be sent to reinforce him. Captain J. H. Wheeler, who commanded Company A of the 1st Kentucky, reported to his commanding officer, Colonel J. V. Guthrie:

According to your orders I proceeded to Guyandotte on 12 of July. On my way down I was hailed by citizens of Virginia at or near Jenkins farm and asked to protect them against three or four hundred rebels. I landed with forty men and dispersed them. On arriving at Guyandotte Col. Woodruff of the 2nd Ky. Regt. informed me that he required my assistance to guard the town of Guyandotte as he knew that he was to be attacked that night. I complied with his request...[140]

F. D. Beuhring of Cabell County was arrested and sent to Wheeling shortly after the battle. Credit: Special Collections Department, Marshall University.

Lieutenant Colonel George W. Neff and a small force of Union soldiers camped on the farm of Albert Jenkins before moving on to Guyandotte. Neff informed Virginia Jenkins that if he caught her husband, he would hang him. Mrs. Jenkins replied that her husband would treat Neff as a gentleman if the two were ever to meet. Meanwhile, the 2nd Kentucky Infantry continuously scouted the area along the Guyandotte River. Skirmishing parties left on foot and returned on "nags" confiscated from farms owned by secessionists. Union supporters' property was carefully respected, while they in turn volunteered goods and information to the Federal soldiers.

Woodruff continued to gather information about the rebel camp from scouts and Union sympathizers. On Friday afternoon, July 12, Woodruff sent Matt Noble toward Barboursville to investigate the camp. Just below the village, Noble was fired on several times by rebel pickets. He escaped to high ground but lost his horse in the process. Noble managed to conceal himself until dark, when he returned to Guyandotte and informed Colonel Woodruff that reinforcements were arriving steadily in the village. Woodruff could not determine the number of Confederate defenders or the strength of their position, but he was certain that he must immediately attack the camp.[141]

At midnight, the men of the 2nd Kentucky Infantry awakened, and Companies A, B, D, F and K were "drawn up in line." Colonel Woodruff instructed them

as to the manner of marching, and cautioned to pay strict attention to the commands of their officers. To company B he said: 'Company B – representatives of Louisville – you about going into your first battle; I know you will sustain the reputation of your Kentucky home; obey the commands of your officers and you will drive your enemy before you.' At the mention of 'Louisville' the boys could hardly suppress their hurrahs..."[142]

Woodruff then turned command of the force of 316 soldiers over to Lieutenant Colonel George W. Neff, who "proceeded in accordance with your orders to take possession of Barboursville." The Union troops began their advance at about 3:00 a.m., marching along the road connecting Guyandotte and the county seat.[143]

It had been a restless Friday night in the village as the townspeople and their "army" of local citizens prepared to resist the impending Union advance. The Wayne County militia had arrived in Barboursville on Friday afternoon. Many of the men from both counties slept on the floor of the Cabell County Courthouse. During the night, frightened pickets reported that the Federal troops were entering the village. Someone accidentally discharged a gun and panic quickly spread through the ranks, causing some of the local farmers to head for home. One citizen soldier recalled, "Wash Gilkinson fainted when we started downstairs." Order was soon restored and the men tried to get some rest. At daylight, many of the defenders were searching for breakfast when word came that the Union regiment was nearing the village. The town's women and children sought refuge at the farm of Grandma Blake.[144]

A Cabell County farmer named James Reynolds stopped for breakfast at the William C. Miller home on Main Street. He and his sons lived up the Mud River on Dry Creek, below Mud Bridge. Reynolds, who was in his late fifties, was on his way to the ridge to join the militia who were gathering there on this foggy morning. Miller tried to talk Reynolds out of joining the younger men, but he persistently rose and headed toward the militia camp, which overlooked the confluence of the Mud and Guyandotte rivers.[145]

The ridge defended by the citizen force was an ideal defensive position, "inaccessible on all sides, and commanding a view for two miles around of a magnificent level plain, with all its roads in full sight, until they dwindled into the distant forests." Prior to the onset of war, workers had begun cutting into the ridge preparing a right-of-way for the C & O Railroad. This left forty-five-foot bluffs on either side of the cut. A few yards from the junction of the two rivers, a covered bridge spanned the Mud River, which the Union troops would have to cross before they could take the town. The militia removed about twenty feet of the planking from one side of the bridge, making the crossing extremely hazardous, as the 2nd Kentucky Infantry would soon discover.[146]

The Border Rangers were present, having marched from their camp at Coalsmouth to Barboursville in ten hours. Merchant George Thornburg of Barboursville stated that before the skirmish, he saw Captain Albert G. Jenkins standing on the corner opposite his store. Jenkins reportedly told another officer that they would meet the enemy outside the town, declaring, "These folks here are our friends."[147]

Although friends, Jenkins seized all the sugar, coffee, bacon, and flour from the store of Matthew Thompson in Barboursville. The Wayne County militia, upon their arrival in the village, "wanted many articles to fil out ther uniforms and haveing no money they walked in to Thomson store and helped themselves to [what] they wanted such as shoes hats pants flannels and various other sundries."[148]

The Sandy Rangers, a cavalry company from Wayne County led by Captain James Corns, also left Camp Tompkins and "marched to Barboursville to meet the foe." These men could be distinguished by the bright red flannel hunting shirts and caps (or bandannas) which they wore early in the war. "Mexico" Smith, who claimed to have commanded a company in the Mexican War, placed some of the Cabell County men in line on the hill. Colonel Milton J. Ferguson quickly rode up and said, "Gentlemen, this will not do, the way you are placed here; drop down, behind the hill and come up and command yourselves."[149]

Meanwhile, on the morning of July 13, 1861, the men of the 2nd Kentucky marched quietly along the road toward Barboursville. According to a Union correspondent who described the event, "It was proposed to make the attack at early daylight, but the deep silence observed along the route, together with the halts to send forward scouting parties, deferred their coming into sight of the enemy until the sun was two hours high." Neff and others, however, stated that they reached Barboursville just after sunrise.[150]

Lieutenant Colonel George Neff, 2nd Kentucky Infantry. Neff led the Federal force at the battle of Barboursville. Credit: Roger Hunt.

As the Federals filed around a hill near the village, the Confederate cavalry, "numbering about 150, under Jenkins, came in sight. Their long swords, glittering with borrowed pomp from the rays of the morning sun, looked truly magnificent." The Confederate horsemen withdrew at the sight of the Union column. Lieutenant Colonel George Neff described nearing the enemy position:

> I found the enemy in force said to be six hundred and ten (610) men, stationed upon a ridge 100 feet in height about 100 yards wide, all sides being almost inapproachable by a bluff bank, covered by and with trees, bushes and stones protecting the road for about ¾ of a mile.[151]

As the head of the Union column approached the bridge, one of the men observed that

> their infantry opened a murderous fire upon us. From every tree, bush, and stone, rifle and musket balls were literally showered upon us. On a hill,

southeast of the bridge, their main body formed in beautiful order, the front rank kneeling and the rear rank standing, and loaded and fired in rapid succession.[152]

One Union soldier, John Jordons of Company B, was killed instantly, and a number of others were wounded. Lieutenant Colonel George Neff reported they "were exposed to a galling fire for the space of about half a mile." As they reached the bridge, "we found the floor torn up, and one of our scouts on horseback rode in, his horse falling a distance of thirty feet, and himself catching on one of the joists." The Union troops frantically sought cover in and around the bridge. Meanwhile, all around the entrapped Federals, "bullets pelted, pattered, and whistled like a leaden hail-storm."[153]

Neff recorded,

I saw there was no means by which I could obtain possession of the place except by storming at the point of the bayonet. I therefore ordered the charge to be made, Company K being on the right. But in consequence of the refusal or neglect of the officers in command of Co. K to make the charge I ordered Co. A to take the right and charge which they did in a most gallant manner.[154]

The men from Cabell and Wayne counties were exultant at their initial success, and cheers and shouts rang down from the ridge. The Union troops from Company A responded with their own yells as they navigated the treacherous bridge deck in single file. As the Federals began to emerge from the covered bridge, they were met with another volley which was aimed too high. The Federals cleared the span and were "yelling and leaping like madmen. They turned suddenly up the side of the hill a charge bayonets, and literally dragging themselves up by bushes and jutting turf." The defenders were stunned by this sudden reversal and began to flee, singly at first and then in expanding clusters.[155]

One Cabell County man, George "Lucky" Savage, who had never seen a bayonet, described his experience: "By Gosh, Almighty, I loaded and fired till the Yankees began to load with butcher knives, then I thought it was time to be going. I turned and found I was by myself." As the 2nd Kentucky Infantry reached the crest of the ridge, they were fired on again with effect by some of the militia. It was their final volley of the day. The Federals charged and the militia "swayed for a moment, a leap was made from their flank and rear, and then the whole body scattered like sparks from a pinwheel..."[156]

George "Lucky" Savage, local resident who fled at the sight of "butcher knives" wielded by the 2nd Kentucky Infantry at Barboursville. Credit: Special Collections Department, Marshall University.

The Kentucky regiment was too winded to pursue the local defenders, but they continued to fire on the fleeing men. Colonel Joseph J. Mansfield fell or was knocked from his horse, but he was retrieved by some of his men, enabling him to make his escape. Another member of the local militia, Dave Dick, fell into the railroad cut, breaking a couple of ribs. Despite the pain, he was able to get up and run as the charge overwhelmed the locals.[157]

A young farmer named Chapman, who had been trapped behind the enemy along the Guyandotte River, broke from his cover and quickly caught up with his comrades. Another farmer mounted his horse, which was tied up in the ravine behind the ridge. Rattled by the excitement, he whipped and beat the poor animal until realizing he had forgotten to untie him.[158]

The Union soldiers claimed the citizen army was "making 'Flora Temple time' when they passed through the town. One of them was heard to shout something about the Federal troops having 'd____d long spears on their guns'." The militia fled into the hills behind Barboursville where they split into small groups. Mary Lunsford, the thirteen-year-old daughter of militia captain Richard Lunsford, lived with her family on Tom's Creek. She later recalled that morning:

> I heard the firing begin at Barboursville, at daylight, or a little after. I was building a fire in the stove. By the time breakfast was ready, men were coming from the fight. We served breakfast to the men. They wouldn't come in; they were so badly frightened, they preferred to wait in the cleared ground. Some ate running...Some had thrown away their guns. Mother asked them why they did it. They replied that it was because they were so heavy, they couldn't run.[159]

John W. Miller, the son of William C. Miller, who had constructed the courthouse in Barboursville, was sixteen years old at the time of the battle. He later wrote:

> My father didn't want me to join the army, because I was so young. However, when I found out that there would probably be a battle within sight of our house, I took a little double-barreled pistol I owned, and started down toward the probable battlefield. Sometimes you could pull one trigger and both barrels would go off, and sometimes you could pull both triggers and neither barrel would fire. Anyway, I felt there was not a man in either army armed as well as I. I would, I firmly believed, take this deadly weapon and go out and put an end to the war. Just before I reached the field of battle, I met the Confederates coming back – fast. I fell in line without firing a shot – and the war went on four long years.[160]

One of the retreating militia, Absalom Ballangee, tumbled into the railroad cut and broke his leg. Miller assisted the injured man up the hill to Grandma Blake's farm. Miller described Ballangee as

> the worst stove up man I ever saw. He had a little muzzle-loading shotgun...It

shot what looked to be about number eight birdshot. It was about the size of a present-day air rifle. I asked him if he thought he had got any of the Union men. He replied, 'I don't think so; I don't think I could quite reach them.'

Grandma Blake put the young man on a horse and took him three miles to a ferry which crossed the Guyandotte near Dusenberry's Mill.[161]

Border Ranger James D. Sedinger reported that the company "marched off the hill in order, without firing a gun and marched back to Coalsmouth without the loss of a man or horse. We took the fire of the regiment best. No one was hurt of the company." Before leaving the area, the Confederate cavalry companies gathered about a mile from the ridge and reportedly "waved their Secession flag at the victors on the hill."[162]

The Fairview Riflemen were sent from Camp Tompkins with an artillery piece to aid the local defenders but "arrived only in time to cover the retreat." The cavalry units withdrew to Coal Mountain, where they planned an ambush. The Kentucky regiment learned of the trap and succeeded in avoiding it, but the men would soon meet again on July 17 at the battle of Scary Creek, where Lieutenant Colonel George Neff was captured by Confederate troops. Border Ranger James D. Sedinger recalled: "the Capt. (Jenkins) dismounted took him by the hand and told him Mrs. Jenkins' words should be made good – that he should be treated gentlemanly and if we remember rightly he was paroled after having his wound dressed."[163]

The Union troops gathered up coats and weapons which had been thrown away by the retreating militia. The latter filled a wagon and included "all descriptions from the old fashioned flint lock horse pistol to a double barreled shot gun," constituting to the regiment "spoils of their victory." A correspondent noted, "Almost every man engaged in the attack has either some weapon, trinket, article of apparel found after the fight…About forty horses, left in the stables by the gallant 'five-to-one-sters,' are now in our possession."[164]

The sword of Colonel Joseph J. Mansfield was discovered on the battlefield by Private Isaac West of the Woodward Guards and brought to Cincinnati. It was described as an "antique looking specimen, rather too clumsy, we should say, for the delicate fingers of a 'chivalry'." It is quite possible Mansfield used the weapon during the battle. One man not listed in newspaper accounts as one of the wounded was Jacob Hurd Smith, who in 1900 was promoted to brigadier general in the United States Army. Smith received a saber cut in the head during the fight at Barboursville and would wear the scar for life. He is buried at Arlington National Cemetery.[165]

Less than a week after the battle of Barboursville, Joseph J. Mansfield was shot from ambush and mortally wounded in Putnam County about four miles from Hurricane Bridge. His son, W. L. Mansfield, recorded that Colonel Mansfield was "wounded in the shoulder, but rode on to a farm house. The messenger sent to take the information to his family, and to return the horse to its owner, carried a short note from him giving comforting assurances that the wound was not dangerous and he expected to be able to return home in a short while." However, Mansfield recognized his wound was mortal and had his will drawn up. He then signed the document, written hastily in pencil, on July 19. It read, it is with great regret that I reflect, that I have been cut off away from home, for no crime that I know of, without an opportunity of a last embrace from my wife and children, yet, as I believe the act which prostrated me was not one of personal malice toward me, I forgive those who did it and hope that no steps will be taken to prosecute them for the same. Dear wife, spare no opportunity to educate our children and accept my best wishes and regards for yourself and inform my children that the last years of my life were spent for the promotion of their interests, and this my last will I bring to a close.

A week later the Mansfield family was "shocked by the information that a wagon bearing his dead body was approaching the town." Joseph J. Mansfield was buried on the Boyd Adkins farm.[166]

Following the battle of Barboursville, Lieutenant Colonel George W. Neff recounted, "After scaling the heights the bat[tal]ion rallied and formed in line on the summit, where we flaunted our flag the day being won by us." An observer noted, "The victorious battalion, when the rebels had disappeared, marched through the town with the banners flying and bands playing airs which the inhabitants never hope to hear again. The Woodward boys planted their flag on the cupola of the Court House, and seemed to regard as a coincidence, that precisely two months after it was presented it was streaming from a spire in one of the hotbeds of secession."[167]

Neff reported,

> I desire to make particular mention of Lieut. Wm. R. McChesney of Co. H who acted in the most brave and gallant manner, also of Capt. A. J. M. Brown of Co. A, Capt. Warner Spencer, Capt. Hurd and Capt. Geo. Austin of Co. B...I also desire to make mention of the gallant conduct of Serg't Major Mitchell, Serg't Smith of Co. A and Serg't Kuhn of Co. K.[168]

*Captain George Austin, 2nd Kentucky Infantry.
Credit: Massachusetts Commandery Military Order of the Loyal Legion and the US Army Military History Institute.*

James Reynolds, the elderly Cabell County farmer, was mortally wounded in the battle. He was treated at the courthouse but died within a day, becoming the only defender lost in the battle. On the Union side, in addition to Jordons, who was killed in the initial volley, Barney McElroy of Company B was shot below the left eye and died the following morning, while a third Union soldier, John Donnovan of Company A, died one week later in Gallipolis, Ohio, from wounds received at Barboursville. At least thirteen other members of the 2nd Kentucky Infantry were wounded during the battle. A newspaper correspondent noted, "The Surgeon is doing all he can for the wounded. Considering the hazard the above list is marvelously small."[169]

The Union dead were buried behind the grave of Joseph Gardner in the Barboursville Cemetery. Their remains were transferred to a national cemetery after the war. Ben Swann of Barboursville recalled that he "visited the scene just after the fight Saturday morning and saw the bridge floor covered with blood. I saw two Yankees buried; I was in jail at the time, the Yankees having arrested me."[170]

Harold Faller, in an August 4, 1929, *Herald Advertiser* article, tells of a horrible incident which supposedly occurred following the battle. The Federals were digging a trench on the ridge when a young civilian stopped to watch them. When asked what they were doing, a Union soldier replied, "We're digging a grave to bury you in." The terrified man bolted away, ignoring an order to halt. One of the soldiers fired and the civilian dropped dead. This was undoubtedly just a folk story, as all sorts of rumors were spread after the battle.[171]

"Lucky" Savage recalled that a

> Mr. Grass, from Wayne, reported that they were killing men, women and children. Others told the same. They said that nearly all were killed at Barboursville. Mother didn't believe him, but the children did. Calvary and Wheeler Lunsford got under some saw logs.[172]

In a July 19 dispatch, General George B. McClellan reported to Colonel E. D. Townsend: "One of Cox's regiments, the 2nd Kentucky, defeated and drove 600 of Wise's men out of Barboursville, Cabell County, on 16th." Obviously, McClellan was incorrect about the date.[173]

Upon learning of the victory at Barboursville, Colonel Woodruff and the remainder of the 2nd Kentucky Infantry vacated Camp Crittenden and marched toward the village. At eleven o'clock they reached Barboursville, where "the entire regiment is encamped here on the scene of the victory." A correspondent noted, "Since we left Camp Dennison, we have been joined by two artillery companies, with splendid brass pieces, and we do not think that five times our number could dislodge us from this Gibraltar."[174]

On Saturday, the day of the battle, the steamer *Victor No. 2* traveled from Ironton to Guyandotte, carrying about thirty Ironton citizens. The boat returned to Ironton that evening and news of the battle quickly spread through the area. Over two hundred men, including an artillery squad, gathered and left shortly after for Guyandotte, disembarking there about midnight. They were ordered to march immediately to Barboursville, along with Captain Flamen Ball's company of the 2nd Kentucky Infantry, which had been left to protect Guyandotte.

About 180 men arrived in Barboursville at approximately five o'clock Sunday morning. They found the 2nd Kentucky encamped on what became known as "Fortification Hill," with an Ironton squad guarding the entrance to the camp with a brass six-pounder. The men "saw the blood stains on the ground; visited the hospital, found two dead in it, laid out, 12 wounded men, one in a dying condition, shot through the body; many buildings in town vacant and open, occupants having fled..." A reporter wrote, "It is singular, from the nature of the ground, that one half of the Federal troops were not slaughtered; but the truth is, the men of the rebel force had no heart at all in their unjust cause, and the rapid and vigorous charge of the gleaming bayonets and the enthusiastic shouts of our men at once struck terror into them."[175]

After eating breakfast, the men marched back to Guyandotte, arriving at 4:00 p.m. before returning to their homes in Ironton. A correspondent observed that in both Barboursville and Guyandotte, "the secession families have all 'lit out,' with the exception of some five or six scions who are in jail."[176]

The victory at Barboursville made the 2nd Kentucky Infantry "for a time the envy of the rest of the command." At least eight recruits joined the ranks of the regiment during their brief stay in the town. On July 15, "we struck tents and commenced the march" to the Kanawha Valley. As the regiment was leaving, "the ladies came out of their houses and bid us good-bye with cheeks streaming with tears." The soldiers of the 2nd Kentucky Infantry were described as "prolific of stories incidental to their brush with the rebels at Barboursville, which they now seem weary of telling." This regiment later fought in some of the bloodiest and most decisive battles of the war, including Shiloh, Corinth, Nashville, Stones River, and Chickamauga, but they would always remember their first fight at Barboursville.[177]

The German Home Guard Company met on July 16, 1861, at the courthouse in Ironton. These men had apparently refused to march to Barboursville along with the relief force from Ironton and had been accused of cowardice by William H. Powell, who later rose to the rank of major general. The company unanimously adopted the following:

WHEREAS, The German Company of Ironton has organized itself as an Independent Home Guard, and tendered their services for the protection of the town and county, and were so accepted, and are, under no circumstances whatever, obligated to do service beyond the county, without their own free will; and,

WHEREAS, At the late expedition to Guyandotte, an attempt was made to force the German Company, in an unreasonable and ungentlemanly manner, to do duty which they neither had the right nor the will to perform; therefore be it

Resolved, That we hereafter intend to go our own way, and do and perform only such service as our Constitution prescribes, and the town authorities command.

Resolved, That we demand of those, and especially of William H. Powell, who used the most ungentlemanly and uncalled for slanders, at the late expedition to Guyandotte, against our Company, a manly and fair apology, through the columns of the papers of this town.

Resolved, That we are determined, if we do not receive complete satisfaction of the several persons, members of other Companies, to hurl the slanders back in their teeth.

Resolved, That we look upon the conduct and expressions of William H. Powell, in heaping these slanders upon our Company, (so long as he refuses to take them back,) as the most ungentlemanly and mean that any man can be guilty of.

Resolved, That we deeply regret that we cannot excuse some members of the several Companies who have taken part in the slanders against our Company but we sincerely hope that they will be honest and frank enough to make the necessary apology.

Resolved, That should we not receive the above satisfaction, we will find ourselves compelled to sever all connection thereafter with the several Companies whose members have been guilty of the charge.

Resolved, That we tender our sincere thanks to the citizens who have approved of our conduct at the late expedition to Guyandotte, and pronounced the slander as undeserving and ungentlemanly.

William Schelling, Secretary[178]

The *Ironton Register* supported the company's decision, saying, "we think the severe censures cast by many upon the German Blues for not going to Barboursville, uncalled for. We were sorry that they did not go, but there was no obligation whatever on their part to do so, and that they are any more 'coward' than the rest of us, who did go, we do not believe."[179]

William Powell, however, responded with a harsh letter to the *Ironton Register*:

I notice, in your issue of the 18th inst., a number of resolutions adopted by the German Home Guards of Ironton, at a meeting held by them at the Court House, on the 16th inst., in which my name is used freely, charging me with having treated them ungentlemanly at Guyandotte, and demanding an apology from me, through the press of Ironton.

Presuming our citizens generally, by this time, fully understand the purpose of the trip taken by our companies to Guyandotte, on the 13th inst., I therefore deem it unnecessary to enter into details.

On the morning of the 13th, a few, myself included, chartered the Victor No. 2, to convey us to Guyandotte and home again. We went up, as is commonly said, on our own book, as an independent squad. Upon our arrival at Guyandotte, Mr. John Campbell boarded our craft, and reported a request from Capt. Ball, in charge at Guyandotte, to send down for all the force that could be raised at Ironton, to be at Guyandotte that night, which was executed by Mr. Campbell, and the steamer Victor dispatched for them – a matter with which I had nothing to do. That evening, at 8 o'clock, Capt. Ball stationed a force from Proctorsville, in charge of his Lieutenant, to guard Guyandotte, and requested our force to join him in the march to Barboursville, detaining the movement of his train until the arrival of the boat with the force from Ironton. Anticipating some trouble on the way, created, in his opinion, the necessity of requesting us to do so – to which all readily assented, except the German Home Guards, the Captain of which remarking at the time, that 'he would go if his company would.' After considerable loss of time, spent in attempting to persuade them to go, by myself and others, finding it in vain, I did charge them (the Captain excepted) with being cowards, undeserving the arms they bore, saying that the authorities at Ironton ought to take them out of their possession, and place them in the hands of those who would be willing to use them in an emergency; and that their refusal to act with the other companies was not only disgraceful to themselves, but those who accompanied, and the town from whence they came; they replying that when they wanted to fight, they would enlist in the regular service, and draw their pay; that they would not go out there to fight, that such was not the object of their organization, which we presume is true, and we have no doubt, judging from the character of their resolutions, but that they have also resolved, never, no, never, to leave Ironton again, except when invaded!

The whole movement was voluntary on the part of all our companies. Men were not compelled to act contrary to their wishes. As to the right or necessity of the request, we leave that with Capt. Ball, to settle with his superiors. I made no attempt to force them into measures, neither did I see or hear any one else do so; and he or they who so report, is or are willful and unscrupulous misrepresenters of the facts. Their refusal to act voluntarily with our other companies made it appear the more cowardly.

I am not desirous of gaining newspaper notoriety, or to create any difficulty between our German friends and myself, and only notice their resolutions in compliance with their request. What I said was said upon my own individual responsibility, free from the influence of any one. I charged them with what I believed to be true of them, and have seen or heard nothing since to change my opinion, in regard to the cause which led them to decline going. We wish it distinctly understood by the German Home Guards, Captain excepted, that we have no apology to make to cowards, those who would forsake their friends in time of probable need, as they did; and further resolve (as it is now our time) that we wish them (the German Home Guards) to understand that any attempt by them, collectively or individually, to enforce the threats embodied in their resolutions upon myself, in any way, will be met promptly and effectually, as long as I have power to raise an arm.[180]

This may have been the first time William H. Powell was immersed in controversy, but the war would provide him other opportunities to perform both heroic acts and infamous actions.

5
Lawlessness Abounds

"Col. Ziegler if you will call in your scouts and cease your violation of persons and property and restore what you have taken and make good what they have lost, and confine yourself to the limits of your camp, and leave to contending armies to decide the question then they would return to their homes.

2d and if you violate these stipulations, we pledge that we will carry the war to the knife, or lay our lives on the altar of our country's liberty.

3d To yield our rights as freemen don't think for a moment we intend to do it. If you will carry out the stipulations in good faith, I pledge myself that our people will do the same."

Hurston Spurlock, Commandant
[Confederate forces in Wayne County], August 1861

The Federal victory at Barboursville did little to protect Union supporters in Cabell County. The absence of Federal troops and a functioning county government resulted in a sustained period of lawlessness in 1861, which would only be curbed, ironically, by the November raid on Guyandotte. During the summer and fall of 1861, Union authorities began raising troops to defend the westernmost part of Virginia, and their efforts would result in the formation of several regiments in the area.

Granville Parker, who would serve as Cabell's delegate to West Virginia's first constitutional convention, informed Governor Francis Pierpont on July 15 that the 2nd Kentucky Infantry, commanded by Colonel William Woodruff, had left the village of Barboursville on the previous day bound for Charleston. "The medicine administered by Col. W. has done much good," Parker wrote, "but the disease is deeply seated & requires further treatments & that promply or a relapse may take place." Parker noted that a "force of 100 to 200 volunteer scouts will hold the Rebels in check until some regular troops can be stationed to protect the Union men but force is indispinsible as a neuclus & protection, for Union men to rally round & organize." Sixty men were being organized in the area to serve in a new Federal regiment comprised of Virginians, and Parker believed if these troops were stationed at Guyandotte or Barboursville, "it will be of great service to the Union men."

Influential Union supporters in the area were forming what was "to be styled" the 4th (West) Virginia Infantry regiment with Guyandotte, "we think the worst secession nest," as the recruiting station. Proctorville, Ohio, was the suggested depot for arms, and Parker believed muskets and ammunitions should be sent immediately, as "the certainty that arms are ready helps much to bring the boys in." He also urged the organization of Home Guard units that could protect the citizenry if the Federal regiments were ordered away from western Virginia. Reminding Pierpont that he and two others were refugees to Ohio "from the odious barbarians of Secession," Parker stated that combatting the guerrilla warfare initiated by Confederates "requires a like mode intensified."[181]

Following the departure of the 2nd Kentucky Infantry, L. W. Wolcott wrote to Governor Pierpont complaining that conditions in Cabell County were worse than ever. "Secession has sprung back again with increased intolerance," he noted, adding that "secessionists are all returning to their homes & what few Union men that are left are leaving." Wolcott then asked, "Cannot a hundred men & a good recruiting officer be placed at Guyandotte as a nucleus for the Union men to gather around."[182]

Reverend Jeremiah Hare, a Union supporter and Methodist minister who served the Walnut Grove circuit in Putnam County, was arrested in Guyandotte by members of the Border Rangers. Guyandotte citizen Edward Smith approached Hare and "punched and picked at him and asked him how he felt and wanted them to shoot him there but they did not do it." While being transported to Camp Tompkins in the Kanawha Valley, Reverend Hare and his captors encountered Captain Milton J. Ferguson. Ferguson

> had a gun on his shoulder, and was then on his way to Wayne for the purpose of arresting some of the most prominent loyal men of that County. He stopped those who were conducting me to the Camp, and after abusing me for the space of ten or fifteen minutes – charging me with being at the head of every thing that was done in the County against the Southern Confederacy – he told those who had me in custody, 'By no means to suffer me to escape, but conduct me safely to Camp; for I was one of the very worst prisoners they had had for a long time.'[183]

In Wayne County, John Zeigler took charge of efforts to advance the Federal military cause in the region, organizing nearly all the Union men in the county into companies and establishing his encampment and headquarters at Ceredo. Zeigler and his friends footed the bill for the endeavor but "is greatly wanting of authority and the propper means of keeping down the Rebels." L. J. Hampton and John D. Mims informed Governor Francis Pierpont on July 17 that Zeigler "has at this time restored peace in Wayne and compelled every Rebel to flee or take the oath of aligiance to the U. S. and your Government." The men asked that Zeigler be placed in charge of a regiment or brigade, requested arms, and pledged to keep the governor informed of events in the region.[184]

John L. Zeigler, a native of Franklin County, Pennsylvania, later moved to Kentucky and worked as a shoemaker in Greenup County. He relocated to Dock's Creek in Wayne County, Virginia, shortly after the county's formation and with his wife Susan, Zeigler raised a large family and farmed the land. It was the good fortune of all Union supporters in western Virginia that he took the initiative to defend the region. The regiment he formed in the summer of 1861, the 5th (West) Virginia Infantry, was the first Federal regiment to be formed in the region and would be essential to maintaining a foothold of Unionism in Cabell and Wayne counties.[185]

Hampton also wrote to William Ratliff on July 17 and informed him that Zeigler had forced secessionists in Wayne County to take the oath or flee to Kentucky. Wash Adkins, court clerk, had selected the latter course of action, taking with him the county court's books and papers. Several prominent Confederates from Wayne County had been captured, including "old Burwell Spurlock," who had been raising a company to serve under General Henry Wise. Hampton wanted a commission for Zeigler "without fail," although "everything can be done right and legal." Guns were needed, and "means to act with." If Ratliff would convince Governor Francis Pierpont to take action, Hampton avowed, "I will insure you that Wayne County will be all right."[186]

On the same day, John Adams penned a letter to Pierpont from Ceredo, stating, "There is a good deal of trouble here on acct. of the war & battle at Barboursville – the rebels feel badly & will seek for personal revenge & this place is surrounded by rebels. This is the only place where the people dared to raise a flag in the Spring & keep it to the breeze until now & it still waves here."

Adams informed Pierpont that citizens from the immediate area had maintained a Home Guard unit for some time and "have endeavored to do all we could possibly do under the circumstances..." Until the 2nd Kentucky Infantry arrived and drove secessionists from the area, he noted, "we had but little peace or rest." The men of the Home Guard company sought arms "to protect our precinct" and wished to be headquartered at Buffalo Shoals on Twelve Pole Creek. Over sixty men were enrolled and officers had been duly elected, with Harvey Dunkle serving as captain. Adams clarified that "we have over 60 on the roll, but perhaps not many over 40 would like to do active service, but the balanse stand ready to assist when needed."

The local Union force had about fifty guns, but Adams requested better weapons. He informed Pierpont that they were very selective in permitting men to serve in the Home Guard, allowing to join "none but those who are true & have been so all thro the troubles."

"We have watched night after night & all for our own protection & those below us on the Ohio River," Adams wrote. "We are some 10 miles up Twelve Pole from Ceredo on the Ohio: The county above us at Trout's Hill is rebel & also on Beech fork: that is the one left our front & our back are rebel districts & we are obliged to watch these movements; please write to me your instructions..."[187]

On Friday night, July 26, 1861, Milton J. Ferguson, "the leading Secessionist of Wayne Co., Va.," approached Ceredo accompanied by a number of supporters. Ferguson had learned that Union men had taken up arms in the fledgling community and he was determined to "straighten up things." Another report claimed his intent was to arrest John Zeigler. Ferguson left his comrades about one mile from town and advanced, but he was halted by a group of armed Union men led by Zeigler, who had been forewarned of his approach. As they called on him to surrender, a stunned Ferguson exclaimed to the Union leader, "Why, Squire, I didn't expect such treatment as this." Zeigler replied, "I know you didn't expect it Jimmyson; I know you didn't expect it." On the following Monday, U. S. Marshal E. F. Gillen of Ironton took Ferguson to Columbus, where he would be confined in Camp Chase Prison.[188]

Zeigler apparently sought to capture Hurston Spurlock, but he "was in a rebel camp & cannot well be taken..." One Union man noted,

Confederate Colonel Milton J. Ferguson. The most prominent citizen in Wayne County, Ferguson was seized by Colonel John Zeigler and sent to Camp Chase Prison in 1861. Credit: Mahlon Nichols (courtesy of Robert Thompson).

> Ferguson was Prosecutor for Wayne County threatened Union men with the penalties of the Bogus treason law of the Richmond Convention. He was also a Col. of militia and used that authority to over awe Union men and is said to have led a command at the fight at Barboursville & Scary. Up in the whole I consider him a much better man for Gov. Pierponts purposes than Spurlock would have been.[189]

William Ratliff, Wayne County delegate for the Reorganized Government of Virginia, wrote Governor Pierpont on July 28 from Catlettsburg, Kentucky. He reported that Zeigler was "doing good work" at what he called Camp Ratliff in Ceredo. Several prisoners had been taken in Cabell and Wayne counties, and Zeigler was organizing companies "as fast as he can...You must try and do something for him. He must have arms and some authority to purchase provisions and clothing for his men. Please don't fail to attend to this for if this camp is attended to it will settle everything from here to Kanawha."[190]

On this same day, L. J. Hampton contacted Pierpont concerning dire conditions in western Virginia. Union men had been forced to flee for their lives from Confederate cavalry that had been left behind when Wise retreated from the Kanawha Valley. These troops were

> committing the most diabolical atrocities on the Union men of that region by

robing & pressing men, tying and whipping them and in some instances taking life and every species of property that they can...in a word lying waste the country. This is <u>reliable beyond a doubt</u>. Some must be done speedily or those counties [Wayne and Logan] & Cabell & Kanawha is lost.

Federal supporters feared forming companies until they were armed, and Hampton suggested sending weapons to Ironton, Ohio, where they would be safe until the units were raised. He wrote, "Ziegler is the only man that has had the nerve to undertake it but he will be overrun and driven out unless he can get arms to enable him to get more men. There must be arms and the proper provisions made to enable him to organise with more men or he will be slaughtered."[191]

Robert Hager and others in Boone County supported the Union, but "all the Judges, J. P.s, Lawers, Shareffs, Country Clerks, merchants, politians & slave holders and drunkards out number us considerable, and are to strong for us." In late May, fifteen secessionists stormed into his home armed with revolvers and Bowie knives, and the sheriff pointed a gun at Hager's wife and seized his rifle. Hager fled immediately to Ohio. He believed that 500 troops stationed at both Boone Court House and Barboursville would be sufficient to quell secession sentiment and establish the Restored Government of Virginia and declared that if the Union men in the region were armed "we could have pese and prosparity onst more."[192]

Confederate legislator and supporter Peter C. Buffington, who would later become the first mayor of Huntington. Credit: Special Collections Department, Marshall University.

On July 31, Mrs. E. T. Sanders wrote from Covington, Kentucky, to the Union commander at Guyandotte. She had read in the *Cincinnati Commercial* that Union troops had seized Guyandotte and captured thirty or forty suspected Confederate supporters. Mrs. Sanders wrote specifically to urge Federal officials to keep an eye on Peter Buffington, who lived two miles below the town. She claimed he was "the first man that caused the first exsitement in that section of the contry" by applying to Virginia Governor John Letcher for weapons to arm Confederate supporters and providing horses to enable Jenkins to complete the organization of his cavalry company. Sanders stated that the Union supporters in Cabell County would not be safe until Buffington was imprisoned or forced to take the oath of allegiance.[193]

Two Union citizens wrote Union Virginia Governor Francis Pierpont from

Catlettsburg on August 2 regarding conditions in Cabell and Wayne counties. William Ratliff had informed them that Greenbury Slack of Kanawha should have been in Wayne to organize the judicial department, but he had not been there, which was a cause for concern. The Union men made recommendations for justices; they also observed that the county sheriff "has been considered a little doubtful," but had agreed to take the oath and was willing to turn over county taxes he had collected. John Laidley, "that old & tried patriot," was recommended as judge and Barboursville native Henry Jefferson Samuels as prosecuting attorney.[194]

Congressman Kellian V. Whaley, who was tasked with raising Union regiments in western Virginia. Credit: Library of Congress.

On August 5, Colonel John Zeigler led four companies of the 5th (West) Virginia Infantry from Ceredo to Barboursville, which they surrounded with pickets just before daylight. Any Confederates there departed during the night, allowing the Federal detachment to seize the town without a fight. Kellian V. Whaley wrote, "He is now holding the place and supporting the Union men until they organize themselves into companies for service and those companies will be attached to the new Regiment for the Cavalry Company."

Kellian V. Whaley was instructed by Governor Francis Pierpont to organize loyal regiments in southwestern Virginia. The congressman assisted in the creation of the 5th (West) Virginia Infantry and began raising a second regiment in Ceredo, to be known as the 9th (West) Virginia Infantry. Whaley had received letters of assurance that men from Portsmouth and other locations would enlist in the new regiment as soon as the organization of the 5th was completed, and he anticipated this would occur in a few days. He also expected that the formation of the new regiment would not take long, as "a portion of the Union men exhibit commendable zeal of earnestness having discovered at length that war is upon them." Whaley requested that the steamer *Victor*, which ran from Portsmouth to Pomeroy, Ohio, be employed to bring troops and stores to the recruit camp at Ceredo.[195]

Restored Government of Virginia Governor Francis H. Pierpont received a letter from an Ironton citizen on August 7, 1861, complaining that in Cabell, Wayne, and adjoining counties, there were "no civil authorities, no law, no protection to the persons and property of either the Loyal or disloyal citizens – all is anarchy and confusion." The writer continued:

Since the retreat of Gen Wise there is no military belonging to the Rebels in this part of the State and while there are some secessionists they have neither the ability or power to do much mischief. There is as you are aware no military power belonging to the Government to control and govern, so that they are emphatically without any government whatever and every one feels disposed to act according to the dictates of his own mind whether they be good or evil. Lawless men, plunderers, thieves, and robbers have no check or restraint upon them in consequence of which, no good citizen feels any security whatever for his life or property.[196]

From Ceredo, Colonel Zeigler complained that his men were "suffering very much indeed now for the want of blankets." The nights were cold and damp, and many of the 700 soldiers in camp had "taken colds." The dangerous conditions in the region required constant vigilance from the Union troops, as they were "protecting our position as well as the neighboring Union men in this part of our County." Zeigler requested funds from the government to pay bills the regiment had incurred for flour, bacon, groceries, and other necessities, and informed Governor Pierpont they were forced to purchase their supplies in Ohio and Kentucky and were "obliged to submit to a discount of 10 to 15 per ct in Va. money."[197]

Citizens praised Zeigler as "a good Unionist and a determined man," but at least one Union citizen believed "he neither possesses the judgement, discretion, nor intelligence absolutely necessary to bring order out of the chaos there existing." Men were flocking from Ohio to Ceredo to enlist in the Union army, "and it is absolutely necessary that some man of military experience, good judgement and great discretion should be sent there to enforce military discipline and to afford protection to the lives and property of the people."[198]

In mid-August Zeigler contacted Hurston Spurlock, commander of what remained of the Wayne County militia, in an effort to procure the return of Federal property. In response, Spurlock declared, "we greatly desire peace in our county and among our old neighbours" and agreed to an exchange of property, but he warned that "if the stipulations are violated we pledge you that we will carry the war to the knife or lose our lives on the altar of our country's liberty – to yield our rights as freemen don't think for a moment we intend to do."

A day later Spurlock, who was the son of Reverend Burwell Spurlock, Wayne County's delegate to the Richmond Convention, addressed a letter to the citizens of Round Bottom:

Dear Friends – I understand that your country is in a state of War against the cecession party – I would suggest the idea of your returning to your homes in peace.

I do assure you that the cecession party will not interrupt your persons or property unless you throw yourselves in a warlike attitude. If you do you will have to abide by the concequences – I do also state to you that there has been

Chaplain Joseph Little of the 5th (West) Virginia Infantry. Credit: L. M. Strayer Collection.

peace measure agreed upon between the t[w]o parties which you must abide by.

That "peace measure" would soon be terminated.

Zeigler informed Governor Pierpont on August 22 that he had hired an Ironton man to construct a breech loading cannon for his artillery company. Nearly five feet in length, the piece could be fired eight to ten times per minute and weighed less than three hundred pounds. He stated, "It appears to be just such a cannon as would be of incalculable advantage in such a hilly country as this is. It is more suited to this country than a heavy cannon on account of the universal bad roads that traverse this region of country."[199]

Captain William Reany was employed by General William S. Rosecrans in the summer of 1861 to provide intelligence in western Virginia. He reported from Camp Pierpont on August 20 that "I have had my boys through this whole section of the country, some as peddlers; and we have two of our boys fishing on Jenkins sandbar." The only Confederate force in the area was at Wayne Courthouse. Zeigler had plans to take possession of the town and Reany declared "he will do it sure if he undertakes it." He described the men of the 5th (West) Virginia Infantry as "bold fearless mountaineers from the hills of Ky. & Virginia. They are a rough hardy set of men, and at the same time they are a verry moral set of men; they had devine worship on Sunday at 10 oclock prayer meeting in their quarters at night, and have class meetings twice a week." Each day, citizens came into the camp at Ceredo to take the oath to support the Restored Government of Virginia. "The Secessionists are getting uneasy here," Reany observed, and "I am satisfied that a rout at Wayne Court House will put a stop to rebellion in this section."[200]

Reany wrote Rosecrans again on August 25 after spending time at Camp Pierpont and informed him that Zeigler had gone to Wheeling to procure blankets and other provisions and would attack Wayne Courthouse upon his return. Confederate Captain Hurston Spurlock had again proposed returning property if the Union scouts were withdrawn to Ceredo and even returned several horses, but Zeigler had not replied. Reany saw the notice posted by Hurston Spurlock but believed "he knows them to[o] well to trouble them."[201]

He also related that the "Rebels have committed several outrages on the Sandy River about 14 miles from the mouth. Last Wednesday they robbed the mails also attacked two Union men who were coming to the mouth of Sandy in a canoe. They robbed them even to the clothes on their back." Reany had learned that Jenkins was in Greenbrier County and that Spurlock had sent a man to try and convince him to leave Confederate troops in Wayne County to resist Zeigler. He noted that court was supposed to be held in Wayne the prior week, but the judge "was afraid Zeigler might come along so he did not open court." Reany also observed that Zeigler "has one company of Tug Fork boys, who can clear out the whole county and they are anxious to try the job on. All they want is blankets and a barrel of hard bread or two."[202]

Following a brief skirmish on August 27, a detachment of fifty-three Union troops of the 5th (West) Virginia Infantry under Captain James E. Smith took possession of Wayne Courthouse. One newspaper wrote, "Perhaps nowhere in Western Virginia has there been a viler nest of secessionists than at Wayne Court House, the county town of the county, lying on the Kentucky line." A number of Confederates were captured, including Hurston Spurlock, Jesse Spurlock, Burwell Spurlock, Stephen Strother, and county clerk Wash Adkins. A. J. Miller was shot and killed "by one of the Tug Fork men" while attempting to escape. Captain Thomas N. Davey sent a telegram to Governor Francis Pierpont on the following day informing him of the seizure of the Wayne County seat. Davey noted that four secessionists were killed and one wounded, and that "all quiet at present."[203]

Stephen Strother was captured at Wayne Courthouse on August 27, 1861. Credit: Stephen Strother (courtesy of Jack L. Dickinson).

After Hurston Spurlock had been arrested by Union authorities at Wayne Courthouse, Kellian V. Whaley informed Pierpont that Spurlock had voted in favor of the Ordinance of Secession and "has been a persistent and violent advocate of the right of Rebellion before and ever since." He and his cousin, Jesse Spurlock, were "men of influence in the county and by their activity energy and indomitable perseverance have succeeded in doing great injury to the Union cause." Hurston Spurlock fought on the Confederate side at Barboursville and Scary Creek, and Whaley believed both he and Jesse Spurlock would be indicted by a Federal court in Charleston. He advised the governor, "In my opinion they are among the last of our prisoners who should be liberated."[204]

A number of Cabell County citizens later wrote to Pierpont requesting the release of James McCorkle, who had been on his way to Louisa, Kentucky, when he was arrested at Trout's Hill. The Cabell Countians declared he had never taken up arms against the Federal government. McCorkle had ten children, and his wife was "compelled to be on her horse nearly every day to hunt corn to make bread and other necessaries of life."[205]

Union leaders believed that Stephen Strother "ought to be kept & tried – he was fighting like a tiger when he was arrested." One month later, however, Adjutant General H. J. Samuels received two letters from a group of Union citizens in Catlettsburg, Kentucky, recommending Strother's release. One described him as "a civil man and good citizen," while others attested that he voted Union in the previous election and "was a member in framing the Wheeling Convention last summer at the round bottom wayne county virginia."[206]

One of the leading secessionists in the area was Reverend John C. Johnson. A newspaper correspondent wrote that Johnson "has been one of the most violent in his efforts to incite this rebellion in our region, forgetting altogether that if he is a follower of his meek and lowly Master, his mission is one of peace." Johnson was paroled with the condition that he remain at Wayne Courthouse, but he fled at the first opportunity "and is, no doubt, now with a violated oath, endeavoring to incite others to rebellion." His horse was seized and "we trust it will be used by those who are not only true to their country, but true to their word and honor."[207]

Jesse Spurlock, one of the men arrested during the encounter, believed it was "through fear the citizens gathered themselves together at wayne Court house to protect themselves and property against an invading foe as they exposed themselves." After learning that Zeigler had pledged that if they would lay down their arms and "molest no one that they should not be molested," the men disbanded and went home, "but thare was still men that was disposed to do devilment in our County and to take and carry off property and such men as these the citizens had to watch."[208]

Ralph Leete and Henry J. Samuels traveled to Camp Pierpont in late August and turned over 500 Enfield rifles received from the New York Arsenal. Samuels informed Governor Francis Pierpont "that in Cabell & Wayne Counties open & notorious rebels, now holding office, are meditating to take the oaths prescribed by the convention of 11th June at Wheeling with the understanding & mental reservation that they are not building at all on their conscience and that they take them under duress." The Cabell County clerk had concealed the records of the county, and Samuels sought authorization for someone to "take charge of the records to safely keep them during the unsettled state of the county."[209]

Deputy Commissary Samuel Almond informed General Jacob D. Cox on the last day of August that Mrs. Bowlin, mother-in-law of Albert Gallatin Jenkins, had arrived at Point Pleasant that evening "expressing her determination to attempt passage through your lines with the intention of visiting her son in law in the Rebel Army." He also reported that steamboats were frequently entering and leaving the Kanawha River without reporting to the Union command at Point Pleasant and that some of them were suspected of transporting goods to the Confederates.[210]

Henry Jefferson Samuels of Barboursville, who had spent a good deal of the year in Ironton, was appointed adjutant general for the Reorganized Government of Virginia in September 1861. He left Ohio in the middle of the month and headed to Wheeling to assume his duties. His brother Alex was a Confederate officer, serving in the 8th Virginia Cavalry.[211]

John S. Carlile, who was leading the movement toward West Virginia statehood and served as United States senator for the Reorganized Government of Virginia, wrote to Governor Pierpont on September 2 hoping to help him "see the importance of the civil power of our state government being asserted at the earliest possible moment in Cabell county." Carlile believed it important to seize the reins of government before the Federal court met in Charleston. He stated that "a few indictments for treason and for tampering with the U S mails against some of the prominent secessionists of Cabell would greatly strengthen in the effort now making to restore and assert the state authority for the protection of the few loyal citizens left in Cabell and to enable the hundreds that have fled from their homes in that county to return." Carlile asserted that if part of the 5th (West) Virginia Infantry could be stationed at Guyandotte and Barboursville "until the Union men of Cabell could return and organize & arm themselves it would enable them in the future to take care of their secession friends."[212]

*United States Senator
John S. Carlile.
Credit: Library of Congress.*

Unwilling to wait for official permission, Zeigler "anticipated the want" of his regiment and ordered the organization of a cavalry company, which he equipped by borrowing from the state of Ohio. Thirty-five men with horses had been organized and Zeigler asked Pierpont to furnish stock and accoutrements for the company. He informed the Virginia governor that "in this particular locality," cavalry was "indispensible." Zeigler also reminded him to send equipment and uniforms for the artillery unit.[213]

On September 10, Kellian V. Whaley informed Governor Pierpont, "We are getting along very well. There is some little sickness in camp owing principally to the fact that our boys are yet without blankets and take cold. Also some dysentery in some of the quarters but as soon as we get blankets we will go into tents & the disease will not likely spread much more among them." Zeigler had not yet returned from Barboursville, but Whaley believed that "secession is on the decline in this section."

Whaley intended to expend considerable energy in raising the new Union regiment, but his frequent absences due to his congressional responsibilities led him to request that someone be appointed to fill in when he was not present at Ceredo. He recommended Abia Allen Tomlinson as someone who could administer the oath to recruits and superintend affairs. Whaley wrote, "Numbers of men would come here &

finding no one authorized to enlist them would get discouraged and go home." Whaley asked that Tomlinson be sent a captain's commission with authority to muster troops into state service.[214]

Whaley observed that a number of three-month volunteers returning to the area after the expiration of their term of service might be convinced to enlist in the new regiment he was raising and asked Governor Pierpont if travel expenses for these men could be paid prior to their re-enlistment. He also noted there was dissatisfaction in the ranks concerning the recent appointments for lieutenant colonel and sutler of the 9th (West) Virginia Infantry. Due to the criticism of Colonel John Zeigler's lack of military experience, it was preferred that a man with previous service be appointed lieutenant colonel. The criticism of Benjamin Starr as sutler, however, had uglier roots: "Mr Star of Cin. being a Jew – The Reg. will not believe but he will use his office to the promotion of his own instead of their interests." The Union soldiers preferred that William H. Copley, who represented Wayne County at the Wheeling conventions, fill this post.

"I have already commenced operations towards the organization of the new Reg.," Whaley wrote, "and hope to have several companies ready to go into camp as soon as Col. Ziegler's is full and would respectfully suggest that we be permitted to move to Cabell County to fill up as soon as we have sufficient strength to maintain the rendezvous, as I am well satisfied that several companies can be organized in that county as soon as they have a permanent rallying point."[215]

Colonel Zeigler was still at Barboursville on September 12 and had been reinforced by 125 soldiers from Ceredo, bringing his total force to 425. Whaley was disturbed that Zeigler had failed to attack a small "rebel camp" six miles south of the village on the Guyandotte River, "but instead has condescended to engage in a correspondence with one Bill Smith one of their leaders who is nothing more than a horse thief and the lowest kind of a character." Whaley believed one company would be sufficient to break up the Confederate camp.

"I shall proceed at once to raise the new regiment," Whaley declared, "as I see the necessity and propriety now more than ever to have one officered by men of military experiences, in regard to whom I shall consult your Excellency when the reg. is nearly full. I shall leave for Camp Pierpoint on the first boat and will keep you advised of passing events."[216]

A portion of Zeigler's regiment was involved in a brief skirmish at Poore's Hill (in the present-day community of Ona) on September 12, 1861. It appears that secessionists began gathering there to oppose the Federal troops that had occupied Barboursville. A detachment of the 5th (West) Virginia Infantry was sent to disperse the local men and a clash erupted. The Union troops placed a small cannon on the knoll which they fired during the fight, twice striking the yard at the Maples, east of Poore's Hill. One excited citizen said the bullets were flying so thick that he could have swung a basket around his head and quickly filled it to the top. Lewis Lusher, one of the secessionists, boasted "that he stood the fire of the Federal troops until he fired ten times when the wind of the cannon ball knocked him down." He also claimed that "he took seven fair fires at the Federal troops, and they might hold it against him & be God damned."

Hugh Willis, a member of the Union regiment, wrote his recollections of this battle after the war:

> I had got behind a persimmon tree, and had fired a couple of shots, when a ball struck the side of the tree and scattered the bark into my mouth and eyes. While I was clawing it out, a comrade next to me, says, 'get away, let me try that tree,' and just as he was aiming, a bullet struck the tree close to his face and filled his mouth with pieces of the bark, that so frightened and annoyed him that he didn't fire.

Some of the Federals were ordered to "make a flank movement" to "get behind the rebs, and we succeeded finely." Reaching the top of Poore's Hill, they charged the secessionists, causing their entire force to disperse rapidly. Willis sprinted after one of the fleeing rebels, forcing him to drop his gun in an effort to get away. Determined not to lose his prey, Willis released his weapon and jumped atop him. Willis observed,

> He was full of steel and very wiry, and I had all I could do to hold on to him. While the tustle was going on, we were both losing breath all the time, and gradually slipping down the hill, until we came to a little bluff or jumping off place, eight or ten feet high, and down that we rolled each fellow nearly fagged out.

> I was so exhausted that I was determined to end the conflict right there, so I ripped out my jackknife, and opened it, and holding it up over the reb, whom I had down, I said, 'surrender or I'll cut your throat from ear to ear,' and then the fellow yielded. He got up and I marched him off to the Colonel. He was a sad looking spectacle for I had torn the shirt clear off of him in the melee. The Colonel took charge of him, and the man afterwards joined our regiment, and made a good soldier. His name was Wm. Peyton.[217]

Willis also captured another local man, Eb Fuller, in a privy: "I surrounded the works myself, demanded their surrender, and the garrison to give up its arms. The reb did but he only had a pocket knife, his gun being thrown away when he entered the fortifications."[218]

The secessionists were scattered, and the Union troops pursued for a short distance before returning to Barboursville with no reported casualties. A citizen by the name of Damron was reportedly killed in the clash, and William Hensley and John Tassen were listed as being captured. No conclusive evidence could be found to substantiate these claims. Documents do show that Thomas T. Adkins, William Hanley, and Will Peyton were captured and imprisoned for participating in the Poore's Hill skirmish. Testimony would implicate several other local residents.[219]

Thomas T. Adkins was charged by Federal authorities with rebellion and secession. He seized a mare owned by William H. Lawrence and "scouted and bushwhacked through the county." According to F. M. Ferrill, "When I went to Porr's hill to compromise with the forces and get them to lay down their arms I saw defendant then cooperating with the rebels. Presley Showans was seen "under arms, with the company that was getting ready to go to Porrs Hill, under Barrett and Shelton." Zachariah Nicely stated he saw Showans "fixing his gun and heard him say he was getting it ready to shoot the damned Yankees."[220]

G. H. Ashworth was charged with rebellion and had apparently been part of a mob that sought to arrest James Webb "on account of his union sentiments." Ashworth was also involved with a company that was being raised at Marine Sanford's to fight against the Union force at Barboursville. William H. Lawrence heard him say "he would blow any mans brains out that would say any thing against the southern confederacy."[221]

J. C. Wheeler informed Governor Francis Pierpont of the encounter in a September 13 letter:

At the request of Hon. K. V. Whaley, who has just left for Camp Pierpoint, Ceredo, Va. I forward to you the latest intelligence from Col. Ziegler's command. Yesterday at 11 o'clock, Col. Ziegler, with a part of his Regiment, attacked 250 rebels drilling in the Turnpike 8 miles east of Barboursville. They fled at the first fire, which killed and wounded several. Eight prisoners were taken, among them Wm. Hensley, their ring-leader; also, John Lawson and Wm. Hanley, son of old Patrick Hanley, also 15 stand of arms, 7 horses, and 2 mules.[222]

On the day following the skirmish at Poore's Hill, Henry J. Samuels, adjutant general for the Reorganized Government of Virginia, informed Governor Francis Pierpont that Colonel John Zeigler had procured the commissioners' books for Cabell County and had been instructed to seize the Wayne County books, which Samuels stated he would take on his return to Wheeling. A week later, Zeigler told Pierpont he had obtained possession of the commissioners' books for both Cabell and Wayne counties and asked for guidance as to whether he should send copies or the originals to the Secretary of State.[223]

Samuels believed Pierpont needed to convince the public that his government was one of the causes for which the Union men were fighting:

Many persons taking their cue from Summers and others of the Kanawha regency ridicule our Wheeling government as an usurpation – and a sham can only be brought to respect it, by an exercise of its power, fear being an argument that they fully understand, and though they claim to be Unionists have been too timid to advocate or fight for it and held themselves ready to take the winning side. I therefore recommend and respectfully suggest that you urge on all the officers to proclaim the cause of your government to be as much the object for which they are fighting as the Union, in fact that they are identical, and procure Rosecrans assistance, to drive the impression into the people.

Zeigler had done his part, and Samuels had "taken measures to have the sentiment of Cabell among Union men consolidated in favor of the Wheeling government."[224]

Captain John Hunt Oley, who had been detailed by General William Rosecrans to instruct and drill the 5th (West) Virginia Infantry, training at Ceredo, issued a report to Governor Francis Pierpont on September 14:

> There are at present seven (7) Cos organized & mustered in the U. S. service with numbers varying from 80 to 95. I think there will be one more Co of 80 men ready by Monday. Officers are recruiting for the other two Cos with good prospects of being able to fill them by the last of next week. A large majority of the men have never been under military discipline & drill before – very many of them never handled a musket before and consequently will need much moulding before they will be ready to take the field for active service as a Regiment.

John Hunt Oley of New York served as drillmaster for the 5th (West) Virginia Infantry at Ceredo in the fall of 1861. Credit: Richard A. Wolfe.

> Since they have [been] gathering & forming they have had much picket & guard duty to do and late had to make two or three necessary expeditions (to quiet bodies of Rebels) of several days each. This has necessarily interfered with their progress in tactics & discipline.
>
> I should say that the men understand & execute the manual of arms ordinarily well, that while some Cos have been drilled in all of the Co movements and understand the principle of them others have not been practiced in them at all.
>
> The Companies have never been drilled in Battalion manouevre as all of the Cos are not sufficiently progressed in the School of the Soldier & School of the Company.
>
> The men as a body are very willing and learn readily – they are a brave & courageous set of men.
>
> The seven companies are now armed with the Enfield rifle, but there seems to

be some question whether they can be kept permanently as the[ir] arms were sent to a committee of citizens for the benefits of the loyal inhabitants of Virginia.

The men have been furnished with one suit of blue flannel clothes.
Two (2) pairs of drawers & shirts
One pair of shoes
One very ___ knapsack
with canteens, haversacks, cartridge boxes & belts camp equipage and I believe all its necessary appendages

The Regiments need immediately
blankets & overcoats very particularly & urgently
50 Sergeants Swords
10 1st Sergeants Sashes
20 Drums & Fifes
Company letters for their Caps
Caps or Hats for the entire Regiment
Blank forms & Books for Companies
Blank forms & Books for Regimental business
Horses & waggons for each Co & perhaps some other little camp fixtures.

Capt. John H. Oley
Instructor of Tactics[225]

Colonel John Zeigler had high praise for the young officer that would one day be one of the founders of Huntington, writing to Governor Pierpont, "I feel it my duty to highly commend to your favorable consideration my friend Capt Oley. He has rendered excellent service in organizing and instructing this Regiment. He is industrious, trustworthy and competent, and will faithfully discharge his duty to his country in whatever position your Excellency may see proper to place him."[226]

In compliance with Special Order No. 14, First Lieutenant James A. Groom of the 10th Ohio Volunteer Infantry sent a report to Captain George L. Hartsuff, assistant adjutant general of the Department of Western Virginia on September 15. Upon arriving at Ceredo, he found two companies filled; five others were mustered in within a week of his arrival. He complained that Zeigler had moved the regiment to Barboursville ten days earlier "to protect a few loyal people, and drive back as many rebels," a move that impeded organizational progress. Groom was able to procure medical stores, distribute clothing and accoutrements, and provide instruction to quartermaster Z. D. Ramsdell on carrying out his duties. He believed that Colonel John L. Zeigler "is a dam good man, but not possessed of any military tact, and in fact, none of the officers are especially distinguished that way. As soon as the blankets and overcoats are received," Groom declared, "this Regiment is ready to 'turn a good hand.'"[227]

However, Lieutenant Groom believed the 5th (West) Virginia Infantry was "not advancing as rapidly as they would away from their present camp." The officers and men were from the immediate area and were "constantly away from duty on furlough, and as long as the distance is that the visits will be frequent." He informed Captain Hartsuff that "the sooner they are ordered from Ceredo, the better it will be for themselves and the credit of the Army." He also noted the impressive work done by Captains Oley and Merriman "under most discouraging circumstances."[228]

On the following day, Captain John Oley wrote to Hartsuff from Camp Pierpont. He was more pessimistic than he had been in his correspondence to Governor Pierpont, writing, "We found the drill here very poor_& the discipline worse than none at all. A very large majority of the officers & men have never been under military discipline & drill before and it seems almost a superhuman task to mould them into shape." In fact, Oley admitted, "if I knew the labor, difficulty & annoyances I should have had to encounter here, I might have declined the place."[229]

Captain George L. Hartsuff, assistant adjutant general of the Department of Western Virginia. Credit: Library of Congress.

Oley, who had been in the area for about two weeks, described Zeigler as "a very brave & courageous man, a kind hearted but determined man, a devoted Unionist and a terror to the Rebels, but the poorest kind of a military man." Like Groom, he complained about the movement of the 5th (West) Virginia Infantry to Barboursville and observed that the regiment was "scouting most of the time."

Early on the afternoon of September 21, 1861, two companies of the 5th (West) Virginia departed from Cassville, returning to Ceredo after a scouting expedition into the southern part of Wayne County. Major Ralph Ormstead, quartermaster of the regiment, Second Lieutenant James Baisden, and others were at the rear of the column. Colonel John L. Zeigler recorded, "They had just left the camp there to return here and had gone a short distance when some assassins who had secreted themselves on the hill-side fired on them killing both instantly."[230]

The bodies of Ormstead and Baisden were taken to Catlettsburg, Kentucky, the home of the two slain Union officers. A newspaper account noted,

> The arrival of the bodies created the intensest excitement in the village, which continued through the next day and until after the funeral. All of the prominent

secessionists of the place were arrested, some twenty in number, and taken to Camp Peirpoint, where they were kept a few days and then sent to Louisville. Lieut. Blaysden's wife was almost distracted. She is said to have fallen upon the grave of her husband, to which she clung with the wildest distress. This, with other similar scenes, aroused the people to the highest pitch of excitement.

An inventory of Ormstead's effects, which were given to his parents, listed a saddle, bridle, a pair of spurs, a suit of military clothing, a belt, and a sash.[231]

On October 1, Colonel John Zeigler informed Governor Francis Pierpont, "Our camp is shrouded in gloom to-day...Major Ormstead was a noble & brave young man, and we deeply mourn his loss." Zeigler also informed Pierpont that Confederate General John Floyd with 3,000 men was rumored to be at Logan preparing to march on Ceredo. He asked the governor to apprise General William S. Rosecrans of the rumor and of the death of the Union officers.

On the previous night, Zeigler had arrested thirteen citizens of Catlettsburg, Kentucky, some of them "men of prominence" who "are supposed to be accessory to the murder of Major Ormstead by giving information &c &c. I will send them up soon." Zeigler recommended the appointment of Abia Allen Tomlinson to replace the slain officer and asked that Pierpont forward a commission for him.[232]

Efforts by Kellian V. Whaley to enlist men in the 9th (West) Virginia Infantry met with some opposition. Apparently, several prominent Ironton citizens tried to discourage Lawrence County residents from joining the new regiment. Major Whaley wrote to the *Ironton Register* in October 1861 to explain why it was in the best interest of the region to support this fledgling unit.

> MR. EDITOR: At the earnest request of Gov. Pierpont, of Virginia, I accepted an order to raise the 9th Virginia regiment, which is designed for service in Western Virginia, between the Kanawha and Sandy rivers. I was requested by the Governor, not to commence recruiting until the 5th regiment, under Colonel Ziegler, was fully organized and mustered in – which has only recently taken place.
>
> I regret exceedingly, while I have been waiting for the completion of the 5th regiment, to see a cold shoulder turned toward the enterprise from your side of the river, which I think is evinced by a recent article in your paper, from your Military Committee, discouraging volunteers from joining this regiment, when a moment's thought must certainly convince every reflecting mind that it is to the interest of the citizens along the border of the Ohio to fill up this regiment, which is for your protection as well as ours – for should Colonel Ziegler's regiment (which is now nearly ready) receive orders to march, it would leave a long frontier exposed to the depredations of marauders, who could cross the Ohio in the night, and do a considerable amount of damage and return, before any force could be organized to repel them – unless you should at once organize a standing force on the other shore, who would be likely to lie there idly,

without hurting the guerillas, as a force on this side of the river would be likely to do.

By special arrangement made with the authorities, this regiment will remain in this immediate vicinity, and it seems to me, if you would consult the welfare of your own citizens, you would encourage them to take service here, in preference to going a long distance, and leaving their own border unprotected; at the same time they would, by serving here, protect their own firesides and homes.

We ask for but a few men from Ohio, to constitute, with those we have already recruited from Virginia, a nucleus around which we can recruit Virginians from the interior, as fast as they can get past the secession forces which hem them in.

As I know of no law, State or National, which would prevent men from your State, unarmed and unsworn, coming here to volunteer, and as it is one common cause in which we are all engaged, I trust that those who may patriotically respond to our call for help, may at least be permitted to do so without any interference or discouragement.

The regiment will be officered by men of military education and experience – the Colonel having been selected by Gen. Rosecrans himself, who has recommended James W. Conine, Assistant Adjutant of the Kanawha Brigade.[233]

Sallie P. Smith of Guyandotte wrote to her cousin Julia Sprague on October 8 and informed her that their "Aunt Patience has been raising flowers this summer amidst all of the war." She noted that members of the 5th (West) Virginia Infantry had passed through Guyandotte on the previous day with a number of prisoners from Barboursville, including Dr. Henry Maupin, Robert Allen, Bob Blackwood, Enoch Blankenship, and three others.[234]

On October 11, Whaley informed Adjutant General Henry Jefferson Samuels, "Secession is gaining in Cabell County every day." A cavalry detachment had been sent into the countryside a few days earlier to make some arrests, but Whaley was critical of Union troops in the area, noting:

A portion Kirks whole company are at home on furlough drinking and cutting up their corne. They have their guns with them. More from other companies are at Catlettsburg engaged in drunkness and debauchery. The people in Cabell and Wayne are disgusted with Zeiglers management and will demand an investigation into his military capacity. I have done the best I could to summon the witnesses to Charleston but Zigler would not send the Cavelry to Cabell to summon the witnesses from there. You ought to feel as deep an interest as any other man for the welfare of the people of your native county and I cannot do any thing for them trameled as I am with the low prejudice of Zeigler. I have written a statement of the facts to the Govenor which you can peruse if you please.

Whaley also informed Samuels,

> People are daily coming to see me from Cabell County asking me to write to you to help deliver them from secession bondage. If I can get a start here I can go to Guyandotte and recruit and get fairly under way before I have to leave for Washington but if the prejudice that is practised upon me here is sanctioned by the Govenor I shal abandon the attempt. If I have to be governed by the unpopularity and military incapasity of Zeigler you will soon hear bad news from your county. Nevertheless I shal do my duty and I believe the people are satisfied that I have done so.[235]

Whaley also contacted Governor Francis Pierpont, recommending that Dr. Jonathan Morris, "one of the finest surgeons and phisicians in this vicinity," be commissioned as surgeon for the new Union regiment. Morris, who delivered Whaley's message, was anxious for the governor's decision, as the exam for the Medical Board of Ohio was scheduled for October 16, and if Virginia did not give him a commission, he would seek one in an Ohio regiment.

Whaley noted that the 5th (West) Virginia Infantry regiment was nearly full and claimed that "Zeigler and some of his officers have been working against the new regiment for some time secretly. They conclude that if a new Regiment is formed that their Regiment will be called away from this point." Complaints had been made against Zeigler by others, and Whaley believed that "a universal demand" called for an investigation into the military capabilities of the officers of the 5th (West) Virginia.

Expressing frustration with the challenges he faced, Whaley informed Pierpont,

> as I have promised the people of Wayne Cabell and Putnam Counties that there would be a new Regiment formed here and officered with competant military men, I shal now endeavor to do so even if I have to abandon my seat in Congress. I did not expect nor would I receive an office as with a little military knoledge I am not vain enough to think I can command a Regiment. It is availability and prosperity that I want to see returned to our state, to see her laws enforced and her people be once more able to go to their Court Houses without being molested.

Whaley believed he could have raised two regiments if he had been permitted and observed that "men are coming in from Cabell and other places almost daily urging me to get my regiment started."[236]

On October 18, General William S. Rosecrans wrote to Governor Francis Pierpont and informed him that he was recommending that Lieutenant James W. Conine be appointed colonel of the 9th (West) Virginia Infantry. Rosecrans expressed his hope that Conine would "proceed at once to Guyandotte & organize this regt."[237]

In October 1861, Union authorities learned that a company of Confederates was being organized at the home of John Jarrell in Cassville, and Colonel John L. Zeigler ordered Lieutenant William Willis to take Company D of the 5th (West) Virginia Infantry to break up the camp. Early on Saturday morning, October 19, part of Company D surrounded Jarrell's house and barn, where a significant number of Confederates were still sleeping.

At daybreak, the Union troops unleashed a deadly fire into the home and barn, killing and wounding a number of the stunned Confederates. One of the Union soldiers, John Bowen, was startled to see a young boy emerge from the home and run directly toward him. Bowen wrote,

> I saw this boy when he first started from the house and saw he did not have any gun and I did not shoot at him as I saw he was coming direct to me and as this boy came up to me and pleaded for protection S. F. Fuller one of our company drew his gun to shoot this boy and I told Fuller that if he did I surely would shoot him. I took this boy with me to Casvill, W. Va. and that is the last I ever saw or heard from him. But it is great satisfaction to me to know that I saved his young life.[238]

John Jarrell was not home at the time of the raid. He acknowledged that the Confederates were encamped on his property but claimed they were unwanted guests. Colonel Zeigler wrote, "We have however only his word for the truth of the latter clause. It is clear, however, that his property was not used for insurrectionary purposes. Since the time of its capture he has voluntarily come into camp and taken the oath of allegiance." The Union soldiers confiscated "considerable property" which was hauled back to Camp Pierpont, and Zeigler sought direction concerning materials seized from those in rebellion against the United States.[239]

The Federals claimed that at least nine of the secessionists were killed and "many wounded." Five prisoners were taken, along with nine horses and nine rifles. Captain Thomas N. Davey of the 5th (West) Virginia informed Governor Pierpont on October 22 that "Col Zeigler went up Sandy yesterday. Another company is scouting up twelve 12 Pole are after the notorious Witcher who leads a band of desperadoes. We shall protect the polls in Wayne & Caball Counties shall clean out as we advance."[240]

Colonel A. Sanders Piatt of the 34th Ohio Infantry informed General William Rosecrans on October 24 that he had ordered Major Freeman Franklin to "Mud Village" to protect the polls as ordered. Franklin reported that "his scouts were fired into by five men yesterday but no one was hurt. This was near Mud as one of his scouting parties was making an advance into this secession district, which appears to me to be emboldened from some cause or other unknown to me, save rumors of a large force arriving upon Guyan." Piatt, who was stationed at Red House, believed it "of the utmost importance" that Mud Bridge be occupied by a Federal detachment.[241]

On October 26, 1861, western Virginians went to the polls to express their sentiment regarding the proposed new state of Kanawha. Captain Thomas N. Davey observed, "The election in Wayne and Cabbell Counties passed off pleasantly and peaceably." Davey noted that Whaley had moved his headquarters to Guyandotte and requested that field pieces for the artillery company be sent to Ceredo. The *Ironton*

Register reported that "Col. K. V. Whaley is forming the 9th Virginia Regiment at Guyandotte; on last Saturday he had 110 men in camp at that place."[242]

Alvin Hatton of Wayne and John Alford of Cabell had been selected colonels of their county militia regiments. J. C. Wheeler notified Adjutant General H. J. Samuels: "Some persons came to me who were organizing patrols and I advised them to suspend & organize under the militia." Wheeler, adjutant of the 9th (West) Virginia Infantry, who had been defeated in the election for delegates to the constitutional convention for the new state of Kanawha, also stated boldly, "We expect to have the 'crack' Regiment of this State."[243]

Kellian V. Whaley wrote Governor Pierpont on October 28 from Camp Paxton in Guyandotte:

We have now removed to this place with the portion of the 9th Regiment we recruited at Ceredo and we are now filling up more rapidly.

We will get quite a number of men yet from Ohio notwithstanding the late regulations at Columbus to prevent it. I attended the election at Cabell Court House & called the citizens together & exhibited to them their duty to rally to their own defense & considerable enthusiasm now prevails in the recruiting service in this county. Secesh is gradually dying out here as far as I can discover yet there are a few gurrilla bands thieving back in the mountains & occasionally make a dash to within 10 or 12 miles of the Ohio & are gone to quick to catch them unless we had a stronger force of cavalry.

Whaley also requested the transfer of Captain E. R. Merriman from the 5th (West) Virginia to the 9th (West) Virginia to serve as a drill master.[244]

Jesse Spurlock wrote to H. J. Samuels from his home at the Falls of Twelve Pole on October 28. He observed that few of the citizens in Wayne County had taken up arms against the government, but "thare is marauding bands or companies scouting and takin property and producing trouble and distress." Secessionists reportedly led by Vincent Witcher had recently ridden through the area seizing horses and a few prisoners, most of whom were released after taking an oath to support the Confederacy. Union troops had pursued Witcher's men to the forks of Beech Fork but could not overtake them. They did seize considerable property from secessionist citizens living in the vicinity of the Wayne County Courthouse. Spurlock opined, "if those marauding bands or companies could be prevented from committing those outrages in our county that we would have peace."

Spurlock also inquired about his son-in-law, Hurston Spurlock, who was confined in Wheeling. Jesse Spurlock informed Samuels that his release "will strengthen the union cause in our county for I am satisfied that he would not do anything to hurt it," and added, "we would greatly rejoice to see him again with his family."[245]

On October 29, B. D. McGinnis wrote to Adjutant General H. J. Samuels from Guyandotte and informed him that he was raising patrols – one for Cabell & one for Wayne. I expect to command the one in Cabell. Wm. Turner I think will take charge of the one in Wayne. Please represent this to the propper authority, and instruct me as to the course to pursue. I shall begin to operate Wednesday to-morrow There are two or three marauding bands roving in these counties, and have plundered a great many families of their households, and other effects as horses, cattle &c. and all within a few miles of Zeiglers camp.

McGinnis, like other residents of the region, was critical of the commander of the 5th (West) Virginia, stating,

Col Zeigler is not the man for the place and if a petition for his removal and the appointment of Capt. James Smith in his stead would be granted, I am confident the entire loyalists of Cabell & Wayne would sign it...Jeff, I can produce the evidence to prove that Zeiglers sympathies and actions were for the rebels until about the time of Col Woodruffs comes to Guyandotte – this evidence will be from his near neighbors.[246]

The number of Union troops stationed in Cabell County increased on October 30 when the 34th Ohio Infantry moved their camp from Hurricane Bridge to Mud Bridge. Private Francis Hale recorded,

we arived at mud at half after seven in the evening after a march of eighteen miles in eight hours. We was awful tiard when we got here. A good many give out and had to get in the waggeons. I thought I would give out my self but did not. I feele awful sore to night but I felt better after I got my supper.

The soldiers slept in a new but unfinished house on beds of hay that "felt like a feather bed to us or to me at least."[247]

The camp at Mud Bridge was a beehive of activity on the following morning. A tragic accident occurred at one of the picket posts when one of the soldiers, Thomas R. Hazard, shot himself. Hazard, eighteen years of age and a member of Company F, apparently had his foot on the hammer of his rifle. When he started to turn around, the weapon slipped off the pile of boards on which he was standing and discharged a ball into his forehead about an inch above his right eye, "taring an awfull hole." Private Francis Hale took the fatally wounded soldier's place at the picket post and observed his suffering. Despite his condition, the Zouave removed several letters from his pocket and handed them to Lieutenant Albert Nesbitt, who gave the documents to the regimental chaplain.

Hale noted that the young man "has no brother or relations to weepe for him here. There is not a tear shead for him," but added that he "was a tolerable good boy." A two-horse wagon was sent from camp to retrieve the wounded soldier. His condition had improved slightly on the following day, but Hale did not believe he would live for long, observing that "his brains is out. I saw part of them buried where he was shot. Part of his scull was found and part of the bullet was found clost with sum hair on it."

The wounded soldier died on November 4 and his body was taken to Camp Red House and on to Cincinnati to be turned over to his parents. His company followed the wagon about a mile out of the camp at Mud Bridge playing music and marching with reversed arms, a first for the company. According to Hale, "it was a sad sene."[248]

On November 2, seven secessionists were brought to the camp of the 34th Ohio Infantry at Mud Bridge. Private Hale wrote, "they ort to hang evey one I think for they are the meanest set of people I ever saw...they only sware them. They take the oath and go and fight again."[249]

On the same day, Captain Thomas N. Davey, adjutant of the 5th (West) Virginia Infantry, wrote to Governor Pierpont concerning his quest to obtain artillery to defend Camp Pierpont. Davey had been sent to Ironton to secure a brass field piece for the regiment's use in their march on Prestonsburg, Kentucky, but was unsuccessful, and the expeditionary force was forced to take the only cannon at Ceredo. Davey noted that due to the absence of artillery, "we shall be very illy prepared to defend our position. Can you not send us two or three six pounders upon the receipt of this?"[250]

On November 3, Francis G. Hale of the 34th Ohio Infantry noted,

> there is a good many rebels a bout here. There has a bou fifty com in and took the oath but they will not ceepe it longer than they can get a good canch to pop one of us over and run. The[y] often fire at us as we go long. They know all a bout our camp where our pickets are posted where they can get in at and not be seene by them. They was a going to fire on them one night.[251]

At Ceredo, the home of Frederik Holden was accidentally destroyed by fire. A short time before, Colonel John Zeigler had taken possession of Holden's dwelling to house Confederate prisoners who were stricken with measles. "It would not do to keep them in camp," stated Zeigler, "as the whole regiment would be exposed to the disease."[252]

Joseph C. Wheeler wrote from Camp Paxton to update Adjutant General Samuels on the progress of the 9th (West) Virginia Infantry. He noted they had "made a prosperous beginning" and praised Kellian V. Whaley for his "untiring energy and exertion." Whaley had only sixty-one men when he moved his camp to Guyandotte, but "since we have been here recruits have been coming in rapidly." Some of these recruits were permitted to return to their homes for a few days to gather supplies and other things they would need for soldiering. Wheeler informed Samuels, "Too much credit cannot be given to Friend Whaley for his indomitable perseverance in contending against the various opposition that has been exerted against this enterprise by those to whose interest is getting up the 5th Regiment. He freely devoted his time & money, to procure for them arms clothing & subsistence, and it is really astonishing that he did not yield to the discouraging prospects which presented itself before our removal to this place." Wheeler implored Samuels for blankets, caps, overcoats, and camp kettles for the men of the new Union regiment: "The weather is inclement & the poor soldier sleeping in the straw, without any covers, are daily attacked with sickness & have to be sent to the hospital."[253]

William Ludwig of the 34th Ohio Infantry, however, wrote on the same day from Mud Bridge, "We have very good quarters. Our Company is quartered in a frame house. Part of the boys sleep on straw beds and part on feather beads...the chickens have stopped crowing in this country..." He also observed,

> We are the first troops that have been through this part of the country. It is the most miserable country ever I saw. We were obliged to return from our scout on account of nothing to eat, and you may judge it is a pretty rough place where a soldier can get nothing to eat. We entered one house found a piece of corn bread one knife without handle one fork with one prong broke and two tin plates.[254]

Captain Thomas N. Davey of the 5th (West) Virginia Infantry wrote from Camp Pierpont on November 5, informing Henry J. Samuels that "our cavalry are now posting up 'notices of the election' in Wayne and Cabbel Counties. On the day of elections the Polls will be again protected by our forces, so that the people may peaceably inaugurate a movement for the establishment of the Government and the sustainment of the Laws..." On this same day, however, seven companies of the 5th (West) Virginia were ordered to the Kanawha Valley, complicating efforts to complete the enlistment of the regiment. Davey noted that this had an immediate effect on loyal citizens in Wayne County: "This afternoon several Union men from the upper portion of the County are here begging for Rifles, for they think that the removal of so much of this Regiment will develope secession influences in their neighborhood. I hope not."[255]

In early November 1861, rumors swirled around Wayne County that Milton J. Ferguson would be released from prison. Reverend Jeremiah Hare immediately wrote Virginia Governor Francis Pierpont stating that "the Union men of Wayne Co. do not want him among them, unless he has become loyal to the Government and is willing to reside there as a law-abiding citizen." He noted that Ferguson had served as prosecuting attorney and was colonel of the militia,

> and the influence of these offices secured to him, together with his talents, and a portion of his means, have been applied to the cause of treason, and to subserve the interest of traitors. He was one of the ringleaders of that unholy cause in Wayne Co. and has been instrumental in getting a number of volunteers for the Rebel army. Your Excellency may rest assured, unless, during his imprisonment, he has renounced his treasonable sentiments, purposes and works, were he now in Wayne Co., he would be instrumental in doing a great deal of harm.[256]

Colonel John L. Zeigler sent a telegram to Virginia Governor Francis H. Pierpont informing him that "[r]ecent developments in the Kanawha Valley suggests the propriety of strengthening my position." He requested that Pierpont "send immediately if possible six brass field pieces also primers balls & grape shot."[257]

At Mud Bridge, Private Francis Hale of the 34th Ohio Infantry recorded:

I am a gain on picket today on in the place where one of our boys shot at a fellow this morning but did not hit him. He run like every thing. He was not farther than forty yards. He was just geting over the fence when he shot at him…they did not see any more of him. Our company went out on a scout this evening. I do not know when they will return.[258]

Companies F and I returned to camp on November 6 from a scouting expedition that took them about ten miles into the countryside. Some of the men spent the night at the home of an "old secesh." They received royal treatment and particularly enjoyed sleeping in feather beds. Appropriated cattle, horses, and sheep accompanied the Zouaves on their journey back to Mud Bridge.[259]

Adjutant J. C. Wheeler of the 9th (West) Virginia again wrote Samuels from Guyandotte on November 6, noting,

The news from the country has been rather flattering recently – a great many secessionists have come into Cassville & taken the oath and several in this county have voluntarily done the same. We arrested a young man named Carter on Mud river who recruited some for a company commanded by his father. Afterwards the old man came in & surrendered to be tried before Dr Rouse U. S. Commissioner who has him under bonds for his appearance this week. The young man was tried before me & put under bonds for his appearance at the Federal court.

Wheeler noted the disposition of the cases of several secessionists who had been detained and recommended the release of Mart Frazier and Matthew Bellamy, who were prisoners on Wheeling Island. He described Frazier as "a great coward & a mercenary kind of a man but I cannot find that he has done any thing serious. Matthew Bellamy has fed some secessionists as they were passing & that is all that can be proved against him."

Wheeler praised the efforts of Kellian V. Whaley, stating his management at Guyandotte had been "unflinching" but "just & magnanimous towards the citizens and I think it has done more to kill opposition than could possibly have been accomplished by brute force. The Major is not mercenary but patriotic. I believe he is willing to spend the last dollar for his country & let his wife & children enjoy but a very small share of his income."

In contrast, Wheeler complained about Colonel John Zeigler's policy of releasing prominent Confederate supporters. Immediately following his return from Federal court, he had observed a detachment of artillery parading in front of headquarters and inquired as to their destination. They informed him they were headed to Barboursville on a scouting expedition. Wheeler asked Zeigler, who was present, "if I should not give them a list of the names of the leading rebels in that vicinity and he consented that I might but looking over my list objected to my giving the names of Maupin, Allen, Wood & several other leading secessionists – his attention however was immediately called to something else & I copied the entire list against whom an affidavit was filed in Wheeling & gave it to the Lieut. in command of the expedition."

Wheeler left for Portsmouth expecting to return before the expedition concluded, but the Union soldiers came back in his absence and all those arrested were discharged by Colonel Zeigler. Wheeler protested, but Zeigler explained that Daniel Frost, speaker of the house for the Restored Government of Virginia, had been present and recommended that course of action. Wheeler "had nothing further to say believing that the action of Col Zeigler does not interfere with the civil prosecution of those men upon the indictments found & to be found against them. In regard to 'inducements' I know nothing about them & have heard nothing on that subject."

Wheeler noted, "But I think probably I do not have so bitter a feeling towards the rebels as...many others do. I have always tried to keep my mind free from the influence of prejudice on all subjects so as to prevent my being misled by it. I hate the treason, but not the traitor so intensely as some others & would punish them more, to stop the treason than to wreak vengeance on them."

Wheeler observed that there was an effort being made to unite the 9th (West) Virginia Infantry with troops being raised in Mason City: "if left alone a short time we can fill this here but if it becomes positively necessary to consolidate that fraction should be sent to this & have the head quarters here to finish recruiting, as the material is about worked up in the vicinity of Mason City and besides two Regiments are needed at present between the Kanawha and Sandy Rivers as the Rebels are concentrating in heavy bodies back of that border." He noted that county elections were scheduled for November 18 and complained about his recent defeat at the polls:

> At the election for delegate from Wayne I was induced a few days before the election to become a candidate and was defeated by a scandalous misrepresentation made in my absence which I had no opportunity to explain that I am not a citizen, my family still remaining at Portsmouth except myself & boy who are both in the army. He is but eleven years old & is a drummer here in the service.

Wheeler closed his lengthy letter with the observation, "We need a cannon here verry much."[260]

A squad of cavalry commanded by Lieutenant William Feazel arrived at Camp Pierpont on the night of November 7 and reported they had put up election notices in every precinct in Cabell County. They also detained sixteen secessionists, who were turned over to the 34th Ohio Infantry at Mud Bridge. One of those captured was Archibald Reynolds, a citizen of Cabell County, arrested at his home by Lieutenant Feazel, whom he criticized as exhibiting "a cruel and inhumane disposition that is not found in the Federal Army else where." A small detachment of Company F of the 5th (West) Virginia Infantry, which had remained in the Tug Fork region, also made their way to Ceredo, bringing several horses. They had recently skirmished with Confederates about four miles above Trout's Hill.[261]

Jesse Spurlock informed Adjutant General H. J. Samuels on November 7, "In regard to the state of affairs in our county I think they are flat[t]ering. I think peace will soon be restored if not already in our county." Spurlock observed that a number of Wayne County men had surrendered to military authorities and been sent home, and declared:

> thare is none of our citizens that is in arms at this time or that is disposed to be found in armes unless it is to protect themselves and property from an invading foe. Such characters as is prowling through our county for gain thare has been such characters and may be some still but I have not heard of them for some time and I am in hopes they have left our county for all of our permanent citizens are down on such men. I have spoken repeatedly and to several of my county men on this matter since I have come home and they all say that they do not wish to do the government any harm but they fear that the government troops will do them harm if they get them...[262]

Spurlock had been indicted, which he attributed to "spite" or "some cenister motive," but his primary reason for writing was to plead for the release of his son-in-law, Hurston Spurlock. He believed Hurston had "ben sufficiently punished for all that he has ever done," and gave an explanation for the charges against him. "We are all weighting with great anxiety for the release of Herston," Jesse Spurlock wrote, "for his wife greeves about him and is distressed on account of her husband." He added, "I am satisfied if you will release him that he will never betray his trust."[263]

On November 8, Captain Thomas N. Davey, adjutant of the 5th (West) Virginia observed,

> I had supposed from the previous reports of our men that secession influences was entirely destroyed in the upper portion of this County, but from recent indications this is not the case; Union men still complain of depredations upon their persons and property. William Ratcliffe, member of the Legislature was in the Office today, and stated, that he had been plundered out of about three hundred dollars worth of property. He is extremely anxious to obtain guns for a 'Patrol Company' and has requested me to correspond with the Governor on that subject which I shall do this evening.[264]

On the following day, Davey informed Governor Francis Pierpont that a patrol company of fifty-three men had been raised, which was to be led by Captain Thomas Damron and First Lieutenant Wilson Damron. The Wayne Countians were "anxious" that their commissions, arms, and accoutrements be sent immediately via Colonel John Zeigler. Davey remarked, "These men think that if they were properly equiped, that they could subdue neighborhood secession influences and be of advantage to the Federal forces throughout the county." He also gave some more details on depredations in Wayne County: "Wm Ratcliffe said to me, that about ten days since one hundred men visited him and took from his premises about three hundred Dolls in stock & mdse. They (the Secessionists) desired very much to 'contraband' him also."[265]

The commander of the 34th Ohio Infantry, Colonel Abram Sanders Piatt, contacted General William S. Rosecrans on November 9 concerning a proposal "to permit hospital nurses for my regiments." Piatt supported the plan, writing,

> I deem the care of the sick of the first importance and there is no hand like that of a kind nurse to soothe the sick bed. My whole regiment is anxious for this. The little cares and attention necessary in pain are more fully given by the hands of woman. I will see that none but proper nurses are installed. All matters in the division at Mud Bridge, Lt. Col. Toland reports to me are progressing as they should. The Rebels that are inciting disturbance there are being properly dealt with.[266]

William Ludwig, a member of the 34th Ohio stationed at Mud Bridge, wrote to his family on November 10, 1861:

> We have just returned from one of them rough scouts. We walked from nine oclock one night through the roughest country ever I saw. We returned with twelve prisoners, some of which are now on the way to Columbus. We are still at Mud Bridge, but I do not know how long we will stay here. I think we shall go into winter quarters soon but I cannot tell where. There are eight companys here and some of them out on a scout all the time.[267]

Ludwig and the members of his regiment observed the Sabbath with a worship service as "the sun shone forth in all her glory." The chaplain invited local citizens to attend with the promise that the pickets would allow them both in and out of camp. A large number responded, and the camp quickly filled with "a good many of the country peopple." The sermon was based on Joshua 5:15 and "the Chaplain give the virgineans fits for not taking up armes for the defence of the country."[268]

At the recruit camp of the 9th (West) Virginia Infantry in Guyandotte, about twenty of the men were on furlough during the second week of November, and another eighteen were sick in the camp hospital. Lieutenant William Feazel, who commanded about thirty-five cavalrymen stationed temporarily in Guyandotte, informed Adjutant General Henry J. Samuels on November 10 that part of the 34th Ohio Infantry stationed at Barboursville was making use of his old law office in the village. Feazel failed to mention that he had that day refused a request from Major Kellian V. Whaley to take his mounted troops on a scouting expedition down the Guyandotte River toward Barboursville. "I did not come here to scout," Feazel informed Whaley, "but to recruit my horses and get them shod." The lack of reconnaissance left the town of Guyandotte open to a surprise attack. It was not long in coming.[269]

6
The Raid on Guyandotte

"There was a sanguinary struggle at the bridge over the Guyandotte river, and those who have since visited the bridge, report it covered with blood, as in a slaughter house."

Ironton Register, November 14, 1861

In early November 1861, Confederate General John B. Floyd ordered Colonel John Clarkson and his cavalry force "to proceed in the direction of the Ohio River, and to strike the enemy a blow whenever and wherever he thought it prudent to do so." Clarkson had led a raid into the Kanawha Valley three weeks earlier, an expedition that provided intelligence and experience that would prove invaluable. Clarkson commanded about seven hundred cavalry from the 5th and 8th Virginia Cavalry regiments, the latter led by Colonel Albert G. Jenkins. Guyandotte was selected as their target.[270]

Departing from Camp Dickerson in Fayette County on November 4, the cavalry experienced "a most tedious and exposed march, without tents or other camp equipage, for one hundred and seventy-five miles, over roads washed away by the unprecedented freshets of this Fall..." One Confederate soldier wrote, "We had a hard time during the whole trip & passed through the most lonely & barren country that I ever saw."[271]

The expedition led the men through Raleigh, Wyoming, and Logan counties and was conducted "with greater speed than the news of their march could be carried by the spies who

Confederate General John B. Floyd. Credit: Library of Congress.

infest the country." One of the Confederate cavalrymen declared, "The march itself was one of the most daring feats of the campaign, and was untiringly prosecuted in defiance of weather and mountain, by swimming rivers and traveling paths on the steep sides of mountains."[272]

A Border Ranger recalled,

> Nothing of interest occurred on this march until we reached Logan C. H., which we did on election day, and, after improvising a ballot box everybody voted the 'straight ticket'...The business of 'scratching' a ticket in those days was not indulged in so generally as at present; but then it is likely that the Devil had less to do with elections then than now.[273]

The Confederates reached Cabell County on the afternoon of November 10. At sunset, they dashed into Barboursville, "surrounding the town before the inhabitants had any notice of our approach." Union troops from the 5th (West) Virginia Infantry had been in the village but departed before the enemy's arrival. The Confederate soldiers arrested several "traitors" and raided a store owned by Matthew Thompson, which had been stocked with new goods. There,

> they found a tresure for they truely was in want of every thing in the shape of clothing such as boots shoes and coats which they found here in abundance and many of [them] said they had received nothing to eat for 2 days so they being raged and hungery they were like wild Deamons so they robed Thomsons store of all the best of his stock and money and then seazed Thomson and dragged him off to Guyandotte...[274]

Upon leaving Barboursville, the Confederates crossed the Mud River and resumed their advance toward Guyandotte, a distance of about seven miles, on the road that followed the Guyandotte River toward its confluence with the Ohio. Many of the men were from Cabell County, and some were preparing to raid their hometown. Border Ranger James D. Sedinger, a native of Guyandotte, recalled, "The boys were all happy then. We were going home for the first time since we left in the spring."[275]

The Union troops at Guyandotte were unaware that the Confederate cavalry was near. One mile from town, Colonel John Clarkson issued orders for a three-pronged attack. A force under Captain James Corns was to seize possession of the suspension bridge, cutting off retreat toward Ceredo. Major Henry Fitzhugh was to ride through Guyandotte and guard the escape route up the Ohio River, while Colonels Clarkson and Jenkins were "to penetrate into the centre of town, and to dislodge the enemy from buildings which they occupied in that quarter." One Confederate noted, "The movements were conducted nearly simultaneously, so as completely to surround the enemy before they were aware of it."[276]

H. C. Everett, whose family lived on a farm along the Guyandotte River, heard the approach of horses and went out to the road with his father, Tarleton W. Everett. He later recalled,

In a short time the column, which was a part of the 8th Va. Cavalry, C. S. A., passed going at a rapid rate. 'Cooney' Ricketts was pretty near the head of the column, his saddle cloth was slipping from under his saddle and as he passed our fence he threw the saddle cloth into our yard and hollered 'How are you, Uncle Talt?' My father, Talton Everett, followed the column down the road towards Guyandotte and just before he got to the town he saw a man crossing the road and hurrying down into a ditch. Father called out, 'You need not run from me, I will not harm you.' The man addressed was Captain William Turner who lived on a farm on the west side of the Guyandotte River opposite the Everett place but at that moment was a Captain in Colonel Whaley's (U. S. A.) recruiting party...Turner recognized my father and made no further effort to conceal himself.[277]

H. C. Everett observed his cousin Cooney Ricketts and the Confederate cavalry passing the Everett home on the Guyandotte River just prior to the raid on Guyandotte. Credit: Special Collections Department, Marshall University.

Sunday, November 10, 1861, was a pleasant and fair day in Guyandotte, although clouds appeared about four o'clock in the afternoon. About 130 recruits had joined the 9th (West) Virginia Infantry, but twenty of the men were on furlough and eighteen were sick and being cared for in the regimental hospital, leaving a force of ninety-two soldiers. Major Whaley had issued an order a few days earlier "recommending all to be faithful in attending public worship." Many of the Union troops were present at services that Sunday evening including one conducted by the chaplain of the regiment, Joseph C. Wheeler. John Barbour, who served in Captain William Turner's company, went to church with a fellow soldier. Turner had urged all of his men to take their weapons with them, but his admonition was widely ignored, and when the attack began, many of the Federals were unable to procure their arms.[278]

Just after 8:00 p.m., as the congregations were returning from worship, a cry rang out, "Corporal of the guard, post No. 5! Corporal of the guard post No. 5! Corporal of the guard post No. 5!" Dr. Jonathan Morris, physician for the 9th (West) Virginia, had just turned onto Guyan Street, which paralleled the Guyandotte River, "when several shots were fired up Second street from below the bridge, the balls whistling past me, some striking Hite's house by my side." Morris recorded,

My first impression was, that our pickets had become alarmed, and fired at something, they knew not what. Paying no attention to it, I walked on, and as I passed Capt. Payne's quarters, I observed the men rushing out of their quarters, and the Capt. ordering them to fall in ranks. I asked what was the matter, but received no reply. I then thought they were all getting frightened, and nothing to be alarmed at, and I very leisurely walked on; but had proceeded but a few steps, when a heavy fire came raking down street toward the Ohio river, the balls whizzing and buzzing over my head and to my left. I then began to feel indignant at our pickets, still supposing it was them firing, and turned around to go up and put a stop to it. As I turned round, I saw a man I took to be Dr. Bailey, coming out of the Quartermaster's Department with a gun in his hand, and started up the opposite side of the street. I walked on until I came near the corner of Hite's house, probably within two feet of where I was when the first shots were fired from the direction of the bridge, and then another heavy fire came raking up street from the same direction. I then knew it was not our pickets...[279]

Dr. James H. Rouse was relaxing at the home of a friend when he heard musket fire. Rouse dashed outside and was informed that the town was under attack. Rushing down the street to his office, he grabbed his minie rifle and seven rounds of ammunition and joined Captain Uriah Payne, who was attempting to rally the Union recruits.

Edward Smith, Absolom Chapman, Wayne McMahon, and J. H. Shoemaker were sitting in chairs on the pavement in front of Baumgardner's Hotel when they "heard an alarm" followed immediately by the sound of firearms up the street near the end of the suspension bridge. After several volleys, one of the men "remarked we had better be getting away or we will all be killed," and the group dashed into the building.[280]

Rebecca Baumgardner, whose father owned the hotel, ran out onto the back porch. Drums were beating furiously, and as she dashed out through a gate, she heard gunfire. Baumgardner ran into the hotel hall where she met Smith, Chapman, and William Rogers coming out of the barroom. Smith suggested taking refuge in the cellar, and the group rushed down the stairs and found Baumgardner's father and the others already there. Her brother Henry came down a few minutes later.[281]

As the Confederate cavalry began storming into Guyandotte, Joe Bragg and Thomas Burks, who were on camp guard duty, were both shot in the thigh. They were the first Union casualties of the night. A drummer attempted to sound a warning but was forced to cease when a bullet pierced his instrument. The Border Rangers had been ordered to capture and hold the suspension bridge across the Guyandotte River. As they charged the wire span, a picket standing about midway across the bridge fired at the Confederates, killing Al Long. Corporal James Sedinger observed, "Some one of the company shot him. This happened as we charged the Bridge. Why he did not throw down and surrender was always a mystery to us. He was a small red headed man – would weigh about one hundred and forty pounds."[282]

Simultaneously, Confederates moved into position in the northern end of the town, and the main force launched its attack on the badly outnumbered Federals, with the

CHAPTER SIX   107

The Guyandotte suspension bridge, scene of bloody fighting on November 10, 1861. Credit: Special Collections Department, Marshall University.

fighting centered in the heart of Guyandotte. One Confederate wrote, "Most of the enemy took to the houses on the borders of the narrow streets, and from the upper windows and doors delivered deadly volleys of fire on the horsemen galloping in the streets below them. In the darkness we never knew where an enemy was, but by the flash of his gun from some hiding place."[283]

Dr. Jonathan Morris

> had proceeded but a few steps from the corner, when Capt. Payne ordered his men to shelter themselves in the alley and behind their quarters, and fire up street. The order was quickly obeyed, and a heavy fire belched forth from behind the building, which sent the deadly missiles whizzing and raking the street to my left. At the same instant I heard up street tumbling, snorting and falling of horses, and I knew the fire had done execution.[284]

Dr. James Rouse wrote,

> our little band knowing nothing but load and fire, stood the enemy's fire and fought in a manner that would have done credit to much older and more experienced veterans. The enemy's shot fell thick and fast on every side, still our men fought with a determination that astonished the rebels themselves, causing them frequently to fall back, but knowing their superior numbers, they would renew their charge with increased fury.[285]

Major Kellian V. Whaley ordered Lieutenant William Wilson to "rally the men in the shade of a house, near the end of the Wire Bridge." Wilson recalled, "We went to two or three groups of men, called them into ranks. I succeeded in getting twenty-five or thirty at said house...I then ordered the men to fire on the enemy and they did so. Our firing told the enemy where we were. Then the battle commenced."[286]

Whaley attempted to organize a defense with the few troops available. The Union soldiers gathered in squads and sought cover in buildings and alleys "and kept up a brisk fire upon the enemy for near three quarters of an hour." The Confederates "were ordered to dismount and to storm the houses, which they promptly did, killing, or capturing, the inmates."[287]

Lieutenant William Wilson of the 9th (West) Virginia Infantry recorded,

We continued to fire for some time. I saw Sine fall. He said he was a dead man. I saw one little man bleeding at the mouth. He cursed and swore, but continued to load and fire...He was grit to the bone – no better soldier when wounded, certain. About this time I was wounded, and the enemy drew nearer. I gave the boys orders to leave, and every man to take care of himself.[288]

Carey Hayslip, who was from Guyandotte, fought fiercely against the Confederate cavalry, paired up with Lieutenant Colonel George W. Bailey. Finally, a squad charged on their position and fired a volley. Hayslip "tumbled over the bank and crawled under some logs that had drifted on the shore and laid there until the enemy left next morning."[289]

Some of the Union troops, including Bailey, attempted to escape across the suspension bridge, but the Border Rangers, stationed at the end of the span, were waiting for them. James D. Sedinger recalled, "We waited until they were in 50 feet of us when we opened fire on them. What became of them after that I never knew, but I think they jumped over the rail into the river..."[290]

Another Confederate wrote, "During the fight a number of the enemy attempted to cross the bridge towards Ceredo, defended by Capt. Corns, who fired into them, killing three, and making the rest leap into the river, drowning all except two, who were captured after they swam ashore. Others who attempted to swim the Ohio were also shot or drowned."[291]

Several Federal soldiers were killed and two were captured after they swam ashore, but another seeking mercy met a brutal end.

Confederate Captain James Corns of Wayne County, who seized the suspension bridge at the outset of the Guyandotte raid. He later commanded the 8th Virginia Cavalry. Credit: Judy West (courtesy of Jack L. Dickinson).

He was attempting to swim across the Guyandotte River, but a Confederate soldier yelled to him that if he surrendered no harm would come to him. As the Federal soldier reached the river bank with arms uplifted, Wilson B. Moore, a former sheriff of Cabell County, suddenly raised his revolver to the man's temple and "discharged its contents into his head, literally blowing his brains out, mutilating his head in a shocking manner." His clothing was stripped from his body, which was left on the bank of the Guyandotte.[292]

John S. Everett, who lived near Guyandotte, was accused of shooting Union soldiers as they made their way to shore. After his close call with the Confederate column, Captain William Turner made his way into the town, where he was soon in the midst of combat. He escaped by mounting his horse and "dashing through their lines," but was forced to abandon his mount at the riverbank with the Confederates on his tail. Turner was compelled to lay in mud and water and attempted to use a tree as cover while his pursuers searched for him. He heard them yelling, "John, Oh John Everett, shoot them d___d devils coming out of the water there," followed by two gunshots. Someone shouted, "There's another just out behind the tree there. Oh, I've sunk that d___d Yankee." Another Federal was shot while crawling in the mud near Turner's concealed position. Turner heard another yell, "I've got one of the d___dad's scalps and a first-rate Enfield rifle." Turner was eventually able to swim across the Ohio River to safety.[293]

Dr. Morris rushed through the tavern of the hotel into the hall and upstairs toward his room with Confederate cavalry in hot pursuit. As he neared the top steps, a volley was fired into the building, followed by "a rush in at the bar-room door, firing away in every direction." Morris entered his room and was greeted by a shower of bullets from the street through the windows. Another volley was fired from the first floor and Dr. Morris prepared to go downstairs to offer assistance. After yet another heavy volley in the hallway below, a voice yelled out, "If there is any d___d Yankees up stairs, come down or we will burn the house down." As he descended, Morris could see the hall "crowded with men and all had their guns pointing at me."[294]

Morris had to step over two dead bodies at the foot of the stairs and observed a wounded Confederate lying in the hall "in great pain." Several of his captors aided him in leading the soldier into a sitting room, where Morris and a Confederate surgeon dressed his wounds. Morris also treated a Union soldier and "dressed the hand of a small boy, who had been shot through the ball of the thumb." Suddenly five Confederate cavalry appeared, and upon learning Morris's identity, said they had been sent to take him prisoner.[295]

As he was brought through the barroom he noted about ten Confederates, including Colonel John Clarkson, opening the trunks they had seized. Half of the group was particularly interested in Whaley's, rifling through the papers and "scattering things in every direction." Whaley himself was on the mind of the expedition's leader; every few minutes Colonel Clarkson would say, "Come, men, hunt that d___d Col."[296]

Meanwhile, Major Whaley sought to rally his few remaining recruits, at the brick hotel on the bank of the Ohio, where I had ordered a box of cartridges for their use. At this place they also fired briskly for a short time. I then returned again to the street to rally what men I could find to the hotel, and near that point was charged upon by a company of rebels commanded by H. Clay Pate. We resisted the attack for a short time, but were finally overpowered by superior numbers and taken prisoners.[297]

A Union soldier described the aftermath:

The rebels rushed upon him crying 'Kill the damned Abolitionist!' and presented their guns, and one attempted to fire at his breast while he was being held by the arms by two men, but the gun missed fire. Captain Pate in a loud voice demanded to know of him where his men were, threatening to kill him if he did not tell...Colonel Whaley refused positively to give him the desired information, replying: 'You will find them soon enough.' The men still continued to threaten his life when Colonel Clarkson rode up and asked if he was Colonel Whaley. Whaley replied that he was not a Colonel, though in command of the post. Clarkson then commanded his men not to kill him and remarked: 'He is a brave man and I design to so report him.'[298]

Captain Henry Clay Pate, who led the final attack at Guyandotte and captured Major Kellian V. Whaley. Credit: West Virginia State Archives.

After the firing ceased, the Border Rangers crossed the bridge into Guyandotte and "kissed all the girls in the town." Several of the women, including Kate Everett, Dollie Russell, and Margaret Ann Rece (the latter two were the wives of ministers), became so elated at the Confederate presence "that they offered up cheer after cheer" for Jefferson Davis until they became hoarse from their efforts. According to another account, "The people of the town received our men with great cordiality, and gave them a fine supper." Sallie Smith recorded that "Ed Smith took 27 of them to his Fathers and made Old Jinny get supper for them and his Father did not dare to say a word."[299]

Confederate Captain Tom Huddleston was accidentally killed while searching the Forest Hotel for Union soldiers. A Confederate soldier recorded that Huddleston was "killed by our own men, who mistook him in the dark for one of the enemy." Another noted that he had "failed to give the countersign upon being hailed." Some accounts declared that Colonel John Clarkson was responsible for Huddleston's death. An observer wrote poignantly, "Capt. Huddleston was a brave man, and so much endeared to his company that when the command left Guyandotte I saw many of his old comrades near his dead body in tears, and others kissed his pale, tranquil face, which they will never see again."[300]

The home of Percival S. Smith was situated on the corner of the town square, just across the street from the end of the suspension bridge. Much of the clash took place directly in front of his house. Concerned for the safety of his son Edward and his family, Smith, who had turned sixty-five less than a month earlier, ran through his garden and across the alley to his son's residence several times during the battle. Each time, Edward's wife Josephine informed him he had gone down the street. About five minutes after the firing ceased, Smith heard a knock at the rear entrance of his home. He rose and upon hearing Edward's voice, opened the door. Edward asked if anyone was hurt and told his father he had taken refuge in the cellar of the Baumgardner Hotel. He then hurried home to check on his family.[301]

Margaret Rece, wife of Reverend John Calvin Rece. She was among a number of Guyandotte women who rejoiced following the Confederate victory and cheered repeatedly for Jefferson Davis. Credit: Special Collections Department, Marshall University.

Hugo Deitz, a Guyandotte citizen, noted the cessation of gunfire and started toward the heart of town to check on his brother-in-law, Roland Clark, who had enlisted in the Union army. Passing down the street, he was hailed by John Hite, who requested aid in moving a wounded Union soldier. Deitz and Hite went to Henry Miller's store house, where they assisted Lewis Peters in transporting the soldier. They attempted to get medical attention for the wounded man but were unsuccessful. Hite returned to his home while Deitz went down to the hotel to check on the condition of John White, who had been wounded. After returning home, Deitz was visited on several occasions by Confederate cavalry, who remarked on their disappointment as to the number of captured guns.[302]

Meanwhile, stunned and frightened Union soldiers attempted to flee the town, using any means possible to escape the swarming Confederate cavalry. Lieutenant William Wilson and a Mr. Riggs of Ironton "passed under the end of the Wire Bridge, making our way up Guyan River." Wilson recorded, "I hobbled along as fast as could, under near the upper end of town; there, we saw a large body of troops, making toward us. I pulled off my boots, threw them into Guyan River, threw in my Enfield rifle, then, together with six or seven more, jumped into the river. I got to a tree standing in the water, sunk my body underwater, keeping my head out, of course." Wilson and Riggs crossed the Ohio into Ohio and climbed the bank on the opposite side. They then walked three or four miles through the woods, following the Ohio River. The Union men later summoned Dr. R. M. P. McDowell, who dressed Wilson's wound.[303]

Joseph C. Wheeler, the adjutant for the 9th (West) Virginia Infantry, escaped by running into a cornfield, losing only baggage belonging to himself and his son, a drummer in the regiment. Father and son walked all night until they saw someone they felt safe to approach about aiding them in crossing the river. The Wheelers were forced to "employ the persuasive chink of the almighty dollar" to convince the man to help.[304]

A Union recruit by the name of Roland Clark, who was a bass drummer for the 9th (West) Virginia Infantry, was cut off from his fellow soldiers. He spied a skiff lying at the levee and attempted to make his escape. Clark managed to start across the Ohio River when he heard a faint cry for help. Turning back to shore, he found a Union soldier who had been in the hospital when the raid began. Clark "clasped the sick man in his arms and carried him aboard, then plying the oars with manly strokes, amid a thick volley of musketry, he made his escape without harm and landed safely on the Ohio shore."[305]

A group of about twenty soldiers fled up to Seven Mile Creek, where they crossed the Ohio River. Captain A. T. Brattin of Ironton hid under a house until the next morning, when he was able to make his escape. While a number of men did manage to evade capture, most were not as fortunate. James E. Wood, a resident of Guyandotte, was reportedly shot in the hand and run over by a horse. He somehow managed to reach the middle of the suspension bridge, where he jumped off and swam to the west side of the Guyandotte River. When he emerged from the water, he was captured by members of the Border Rangers.[306]

Lying at the wharf in Guyandotte was a keel boat loaded with wheat owned by William H. Langley. John Lawson, a miller employed by Langley, was in charge of the craft, assisted by three deck hands from Gallipolis – Thomas Berridge, Andrew Langley, and John Blagg. On the evening of November 10, Lawson and Berridge attended church in Guyandotte while Langley and Blagg remained on the boat.[307]

Dr. James H. Rouse had joined in the firing on the charging Confederates, but he soon ran out of ammunition and was in danger of being trapped between two Confederate detachments. He fled toward the river and jumped into Langley's keel boat. Several other citizens joined the men already aboard, and the group shoved the boat into the Ohio River in an effort to escape. A large force of Confederates suddenly appeared on the riverbank and opened fire on the craft, threatening to kill all aboard unless they returned to the Virginia shore. Langley and Blagg jumped into a skiff attached to the keel boat and rowed frantically across the Ohio while "a continuous shower of bullets" flew all around them. As they landed on the Ohio shore a bullet struck within a few inches of Blagg.[308]

Rouse and the remaining men attempted to follow the skiff in the keel boat but were thrown into the river when the oars came loose. The boat and those aboard were captured, but Rouse swam back to shore and hid in a cave along the river bank for about four hours. He was finally forced to seek assistance due to his wet clothing. He surrendered to Edward G. Vertigans and was taken to the home of A. J. Keenan, a southern sympathizer, where he was given some dry clothing and a pallet on which to sleep.

Rouse was later taken to the hospital for the recruitment camp, which had been converted into a guardhouse. There he saw fellow prisoners T. J. Hayslip, A. G. White, and Dr. Jonathan Morris and observed

Dr. James H. Rouse was captured at Guyandotte and wrote a detailed account of the event and his subsequent imprisonment. Credit: Special Collections Department, Marshall University.

> a sight I trust in God I may never see again. There lay our wounded and sick in heaps upon the floor crying for water to quench their thirst and begging the rebels to allow them to have their wounds dressed (their surgeons were there with their hands tied) to which appeals the rebels would only reply that if they did not make less noise they would send them to a hotter climate to have their wounds dressed after the most approved plan.[309]

Dr. Morris observed that about sixty citizens and soldiers had been captured and that five of the men were wounded. He asked a Confederate captain to untie him so he could render assistance, but the officer replied, "He would see us all in h_ll first." Morris later appealed to Captain George Poague of the Valley Rangers, whom he described as "a large, rough, ugly looking customer." Poague listened patiently and replied, "certainly, sir, certainly, sir," before untying his arms. Morris marveled at his response, stating, "The term *sir* startled me more than the sight of the ghastly dead or the flowing blood of the wounded, for I had heard nothing from them but 'd__d Yankees,' 'd__d Negro thief,' &c. from the time I first descended the stairs."[310]

Guards accompanied Morris to his former office, where he "found everything demolished or carried away, my bandages were all gone, lint trampled under foot, bottles broken to pieces, and everything in a state of chaos." He still managed to dress the prisoners' wounds and was informed that there were at least two other wounded men that could not be moved. A guard of three marched Morris down the street and into the Ricketts home, where in the front room he saw two or three dead Confederates and three others wounded. He was quickly ushered out and led to the quarters of Captain Uriah Payne.[311]

There he found a Union recruit whose thigh had been "terribly shattered." Morris wrote, "The poor fellow must have been suffering severely, but manifested heroic fortitude; he bore it without a groan, and even talked cheerfully about amputation. All that I could do for him that night, was to confine his limb in a straight position, and let him await an opportunity to amputate." After giving the soldier a dose of morphine, Dr. Morris crossed the street to aid another wounded man who was shot through the upper part of the right knee. It was a severe wound, but Dr. Morris believed early amputation would save his life. "It was truly agonizing," Morris recorded, "to hear his groans, and the great burthen of his mind was, that he would not live to see his wife, who I believe lived in Millersport."[312]

John Hite provided a pine box to make splints and some material that Dr. Jonathan Morris constructed into bandages. A Confederate surgeon assisted Morris in dressing the wounds of the Federal soldiers. When Dr. Morris returned to the former hospital, he treated the Felix brothers of Barboursville, one of whom was shot through both arms and the other wounded in the mouth.[313]

Meanwhile, the victorious Confederates posted pickets around the town and spent most of the night rounding up prisoners. Among those captured were Major Kellian V. Whaley, Captain Landford Thomas, Quartermaster-Sergeant T. J. Hayslip, and Sergeant Major Thomas Ross. Also seized was Captain Uriah Payne, who had been one of the first three men to plant the Stars and Stripes at Monterey during the Mexican War. One Confederate recorded, "Only some forty of the whole saved their bacon."[314]

Rouse declared that John Hite, Elijah Ricketts, Jennie Ricketts, the Baumgardners, T. C. Dusenberry, John Ong, Isaac Ong, Kate Everett, and the Scott family all aided the Confederates in rounding up Guyandotte citizens that supported the United States. Rouse observed that the Confederates, "taking advantage of the information thus gained, proceeded to arrest all the Union men and place them under heavy guard, taking some of them out of their beds and not allowing them time to don their clothing, compelling them to stand in the street all night with their hands tied, and would not permit them to go to the fire to warm their cold and chilled limbs."[315]

After the fighting concluded, a cavalry detachment rode out of town along the Guyandotte River with revenge on its mind. The war created many tense confrontations between neighboring families who held contrasting views and were now on opposing sides. Two such families, the Fullers and the Sheltons, resorted to violence to settle their differences.[316]

Henry Shelton, a prominent resident of the county, had formerly served in the House of Delegates and had been a colonel of the militia. He was a slaveowner, and his prominent home and farm stood along the James River and Kanawha Turnpike about two miles west of Barboursville. When war erupted, several of his sons joined the Confederate army. A little over a mile west of the Shelton home, overlooking Russell Creek, lived the family of Achilles Fuller, a native of Massachusetts.

In the fall of 1861, Fuller's youngest son Albert decided to join the Union army at Barboursville. Accompanied by another youth, William Ward, Fuller marched down the turnpike armed with a musket and bayonet. As they passed by the Shelton home, Henry Shelton appeared and engaged the young men in conversation. Shelton shared some cider as they sat and talked, but eventually the discussion centered on the war and

Henry Shelton Home. Shelton was murdered in front of this home in the summer of 1861. Credit: Special Collections Department, Marshall University.

grew heated. One story is that Mrs. Shelton took the weapon inside the house out of caution, but it is likely that Shelton simply seized the musket.

An enraged Fuller hurried up the turnpike to Barboursville to report the incident, and a company of Union cavalry was sent to arrest Shelton. Meanwhile, William Ward hurried to the home of Achilles Fuller and reported that Albert was being held against his will. Some secessionists suspected that the younger Fuller served as a messenger for Union forces in the area, and one rumor was that Shelton planned to turn him over to Confederate authorities.

Achilles Fuller and his son John, who lived nearby, took down their hunting rifles and marched up the road to the home of Henry Shelton. Shelton was sitting on the stone mounting block in front of his house when they arrived. One account claimed that Henry Shelton fired and missed, and John Fuller responded by shooting Shelton. Most, however, declared that the Fullers, without provocation, fired several shots, killing Henry Shelton. A short time later, the Union cavalry arrived with Albert Fuller. His brother John returned with the cavalry to Barboursville and then reportedly fled to Ohio. No action was taken against the Fullers by either county or state authorities.

On the night of November 10, 1861, George Shelton led a cavalry detachment that crossed the suspension bridge at Guyandotte and rode three miles to the brick home of Achilles Fuller along the James River and Kanawha Turnpike on the bank of Russell

116   DISORDER ON THE BORDER

Achilles Fuller Home. Fuller was murdered at his front door on the night of November 10, 1861. Credit: Special Collections Department, Marshall University.

Creek. It is unclear when Shelton learned of his father's murder, but the young man had undoubtedly become obsessed about the opportunity for revenge.

One of the Confederate horsemen, probably Shelton, dismounted and advanced toward the front door. Achilles Fuller, dressed for bed and armed with a candle, opened the door and called out, "Hello, what is wanted, hello!" Suddenly, shots rang out and Fuller fell dead in the bloodstained doorway. The *Wheeling Intelligencer* called it "a cold blooded murder," but the *Richmond Enquirer* deemed it "the just fate of a traitor and a murderer."[317]

Albert Fuller, described as "an unruly boy," was taken prisoner that same night. When John and Allen McGinnis went to the home of Achilles Fuller after his murder, his wife "urged Allen to follow the Confederate troops and try to get her son Albert released." However, Albert Fuller was sent to prison in Richmond, where a number of refugees from Guyandotte (Peters, Poteet, Beekman, Wilson) testified against him. A Confederate official reviewed the case and wrote,

> I think Fuller ought not to be discharged but from the imperfection of the testimony I cannot advise where he should be sent for trial. I think he was the cause of Shelton's death and ought in some way to be brought to justice either by the State or Confederate authorities; but the seat of justice of the

Confederate States for this district (Charleston, Kanawha County) and the committing of the offense are both in the possession of the enemy. I would suggest the propriety of an act of the Legislature of Virginia authorizing the trial in some other county.[318]

Casualty estimates of the battle at Guyandotte vary, but it is known that at least three Confederates were killed and less than a dozen troopers were wounded. Nineteen of their mounts were killed or disabled during the raid, but the Confederates captured thirty-two cavalry horses to more than replace their losses. Adjutant Wheeler estimated Federal casualties at ten or twelve killed and twenty to thirty wounded. Nearly one hundred Union men, both soldiers and civilians, were captured by the Confederates and sent to prison camps.

Numerous reports claimed that the citizens of Guyandotte knew the Confederates were going to attack the town that night. When the fight at Guyandotte erupted, Doctor Jonathan Morris observed that "in the secession houses *not a light was to be seen*."[319]

Throughout the country, citizens and soldiers alike were outraged at the reports that the secession residents of the town had aided the Confederates in their attack. The *Zouave Gazette* reported on November 15 that the Confederates and townspeople used

> trickery to massacre our troops in cold blood...(They) were very kind to our troops on last Sunday evening and invited them to their houses on various pretexts, and all who were off duty accepted the invitation...signals were displayed from every house where the federals were...[320]

A correspondent for the *Ironton Register*, in an early account of the raid, claimed that "citizens, in the late 'massacre,' fired from their houses upon our men seems to be well attested – at least from H. W. Hite's (now prisoner at Columbus); and our men say that the Scott *women* fired upon them! E. A. Smith (prisoner) is reported seen in the streets with a revolver firing on our men." Alzira J. Scott disputed this claim, however, writing: "As for the ladies of Guyandotte shooting at the Federalists, I will guarrantee that to be false, for their own weapons are their tongues, and I must admit they are good at using them."[321]

On November 11, Ralph Leete of Ironton wrote a lengthy letter to Ohio Governor William Dennison Jr. detailing the events in Guyandotte. He observed,

> The evidence, I was told by our people who have returned from there, is clear that there was a concert of action between the people of Guyandotte and Jenkins, as to the surprise and attack – that even the women were wild with joy, while Jenkins men were put[t[ing to death the unarmed recruits of Mr Whaley – and that the indignations heaped upon Whaley and his fellow prisoners after they were bound, were all that barbarism could suggest.[322]

There is no solid evidence, however, that the secessionist citizens of Guyandotte had foreknowledge of the attack. John Lawson, who was captured and soon after released, stated, "The reports of women firing upon our soldiers from the houses, and the hallowing 'take no prisoners, give no quarter' were false." Lawson also declared there were "no preconcerted arrangements or preparations made between citizens for the appearance of the enemy," and believed "probably one or two persons but not more, may have been aware a few moments before of the enemy being in the vicinity."[323]

The primary reasons for the success of the raid were the overwhelming numerical advantage of the Confederates and the failure of Whaley to station pickets a sufficient distance from Guyandotte. As one Confederate soldier wrote, "Although a night attack was deprecated by our officers, yet the surprise to the enemy was found to be so complete as to invite an immediate descent on them." Colonel John B. Floyd, who had engineered the expedition, wrote that "Colonel Clarkson executed his mission in the most satisfactory and gallant manner, and merits the highest commendation." Major Kellian Whaley, however, was criticized for failing to post pickets, and the camp was described as being "in a criminally careless condition."[324]

Confederate supporters lauded the raid on Guyandotte, stating, "A night attack by cavalry is the most startling feature of war, and generally condemned as military gambling by the red tape soldiers of the schools, has not been tested during this campaign, except in this instance, with its brilliant results. In fact, the whole of this march and attack could only have been so successfully conducted, by energy far in advance of the tedious regularity of West Point cadets." The *Richmond Enquirer* believed it was one of the most daring encounters and "complete defeats over the enemy which has yet shed lustre on our arms," and added, "The Lincolnites were totally annihilated." Cavalry horses, saddles, clothing, ammunition, 200 Enfield rifles, medicine, and other military stores worth at least $30,000 had been captured.[325]

Although Confederates and their supporters in Guyandotte rejoiced at the victory, retribution was only hours away.

7
Reaping the Whirlwind

"Guyandotte...has always had the reputation of being the 'ornaryest' place on the Ohio River. It was at 'Guyan,' where counterfeiters, horsethieves and murderers 'did most congregate.' It was a Vicksburg on a small scale. It was the first town on the Ohio River to display a secession flag, and has always been the worst secession nest in that whole country. It ought to have been burned two or three years ago."

Wheeling Intelligencer, November 13, 1861

On the morning of November 11, Mrs. Hite, a longtime resident of Guyandotte, paid an early visit to Percival and Mary Ann Smith. She greeted her friends and commented, "Our troubles are over; we won't be bothered with the dirty Yankees anymore." Mr. Smith responded gravely, "Our troubles have just begun." Indeed, the town of Guyandotte was about to be afflicted with the wrath of vengeance.[326]

Hugo Deitz walked to the end of the suspension bridge later that morning and discovered John Hite and James Shoemaker standing between the piers of the span, seeking protection from gunfire projected from the Ohio side of the river. The men also discovered the bodies of three Union soldiers still lying on the bridge. At Hite's suggestion, the men carried the corpses to Hite's storehouse. During the unpleasant task, Hite remarked, "Hugo, this is a desperate state of affairs. I am sorry this has happened. I don't know where it will end."

Guyandotte citizen John Hite.
Credit: Special Collections Department, Marshall University.

Deitz was directed by Hite and Edward Smith to make some boxes in which to bury the Federals. They offered to pay him for his labor, but Deitz stated he would do the work if someone furnished the lumber and nails, and the men agreed.[327]

Although Union soldiers and supporters suffered through a night of hell, the Confederates had enjoyed a homecoming of sorts. They now prepared for their departure from Guyandotte. The prisoners were brought together and "tied two and two, about fourteen inches apart and filed out in the street; when we got out so as to form a straight line, a ¼ inch rope was made fast to the cord that bound the two first together, carried back to the next two, wound around the cord by which they were fastened, and so on through the whole line." The cords were furnished by a Guyandotte citizen, S. M. E. Russell. The regimental history of the 9th (West) Virginia Infantry recorded, "the boasted chivalry of the Old Dominion, exhibited itself, as slave dealers in the Southern cities exhibit their human chattels on the streets when taking them to market."[328]

Before the column left Guyandotte, Mary Hiltbruner, whose son Stephen was one of the prisoners, approached the Confederates and asked permission to take a few of the Union men to her home for breakfast before leaving. When refused, she

> told them defiantly that they would reap the bitter fruit of their cowardly act. Then, turning to her son, who appeared somewhat desponding, she said, 'Stephen, cheer up, and my prayer is, that you may live to return and show these fellows that you are able and willing to defend your country to the last.' She then hastened out to bring us some refreshments, but before she could return we were hurried away.[329]

The wounded men were mounted on horses and the march began at a full run. The prisoners were forced to stay in the middle of the road, where the mud in some places was four to ten inches deep. The civilian prisoners were called "Tories" and required to march behind Major Kellian Whaley at the head of the column, while the Union soldiers were simply "Damned Yankees."

Dr. Rouse recalled, "we had not traveled far, when to our great surprise and chagrin a detestable Miss answering to the name of Jennie Everett, as if to add insult to indignities, made her appearance, regaled in her secesh costume, cheering the rebels in what she supposed to be a glorious victory."[330]

As the column neared Barboursville, the men "heard the boom of the cannon at Guyandotte." An attack was expected at any time from the 34th Ohio Infantry, stationed at Mud Bridge. One member of that regiment wrote that the Union troops had learned of the approaching Confederate column well in advance of their arrival in Cabell County:

> Last Sunday morning we had the report that there were eight hundred Cavelry advancing on us. Our Company was immediately sent out to a hill two mile from camp where we worked all day throwing up breastworks of logs and bush. We lay there untill the next morning when we heard that they had made an attack

[on Guyandotte]...we had a position behind our works strong enough to keep back five times our number.[331]

According to this soldier, the 34th Ohio was informed of the approaching Confederate cavalry force on the morning of November 10, half a day prior to the attack. Yet, no similar message was sent to Guyandotte, a more vulnerable target, and the Ohio soldiers failed to pass on the warning. On November 11 Major Freeman E. Franklin of the 34th Ohio "had the honor of leading a detachment to intercept them, and was only half an hour too late, but as they were cavalry and our men infantry, we could not overtake them."[332]

The Union captives were untied and mounted on horses with their captors just before reaching Barboursville. The Confederates marched through the village "on Duble quick," gathering up a few more prisoners that had been left tied by the roadside, while Captain Vincent "Clawhammer" Witcher "gave Thomson store another radeing and committed many other depradations." As they passed by Matthew Thompson's home, the Confederates refused to allow the local merchant to stop, instead "draging him with them on foot in his debilitated condition after stealing his horse bridle and saddles." The prisoners dismounted outside the town and resumed the grueling march.[333]

Among the Union prisoners, Dr. Rouse noticed William Douthit, William Hinchman, and Thomas Kyle,

> all of whom had served their country in a civil capacity until now their heads being silvered over by the frosts of over seventy winters, when it is made by the wanton rebels a crime to serve our country in any other capacity or way save that dictated by themselves, these aged men were caused to suffer in common with the balance, and it was truly heart-rending to see them, with feeble health and broken constitutions...[334]

A messenger arrived from Guyandotte and reported to the Confederate commanders that the town had been burned and that Union troops "were murdering the citizens in the streets, regardless of age or sex." The enraged Confederates were ready to take revenge on their prisoners, but fortunately another message arrived with a more accurate account of what had transpired at Guyandotte following their departure. Two civilian captives from Gallipolis, Ohio, were released before the column reached Chapmanville after it was discovered that they had only been in Guyandotte to purchase wheat.

Major Kellian V. Whaley made a daring escape during a stop in Chapmanville. Awakening at about three in the morning, he discovered that all of his guards were fast asleep. Whaley grabbed his shoes and the hat of Captain Vincent Witcher and carefully made his way out of the cabin. He then ran two hundred yards to the Guyandotte River and was forced to swim through the bone-chilling water to the other side. For the next few days, he kept hidden during daylight hours and traveled at night until finally reaching the Wayne County home of Absalom Queen, a staunch Unionist. Queen and his men escorted Whaley to a Union post on the Big Sandy River.[335]

The remaining prisoners were force-marched through rugged terrain. Several casualties occurred during the trek. John Ross, who had reportedly killed a man in a drunken spree some time earlier, was ordered to be hanged. After pleas for his life were ignored, Ross attempted to escape but was shot and left by the side of the road. A soldier by the name of Adkins died a week after the march began, while a third captive, John Coffman of Lawrence County, Ohio, became ill and died on December 11.

The route of the column followed the Guyandotte River, and stopping points were at the following locations:

Night 1: home of Henderson Drake, Ten Mile (present-day Lincoln County)
Night 2: Chapmanville
Night 3: Logan Court House, departed at midnight, four miles to old mill
Night 4: Huff's Creek, near junction with Guyandotte River (Man)
Night 5: log house, Guyandotte River, six miles above Wyoming Court House
Night 6: over Guyandotte Mountain
Night 7: church, New River
Night 8: Pearisburg
Night 9: Pearisburg
Day 10: caught train at Newbern

At Newbern, Virginia, the Federal captives were ordered into cattle cars which transported them to confinement in Richmond and other southern prisons. On November 23, a Richmond newspaper noted that "the Danville train arrived with nearly 100 Lincolnites from Guyandotte, Virginia...the prisoners were subjected to the tallest kind of marching." Another observer described the Union men from western Virginia: "The entire party were strikingly unintelligent in looks, and their toilettes having been necessarily neglected during their extension to Richmond, they presented a decidedly unpreposs[ess]ing appearance."[336]

About 8:00 a.m. on Monday, November 11, as the Confederates began withdrawing from the town of Guyandotte, the steamer *Boston* appeared on the Ohio River. Aboard were about two hundred soldiers of the 5th (West) Virginia Infantry under the command of Colonel John Zeigler. These troops had been encamped at Ceredo. The *Boston* came ashore at Proctorville long enough for a number of Lawrence County Home Guards to board.

Proctorville was bustling with activity. The town had been fired on by Confederates from across the river in Guyandotte, and the gathered Home Guards returned the fire, excited to a fever pitch. The Lawrence County men boarded the *Boston*, and the steamer then headed toward the Virginia side of the river. As the boat neared the shore, a small cannon aboard was fired a number of times. One ball went through the brick home of a secessionist. J. C. Wheeler, adjutant of the 9th (West) Virginia Infantry, reported that "the hypocritical secession citizens, who had been instrumental in setting up the attack, came on the bank of the Ohio with a great number of white flags, which they waved with great apparent earnestness."[337]

The Union troops and members of the Lawrence County Home Guard disembarked above Guyandotte, near the home of Robert Stewart, a secessionist. Rumors had reached the Federals that fleeing soldiers of the 9th (West) Virginia Infantry had been fired upon from this home. The torch was applied, and the residence was soon engulfed in flames. A son of Robert Stewart was taken prisoner by the soldiers before they moved into the town of Guyandotte.[338]

Fear and rage consumed the soldiers and citizens from Ohio, who believed the townspeople had been active participants in the previous night's raid. Perhaps the seeds of animosity toward Guyandotte had been planted five years earlier when Alfred Proctor was attacked on the Ohio riverbank. Regardless, when the men entered the town, they deliberately began burning homes and businesses.

The two-story brick residence owned by Virginia Ricketts (Cooney's mother), located on the corner of Main and Bridge streets, was burned, as was the Hite dwelling. Henry H. Miller, who was a captain in the militia before the war, lost his home and his store. The Buffington Mill was burned, along with a smaller mill run by Roseberry and Eastman. Among the many businesses razed on November 11 were the Beekman and Enshimer Clothing Store, Hiltbruner's Store, and a dry goods store run by George Holderby and St. Mark Russell, Jr. The *Ironton Register* reported, "As near as we can judge from one-half to two-thirds of all the houses in town were burnt, probably safe to say over one hundred houses." Another account noted, however, "Some fifteen or sixteen houses were burned at Guyandotte; the majority of the buildings in the town were not burned. The burnt district, however, comprises the most valuable business houses and dwellings."[339]

Ruins of Buffington Mill, burned on November 11, 1861.
Credit: Special Collections Department, Marshall University.

When Union soldiers set fire to a pile of cooper's shavings, they were stunned speechless by the sudden emergence of a member of the 9th (West) Virginia Infantry, who had used them as a hiding place. The soldier was described as "almost wild." Soldiers who came to burn the Thomas Carroll home on Guyan Street found that Mary Carroll had barricaded herself and her children inside the home, saving it from destruction. The home of Dr. A. B. McGinnis was saved by a Union man named Lecky. In addition to the Carroll and McGinnis homes, the homes of John Russell, Victor LeTulle, and Percival Smith were also saved.[340]

Charlotte Temple Douthit, whose husband William and son John had been arrested and taken prisoner by the Confederate forces only hours before the Union men arrived, was not as fortunate as Carroll. She later remembered:

> I carried my goods out of my house and across the bridge with my own hands after the soldiers had set the torch…Early in the war we became frightened and went across the river, but we didn't like to stay there, and determined to come home. We had only been back a little while and my husband had just gotten a new stock of goods when the fire came…
>
> I was standing at the front door when two soldiers came and told me I had better save what I could for they were going to burn the house. I told them not to do that as we were union sympathizers, but they wouldn't heed me, saying they had been given orders to fire every house. I and my sons might have saved the buildings if I had not thought they were determined to burn it. Some buildings were saved by people who threw water on them after the soldiers had gone.[341]

The Guyandotte Baptist Church on Richmond Street was also destroyed. The church history recorded, "The Union soldiers efforts were not successful to burn the church…until the third time when they tore off the shutters and stuffed them with straw in the belfry to start the fire…"[342]

Adjutant J. C. Wheeler reported that "armed citizens from Ohio set fire to the town." It is more likely, however, that Colonel Zeigler and his men initiated the conflagration. In an affidavit made on October 18, 1906, Joshua Suiter, who participated in the events which took place on the morning of November 11, 1861,

Joshua "Doc" Suiter, who later wrote a justification for the burning of Guyandotte. Credit: Cabell County Annals and Families.

testified,

> that in the year 1861, at a time when Gen. A. G. Jenkins, then a captain in the Confederate service made a raid upon the town of Guyandotte in said Cabell County, a large sidewheel steamboat carrying several companies of the Fifth Virginia Infantry, U. S. A., then stationed at Ceredo, West Virginia, landed at Proctorsville, on the Ohio river, and took aboard about as many as a company of what was then known to this affiliant as members of the Ohio State Militia; and that this affiliant, along with other non-enlisted men and boys also went aboard said steamboat; that said steamboat went up the river to a point one mile above the said town of Guyandotte, when the said United States soldiers, and the other militiamen and citizens of Ohio entered the same; that great confusion prevailed in said town and it was not known whether the said Confederate forces had abandoned their said raid or not, and that the report was abroad that a number of soldiers and others had been killed; that the streets of said town in the business portion, were filled with goods and merchandise from store houses and that it was generally thought that the said Confederate forces would return and seize said goods and merchandise; that the said United States officers and soldiers were in command and direction, and that the greater portion of the dwellings and business houses in said town as well as said goods and merchandise were, that day, consumed by fire, which said fire was made as this affiliant remembers and believes on the grounds of military necessity; that included in the buildings so burned, were all of the buildings then situated on the east side of Guyandotte Street between Bridge Street and the Ohio river.[343]

Colonel William Bolles of the 2nd (West) Virginia Cavalry risked his life to halt the burning of Guyandotte on November 11, 1861. Credit: History of Scioto County, Ohio.

While Suiter claimed that "military necessity" forced the burning of the town, it is almost certain that the anger caused by the attack, and the suspicion that the townspeople had foreknowledge of the events triggered the decision to burn the town. The majority of Guyandotte's citizens favored the Confederacy, and their assistance in rounding up Union soldiers and sympathizers in the aftermath of the raid was another contributing factor.

Colonel William M. Bolles of the 2nd (West) Virginia Cavalry, a resident of Ironton, arrived on the scene and attempted to stop the destruction. Several of the Union men threatened to shoot him, but he persisted in his efforts and helped bring a halt to the devastation. His efforts to protect Guyandotte, however, were criticized by many Federal supporters. The *Jackson Standard* wrote sarcastically,

> Of course, every other Secessionist rejoices at the regular manner in which Col. Bolles acted. The Colonel understands his duties. He was there to see that no traitor suffered, either in person or property. We hope the colonel did not suffer the escape of any negroes belonging to the traitors. If he can satisfactorily show that he did not suffer one of the slaves of our 'Southern brethren' to escape, we move that he be promoted. Let him be appointed a Brigadier General.[344]

Alzira J. Scott, a Guyandotte resident and Confederate supporter, recorded that Zeigler's men and the Ohio citizens arrived about an hour after the departure of the Confederate cavalry. In a letter to an Ohio newspaper, she captured the immediate consequences of the town's conflagration, writing that

> in opposition to the prayers and entreaties of the Unionists on both sides of the River, they went about the demoniacal act of burning the town, turning defenseless women and children out of their homes, to endure the inclemency of the frosty weather; it was a scene calculated to melt the heart of the most hardened, to see homeless creatures build fires on the commons to keep their little ones from freezing during the bitter cold night that followed the conflagration. True, there were houses enough to shelter under, but the rage and threats of the men that burned the town was so great that the females were afraid that they would come and set fire to the houses in the night and that they would not be able to save themselves and children from the flames.

Ralph Leete of Ironton wrote Ohio Governor William Dennison on the day Guyandotte was burned and described the confusing situation:

In the afternoon yesterday (Sunday) several steam boats passed up but on nearing Guyandotte the[y] sounded to, and came back to Ceredo, and to this place. Early this morning one of them the Grey Fox took around 110 armed citizens from this place and 140 of Col Lindseys men from Ky opposite and proceeded to Guyandotte. They however had been proceeded by 400 troops from Point Pleasant and 150 of Col Ziegler's men, in command of Col. Ziegler himself. After an enquiry into the facts the town of Guyandotte was set on fire by Col Zieglers men at 10 oclock this morning, and at 5 this afternoon it was in ashes.[345]

Leete noted his approval of the action, writing, "The destruction of the place was not perhaps, wise or politic, yet if the destruction of Sodom was justifiable, on the same ground may the destruction of Guyandotte be justified for there was but one true

Union man in the place." He observed that the town's population was about 1,100, and that the conflagration "made verry nearly an entire wreck of the place, destroying all the valuable buildings."[346]

Zeigler's men found seven bodies in Guyandotte, which they transported to Ceredo for burial. The two initial casualties of the raid, Joe Bragg and Thomas Burks, were also moved to Camp Pierpont, where both men had a leg amputated. Bragg and Burks died shortly after the procedures.

Among the dead was Dr. George B. Bailey, whose body was found near the mouth of the Guyandotte River. Bailey had attended West Point for a short while and had been a boyhood friend of Ulysses Grant. His father, a prominent physician, had gotten him admitted to the United States Military Academy, but he failed his first semi-annual examination. The elder Bailey procured a tutor for his son and was able to get him re-appointed, but he was apparently expelled during his second year and chose not to return when offered the opportunity. His place at West Point would be filled by the future general and president.[347]

George B. Bailey, killed at Guyandotte on the night of November 10, 1861. A childhood friend of Ulysses Grant, Bailey fought at First Manassas and was appointed lieutenant colonel of the 9th (West) Virginia Infantry. Credit: Portsmouth Public Library, Portsmouth, Ohio.

Bailey's remains were delivered to his family at Portsmouth and on November 13 were taken to Brown County, Ohio, his former residence.

A large number of citizens, including the Mason and Odd Fellows, together with Colonel Kinney's Regiment and the remaining members of his old company, escorted his remains to the boat and visibly testified their deep sorrow at his death, and their sympathy for his bereaved family. He was a superior officer, thoroughly versed in military tactics, and well understood, and was peculiarly adapted to the task of organizing and disciplining the volunteers. Let us long cherish his memory as a gallant soldier and valuable citizen-and as one who nobly sacrificed his life in defence, and for the honor, of his country."[348]

One newspaper tribute noted that the death of George B. Bailey, "occurring as it did while bravely performing his duty as a soldier and officer, cast over our city a deep and heartfelt sorrow. During the period of his residence in this place, he made many warm friends, and was universally respected as a citizen and gentleman."[349]

Describing his military service, his obituary noted,

When the Fall of Fort Sumter startled the country, and the President called for volunteers, he was the first in our State to offer a company to the Government. He received a dispatch, accepting his services on the evening of Tuesday April 16, 1861, and the next day, at 11 o'clock, A.M. his company was on its way to Columbus-the first to leave their homes in the State of Ohio. From appearances about Washington at that time, he expected to be in active and dangerous service in a few days. He commanded his company at the massacre of Vienna and the equally unfortunate battle at Bull Run. On his return, he accepted the position of Lieutenant Colonel of the 9th Virginia Regiment, stationed at Guyandotte, and immediately devoted all his energies to its welfare and success. In the attack at that place although suddenly surprised by a vastly superior force, he fought with heroic bravery. With musket in hand, he acted the part of a private soldier and sacrificed his life rather than surrender.[350]

His widow, Margaret J. Bailey, wrote to Virginia Governor Francis Pierpont a few weeks after her husband's death to ascertain whether Bailey had been commissioned as a lieutenant colonel. She had been unable to find the commission in his papers and observed that if he had one, "it was burnt with his other effects when the town was burned, the day following the attack." She noted his death at Guyandotte and added, "By this sad event I am thrown upon the mercy of the world with a family of five small children."[351]

Pierpont later received a letter from John Glidden of Portsmouth, Ohio, concerning Bailey's pension. His widow was left with nothing except some outstanding accounts, and she had five young children to raise. Glidden informed Pierpont he was making application for a lieutenant colonel's pension, writing,

He went to Guyandotte & took command of the regiment there forming then by an understanding with Hon. K. V. Whaley that he should hold the position of Lieut Col and our understanding here is that he had already recd the appointment from your excellency. In either case in justice she is entitled to pension but as there is now no law to provide for such cases it must be obtained through a special act of congress and to effect that your testimony is necessary as to his promised rank.

By doing this, Glidden declared, "you will confer a great favor upon the needy widow of an efficient officer and brave man who sacrificed his life in the defense of your commonwealth and its loyal inhabitants."[352]

The House of Representatives passed a bill in 1862 securing one month's pay and pension to Margaret Bailey, widow of George B. Bailey. The pension was set at $30 per month, reflecting Bailey's rank of lieutenant colonel.[353]

As the destruction began to wind down in Guyandotte on November 11, the Union troops identified and arrested sixteen of the town's secessionists and placed them on a boat to be taken to Camp Chase Prison. Just as the steamer began pulling away from shore, Captain William Turner appeared and noticed that among the secession prisoners was Tarleton Everett. Remembering their encounter on the prior evening, he ordered that Everett be released, stating "You saved me last night and I have saved you today."[354]

The steamboat *Liberty*, which was bound for Cincinnati on the night of the raid, was hailed above Guyandotte by Union citizens who warned of the danger ahead. The pilot turned back and headed north to dock at Gallipolis. The 4th (West) Virginia Infantry, stationed at Point Pleasant, immediately proceeded by steamboat to "the scene of action," where they found a large force from Ceredo and elsewhere "already assembled."[355]

In Marietta, a message arrived that a large Confederate force had taken Ceredo, captured a steamboat, and blockaded the Ohio River. There was "intense excitement" in Marietta, Gallipolis, and other Ohio towns along the river. Another dispatch from Portsmouth laid these rumors to rest, but Union civil authorities responded to the threat by throwing up embankments and instituting other defensive measures.[356]

At Ironton, the first alarm of the Confederate raid came shortly before midnight with the firing of a cannon and the ringing of bells. About 100 armed citizens of Ironton traveled to Guyandotte on the following morning, but by the time they arrived, "the work there was over, and they stopped a few minutes to see the ruins." An attack on Camp Pierpont at Ceredo was perceived imminent, and a force from Ironton arrived to lend a hand in defending the town.[357]

Colonel John Zeigler, alarmed that the Confederates would advance on his small force at Ceredo, requested reinforcements from the area citizenry and began erecting breastworks. For several days, hundreds of men busied themselves with heavy labor as they prepared for an attack on the community. According to a newspaper account, the 41st Ohio Infantry reinforced the Union troops at Ceredo shortly after the Confederate raid. The Guyandotte citizens seized by Union soldiers on the day following the raid were sent to Camp Chase through Ironton and Portsmouth, "at both of which places the citizens made hostile demonstrations, and it was with the greatest difficulty that they (the prisoners) were protected."[358]

Across the river from Guyandotte, Lawrence County officials issued a proclamation on Tuesday evening, requiring all able-bodied men between the ages of 18 and 45 to muster at South Point with arms, ammunition, and five days' rations. The response was quick, and the Ohioans began gathering at South Point and Ceredo. The *Ironton Register* opined, "Unquestionably, Ceredo will be attacked and destroyed, if in the power of the rebels."[359]

On the night of November 11, the steamer *Telegraph No. 3* went to Green Bottom and returned on the following day with several hundred bushels of corn, 150 hogs, and other items seized from the Jenkins plantation. The corn was picked and husked by the Union soldiers and the "41st was confiscating all of Jenkins' movable property." The Gallipolis paper wrote that "it is fit that he should thus be made to feel the same punishment he has been so ready to inflict on others…It is high time some such lessons should be administered to these scoundrels, who, not only commit every crime known to the decalogue, but violate every rule of civilized warfare."[360]

Messengers informed Colonel Zeigler on November 12 that an attack on Ceredo was imminent. About 125 armed citizens traveled from Ironton to Ceredo to help

130   DISORDER ON THE BORDER

defend the town. The *Ironton Register* recorded, "All quiet at Ceredo today (Wednesday) at noon; force there now strong enough to repel any probable attack."³⁶¹

On the same day, citizens in the Northern panhandle town of Moundsville learned of the Guyandotte raid. A resident wrote,

> Soon our streets were filled with excited men and women. Four secessionists were knocked down and three of them put to jail. A committee of Union men, laboring under the wildest state of excitement, passed from one secession house to another, peremptorily ordering them to pack up and leave. At 12 o'clock today the prisoners will have a hearing. The excitement still continues unabated. Nothing can be heard but 'Guyandotte must and shall be revenged!'³⁶²

On the evening of November 13, a steamer transported more home guards to Ceredo to reinforce the community. As it traveled up the Ohio River, the boat passed the ruins of Guyandotte about three o'clock Thursday morning, and George Sprecher of the 34th Ohio Infantry noted, "it very darke and cloudy there might have been a few houses standing but I could not see none. I could see the burning of the heavy timber all over where the town had been..." Colonel Joseph J. Lightburn of the 4th (West) Virginia Infantry telegraphed Governor Francis Pierpont: "Send me two 2 pieces of artillery with ammunition. Guyandotte has been taken Ceredo threatened with three thousand 3000 rebels Gallipolis and Pt Pleasant in danger."³⁶³

While the *Wheeling Intelligencer* stated that Whaley and his recruits "were about the only decent, honest men who had ever staid in Guyandotte over night," the *Ironton Register* defended the town to a limited degree, stating the paper was "altogether too hard on Guyandotte."³⁶⁴

Some Union newspapers recognized the dangers of the town's destruction:

> Most all the Union men from this side the river and the greater part of those on the other, were greatly incensed at the burning of the place. It was a waste of property which was now completely in the hands of the Union forces, and could have been saved for paying the expenses of the war. Such deeds should be condemned, and those who will engage in them should meet their just punishment. In this the innocent are made unnecessarily to suffer. The secessionists will do the same thing in retaliation to a greater extent than they would do were we not to commit any such acts, besides it greatly endangers the bordering towns on our side of the river, as well as those on their own where Union sentiments prevail.³⁶⁵

Still, the response throughout the North supported the razing of the Cabell County community. The following was published in the *Ironton Register*:

> Our neighboring town of Guyandotte, Virginia, opposite the upper part of this county – a town of about 1,000 inhabitant[s], when the war began – was the theatre of tragic events and terrible scenes, last Sunday night and Monday. The

town is two-thirds in ashes – hotels, business houses, and dwellings, all in one dreadful ruin. The people – nearly all of the bitterest and most violent Secessionists and Rebels, with scarcely 'ten righteous' among them, far in *advance*, in rebel work, of any in all Western Virginia – the people have met with a terrible retribution, awfully severe, yet the fruit of their own works. What a *reward* is theirs! Ten of the leading men now prisoners, in jail, their stores, hotels, and fine residences, in total ruins, their families wanderers.[366]

Below are a few of the editorials that appeared in northern newspapers endorsing the destruction of Guyandotte Much of the animosity derived from the belief that the citizens of the town had forewarning of the attack.

"Among the works of christianity of this century the destruction of Guyandotte, Va., will doubtless have a place."
Cleveland Morning Leader, November 15, 1861

"Guyandotte's machinations hath kept the border in constant alarm; its people hath sown to the wind, and already reaped the whirlwind..."
Ironton Register, November 21, 1861

"The destruction of that hot bed of secession and scene of murderous treachery, Guyandotte, is a step in the right direction. If the inhabitants had half sense, they must have known that their conduct in assisting in a massacre of our troops, would provoke the most summary retribution. Every place where such bloody treason is practiced should be laid in ashes, and all the assassins caught should be promptly shot or hung. It is time to make war troublesome to those who insist upon it."
Cincinnati Commercial, November 1861

"The cold blooded massacre of our troops at Guyandotte, the particulars of which will be found in the telegraph this morning, is enough to send the blood hissing through the veins of the coldest loyalist in the land. The brutal villains outstripped all the early atrocities of savages. They deliberately murdered our poor, unarmed soldiers while sitting at their own firesides, their invited guests. Such cruel barbarity is unrecorded in the annals of civilized warfare. It ought to call down on the perpetrators the most terrible vengeance."
Wheeling Intelligencer, November 13, 1861

"The burning of a town in war is rather an act to be excused or palliated, as that of soldiers infuriated by protracted resistance and great slaughter, impossible to be restrained by their officers, than to be advocated. The rules of war might justify the burning of Guyandotte. The loyal Virginia troops were there only for the preservation of peace and the protection of the inhabitants. The inhabitants entered into a conspiracy with the rebels to decoy the loyal troops into their houses under pretense of hospitality, while the rebel cavalry entered the town and were guided by signals to those houses. There could hardly be a stronger provocation...The loyal soldiers who were occupying the town were Virginians, who were naturally more exasperated at such treachery from their own people, to who they had done nothing but to protect them. They also understood the character of the inhabitants, who are represented as the most virulent Secessionists. It is evident that rebellion must be made a costly amusement or it will never be put down. A policy which exempts rebels from retaliation sacrifices loyal men...But we refer to the policy which holds the inhabitants of a town accountable for the safety of the persons and property of loyal men, and makes their losses good out of the property of the secessionists; which also holds the town accountable for its loyalty."

Cincinnati Commercial, November 1861

"Served Them Right – The disposition made of the town of Guyandotte, Va., by Col. Zigler, was the right one. The inhabitants had conspired with the secessionists to murder in cold blood all the Federal soldiers who were stationed there. How many were thus assassinated we are not informed, but we have the satisfaction of knowing that the town which harbored such wretches was speedily reduced to ashes. One such example is worth ten thousand oaths of allegiance, and will administer a wholesome lesson to the dastardly rebels of Western Virginia. Let them know that they will meet with no mercy if they perpetrate such crimes, and they will hesitate long before they put their necks and property in such danger."

Cleveland Morning Leader, November 14, 1861

A steamer filled with about 300 men of the 41st Ohio Infantry under the command of Lieutenant Colonel John J. Wiseman moved up the Ohio River about a week after the raid on Guyandotte. A correspondent wrote,

At Ceredo we found a detachment of Zeigler's 5th Virginia fortified and ready for an attack...Passing Guyandotte, we had a full view of the town, which is now nearly deserted. A few of the inhabitants came out and cheered us as we passed, but there was little enthusiasm in their voices. There was the skeleton village, the embers of some sixty or seventy buildings yet smoking, and the people in a terrible fright.[367]

The boat continued on and stopped at the landing near the home of Colonel Albert Gallatin Jenkins. Some of the soldiers put out a plank, and four companies of the 41st Ohio rushed toward the house. Skirmishers searched the hills in the rear of the residence but found nothing. Virginia Jenkins informed Wiseman that her husband had not visited his home in six months and stated that most of the property was owned by her father, Judge James Bowlin of St. Louis. Bowlin, who claimed to be a Union supporter, told the soldiers that had he arrived in Green Bottom two days earlier, he would have kept Jenkins out of this "accursed muss." Wiseman and his men confiscated ten horses, some pigs, corn, and "about fifteen barrels of splendid apples."[368]

A writer for the *Cincinnati Daily Commercial* described the property:

The Jenkins estate, owned by three brothers, Albert, the 'Doctor,' and Jefferson, (all in the rebel army) stretches along the river shore a distance of three miles. Fields of wheat and corn stood ungathered, and unhusked. There was an abundance of everything about the house. The house is a substantial two story brick, very spacious and comfortable, and surrounded by fine old oaks and sycamores – a very desirable country residence.[369]

He added,

There was something suspicious in the fact that in every house visited in the neighborhood not a man was to be found, though the women and children were at home to receive military calls. And after our boat steamed out, at two or three houses, a mile or two above, several horses saddled and bridled, were seen standing at the bar[n]s, and men furtively standing about.[370]

About 4:00 p.m. on Saturday, November 16, the citizens of Ironton were alarmed by the sound of cannon fire on the river:

'Secesh!' was the first exclamation. Men and boys started on a brisk trot; heads popped out of every window in sight; some of the more timid merely venturing out of doors, and coming to a dead halt, undecided which way to run, while 'Jenkins Cavalry' was vivid in the imagination of many. The suspense was soon broken by the appearance at the wharf of the magnificent steamer *Telegraph No. 3*, having on board the 41st Regiment of O. V., and a part of a battery of Artillery, and several secesh trophies captured off Jenkins' place, among them a pig, which we are now owner of. The Regimental band blowed, and everybody...crowded upon the Square, while the soldiers debarked, marched up the levy and formed on the Public Square, which was done in excellent military style. The boys were housed in Greenwood's brick, on Second street, and Creuzet's unoccupied house on the lower side of Court. The arrival of the Regiment produced a great and perceptible change in the countenances of many whose minds dwelt for the past week only on the terror of sesech Border Cavalry. Bully for the bloodless 41st.[371]

Major Abia A. Tomlinson of the 5th (West) Virginia Infantry sent a telegram to Governor Francis Pierpont on this date: "We are reliably informed that the rebels numbering about twenty five hundred are at Wayne Court House and along the Tug fork of Laurel River. The cavalry that attacked Guyandotte are there."[372]

John Lawson and Thomas Berridge, the two citizens released by the Confederates on November 12, returned home to Gallipolis, Ohio, on November 20. Lawson noted they had nothing to eat on their trek except raw turnips, cabbage, and beef. They had been granted their freedom about thirty-five miles from Guyandotte due in part to

Lawson's acquaintance with several of the Confederates. He described the cavalry force as "well drilled, poorly armed, mostly with shot guns and rifles, bowie knives and pistols, and the most daring and determined set of men he ever saw."[373]

On November 23, 1861, the *Wheeling Intelligencer* reported: "Passengers by the steamer *Liberty*, which arrived last evening, report all comparatively quiet along the Ohio. The steamer *Telegraph* was still lying at Gallipolis, making semi-occasional trips between that place and Jenkins' farm, where two or three companies of the 41st Ohio are encamped."[374]

An article in the *Gallipolis Journal* opined,

> The case of Mr. Jenkins shows the terrible influence of this treason and rebellion on those who yield to it. Wealthy, respectably connected, popular and influential, he had everything to gain by the existence of the Union. Ambitious of higher honors, he has sacrificed wealth, friends, influence, reputation, everything, and become an outcast and vagabond, only feared for his ability to commit crime, as he is detested for his evil proclivities. He is not alone, however, for thousands like him are now upholding this tremendous evil, and running a course whose end is destruction, swift, sure and terrible.[375]

Several of the Union prisoners captured at Guyandotte wrote home from Richmond following their arrival in the Confederate capital. Sergeant Major Thomas Ross penned a letter to his wife on November 30 to update her on his situation:

> We arrived here over a week ago. I hope you will try to bear up under this trial. It is only the fate of war. You may be thankful that I am alive. I thank kind Providence that while others were falling around me amid showers of bullets I escaped uninjured. I trust that there are those who will render you all the aid necessary until I am released. I think as soon as Congress meets, there will be something done towards an exchange of prisoners. I do not know how long we may remain here. On Monday and Tuesday of this week a good many were sent to Alabama...[376]

On December 1, Granville Pollock observed,

> The prisoners taken at Guyandotte on the 10th of November, some ninety odd, are all here and well. We are faring as well as prisoners could expect, I suppose. I do not know from experience, as I was never in a prison before. There are a number here from all parts of the North, and it looks as if we would have to stay here some time. We will have to be patient and trust in God...[377]

A few days later, Lieutenant James E. Wood wrote to H. J. Samuels from Richmond concerning the needs of the Federal prisoners: "You are aware of the capture of troops & citizens at Guyandotte Va on the night of the 10th of Nov. As the same were marched off without having time to obtain any clothing except what they had on their backs you can judge of their present destitute condition..." Wood noted that the men captured at Guyandotte consisted of thirteen troopers from Company F of the 1st (West) Virginia Cavalry, forty soldiers from Company A of the 9th (West) Virginia Infantry, seventeen belonging to other companies of the 9th (West) Virginia, and twenty citizens of Cabell County and Lawrence County, Ohio. He observed,

> A great many are in need of shoes, shirts, drawers coats pants &c. In fact any thing in the shape of clothing is wanted, and in order to supply some of the necessaries of life money is wanted. Our object in writing to you is to have you to attend to the above wants and render us all the relief in your power by negotiating with the Secty of War on the subject. Your prompt attention to the above will meet with our warmest thanks.[378]

J. C. Wheeler, adjutant of the 9th (West) Virginia Infantry, wrote to Virginia Governor Francis Pierpont on November 29. Wheeler had discovered that a number of citizens arrested in the aftermath of the raid on Guyandotte were actually Union supporters and requested their release. Henry J. Samuels, adjutant general for the Restored Government of Virginia, also received a great deal of correspondence from citizens in his home county impacted by the event.[379]

Eliza Morey of Barboursville contacted Samuels on November 24. Her husband Frank had been taken prisoner, and she admitted that "if Frank never comes back I [k]now not what to do." She observed that "true Union men is scarce in this town," and added, "it has ben very gloomy here since the Jenkins outrage. The rebels cheered him loud and long and cried when he left because he could stay no longer. Every face now wears a gloom..."

Morey also informed Samuels that his brother Alex was reportedly at Logan Courthouse and was very ill. She believed "if this is true it would be a good time to take him out of bad company and not let him run at large like other rebels."[380]

Matthew Thompson, the Barboursville merchant whose store was repeatedly robbed by Confederates, was the subject of several letters. B. F. McCune wrote on December 11 that he had not heard from Thompson since his capture, "but I hope he will be guided by Providence while he is in the hands of the enemy and be permited to arrive safely to his home and to his distressed companion but at the same time she has met all her misfortune like one who is in submision to the will [of] Devine Providence." Thompson's wife Elizabeth wrote to Samuels four days later and asked him to send Dr. Henry Maupin to Richmond to arrange for the exchange of citizens taken at Barboursville and Guyandotte. She observed poignantly, "I am here a lone woman in distress and I hope you will befriend me in this the saddest hour of my life."[381]

Emily Morris, the wife of Dr. Jonathan Morris, contacted Samuels on December 27, confident "that you will render me all the aid in your power and God grant it may be successful." Morris had not heard from her husband since he was captured at Guyandotte. Dr. Morris had no winter clothing, and his wife expressed dismay that he had not been exchanged as was customary with surgeons. She had read a recent appeal from prisoner James Wood "which makes my heart ache," and another from the quartermaster "which is enough to craze one as uneasy and been in suspence as long as I have." She asked Samuels "to relieve a distracted wife."[382]

On January 8, 1862, Morris wrote,

> I presume you have heard of the release from Richmond and the arrival home of eleven of those persons captured at same time with my husband. One of them came to see me being requested to do so by the Dr. His account of the treatment received by them is enough to craze any who have friends there. He says the tobacco house in which they are is so low they cannot stand upright. They are badly clothed and worse fed.[383]

More than a dozen Cabell County citizens were freed and permitted to return to their homes on December 4, 1861. Dr. Morris and several others were released on February 22, 1862, after signing the following oath: "We, the undersigned, in the service of the United States, prisoners of war, pledge our word of honor that we will not, by arms, information or otherwise, during the existence of hostilities between the United States and Confederates States of America, aid or abet the enemies of the said Confederates States, or any of them, in any form or manner, until released or exchanged."[384]

When the prisoners were released from prison, they were forced to see a number of Confederate officials to obtain passports and discharges. No clothes or funds were provided by authorities, and the men were forced to find their own way home. Several natives of Cabell County living in Richmond, particularly W. L. Peters, Hugh Petit, and Albert Laidley, aided them in obtaining their releases and provided funds to help defray expenses on their lengthy trip home. Other former neighbors, such as Asa Wilson and Lewis Beekman, testified against the Union men from Cabell County; their statements led to long periods of confinement for at least two of them.

Colonel John Paxton of the 2nd (West) Virginia Cavalry penned a request to Samuels on December 20 from Guyandotte for muster out rolls and asked if the battalion organization had been completed. He also noted that "Jenkins and band said to be 3000, is near 'Trouts Hill' 3 of our companies are reconoiting near them. We need a general very much in this county, as we are on the extreme wings of two departments."[385]

Adjutant J. C. Wheeler wrote to Samuels on December 29 concerning Union prisoners, particularly the case of William Hinchman:

> I was just talking with Mrs. Hinchman who in addition to the affliction of having her husband a prisoner among the rebels, is now waiting upon her aged mother who from a fall down stairs is in a dying condition. She has been informed that the proposition has been made to exchange Mr. Bumgarner or Mr. Rickets for Esqr. Hinchman...neither one have sufficient influence to secure his release as Mr. Hinchman is known to be a man of influence in his county and will not be exchanged except for some prominent secesionist. I think myself she is right in that matter, and some more prominent men should be selected to

exchange for him. We are sorry that we are unable here to do any thing for the release of our friends and acquaintances suffering in Richmond more than to urge upon the authorities at Wheeling to hasten that matter as soon as possible but knowing your sympathy for your unfortunate fellow citizens we have full confidence that you will promptly do every thing for their release that can be done.[386]

On December 30, Percival S. Smith of Guyandotte noted that a number of Union men captured during the Confederate raid had arrived home from Richmond, but William Hinchman had not been released. Smith asked Samuels to "please do all you can" to aid Hinchman.[387]

William Hinchman, who was 60 years of age, was examined by Confederate authorities in Richmond. He had opposed secession and voted for a member of the Wheeling Convention, and a Confederate official observed, "His general character is good." He also, however, recommended that "as Henchman has voted for establishing the revolutionary government of Virginia he ought to be turned over to the State authorities to be tried for treason against the State."[388]

Thomas Monroe wrote to Governor Francis Pierpont on January 4, 1862, concerning Hinchman. Although a number of the citizens had been released, Hinchman, "a man of sterling worth, and unwavering loyalty," remained in prison "without any probability of his release." His wife had learned he was to be sent to an interior county of Virginia to be tried, presumably for treason. Monroe learned that Hinchman had been targeted because during his examination, he admitted to voting for the new state. "If I understand him," Monroe wrote, "I think he is among the last men to evade and I judge, if he could soon be released, as were the others, by taking the oath of loyalty to the Southern Confederacy he would refuse his liberty on that ground." Monroe was concerned about Hinchman's fate: "In the state of mind prevailing in those counties that are disloyal, I presume he might be severely dealt with, if he was brought to trial. He is disliked exceedingly by those who are disloyal." Friends of Hinchman recommended that hostages be held for his safe return, but the governor, Monroe was assured, "will know better than I can what course will be proper."[389]

Charles Roffe, who lived near Dusenberry's Mill, was seized as a hostage for Hinchman and eventually paroled. Roffe asked General Jacob D. Cox for his release on January 5, 1862, and enclosed affidavits and certificates of Cabell County citizens John Mills, Thomas Thornburg, and Greenville Harrison, all of whom swore that Roffe was loyal to the Union.

Roffe also pledged his continued efforts to procure the release of William Hinchman. His parole was extended until January 22, 1862, but he was required to report to Federal headquarters at Louisa, Kentucky, a distance of more than fifty miles. Roffe wrote, "I have to pass through a section of country that several persons have been shot during the last 6 or 8 months. The distance I have to ride, and the risk in travelling throug[h] this hostil[e] section, my ill health & the unfavourable weather at this season of year, are the causes that prompt me to ask to be relieved from being held as a hostage." His efforts on behalf of the elder Cabell County citizen were in vain, as

William Hinchman died on October 2, 1862, while imprisoned in Salisbury, North Carolina.[390]

On the last day of 1861, J. C. Wheeler contacted Samuels from Camp Paxton concerning Stephen Hiltbruner, who had been captured at Guyandotte and taken to Richmond. Hiltbruner's father was "greatley distressed" and thought Samuels had a friend named Calvert that might be able to arrange his son's exchange for Robert Holderby "or some other active rebel whom you might select." Wheeler had nothing but praise for Stephen Hiltbruner:

> I will say that we had no braver or better boy in our Regiment than Stephen. He was our Commissary Sergeant, and was industrious & attentive to business & during the fight he fought like a tiger & carrying a box of cartridges into the hotel he was fired upon by a dozen Rebels.[391]

Charles Roffe, who lived near Dusenberry's Mill, was seized as a hostage for Union citizen William Hinchman of Cabell County. Credit: Special Collections Department, Marshall University.

Adjutant General H. J. Samuels received letters from several Cabell citizens after the raid asking for assistance and describing conditions in the county in the aftermath of the Guyandotte affair. A. M. McGinnis notified H. J. Samuels that his family had been threatened and requested protection for himself, his kin, and his property.

When the Confederates raided Guyandotte, his sons John and Dr. Allen McGinnis went to the home of Achilles Fuller, who had been murdered. His widow urged Dr. McGinnis to follow the Confederate troops and try to get her son Albert Fuller released. John McGinnis ran into a Union man "who ordered him not to come on that side of the river and told him that him & the Dr. was marked men and leave if they wanted to save their lives." John rushed back and reported the encounter to his father, who ordered him to depart and to inform Allen that he was not to return until he sent word.[392]

John caught up with the Confederate cavalry and accompanied them as far as Logan Courthouse. He saw his brother, who "told him if he would come back and get up a pet[it]ion he thought the citizens could be got back." When Jenkins learned of the threat against the McGinnis family, he informed the doctor "he would aid him in any thing that was honorable."[393]

John McGinnis's return to Guyandotte angered Union supporters in the area. His father encountered Clem Poteet in the road, and Poteet inquired repeatedly about John. When McGinnis asked why they couldn't all get along, Poteet exploded and blamed McGinnis's "goddamed 'Cecesh' sons," calling them "a damed set of roages & thieves." Poteet threatened that if John or Dr. Allen came back "they will go up dam quick." When McGinnis asked what John had done, Poteet avowed that when the Confederate cavalry had approached Guyandotte, John and the doctor met them and informed them of the number of Union troops in the town. McGinnis responded that John did not leave the house that night. Poteet retorted that

> I was a liar. I replyed if you say he did you are a dam liar. He made some threats. I told him to shoot that [I] had no armes so he could crack away but not to go under the bank or behind a tree or log to do it but do it in open day and in the road. We had many contradictions when we parted. He told me to keep my self on my own side of the river or I might be missing.[394]

Samuels also received requests for assistance from Cabell County residents arrested by Union authorities. James Stewart, the teenaged son of Robert Stewart, whose home was the first burned by the Federals on November 11, had been seized by Federal troops. His father wrote to Henry J. Samuels on November 14, requesting his aid:

> Before burning my house the soldiers took a great many things out of it, among which was my papers. My son who was taken to Columbus had in his pocket a part of my notes. They were taken from him between Guyandott and Ceredo. I have since heard that my papers were in Colo Zeiglers possession. I yesterday saw Colo Boles he directed me to write to you. Now if you can do any thing for me that will enable to get my papers I would take it as a particular favour. I had notes and accounts to the amount of between five and six thousand dollars and several deeds &c.[395]

Stewart wrote to Samuels again on December 28, seeking help for his son James, who was a prisoner in Wheeling or Columbus:

> I do not know which, as he expected when he wrote last to be taken to Wheeling in a few days. What the charges are against him I do not know. I have heard it was for shooting a soldier that should have passed our house on the night of the fight in Guyandotte. The same charge was made against me by some enemy and I have understood my property was burned under that impression which was utterly false. Colo Zigler investigated that matter and was satisfied that no man was shot near my house. I went before Col. Piatt and had my case investigated and he permitted me to go home. I hope you may be willing to do something toward procuring his release as he did nothing at all in the fight and is only 16 years old.

Stewart added, "Eight of the citizens taken by Clarkson from Cabell have been released and I have understood that James was held as a hostage for John Douthit who is released."³⁹⁶

Residents of the county also sought the release of Robert Reynolds of Cabell County. Reynolds had voted in favor of secession but did not take up arms when the war erupted. On November 10, the day of the raid on Guyandotte, Reynolds was arrested at his home by order of Colonel John Zeigler. He was later sent to Camp Chase, leading several of Cabell's Union citizens to send a letter to General William S. Rosecrans requesting his release. They noted the need of his family and stated they were satisfied that if Reynolds took the oath and returned home, "he would remain a loyal & good citizen."³⁹⁷

S. M. E. Russell, Jr. informed Samuels on December 27 that about fifteen of the Cabell County residents seized during the Confederate raid had returned from Richmond. Matthew Thompson had also been freed but was ill and unable to return with the other Union men. Russell reminded the adjutant general that his father, St. Mark Russell, was still incarcerated at Camp Chase as a hostage for some of the Guyandotte citizens and asked him to "take his case into consideration." A group of Guyandotte citizens submitted a petition on Russell's behalf, stating they had known him for many years "and have associated with him daily since the commencement of the present troubles" and certified "that he has never taken up arms against the general Government to our knowledge and that he has remained a private citizen..."³⁹⁸

On December 30, Governor Pierpont received a letter from the Guyandotte men who had been arrested on November 11 following the raid and sent to Camp Chase in Columbus, Ohio:

> The undersigned, citizens of Cabell County Va respectfully petition your excellency to request the proper authorities to have us transferred from the prison at this camp and placed under your own control at Wheeling rather than sent to the military prison at Sandusky, whither we have heard we would probably be sent in a short time. As Virginians we think it not unreasonable to prefer and to ask that we should be under the control of the authorities of our own state so long as it may be thought necessary that we should be kept in confinement.³⁹⁹

J. C. Wheeler contacted Samuels in late January concerning some of the prisoners. A mutual friend, Skelton Poteet, had asked Wheeler to see if a Confederate soldier held as a prisoner, possibly George Russell, could be exchanged for his son James. If Samuels agreed, a message needed to be sent immediately to Robert Holderby, who was reportedly headed to Richmond to be exchanged for Stephen Hiltbruner, so that James Poteet could be released at the same time. Thomas Poteet wrote Samuels on January 20 from Catlettsburg requesting the same favor.⁴⁰⁰

Alexander Johnson, another mutual friend, visited Wheeler in Guyandotte on January 25 and inquired if an exchange could be arranged for his son, David Alexander Johnson, imprisoned in Richmond. William Bramlett, a soldier in the 8th Virginia Cavalry who was incarcerated at Camp Chase, was suggested as the Confederate half of the swap. Lou Peters, the Guyandotte painter who had moved to Richmond, was attempting to facilitate the release of Stephen Hiltbruner and William Hinchman, and Wheeler proposed that he could also bring back Bramlett. The elder Johnson wanted Bramlett released without having to take the oath so that his son could do the same and resume his military service.[401]

William Dusenberry rode toward Barboursville after dinner and met up with Lewis Childers, Green Childers, John L. Bowen, Perry Peyton, and G. W. Savage, Confederate sympathizers who had just been released from prison in Wheeling. When he reached the village, Dusenberry saw Mott Jewell and Tom Scales, who had also been imprisoned. The paroled prisoners had a difficult time finding someone in the area to take their bond. Dusenberry received an appointment from Wheeling as a tax collector, but the bond was $30,000 so he refused it.[402]

J. C. Wheeler wrote Samuels on January 26 from Camp Paxton regarding the fate of John Alford, a Union supporter seized at Guyandotte during the Confederate raid and imprisoned in Richmond. Wheeler was incensed after reading a document copied from Richmond papers that Alford was one of six prisoners presented to Confederate Secretary of War Judah P. Benjamin as "traitors that ought to be hung."[403]

Wheeler learned that John W. Hite had been held for the release of Alford. He urged that Hite be re-arrested and "immediately confined in jail and suffer whatever fate John Alford does." Wheeler also believed Dr. Virginus R. Moss should not have been released, as "he has shown himself as dirty a rebel as any in the Confederate Army...he is as bad a man as Wils. Moore." Wheeler pleaded, "in the name of justice & humanity let something be done to save as good a man as John Alford whose only crime is having discharged his duty to his country without fee or reward of any kind."[404]

Efforts continued to procure the release of Guyandotte citizens arrested on November 11 and imprisoned or held as hostages. On December 23, 1861, Adjutant General H. J. Samuels wrote a pass for Edward Smith, a Guyandotte citizen who had been sent to Camp Chase. Smith was paroled but required to live in Ohio. Samuels issued permission for him to return to Guyandotte to remove his family to their new location and noted that he was "entitled to protection."[405]

On December 4, Charles Everett, who had been taken to Camp Chase, proposed to give bond and sought to obtain evidence and determine the charges against him. He wrote, "I have been told that I am charged with dif[f]erent things, though I know not, what I was arrested for." Everett was willing to take the oath of allegiance and listed several persons who would serve as security.[406]

Other individuals, however, gave testimony against his release. T. J. Smith swore that Everett "told me that I should be obliged to come over to secession or we will sooner or latter have your scalps." Everett "also said he had 500 acres of land to spare & would give 100 acres each to 5 men who would go & fight for the S Confederacy."[407]

David Earls testified that Everett loaned horses to several members of the Confederate cavalry. He also heard Everett say he "was in favour of the S Confederacy & should support it." In July 1861 Earls observed Everett and Robert Reynolds go into Everett's house for shot and powder before the men departed on Everett's horse, "which he took out of the plow to accommodate him. He told me he was going to Jenkins Camp."[408]

Jacob Baumgardner, Charles T. Everett, Peter Everett, David Frampton, Elijah Ricketts, St. Mark Russell, and James Stewart were all discharged from Camp Chase Prison in Columbus on January 1, 1862. Frampton was released despite testimony that he had informed Robert Seamonds "that all Union men who came over the river might be killed. He also said he would give my horse & my brothers horse to the secessionists & in a few days after my horse was taken out of the pasture. He always talked in favour of secession."[409]

Another Guyandotte resident imprisoned by Federal authorities, William C. Rogers, wrote to Major Joseph Darr on December 19 concerning his case. "I do not know that I have been properly advised as to the cause of my arrest or the nature of the charges against me," Rogers claimed. He had been seized on November 17 by order of Colonel John Zeigler and charged with "aiding the Rebel Troops." Rogers refuted the claim, declaring he had "never in any wise voluntarily rendered aid to them." He owned a team and kept a livery stable in Guyandotte, and his stable and provender were used by the Federal troops stationed in the town until the night of the Confederate raid. Rogers wrote:

On the next morning, my waggon and team was taken by compulsive means under the pretext of burying the dead, but in fact to convey away spoils. Upon inquiry I was informed that I could get my team and waggon after they had used it one day drive. I went with it and according to promise it was returned to me and I returned home on the following day. Col Whaley who was a prisoner and was with me at the time knows these facts. It is also known by him that I received and executed his orders while he was commandant of that post and I gave to him and his command any aid in my power...

I will comply with any terms within my power that will give satisfactory evidence or guaranties of good conduct and loyalty in view of the very critical condition upon the border exposed to arrest by either party. I have avoudid any or either extreme, and have rendered quiet obedience to all authority especially when upheld by Bayonets. I sought to avoid sacrafice and loss – my property was of such a nature as rendered it liable to be carried away at any day – my property sacrificed by both parties, but property has no value compared with liberty – especially when I feel that my liberty is restrained without sufficient cause.[410]

On January 8, 1862, Colonel Joseph A. J. Lightburn wrote from Ceredo concerning Confederate prisoner Francis Bing of Wayne County. He noted that Bing joined the Confederate service on May 28, 1861, and was captured while a member of Jenkins's cavalry near Louisa, Kentucky. Bing confessed to have fought at Scary Creek and Carnifex Ferry, and Lightburn wrote that "from the marks he received in capturing him I should judge him to be a brave man."[411]

Bing had been granted parole but was required to reside in Ohio until the end of the conflict. On April 22, 1862, Bing informed Darr that he wanted to return to Wayne

County, writing, "There are men there, that in my absence, are making and circulating reports about me that I want to clear up." Darr denied his request in early May, but Bing wrote again on July 16 from Rutland, Ohio, to plead his case. "I took the oath of allegiance," he declared, "not for the sole purpose of gaining my liberty, as many doubtless do, but because I thought that it was my duty and when I took the oath I took it with the intention and determination of living to its terms, which I have done in every sense as the word and which I intend to do under all circumstances, wherever I may be."

Still, Frank Bing desired to return to his home in western Virginia: "My reasons for wishing to go back are, that my health is very poor, and has been since I have been here and I wish to be there in time to get in a fall crop." On July 18, a notation on his file recorded, "Permission not granted." Bing must have ignored the restriction, since he enlisted in the 16th Virginia Cavalry regiment on April 11, 1863.[412]

Francis Bing of Wayne County. Bing was captured and imprisoned during the first year of the war. After being paroled, he joined the 16th Virginia Cavalry. Credit: Evelyn Booth Massie (courtesy of Jack L. Dickinson).

During the first week of January 1862, Virginia Governor Francis Pierpont received a number of brief letters from Cabell County residents who had been confined at Camp Chase. The correspondents simply informed Pierpont that they had returned safely to Cabell County and were reporting to him as a condition of their parole.

Some of the imprisoned Union soldiers began returning to Cabell County from Richmond in early 1862. On Thursday morning, March 6, 1862, Dr. Jonathan Morris arrived in Wheeling after several months of captivity in the Confederate capital. He discovered that Francis H. Pierpont was not in the city, and "was very much disappointed in not having the pleasure" of meeting the governor. Dr. Morris learned that the position of surgeon for the 9th (West) Virginia Infantry had been reserved for him and asked Pierpont to send the commission to his home in Ironton. Morris, who had only recently been released from prison, declared, "I wish to join my Regmt as soon as posible."[413]

Sixteen Federal soldiers from Cabell County and Lawrence County, Ohio, incarcerated at Salisbury, North Carolina, were released in May 1862 as part of a prisoner exchange. Hillary McVickers of Barboursville also returned home in June 1862 and wrote to Adjutant General H. J. Samuels to ask,

what prospect there is for my getting paid or any part of my wages. I was one of those captured at Guyandotte having just returned home (and as you are doubtless aware paroled). I am unable to perform labour and must if possible have something to subsist on. If I can only get part, that is due me, it will aid me greatly. Please give this matter your earliest attention and advise me what to do, as soon as possible.[414]

Thomas Ross of Ironton, who had been captured at Guyandotte and imprisoned in Salisbury, North Carolina, informed Samuels on June 30 that he had returned to the area. He noted that his health was "rapidly improving" and stated he was ready "to return to the field & meet the enemy once more – or to the service in any other capacity as soon as called on."[415]

Hamilton Smith of Ironton, who had served as a baker for the 9th (West) Virginia Infantry and was captured at Guyandotte, returned home in February 1863. He had been confined at Libby Prison in Richmond and was later incarcerated at Salisbury. His story mirrored those of his fellow prisoners: sleeping on the hard floor, eating "meat full of carrion" and soup swarming with dead worms, and being treated more like dogs than men. A newspaper correspondent believed "his emaciated appearance, his pale countenance, contrasted with his jaundiced eye, tells a tale of long suffering and woe."[416]

On July 5, 1864, United States Military Agent R. L. Stewart wrote to Samuels concerning William Massie, who had volunteered in Company H of the 9th (West) Virginia Infantry on August 18, 1861, and had been captured during the raid on Guyandotte. Imprisoned in Richmond and Salisbury, Massie escaped and returned to his home in October 1862. When he reported to General Jacob D. Cox at Point Pleasant, he was told to remain at home, as he had not been officially mustered into the 9th (West) Virginia Infantry. On two occasions, Massie actually traveled to Fayetteville where the regiment was stationed, but "no officer came." Massie was then drafted and paid his commutation fee. Stewart inquired, "Now he wishes to know if he is to be considered a member of the 9th Va. Can he be held under his enlistment? If so, is he liable to draft? I write at his earnest solicitation and have given you the facts, from which you can readily perceive his peculiar situation."[417]

Kellian V. Whaley would later write,

During the short time I was organizing the Regt, I furnished considerable money for poor officers, without the expectation of receiving anything in return; during the time of the confinement of the prisoners I sent considerable money to the families of quite a number of them, a small portion to your wife. On the return of the prisoners from Salisbury & Richmond, the portion that came to Washington can speak for themselves as regards the amount received from me, the efforts I made to get them mustered into service here, to receive their back pay and ration money. You know how I succeeded, and also in having the Paymaster General telegraph to New York to have the squad, of which you was one, then in that city, paid their money also. The time I have occupied, the attention I have given, & the claims of the widows of those killed in battle, for their bounty money, is I believe appreciated by a large portion of these unfortunate men, taken while fighting under my command at Guyandotte. Brave men! I will never forget them, for they believe I have done the best I could, and they are satisfied; and do not follow me like evil spirits...in feeble health, with arduous duties to perform.[418]

8
The Darkest Hour of our Perils

"I beg leave to trouble you with a few lines asking for protection. If we do not get protection, and that soon we will have to give up our farms & property to the rebels, and get our families away as best we can – we can hold out but little longer. The troops in Cabell has afforded but very little relief in the upper part of the county. When they send out a company it is only for three days, which are taken up in marching to Hamlin and back to camp. The rebels always know of their coming, flee to the hills from which they watch their movements, and as soon as they are gone return to their homes & lurking places so that the Union men are obliged to leave their families and go with the troops to save their lives, leaving their families & property at the mercy of the rebels."

James C. Black, present-day Lincoln County, December 25, 1861

Cabell Countian P. H. McCullough wrote on November 15, 1861, "Since Col Clarksons ar[r]ival here & exodus this county has been overwhelmed with grief & consternation. Mutual confidence has taken its exit & none feel safe from sword & fire." The presence of the 9th (West) Virginia Infantry in Guyandotte had led to "hopes that mutual kindness & mutual confidence would soon return" and that "recrimination would cease to exist but my God who can now anticipate the end." He added, "As to my own part I have never done any thing but vote for the Ordinance, have never been in arms, have not had a gun for 20 years about my house & intend to hold my self aloof the storm that is now entombing so many of our friends & acquaintances." McCullough also observed, "The part of the town of Guyandotte that escaped the fire is almost totally deserted & so it is with Barbersville."[419]

Colonel William Bolles of the 2nd (West) Virginia Cavalry informed Adjutant General Henry J. Samuels on November 16 that he had visited Guyandotte and believed that

> a force of mounted men should at once be placed in that region. I would be very

glad to occupy Guyandotte Barboursville & such other points as might be deemed best & sweep over that portion of the state between Big Kanawha & Big Sandy. That section is the more important, as the supplies for Genl Nelsons column are being taken up Big Sandy. If it should be thought best to order my Regt there, as there is some difficulty in procuring reliable Cavalry arms, if one half the Regt could be supplied with the Enfield musket instead of the Carbine they could act as mounted Rifles viz effectively induced, while the other half could act as Light Cavalry.

Bolles also observed that there were more than twelve thousand bushels of corn and plenty of hay at the farm of Colonel Albert G. Jenkins and that Confederate troops were rumored to be in the area.[420]

In a November 20 letter, Cabell County resident Charles Wilgus declared that Adjutant General Henry J. Samuels was in a position to help the Union men of Cabell, Putnam, Wayne, and Logan counties and questioned why no forces had been placed in his hometown to protect the Guyandotte River Valley: "At the town of Barbersville, at the mouth of Mud river is one of the finest location[s] for a camp and am made by nature as strong for defence as almost as any in Western Va." He also believed a supply depot and custom house should be placed at Guyandotte, which he considered crucial to the Confederates:

an irregler male has been carried up this river from Guyd to Richmond Va and also to Floyds army and as long as this vally is left open for a public highway for the rebles this counties will never be restored to peace. You can see of what importance the rebels hold Guyandott as a port of entry for them, as soon as Mr Whaley & his small band had posesion Jenkens & his outlaws captured kild & skatered his forces. I was told that powder and percussion caps was stored in a celler in Guyd to suply the rebeles wich they recd.

Wilgus observed that the 5th (West) Virginia Infantry was stationed at Ceredo and the 34th Ohio Infantry at Mud Bridge, leaving the "valy of Guyan open for the use of the reble highway and one turnpike road open on each side of Guyan for their travel." He told Samuels, "I do hope that Governor Peirpoint & you will take active measures to have the forces placed so as to close this valy & post against the rebels."

Wilgus complained that "roving rebles" were killing, robbing, and seizing Union men, and that

If this is sufferred to go on the way it has been this part of the country will soon be cleard of all its good and law abiding citizens. The Union men and families are daly leaving Va to seek peace and safety on this side of the river. The no[.] of men & families that are daly leaving the State of Va is large.[421]

Thomas Thornburg contacted Samuels on November 23, describing the aftermath of the Confederate raid on Guyandotte, which had brought "distress and destruction upon all of our people." Thornburg had moved his family to an old mansion to spend the winter

> if permitted to do so. God deliver me from the horrors of Civil war. Would to God it were ended. It is intirely useless for me to attempt to give you an idea of things here...every body living in fear. If one thing could be stoped on both sides it would allay the excitement in some degree the taking of persons and sending them of[f] and taking of property. If this is not done women & children must suffer. I cannot [believe] for a moment the Federal Government will countenance some things that has been done in Cabell for instance the taking of the last horse that a man has and that to[o] from good Union men. Such has been done.[422]

Thornburg added,

> You no doubt have heard of the particular of the destruction of Guy[andotte]. Jeff it was shameful. The citizens of Guy. are clear of all blame in the matter and I have not seen the first man but what condemns the course of Col J Clarkson. They the citizens were in more peace, and better contented than they had been for the last 3 months...[423]

Eliza Morey wrote to her old neighbor H. J. Samuels on November 24, informing him of the "cowardly insults on the citizens of Barboursville" by the Confederate cavalry under Clarkson and Jenkins, who "took Mr Morey Fridle Mr Cile Mr Thompson from this place and treated them like beasts." Morey blamed the outrages on the "leading rebels" of Barboursville, and believed her husband was arrested because he "voted the new state ticket. That is his crime."[424]

Certainly, the town and the townspeople of Guyandotte had suffered, but the raid caused fear that continued to reverberate throughout the entire region. M. A. Cruikshank wrote from Catlettsburg, Kentucky, on November 30:

> We live in a state of chronic panic here – Every day we are told 'Jenkins is going to burn the town tonight – he is on the way with 800 cavalry!' but we are getting hardened to it and pay no attention to the story. The day after the massacre at Guyandotte there was a great fright and 12 muskets were our only defense. We had sent every gun & every man up Sandy...[425]

J. C. Wheeler, adjutant for the 9th (West) Virginia Infantry, stationed at Guyandotte, informed Governor Francis H. Pierpont on December 11: "We are here with a few of our men, who are coming in as fast as they get the word...The stables for the Cavalry are progressing rapidly and they are expected down tomorrow. Two companies of the 10th Reg. are also expected here tomorrow." Wheeler also requested permission to propose an exchange of prisoners with Allen McGinnis, whose son was a doctor serving with Jenkins in the Confederate army. "We are very anxious here for the return of our men," Wheeler wrote, "and if any thing can possibly be done for their restoration to their families let it be done immediately. You can scarcely conc[ei]ve Sir, of the suffering that has been brought upon the people of this section by the war and heretofore the bulk of that suffering has been endured by the Union people." He added, "We have had all sorts of rumors about a threatened attack upon this place recently by Jenkins' force but this time although there is but a small force they are well prepared to give them a hot reception."[426]

Carey B. Hayslip of Guyandotte was recommended by Wheeler as first lieutenant for Company A of the 9th (West) Virginia. Described as "a sprightly ingenous young man with a tolerable good education," Hayslip had already been pegged as a possibility for the position; one of the other aspirants was in prison while another was too severely wounded to serve. Wheeler stated, "It is the opinion of every one that Carey deserves a commission for his gallant conduct in the Battle of Guyandotte."[427]

Hayslip's father, who had served as the quartermaster's clerk, was captured by the Confederates on November 10 and sent to prison in Richmond, "leaving the family in destitute circumstances." Although the company's rolls had been lost and the unit numbered less than forty following the raid on Guyandotte, Hayslip was providing quarters for the men of his company and "attending to their wants." Wheeler observed, "Carey has rec[ei]ved considerable credit for his conduct in the battle. The Brigade officers here have a high opinion of him & for several reasons they think he ought to be commissioned. Among them his father is a prisoner and also a Brother Mason – and the family have claims upon us – but besides he is competent and will make a good officer."[428]

Wheeler wrote to H. J. Samuels from Camp Paxton in Guyandotte on December 16 and noted that the "Barboursville jail is full of secesh prisoners – I tried one of the Gurrilla's yesterday & sent him on to the Federal court. I have to go to Barboursville next Friday to try the rest." Wheeler also shared a rumor that Colonel Albert G. Jenkins had proposed an exchange of citizens from Cabell and Wayne counties and suggested that Samuels "ascertain what kind of a proposition we can make & let me know."[429]

The companies for a new Union cavalry regiment for Virginia were from Lawrence, Meigs, Vinton, Jackson, and Muskingum counties in Ohio. It was seen as "highly probable" in September 1861 that the unit would be an Ohio regiment. The *Ironton Register* agreed, writing, "Right! – for the men are from Ohio, and Ohio should have the credit." Eventually this Union outfit, however, was credited to Virginia and named the 2nd (West) Virginia Cavalry.[430]

An article in the November 18 issue of the *Wheeling Intelligencer* recorded, "We learned yesterday that it is the intention of the authorities to send the 2d Virginia cavalry, now at Parkersburg, into the Guyandotte country to look after Jenkins and the secesh in general. The 2d Cavalry are now at Parkersburg lying idle, and want to be assigned to active duty."[431]

By noon on December 15, the troopers of the 2nd (West) Virginia Cavalry had boarded steamboats at Parkersburg, and the regiment was soon en route to Guyandotte. After spending the night aboard the steamers, the soldiers disembarked at daylight on the morning of December 16. As the men began preparing their quarters, they were surrounded by the destruction that had befallen the town only a month before. George D. Pyle described Guyandotte as "a very pretty place," but added that the "best part of the town" was destroyed by fire. Pyle observed a stable that was "perfectly riddled with bullet[s] w[h]ere the secesh fired at the union men that were quarterd in it at the time of the fight." Junius Jones noted that "our mess got a very nice house." He also wrote that "the best part of the town was burnt down and the remainder looks prety shaby." Jones stated, "the people of this place are not very friendly toward us for they are nearly all secesh." One or two of the women in Guyandotte "make themselves so bold as to exhibit a sesech apron." Apparently one or two of the Zouaves "took the job of taking care of it for her." At Guyandotte they joined with the 9th (West) Virginia Infantry, which had begun its reorganization. A regiment was stationed on each side of the Guyandotte River.⁴³²

Junius Marion Jones, 2nd (West) Virginia Cavalry. Credit: West Virginia State Archives.

J. C. Wheeler wrote to Samuels on December 17 concerning the Home Guard Company of Absalom Queen of Wayne County, whose aid had proved crucial in the successful escape of Major Kellian V. Whaley. In addition to providing Samuels with a roll of the company, Wheeler informed him that Queen wished to be commissioned at once and requested that their uniforms be sent to them: "This will be necessary to their efficiency as they do not approach our lines without them." Wheeler also noted, "There are rife rumors in regard to the capture of Lafe Moore & his Regiment and the advance of a large force to this place to attack us. The advance guard of 500 are reported at Trouts Hill. We are expecting a fight."⁴³³

On the morning of December 17, Captain J. L. Wallar, who commanded Company A of the 2nd (West) Virginia Cavalry, led his unit from Ceredo to Trout's Hill. There they learned that a group of nearly fifty Confederates had been in the town on the previous day. Complying with Lightburn's order, they took possession of the books of the county clerk at the courthouse and sent them under guard commanded by Sergeant Elihu Robinson to headquarters at Ceredo. Company A linked up with troops under Major Rollin L. Curtis and on the following day marched to Louisa, Kentucky. On the third day of the expedition they traveled to Catlettsburg, Kentucky, and the combined force returned to Ceredo on December 21, losing only one horse which succumbed to disease.⁴³⁴

A few days later, Colonel Joseph A. J. Lightburn ordered Wallar on another scout into the countryside of Wayne County. Captain Wallar marched his company seven miles beyond Trout's Hill to a location along Twelve Pole Creek known as "Stephens far[m]." During the day the Federals arrested Benjamin Smith, who admitted his sympathy for the Confederate cause and was sent under guard in command of Sergeant Robinson to the regiment's headquarters in Ceredo.

On the following day the company reached the mouth of Lynn Creek, where Wallar directed Lieutenant C. H. Hudson to lead thirty men to Adkins Precinct while he continued with the remainder of the troops to Ross Precinct. Believing that Confederates were in the nearby woods in force, Wallar sent for Hudson's command. Hudson complied, but left a detachment of seven men under Sergeant George Shoemaker at the home of Union supporter William Nixon with orders to protect the family. Hudson and his men marched back toward Wallar but were fired on by the enemy, wounding a horse. After Hudson and Wallar linked up, they found no Confederates in the immediate area, so they headed toward Nixon's home.

Two miles from their destination, the Union troops heard gunfire and rushed forward, coming onto the scene of a skirmish which had been underway for nearly two hours between Shoemaker and his men and about thirty to forty Confederates. Wallar dismounted and ordered his men into the woods, where they drove off the enemy, killing two, wounding several others, and capturing two men – Nathan Clay and his father – who were charged with "being in arms against the U. S. Army." Union guide David Holt was wounded in the arm. The Union force camped overnight at Nixon's before marching to Trout's Hill on the following day and returning to Ceredo a day later.[435]

Captain William Turner, who had escaped capture during the Confederate raid on Guyandotte, was commissioned as captain of independent scouts by Virginia Governor Francis Pierpont. Turner posted an advertisement in the *Ironton Register* calling for one hundred "snake hunters." The enlistees would serve for three years as scouts in western Virginia "or where needed." Turner wrote:

> I want persons who have been exiled by the rebels, to join and help drive the rebels from your homes. If you refuse, you are not worthy of the name or home of a Virginian. I know a number of Ohioans who are just the kind of men I want – brave, energetic men. Fall in! I want men who are *men*; who will fight to the death; who hate rebels worse than snakes; who have 'do and dare to' in them. Every man, whether private or Captain, will be expected to do his duty. You will be expected to make no hard march, go in no unnecessary danger, to suffer no hardship, or risk your life where old Bill won't go. We have the very best arms now made, plenty of clothes, &c. You will be sure of your pay and bounty, and stand a chance to pop a rebel or so. No kid glove gentry, no cowards, no secesh peace men wanted.[436]

Lieutenant Colonel John Paxton of the 2nd (West) Virginia Cavalry penned a letter to Governor Francis Pierpont on December 24 and informed him,

We are still short 200 horses. 560 Enfields is all we have. We have armed the balance of our Reg. with pistol carbines. We all have good health (except myself) are comfortably situated and have plenty. 3 companies of our men had a scout as far as Louisa Ky. found no force. We think there is no force in that direction nearer than 100 miles. Our houses are in good condition and are well fixed.[437]

On Christmas Eve, some of the soldiers were visiting young ladies in Guyandotte when they heard the sounds of their pickets firing. Junius Jones and Oscar Sanders of the 2nd (West) Virginia Cavalry rushed to their quarters, grabbed their weapons, and were ordered to mount their horses. After filing into ranks and riding around to headquarters, the cavalry were ordered to dismount and were dismissed, enabling Jones, Sanders, and other fortunate soldiers to return to their social engagements.[438]

James C. Black wrote to Adjutant General H. J. Samuels on Christmas Day from Barboursville:

We want a force stationed at Lykins mill to subdue the rebel forces in that section of the county. They are represented to be 100 strong, and some small squads besides the 100, in different places. They took several Union men last week and a number of horses. Some 10 or 15 Union men are now in Barboursville from Hamlin who are heads of families, and several other young men. We are destitute of arms, and dare not go home.

I hope you will order 100 men to Lykins mill, say 80 Infantry, & 20 Cavalry, which I think will be enough at present. There are 5 small houses & a meeting house near to the mill with stables for some 15 horses, a saw & grist mill & plenty of grain and hay for 100 or 200 men all winter.

Please send us soldiers immediately for we are in a distressed condition.

Written in haste by your friend.[439]

Samuels referred Black's letter to Assistant Adjutant General George L. Hartsuff with the observation that a few companies stationed at Hamlin would be "very advantageous to the restoration of peace & order & would be an advance in the direction of the enemy."[440]

In response to instructions from Governor Pierpont, William Copley sent advertisements to the districts of Wayne County for the purpose of holding an election for county officers on December 26. On election day some precincts that did not have Federal troops present for protection did not open due to fear of Confederate interference and intimidation. Abel Segur, William Hendrick, William Bartram, David Bartram, Benjamin Davis, James Roman, and Joseph D. York were elected justices of the peace, and Copley informed Pierpont, "we will try to elect the full bunch some other time." On the same day in Cabell County, E. D. Wright, James H. Poage, and

John Ferguson were elected magistrates in District One, Thomas Joy and William Fielder for District Two, and John M. Blake for District Three.[441]

The following letter, written by a member of the 2nd (West) Virginia Cavalry, was reprinted in the *Ironton Register*:

Camp Paxton, Guyandotte, Virginia,
December 27, 1861

DEAR AUNT AND UNCLE: As I have a little time now, I will write you a few lines, although news and items are very scarce. John and I are writing at the same table; he is writing to my cousin; he has been up since 12 o'clock, and has got the start of me, and used up what little news I did have; so I have nothing to write, unless I turn my pen into a drawing pencil, and give you a description of our surroundings.

Instead of five of us being cooped up in a tent six feet square, covered with canvas, thirteen of us occupy a room up stairs, as big as all down stairs, in which we can conveniently stow away all our plunder, and still have room to spare. All around are nails driven in the wall. On these hang our death-dealing weapons – for each man, one sabre, one carbine and one revolver; also our clothing, such as gum coats, over-coats, roundabouts, stable cks, haversacks, canteens, boots, shoes, &c.

About midway of the room, but near the wall, is a common school desk, which is covered with books, tracts, newspapers, pencils, inkstands, &c, and conveniently near is a bench, capable of seating about three persons; and if at the present moment you could look into our room, on the seat near the desk you would see your affectionate nephew, sitting, not according to Spencer, squarely fronting the desk, but taking it in rather an ungraceful, tailor-like attitude and lying around the room, stretched upon their blankets are some of the Corporals and Sergeants of the 'Black Horse Company.' If you were sufficiently near – say within 100 yards – you could hear the melody made by the nasal organs of the sleeping patriots, even above the whistling of the wind, the rattling of the windows, and the confused murmuring of many voices, as they are driven along on the fierce piercing wind as it hurries by.

Our dining room is down stairs, and in it we have an old cannon stove which we confiscated a few days after our arrival here, and appropriated to our own use.

Our stables are nearest to and fronting the river, of which we are quite proud.

Some time ago, I saw an article in the *Ironton Register*, referring to the 5th Virginia boys, the purport of which was that the greater portion of them spent the most of their time in Ironton, and expressing the hope that such would not be the case with the 2d Virginia Regiment; and if we judge the future by the past, that wish will be gratified with a vengeance, for now-a-days such a thing as a leave of absence is a nonentity. But there is always a bright side to every thing, and the pleasing side of this is, if the 2d Virginia can't go to Ironton, Ironton can and does come to the 2d Virginia. And if the *Register* editor wished to make a comparison, he might say, 'Whereas, many of the Virginia soldiers used to be seen on the streets of Ironton, the sidewalks of Guyandotte are now thronged with Irontonians of all classes and sizes, from the full grown man, who is himself big enough to go to war, to the infant child, who cannot lisp its Pa's name.' Old and young, rich and poor, male and female, are constantly promenading our streets, and the cry is, as every boat upward bound lands in, 'Still they come.'

I should judge from my feelings it is somewhere between three and four o'clock in the morning, and yet no cry, 'to arms! to arms!' has gladdened our hearts or given us occasion to break in upon the never-varying monotony of the snorers melody.

The Captain and Lieutenants have been up nearly all night, but I think they are now closely wrapped in the mantle of Morpheus. Our horses have been saddled all night; they will be glad to get rid of their useless burdens.

The first time we crossed the suspension bridge, we went in double file, the whole company at once; when the head of the column got about one-fourth of the way across, my horse commenced to stagger from side to side, as if he had the blind staggers. I was about to dismount, when looking up, I saw all the rest of the horses in the same predicament. Upon looking for the cause, I saw the bridge swinging about a foot out from a straight position, and as we passed along, sinking from four to six inches under us. I began to think the bridge was coming down, and more than one cheek that before was florid with health, now vied in whiteness with the paper on which I write. Since then we have crossed it in single file.

We had a very nice Christmas dinner up here; it consisted in part of baked chicken, apple pies, and doughnuts made by our cook.

I have written in a hurry, as I wished to get through before roll-call, which is at half-past 5 A. M. My love to all.

Your affectionate nephew,
J. B. C.[442]

On the last day of 1861, United States Marshal E. M. Norton wrote Provost Marshal Major Joseph Darr in Wheeling concerning Confederate prisoner Robert S. Holderby of Cabell County. Holderby, a member of the Border Rangers, was hospitalized, but his mother Susan Holderby insisted that he be moved to the jail. Her efforts unnerved Norton, who was "almost worried to anger at the importunity of his mother for his release." He asked Darr for Holderby's release and a number of soldiers to "carry him hither."[443]

Colonel Joseph A. J. Lightburn, commander of the 4th (West) Virginia Infantry, wrote to Captain George H. Hartsuff on New Year's Day concerning a prisoner, Nathan Clay. Clay, who was 21 years of age, lived on Twelve Pole Creek in Wayne County. He was "ordered out by the militia to serve in the Confederate Army" in July 1861. He and his father were captured by Captain J. L. Wallar's company of the 2nd (West) Virginia Cavalry in Wayne County on December 26. Lightburn stated he had no place to keep the prisoner except at the hotel, and he wished to avoid that expense. He included Clay's statement:

> I suppose I was arrested because charged with being a Secessionist. I did not vote for Secession did not vote at all.
>
> I was near the Trouts Hill fight probably a mile from the place. Had my gun. Trouts Hill is about 12 miles from my home. I was at Barboursville at the fight. Called there by Colonel Ferguson of the 147 Regt Va Militia. I was near the Mud River fight called there by Capt. Smith of Virginia Militia. I did not happen to be near enough to either of the fights to fire a gun and did not fire at any one. I have never seen any of the 5th Regt. Virginia Vols. U.S.A. while out scouting. I saw the 5th Regt. at Trouts Hill but not near enough to fire at them. Never heard of any of the officers of the 5th Regt. being shot.[444]

One of Clay's neighbors, William Nixon, believed he was guilty of treason, and gave a deposition to Federal authorities:

> That since harvest I think that Nathan Clay has done nothing but scout about with secessionists. That he was elected a sergeant in a militia company. The report in the neighborhood is that he intended to pass the winter in scouting and picking off Union troops. He has been reported to be present at every fight there has been in the country about. He is reported to have been in the Rebel Army at the Barboursville, Trouts Hill & Mud Bridge fights.[445]

Nathan Clay wrote Provost Marshal Major Joseph Darr on January 17 to inquire "upon what terms I can get my release." Clay was willing to take the oath of allegiance and remain loyal to the United States Constitution. He hoped he would be permitted to visit Darr in the near future.[446]

His wish was apparently granted. Clay "took the oath of allegiance for the sake of getting out of imprisonment and not because of any duty to the United States Gov." He obtained his release after three weeks of incarceration and returned to his home in Wayne County.[447]

In January 1862, Colonel Milton J. Ferguson, incarcerated at the Athenaeum

Prison in Wheeling, sent the following letter to Adjutant General Henry J. Samuels of Cabell County concerning Confederate prisoners of war from Cabell and Wayne counties who were detained there:

> I enclose to you the list of prisoners from Cabell and Wayne now confined at this place. It is somewhat irregular and informal, being very hastily drawn. Allow me to suggest that for correct information of the charges against the men you can obtain the same information by consulting the persons themselves. I have given the substance of their statements, and my own knowledge of the men and circumstances, intending to approximate, as near as I could, their cases.
>
> John D. Mays, with being in arms at Charles Morris, and with intent to resist Federal troops; Thomas T. Adkins, with being in the Poor Hill skirmish; Blackburn McCoy, never heard of any charge, no examination; Wm. T. Childers, being in arms at Jas. Keyser's, Wayne County; Greenville A. Childers, being in arms at Barboursville; Mott Jewel, joining the home guard at Dusenbury Mills; George A. Hatton, with feeding the secessionists; G. W. Savage, being in arms at Barboursville; Perry Peyton, seen in arms at C. Summers, at Cabell; Benjamin France, with being in arms at J. Keyser's at Wayne; H. G. Ashworth, carrying arms; Wm. Curry, watching the roads at home; Jerome Shelton, sympathy with secessionists; Geo. P. Brown, charges unknown to Brown; Joseph Barbour, with joining the home guard; Peter Bledsoe, charges unknown; Eden Wyson, charges unknown; Lewis Elkins (sick), been in Confederate army; John L. Bowen, with volunteering; A. J. Bates, being in arms at Wayne Court House; Nathan Clay, being in arms with the militia; William Hanley, being in arms, Poor Hill in Cabell; Samuel Smith, being in arms at James Keyser's, in Wayne; Francis Bing, Sergent Co. A 8th Virginia Cavalry; Hurston Spurlock, commanding against federal forces; Milton J. Ferguson, commanding against federal forces; Sol Hensley and Emerson Chapman, in jail but not with us.[448]

One of the prisoners listed by Ferguson, Confederate Captain Hurston Spurlock of Wayne County, contacted Samuels on November 11 asking for assistance in obtaining clothing, noting, "I was arrested in warm weather and I was thinly clad and not being permitted to procure clothing from home and being a long way from home and without money and the weather growing cold it becomes necessary for me to make this application."[449]

Sallie Smith wrote to her brother Irving on the second day of the new year and told him that several of their fellow citizens from Guyandotte who had been sent to Camp Chase, including John Hite, Henry Miller, Eli Walton, and her cousin Ed Smith, had been released. Miller took the oath to support the constitution and the Restored Government of Virginia and was permitted to live in Virginia, but he chose to move to Cincinnati. Sallie Smith wrote, "His wife and daughters will have to keep their mouths shut. Good for them."[450]

Hite and Walton declined to take the oath to the Restored Government and were forced to live in Ohio. Ed Smith initially refused, but after returning home he concluded that he would rather live in Virginia than in Ohio, so he wrote to Governor Pierpont asking for another opportunity. He told Sallie that "going to Columbus has made a good Union man out of him."[451]

Smith observed that the Guyandotte Methodist Episcopal Church, South, was being used as a granary and noted, "O but the Southerns are mad." She also related that the home of Peter C. Buffington was occupied by the company of Union Captain William Turner and that they were "camping in his house and sleeping in his feather beds and using his fine furniture."[452]

On January 6, 1862, Thomas Thornburg wrote to H. J. Samuels from Barboursville describing conditions in the county:

We keep in a continual state of excitement here. Scarcely a week of quietude passes over us. On Saturday morning the 3d in the midst of perfect quiet, Jim Dundas, Jim Sedinger, Leonidas Love, and a stranger, dashed into town, ran into the clerks office where Green, John Alford and Tom Merritt were making out the Books, seized the books and skedadled in double quick, doing no other damage... all alarmed believing that a Confederate force was near – a runner started for Ceredo and that night Witcher company followed them to Mahones on Mud who informed them they were about 8 hours ahead, when they stoped and returned believing __ further race useless. Green and John broke for Ohio, but came back yesterday as two companies of the 5th Vir were in town to protect the court. All Sun returned to Ceredo and were again quiet, but a continual fear of the approach of Confederates in will never have peace here until a force at Logan C. H. to stop the thoroghafare.[453]

Thornburg also observed, "I suppose the fate of the state of West Virginia is sealed. This I think right, all or none for the present is my motto."

Expressing frustration at the slow progress by the Union armies, Thornburg wrote,

Jeff my heart sickens at the prospect before us. I begin to fear for my country that all is lost. I have always had an abiding faith that the Federal Govrnment had power sufficient to put down the Rebellion but I must say to you in candor that my faith is becoming shaken and I fear the worst of consequences. All is dark and gloomy. Can it be possible that the great govrnment of ours must fall...I shall continue to hope for the best. Perhaps it may be that we are now in the darkest hour of our perils.[454]

Samuels received correspondence that same day from John Laidley, who related that some of the Union men captured at Guyandotte and imprisoned in Richmond had returned. They had been aided in their quest for release by Laidley's brother Albert, a delegate in the Confederate legislature. The Guyandotte citizens sent to Camp Chase

Lamartine, the home of John Laidley. Credit: Cabell County Annals and Families.

had also returned. Due to feeble health and a "town full of soldiers," Laidley usually kept to his home but had ventured out to discover an election was being held for judge and county officials: "what votes were given, for judge, was generally for you & county officers elected is bad enough it was not as attended to..."[455]

Laidley also questioned the government's authority to seize property owned by secessionists:

> As I do not understand the rights of the Government or whether is any legal authority in the soldiers to seize property of those charged, with being disloyal but Wm Turner, Capt with his men, are camped in P. C. Buffingtons mansion using any thing they have found use for. Has lately seized a jack of Alberts & have I infer they will seize every thing they can find of his property. What is it that sin cannot effect?[456]

The home of Dudley Smith was one of the buildings burned in Guyandotte on November 11, 1861, and his family was forced to resettle across the river in Quaker Bottom, Ohio. His daughter, Sallie P. Smith, wrote to her cousin on January 10, 1862, after a brief visit to Guyandotte.

> I tried to write to you on Christmas but could not. My mind was so flustrated I could think of nothing but my home and the pleasant Christmases that I had spent in Guyandotte but alas they are gone never more to return. I have visited the ruins of my once hap[p]y home twice. It gives me the heartache to look at Guyandotte much less to visit it. I took Josie and Georgia over to Guyandotte about two weeks ago to see the place. They had not been there since the morning after the battle. Josie cried to come back. She could not believe that it was where we lived and poor Georgia cried herself almost sick. It seems to me if we had a house there I could not bear to live there as much noise and confusion the place is more like a city than it is like the Guyandotte of old. There is about twelve hundred soldiers in and about the town, and they are daily and hourly expecting an attack. Nearly every night we hear the long roll and the bugle but so far they have all proved to be false alarms. I hope they will continue so for I don't want to see nor hear any more battles.
>
> You said it would have been better for me to have staid longer. Perhaps it would have been better for me, but not better for my Father for I believe if I had not been there my Father would now bee [sic] a prisoner in Richmond and that I could never bear. They may take property and strip my clothes from my back if they only leave my Fathers and Brothers I will try and be reconciled to my loss.[457]

Smith noted that several of the Union citizens seized at Guyandotte had returned from Richmond "and such treatment as they had you nor any body else ever hear of." Her father went to visit William Douthit, who had suffered a great deal during his confinement. The prisoners had been given three ounces of meat without salt each day and five ounces of bread "and that just thrown to them on the floor." There were no beds, so the men had to sleep on the prison floor and use their boots as pillows. Douthit's feet, however, "swelled so bad that he never had his boots off from the time that he left until he came back again." Douthit declared "that no mortal tongue can tell how bad they are treated."[458]

On January 15, 1862, W. H. Langley wrote to Governor Francis Pierpont concerning policies regarding the purchase of wheat. An employee sent to Barboursville for that purpose discovered that he could purchase the grain, but Colonel Abram Piatt, commander of the 34th Ohio Infantry, "would not allow any wheat to leave there" without an order from the governor or General William S. Rosecrans. Langley related,

> We have been this season and for several years past receiving considerable wheat from all parts in Va from this place down to Sandy and back as far as to Barboursville and was not aware until today that there was any change in the state of things to prevent our continuing to do so, and do not yet feel satisfied that such is the case, but as we do not wish to attempt to do any thing wrong,

you will confer a favor of informing us whether we have the right to purchase, receive and pay for the wheat. If so you will further oblige us by sending us an order or a permit that will satisfy Col. Piatt or any other officer in command there or at Guyandotte that we have the right or privilege of bringing the wheat away or having it brought to the mouth of Guyan river by the parties from whom we purchase it.[459]

Langley's complaint was not the only one Governor Pierpont would receive on this matter over the next few months.

On January 22, Junius Jones informed his parents,

We are doing nothing at present on account of the wet weather; we have a great time in going to and from the stables. The water and mud is over boat top in many places where we have to wade through. If the river raises much higher we will have to move to the hill and pich our tents again which woldnt be very pleasing to us at present.[460]

Rumors that the 2nd (West) Virginia Cavalry was to be disbanded spread rapidly but were without foundation. Six officers had been sent to Wheeling to receive their commissions before spreading into parts of western Virginia to recruit for the regiment.

Major General George B. McClellan, commander of the Army of the Potomac, wrote to General W. S. Rosecrans on February 6 concerning correspondence from Cabell County: "Colonel Piatt telegraphs to Secretary of War from Cabell court-House that rebels are coming with artillery, and asks for one regiment, and one battery from Ohio. I think it a stampede; but if it is not, call on Ohio..." The alarm indeed proved to be false.[461]

Over 2,300 Union soldiers were stationed in Cabell County at this time and another 868 in Ceredo. Six companies of the 9th (West) Virginia Infantry (566 men) and eleven companies of the 2nd (West) Virginia Cavalry (744 men) protected Guyandotte, while ten companies of the 34th Ohio Infantry guarded the county seat of Barboursville. Sickness was prevalent in Guyandotte during the winter of 1861-62. At least fifteen soldiers died in the town during the first few months of 1862.

Union General George B. McClellan. Credit: National Archives.

Colonel William Bolles, who commanded the 2nd (West) Virginia Cavalry, penned correspondence to Governor Francis Pierpont on February 7 concerning his regiment: "I have learned that two Companies have been assigned to my Regt and that a Major has been appointed. A Foreigner. I beg most respectfully to protest against this appointment and sincerely hope if it has been done that you will revoke it."[462]

Junius Jones wrote to his parents from Camp Paxton on this same date, informing them of his activities:

> Well we are still in Guyandott[e] yet but we intend to leave as soon as the weather will permit. We were all packed up once to leave but the boats that intended to take our wagons, could not carry them. The weather was so bad the next day that the march was put off. I expect we will move from hear as soon as the weather will permit.[463]

Virginia Everett Ricketts of Guyandotte. Credit: Jack L. Dickinson.

Jones noted that the horses "have cut up the roads in town hear so that a person on foot cant hardly navigate the mud before we get to our stables."[464]

Tarleton W. Everett of Guyandotte contacted Adjutant General H. J. Samuels on February 7, 1862, concerning a housing issue that sparked partisan sentiment and resentment. Everett had visited his sister, Virginia Ricketts, who informed him that Lieutenant Colonel William C. Starr of the 9th (West) Virginia Infantry had stopped by to inform her that the building in which she was living was to be used as a hospital for sick soldiers. Ricketts, whose domicile was burned on November 11, 1861, was living in a house owned by Lucien M. Wolcott. Federal authorities noted that the home belonged to a Union man and that Ricketts "has no right to stay in it." Fortunately for Ricketts, who was the widow of a Mason in high standing, Colonel William Bolles of the 2nd (West) Virginia Cavalry intervened, but Everett feared that if Colonel Bolles and his regiment were removed from the area, "that family is left without a shelter – every house stable and shed is full."[465]

Everett sought to use his Masonic connection to Samuels to prevail upon him to prevent Starr from removing Ricketts from the residence:

> I now appiel to you (in view of the three great lights before us and all that binds us to gether in brotherly love and frenship and in view of that borne from

whence no travelar has never yet returned) to know whether by your infloence you can not have provisions made for the sick soldiers without depriving her and her little ones of a shelter at any rate untill the weather gets better.

According to Everett, Ricketts "would have been turned out to the enclemency of the weather the second time as her house and house hold goods were nerely all distroyed by the burning."[466]

Everett admitted that Ricketts had two sons serving in the Confederate army but closed with an emotional plea:

Samuels have some provision made for the soldiers. Do not suffer these women and children to be thrown without mercy out in the world without a shelter or food to perish that the vultures of the air may devour them. You may think this is from a Sesesh and through it aside as unworthy of notice, but be assured that I do it beliving it to be my duty and in the feare of that God before whome I shall soon appear to give an acount of the deeds done in the body.[467]

One week later, Lieutenant Colonel William C. Starr contacted Samuels to defend himself. His commanding officer, Colonel Leonard Skinner, had received a letter from "some one in this Heavenly place" complaining that Starr "tried to turn some body out of their house – 'Widows – children &c.['] Now I am going to plead guilty, if that will help the writer make out a case." Starr then criticized efforts to placate secessionists:

Lieutenant Colonel William C. Starr, 9th (West) Virginia Infantry. Credit: L. M. Strayer Collection.

Our men are very much crowded in their barracks & we have had measles & mumps in the companies without the means of separating them. I applied to the Post Q. M. for hospital but he had no house. We accidentally found two large second story rooms in a house owned by Lucien Wolcott on Bridge St. next door and East of P. Smith's. Mr. Rickets & his widowed daughter & her children lived in the lower rooms, leaving the upper story vacant. The Post Q. Master immediately assigned us the said upper rooms and was about sending his carpenters to put bunks up for the sick men, when Col. Bolles came around and forbid us using the house.

Old Col. Everett & Mr. Rickets made a great fuss & accused us of trying to turn a poor lone widow & children out of house & home, but no body wanted to turn her out and we so stated it. But she said she could not live with soldiers in the house &c. &c.

Now Genl we were somewhat out of humor to think our poor boys had to stay with forty men in the same room, sick, fever burning them up and having to endure the noise and foul air – while the well men had at the same time to run the risk of taking disease from those already sick. All to accommodate a darned old secesh (Rickets) who I am told owns one or two houses in town which he is renting.

Starr claimed that Colonel William Bolles, who was commander of the post at Guyandotte, had been of little assistance in his search for a building suitable to be used as a hospital. Bolles "vacated a miserable dirty house and told us to take it for a hospital. Our Surgeon pronounced it entirely unfit for well men." The 2nd (West) Virginia Cavalry, which was headed by Colonel Bolles, had two hospitals, one of which was unoccupied. Starr noted, "They call it their Veneral Hospital." He closed his bitter missive by informing Samuels, "We have at last obtained a house and don't thank any body for it."[468]

Two days after the Confederate raid on Guyandotte, Virginia Governor Francis H. Pierpont wrote to General William S. Rosecrans, requesting that he order a regiment "to take all the movable property" on the farms of Albert G. Jenkins and his brothers. "They have already sold six thousand bushels of wheat and got the money for it," Pierpont related, and asked that he "save the ballance," estimated at forty thousand bushels.[469]

A Portsmouth corn trader, Socrates Glaze, was determined to sell the crops harvested at the Jenkins farms. Shortly after the raid on Guyandotte, Glaze informed Captain Oliver P. Evans of the 34th Ohio Infantry that he had purchased the corn from Albert Jenkins's father-in-law, James B. Bowlin, who had agreed to load it onto Glaze's boat. Glaze wrote, "I want you or some of the officers to come and take possession of the Boat and corn, and I will pay you for it…" Glaze offered Evans $1,000 "in good current funds bankable in Ohio." "This will be old corn," Glaze noted, but if the process worked, "we will gather the new crop of corn and dispose off [sic] it in the same way." The Portsmouth merchant closed his letter by warning Evans, "do not let this letter ever come to light for Jenkins friends would way lay me the first time I am up this way."[470]

Glaze wrote to General William S. Rosecrans on December 14 to complain about his deal with Bowlin, who now refused to load the corn onto Glaze's boat. Bowlin also refused to let Glaze take the corn until he had received payment. Glaze asked, "what shall I do; take it by force or let it be," and requested that Rosecrans respond by telegraph.[471]

On January 11, 1862, Glaze wrote Major Joseph Darr concerning previous correspondence and requested authority to seize the furniture and bedding belonging to Albert G. Jenkins from his farm at Green Bottom and send it to Wheeling. The materials were being used by James B. Bowlin, and Glaze declared that while he claimed to be a good Union man, Bowlin "has correspondence with the Rebels, and lodges and feeds them…" Glaze had hired workers to gather the corn and planned to visit the plantation on January 15 to oversee the work and collect rent from the tenants.[472]

At the end of January Glaze came to Guyandotte to retrieve some tools taken off the boat by "Government officers." He spoke with Captain Vincent Phelps, assistant quartermaster, who told him to see Lieutenant Sayres G. Paxton, regimental quartermaster for the 2nd (West) Virginia Cavalry. Before Glaze could find Paxton, however, Colonel William Bolles, who commanded the regiment, found him.[473]

Bolles was aware of Glaze's efforts to "bribe" Captain Evans and was angered by the merchant's complaints to General William S. Rosecrans about the sale of corn from the Jenkins farms. Glaze claimed that when he encountered Colonel Bolles, he asked him where to find Lieutenant Paxton. Bolles recalled the discussion differently, writing, "when he first called upon me and proposed to take the corn, and have it worked up into whiskey, and turn the whiskey on to the Government, I spoke sharp to him, and advised him to keep away." Bolles went into his sleeping room, but Glaze soon followed and renewed his efforts to convince the colonel to approve payment for the corn. Bolles became enraged, accusing Glaze of "writing [a] damb pack of lies" to Rosecrans and ordering him to leave. When Glaze refused, Colonel Bolles called the guard and directed him to take the merchant to the guardhouse.[474]

Glaze was kept in confinement for half an hour and was then only allowed a few moments to speak with the quartermasters concerning his complaints. Bolles instructed the Officer of the Guard to have a soldier escort Glaze to his skiff as soon as his business was conducted. Bolles wrote sarcastically, "I doubtless [erred] in disgracing the Guard House by sending such a man to it, and that I ought to have made my servant take him out, instead of a soldier, but at the moment I forgot proprieties."[475]

Glaze informed General Rosecrans of the incident on February 1:

> I should have writ[t]en to you sooner, for to let you know how business is conducted in Guyandott Va…the abuse I received from him in that short time is two much for any person to bear; Gen I wish for to know if private persons on business are to be treated in this way by officers under you. If there is any military law for to handle him, I call on you for to have it put in force…[476]

Glaze claimed that the property taken from the Jenkins farm included fifty-two fat hogs, seventy-six head of cattle, and thousands of bushels of corn. He complained that he had only received $100 for nearly two months' work and warned, "there is some men there neads watching…"[477]

Abraham Smith, the younger brother of Sallie P. Smith, enlisted in the Union army despite the opposition of his family. He was the drummer for Company D of the 5th (West) Virginia Infantry for a short time until his father brought him back home. Aber, as he was known to family and friends, declared that if he had been at Guyandotte during the raid, "I'll bet that they would not of taken me to Richmond like they did some of the other Lincoln Kangaroo's."[478]

He noted in a letter to his cousin on February 16 that his father, Dudley D. Smith, was "keeping store" in Proctorville and that his Uncle Edward Smith had returned from Camp Chase Prison in Columbus, Ohio. He proclaimed, "that was the worst thing that Governor ever done to take them Secession prisoners there and hold them two months and let them go again." Abraham Smith had little sympathy for his uncle, writing, "if had of got justice done him he would have had his neck in a halter." He added that "his wife is as bad as Ed."[479]

Captain William Turner wrote to Adjutant General H. J. Samuels on February 20, 1862, informing him that "the horse steeling is yet pervaling in Wayne and Cabbell." Captain James E. Smith had skirmished with guerrillas on Fourteen Mile Creek, capturing James Adkins, mortally wounding Henry Harris, and killing George Ephison. Turner reported that "one thief is out of the way." Adkins was sent to Wheeling and several other Confederates turned themselves in to civil authorities.[480]

Turner expressed displeasure that his company was to be incorporated into a regular regiment, declaring that the men "has becom disatisfyed it was not to be confined in no ridgement." Turner claimed that if he had Company B of the 5th (West) Virginia Infantry, "we can clean Logan an other countys. We can brake up all bush whackers horse steeling witcher scouts in 40 miles of the camp still steeling. I have run him close." Turner's company had just returned from a twelve-day expedition, but his activities were discouraged by Colonel Leonard Skinner of the 9th (West) Virginia Infantry, who "ses I have no bisiness to be scouting till he gets his ridgment full."[481]

Turner had raised sixty-two men and collected about $300 in taxes in Wayne County. He planned to start his militia force to the head of Twelve Pole Creek in pursuit of John Plymale and James Ferguson and "clear wayne county of Rebels." Turner also claimed that he had more friends in the county than ever before the war: "Some men who was Rebels an would of kill me six months ago would die for me I know." According to Turner, John Baumgardner, who was appointed to organize the militia in Wayne County, "is not doing eny thing with it. You had better appoint some one other person." Baumgardner was also accused of seizing property owned by secessionists and using it for his own use:

> Bumgarner lives in Kentuckey. When he goes to take property he ses it is for taxes he has nuthing to do with it. He is takeing property threw fals pretence...men indited for treson. He is a coured. He has never arested but on man he was a criple Jamison Spurlock an he tuck with him 25 men to take him. The truth he is too lasey to do anything. He has taken Colonel Grays negroes and useing them for his one use.[482]

J. C. Wheeler, adjutant of the 9th (West) Virginia Infantry, referred to Turner as "an old Union Scout who hates those of secession proclivities with a perfect hatred, and is from their neighborhood and who is thoroughly acquainted with them & has been during this whole rebellion." When the 2nd Kentucky Infantry arrived in July 1861,

Wheeler wrote,

> the leading citizens of Cabell & Wayne Counties to rouse the citizens to resistance industriously circulated the report through the counties that these were an unauthorized band of robbers principally negroes & mulattoes come into the country to rob steal & burn & to ravish the women & these men take no papers & relied upon this information which appeared to be from respectable source and armed themselves for the purpose of resistance.[483]

Although his brother believed the rumors and took up arms, William Turner "concluded to see for himself & went to Guyandotte, and ascertained the falsity of the report..." He informed his brother and neighbors that the troops of the 2nd Kentucky Infantry, who occupied Guyandotte, "were regular federal soldiers & their friends..." These local men laid down their weapons and had done nothing against the Federal government but "as far as they have acted at all they have acted with our side of the question."[484]

Citizens in the region were divided in their opinions of Captain William Turner. Stephen Spurlock, who had initially advocated resistance at Barboursville in July 1861, believed Turner had

> succeeded admirably in bringing Rebels back against the union. They are coming to him by dozens and taking the oath of fidelity to the Constitution & the union in accordance with Governor Peirpoints administration. And if there was money in the county the people would no doubt pay their taxes. All this favourable change may be ascribed to the patriotic prudent, and gentle manner in which Capt Turner has so wisely managed this affair in the part of Wayne County where I reside. He justly deserves a full mead of praise. He has done more in two weeks past than many officers would have done in three years to bring the people into the union and Constitution. And let it be remembered that he has done it by kindness and gentleness toward his fellow man. Secession on the Border of Virginia has no efficient power & therefore the people must and will submit as I have already done.[485]

Jesse Spurlock, however, declared that if Turner "should sucksced in making up his Company and should be commissioned for gods sake have him removed from Wayne for I believe he will do the cause more harm than good for thare is a great hatred against him." Spurlock's opposition to Turner was undoubtedly influenced by an encounter between the two on November 10, 1861, the day of the Confederate raid on Guyandotte.[486]

Spurlock recounted that he had run into Turner and after exchanging pleasantries, Spurlock asked Turner if he knew who had him indicted and for what charges. Turner said he was responsible for the indictment and after Spurlock tried to defend himself, Turner "flew in to a fit and gets off his horse and thowes his bayonet on his gun and raises his gun at armes length and with the bitterest oaths he swore that if I disputed his word that he would sacrifise me on the spot." Captain Turner then began personally abusing Spurlock despite the efforts of the latter to defend himself against the accusations.[487]

Jesse Spurlock claimed that Turner's hostility stemmed from a debt. Turner had purchased Spurlock's mill three years prior, but Spurlock held the deed of trust, and Turner still owed him a large amount of money. In fact, Spurlock believed Turner's actions "plainly showes conclusively that he had made the last payment he ever intended to make."[488]

Turner's hostility was undoubtedly driven in part by the actions of Spurlock's cousin and son-in-law, Captain Hurston Spurlock, who was one of the most noted Confederate leaders in the region. According to Spurlock, Turner sought "to dictate for me and my family how we are to do and whome we shall assosiate with." Spurlock believed Turner's "whole object is to do me the most harm he can in the most available manner and unless thare can be something done to stop this man in his cause I feel entirely unsafe to remain at home for he is viewed as a dangerous man a very spiteful man." He asked Samuels to "use your influence in that way as will prevent this man from doing me the injury that I think he is disposed to do..."[489]

On February 23, Sallie Smith wrote to her cousin from Quaker Bottom, where her family continued to reside following the destruction of their home in Guyandotte. "Spring is here," she observed,

and with no better prospect than the past for us. We have no home no clothes & in fact no nothing. Some times when I think of our situation and of our prospects for the future it nearly distracts me. You know that my pathway through life thus far has not been strewn with flowers and now what can I expect or look for. I try to be as cheerful as possible before Pa & Ma for they feel bad enough without me reminding them of their loss.[490]

Granville Parker, Cabell County's delegate to the constitutional convention for the new state, wrote to Governor Pierpont on March 7 requesting the proper paperwork with which to hold an election for delegate from Cabell County on the first Thursday in April. He informed Pierpont, "Our people like the Constitution quite well, but are much disappointed that the gradual emancipation clause was not either put in or submitted to them." Friends of several Union men still

Francis H. Pierpont, governor of the Restored Government of Virginia. Credit: West Virginia State Archives.

imprisoned in Richmond were "very much vexed" by the fact that several Confederate supporters who had been seized as hostages and sent to Camp Chase had been freed but were making no effort to procure the liberation of the Union men. Parker also noted that "Col Bolles is not liked. There is much complaint by Union men. They say he favors the Rebels much more than Union men."[491]

On March 14, 1862, Joseph Gaston of McConnelsville, Ohio, contacted Virginia Governor Francis Pierpont to inquire about leasing the property owned by Albert Gallatin Jenkins at Green Bottom. Gaston informed Pierpont, "I am acquainted with the property, and if it can be leased, or permission be had to farm it, I would like to know immediately, so that operations might commence at once." It does not appear that Gaston was successful in his endeavor.[492]

Military authorities seem to have offended Governor Francis Pierpont with their efforts to clamp down on goods being purchased to support the Confederate cause. Pierpont penned an angry missive to Captain George L. Hartsuff on March 20, complaining, "I learn that the military in Cabbell County and in that region have undertaken to interfere with the common trade of the rejun. The people there are not permitted to send their grain to market on the Ohio and in their neighborhoods. I wish you would issue an order directing the soldiers to attend to their own business and let the people pursue their lawful vocation."[493]

In March 1862, a member of the 2nd (West) Virginia Cavalry, stationed at Guyandotte wrote:

> Business now seems to be the order of the day; preparation for duty is strongly advocated, and insisted upon by our officers in command, and all seem to be going to work in good earnest, to fit their men and horses for active service. The spring is opening much to our disadvantage, in consequence of so much rain, still all are industriously at work, and our regiment presents a much better appearance than at first.
>
> Searching for and seizing liquors, has been a daily occurrence. Officers of the day are constantly on the lookout; much has been captured, of late; every effort has been resorted to, to conceal it, as we find it sometimes put up in oyster cans, &c., &c. The constant opposition to, and brilliant victories achieved over 'Old King Alcohol,' has so much diminished his favor, as to render him not a very formidable foe at present.
>
> The health of our regiment is very good at present; will compare favorably with any regiment in the service, under similar circumstances; number of sick in hospital, to date, 22, of which two cases only are serious; 20 reported sick at company quarters, unfit for duty, not ill enough to go to hospital, general health improving.
>
> Our hospital is, undoubtedly, in excellent order, everything about it indicates cleanliness and comfort; the inmates are well provided for, and taken care of;

everything about it indicates a systematic plan of operations and too much cannot be said in commendation of Surgeon Neal, and his Corps de Hospitalians, for their attention to our sick.

Pay Master still invisible; grape vine telegraph says he's drowned.[494]

A member of the 4th (West) Virginia Infantry wrote on March 22, "We have been in Ceredo since December last, and when the weather would permit every available moment has been devoted to drilling, and consequently we are well prepared for the coming spring campaign."

He added,

Circuit Judge James H. Brown, later one of the first justices of the West Virginia Supreme Court. Credit: Terry Lowry.

The Paymaster made his appearance in this section of country last evening. He is now paying off the 2d Virginia Cavalry at Guyandotte, and will be with us next week...Circuit Court met here on the 20th inst., Judge Brown, of Kanawha, presiding. The county seat is located at Trout Hill, in the interior of the county – but the records were removed to Ceredo for safety some time since. But few of them are missing, the more important ones being saved. The attendance at Court is large. The Grand Jury empannelled was composed of the most respectable and intelligent citizens of Wayne County, the county having been rid of the prowling bands of Secessionists who invested it during the past months. The people are beginning to come forth and once more resume their usual avocations. From information derived from those at Court, I think large crops will be harvested here next summer. Business has been almost entirely suspended in Ceredo – the residents of the town having mostly left. Those who remain, contemplate a revival of business here when Spring opens.[495]

In late March, a Union soldier wrote, "Muddy roads, disagreeable weather, and visitors without number, are still the remarkable features in Guyandotte. This morning, whilst we were receiving our pay, a fashionable March snow was falling, and this afternoon, to the immense satisfaction of the privates, there is just enough rain falling to prevent the possibility of there being a dress parade."[496]

Colonel Leonard Skinner wrote Governor Pierpont on March 26 to request that William L. Grant and James H. Hysell be commissioned as surgeons for the 9th (West) Virginia Infantry. Eight companies of the regiment had been raised, two more were nearly filled, and there were "a good many sick men at this time." Skinner believed it urgent that the two doctors, who were currently serving as surgeons for the regiment, be appointed permanently.[497]

Superior Court opened in Barboursville on the afternoon of March 27. On March 31, William Dusenberry was at the home of Charles Morris, where he saw Conwelsey Simmons, George Dolen, and Charles Shoemaker, Confederate supporters who had "returned from the back counties where they went when the Federal Army came in & have now returned to give themselves up & take the oath of allegiance. Simmons is very fearful they will imprison him…" Dusenberry agreed to ride into Barboursville with the men to see if he could assist them and met Calvary Swann along the way. The commander of the post was absent, but on the following morning, Dolen, Shoemaker, Simmons, and Swann took the oath of allegiance to the federal government and to the Restored Government of Virginia in the quarters of Captain Thomas Neal. Bond was set at $2,000 for Simmons, $1,500 for Swann and Shoemaker, and $1,000 for George Dolen.[498]

On March 31, Kellian V. Whaley contacted Governor Francis Pierpont from Washington concerning two of his former surgeons:

> I have just recd a letter from Guyandotte stating that there was an influence against Drs Morris and Rouse as surgeons in the 9th Va Regt. Both were appointed by me as surgeons before the two regiments were consolidated, they were taken prisoners the night of the fight and sent to Richmond and have both returned, and I can see no reason why they should not be commissioned. Dr. Rouse's drug store was totally destroyed by the Rebels and leaving him without a dollar to start business again. Dr. Morris passed an examination before the medical board at Wheeling before his capture, and has certainly suffered enough without being deprived of his plase and it was a positive agreement between the officers of the 10th & myself that the appointments I made should be confirmed by them, and I expected the arraingement would be carried out in good faith, and I hope your Excellency will see the justice of my application to have them commissioned.[499]

An election was held throughout the counties of the proposed state of West Virginia on April 3 to ratify the constitution. The polling took place in Guyandotte under military authority. Of the 201 votes cast on the constitution, only one opposed it. Twenty-three of the voters were civilians, while the rest were members of the 9th (West) Virginia Infantry or the 2nd (West) Virginia Cavalry, "residents of Cabell and other counties within the proposed new state." Of the total number of voters, 177 "ordered their names to be signed to the instruction for the gradual emancipation clause," while the other twenty-four "withheld their names." Twenty-one of the twenty-three civilians voted "for the instruction."[500]

In Barboursville, William Dusenberry was forced to act as clerk for the election, with Greenville Harrison and S. A. Childers serving as commissioners and Johnson Lusher as conductor. Dusenberry recorded that of forty-five votes cast, only two men, Underwood and Al. White of Guyandotte, voted against the new state and that the majority also supported the question on gradual emancipation. The polls were adjourned about 4:00 p.m.[501]

Granville Parker described the election in Cabell County in a letter to the *Wheeling Intelligencer*:

> During the election, John Laidly, Esq., lately elected Commonwealth Attorney for Wayne and Cabell counties, and father of Albert Laidly, now in Letcher's Legislature at Richmond, appeared before the Commissioners under great excitement, and declared that the taking of the vote on the instruction was unauthorized and improper, throwing the weight of his influence and character against it. I think, however, he failed to convince any voter at that poll that the people have not the right to instruct their servants, whether the latter be black or white, whether field or legislative. He voted for the Constitution, but vociferated a very emphatic *No*, when asked as to the instruction and retired.
>
> Polls were opened at four other precincts within the county, and poll books and printed instruction furnished. The result I have not learned. Detachments of cavalry were sent to two precincts. No disturbance occurred except at one, where two secesh undertook to disturb the election, but were at once arrested. James H. Brown and John Laidly, visited by John Hall, President of the Wheeling Convention, while holding court in Wayne county, exerted their influence to prevent any expression of the people on the 'Gradual Emancipation clause' in that county; and though I sent Lieut. Col. Lightburn, of the 4th Virginia Infantry, a copy of the printed instructions two weeks before the election, with a letter stating the necessity of taking the sense of legal voters under his military charge, I learn it was suppressed altogether at his camp, though 300 to 400 voters are there. Messrs. Brown and Laidly were also acting both in their private and official characters against the instructions while holding their court at Barboursville. I shall write fully as soon as I get returns, and also what Judge Brown's court did while in session in Cabell and Wayne.[502]

The quartermaster of the 4th (West) Virginia Infantry, stationed at Ceredo, wrote to the Point Pleasant *Weekly Register* on April 7 to inform readers of the condition of the regiment. He noted that twelve members of the 4th (West) Virginia had died since the unit's inception but called it comparatively an "extremely low figure" credited to good sanitary practices.

> Many single companies in other regiments, have buried more men during the

same period of service than our entire regiment. This speaks well of the medical staff, and it must be gratifying to those who have friends connected with us to know that their health is entrusted to such faithful hands, and also to feel assured, that if it should fall to their lot to meet with any casualty on the field, they will have the benefit of all the facilities that skill and industry can afford to make them comfortable.[503]

General Jacob D. Cox informed General John C. Fremont on April 5: "At Guyandotte the Ninth Virginia Volunteers have two bronze smooth 6-pounders, with full equipments, recently sent them from Washington. They are ordered to man the guns with a detachment from the line."[504]

A. M. McGinnis wrote to Adjutant General H. J. Samuels in April 1862 describing another feud in Cabell County. McGinnis was apparently having trouble with Skelton Poteet and had sent sons Allen and John away "to prevent another H W Shelton and A Fuller case." McGinnis then met with Poteet,

> and he commenced in his usual strain of abuse made many charges that I knew to be false among the rest said I went to Thos Thornburgs with a saddle bag full of letters to send to the Secesh army. I replied he was mistaken that I was as much Union as he was and much more loyal for he was a law abiding man & good citizen. He then swore he would arrest me the next time he caught me over there

and declared that such men "should be shot." McGinnis also believed that Colonels Bolles and Paxton of the 2nd (West) Virginia Cavalry "make more Union men out of 'Secesh' than all the rob[b]ing and arresting parties that could be sent or come here."[505]

J. B. Baumgardner wrote to Adjutant General H. J. Samuels on April 6, requesting Enfield cartridges for the Home Guards in Wayne and Cabell counties. He noted, "Rebels again have made their appearance in this county and are committing depredations of the vilest kind. They are taking and confiscating all property belonging to Union men that they can lay their hands on. 'Clawhammer' is now in Cabell (true to his instinct) stealing and plundering every thing that comes in his way."[506]

Junius Jones of the 2nd (West) Virginia Cavalry went to Barboursville on April 9

Cabell County public official J. B. "Fatty" Baumgardner. Credit: Special Collections Department, Marshall University.

with several members of his company. The road from Guyandotte to Barboursville followed the Guyandotte River and featured some very good bottom land. A number of nice farms adjoined the village, but Jones believed the ones in Barboursville were "not the best," though he thought if the land was drained it would make very good wheat and corn country.[507]

In a letter to his parents, Jones described the people of Barboursville as "very clever and sociable, especially the Union portion." He informed them that "the town is built on an uneven vall[e]y on the east bank of the river. It has about 500 inhabitants 6 or 7 stores (only one of which has any goods in) three taverns a blacksmith shop and is the county seat of Cabell Co. & a very good courthouse and jail." He noted that "a number of houses have [been] severely handled by soldiers using them as quarters and stables."[508]

Jones was especially enamored with the Morey family, formerly of Boston. Frank Morey was a painter and leather dresser, and his wife Eliza was "a very fine woman." Two of their four daughters were grown, but the two younger girls, Cynthia and Frances, lived at home. One of them "was a very smart child and caused a great deal of mirth wherever she was & was a joy to the whole family."[509]

On April 10 John Laidley noted the difficulties faced by civil authorities:

We are progressing verey slowly, in organizing courts – there seems to prevail a general dread of the guerrillas and those whose aid is so important from their acquaintance with business will not appear [&] cannot be mooved. We had a county court on Monday. The sheriff failed to give bond & court was adjourned until this day for his accommodation. I did not go up as I had but little faith in his success. Turner, sheriff elect in Wayne has also failed to give bond having been mustered into the regiment at the head of his company & presume will abandon the collection of the revenue under his office of collector.[510]

With the onset of spring, guerrilla activity in the county had increased. That night, three horses owned by William Hinchman and Elisha Deal were stolen. Circuit court was held in Wayne County on March 20, in Cabell County on March 27, and in Putnam County on April 8. The Point Pleasant *Weekly Register* reported that "upwards of a hundred indictments were found at the first, nearly as many at the second, and more than half as many at the third."[511]

Excitement again filled the streets of Guyandotte on April 18, 1862. On this occasion, however, the incident did not produce bloodshed but instead the conflicting reactions of anger and humor.

At 11 o'clock last night, we were again called to arms by the beating of the long roll in the camp of the 9th Regiment of Virginia Volunteer Infantry, just below the Guyan River. The three remaining companies of 2d Cavalry were, as usual, ready and anxious for a fight; reported in the roads leading into town above the Guyan river, leaving the roads below in charge of the 9th Virginia. The alarm having been caused by the fireing of several gun, some half mile below the 9th

Virginia camp, on the road leading to Ceredo, for a short time all felt as though a battle was inevitable; and whilst the boys of the 2d Virginia Cavalry stood their ground like men, many of the 9th Virginia were discovered, skedaddling through the dark in every direction, than toward the supposed position of the enemy; many running and taking a Sam Patch leap in the dark over the river bank, of about 28 feet, as per examination this morning; whilst others were seen running about with their coats under their arms, in their bare feet, in a state of bewilderment; others jumping into the Guyan river and swimming across into our camp. One man reported drowned; others cutting boats loose, and pushing out into the river; 6 men out of one of the companies reported missing this morning. Some one (name not ascertained) had a trading boat near the wharf, who, upon hearing the alarm, ran out on shore to let go his line, and when in the act, was discovered by a colored boy standing on the bank, who yelled out 'Halt,' the boatman immediately straightened up without taking time to untie his line, ran the stream, and away he went, leaving his line, to prove his cowardice…We soon learned that all was a hoax; nevertheless, it served to try the nerve and point out cowards; we are glad to say, that last night, as on all former occasions, the boys of the 2d Virginia are always that.[512]

This letter, signed "Invincible", was written by the controversial William Powell. It appeared in the April 24 issue of the *Ironton Register*, but was strongly denounced one week later by two letters written by members of the 9th (West) Virginia Infantry. One of these rebuttals is printed below:

In your issue of 24th inst. we are sorry to see a communication from this place, from somebody who boasts the soubriquet of "Invincible," giving an account of the bit of sport that came off one week ago.

We are sorry that an officer of the 2d Virginia Cavalry should so far forget the attributes of a military man, or a gentleman, as to undertake to destroy the reputation of another, in order to improve the damaged reputation of himself. It seemed very much as though he would cowardly shoot a prisoner, if he had the chance. It may possibly prove a paliative to a guilty conscience. Yet the place and execution are both pusilanimous, and unbecoming a soldier.

The alarm was planned at our own (9th Virginia Regiment) head quarters, and the firing was by one of our own companies, detailed for that purpose. Our Regiment was promptly into line, except two privates, that did jump off the bank, for which they were court-martialed and disgraced. Many of our sick, that had not been on duty for weeks, shouldered their rifles, and fell in. It is true that the firing came from the west side of our camp. Then why did the 2d Cavalry, without taking time to secure their horses, take the opposite direction? and it is reported that 'Invincible' threw his company as near the woods and hills as possible! He says, 'the 2d Cavalry, as usual, were ready and anxious for a fight.' Were they seized with diarrhoea, as on a former occasion, while standing in the ranks? Or did they ever put two saddles on one horse, and enquire for a third? Did 'Invincible' ever see a fight? Did his men ever take a couple of prisoners? And did their Captain shoot them in cold blood with his revolvers? Did 'Invincible' start the report that one man was drowned – others cut boats loose – or that six men were missing – or that any of our men swam Guyan river? He is so ready at falsehood, that we suspect he did. The trading boat was cut loose from their own camp…Why is it that the citizens of Cabell county have petitioned that the 2d Cavalry be removed from this region, on account of the poor protection they furnished the Union men, and the consolation they gave to the uncombed men and red headed women on the other side. We speak only of the rank, not the file.

Our acquaintance with 'Invincible' is very limited. We have had him frequently pointed out to us as the unhappy murderer of men who had thrown down their arms and surrendered themselves prisoners of war, in a little, and the only skirmish in which he was ever a participant. We pitied him then, but now, since he has added lying to the sins, we both pity and despise the poor, avoided poltroon.[513]

Perhaps the best account of the events was given by the quartermaster of the 4th (West) Virginia Infantry, who happened to be an eyewitness:

Editor Register: As there is no interesting news from Ceredo, I propose to give you a few items relating to a little piece of fun that came off at Guyandotte a few nights since, in the shape of a 'surprise party.' It appears some of the fun-loving soldiers concluded to surprise a party of young ladies at a neighboring house, for the purpose of a social dance; when some of their less disposed comrades, who were probably somewhat effected with the green-eyed monster, took exceptions to the proceedings, and followed for the purpose of surprising them. Accordingly a party numbering some twenty or thirty, took their muskets and repairing to the place where the young folks were enjoying themselves, – fired volley after volley over the house. The inmates supposing themselves to be attacked by the Secesh, commenced beating a hasty retreat, using every means in their power to facilitate their flight, making their egress through windows and every other accessible outlet. In short, there was a grand skedaddling for camp. Some of the boys are reported to have tumbled end over end, some thirty feet down the bank of the Guyandotte river. By this time the town was thoroughly aroused – the drums beat the long roll, and the bugle sounded to arms. Everybody crying, 'rally, rally! The Secesh are upon us! The Secesh are upon us again!' While from camp could be heard the loud commands of the officers, shouting 'fall in, fall in,' &c. The cause of the alarm was, however, soon discovered, when all quietly returned to their quarters. The only casualties arising from the affair, was the collission [sic] of two cavalry companies, which resulted in the death of two horses; and more or less injury to their riders; besides a score or two of men being shot in the neck with a pint flask charged with liquid fire...[514]

The criticism of Major William Powell stemmed from an incident that occurred in January 1862, when he was involved in his first skirmish near Paintsville, Kentucky. He became separated from most of his company and stumbled onto a couple of unarmed Confederates who had lost their horses. Powell recalled, "having no men to spare to guard any as prisoners – the forces being in action – and knowing that their force was much greater than ours, and not knowing what moment we might be overpowered and made to retreat, I shot them and passed on, in the conscientious belief that I had discharged my duty to the Government, as well as to the rebels." Although various writers branded him a murderer for his actions at Paintsville, his commanding officer, Colonel William Bolles, defended Powell, stating, "No man ever led his command into action in more gallant style, and many an officer has received public thanks and promotion for much less services."[515]

Union Major William H. Powell, 2nd (West) Virginia Cavalry. Powell would be brevetted as major general after the war and was awarded the Medal of Honor for his actions at Sinking Creek in Greenbrier County on November 26, 1862. Credit: Richard A. Wolfe.

The 2nd (West) Virginia Cavalry left Guyandotte at two o'clock on Monday, April 28, 1862. The troops rode to Barboursville, where they joined two companies of the regiment which had been stationed for a short time in the village. The regiment encamped there for the night, arose at six the next morning, and marched to Camp Piatt. The 9th (West) Virginia Infantry also left in April for service in the Kanawha Valley. Both regiments lost a number of soldiers to sickness during their stay in Guyandotte. Among them was Private John Hardee, who died of pneumonia on March 24, 1862. Hardee, whose home was across the river in Lawrence County, Ohio, was only sixteen years of age.[516]

The men of the 9th (West) Virginia were delighted at the opportunity to see some action. One soldier informed a local newspaper that the regiment had "been engaged all spring in guarding from encroachment the rubbish and ruins of disloyal and not-to-be-pitied Guyandotte, Va..."[517]

William Dusenberry attended Federal court in Charleston in late April. On May 1, Dusenberry and John Witcher, soon to be a prominent Union military leader, met with

General Jacob D. Cox, who "told us we should be protected in our County." The departure of nearly all Union soldiers from Cabell County would instead leave the region decidedly unprotected.[518]

resulted in the death of two horses; and more or less injury to their riders; besides a score or two of men being shot in the neck with a pint flask charged with liquid fire...⁵¹⁴

The criticism of Major William Powell stemmed from an incident that occurred in January 1862, when he was involved in his first skirmish near Paintsville, Kentucky. He became separated from most of his company and stumbled onto a couple of unarmed Confederates who had lost their horses. Powell recalled, "having no men to spare to guard any as prisoners – the forces being in action – and knowing that their force was much greater than ours, and not knowing what moment we might be overpowered and made to retreat, I shot them and passed on, in the conscientious belief that I had discharged my duty to the Government, as well as to the rebels." Although various writers branded him a murderer for his actions at Paintsville, his commanding officer, Colonel William Bolles, defended Powell, stating, "No man ever led his command into action in more gallant style, and many an officer has received public thanks and promotion for much less services."⁵¹⁵

Union Major William H. Powell, 2nd (West) Virginia Cavalry. Powell would be brevetted as major general after the war and was awarded the Medal of Honor for his actions at Sinking Creek in Greenbrier County on November 26, 1862. Credit: Richard A. Wolfe.

The 2nd (West) Virginia Cavalry left Guyandotte at two o'clock on Monday, April 28, 1862. The troops rode to Barboursville, where they joined two companies of the regiment which had been stationed for a short time in the village. The regiment encamped there for the night, arose at six the next morning, and marched to Camp Piatt. The 9th (West) Virginia Infantry also left in April for service in the Kanawha Valley. Both regiments lost a number of soldiers to sickness during their stay in Guyandotte. Among them was Private John Hardee, who died of pneumonia on March 24, 1862. Hardee, whose home was across the river in Lawrence County, Ohio, was only sixteen years of age.⁵¹⁶

The men of the 9th (West) Virginia were delighted at the opportunity to see some action. One soldier informed a local newspaper that the regiment had "been engaged all spring in guarding from encroachment the rubbish and ruins of disloyal and not-to-be-pitied Guyandotte, Va..."⁵¹⁷

William Dusenberry attended Federal court in Charleston in late April. On May 1, Dusenberry and John Witcher, soon to be a prominent Union military leader, met with

General Jacob D. Cox, who "told us we should be protected in our County." The departure of nearly all Union soldiers from Cabell County would instead leave the region decidedly unprotected.[518]

9
Piatt's Zouaves

"...we then went on to the mill where they say the two boys was killed the Zouaves. There was a woman a runing the mill. The boys tryed to make her tell where they was beried but she would not tell. The boys threatened to shoot and drawed there gunes on her but she would not tell. There was three wimen at the house but they swore they did not see them nor did not know any thing of them... The boys just went in on ever thing chickens and mollases and every thing that they could get. They burnt the fence up and all the wood. They would have burnt the mill and the house if the captain had not cept them from it."

Francis Hale, 34th Ohio Infantry
Gilkerson's Mill, Wayne County, December 30, 1861

In October 1861, the 34th Ohio Infantry regiment arrived in Cabell County, where they would remain for the next six months. Named Piatt's Zouaves for their colonel, Abram S. Piatt, and for a class of light infantry regiments of the French Army, their unique uniform consisted of a dark jacket with red trim, sky blue baggy trousers with two vertical stripes of red tape, tan gaiters, and a red fez with a blue tassel. The regiment was raised at Camp Lucas in Clermont County, Ohio, moved to Camp Dennison near Cincinnati on September 1, and advanced two weeks later into the Kanawha Valley in western Virginia. At the end of October, the 34th Ohio moved their base of operations to Mud Bridge in eastern Cabell County.

The Zouaves were scattered at posts throughout the area. Three companies were at Winfield, five companies were stationed at Mud Bridge, and two companies occupied Barboursville. Writing from Mud Bridge on November 14, William Ludwig of the 34th Ohio noted,

We have accationally a case of fireing on our pickets. But there has been none for the last weak past. The boys wood like no better fun than to have a nice little fight, for they are just spoiling for one. The Secesh up in this part of the Country shudder at the very name of the Thirty Fourth. We have traveled ten miles without meeting a man. Whenever we do meet one he has either been sick all summer or he is lame. We cannot get one of them to say he is all right...[519]

Lieutenant Ethan A. Brown wrote to a Cincinnati newspaper in early November and described the regiment's activities:

> We are now at a point called Mud Bridge. Parties go out daily ten and twenty miles into the country, and bring in more or less prisoners; but what use is it to take prisoners when, upon simply administering an oath, they are turned loose again, not only to pick up their rifles and fight, but to give all the information they can gain while in our camps to the enemy? This 'swearing in' business, or 'taking the oath,' as it is called, is as the boys say, 'played out.' It is a humbug, not to say a mockery. Many of the very men who took the oath last summer, when Col. Woodruff was through here, have been acting the part of, and associating with, 'Secesh,' ever since he left.[520]

Sergeants of Company A, 34th Ohio Infantry, taken at Tompkins farm near Gauley Bridge in Fayette County shortly after their departure from Cabell County. Credit: L. M. Strayer Collection.

Brown's complaint was a common one among the Ohio soldiers. Francis Hale claimed the local citizens "know all about our camp where our pickets are posted where they can get in at and not be seene." On several consecutive days Union pickets fired on citizens who got a little too close to camp. Although most secessionists were released after taking the oath of allegiance, others refused. These men, along with those arrested while armed, were placed in the guardhouse and eventually sent to Camp Chase or to the Athenaeum in Wheeling.[521]

Brown described another excursion his company had undertaken, stating sarcastically that "although some brilliant strategic maneuvering was performed, we bagged no game." The company traveled six miles from Mud Bridge to a house known as "secesh headquarters" where they expected a fight awaited them. "With stealth and circumspection we surrounded the house," Brown wrote,

> and at the call of the bugle all advanced at 'double quick' up to the secesh house. The Captain told me to go in and bring out the prisoners. I proceeded to obey

the order. With gun cocked and bayonet fixed I knocked at the door. My call was soon answered – not by a volley of musketry, nor by a racket within and a rush out at the back-door, but by the appearance of a beautiful young lady.

Undoubtedly warned of the approaching Union column, the Confederates were nowhere to be found. As Brown noted wryly, "we found no secesh of the masculine gender." In response to Lieutenant Brown's interrogation, the woman stated that the men were absent from home, "that they were 'secesh,' and expected to fight for the South – that she was of the same mind, and would fight too, if necessary." Brown described her as "a very spunky little piece of humanity, and that she was pretty there is no mistake." The woman lived on Big Sandy but her romantic interest had been shot in both legs at Scary Creek, and she had moved to the area to help nurse him back to health.[522]

Lieutenant Ethan Allen Brown, 34th Ohio Infantry. Brown was mortally wounded at the battle of Fayetteville in 1862. Credit: Terry Lowry.

Ludwig wrote from Mud Bridge on November 18 that a Confederate attack had been anticipated on the previous evening,

but they would not have found us asleep. There are Seven companies here and will show them a good fight to the last man that is the Zouave still. Fight or die. We were called out twice last night, and never did I see a set of men take it so cool as they did. We were in line and had the skirmishes thrown out in less than ten minutes. Our company being the left flank some of the companys made for the Brestworks we have thrown up on the side of a hill others guarded the road while Co. G made for the opposite hill.

The Union troops scouted the hillside for about an hour but found nothing and returned to Mud Bridge. Ludwig recorded, "We had hardly got in when another alarm was given which as the other proved false as the picket saw crawling uppon him. Today three companys leave for Barbersville a little town between here and Gandotte as a gard for the election. But I expect they will be back some time tonight..."[523]

On November 22, Private Francis Hale of the 34th Ohio recorded that "a part of boys went out on a scout. They was about 18 miles from camp there was two virginians along the[y] camped in 2 1/2 miles from one fellows home. He started to go hom[e] had got near there whe[n] a bushwhacker shot him in the mouth and killed him dead. They buried him there."[524]

Snow began falling on November 23 and continued for the next few days. The Zouaves enjoyed "snowing one another like every thing." The men anticipated a move to winter quarters but were still unclear as to their destination, although they hoped "it will be to some good place to keepe warm and dry."

At nine o'clock on the night of November 25, the 34th Ohio Infantry left Mud Bridge and marched west a little more than ten miles to the village of Barboursville. Despite constant snowfall, the road was muddy and difficult to traverse. As they crossed Poore's Hill, the site of a September skirmish, four prisoners guarded by Private Francis Hale shared stories about the encounter, including one that claimed a Union soldier put a cannon on his shoulder and fired it at the secessionists. The Zouaves reached their destination about 2:00 a.m.[525]

William Ludwig wrote from Barboursville on November 27:

We arrived here night before last. We are in good quarters in houses. John Brunson and I have a room to ourselves. We have a nice little coal stove a writing desk, and a nice little bunk in one corner. The room is ten feet square. Each mess has but one room. A good fire place to cook in and every thing handy. The town is about as large as Brookville. There is a splendid Corthouse here in which there are two companys quartered. This is the place where the 2nd Ky. Reg. had thier first fight some of the boys have been all day picking up old bullets which they find on the battle ground. Three hundred of the Ky. boys cleaned out seven hundred Secesh and they up on a hill. The town is on the G[uy]andotte River, well situated on the junction of four roads commanding the whole country around...[526]

Another member of the regiment described Barboursville as "a beautifully located town and if it was in a free state it would make a flourishing place of business. It contains about 500 dwellings and one court house, one jail, one church, one school house, one Masonic lodge with over 100 members. The school house is the first I saw in Virginia..."[527]

On November 29, Francis Hale of the 34th Ohio recorded in his diary that "three of our men has just got back from guyandott. They say it is awfull bad for the union men the way they burnt up the town. The boys sayed ther is to be 5 hundred of cavelry to winter ther. They say things looked very bad there now bullet holes through every place pretty nigh."[528]

A small skirmish took place near Dusenberry's Mill sometime during the first year of the war. It is probable that the Federal troops involved in this brief encounter were members of the 34th Ohio Infantry. The clash was later recalled by Confederate Sampson Sanders Simmons, a member of the Border Rangers:

We got as far as Uncle Sanders' and Dusenbery's Store, about two hundred yards above where the bridge now stands. The Federal soldiers were up on the hill above Uncle Charles Morris' house. I had stopped at the mill to talk with the miller, Jack Lloyd, but dodged behind the other boys; but the Yankees fired on me. One bullet came so near that it struck the road near my feet; another bullet struck the store about fifteen feet away.

One local man, John D. Mays, was captured and sent to prison.[529]

A detachment of Zouaves departed from Barboursville on Friday evening, December 6, searching the countryside for enemies of the Union. During their expedition, they were fired on by secessionists. Their guide

> got a rifle ball through the left arm, it is called a flesh wound but it scraped the bone close enough to crack it, the ball went in the inside of his arm just below the shoulder behind and came out in front just above the elbow. The fellow that shot him was secreted in some bushes up on the hill side and waited till Harrison had passed and then run up the mountain and cleared himself. Harrison saw him running and knows and swears he will have that shot back with interest as soon as his arm gets well enough. The fellows name is Adkins. There are six brothers of them in the Secesh army and our scouts brought 3 of them along as prisoners on Monday evening but the one that shot Harrison made his escape and tis well for him he would never have been brought in a prisoner.

The Zouaves returned to camp on Monday, December 9, with nine prisoners and four horses.[530] An illustration and slightly different description of this expedition appeared in the December 28, 1861, issue of the *New York Illustrated News*:

> Herewith I enclose you a lively sketch of a surprise, and a brilliant charge with the *bayonet*, by the *mounted* Zouaves, 54 in number, of the 34th Regiment O. V. (infantry), the only mounted Zouaves in the world.
>
> Information was brought in, that the rebel Jenkins was, with a squad of his cavalry, on his way toward Guyandotte, to meet his wife and escort her to his rebel quarters. A detachment of mounted Zouaves was dispatched to intercept them; when, early in the morning of the 5th inst., they suddenly surprised them (mostly dismounted), in a very romantic spot in the mountains, called the 'Devil's Elbow,' in Cabell county, Va. The place was of a highly picturesque character, and awfully grand; for hanging, high over head and on each side, were huge heaps of shapeless rocks, which the artist has faithfully portrayed in his sketch.
>
> The rebels when first discovered, were treated with a Zouave yell, and charged with the bayonet *upon horseback*, the Zouaves having no sabres. Three only of the rebels showed fight; the rest fled in dismay, leaving twenty-five horses, and three prisoners, all wounded, in our hands; four of the Zouaves were slightly wounded.[531]

Skirmish at Devil's Elbow, Cabell County.
Sketch from New York Illustrated News, December 28, 1861. Credit: Terry Lowry.

In mid-December, Francis Hale of the 34th Ohio recorded that "we have the guardd house pretty nigh full of secesh prisners. They are an awfull hard set or looking set dirty & raged. They would make a good band of cut throats by their lookes I presume..." A few days earlier, a secessionist had come to Barboursville to visit one of the prisoners. Unfortunately for the local Confederate supporter, he was recognized by a resident of the village who informed Colonel Piatt of his sympathies. The man arrived at headquarters on December 14 to request a jail pass to visit a prisoner, "but when he got in the jail he could not get out and was cept a prisner for to go to Columbiss for to stay there a while I gess."[532]

George Sprecher of the 34th Ohio wrote from Barboursville a day later, noting,

> it is nothing uncommon to see some proud soldier walking the pavement of this splendid county seat in all the pomp splendor of an Eastern nabob dressed from head to foot with 1 hat, 1 shirt, 1 pair of drawers while the rest of his wardrobe is hung on the fence to dry after washing, and when he washes his shirt and drawers he will wear his pants and roundabout and this [way] he has a change of clothing all the time.[533]

Sprecher observed, "The weather has been beautiful more like spring than

Sketch of 34th Ohio Infantry marching down Main Street, Barboursville.
Credit: Terry Lowry.

December, the scouting goes on fine and our scouts bring in from 2 to ten prisoners a day, last evening they brought 4 as hard looking customers as I ever saw and they drove 7 fat steers, 1 yoke of oxen, 5 horses, one fine carriage and one buggy and a number of other articles." That night he attended a Masonic Lodge meeting conducted by Minerva Lodge No. 51 at Barboursville. Although only ten members of the lodge and four visitors from the 34th Ohio were present, the men "had quite a happy time" and Sprecher informed his wife that "it was the pleasantest evening I spent since I left home."[534]

The men of the 34th Ohio Infantry complained about the lack of furloughs for the regiment, but the officers anticipated that granting leave to a large portion of the men would leave them exposed to a Confederate attack:

> the Secesh would gather a mighty force and come down on us and wipe us out for they hate the Zouaves and fear them as bad as the Devil does holy water. Col. Jenkins sent us word on Friday that he would eat his breakfast in Barbersville or in Hell on this (Sunday) morning, now it is about sundown and Mr. Jenkins has not yet appeared with hosts for his breakfast at this place, whether he got it at the place or not I don't know...[535]

On the same day, Major Freeman E. Franklin of the 34th Ohio wrote to the editors of the *Tiffin Weekly Tribune* from Barboursville, noting,

> It is the best part of Western Virginia that I have seen. We are comfortably quartered, and have only 20 men sick in our whole Regiment. We have lost five killed and four from sickness; the balance are all in good spirits and spoiling for a fight.[536]

In a letter to his wife, George Sprecher described the regiment's daily routine:

> it is 5 o'clock revile and roll call, 6 o'clock breakfast, 7 o'clock surgeons call, half past 7 guard mounting, 8 o'clock squad drill, 9 o'clock company drill, 11 o'clock cook dinner, 12 dinner, 1 battalion drill, 4 dress parade, supper between that and 6 o'clock, 6:15 roll call, 8:50 tattoo, 9 taps, out all lights except the hospital and headquarters...[537]

On Sunday, December 15, the 2nd (West) Virginia Cavalry arrived in Guyandotte. Two hundred men of the regiment left on the following day, passing through Barboursville on their way to Louisa, Kentucky. On Wednesday, December 18, John Castelow and John L. Cerbe of Company D of the 34th Ohio were sent with a local guide named William Collins toward Wayne Courthouse to request that a detachment of the 2nd (West) Virginia Cavalry move their camp closer to Barboursville. Collins, a farmer who was born in Cabell County and lived on Madison Creek, had enlisted in the regiment at Camp Toland only three days before the fateful mission.[538]

The three Zouaves were on Beech Fork in Wayne County about sixteen miles from Barboursville when suddenly a militia force from the area fired on them. The Ohioans returned the fire but were overpowered before they could reload. While the guerrillas were searching the Union soldiers, Collins jumped on his horse and rode off. After a chase of about two miles, the local men caught Collins, who was wounded in the encounter, and took him to Gilkerson's Mill, where the two other Zouaves had been moved. On the following morning, the militiamen debated what to do with their prisoners. Some advocated sending them to Richmond, some to a Confederate camp at Logan Courthouse, but others argued that the Yankees should be murdered. According to a Union account, Helena Gilkerson "wished one to be killed on her porch, so that she could dance in his blood."[539]

Sketch of the murder of Piatt's Zouaves on Beech Fork in Wayne County, December 1861. Credit: Harper's Weekly.

On the following morning, December 20, the secessionists took one of the Zouaves up a run about a quarter of a mile from the mill and tied him to a tree. Bill Prichett, Lew Prichett, Isom Miller, and a man named Stevens walked a short distance from their prisoner, then turned and fired until the Union soldier was dead. Robert Mays and the other bystanders went back to Gilkerson's, retrieved the other Zouave, and brought him up the run. When they neared his murdered comrade, he stopped, "unbuttoned his Zouave jacket and tore open his shirt" and said, "My God! if you intend to kill me, shoot me through the heart, and don't mangle my body." Mays stepped forward and volunteered to escort the prisoner to the Confederate camp at Logan, but the other men bound their captive to a tree and shot him repeatedly until he was dead.[540]

The men then returned to Gilkerson's Mill, where they cruelly teased the wounded Collins, telling him he was about to be killed. Collins replied, "For God's sake let me alone: I am dying as fast as I can; let me alone." About noon, they dragged him off the porch and drove him down the run a short distance. One of the Pritchetts "said they were to see who could hit nearest his heart without killing him." The brave Collins was shot multiple times and died instantly.[541]

Eight or nine local residents heard the gunfire and crossed over the hill until they reached the scene of the murders. William L. Johnson, who had fought with the militia at Barboursville, noted he "saw two of them dead and the third man wounded. When we got in sight, and saw the bushwhackers dressed in the blue uniforms which they had taken from the Zouaves, George saw that we were about to shoot at him and his companions, and he said 'Boys, don't shoot; these are our boys'." After a brief conversation, Mays "said he wanted them buried right, and the bushwhackers agreed to let all the men there look at them. We found them buried behind a root and covered up with leaves and chunks. We then buried them, in the same place, a little better..." The bodies of the Union soldiers were reportedly later moved and dropped into a nearby crevice that became known as the Zouave Cave.[542]

According to William Johnson, Collins was one of the soldiers that was already dead when he arrived. The local men apparently knew William Collins. In fact, Johnson informed the bushwhackers that "they had killed a man with whom I had slept many times." Stevens responded, "How come you so sharp." The wounded Zouave was marched off and his guards told Johnson they were taking him to headquarters. Within a few minutes, however, Johnson heard a gunshot and he soon crossed paths with the local men, who were without their prisoner.

Thirty soldiers of the 34th Ohio Infantry left Barboursville on the night of December 18 on a scouting expedition and returned the following afternoon. Another detachment marched out on the morning of December 20 to corral horses along Mud River. A Confederate cavalry force was reported to be nearby, and the Zouaves set an ambush, but the enemy did not appear. The Union soldiers also did some rabbit hunting and saw quite a few but were unsuccessful as the intended victims "run faster than [in] Ohio." On the following day a detachment was sent in pursuit of a man named Rece who fled the area with about twenty horses. The Federals pursued as far as the Falls of Guyandotte, but Rece had "to mutch of a start of us." These scouting parties were probably part of a desperate effort by the regiment to find their missing comrades. Information regarding their fate must have been ascertained, as a member of the 34th wrote one week after their disappearance, "We have got all the murderers names, and know where they live."

One resident of Cabell County, Jerome Shelton, was arrested by troops of the 34th Ohio at Barboursville and sent to Wheeling. In response to an inquiry from Adjutant General Henry J. Samuels, Lieutenant Colonel John L. Toland wrote on December 23 that it "seems to be the especial terror of that neighborhood that there is a possibility of his being released. This has been expressed by a number of citizens." Toland noted he would be tried within a day or two, and if sufficient testimony was brought against him, Shelton would be sent to prison in Wheeling immediately.[544]

Shelton was an outspoken secessionist. He had favored the Ordinance of Secession, and one of his neighbors noted that "men who were understood to be secessionists made Mr. Shelton's house their regular stopping place." Shelton was charged with repairing a bridge for Jenkins's cavalry, robbing a Union man named James Woods, and "getting up a company for the Porr's Hill battle." Several of Shelton's neighbors bore witness against him, including James C. Bias, Joseph Dick, James W. McMillian, Joseph Newman, and Winston Noel.[545]

Bias testified, "When I have told him that we ought to fight for the government under which we had been born and raised he replied that he ought to fight for his state." Shelton also informed neighbors that if they were loyal to their state, they should enlist and go to Poore's Hill to attack the Federal forces. Bias claimed that

CHAPTER NINE 189

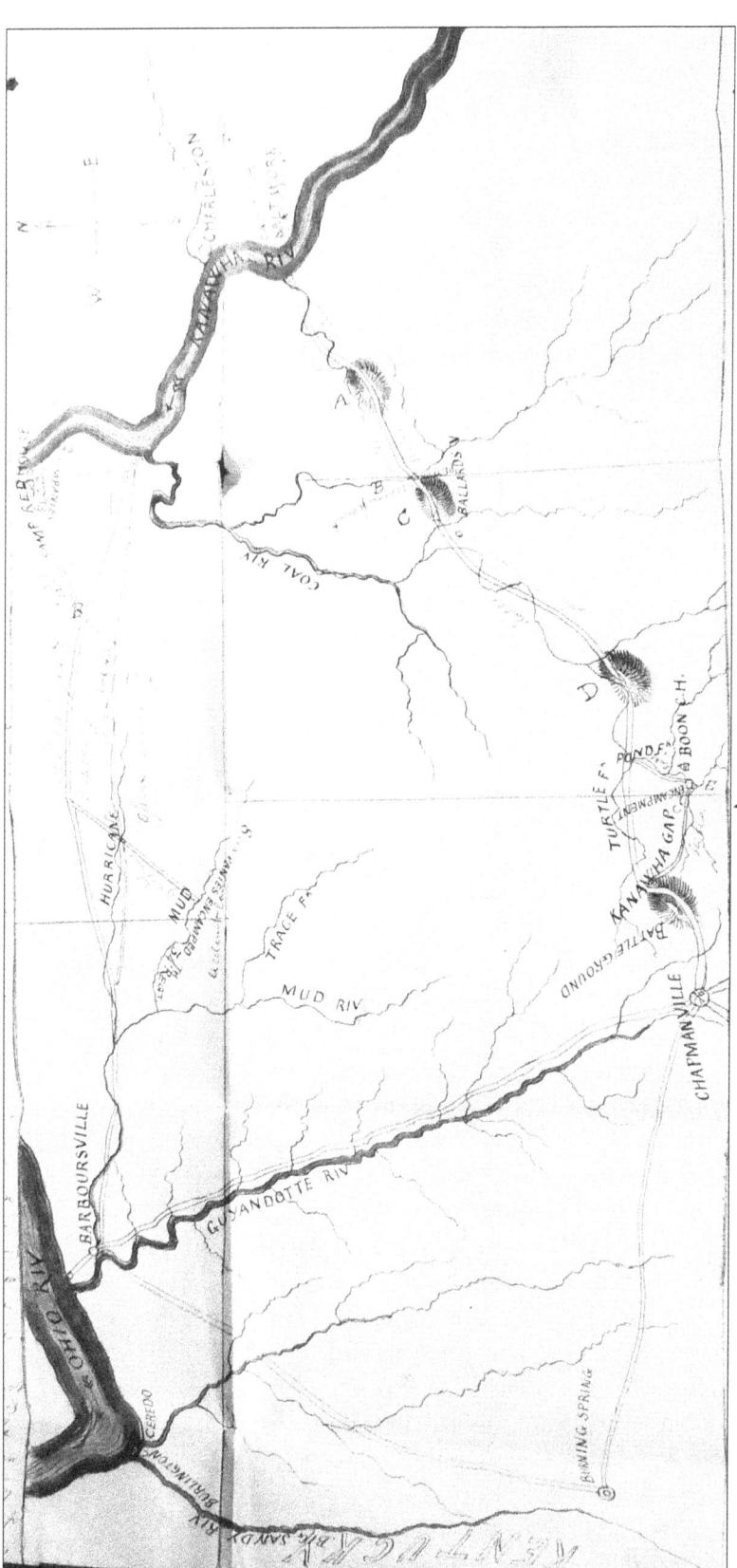

Map included in correspondence of 34th Ohio Infantry, National Archives. Credit: Terry Lowry.

Shelton "laid out in the woods when the union troops were passing through. I have heard him say that he did not wish to be taken by the union troops."[546]

Newman attested that he had seen Shelton at the 1861 fight at Poore's Hill and that he had brought twenty or more men there to fight against the Union troops. James McMillian was present when Shelton signed up a number of the men for a company. He recalled, "Jerome told me if I would join the company he would give me back a gun I had sold him – also a horse saddle and bridle – and that my wife might go to his corn crib and get all the corn she wanted. And that if I did not...it would be my own fault."[547]

On December 27, J. C. Wheeler of the 9th (West) Virginia asked Samuels to provide General William S. Rosecrans with a list of Confederate prisoners. Wheeler stated he would "not be able to do much for Jerome Shelton [a pre-war business partner of H. J. Samuels] I fear as the military authorities at Barboursville seem inclined to make a final disposition of the prisoners they arrest and are not disposed to make any compromise with those who have in any way aided the Rebellion." Regarding this force at Barboursville, presumably the 34th Ohio Infantry, Wheeler wrote, "They have no policy & they ought to have to secure the restoration of peace & quiet."[548]

A scouting party under Lieutenant Samuel West encountered a small group of Confederates on Christmas Day about ten miles from Barboursville. A skirmish erupted and the rebels were driven off, leaving three killed and five wounded. None of the Union soldiers were wounded.[549]

Camp Toland was relatively quiet, as no drill was held, and many of the men walked to Guyandotte to visit the Virginia soldiers occupying the town. Some of these troops brought back the rumor that an attack by a Confederate cavalry force was imminent. Private Francis Hale recorded that when he attended church that night, "I took my gun a long and other fixings so that if we was attacted I would be ready."[550]

During the winter months, battalion drill was held in the village of Barboursville despite the extreme cold. Hale noted "the boys did not do right some times and then the Liewtenant Colonel woul[d] cuss for surtain." Some of the soldiers refused to emerge for drill until they were threatened with admission to the guard house.[551]

The camp of the 34th Ohio Infantry was "in a stir" on December 28 as word arrived from Guyandotte that Captain Vincent Witcher was in the vicinity of Mud Bridge. The 2nd (West) Virginia Cavalry started in pursuit, and Company F of the 34th left Barboursville that evening about 7:00 p.m. The latter unit headed toward the Mud River, then crossed the countryside until reaching Dusenberry's Mill on the Guyandotte River. After crossing at the mill, half the company followed the road to Beech Fork and stopped at the home of a Union sympathizer.[552]

After spending the night and enjoying a quick breakfast, the Ohioans started toward the next home, occupied by the Collins family. When a woman answered the door, the soldiers asked to speak to the man of the house, but she stated he was not home. While they were conversing, her husband was seen "going up the hill double quick." The Federals yelled for him to halt and he complied and was taken prisoner. According to one of the soldiers, "his wife cried very hard when we left her. She had a small child in her armes."[553]

Marching along roads frozen and rough, the men continued on along Beech Fork and up Raccoon Creek. At one house, a man was observed running away and was ordered to halt,

> but he run on. We fired as he got over the fence. There was two men on horse back. We fired about fifteen rounds at them but we did not kill any of them. The men farley flew on horse back.[554]

Private Francis G. Hale observed, "we are now where one of our men got wounded about three weekes ago. We are in a dangerous part of the country."[555]

The Zouaves stopped for the night at the home of a secessionist named Davis near the Falls of Guyandotte where they were met by the other half of the company. On the following morning the men were eating their breakfast (one of them "killed a hop") when they were fired on by a man from a large hill nearby. The ball fell short and hit the house, and the secessionist quickly disappeared. As three of the Union soldiers went to get their horses, they discovered two men building a house who fled at the sight of the Federals. The Zouaves fired and "hit on[e] they think he fell and put his hand up to his back and crawled a piece."[556]

The company continued on to Gilkerson's Mill, the site of the murders of their fellow soldiers. Hale noted, "There was a woman a runing the mill. The boys tryed to make her tell where they was beried but she would not tell. There was three wimen at the house but they swore they did not see them nor did not know any thing of them." Detachments began searching the property, and although they did not find the bodies, they discovered lots of blankets and a shawl that had been hidden under some rocks on a hillside. They also found a bed sheet full of tobacco hidden under a shock of fodder in a nearby corn field.[557]

Anger at their inability to locate the bodies of their comrades surged through the men, and they "just went in on ever thing chickens and mollases and every thing that they could get. They burnt the fence up and all the wood. They would have burnt the mill and the house if the captain had not cept them from it." About nine o'clock that evening, a firearm was accidentally discharged, shooting a member of the company through the leg, a mishap that would hasten the termination of the expedition.[558]

On the last day of 1861, the company ate breakfast and again sought to elicit information from the women of the house. Hale observed, "We tried a good many ways. Some of the boys threatened to shoot them and cocked there guns and pointed them at them. They would not tell and said they did not know any thing of them only that they was sent to head quarters." Two young boys informed the soldiers that another youngster who lived about two miles away knew where the Zouaves were buried. A detachment was sent for the young man, but he had fled into the woods, and although they interrogated his mother, they did not learn the location of the bodies.[559]

After procuring a litter for their wounded comrade and securing their prisoners, the company of the 34th Ohio began their march back to Barboursville. A wagon met them about halfway on their return, and the entire detachment made it back to camp by 9:00 p.m. Hale recorded that at every hous along the road there husban had gon to Logan or to twelve pole or she was a lone widow taking care of these poor orphan children or the man of the house had gon out she did not know where he had gon. I saw many a heartrendering seene while I was gon husband parting with his wife and children. I came near crying my self lots of times wife thinking we shot her husband.[560]

A member of the 34th Ohio wrote to his brother from Barboursville on New Year's Day 1862:

I was at a fine dinner given by the Capt. last Sunday. It was a grand affair, and well gotten up, in good style...there is nothing new going on here except now and then. A scout returned last night brought in a few prisoners. We had at one time thirty two Secesh in the Gard house. That was about three weeks ago. There are now fourteen out of our company home on ferlough. Things are so dull here that I can find nothing to write.[561]

The men rested all day, exhausted after the difficult expedition, although some found the energy to shoot firecrackers to celebrate the new year. In the evening, the captain of Hale's company sponsored an oyster supper at the Cabell House, at which the troops enjoyed coffee with cream and sugar, and "segars."[562]

On this same day, William F. Dusenberry of Cabell County wrote,

I am still at this place with my family...The Civil War now distracting our country has ruined our business and is causing everything along the border here to be destroyed. Being a Union man, I do not know what moment I may be stripped of everything and driven from my home. My greatest wish is that before this day 1863, peace and harmony will be restored, and we will be united and happy again.[563]

Dusenberry had moved to Cabell County from New York and purchased the mill built by Sampson Sanders which became known as Dusenberry's Mill. His diaries provide insight into daily activities during the Civil War.[564]

The 34th Ohio Infantry held no company drill on January 2, 1862, as some of the officers had been granted furloughs, and the others were "busy." The weather remained cold and wet, and two Zouaves died of typhus fever during the first week of January. A bakery for the regiment was completed on January 5, enabling the men to have fresh bread.[565]

Sometime during their stay at Barboursville, Lieutenant Colonel John Toland noticed that a large number of his men were intoxicated. Alcohol had been banned, and he was for a time unable to determine where the men obtained the spirits. His officers finally learned that the source was a man who sold the liquor from a little log hut located on the bank of the Guyandotte River near the village. Toland sent his orderly to retrieve Corporal Henry Minshall of Company G of the 34th Ohio, who was dispatched to take ten men to the cabin to seize and pour out the whiskey. The industrious Corporal Minshall ordered his men to "string all the canteens they could find around their necks." When they arrived at the hut, the liquor was "poured out" and the detachment then returned to camp.

Minshall reported to Colonel Toland and informed him the mission had been completed. However, Toland noticed a canteen around the corporal's neck and the smell of alcohol in the air. After Minshall twice insisted they had poured out the whiskey, Colonel Toland finally asked, "And where did you pour it, sir?" Unable to evade the direct question, Minshall admitted it had been transferred to his men's canteens. Angered at first, Toland soon smiled and asked Corporal Minshall if the canteen around his neck contained the confiscated beverage. Minshall allowed that it did and offered some to the colonel. Toland responded, "I don't care if I do," and took a healthy swig. "Not a bad article—not a bad article; but, Corporal, next time I send you to pour out whisky I will tell you *where* to pour it."566

Lieutenant Colonel John Toland, 34th Ohio Infantry. Toland would be killed at Wytheville, Virginia, in 1863. Credit: Massachusetts Commandery Military Order of the Loyal Legion and the US Army Military History Institute.

Five soldiers from the 34th Ohio Infantry arrived in Wheeling on January 3 on the steamer *Ben Franklin*. In their charge were ten "rather scaly looking prisoners" captured in Cabell County. The *Wheeling Intelligencer* reported, "They are said to be the worst kind of Bushwhackers."567

In early January 1862, the 34th Ohio continued to scout throughout the region. Company A was stationed at Red House, Company B at Camp Paxton in Guyandotte, and Company G at Mud Bridge. On January 6 a detachment of fifteen soldiers of Company K returned with nineteen prisoners, along with horses, mules, and blankets. That afternoon, Company G, which had marched from Mud Bridge to Camp Toland in Barboursville, left with a wagon and rations to sustain them for several days. On the evening of January 8, they arrived at Lykins Mill, twenty-eight miles from Barboursville, where they established Camp Broadwell. Company G remained at Lykins Mill until January 31, when they moved eighteen miles to Camp Franklin at Mud Bridge. They would not rejoin the regiment in Barboursville until February 7.568

John Lykins, who owned the mill, was arrested by members of the 34th Ohio Infantry and tried for insurrection and rebellion against the United States government. Several of his neighbors noted that Lykins was known to be a secessionist. One wrote, "I am certain that he would not have aided a union man in defense of his property." Several testified that armed men had gathered at his mill during the first week of July, and Lykins reportedly declared "there were five guns loaded," to be used against Union troops. Another neighbor, Jeremiah Witcher, claimed that Lykins "has always been exceedingly cool when the Union troops have been here – but when the Southern troops are here he generally came out and expressed himself fearlessly as a secessionist." When cross-examined by defendant Lykins, Witcher admitted he had never seen him in arms against the United States government. James C. Black claimed that Lykins "expressed himself in a very angry manner when he heard of the success of the Federal forces, and said that the newspaper reports concerning them were all lies. These expressions were uttered about the time of the fight at Philippi."[569]

Lykins was sent to the Athenaeum Prison in Wheeling. He wrote to Major Joseph Darr on January 10, 1862, seeking his release:

I have never been in arms against the Federal Government. I have never been a secessionist. I have been told that the only circumstance that attaches suspicion to my case is the fact that a rumor existed that I was present at the 'Poor's Hill' skirmish – there is not the least foundation for this rumor. I went to that place a day or two before the skirmish, and took my sons home from that place.

Adjutant Gen. Samuels knows me very well, and I have been waiting some days to see him, but as yet, I have not been favored with an interview with him, and I learn from prisoners here that you are the proper officer to address this communication to. Can I expect a release soon?

Darr referred the case to Henry J. Samuels, who wrote,

The old man is not very influential in his neighborhood. His sons are under his influence. He has some 9 or 10 of them. He would not vote on secession. As to his conduct I know nothing. If he gives bond it would probably be best to let him go.[570]

It is uncertain when Lykins was released, but at least six of his sons served in the Confederate cavalry during the war.

George A. Holton, a neighbor of Lykins, was charged with "receiving and keep bacon for Secession troops, also going in arms to assist in arresting James Webb and encouraging William Morris to shoot Zachariah Nicely and furnishing gun for Porr's Hill battle." Holton was a noted secessionist who stated that "if his house burned there would not be a union man's house left in the neighborhood."[571]

During a conversation with William Morris at Lykins Mill, Zachariah Nicely "asserted that he (himself) was as good a Union man as any body." Morris reacted angrily, telling Nicely "that if he repeated the assertion he Morris would shoot him, and went to the house for his gun." Samuel Bragg and George Holton encouraged Morris to shoot Nicely, and then threatened to turn him over to Confederate military authorities. Holton had also been armed and a part of the mob that went to arrest

Union supporter James Webb.

William H. Lawrence claimed to have seen an armed Holton "watching the roads" in early November 1861. Holton told him it was the only time he had taken up arms. William Mahone recalled, "The body of men was the citizens call under the militia Laws, and I think Holton was a member." During cross examination by the defendant, however, his neighbors admitted that he had always expressed himself in favor of peace and claimed to be a Union supporter.[572]

In Barboursville, where the majority of the 34th Ohio Infantry was encamped, sixteen secessionist prisoners were locked up in the guard house awaiting trial, and civilian access to the camp was limited. Two members of the 34th Ohio went undercover on January 8, 1862, posing as Confederate prisoners to gather intelligence from the detainees. Although their identities were eventually discovered, they learned a great deal of information including the reported location of the bodies of the three Zouaves murdered at Beech Fork on December 18.

On the following day, one of the secessionist prisoners, Robert Mays, attempted to escape. The guards repeatedly ordered him to halt, but Mays ignored them and was shot in the right hip with a rifled musket. The bullet went completely through his body and he lay mortally wounded. According to a member of the 34th Ohio, "he was one that helpt to burie the men that was killed on beachfork…he said he thought it was death if he stayed so he tried to run of[f]." Mays, who lived on Beech Fork, died on the following evening, but not before giving a death-bed confession describing the murder of the Union soldiers. Another member of the regiment wrote, "Every effort possible was made for his recovery, but it seems that his fate was determined upon by the powers that be." On January 10, groups of Zouaves passed by Dusenberry's Mill, including a large number aboard a four-horse wagon headed to Beech Fork, undoubtedly in search of their murdered comrades.[573]

On January 9, Captain Herman C. Edwards led Company H to Gilkerson's Mill on Beech Fork, the scene of the murder of the Zouaves. While there, the troops were fired on by three guerrillas but were unharmed. They remained there three days before returning to Barboursville on January 13, "having performed a march over almost impassable roads and in extremely bad weather from the effects of which one sergeant, Samuel Balser, died and much sickness resulted."[574]

Private Alonzo Peitzel of the 34th Ohio Infantry described conditions and regimental activities in the region in a January 11 letter:

> It is very muddy here at present, making it very disagreeable getting around. On this account, drill, both company and battalion, is suspended at present; even dress parade is sometimes omitted. Two companies are at present out scouting, near the head of Guyandotte river. A scouting party of fifteen men that were out last week, brought in twenty-one prisoners, several of whom belong to the Secesh army, and had come home on furlough.

Peitzel also remarked, "The health of the regiment is very poor. Bad colds and fevers are very prevalent…"[575]

William Dusenberry and a few fellow Masons went to the lodge in Barboursville on January 11 to prepare for a meeting to be held that evening. The stove pipe had come apart and the room was covered with soot and smoke and filled with gas. After fixing the pipe and cleaning the room, the men went to Hatfield's to wash and returned to the lodge about six o'clock. Captain John W. Shaw of the 34th Ohio delivered a short address and the meeting adjourned at eight. Colonel Abram Sanders Piatt, who had returned to Barboursville earlier in the day, gave Dusenberry a general pass, and then Captain Shaw passed he and Charles Sweetland out of camp while Charles Dusenberry, William's brother, rode out with the flying pickets. William Dusenberry returned to the village on the following day, and after gaining admittance from the officer of the day, he was successful in obtaining the release of "old Elijah Adkins" from the adjutant of the 34th Ohio.[576]

Regimental surgeon W. R. S. Clark wrote to the "Ladies of Bucyrus and Vicinity" on January 26 to thank them for supplies of clothing and hospital stores sent to the troops stationed in Cabell County. "Could you know the change in the appearance and comfort of our Hospital," Clark wrote, "you would be fully repaid for your labor." He added, "We can now make our sick as comfortable as at home, except the care and attention of the sister, mother or wife." He relayed the thanks of Captain John W. Shaw for clothing sent to his company and Shaw's promise that "it shall never be taken by a traitor to his country."[577]

A soldier of the 34th Ohio wrote from Barboursville on January 28:

We have occasionally heard a rumor in camp about our friend Jenkins, but he is like the pay-master always coming but never gets here. The weather is very mild now, and we have mud in abundance. The back-water from the Ohio River cut of[f] all communication between our camp and all other places for four days, but the road is again open without much damage being done. Our labor consists of drilling and scouting, which takes up our time. The latter does not avail us much as the 'sesesh' are about all run out of Western Virginia. Occasionally our scouts get after a stray one that has deserted the ranks in Eastern Va., and has come here to seek peace and quiet in the mountains during the winter. We prefer to give them quarters in Camp Chase, Columbus. They are much safer there.[578]

On the morning of January 30, three of the Zouaves rode to Dusenberry's Mill and retrieved a wagon bed they had left for safekeeping. The Union soldiers also picked up ninety-two feet of walnut lumber from the mill.[579]

Colonel Abram Sanders Piatt, who commanded the 34th Ohio, wrote to Ohio Governor David Tod on January 31 from Camp Toland in Barboursville: "Without alarm prudence dictates that a reenforcement should be sent here. The information received here shows that the enemy are looking to this point as the place to retrieve their lost fortunes." Piatt suggested a regiment and company of artillery be sent to support his force, which was scattered throughout the area. He also requested fifty men to fill up his regiment and twenty-five wagoners. Piatt added, "We are determined to do our duty, reenforced or not."580

On his return to Cabell County from Wheeling, William Dusenberry was informed by the chaplain of the 34th Ohio that some of the regiment and a part of the 2nd (West) Virginia Cavalry had gone up Mud River in pursuit of a secession force reported in the area. Dusenberry reached Guyandotte on the following day and found "considerable excitement arround here at the report of Rebel Troops being above here."581

On February 4, Captain James L. Wallar of the 2nd (West) Virginia Cavalry wrote Colonel Joseph A. J. Lightburn from Ceredo concerning a prisoner, Calvin Adkins, "represented as a violent Secessionist by the Union men of his neighborhood." Wallar had earlier arrested James Collins of the 34th Virginia Infantry Battalion, who fingered Adkins as having participated in the fights at Barboursville and Trout's Hill. More importantly, Adkins lived within a half mile

Colonel Abram Sanders Piatt, 34th Ohio Infantry. Credit: Massachusetts Commandery Military Order of the Loyal Legion and the US Army Military History Institute.

of where the Zouaves had been killed in December and admitted that he had seen them while they were prisoners in the hands of the guerrillas. Wallar wrote, "his (Adkins) whole course while a prisoner in my hands, convinced me that his object was to deceive me as to the persons who committed the murder and also as to the position and strength of the enemy."582

Adkins and fellow prisoner George W. Cole, both of Wayne County, would be released from the Athenaeum in Wheeling due to the efforts of William Ratliff, delegate for the Restored Government of Virginia. Ratliff declared that he had known the men "from infancy" and they were "harmless and inoffensive." Both had voted against the Ordinance of Secession, but secession leaders in the area, according to Ratliff, "artfully misrepresented the intentions and the conduct of the federal forces in that region, detailing reports of robbery & rape, plunder & rapine so as to mislead many good men and true to the government."583

A soldier of the 34th Ohio reported on an incident that occurred in the village of Barboursville on the morning of February 5: "Just at day-break, we were aroused by the Long Roll. Co. E was, as usual, the first on hand to rescue whate're it might be. When we were in line, it was discovered that a fire had broken out in one of the large barns, which contained our best horses. We broke ranks and rushed to the barn and soon extinguished the flames." Although the excitement quickly subsided, the soldiers' efforts to resume their slumber was interrupted by a messenger from Mud Bridge, where Company G was stationed, who reported a threatened attack on that post.584

George Sprecher of the 34th Ohio described additional events of February 5:

We had a lively day yesterday. The way it was the Broadwell Tigers were stationed at Mud Bridge they sent in a messenger stating that they were about to be attacked by Miller with 400 cavalry but before the attack was made a messenger came and stated that Captain Rathbone had arrived at Mud Bridge with Co. A. Col. Piatt sent a message to Guyandotte for as many cavalry as could be spared and about 1 o'clock p.m. Capt. Shaw with Co. E started to Mud Bridge. Toward evening Col. Piatt, Surgeon Ayres and Orderly Kirk started for the scene of action. About sundown 4 companies of cavalry come from Guyandotte and about an hour afterwards Major Franklin mounted his horse and took command of the cavalry and started for the scene of action and this morning about 2 o'clock 2 more companies of cavalry came through here on their way. They are determined to catch them this time if they have to follow them to Logan Court House. There they will be sure to get a little fight for there are from 10 to 12 hundred Secesh who have their head quarters and it is the only foot hold they have in W. Va. any more and I think if there is any fight in them they will sho[o]t it there. Captain O. P. Evans of Company B is in command here at Camp Toland just now. We have not heard nothing from the fight if it was a fight nor from the race if it was a race. Everybody is wondering and surmising as what might be the result. If the Secesh came early in the day and stood up to those companies as they should according to their number they may have been considerable shedding of blood for the messenger took back positive orders to our men to hold them in check until reenforcements should arrive. Whether there was an attack made or not by the Secesh they will be driven out of the neighborhood or taken prisoner and locked up where they wont bother us any more...[585]

Colonel A. Sanders Piatt sent an urgent dispatch to Secretary of War Edwin Stanton on February 6 declaring it was "necessary" to send an Ohio regiment and artillery to Barboursville immediately. He informed Secretary Stanton dramatically, "They are coming upon us with artillery."[586]

Stanton contacted General George B. McClellan, who wrote General William S. Rosecrans later in the day:

Colonel Piatt telegraphs to Secretary of War from Cabell Court-House that rebels are coming with artillery, and asks for one regiment and one battery from Ohio. I think it a stampede; but if it is not, call on Ohio. I am anxious to send all Ohio troops just now to Buell to support attack on Fort Henry, so do not take troops if you can avoid it.[587]

Rosecrans was receiving daily reports from Raleigh County and frequent ones from Colonel James Garfield, who was stationed on the Big Sandy. He told McClellan there was "[n]ot the slightest foundation for Colonel P[iatt]'s apprehension. If he wants to lead a brigade he ought to give the real reasons..." Rosecrans wrote again to his superior later in the day including the observation, "Sixty or seventy guerrillas in wilds about Barboursville."[588]

Meetings held by the Masonic Lodge in Barboursville continued despite the tumult of war. A number of the 34th Ohio Infantry were Masons, and they joined the local men on regular occasions. On February 8, a resolution was passed permitting the chaplain of the Zouaves to hold prayer meetings in the Lodge room, but local merchant William Dusenberry cast the sole vote against it, stating he would have "done so in face of the whole Regiment."[589]

Captain James E. Smith, commanding 21 soldiers of the 5th (West) Virginia Infantry, surprised a Confederate cavalry detachment along Lynn Creek in Wayne County on February 8. The troopers were reportedly feeding their horses from the crib of a Union man when the Federals struck. A number of Confederates were killed, several others wounded, and the remainder captured. Nearly thirty horses were also seized. According to newspaper accounts, Smith lost one killed and one wounded. These same articles report that the skirmish was on Linn Creek in Logan County.[590]

The Federals returned to Guyandotte with their prisoners on February 12. Reported to be among the Confederates killed in the fight was a man named Stevens, who "was one of a party of a dozen who not long ago captured three of Piatt's Zouaves took them out in the woods tied them up to trees and shot them." Stevens was described as "at least sixty years of age and a most desperate character." Seized was a "very extraordinary gun, six feet long, which formerly belonged to Stevens and the barrel of which he made himself out of old horse shoes," which was placed in the office of Adjutant General Henry J. Samuels in Wheeling.[591]

George Sprecher of the 34th Ohio wrote his wife from Barboursville on February 15 and informed her that "it snowed yesterday and last night and part of the time today and the snow is nearly an inch deep now. It melts nearly as fast as it falls but it makes the surroundings look beautiful, hills covered with snow like great white blankets and they show the evergreen, pine and mistletoe to better advantage then they could be seen where there was no snow on the ground..." The Ohioans celebrated Union victories at Roanoke Island and Fort Henry, and Sprecher wrote jubilantly, "if victory follows victory for six weeks more like it has the last six weeks Secesh will be played out." Noting the threat of intervention on the side of the Confederacy by France and Great Britain, Sprecher added:

> Then if England and France wants to pitch let them come. They never can come at a better time for our army is now well disciplined and well armed and England and France together can with all their forces never get 20 miles from the coast any place in the U. S. till they find themselves buried in bloody graves. But it is folly to think of England and France meddling. They will consult their own safety and stay at home.[592]

Washington's birthday was celebrated in the village of Barboursville on February 22. "We fired a national salute at four o'clock in the morning," a soldier of the 34th Ohio wrote. The Zouaves illuminated the town, and "every window in their quarters & the Courthouse had a light on every pain of glass. It looked beautiful." One Ohio soldier

Susan Holderby, owner of "Buena Vista" and the largest slaveholder in the Guyandotte district of Cabell County. Two of her sons, Robert and George, were Confederate soldiers, and her daughter Susan was married to Thomas Jenkins, brother of Albert Gallatin Jenkins. Credit: Cabell County Annals and Families.

observed, "The citizens were astonished; they had never seen the place illuminated before." A fine supper, including "pleanty of oysters," was served, followed by toasts and speeches by the officers and dancing with comic songs. According to one of the local men, however, the officers were "much disappointed that our women folks did not come down."[593]

Although there were not a large number of enslaved people in the region at this time, an incident occurred in Cabell County which reflected a national policy that would change considerably over the subsequent year. Susan Holderby, a widow who lived at "Buena Vista," four miles from Barboursville, called on General William S. Rosecrans in late February 1862 to complain about interference with her slaves by a Union officer. Apparently two women, Isadore and Ginny, had run away from Buena Vista and taken refuge in the camp of the 34th Ohio Infantry at Barboursville two months earlier, and at least one was employed by Major Freeman E. Franklin as a cook.[594]

Holderby, whose sons were Confederate soldiers and whose daughter was married to Thomas Jenkins, the brother of Confederate Colonel Albert Gallatin Jenkins, twice attempted to reclaim her slaves and applied directly to Franklin, but soldiers denied her the opportunity to see them. She then contacted the deputy marshal, whose efforts to gain assistance from the Zouaves were met with resistance "owing to threats which the soldiers had made" and denied by Major Franklin, who declared his men would not be made available in the event the marshal needed their aid. On February 21, Holderby filed a complaint with Hannibal Forbes, United States Commissioner for the Western District of Virginia, declaring she would be unable to regain her slaves "unless some higher military authority interposes."[595]

Captain George L. Hartsuff, assistant adjutant general for the Department of Western Virginia, wrote to General Jacob D. Cox on February 28 and directed him to instruct the offending officer as to his duty and "to take such steps as will insure obedience to these or the punishment of the offenders." Rosecrans himself wrote, "Send a copy of this to Col A. Piatt and direct to use all proper efforts to see the woman righted & to report the result."[596]

Cox contacted Franklin immediately, instructing him to comply with the rules and articles of war and impressing upon him the special circumstances created by the conflict. "The subject of our relation to the civil government of western Virginia is one

*"Buena Vista," plantation of Susan Holderby.
Credit: Cabell County Annals and Families.*

of great delicacy," General Cox wrote,

> in view of the fact that the ordinary civil government is to be thoroughly respected in the performance of these acts which may be in accordance with his powers and duties under the Federal laws or those of Western Virginia. We are not here to abrogate the existing laws of the land or to obstruct their operation and any act of a military officer which could be reasonably regarded as doing this would subject him necessarily to severe discipline.[597]

General Cox also addressed the obligations of the military regarding enforcement of the institution of slavery, writing:

> In regard to slaves, my instructions to officers under my command have uniformly been to avoid all interference with the relation between them & their masters, if their masters are peaceable citizens of the country bearing the civil laws to regulate the matter previously as if no army were here. I do not believe it to be the duty of any officer or soldiers to assist in the recaption of fugitive slaves, and should regard it as unmilitary and improper for him to do so but he is scrupulously to abstain from interposing or allowing the men of his command to interpose obstructions in the way of the proper civil officers performing what they may regard as their duty under the orders of the ordinary civil magistrates and courts.

Major Freeman Franklin, 34th Ohio Infantry, became embroiled in a slavery controversy with Susan Holderby of Cabell County in the spring of 1862. Credit: L. M. Strayer Collection.

Franklin was warned that if he or his men interfered with the duties of a United States marshal, county sheriff, or deputies of either, they would be held accountable to both civil and military courts.[598]

On March 8, Holderby wrote Rosecrans again informing him that her slaves had not been seen in Barboursville since she had been rebuffed by Major Franklin. "I think we may reasonably conclude," she noted, "that they have been sent away, or concealed through Major Franklins agency, but if this cannot be proved, it was certainly his fault that they were not placed in my possession when the Marshal requested aid from him in taking them. I would be glad to hear from you upon the subject."[599]

After receiving correspondence from United States Deputy Marshal Hibbens declaring that Franklin did not interfere with the performance of his duties, General Rosecrans sent Susan Holderby a packet of documents and apparently accused her of perjury. Holderby responded on April 8, claiming she "was at first too indignant to reply to them; but upon reflection I have concluded that as the charge made against me is a very grave one; simple justice to myself demands that I send you an answer..." She claimed to have witnesses to her interaction with Marshal Hibbens and her encounter with Major Franklin. Regarding the latter, Holderby wrote, "I am able to believe that a man who would either steal or harbour a negro might with as few pangs of conscience forge even more than a 'portion' of a letter." She added, "I feel it will take more than the evidence of a man having the character and lineage that U S Dept Marshal Hibbens does to convict me of perjury." Holderby closed by asking why the marshal had not "been severely dealt with for the non performance of his duty."[600]

In March 1862, the Department of Western Virginia, which Rosecrans directed, was converted to the Mountain Department, which was commanded by General John C. Fremont, and the future commander of the Army of the Cumberland was temporarily out of a job. Holderby's request for the return of her slaves was forwarded to Major Joseph Darr, Provost Marshal of the Mountain Department, and it is unclear if she ever succeeded in her efforts.[601]

A member of the 34th Ohio Infantry wrote from Barboursville on March 2:

The present indications are, that we will move soon, but when, where, or how, nobody knows, but there is any amount of guessing. The men are required to drill henceforth, with their knapsacks on battalion drill, to get used to the fatigue. The new uniforms are at hand, and will be distributed tomorrow. The health of the camp is very good, only fourteen in the hospital, and none dangerously sick.[602]

Another soldier of the regiment wrote, "We have been here so long that many of us feel the force of the language used by a German servant to a Captain, while at Mud Bridge, recommending a move as they were beginning to owe too much." He noted the new uniforms

General William S. Rosecrans, who commanded the Department of Western Virginia. Credit: Library of Congress.

are a much better article than the former ones, the leggins are longer, and lace up instead of buckling. The boys all look as neat as a new pin in their new uniforms on dress parade. We are now comfortable, and fully equipped for any emergency, and all we ask is to give us something to do, and you shall hear a good report of the 34th.[603]

William Dusenberry opened the Masonic Lodge in Barboursville soon after dark on March 15. A large group gathered for an initiation ceremony, among them nearly a dozen officers and privates of the 34th Ohio Infantry. Following the formal meeting, most of the men went to Hatfield's and had an evening meal before returning to the lodge. The gathering did not conclude until nearly midnight.[604]

The 34th Ohio Infantry received orders on March 17 to march for the Kanawha Valley at 8:00 a.m. on the following morning. William Dusenberry rode to Barboursville where he visited several officers and sites and noted "the Zouaves were awful noisey." Dusenberry spent the night in the quarters of Captain John W. Shaw, and on the following morning, he worked his way through the camp gathering items left behind by the Ohio soldiers, including a saw, bucket, basin, teapots, an axe, some sacks, and several empty barrels. The Zouaves left Barboursville at 1:00 p.m. and marched to Guyandotte. A member of the 2nd (West) Virginia Cavalry observed, "The Zouave regiment that was stationed out at Barbersville passed through heare on there way to gaully. There are a prety rough lot but they will all fight." One company of the 2nd was moved to Barboursville on March 20.[605]

Residents of Barboursville had grown frustrated with the actions of the 34th Ohio

Infantry, and some were glad to see them leave. Two days after their departure, Adjutant General H. J. Samuels, a native of the village, wrote to Brigadier General William S. Rosecrans, commanding the Department of Western Virginia, listing a litany of charges against the Ohio regiment:

> It has been charg'd against the 34th O. V. at Camp Toland
>
> That they do take the horses of the people, and convey them away sell them and appropriate the money & also take and appropriate other property
>
> That they harbour slaves in their camp, and by their protection said slaves escape and run away
>
> That they use the slaves of persons as servants against the master consent
>
> That they refuse to render aid to U S Marshalls in executing orders & process of U S Court, That they have destroyed the records of the county in part and did so by breaking down the doors where the records were kept in the Court House, have destroyed the desks tables benches jury boxes & doors of Court House and in fact every species of furniture in the Court House and all in a spirit of wantoness and malicious mischief
>
> That the people of all parties fear the soldiers & are afraid to make complaint to the field officers
>
> That personal abuse of citizens, goes without reprimand or punishment
>
> As to the truth of the charges I shall not express an opinion, except as to the vandalism comitted upon the Court House & furniture & public records which I examined for myself and know to be true – The other charges are generally made to seem to be the personal opinion of the people.

Charles L. Roffe noted, "I am just from Cabell County & know the charges above made are believed to be true by the people of Cabell."[606]

Two weeks later, Thomas Thornburg of Barboursville wrote to Samuels confirming the citizens' complaints, stating "that the wanton destruction of property by them will I fear unbalance the good that they accomplished. Five hundred dollars will not pay the damage to C H & Jail beside the destruction to clerks office which I fear is irreparable. Every body rejoiced when they left..."

Thornburg added that following the departure of the 34th Ohio, a portion of the 2nd (West) Virginia Cavalry was stationed in Barboursville. These troops were viewed in a more positive light, but citizens did complain that they had made "stables of dwelling houses, for instance W B Moore V R Moss & Jim Lusher's..." Thornburg believed "this should not be done if for no other reason than the comfort of those who reside in town." He described Barboursville as "a perfect reck," and stated that "nothing can renovate it but fire." He also noted,

> The country is much more quiet. People are disposed to go to work and earn an honest living. The court was held without an interruption. Grand jury made numerous indictments for all kinds of offences. The Election yesterday very quiet but few voters out, what the result I do not know.[607]

A number of secessionists from the area who had fled when the 34th Ohio Infantry was ordered into Cabell County had returned. These men, including A. J. Keenan, Sanaford Scott, George Dolen, Charles Shoemaker, C. M. Swann, and Conwelsey Simmons, reported themselves to headquarters in Barboursville on March 29, took the oath of allegiance, and were permitted to return to their residences. They informed authorities that they were unaware of any Confederate plans for a raid into Cabell County and believed that the only thing preventing a return of refugees was their fear of being arrested and sent to Camp Chase prison.[608]

On the other hand, Union supporters in Cabell County dreaded a repeat of the Guyandotte raid and the possibility of imprisonment in Richmond. Thornburg noted, "the fate of Kyle[,] Hinchman and Alford is enough to alarm all." He requested information on the Union men from the county who remained incarcerated in the Virginia capital, observing that few had returned home. He believed a Union force at Logan Courthouse "would in a great degree quiet the people here."[609]

Thornburg also expressed satisfaction that Captain William Turner and his men had been arrested by Colonel John Paxton for their conduct: "what course he persued with them I do not know but this I do know, he has the thanks of the entire community for prompt manner he dealt with them, they should have been attended to sooner." In closing, he directed Samuels to send his reply to Cabell Courthouse, as "we have a Post Office again."[610]

The 34th Ohio Infantry was stationed in Cabell County from October 1861 through March 1862. The regiment participated in the fighting around Princeton in mid-May 1862 and suffered heavy casualties at the battle of Fayetteville on September 10. The Zouaves fought through the remainder of the war and would be consolidated with the 36th Ohio Infantry on February 22, 1865.[611]

The final resting place of the three Zouaves murdered on Beech Fork in December 1861 remains unresolved. No official records were found, but family lore may shed some insight. The Zouave Cave, where the bodies of the dead soldiers were reportedly placed shortly after the murders, became a popular spot for picnics. Oral tradition relates that after a public official learned that people were collecting bones as souvenirs, he had the remains removed to the Charles Adkins Cemetery (now Mars Cemetery) nearby.[612]

10
Outrages and Fiendish Acts

"The females of Guyandotte are ten times worse than the men and they are bad enough the Lord knows. The Federal Court is now in session at Charleston and it is thought that some of the females in Guyan will be arrested by the Ceredo men and taken there and tried. I do hope that some of them may be hung or imprisoned for life."

Sallie P. Smith, Guyandotte, October 4, 1862

In the spring of 1862, the thousands of troops that had wintered in Cabell County moved eastward into the Kanawha Valley, and the lawlessness that prevailed prior to their arrival returned and expanded. Union supporters in the portion of Cabell County that would in five years become Lincoln County were particularly vulnerable due to the lack of military or civil authorities. A group of citizens in Hamlin wrote to Restored Government of Virginia Governor Francis H. Pierpont requesting assistance, noting that small squads of guerrillas, "of the lower class of citizens," were robbing residents and stealing horses. While some of these men had enlisted in the Confederate army and were home on leave or to provide intelligence, others were bushwhackers taking advantage of the unrest to prey on their weaker neighbors. Particularly disturbing to the Union supporters was that both groups were fed, armed, and encouraged by "men of property," men who had taken the oath to uphold the constitution and were protected by the Federal government while "secretly supporting a reign of teror against loyal subjects, especially those that have been most active in suppressing the rebel[l]ion."

Some of the Union populace in the Hamlin area were in particular danger due to their uncompensated service as guides for Federal scouting parties. Several had been compelled to flee to Ohio taking whatever property they could along with them, and others would be forced to follow if Federal protection were not forthcoming against the rebels, "who are daily threatening our lives thus greatly reducing the Federal force and influence in this part of the state." As the correspondents to the governor noted, "it has only been by the influence and active exertions of the above named loyal men, who risked their lives and lost a part of their property, that the Union cause has been maintained in this part of the state."

The Union men believed that ample resources had been available to put down the rebellion in southern Cabell County, but they had not been used effectively. Secession sentiment was cowed when Federal troops were stationed in the area, but as soon as they were removed, "the rebels are more vindictive and desperate against their Union neighbours than before."

When the 34th Ohio Infantry was stationed at Mud Bridge, detachments were sent fifteen miles to Hamlin in search of guerrillas on a number of occasions with limited success. The Union troops started after dark and marched through the night, but the guerrillas always learned of their approach and escaped to the woods before the Zouaves arrived in the town. With "little skill in bushwhacking," no knowledge of the people or the area, and constrained by orders to return to camp on the third day, the Federal soldiers were unable to pursue the guerrillas into their strongholds and usually returned to Mud Bridge with little to show for their efforts. They were always accompanied on their return by Union supporters in the Hamlin area, who went along "to keep from being captured or killed by the secesh as soon as the troops left." The only successful mission was launched by a sergeant and two citizens who left Barboursville in the evening, followed the Guyandotte River to Hamlin without being discovered, and captured Jerome Shelton and five other secessionists the same night.

Although it was recognized that large forces were necessary to meet other large forces and "hold places of deposit and distribution," the local citizens "have learned by experience that they are too slow in their movements, and too much exposed to observation to catch small squads of secesh bushwhackers." It was also impossible to supply a sizable body of soldiers with food and forage in a region without wagon roads and with a sparse population. Dressing and cooking meat took time, and some of the Union troops became impatient and were "disposed to plunder from union men & secesh without discrimination," acts that were "discreditable to the soldiery, and injurious to the union cause."

The Union men requested that Governor Pierpont appoint a scouting agent to investigate conditions in their region, make arrests as necessary, and return stolen horses and property to their rightful owners. The agent would be required to make frequent reports, turn prisoners over to military or civil authorities, and secure the testimony of witnesses. This position "would give much saf[e]ty to the property and persons of our citizens and at little expence..."[613]

On May 10, 1862, Colonel Albert Tracy, assistant adjutant general to General John C. Fremont, informed Colonel Joseph Lightburn, stationed at Charleston, that Governor Pierpont had received reliable intelligence that Jenkins and his Confederate cavalry force "are on the headwaters of the Guyandotte and the rivers that interlock therewith, and that guerrilla parties are forming within 50 miles of the Ohio River, who have already shot and killed peaceable citizens in Wayne and other border counties." Pierpont informed Tracy that the residents of Point Pleasant, Gallipolis, Ironton, and other Ohio River communities "are in great fear of the long-threatened vengeance of Jenkins and Clarkson, and are moving away in considerable numbers."

Tracy warned Lightburn to stay vigilant, writing,

Every precaution should be taken to prevent any repetition of the Guyandotte massacre, and to quiet the apprehensions of the loyal inhabitants of that section. To this end every effort should be made by frequent and sudden attacks, by rapid marches without transportation, by surprises and severity, to destroy all bands forming and organized in your district, and by terrorizing these marauders finally to uproot the whole system.[614]

J. B. Baumgardner wrote to Henry J. Samuels on May 14, 1862, and presented a petition to raise a "patrol company" for Ceredo and Wayne County. Baumgardner informed Samuels that he and five other Union men had been standing guard in the town since the departure of the 4th (West) Virginia Infantry. "We are the only ones that have taken any interest in it," Baumgardner stated, as "the rest seem to be afraid to do any thing."[615]

Samuels also received a letter signed by a number of Ceredo residents. They had a similar plan to form a company to scout throughout Wayne County for the purpose of eliminating the band of guerrillas that were wreaking havoc in the area. They informed Samuels that "excitement reigns supreme throughout the county," and in fact, "there is more excitement in this county now than was during last summer." Some of the most respected Union citizens in the county "have been shot down at the door of their own domicile by these ruthless midnight assassins who are continually stalking through the county seeking whom they may destroy."

Due to the lack of Federal troops and civil authorities, there "seems to be no power at present to arrest them in their fiendish acts." Many Union supporters, some of them destitute, had moved to Ohio, and if conditions did not improve, "the county before one month shall have passed, will be almost entirely deserted." "All we want is arms and encouragement from the state," the Wayne County men wrote, "and we pledge ourselves never to stop until the last vestiage of these 'Fiends of Hell' shall have been swept from the face of our county." John Laidley recorded that the people in western Virginia "are more afraid of the guerillas than ever was the people of Indians."[616]

The last of the Union troops stationed in Guyandotte departed by steamboat for the Kanawha Valley in the early morning hours of May 17. As they left the town, the sounds of their cheering awakened the citizens. William Dusenberry noted that when he crossed into Guyandotte later that morning, "the place looked deserted as there was not a soldier there." He also recorded that "the people are much worried for fear the Southern troops will come in."[617]

Dusenberry rode into Barboursville on the morning of May 18 and spotted John Alford, who informed him he had escaped from prison in Richmond on the previous Sunday night. On the following evening, Lewis Hatfield informed Dusenberry that 1,700 Confederates had taken Charleston and were expected in Cabell County by nightfall. A number of Union men left town in fear, but it was a false alarm.[618]

On May 25, 1862, Captain John Young of the 11th (West) Virginia Infantry led an expedition into Cabell and Boone counties. It is unclear which part of the county they passed through, but it most likely was present-day Lincoln County. Young's company was temporarily assigned to the 13th (West) Virginia Infantry by Virginia Governor

*Captain John V. Young led a Federal expedition through Cabell and Boone counties in late May 1862.
Credit: West Virginia State Archives.*

Francis Pierpont in August 1862, although they were technically detailed to the 11th (West) Virginia.[619]

Captain William Shannon of the Wayne County militia wrote to Adjutant General H. J. Samuels on June 24, 1862, requesting guns, powder, lead, and molds. He observed that "thay is som out ragis commited in this county. I have mad som arests and som of the Rebels have left the county." Shannon also asked Samuels to "excuse bad spelling."[620]

Three days later, Conwelsey Simmons stopped by the home of William Dusenberry and reported that one of his horses had been stolen on the previous night. Simmons accused Captain William G. Smith of the 9th (West) Virginia Infantry of taking the animal and "went on at a great rate demanding protection from the government &c." Dusenberry stated he did not believe that Smith was the culprit and informed Simmons he could "do nothing in the matter."[621]

In early July, citizens of the county eagerly awaited news of the fighting around Richmond, which threatened the capital of the Confederacy. "A great many" traveled to Barboursville to learn the latest. According to William Dusenberry, "the Secesh are claiming a victory there. The Union men are much worried & anxious to hear how things are situated about Richmond." He also noted the failure to celebrate the nation's birthday: "An awful dull fourth of July in these reagons. Too much Rebellious sentiment to celebrate our national anniversary like old times."[622]

County court was held in Barboursville on July 7. As the citizens gathered, a newspaper was read which included an extensive account of McClellan's defeat in eastern Virginia. Dusenberry recorded, "it rather made us feal gloomy," a feeling magnified by secession supporters who "are blowing a good deal." There was a great deal of restlessness in Cabell County one week later due to a report that a number of Border Rangers were in the area and "intend to take some prisoners & horses out with them." A week later Dusenberry recorded there was "great excitement" in the area after a report that Confederate Major Vincent Witcher was due to arrive, causing several Union supporters to cross the river into Ohio.[623]

On July 15, 1862, John Laidley wrote from Guyandotte to his friend Henry J. Samuels concerning information he had received "that is to be relied on – beyond question":

Last week there were six soldiers privates in the company, lately commanded by A. G. Jenkins, now Lt. C. Everett, citizens of Guyandotte, that returned to the village. They reported to their friends that their object was to reconoiter and finding that there was no Federal troops in the Guyandotte & 12 Pole Valley they would return and make their appearance next week, between Monday & Friday. Their object was to break up the county organisation of courts & therefore they would capture and carry off all the efficient officers. This is to apply to Cabell & Wayne – that I stood at the head of the list – a few of the Justices Clerks & Sheriffs.

Today I was at Ceredo & there learn that there is carried on a regular current of visitors from the families of those in camp and all betray the same feeling sanguine in retaking Cabell & Wayne. I had resolved to leave home and abandon the ship, but meeting with L. T. Moore he has undertaken to procure some 2 or 3 companies from Louisa & Catlettsburg to come up for our protection for a short time and it is perfectly manifest that unless there are troops stationed in those two counties, we cannot hold any more Courts nor collect county or state revenue.[624]

Laidley noted that the "Rebels have uniformly betrayed more confidence & become impertinent." Unless he received some assurance that protection would be sent to the area, Laidley declared, "I will have to prepare to leave home." William Turner's company was not in the area, and Laidley believed they offered little protection even if they were. Laidley planned to write Governor Francis Pierpont but observed "that will take more time to procure aid than will be safe for us." He asked Samuels to send troops immediately.[625]

Dudley I. Smith informed his aunt on July 20, "There is a good deal of excitement here about Jenkins men coming in Guyandotte. They have swore that they would burn this place." The rumor was that the Confederates were seeking to seize a steamer with ammunition and provisions. Smith, who was living in Proctorville, added:

Times look pretty gloomy here. Union men from the Va side come over & stay of nights here. They are afraid to stay there. There has been a good many houses going up here, a mill & the store I am going to clerk in but the excitement has got so high that they are afraid to build.[626]

His uncle had returned to Guyandotte, "yet he said last week if there was not some Government troops sent there he would leave." A young cousin staying with the Smiths in Proctorville was haunted by the specter of another Confederate raid. Smith wrote, "She was talking about Jenkins last night. She said she wished she was dead. Ma asked her why. She said if she was dead that Jenkins could not kill her."[627]

On July 25, General Jacob D. Cox, stationed at Flat Top Mountain in Raleigh County, notified Colonel George D. Ruggles, chief of staff for the Army of Virginia, that he sent two companies to Guyandotte "where there is fear of guerrillas." Colonel

Joseph A. J. Lightburn wrote to Cox on July 27 informing him of a communication he had received from Dr. Edward Naret in Buffalo, which claimed that the "brothers Jenkins are now at home. Secessionists are much excited, and threatening Lieutenant Watterson, commissioned by Governor Pierpont. He states that threats are being made daily by the rebels that now is their time to do mischief, that the Yankees must go up." Naret added that "Jenkins was on his place and also his brother Jeff. Several of their men who had not been seen since the beginning of the war are at home, threatening their neighborhood..."[628]

Cox responded impatiently from Flat Top on the same day, writing,

Colonel Joseph A. J. Lightburn.
Credit: Terry Lowry.

> Who are the Jenkinses Dr. Nare[t] refers to? If they are at A. G. Jenkins place, near Guyandotte, your two companies there ought to catch them; but I do not believe they are there at all. I will order a company of cavalry down to you. Your detachments must all be kept busy, and not remain quiet in such posts as Chapmanville, Guyandotte, &c., but keep so active that they will know everything going on within 30 miles of them.[629]

General Cox also ordered Lightburn to send detachments to Buffalo, Ripley, and other locations

> to show that we are alive, and let it be everywhere understood distinctly that the secessionists of the neighborhood will be held responsible for mischief done by guerrillas both in property and person. If persons are threatening, arrest them promptly and keep them confined at Charleston till they can give good security for their behavior; activity, energy, and, if need be, severity must be used to make them understand through the whole valley that it is best for all disaffected persons to keep quiet.

Lightburn asked Cox if he did "not think it advisable" to send a company of cavalry to the area to operate as scouts, but he was directed to await further orders.[630]

William Dusenberry traveled to Wheeling in late July and met with Adjutant

General Henry J. Samuels at the State House on July 29. He received a second lieutenant's commission to recruit for the 13th (West) Virginia Infantry and then went to the office of Major Hill, where he was sworn into United States service. After dinner and a glass of beer with Samuels and his wife, the men walked over to the Athenaeum, where Confederate prisoners were held. Dusenberry saw Charley Harler, Ten Adkins, and the Lusher boys, all of whom asked him to deliver correspondence to their families in Cabell County.[631]

The Lusher boys, Charles, John, Robert, and Lewis, sons of Irwin (or Irving) Lusher, were all arrested by Federal authorities during the first two years of the war. In *United States vs. Charles Lusher*, Henry Worrell, a Union soldier captured at Guyandotte, testified that Charles Lusher guarded the prisoners on the first day of their march. Charles, the youngest brother, who was in bad health, wrote Adjutant General H. J. Samuels from the Athenaeum on March 19 asking him to visit. On the following day, Samuels wrote, "I am satisfied that the charges against Charles Lusher a prisoner in Athenaeum is not true to wit that he was in the Battle of Guyandotte. I think he has never belonged to any military company, and was when taken fleeing from fear of our troops." Samuels noted that one of his brothers was probably mistaken for Charles and recommended a $1,500 bond be given. John Lusher of Barboursville agreed and also pledged to pay the return cost of transportation for Charles Lusher from Wheeling to Guyandotte.

Captain William Turner suspected Robert Lusher was a secessionist and had spoken with him in August 1861, but Lusher swore he had taken the oath under Colonel William Woodruff a month earlier. Still, Turner pursued Robert for several months until finally arresting both he and his brother Lewis on July 15, 1862, at the home of their father. Louie Kingsolver attested that he had seen Robert "going down to Guyandotte with the Southern Cavalry, but I did not see him coming back." Despite his testimony, Adjutant General Henry Jefferson Samuels recommended the release of Robert M. Lusher on August 11. Robert M. Lusher enlisted in the 16th Virginia Cavalry on September 16, 1862, in Cabell County and was captured there on April 3, 1863. He was sent to Camp Chase but was exchanged the next month. Robert Lusher surrendered to Union authorities in Charleston and took the oath in February 1865.

John Lusher was captured on June 19, 1862. On August 11, Samuels recommended his release, but testimony from several residents of Cabell County caused him to change his mind. Stephen Paine said he saw John Lusher with Boston Thompson's horse and heard him say he had taken it from him. Union authorities seized Lusher and the horse, which was returned to Thompson, and Elisha McComas swore that John "made his escape from the custody of the Union troops." Samuels noted, "If the facts are as these affidavits disclose I decline to endorse."

Lieutenant William Feazel of the 13th (West) Virginia Infantry wrote to Major Joseph Darr on August 16 concerning John Lusher. Several citizens had sworn they had seen him armed with an Enfield rifle, but Feazel had spoken with other Union neighbors who believed it was another case of mistaken identity and that they had seen not John, but one of his brothers. Feazel informed Darr he would come immediately to Wheeling and sign a bond for John Lusher. "He is my wife's brother," the Union officer wrote, "and for her sake I will vouch for him." Despite Feazel's plea, John Lusher would not be released until January 13, 1863, when he was ordered to report to Darr.

Lewis Lusher, the oldest of Irwin's sons, was arrested by the 9th (West) Virginia Infantry on July 15, 1862, at the home of his father and charged with "aiding Rebels." Captain William Turner observed that Lewis Lusher was "accused of being a notorious horse thief." Several Union citizens and soldiers testified that they had seen him at various times "running around with a gun." One "saw him arrest a Union man and search him for letters &c. and took him to Poors Hill some time in October." Several noted his involvement in the Confederate raid on Guyandotte. Louis Kingsolver stated, "I saw him going down with them [the Confederate cavalry], and I saw him coming back again with a suit of northern military clothes, with a big blue overcoat in arms." Samuel Beall of the 9th (West) Virginia Infantry saw him in the same Union attire and heard him tell "a Rebel lady that he had taken the coat from one of the Yankees, and it was nothing but fun."

Lusher told Elisha McComas that "on their arrival at the premises of Chas. L. Roofe, that Col Clarkson observed 'there is a good horse, boys, any of you may take him that wants him.'" Lusher leaped off his mount and "took said yellow horse off with him." McComas later saw Lusher and one of his brothers, both armed, "in company" with the Border Rangers. Lusher was not riding Roffe's yellow mare or the bay horse he had previously ridden. When McComas asked what he had done with his steed, he replied, "I have been trading horses."

McComas claimed he had no knowledge of either Lewis or Robert serving in the Confederate army but declared that Lewis Lusher had admitted his participation in the fight at Poore's Hill. On August 11, 1862, Adjutant General H. J. Samuels wrote, "Lewis Lusher & Charles Harler must get the loyal men of that county to endorse for them as the last I heard of them from there the loyal men were down on them." Lewis Lusher was sent to Camp Chase on the following day.

Rodolphus Bukey reported on July 30 that things were quiet at present in Cabell County. Two companies of the 4th (West) Virginia Infantry were stationed in Guyandotte, "a kind of a bate for the confederates." Bukey noted that "we have reports every day of their scouts being in the county. I have no doubt in my mind but there will be a brake on Guian if there is not more force put there..."[632]

County court was held on August 4. A majority of the court favored giving a $25 bounty to each volunteer credited to the county, but John Laidley claimed they "had no right to make the levey." Rodolphus Bukey of Guyandotte had the Stars and Stripes "hoisted on his house" during the day.[633]

During July and most of August 1862, companies B and H of the 4th (West) Virginia Infantry were stationed at Guyandotte. Things were peaceful in the town until 4:00 a.m. on August 11, when Lieutenant Colonel W. H. H. Russell received a dispatch reporting that the two companies of the regiment stationed at Chapmanville had been captured by a Confederate cavalry force estimated at six hundred troopers. A rumor spread through the town that an attack was imminent and "that we better look sharp here."[634]

Leading citizens in nearby Ironton received the following dispatch:

HEADQUARTERS, CAMP GUYANDOTTE, VIRGINIA, AUGUST 11, 1862.

To Col. Parker, Mr. Wilgus, and others –

GENTLEMEN: Our pickets have been driven in from Chapmanville, Logan County, by a force of six hundred Rebels, and they will doubtless make a dash at this place. I expect them here within the next twenty-four fours. You will oblige me by sending out couriers immediately to the different companies of State Guards in your vicinity; with orders to report to me at this place without delay. My orders are to hold this place at all hazards, and this I intend to do so long as I have men to fight. My force here is but one hundred and fifty effective men. If you can send me two hundred good men, all is safe. For the honor of your State, let me urge you to send your men on this side of the River, and not allow the traitorous hordes to pollute the soil of Ohio with their footsteps. Let all fighting be done in Virginia.

Let there be no delay in getting your men together, as the Rebels are perhaps even now on their way to this place. Whatever you do, do at once. All depends on my getting men in time.

Respectfully, your obedient servant,
W. H. H. RUSSELL
Lieut. Col. 4th Reg. V. V. I. U. S. A. Commanding Post[635]

Sallie P. Smith recorded,

The good citizens of Proctorsville sent a message to every town and villag[e] in the county and by five oclock in the evening there was about one hundred men here. Most of them went over the river staid all night. About midnight there came from Ironton one hundred & 10 men and two cannons: they fixed them selves for battle, but no enemy came. I wish they would have come last night for they would have met with a warm reception.[636]

On the following morning, the citizens of Lawrence County returned to their homes and the cannon were taken down to the river and loaded on the first steamer. Smith wrote,

I feel very sorry they are going away so soon. I feel confident the Rebels will be in Guyandotte in a short time if our soldiers there are not reinforced. That Rebel Regiment is as well posted in Guyan affairs as I am and better too. The one that the Guyandotte boys belong to.[637]

About noon, as she was finishing her letter, Sallie Smith was interrupted:

I am so excited that can scarcely write. Since I have been writing those cannon and men have left for Ironton, and about five minutes ago two women came into Guyandotte having walked twelve miles to inform the soldiers that the Rebels are coming to night. The soldiers have posted a man after those cannon and men from Ironton. I don't know whether they will overtake them in time or not. I hope so at any rate.[638]

The Confederates, however, failed to make an appearance, and a sense of normalcy returned to the town. The *Ironton Register* remarked that "a repetition of these favors would be too much of a tax on the patriotism of our 'Militia'." It is clear that the Guyandotte raid had left a deep impression on the citizens and Union soldiers in the border region, one which would remain until the end of the war.[639]

Captain John L. Vance, Company B, 4th (West) Virginia Infantry. Vance took command of the post at Guyandotte in September 1862. Credit: Terry Lowry.

Russell commanded the post until relieved and replaced by Captain John L. Vance of Company B. Near the end of August, Colonel Joseph A. J. Lightburn ordered that Guyandotte be abandoned and that the Union units report to his headquarters on the Kanawha River.[640]

On August 13, William Dusenberry returned from Guyandotte to his home above Barboursville, where there "was a great deal of uneasiness" about a possible attack by Confederate raiders. Feeling it unsafe to remain at home, about nine o'clock that evening Dusenberry saddled his horse and rode to Barboursville, where he met with Greenville Harrison and John Witcher. While they were discussing the situation, Captain John L. Vance and another soldier from Guyandotte in citizens' attire appeared and informed them they had scouted as far as Sol Midkiff's and had not found evidence of the enemy.[641]

On the morning of August 17, William Dusenberry finished breakfast and walked down to his garden. As he began to gather some vegetables for dinner, his wife rushed up and "told me the Secessionists were at the house & for me to hide." Dusenberry sent her back to grab his coat and vest and then made his way toward the Guyandotte River, where

> just as I got there I saw the men fording the river. There was eleven riding & four on foot, no two of them dressed alike. Some of them had some part of the federal uniform on. They were a hard looking set.

The men stated they were appropriating Dusenberry's colt, but Cynthia Dusenberry informed them the horse was lame, and when "one asked her if he was a good Secesh horse she told them no there was no Secesh about that horse nor her either." The men then rode off and soon ran into Ben Swann, who was relieved of his mount.

Meanwhile, Dusenberry stopped at Barboursville and informed some of the citizens about the raiders before riding on to Guyandotte with John S. Witcher. On the following day he met the Bowdens, who informed him that on Saturday night, August 16, this same group of armed men was at their home. They had reportedly killed a man named Bill Brumfield in the afternoon and fired their weapons by his house that night. On August 26, the Federal troops remaining in Guyandotte departed. Court was to be held on the following day but the judge left with the soldiers.[642]

William Dusenberry, who had received a second lieutenant's commission to recruit soldiers for the 13th (West) Virginia Infantry exactly one month earlier, rode to Guyandotte on August 29 and then crossed over to Proctorville, where he found J. B. Baumgardner and 41 recruits from Wayne County. They all boarded a steamer for Point Pleasant and "cheered all the way up the river as long as it was light." Two little boys from Proctorville played fife and drums and received generous donations from those aboard the boat. On the following day, Dusenberry and fellow recruiter Brown reported to Lieutenant Colonel William Hall, who gave them permission to return home and attempt to fill their company. That evening Dusenberry spoke with Kellian V. Whaley at the hotel concerning affairs in the country. County court was held in Barboursville on the first day of September.[643]

In August of 1862, a large part of the Federal force occupying the Kanawha Valley was moved to Washington. In response, Confederate General William Wing Loring began planning an advance into the region and ordered Brigadier-General Albert Jenkins to move his cavalry force northwest from their camp in Monroe County. Seven companies from the 8th Virginia Cavalry and five companies under Captain W. R. Preston began the march, a total of about 550 soldiers. They left Salt Sulphur Springs on August 22 and raided a number of towns including Buckhannon, Weston, Glenville, Spencer, and Ripley, before reaching the Ohio River at Ravenswood.

On September 4, Jenkins and his men crossed the river and became the first Confederate soldiers to plant their flag on Ohio soil. The main body of troops captured Racine, Ohio, while a smaller force continued

General Albert Gallatin Jenkins.
Credit: National Archives.

down the river on the Virginia side. They reunited the following day about six miles from Point Pleasant before marching to Buffalo. Two days later, they camped near Green Bottom.[644]

When Union Colonel Joseph A. J. Lightburn learned that the Confederates were marching toward Barboursville, Colonel John C. Paxton, who commanded the 2nd (West) Virginia Cavalry, received permission to lead a force in pursuit. He gathered eight companies, six of the 2nd (West) Virginia Cavalry and two of the 4th (West) Virginia Infantry (one source reports the infantry companies as being from the 11th (West) Virginia Infantry), and moved down the west bank of the Kanawha River until they were a few miles below Charleston. At this point, they marched west up the turnpike toward Barboursville.

On Sunday, September 7, Colonel John A. Turley of the 91st Ohio Infantry was informed that the Confederate cavalry was approaching the area. He called out the Home Guard to "assemble, organize and drill," and requested that the women return immediately to their homes. At least six companies reported to the Lawrence County Courthouse "armed and equipped and ready for the contest." It was rumored that the Confederates had crossed the river at Guyandotte and were intent on burning Ironton.[645]

A newspaper correspondent reported, "The arrival of a courier and the packet Swan settled the matter that Guyandotte was in possession of the rebels. At 10 o'clock P. M. a volunteer Company under Potter manned the Doc Trimble and were sent on steamer Swan to guard the ford just below Guyandotte."[646]

Colonel John A. Turley, 91st Ohio Infantry. Credit: Frederick H. Meserve, Historical Portraits, New York State Library (courtesy of Terry Lowry).

Earlier that day, Company B of the 2nd (West) Virginia Cavalry, at the head of the Union column, stopped at the farm of Abia Rece near Mud Bridge. While they were eating, some mounted Confederates suddenly fired on the Federals from long range. The Union troopers quickly saddled up and chased after them, and when the Confederates turned to confront their pursuers, Captain Charles Hambleton "charged upon them, driving them toward Barboursville."[647]

The Union soldiers halted after capturing two enemy cavalrymen, James Poteet and Lon Love. Major William Powell, in charge of the advance, "learned from the prisoners that the enemy's force consisted of between 1000 and 1200 cavalry under the command of Jenkins and that they were in camp near Barboursville, and had been there twenty-four hours, resting and shoeing their horses."[648]

Powell and his officers conferred at length as to their next course of action. It was

Abia Rece Home, Mud Bridge.
Credit: Special Collections Department, Marshall University.

getting dark by then, but Colonel John Paxton arrived and ordered Powell forward with Company B. As the Federals entered Barboursville, they learned that Jenkins was using the home of William C. Miller as his headquarters. According to the regimental history of the 2nd West Virginia Cavalry:

> Upon nearing the house a charge was made upon it. It was found to be guarded by at least 50 Confederates, which fact could not be observed by the charging column on account of the extreme darkness of the night. The rebel guard fired and fled, and while the house was surrounded, Jenkins and staff escaped by the rear of the house through the garden. This caused the entire rebel force to abandon their camp and flee up the Guyandotte River.[649]

In the charge, Sergeant Braxton P. Reeves of Company B, "one of its bravest and best men," was killed by Confederate fire. His body was placed on the porch of the Miller home until Reeves's company returned following the skirmish. After Paxton determined that the Confederates had left the area, the regiment moved on to Guyandotte, where the body of Sergeant Reeves was forwarded to his friends.[650]

Border Ranger James D. Sedinger's recollections of the second Barboursville engagement differ greatly from the Union account. It is quite possible that they were describing separate clashes between the two cavalry forces. Sedinger recorded:

Ten men in charge of an officer were sent from Buffalo to Mud Bridge, now Milton, with orders if anything was wrong in Cabell to report to the General at Green Bottom. The 10 men that went to Milton continued on down the turnpike to within a half mile of Barboursville. There they met two citizens in a buggy whom they knew, who told them to go back for God's sake as the town was full of Yanks. After finding out from the citizens all that they knew was that they saw an officer and 8 or 10 men turn the corner and they supposed they merely the advance of some regiment coming to take possession of the town we concluded to ride into town and take a look at them. We rode in as far as Thornburg's store on top of the hill where the officer ordered a charge having seen a blue coat. We found them at Hatfield's hotel. About half of them went over the river bank and the rest ran in all directions, the boys firing at them as they ran. We caught two of them before they could get out of the hotel. Lieut. Brown the officer in command of the Yanks hid in a bake oven in the back yard of Oscar Mathers' house. This was the Sabbath day and church was going on at the time in the Southern Methodist church. Three or four bullets struck the building. The preacher did not have time to dismiss the congregation. It was found getting towards home as fast as they could possibly go without waiting for the benediction. The boys felt good over the result of their charge.

Captain C. E. Hambleton, 2nd (West) Virginia Cavalry, who led a charge on enemy forces at Mud Bridge in September 1862. Credit: History of the Second Regiment West Virginia Cavalry Volunteers, During the War of the Rebellion.

We went on to Guyandotte and charged the town. There we found no one but citizens. Told them to stay at home and they should not be disturbed. We went around town shook hands with every one and felt as if we were at home once more. We waited for the Command to come down the Ohio from Green Bottom. We rejoined the Co. and went to Barboursville where a scout from Hurricane came down and reported to the General that Lightburn and all forces in the Kanawha Valley was retreating by the way of Barboursville. He left one Co. of Cavalry to watch them and fell back up the Guyan river and made a forced march through Wayne Co. up 12 Pole into Logan Co.[651]

On Monday, September 8, the Ironton area Home Guard continued drilling until the early afternoon when they boarded the steamers *Victor No. 3* and *Swan*, disembarking at Burlington, Ohio. Captain J. M. Merrill took a few men farther up the river to Proctorville. Artillery was placed at Guyan riffle and Twelve Pole bar, the two most fordable places on the Ohio, guarded by volunteers from the vicinity. That evening a note was sent from Guyandotte under a flag of truce:

MR. CHAS. WILGUS – Sir: I am authorized to say to you by Brig. Gen. A. G. Jenkins that the policy of this Government is not to destroy property and the only Course for the Citizens of Lawrence Co. to persue is to attend to there Own domestic Conserns Stay on your Own Soil as long as armed, as we intend Contending for Our Own he assures you that he will not Molest you or your property, without Citizens and property is disturbed on this side of the Ohio by Citizen's from your place or Community distroy or Molesting property of Citizens on this, we pledge you further that we will not give you uneseness by Our preasants without armed forces attempted to invade us I think you Can govern in a great degree the Community in which you live no more your friend &c., by Order of A. G. Jenkins Brig Gen

John S. Everett[652]

At about one o'clock Tuesday morning,

the clattering of troops over the bridge and on the turnpike caused an unusual excitement which only satisfied our boys that a new levy had arrived. Their anxieties on this subject however were soon allayed by the arrival of J. M. Merrill, of the 2nd Virginia Cavalry, announcing the fact that Guyandotte was in their possession. The cannon was then fired four times and most of the home guards from Ironton crossed and spent the rest of the night in social chat with our 'brave Soger boys.'[653]

The Union women of Guyandotte prepared breakfast for the soldiers early the next morning. They refused to accept payment for the food, even though in most cases it was all that they had. The troops spent the rest of the morning resting, currying their horses, and procuring forage.
At two in the afternoon, it was reported that Jenkins was approaching Guyandotte with 1,200 cavalry and three infantry regiments. At the request of Proctorville's citizens, a courier was dispatched to bring up the brass six-pounder from Burlington, while another messenger went on to Ironton to spread the alarm. The artillery company boarded the *Naomi* and arrived at midnight, "planted their cannon in a principal street and awaited the enemy determined 'to die if need be' rather than surrender."

Colonel John Paxton, 2nd (West) Virginia Cavalry. The 1861-62 winter camp at Guyandotte was named for him. Credit: History of the Second Regiment West Virginia Cavalry Volunteers, During the War of the Rebellion.

The steamer *Swan* was heading toward Guyandotte carrying passengers and provisions for the 2nd (West) Virginia Cavalry when the ship's captain was persuaded to return to Ironton. There the boat was loaded with six companies of the 91st Ohio Infantry, and after much delay the troops reached Guyandotte about three o'clock Wednesday morning. Colonel John C. Paxton, commander of the 2nd (West) Virginia Cavalry, was so alarmed by reports of the strength of the Confederate cavalry force that he ordered the cannon sent back to the Ohio side of the river. The ford was also examined for a possible escape route.[654]

On Wednesday, a "heavy force scouted the country far and near all forenoon, but found the enemy had skedaddled." Colonel Lightburn's command, however, was forced to withdraw from the Kanawha Valley. Lightburn reported, "The Second Virginia Cavalry, under Colonel Paxton, did good service in keeping Jenkins' force at bay, thereby preventing an attack in our rear. I wish, also, to state that Colonel Paxton, with 300 men, attacked Jenkins' whole force (from 1,200 to 1,500) and drove them from Barboursville, which no doubt, kept them from an attempt to harass our retreat..."[655]

Confederate General Albert G. Jenkins sent correspondence to the commanding officer of the Home Guards of Wayne County on September 12. In response to a request to return property, Jenkins declared he was willing to do so "whenever you shall return to the southern men of Wayne Co. the property which has been taken from them on account of their allegiance to the State." Jenkins also stated that he would release the prisoners seized in Wayne County after he was assured that Wayne County citizens arrested by Federal officials were freed and "that hereafter no more similar arrests shall be made." He added,

> I abhor a war on private persons and on private property, and in this I do but represent the feelings and policy of our own government. We have been compelled to pursue a different course at times as the only means of securing us against the aggressions upon private rights and private property, which has marked the conduct of many of your military commanders.
>
> We would hail with great delight the return of your people to a more civilized mode of warfare and are ourselves ready to conform to the same in every

possible respect.[656]

James Bartram wrote to Adjutant General H. J. Samuels from Ironton on September 13:

> I presume you have heard ere this of the frequent alarms in this section of country, caused by the reports of the Rebels advancing towards the shores of the Ohio. The 'Jenkins Raid' on 'Guyandotte' caused great alarm in this quarter, as well as up the river. We had a general turnout and prepared to meet the enemy, but when some of our troops reached the seat of war (Guyandotte), the enemy had left, and then the excitement subsided, and every thing appeared to be quiet...We have frequent alarms caused by the many reports circulated throughout the country, which causes the excitement to be quite general, and I presume we will be liable to the annoyance consequent to the reports in the occasion of alarms as they may occur.[657]

On September 18, the editor of the *Ironton Register* wrote:

> Our absence from town, shouldering a musket in defence of the border, accounts for the scarcity of local news in last issue. This week we have endeavored to bring up arrears. Hope our friends will be indulgent since we did better than many of the papers on the border. The Sandy Valley Advocate suspended, and the Pomeroy Telegraph came to us on half sheet. The scarcity of hands and the embargo on business at Cincinnati gave us much trouble, but by taking a journey to another city we secured the material necessary to keep the machine going.[658]

The steamer *Glenwood* departed from Gallipolis, Ohio, on the morning of September 22 bound for Cincinnati. Aboard were citizens and soldiers including the Portsmouth Artillery, which had mustered in only nine days earlier at Gallipolis as the 18th Independent Battery, Ohio Light Artillery. As they crossed into Cabell County, some of those aboard noted "a cloud of dust on the road back from the river some distance" on the Virginia side. The word spread, and soon the deck was filled with armed artillerymen.

About six miles above Guyandotte, at Martin Hull's Landing, a man hailed the steamer. Unsuccessful in his quest to convince the boat to land, he started up the bank, but at that moment a number of Confederates (estimated at between five and fifty) emerged from the bushes and fired a volley at the *Glenwood*. Several balls struck the boat, but the soldiers of the artillery company returned the fire and forced the guerrillas to withdraw. Lieutenant Henry A. Regnier, who commanded the twenty-five artillerymen, was praised for his leadership, "frequently urging the boys to keep cool, not to unnecessarily expose themselves, and to make every shot tell." Men in the pilot house swore they saw one of the Confederates fall and the horse of another "rear and plunge as if hurt."

Prior to the attack, one of the civilians had taken refuge in the cabin to pen some letters. Suddenly her mother and another woman burst in from the bow, screaming "The Rebels! The Rebels!" The volley from the Confederates followed, knocking out half the glass in the cabin. The woman recorded, "Pa was cut by a bit of glass, but, strangely enough, no one else was hurt..." Two balls were found, one which passed through a stateroom and into the cabin, and the other embedded in a mattress on which a woman had been reclining only recently. Another attack was expected, but the Union men supposed "the first reception they received from us was sufficient, and concluded not to come again." The steamer later landed safely at Portsmouth, Ohio.[659]

Peter and John Harshbarger, sons of David Harshbarger, served in the Union Army during the Civil War. In September 1862, Peter Harshbarger, who joined the 5th (West) Virginia Infantry, wrote letters to his father and brother from a camp near Washington D. C. On September 17, 1862, the same day brother John enlisted in the 3rd (West) Virginia Cavalry, Peter wrote to him:

> I feel worse now about you all and your safety than I do for my self but I cant help you any as I am called away too far from you all. I suppose if all accounts be true it is distressing times amongst you all as we have the news that the rebels are in force on Knwawha valey and that Jenkins has bin on his farm and I no if it is true that it is searious times among you all that is loyal people..."
>
> I expect to receive the news of every thing you have being taken and what they cant take to be distroyed...well John you may be a prisoner before this reaches you but I hope not and I hope you and pop may keep your skirts clear from the hands of the deamons...[660]

In a letter written to his father at Mud Bridge – undated, but probably penned shortly after his correspondence to John – Peter wrote:

> It is with mutch pleasure that I seat myself to drop you a few lines in these perilous times of our country. I no if all reports be true that you are all sufering great uneacynes for fear of your property being distroyed and for your own safety...I am afraid the next I hear from you that the rebels will clean you out off every thing you have and very like cary you away prisoner but I hope you will keep out of their way. If they strip you ove all you have I expect to be payed off tomorrow and I will have $100 which if it will be needed for to relieve any ove your wants you can have it but I hope and trust to god that you may not be distressed as bad as I imagined that you might be...I think the war will not last an other winter. We have nearly a million of soldiers in the field and the rebels are tyerd of mareland and I do not wonder. Well I hope you will all escape the vengence of the traitors. I hope ere this reaches you that our Regt. may be on its way to Cabell and wayne countys relief. If we ever get back there we will make traitors rue the day they ever caused that country to be invaded again. May god bless and guide us and protect us through this life so as when we come

to die that we may be prepared to meet each other in a better world. If we are never more permitted to meet on this earth may we ever be constant to our maker.[661]

On the night of September 21, a Confederate cavalry force under Major Vincent Witcher reportedly raided both Guyandotte and Barboursville. About 10:30 p.m., between twenty and forty Confederates crossed the Guyandotte suspension bridge on foot, leaving their horses on the west side of the Guyandotte River. The rebels took about $500 worth of goods from two Guyandotte merchants, a Mr. Bay and Sidney Bowden. Before reaching Guyandotte, some of the Confederates attempted to capture Sheriff D. P. Ferguson, who awakened when they endeavored to force open his front door. He quickly jumped out of bed and dashed into the woods "with nothing but his shirt and drawers." The Confederates took a hat and $28 in cash from Ferguson's home before leaving.[662]

On that same Sunday night, twenty-eight Confederates dashed into Barboursville. They stole a horse from Andy Dick and took all the leather from Westhoff's tannery before following the Guyandotte River out of town.[663]

On the following day, Reuben Lunceford and Samuel Johnson were on Johnson's farm opposite Symmes Creek when a squad of Confederate cavalry suddenly appeared, capturing both men. After disarming the civilians and seizing two horses, the raiders departed, but this same group fired into the steamer *Glenwood* as it passed by. On Tuesday, Confederate cavalry was seen as far down as Burlington and "trouble is anticipated again on the Border."[664]

Colonel Joseph Lightburn wrote General H. G. Wright on September 23: "Our transportation is interrupted on the ohio river at Guyandotte. I have no more force here than will hold this point – could a force be out there or would it be practicable." Wright informed Lightburn on the following day that he had no troops to send, but he had telegraphed Ohio Governor David Tod "asking him to send any force he can to Guyandotte."[665]

A squad of forty Confederate cavalry commanded by Lieutenant Thompson, brother of George Thompson of Burlington, Ohio, rode into Ceredo on September 27 and seized Wayne County Sheriff William Nixon, his son, and two other men. Nixon had been collecting taxes and was robbed of $845 in cash; eight horses were also appropriated. According to an account of the raid, the Confederates "claim to have 1400 men at Barboursville, and expect to winter on the border, making their headquarters at Ceredo. Time, however, will show..." In the same issue, the newspaper published a copy of General W. W. Loring's proclamation, "To the People of Western Virginia," which, they noted, "does not correspond with their acts yesterday."[666]

A Guyandotte citizen described the desperation in the region in a letter to the *Wheeling Intelligencer*:

> The section of country is literally overrun with bands of thieves; no person is safe at any time, nor will they be until a force is sent here to stay and keep them in check. This thing of sending Federal troops here for to stay a week or two

and leave again for some other portion of country is all a farce; for as soon as they leave the secesh rabble commence their depredations. Unless a Federal force is sent into this country and that immediately the loyal citizens will be utterly ruined. Nearly all of the horses in the county have been stolen. Those who have any left are sending them across the river into Ohio.[667]

In October 1862, A. M. McGinnis contacted Adjutant General Henry J. Samuels concerning recent hardships. Two horses had been taken from his pasture by Union soldiers from the 2nd (West) Virginia Cavalry. McGinnis followed the regiment as far as Barboursville hoping to procure their return, but he was stopped by the rear guards who threatened to shoot him if he pursued farther. After persuading E. D. Wright to accompany him, McGinnis continued his quest to the top of Coal Mountain, where the men learned that a battle was raging in Charleston, forcing their return to Cabell County.

McGinnis had suffered greatly from the moment the first Union troops appeared in the county more than a year earlier, losing cattle, hay, and oats. Following the Confederate raid in September 1862, McGinnis was in Guyandotte "butchering for the town" when two companies of the 4th (West) Virginia Infantry forced him to furnish beef for them. As McGinnis noted,

> I run a risk in furnishing them beef. The Rebels say they will take my oxen for furnishing the Yankees beef. I thought nothing wrong in furnishing them beef for it is an easy matter for an armed force to take that or any thing else they want whether the citizens are willing or not. But that fact is too little considered by both sides.

Despite the heavy sacrifices he had made, A. M. McGinnis reiterated his support for the Union, stating he would "freely give it all to see the government of my choise stand erect in peace once more."[668]

According to the *Ironton Register*, on October 2 "there was a little skirmish between some bushwhackers who had entered Ceredo, Virginia, and the Home Guards opposite. The parties were separated by the Ohio river, yet our guns being of an improved kind, carried that distance and the result was, that two rebels were killed. Since then they are a little wary, and do not appear in full view."[669]

Sallie P. Smith penned a letter from Quaker Bottom on October 4 and gave a melancholy description of her hometown of Guyandotte: "It is five months today since we left home and the sad changes that have taken place in that short period. It does not look like Guyandotte did when we left it! It is the most forsaken melancholy looking place that ever I beheld or want to behold."[670]

Secessionists in the area were quiet at the moment due to the presence of the 5th (West) Virginia Infantry. The rumor was, however, that the regiment was to be ordered to the eastern theater. "If they leave," Smith declared, "I don't know what will become of us. We live in fear as it [is] and when they are taken away I reckon we will cease to live at all." Men from Cabell and Wayne counties who had enlisted in the Confederate army "say that their companies are going to winter in those two counties or have a hard strug[g]le for it the last of this month or the first of November."[671]

Smith noted the sacrifices of her family, writing, "I don't think that any mortal could pen half that they have endured and all because they were for the Union." And yet some of their relatives in Guyandotte strongly supported the Confederacy, causing friction within the family. Sallie Smith informed her cousin that her Aunt Mary and another relative "are not very friendly on account of this trouble." Sallie's cousin Edward Smith passed by her house earlier in the week and "he would not speak to me. I presume it is because I just came from Ohio." She declared that his wife, Josephine "Josie" Smith, "has acted more than any of the men. She drew a pistol on some of Col. Woodruff's men."[672]

Sallie P. Smith related that "Old Mr. Hinchman says that he has not slept this summer only what he slept standing at his door with a pitchfork in his hand. The secessionists were determined to take his oldest son in the army but so far he has kept them from it." Before she could complete her letter, her brother Abraham arrived from Guyandotte and related a report that Confederate cavalry would attack the town on the following day. Smith said, "if they do come the secessionists will all raise their heads and the poor Union men, I don't know what will become of them!"[673]

11
Welcome to Western Virginia

"This miserable rebel town wears the aspect of deep mourning. The few remaining inhabitants have the appearance of those who had just returned from an eighteen months' funeral, at which all their relatives had been buried, and they had returned to find their homes and firesides devastated by general ruin.

Almost every man whom you meet in the street reminds you of Rachel weeping for her children. And though they all protest that they are Union men, yet the confused and unfamiliar manner with which they use the epithet Union, soon satisfies you that their assumed garment of Unionism but illy fits the awkward wearer."

Description of Guyandotte
Major Samuel S. Boyd
Surgeon of the 84th Indiana Infantry, October 1862

Union forces sought to re-establish control in the Kanawha Valley following Loring's September 1862 raid. Colonel Jonathan Cranor, who commanded the 40th Ohio Infantry, headed the Third Brigade of the Kanawha Division of the District of Western Virginia, which consisted of his regiment, the 84th Indiana Infantry, Mitchell's battery, and a squadron of Ohio cavalry. When the Union troops, stationed at Camp McFall in Gallipolis, Ohio, learned they would be sent to western Virginia, one of them wrote, "The rebels is scarce here but up where we are going there is plenty of them and we are going up there to thin them out or get thin[n]ed out our selves."[674]

On October 12, 1862, the 40th Ohio and 84th Indiana drew three days' rations in preparation for their movement into Virginia. Both regiments crossed the Ohio River at three o'clock on the following afternoon and camped opposite Gallipolis. On Monday, the column departed, and the march from there to Guyandotte was through rugged terrain. One member of the 84th Indiana noted, "About half of the way we had to march through farms and along the sides of hills where no mortal had driven six mules since Adam's fall or the late rebellion." The trek left the soldiers exhausted and their feet blistered.[675]

About 4:30 p.m. on Wednesday, October 15, they arrived at Green Bottom and camped on the farm of Albert Gallatin Jenkins. Fences were torn down and "we burnt a lot of his rails to cook with & fed on his hogs." Corporal George Woodbury complained that Colonel Cranor "would not let us dig a few sweet potatoes to eat when we had not had nothing to eat for three days but water and dry bread. He was afraid that Colonel Jinkens would come in on us when we had two to one of them and I don't suppose that thay was in ten miles of us at that time..."[676]

On the following day, the Federal troops marched briskly to Guyandotte, arriving about sundown. They immediately pitched their tents and "stacked arms on a lovely camping ground." One of the soldiers observed, "there has been a lot of houses burnt in this town by our foes last spring. They were bri[c]k houses."[677]

Another described their new home: "Guyandotte is a small, sleepy town which lies at the mouth of the Guyandotte River, once beautiful but now ready to 'fence in.'" Private James Clover of the 40th Ohio wrote, "There was some Rebels here but they got out of the way pretty quick. I do not know how long we will stay here. They say that the Rebels is up the Guyandotte River at a little town called Barbersville. Our cavalry have gone up there today to see if they was there." Clover noted the brigade included four pieces of artillery and observed the men "have plenty to eat and plenty to wear." Another soldier related that the Ohio River was so low that wagons forded just below the camp of the 84th Indiana.[678]

General Jacob D. Cox sent a telegraph to Major N. H. McLean on October 15, writing, "I find that Gen Milroy has sent a brigade to Guyandotte to look after Jenkins there. I shall not recall it at present..."

Major Samuel Boyd, surgeon of the 84th Indiana Infantry, wrote,

> This miserable secession town where we are now stationed, as most of those familiar with the history of the war, will remember, was mostly laid in ashes more than a year ago by Colonel Zeigler. Nearly all of those remaining are a stench in the nostrils of Union-loving men. Forage and provisions are very abundant here, however, and *dirt cheap*.[679]

Major Samuel S. Boyd, surgeon of the 84th Indiana Infantry. Credit: Cathy Callen.

The 84th Indiana was given the name "the traveling 84th" since, as one soldier recorded, "we have been on the march so much." Like most soldiers, the men of the 84th Indiana Infantry were concerned about being paid for their services. One of them wrote, "Well Sally some of the boys think we wont get any mony till the war is over. Some of us have made it up that when we get our mony that we will tell Capt that we are going home & risk a court marshall. They may take some of our wages."[680]

Shortly after their arrival in Guyandotte, Sergeant Isaac Little of the 84th Indiana wrote,

> there is a force of 60 or 75 cavalry goes with us & a battery of 6 pieces of cannons. We could make a noise if nothing else. I want to try it any how. This kind of fiting wont whip the rebels soon but I heard that Col Cranor had 500 dollars but that peace would be made in 60 days. The 40th Ohio all think it will soon be over. I dont care how quick.[681]

The Indiana soldiers made a gruesome find in the town. Little wrote, "When we came here there was the liver of a man hanging on the bri[d]ge or under it. It was dried out so some of our boys buried it. It was a union mans liver so you may know what kind of a place we are in."[682]

On the night of October 16, scouts reported "that there was about 8,000 rebels about 12 miles from here & he thought they were advancing." Sergeant Isaac Little observed, "Some of the boys was a little excited but I have got use to such alarms to loose [sic] much sleep."[683]

"I guess we will stay here a few days to rest," Little wrote on October 17. On the same day Private John Turner of the 84th Indiana related, "We are in Virginia now where the rebels is thick. This part of town has all been burnt out by union troops. Yesterday there was a squad of rebels in this town and there was four of them come up the river and saw us and they come up to this town and told them that we was coming and they all left here with a hurray and went up the big Sandy river."[684]

Sergeant Isaac Little of the 84th Indiana Infantry recorded that "there is plenty of cecesh here. We are camped close to one old man that shot a Union soldier that was wounded last spring. After he was wounded he was cralling up the river bank by his house when the rebel shot him dead. Then the Union men burnt his house. He lives in a small home close by." Some of Little's fellow soldiers went to the home of the unnamed secessionist and found three hundred barrels of apples in the cellar. The men took all they wanted and were "carrying apples to camp all day yester day." They also seized cans of peaches, crocks of apple butter, and some chickens and hogs. Two of Little's company went to the residence on the evening of October 17 and found a bucket of milk on the table which they appropriated and "fetched it to our tent so we had milk in our coffee."[685]

The secessionist who suffered from the appetites of the Indiana soldiers complained to Colonel Jonathan Cranor and sought to have them punished for their transgressions. Cranor told the man the soldiers were not permitted to go beyond the guard lines and sent him on his way. As the Confederate supporter passed through the Union camp, "the boys were so mad they could hardly keep from shooting him. His age is all that saved him," Little wrote. "I felt a little like hurting him my self."[686]

A detachment of Union troops from the 84th Indiana Infantry embarked on a scouting expedition to Barboursville on October 18, but "nothing of importance occurred." That evening they returned with seven prisoners, forty head of cattle, four mules, and several weapons.

Charles Wilgus wrote to Henry J. Samuels on the same day, noting the presence of Union troops at Guyandotte, but he expressed his fear that they would not remain in the area:

> I hope that Govr Pearpoint and you will use all your influence to keep troops at Guyandotte or Barbersville, as it is the only way to restore peace in these counties. The Union families of Cabell Wane & part of Logan is robed by the rebels, untill they are in a sufering condition. The Govr you have taken deep interes in placing troups to protect these countes. An had the troupes of been suffered to remain whare you raised and placed them then would today be a diferent state of thing in the above counties of Va.[687]

Sergeant Isaac Little observed,

> You wont believe the difference in this side of the river & the Ohio side. Here they all look sour at us & over the river they wore handkerchief & shake hands with us. The verry ground looks better nice farms & orchards there & here there is nothing hardly only where a rich man lives but the most of them are in the army or have left here.[688]

Partly as a consequence of this stereotyping, the citizens in Cabell County also suffered from the actions of the soldiers sent to protect them. Sergeant Little wrote, "I seen some of the boys taking cans of peaches out of the rebels house. One fellow had a big crock of apple butter. It looked hard but they do as bad to our folks when they get the chance. Well I believe I will go on a Scout this evening & get some thing good to eat."[689]

Little later described a similar incident: "There was two shocks of wheat standing close to our camp that belonged to that old Devil of rebel. We took most all to sleep on in our tents & the rest was fed to hungry horses."[690]

The Indiana soldiers enjoyed a pleasant Sunday morning in Guyandotte on October 19 and had the good fortune of hearing the church bells ringing across the river in Proctorville. Upriver in Point Pleasant, the quartermaster of the 5th (West) Virginia

Confederate Lt. Colonel Vincent Witcher of Wayne County. Credit: Scott Cole (courtesy of Jack L. Dickinson).

Infantry, Z. D. Ramsdell, ran into Congressman Kellian V. Whaley and the two paid a call on General Jacob D. Cox. Cox issued orders for the regiment to "proceed to Ceredo & garrison that Post." Ramsdell drew six four-mule teams and began loading supplies for the move. The teams crossed the river into Ceredo at 3:00 p.m. on October 19, and Ramsdell found Colonel John Zeigler and 150 soldiers encamped in the town.[691]

On October 20, the Trough Fork Company of the 167th Regiment of Virginia militia skirmished with Confederates under Major Vincent Witcher in the upper part of Wayne County near the Logan County line. Captain William T. Caldwell, who commanded the militia company, reported that his forty-one men fired nine volleys at the Confederates but "had to give way to superior numbers," which he estimated at four hundred. Captain Caldwell reported killing three of the enemy and wounding four, but the company lost one man killed, Second Lieutenant James Maynard, and another wounded.[692]

The presence of Union troops in Guyandotte led to complaints by residents of the town and resultant actions taken by Colonel Jonathan Cranor. Special Order Number 13, issued on October 19, stated, "Complaints having been made to these Hd Qrs that the troops of this command are committing depredation upon the property of citizens, killing hogs & appropriating to their own use. The Commandants will ferret out the guilty parties & have them as well as the Captains or commandants of their respective companies report immediately to these Head Quarters." Three days later, Cranor forbade females from quartering within camp limits. General Order Number 3, issued on October 27, dealt with sanitation issues in the camp:

Colonel Jonathan Cranor, 40th Ohio Infantry and commander of the brigade at Guyandotte in the fall of 1862. Credit: Massachusetts Commandery Military Order of the Loyal Legion and the US Army Military History Institute.

> Commandants of companies will be held responsible for the cleanliness of their men in quarters and around the same; and it is further ordered, and a strict adherence thereto will be expected – that if any officer non-commissioned officer or soldier who shall be caught attending to the calls of nature any nearer to the quarters than has heretofore specified, shall, if a commissioned officer, be subject to a reprimand; if a non-commissioned officer he shall be 'reduced'; if a private he shall be put on extra duty for the first offence, for the second, put in the Guard House.[693]

Discipline was distributed as necessary, and on October 23, one of the soldiers received a harsh punishment. "Well I saw a man bu[c]ked & gag[g]ed to day for the first time in my life," wrote Sergeant Isaac Little. He added:

> I would not be in that fix for 50 dollars. The man got a letter from home & his wife was sick so he went to Cranor & asked for a furlough but he could not get it & he said he would go & got mad & stubborn. They put him in the guard house & then he would not come to order so they fetched him here to camp & told him to cut wood & he would not do it so they buked & gaged him. It look hard but he did not do right. He ought to said nothing after he could not get a furlough & just sliped of[f]. That is the way I will do.[694]

The men of the 84th Indiana Infantry were uncomfortably ensconced in tents, with sixteen men in each. Two of the soldiers were designated each day to cook for their mess mates. Typical fare was coffee, crackers, beef soup, molasses, fried apples, and fried pig meat, "as salty as the dickens." Isaac Little noted the enjoyment of another fruit: "Well I have eat more pawpaws since I left Gallipolis than ever I eat in my life. There is hundreds of bushels of them along the river."[695]

Some of the soldiers entertained themselves by putting pieces of newspapers in envelopes and mailing them to their friends and neighbors. Little confided this secret to his wife and urged her, "dont tell any body about it so they will know who sent them."[696]

"The health of the Regt is pretty good," Little declared, "better than awhile." He noted that "Sam Fraze is not well. He looks bad. He has a cough. You need not tell his folks for it would make them uneasy." Most of the sick had been left at or sent to Gallipolis. A week later, the surgeon of the 84th Indiana wrote,

> The health of the camp is improving rapidly. From over one hundred on the sick list a few days ago the hospital reports show less than fifty names to-day. Our hospital is one of the best private residences in town, which has been abandoned by its rebel owner. We have made enough temporary bedsteads or 'bunks' to accommodate all the patients, and have otherwise furnished the house so as to give it the air of rude comfort.[697]

The men shared a common zeal – preservation of the Union – and applauded efforts to bring Union supporters into the army. One wrote, "Bully for the drafted quaker but we aint fighting for money it is for the union." He added, "I recon Nate Smith wishes he had come with me. I am glad that they are drafted."[698]

One Indiana soldier noted the advantages of remaining an enlisted man: "Lafe Steel has got his comision as 2nd Leftenant. Some of the boys don't like him but I think he will do very well. There is a heap that wants office but I tell you it don't pay after all unless it is a big office. Let a civil private like me get the good side of the officers & he is in the best place of all." He was also happy to learn that some of his neighbors had been drafted into military service: "I never heard such hurowing when I read the names to the crowd...bul[l]y put them through."⁶⁹⁹

Sergeant Isaac Little wrote to a friend about the difficulties of the soldiering life:

> Well George I honestly dont think you could stand it long to soldier. You could make out first rate till it got to raining & you had to march & carry a big knap sack through the mud ancle deep & lay down to sleep with you cloths all wet & have to carry all you eat for 3 days. It is true there are some fine & easy times for a soldier & we are having them now but it may change in a few days. As a general thing a soldiers life is a hard life. I have seen many a poor fellow give out & lay down by the side of the road but you might stand it the best kind & you might be in the hospital in two weeks.

He added this recommendation: "George you can do your share raising stuff to sell to feed the soldiers. Raise lots of potatoes for they are the best thing a soldier can get."⁷⁰⁰

Yet good food always seemed to be at hand. In a letter to his wife, Little observed that some of his company had just appeared with "a fat pig" and that "we will have a good din[n]er." He noted that they had turkey and several chickens for breakfast, and exclaimed, "if we dont live fat I never did."⁷⁰¹

The small hills rising above the Ohio River around Guyandotte were impressive to the soldiers from Indiana. Little informed his wife, "I would send you a little rock. I seen some yesterday about a quarter of a mile long & about a hundred feet high. There is hills about ½ mile high nearly strait up." Climbing up the rise, he saw "lots of names cut on a big rock." Expressing regret that he did not have the time and tools to carve his own name, Little pledged to return if he had the opportunity.⁷⁰²

Battalion drill was conducted during the day of October 23, and the soldiers were able to practice their marksmanship. All of the men shot at targets positioned at a distance of 168 yards. Some of the men hit the paper, while others missed by twenty feet. Several of the Hoosiers found time to use grind stones to carve rings from mussel shells found on the banks of the Ohio River. About fifty rings were produced each day, and there was "the great call for files to make rings."⁷⁰³

The soldiers made efforts to improve their temporary housing. Little wrote, "We went in to town to day & got a small stove & put in our tent so it looks like a house. We can make it to[o] warm in a short time. Some of the boys have got furnaces in their tents & a chimney on the out side but it aint half as good as ours."⁷⁰⁴

Cox responded to a Cranor request on October 20, writing, "Your expedition to Logan and Wayne Counties, and the Big Sandy country, are approved and you are ordered to prosecute them vigorously." Cox informed Major N. H. McClean that

> Colonel Cranor reports from Guyandotte no rebels in that immediate vicinity, but from '2,500 to 4,000' reported in Wayne and Logan Counties. He is sending reconnoitering parties, and will soon report the foundation for these probably exaggerated reports. The Fifth Virginia, which was irregularly furloughed en masse by General Milroy, is collecting at Ceredo. Cranor has with him at

Guyandotte the Fortieth Ohio, Eighty-fourth Indiana, and a squadron of cavalry...⁷⁰⁵

The soldiers encamped near Guyandotte were required to have passes to enter the town. On a quiet Monday morning, October 20, George W. Miller of the 84th Indiana Infantry received a pass and "went up town." He looked at the suspension bridge over the Guyandotte River ("a splendid Bridge") and noted that the "best part of the town" was burnt by Union troops due to "misstreatment to our men."

On the following day, thirty-four soldiers from Company H of the 84th Indiana went up the Ohio in search of secessionist supporters who were reportedly selling whisky and groceries to Confederate soldiers. They moved six miles up the river and surprised a few men lounging on two flatboats. Captain G. M. Carter and twelve soldiers seized one of the vessels, which had "a right smart grocery on it." Lieutenant William H. Focht and the rest of the men gathered up the owner of the boats and seven others and began rowing back to Guyandotte. One of the troops wrote, "the wind blew hard so we had hard work. We got to camp a little after dark & tired & hungry. That is the first battle we have had and not a gun fired."⁷⁰⁶

On Thursday, October 23, Isaac Little wrote his wife: "Well we are going on a scout to morrow up to Barbersville. The rebels are pretty thick. The 40th are going. I dont know how long we will be out but I will write to you as soon as we get back." Instead the majority of the force at Guyandotte would be moving the following day into Kentucky. George W. Miller was detailed for picket duty and traveled about half a mile from the town, which afforded him the opportunity to gaze upon the Federal camp. Every Thursday afternoon, the troops were permitted to fire their weapons, and Miller listened as the Union soldiers enjoyed the opportunity to do so.⁷⁰⁷

On October 24, the surgeon for the 84th Indiana Infantry, stationed in Guyandotte, wrote a depressing description of the community:

> All business is suspended. No one comes to town except a few poor women of the vicinity, who bring in the most shadowy ghosts of India rubber pies to sell to the soldiers.
>
> Not a good horse is to be found in all this region, except those belonging to our army. The rebels have pressed them into the service long since.
>
> Our scouts have captured sixteen rebels who are here under guard. Two of them, a Doctor and a Minister, are rather intelligent men; but the rest of them are of the butternut species.⁷⁰⁸

General Jacob D. Cox informed Colonel Jonathan Cranor on October 24 that information indicated that Confederates had concentrated near Charleston. Cox wrote, "If everything is quiet between you and the Sandy, an expedition, scouting carefully toward the mouth of Coal River, will have a good effect in gathering intelligence which may be valuable, as well as clearing that region of guerrillas."⁷⁰⁹

While stationed at Guyandotte, the 40th Ohio Infantry was bombarded with calls for protection from citizens in the Big Sandy Valley. In response, Colonel Jonathan Cranor moved the majority of his brigade to Catlettsburg, Kentucky, on October 24, intending to march through Grayson and Louisa before crossing through Trout's Hill on their return to Guyandotte. Twenty-eight men from each company made the march, every soldier carrying six days' rations.

Meanwhile, in Guyandotte, a scout arrived about noon with the news that 12,000 Confederates were "moving on this place." A member of the 84th Indiana Infantry described the scene in the town:

> In the afternoon, a rumor spread like a whirlwind in the almost deserted camp, that a rebel force, resting securely in the hills, only awaited night to attack the camp. An old citizen who came excitedly into camp reported that the enemy was within three miles of our pickets and would certainly attack us by sunset. Startled, our little remnant of fighting men looked after their cartridges and rifles. A council of the remaining officers of the 84th and 40th Ohio was called; but could not agree upon any plan for the safety of the camp. The men were at once put to work to fortify a position on the bank of the river, and a courier was also dispatched for the return of the scouts. The fortifications were completed and manned, awaiting the attack…

Upon their arrival in Catlettsburg, the Union troops began searching hotels and other buildings for indoor lodging. About 9:00 p.m., however, Cranor received the message from Guyandotte about the threatened Confederate attack. Sergeant Isaac Little wrote,

> I had just laid down on my blankett by a fire & just got to sleep when I heard the Old Call (Co H fall in) then we all jumped up & started back on quick time. We had to pull of[f] our shoes & stocking & wade big sandy. It was about knee deep & as cold as thunder but we went through safe then we started on quick time for Guyandotte. That is [w]here we took the lead & the 40th Ohio in the rear we put them through. I heard they said they would rebel before they would go so fast again.

Upon his entrance into Guyandotte at 2:00 a.m. on October 25, Colonel Cranor "ordered us across the Guyandotte River to a stronger position and sent our luggage across the Ohio." The Union soldiers put on their accoutrements, crossed the suspension bridge, and "layed on our armes all night" in a large field on the west side of the Guyandotte River. Little wrote:

> When we got here the boys was excited a good deal. They had worked all night digging trenches. When we got here we rested ½ hour & then got in line. The officers said the rebels were coming so we marched over the Wire bridge across Guyandotte creek in to a field & slept on our arms. This morning we marched

back here & eat breakfast & I fell to writing. Soon as I get done I am going to sleep some.[710]

One Federal soldier noted, "The long-looked-for but dreaded morning finally dawned; but no musket shot announced the approach of the enemy. The report was false and the Brigade, weary with watching and heavy labor, returned to quarters to rest." Cranor was "greatly chagrined" to find that he had abandoned his expedition due to a false alarm.[711]

The *Ohio State Journal* reported that the surgeons of the 84th Indiana Infantry moved their hospital stores and sick soldiers across the river into Ohio, adding, "Many of the poor fellows, frightened out of their wits by the terror of the surgeons in charge, plunged into the river and waded to the other side. The whole affair turned out to be nothing more than a slight scare of the officers of the brigade, the heaviest part of which rested on the Surgeons of the 84th Ind."[712]

One of the surgeons of the regiment refuted this claim, writing,

The simple summing up of the whole matter is this: After the return of Col. Cranor at 2 o'clock at night, the surgeons of the 84th Indiana, according to orders, placed the sick (nine men) in the ambulances, and had them taken over the river; the hospital wagon and stores remaining in Guyandotte. As the hospital was situated between the camp and the point of expected attack, this movement was deemed a prudent precaution for the safety of the sick. No surgeons were terror stricken, and no poor sick men plunged into the river and waded to the other side.[713]

Isaac Little observed,

I dont believe we will get in a fight at all for I think Cranor is a little wild about fighting but we may get one yet if the rebels make the attack. Well I believe the war will be over in 3 or 4 months for we heard the Democrats had got the majority. If they have in Congress they will compromise some way. It is the opinion of most of the people here that the war will be over soon.[714]

The alarm resulted in increased vigilance in the town of Guyandotte. More rifle pits were dug, and cavalry pickets remained on duty night and day. Rain and snow fell throughout the day on October 26, but the Union brigade kept on high alert, still expecting an attack. Company B of the 84th Indiana Infantry was sent on a scouting expedition to Barboursville but found no Confederates. Another company marched to Dusenberry's Mill and back, encountering no enemy but capturing a few horses and cattle.[715]

The first frost of the season occurred on the night of October 20, and the first snow followed five days later. On the morning of October 26, Major Samuel Boyd wrote, "This morning puts on the air of dark, dreary, drizzly winter." The troops battled the cold in various ways. Boyd observed, "The men are building what they call brick stores in their tents, which will add largely to their comfort these cool nights."[716]

The soldiers of the Third Brigade settled into the monotonous routine of soldier life. Reveille sounded at 6:00 a.m. and the troops then policed the camp. Breakfast was served at 7:00, surgeon's call was at 8:00 and guard mounting at 9:00. Company drill was held from 9:30 until noon when the soldiers ate their dinner. Battalion drill was conducted from 2:00 until 4:30 followed immediately by supper. Dress parade was held at sunset, tattoo sounded at 8:00 and taps at 8:30 p.m. Lights and campfires were to be extinguished and talking was to cease at taps.[717]

Seven companies of the 40th Ohio Infantry and the 84th Indiana Infantry, along with thirty cavalrymen, departed from Guyandotte on October 31 to open communications with the Federal post in Charleston. The Union troops reached Barboursville later in the day and that evening were quartered in a church and dwelling houses, to the dismay of the village's Confederate supporters: "The ladies there flew into the wildest rage at the presence of the hated 'Yanks' and mingled tears and threats of vengeance; but their entreaties were lost on the officers." The next day, the Union force marched to Hurricane, which the soldiers noted, "bore the marks of war." One wrote,

> The bare chimneys - monuments standing over the ashes of once peaceful and happy homes - and the absence of all able bodied men told the sad story of a town which was one of the first to reap the bitter fruits of war. And this was only a sample of the towns among the Western Virginia hills. The infantry command remained in town under strict orders, while the cavalry scouted towards Charlestown. On the third day the cavalry reported; and on the fourth, the whole force returned to camp.[718]

Back in Guyandotte, another Union soldier described his experience in one of the Methodist churches in Guyandotte:

> I went to church last Sabbath, and listened to the only minister located here at present. The sermon was tolerable, and the closing prayer most decidedly Union in sentiment. But how cold the assembly and surrounding influences. Not more than five or six women were present, and they seemed to be brought out by nothing higher nor holier than a frigid penetrating curiosity. The stiff uniforms of the men, and the sound of the drums in camp, seemed to stand guard against the admittance of a calm and holy aspiration.
>
> High above the door of the best edifice in town is engraved in ominous perspicuity METHODIST CHURCH SOUTH – the *mene mene tekel* of Rebeldom. It has been used for stabling Union horses for more than a year past, and though much of its ancient splendor has departed, yet Christianity has not suffered thereby.[719]

On the evening of November 1, Company K, "which had never been with the

Regiment since it left Richmond" [Indiana], landed at Guyandotte and reunited with their comrades creating "quite a pleasant excitement in camp." The steamer also brought supplies, including oil blankets, which one soldier recorded "would be quite a comfort in stormy weather."[720]

One of the men from the 84th Indiana Infantry informed his wife that he had nothing to eat but half rations of hard bread. The regiment's surgeon, Major Samuel S. Boyd, refuted this claim, stating,

> Now I declare of a verity that there is not a single fact on which to ground a cause of complaint as to the sufficient supplies of wholesome provision in this Regiment since it left home. It is true that if the sick could get more fruit and veg[e]tables they would eat their rations with a better relish. But they do not suffer for want of proper diet.

Boyd suggested that if friends at home in Indiana wished to aid the sick, they could "assist us the cheapest and most certainly, by sending us dried fruits." The regiment had five boxes of hospital stores and medicines broken open and stolen at Portland, Ohio, and the doctor believed, "Anything that can be eaten on the ground or worn for clothing stands but the shadow of a ghost of a chance of reaching us."[721]

Although 860 cases were treated at the regimental hospital in October, the number of sick soldiers in the 84th Indiana was declining in early November. Typhoid fever, however, was becoming prevalent and resulted in the death of Charles Brown, the first member of the regiment to die since they went into the field. Twenty-eight men were confined to the hospital and thirty others were ill but remained in their quarters. The regiment's chaplain traveled to Ohio twice a week to solicit supplies for the residents of the hospital. "Being a Methodist itinerant preacher," Boyd noted, "he is an excellent judge of yellow-limbed chickens, and good things in general for the inner man."[722]

The chaplain delivered his first sermon "since reaching his field of action" in Guyandotte on November 2. An observer noted, "He preached in the Methodist church to a large congregation of blue uniforms, besprinkled with a very few pieces of calico from this almost deserted region. There were not as many civilians present as just men required to save ancient Sodom."[723]

Many of the soldiers, however, spent the Sabbath taking care of more earthly business. "Sunday is letter writing day in camp," observed Dr. Boyd. "I have just taken a walk among the 'boys,' and found them in every conceivable attitude, except standing on their heads; and all seem equally intent on the one object inviting an epistle to the dear ones at home. Tomorrow's mail will carry from the 84th more than one thousand letters, conveying thousands of tender messages to soothe the waiting, anxious minds at home." The soldiers of the regiment had sent out 1,200 letters on a previous Sunday, prompting the postmaster to state that "the 84th cant be beat for writing."[724]

General Jacob D. Cox directed Colonel Jonathan Cranor to "keep some infantry and cavalry at Hurricane Bridge with instructions to scour the country on both Mud and Hurricane Creeks, and over to Winfield, on the Kanawha." A Confederate force was on the Big Sandy River and Cox hoped Cranor would "endeavor to devise some plan by which you may destroy them or drive them beyond the mountains."[725]

Thomas Merritt of Barboursville, who was serving as deputy clerk for Cabell County, wrote to Adjutant General H. J. Samuels on November 6, 1862, seeking government employment but also revealing information about the theft of vital records from the courthouse. Merritt informed Samuels that court was convened on November 3, but "there was little business done as some of Jenkins's men destroyed some of our papers – they cut all of Judge Brown's proceedings out of the record Book and W B Moore & some others took a great many papers from the office not known yet what they were but I suppose they were mostly bonds deeds of trust &c." Merritt observed that the Confederates were "still prowling through the hills stealing horses &c and committing now and then other depredations. Our county here is almost in one perfect waste. A good horse would be as hard to come at as peace..."[726]

The Union brigade was preparing to depart from Guyandotte, but efforts continued to combat sanitation problems in the camp. On November 11, Colonel Nelson Trusler, who commanded the 84th Indiana Infantry, issued orders that all cooking was to be done on the south side of the camp beyond the tents, that each company dig sinks in which to place the offal and water used by the company, and that new sinks be dug each week. The order also required that the straw used in the tents be changed on a weekly basis, and the litter that accumulated was to be buried or burned. At 10:00 a.m., the soldiers of the brigade were mustered and paid for their service through October 31. A case of measles had been discovered on November 3; five days later the number of soldiers confined in the hospital of the 84th Indiana had risen to ten.[727]

*Colonel Nelson Trusler,
84th Indiana Infantry.
Credit: A Biographical History of Eminent and
Self-Made Men of the State of Indiana.*

Civil unrest would increase when the Union troops stationed at Guyandotte were removed from the area. On November 13, John Laidley noted, "A heavy blow is hanging over us yet." No circuit court had been held in September, but a term was scheduled to begin on November 20. Laidley believed the prospect for holding court was "very uncertain," and unless Union soldiers remained in Cabell County, "we dare not attempt to hold a court."[728]

Despite Laidley's warning, the brigade's departure from Cabell County was imminent. Sergeant Isaac Little wrote on November 13, "this evening while out on dress parade there was an order read that we were to be ready to march at 9 oclock in the morning which will be the 14th of Nov. I dont know where we will go." Five boats

Lieutenant Colonel Samuel Orr, 84th Indiana Infantry. Credit: Cathy Callen.

full of soldiers passed Guyandotte during the day, and rumors spread that Colonel Nelson Trusler would take command of the brigade.[729]

That evening the field officers of the 84th Indiana Infantry were serenaded by their men with vocal and instrumental music. Colonel Trusler was absent, but Lieutenant Colonel Samuel Orr, Major Andrew J. Neff, Reverend Silas F. Stout, and Captain William Burres were called on for speeches, and each complied. A correspondent observed, "The length of this letter prevents me from giving the substance of either of their speeches, but suffice it to say that they were frequently cheered while speaking, and at the conclusion of each, three rousing cheers were given for the speaker."[730]

On the following day – Friday, November 14, 1862 – the soldiers of the 40th Ohio Infantry and 84th Indiana Infantry regiments struck their tents and marched out of Guyandotte at 10:00 a.m., reaching the mouth of the Big Sandy River later in the day. Despite the departure of Union troops from Guyandotte, Federal military activity continued in Cabell and Wayne counties. A part of the 13th (West) Virginia Infantry was organized in Barboursville during October 1862, and elements of this regiment would be stationed in the county during most of the next two years. Lieutenant John S. Witcher of Barboursville began forming a cavalry company in Ceredo in December which would later become Company G of the 3rd (West) Virginia Cavalry. This unit included a large number of men from Cabell County. During the next year and a half, they were attached to the 5th and 13th (West) Virginia Infantry regiments.

A Confederate cavalry force commanded by Colonel John Clarkson departed Chapmanville on November 14 for an expedition into Wayne and Cabell counties. Following the Guyandotte River "over a rough and difficult road," Clarkson's men encountered a detachment of Federals on the

Major Andrew J. Neff, 84th Indiana Infantry. Credit: Cathy Callen.

following day and quickly routed them from the field. Continuing the advance until they were within a few miles of the Ohio River, the Confederates broke up a number of Home Guard units in the area, took several prisoners, and drove off sizeable quantities of cattle, horses, and hogs.

They also had an encounter with Union troops in Wayne County. According to Confederate General John B. Floyd, "A strong guard of Yankee troops, acting as a guard for the Peirpoint assessor for the county of Wayne, was attacked and dispersed after a short skirmish, in which were killed and wounded some of the enemy, and we took a few prisoners." Clarkson's force would later clash with Union troops across the river in Kentucky before linking up with Floyd at the mouth of Pigeon Creek in Logan County. The operation resulted in the enlistment of a number of recruits in Cabell, Logan, and Wayne counties.[731]

At about noon on November 15, Cabell County resident George Alford was arrested by Lieutenant William P. Cunningham of the 13th (West) Virginia Infantry while cleaning wheat. Alford was taken to Charleston where he swore he had not voted for the Ordinance of Secession and had never been a Confederate soldier or guerrilla. During Loring's occupation of the Kanawha Valley, Confederates under Captain Peter M. Carpenter arrived to conscript him, but he avoided them, and they did not return. Alford had taken the oath of allegiance in the spring of that year but declared he had no objection to taking it again.[732]

That night, Lieutenant John S. Witcher, with twenty-five members of his company of the 3rd (West) Virginia Cavalry, "composed mostly of recent refugees" from western

Lieutenant William P. Cunningham, 13th West Virginia Infantry. Credit: Richard A. Wolfe.

Virginia, launched their first excursion into Cabell County. According to a newspaper account,

> They were absent about sixteen hours, travelled thirty-six miles, captured three horses, belonging to leading rebels, and the notorious bandit, "Pres. Hodges," who has been committing all sorts of enormities during the last year, and has heretofore contrived to elude the efforts of all the Zouaves, and Capt. Smith included. His house, situated near Howell's Mill, had been repeatedly surrounded and searched without success. Lieut. Witcher's forces arrived about one o'clock, Saturday night, surrounded the house and ordered the inmates to strike a light. A female responded and while she was heard stirring about at one end of the house raising a light, which took a long time, there was

a rattling of boards heard at the other end, by one of the guards. When the light was at length struck, Lieut. Witcher and part of his men entered. Mrs. Hodge received us with apparent kindness and to an enquiry for her husband, replied he was not at home. The Lieutenant, not satisfied, ordered the house to be searched, to which the wife readily consented, and assisted, until, at the Lieutenant's suggestion, a search was made under the bed, and reported that there were short pieces of boards in the floor, apparently loose. At this report the madam's countenance fell, and she left us and sat by the fire. The Lieutenant ordered the boards removed, and at once our good-natured and gallant Charley Shipe, with torch in hand, stretched at full length under the bed, popped his smiling face down the hole, and exclaimed: 'Here he is, with eyes shining like a wildcat.' A thrill of joy and triumph ran through us all, except the wife; she sighed as if all was lost.

Being ordered, the God-for-saken monster slowly emerged from his hole, and from under the bed, where he had eluded for a year past all search, and often heard the tramp of brave but baffled soldiers—to confront in that dim torch light his own neighbors, whose fathers, brothers and friends he had waylaid and shot in cold blood, for no other cause than their steadfast loyalty to the Government; whose property he had plundered and peace and happiness he had maliciously destroyed. He at first assumed to know none of us, and to be cold and defiant. But when Orderly Sergeant Lesage introduced himself as the son of Capt. Lesage (our brave and patriotic citizen whose services we appreciate) whom he had waylaid and lost; and Mr. Hinchman, the son of that aged, worthy and uncompr[o]misingly loyal citizen, whose captivity and suffering he had helped to aggravate, and others sustaining similar relations—his soul and that of his confederate wife sank beneath the weight of conscious guilt. To-day Lieut Witcher handed the monster over to Col. Zeigler at Ceredo, who we trust will deal with him according to his deserts—to be determined by the government's present policy, and not its former, which has crucified loyalty for the entertainment and sport of rebels—by 'swearing copperheads and letting them go.' From our intimate knowledge we hope to be able to do that among our native hills, which our brave country of other States—from a want of that intimate local knowledge, heretofore have failed to accomplish, viz: To out guerrilla and subdue the guerrillas.[733]

Witcher was deemed the right man for the job, as he "knows how to draw rebels from their holes." The young officer had his detractors, however, even within his own company. In a letter to Governor Francis Pierpont "from every man in the company," members of the 3rd (West) Virginia Cavalry criticized his lack of military experience and his failure to actively recruit for the regiment. They also complained that Witcher's quarters were distant from the company and that he was never present for roll call. The cavalrymen expressed their desire to elect their own officers and their choice of James Bazell to be commissioned as their captain.[734]

On November 21, Captain James W. Johnson, who commanded Company A of the 13th West Virginia Infantry, led 22 men on a scout from their camp at Winfield toward Mud Bridge. They returned on November 24. Colonel John Zeigler and the 5th (West) Virginia Infantry occupied Ceredo and were kept busy fighting off the raids of Lieutenant Colonel Vincent Witcher, "whose bands infests Wayne county."[735]

Venerable resident John Laidley wrote from Guyandotte on December 15: "Whatever may be the political prospects of the Union – as far as this county is concerned, it cannot be much worse."

On December 17, 1862, C. H. Mullen, a resident of Cabell County who was imprisoned at the Athenaeum in Wheeling, wrote to Adjutant General H. J. Samuels, refuting the charges against him:

> When I was out a few moments ago before an examining officer he asked me if I was a guerrilla – I told him positivly that I was not but that I was a militiaman. I ment that I belonged to the militia when it was organized but you know & I know that there has been no organization in Cabell since the beginning of this war. The officer said that my charge was bushwhacking, which I believe to be something of his own getting up. I will go before a J. P. and swear that I never was at any time on the hills bushwhacking neither have I ever bin in arms against the Federal Government. The officer persisted in calling me a guerrilla when I am not & I will swear it and prove it besides I want my case attended to and if you have any charges bring them forward also your witnesses against me.[736]

A letter sent from Ashland in Cabell County to Fritz Walker of Kanawha Salines on December 29, 1862, initiated the process of freeing another local citizen from prison. John G. Miller of Barboursville, who had been arrested by Union authorities and sent to Camp Chase, was "in a feeble state of health & frame of mind," and his family was "in great distress." Miller, a native of Germany, was fifty-four years of age, and the correspondent claimed he was unjustly incarcerated due to "envy, malice and spite." He implored Walker to aid Miller, writing, "I could think of no one on whom he could better depend than the playmate of his boyhood when the tie of home country and kin are so nearly blended!"[737]

This passionate missive must have moved Walker, for on January 6, 1863, he wrote a lengthy letter to Major Joseph Darr, the provost marshal in Wheeling, echoing the anonymous correspondent's request. Miller had come to the United States with Walker in 1820 and had lived in Cabell County since that time. He had "soon outworked and outwitted many of his neighbors and as this world is full of envy, many became his secret enemies." Miller eventually supported the Democratic party and was outspoken in his opposition to the Know Nothing party, "which still increased prejudic[e]s against him." He was accused of supplying cattle to the Confederate army during the Jenkins raid of 1862, but Walker believed that this charge alone did not justify Miller's incarceration.[738]

Walker was apparently an old friend of Major Darr and his family and called on him "to use your influence" on Miller's behalf. He noted that Governor Francis Pierpont and others could vouch for his loyalty and that Henry J. Samuels had known Miller since his boyhood. Walker closed by observing, "The most responsible for our troubles which we are surrounded with are least punished. The leaders of the Rebellion should be made responsible. Those that have been mer[e] followers from pre[j]udice or ignorance should not be held so responsible." Walker's letter must have done the trick, as James Wilson posted a bond of $1,000 for John G. Miller on March 31, 1863.[739]

Dozens if not hundreds of men from Cabell and Wayne counties on both sides would be incarcerated during the war. Unlike Miller, many would never return home.

12
The Plough Stands Still

"The loveliness of the day together with other things has caused my mind to fluctuate back to the days of yore, when you and I were handsomely situated in the old County of Cabell surrounded with only friends and all the embellishments of civilized life. But now what a striking contrast. Houses void of inmates. The plough stands still in the fields while thorns and thistles incumber the soil. The workshop is closed. The church going bell has seaced to call the once happy people of this Republick to worship God. And the Church itself, if not consigned to the flames, has become a barracks for the rougheon soldier. May God hasten the day when the Vulture of Carnage shall seace to hover over a civilized land."

George Hackworth, Confederate prisoner at Fort Delaware, April 28, 1863

On Saturday night, January 3, 1863, a small detachment of Confederate cavalry rode into Barboursville and stole the county's tax books from Greenville Harrison, commissioner of revenue for Cabell County. One account recorded,

> Nobody was interrupted and no other papers taken. It seems to us strange that half a dozen men could ride into a place like Barboursville and do such a thing with impunity. The people there must be peaceable or very easily scared...Some alarm existed at Guyandotte when intelligence of the 'raid' reached there. The available force there wasn't under arms. Said available force consisted of a squad of Capt. Baggs men, who were so drunk they didn't care whether it snowed or not. Under these circumstances Guyandotte was thought to be safe unless the half dozen should advance on it.[740]

In response to the most recent courthouse raid, the Cabell County Court met at Barboursville on Monday, January 5. Justices Samuel A. Childers, Roland Bias, John M. Blake, and John Ferguson adopted the following resolution:

> Whereas, the county of Cabell is exposed to the marauding incursions of the rebels; that the authorities have been unable to hold court in Barboursville

without procuring from the United States troops a guard, and as they are advised that the Commissioner of the Revenue, on Saturday last, while engaged in the Clerk's office, a part of the court house, forceably took the books from the officer, and from the fact that protection can be more conveniently had to attend court in Guyandotte, it is ordered to be certified to the Governor to request him to issue his proclamation authorizing the courts of Cabell County to be held in the Town of Guyandotte, until further orders. Signed. S. A. Childers.[741]

"Since then," John Laidley informed Governor Francis Pierpont on January 23,

the Rebells [sic] have remained in the vicinity of the Court-House, broke open the Clerks office, and destroyed a large amount of office papers, the amount of the injury not yet ascertained.

Not having a regular Clerk, we are dependent upon a young man, who transacts as Clerk pro-tem, all the business that is done in this county & also in Wayne County – but he was not to remain at the office.

It is advisable to hold a term of the circuit court on the 27th March next – if you will authorize us to do so in Guyandotte and also to prepare the books & papers. At present, as long as any suits are instituted against a part of these Rebels, or any are indicted, they directly enter the office & destroy the records or papers.

Permit me therefore again to request your assistance, for without that, or some other more efficient proposition, we cannot attend to the public business.[742]

Pierpont authorized the transfer to Guyandotte, and the town would remain the county seat until the end of the war. The county court met in Guyandotte from March 2 until July 1863 and was then replaced by a board of supervisors under the constitution of the new state of West Virginia.

Union citizens of Wayne County met at the courtroom in Ceredo on February 10, 1863, "to give expression to the sentiment of the people" on the subject of the new state. John B. Bowen was selected to chair the meeting and C. B. Webb to serve as secretary. Benjamin D. McGinnis succinctly stated the purpose of the meeting and moved for the appointment of a committee to report resolutions. Bowen nominated McGinnis, Lieutenant Z. D. Ramsdell, Abel Segur, John F. Barbour, and Thomas Adams to the committee, and after a brief conference, they reported the following resolutions:

Resolved, That we believe that the division of the State of Virginia is one of [the] most important measures which our Legislators have acted upon of late years, and that the establishment of a new State as proposed, will contribute to the interest and prosperity of every inhabitant of West Virginia.

Resolved, That we feel it to be our duty to use all our influence and all honorable means from now till the day of voting, to secure as large a vote as possible for the adoption of the Constitution framed by the Convention at Wheeling, and lately amended and approved by Congress now in session.

Resolved, That though there may be an honest difference of opinion as to the time when the new State movement should have been initiated, now is emphatically the time for us to exert every effort to complete the work the Wheeling Convention commenced and continued; and that now, if ever, is the time when we should throw off the yoke and burden which Eastern Virginia has so long imposed upon us, in enormous taxation and unequal representation, in total disregard of our just rights and our claims to a fair proportion of the benefits of the Public Revenue.

Resolved, that our delegate to the Wheeling Convention: W. W. Brumfield, Esq., be respectfully requested to use all his influence and labor to the best of his ability to secure the success of the new Constitution and the organization of the State Government of West Virginia...

J. B. Bowen, Chairman
C. B. Webb, Secretary[743]

Confederate guerrillas struck Union civil officials in Putnam County in early February 1863. Deputy Sheriff Morris was captured and confined by Confederate authorities and James B. Edwards, commissioner of the lower district of Putnam, was seized on February 10. The guerrillas took custody of Edwards's books and papers and threatened to compel him to take the oath of allegiance to the Confederacy, but after refusing, he was set free and permitted him to go home.

At least one of the guerrilla units in the area was headed by Lieutenant William Keaton of Herndon's Battalion of Confederate cavalry. On Sunday night, February 8, 1863, Keaton and his men visited the residence of Calvary Gibson, who lived on Hurricane Creek. When Gibson saw that his house was surrounded, he started to get dressed, but the Confederates fired into the domicile, the bullets nearly striking his wife. They then broke open a window sash and swarmed into Gibson's home. His wife recognized several of the assailants as former neighbors, including Emmerson Chapman, who had been "raised in a manner" by the Gibsons. Calvary Gibson cried out, "for God's sake don't murder me," but Chapman crushed his skull with the butt of a gun, and seven shots were fired into his body, "blowing out every vestige of life, and mutilating the remains in a terrible and sickening manner." Gibson's daughter ran into the room screaming to her mother, "'they've killed Pa, they've shot Pa,' and got in the way of this brute C. S. A. Lieut. Keaton, and he threw her into the fire. The wife and mother sprang to the child exclaiming, 'Don't burn up my child after killing my husband.' Keaton said: 'shut up, you d___d union b___h, or I'll kill you too.'"

According to another account, the Confederates

> shot seven bullet holes through him, bayoneted him several times and to make the crime more hideous, they with the butts of their guns broke his skull in until the hammer of the lock was buried in his brains up to the barrel, all this was being done while he was begging for his life, and to make the crime of a deeper dye, caught the wife of the murdered man, and choked her until she was insensible, and to complete the outrage, they threw a small child of the family, into the fire (there was no charges against this man, only he was a liberty loving and law abiding, Union man.) They passed on, captured the Captain and one of the members of the Home Guard, both said to be murdered afterwards, they also left the country destitute of horses.

In response, Captain John C. Witcher and six cavalrymen left Ceredo at 1:00 p.m. on March 18 and rode twenty-five miles through "drenching rain" to Poore's Hill, where they encamped for the night in a barn without supper and soaked to the bone. A correspondent recorded,

> Next morning we resumed our march and brought up in the Keaton settlement, a distance of 40 miles from camp. Here is the place that a few days ago a company of the 13th Virginia was fired upon from the bushes in retaliation for which a house or two soon disappeared. Here we found that a horseman had lately passed; we followed the trail up a by-path and a short turn in the way bro't us (six in number, not including Lieutenant Witcher) upon a log house, at which were hitched four cavalry horses. A charge was ordered, four men came hastily out, armed and equipped; after a slight resistance and the exchange of a half a dozen shots, they were captured. They seemed well rationed as among the haversacks were found two cooked chickens, two or three suspicious looking black bottles, &c., &c., all of which were duly confiscated, when de Lincum sogers come up. This proved to be a very important capture, as among the squad was the leader of the gang, Lieut. Keaton, a desperado, that has been annoying the citizens of this part of Virginia for twelve months past, and has eluded vigilance, heretofore of the military authorities.

Lieutenant William Keaton and the other prisoners were sent to Wheeling for incarceration on the following day.[744]

An election was held in Cabell County in March 1863. A newspaper account reported:

> The vote cast in Cabell county on the 26th, and by adjournment, the 27th and 28th insts. was, for the 'Amended Constitution' 106, and against it, none. These were civilians mainly. Our county has near 300 citizens in the Union army who has voted elsewhere, and as far as heard from, in favor of the Amended Constitution. The vote would have been much larger if there had been any

assurance of present or future protection.

Lieut. Witcher with his company of cavalry had been at Barboursville during the three days previous to the election, but returned to Ceredo on the morning of the 26th, the day of the election. Maj. Phelps with two companies of the 5th Virginia Infantry came to Guyandotte Wednesday night, but returned to Ceredo in an hour or two afterwards, and Judge Brown, who was to make us a speech on the morning of the election and open his court on Friday – returned to Ceredo with them. The reason assigned for this counter order was an expected attack on Ceredo, or some town on the Sandy river. Lieut. Cummins with 22 of Capt. Bragg's men, they having fortified the town hall in Guyandotte and given protection to our section for the last four months – were our only protectors on that day. A raid was expected, but the polls were opened and 87 votes were cast and the voters mostly returned home on that day. The residue were cast during the adjournments.

About 11 o'clock Friday morning Major Phelps and his two companies returned with Judge Brown, who opened the court and continued till Saturday afternoon when all left, the civil and military. It has since appeared that the rebel bands were on the way and intended to have prevented the election in Cabell, Wayne and other counties. We are thankful they did not succeed altogether, though the alarm diminished the number of voters considerably – We trust West Virginia has become a fixed fact.[745]

On March 27, a public meeting was held at Barboursville during a session of the circuit court. J. H. Prague was called on to chair the gathering, and B. D. McGinnis was appointed secretary. W. H. Tomlinson of Mason County was introduced and "delivered an able and patriotic address." Tomlinson "alluded to the state of the country, and enforced the necessity of selecting men of sound hearts and wise heads to fill the several offices of the new State; none but men of true patriotism and unflinching devotion to the general welfare of the people, would he consent, to hold any office or post of honor in the State." John Laidley was called on and "gave a telling speech upon the subject of appointing efficient officers in the various Departments of State." At the close of his address, Laidley submitted these resolutions, which were unanimously adopted by those in attendance:

Resolved, That Messrs. E. D. Wright and W. H. Copley be appointed delegates, and W. H. Tomlinson of Mason, as alternate, to represent Cabell county in the Convention to be held at Parkersburg, to nominate candidates for offices in the State of West Virginia.

Resolved, That our delegates be instructed to support and vote for the nomination of Judge Jas. H. Brown of Kanawha, for the office of Judge of the Supreme Court of Appeals…[746]

Union Captain John Witcher's company continued to harass Confederates who remained in the area. One member of the unit declared:

> If we are allowed to remain in this portion of West Virginia we guarantee our work speedily and well done, for they (the rebels remaining in the country) cannot dodge us, as we know every bridle path, rock, house and hollow log in Cabell, Wayne and Logan counties. Our list of rebels captured this last winter, is one Captain, three Lieutenants and sixty privates, about forty horses, and a large portion of small arms. What company of sixty-five men can boast as much.[747]

On March 18, 1863, four hundred Confederates of the 8th and 16th Virginia Cavalry regiments under General Albert Jenkins began a raid aimed at Point Pleasant. Jenkins had issued a general order on the previous day from the cavalry camp at Abbs Valley, which read:

> I. Regimental & company officers will march in their proper places near their men & no soldier or officer will leave his place in his company without the permission of the commanding Regimental officer.
>
> II. No species of property along the road whether belonging to Union men or others, will be taken by the troops without special orders.

Howell's Mill. Credit: Special Collections Department, Marshall University.

III. Regimental & company officers will see that their men abstain from burning rails & depredating on property along the road.

IV. The firing of guns along the march or in camp will be immediately punished.

V. Whenever an engagement shall occur with the enemy whether brought on by the enemy making a sudden attack on the march or otherwise, the men are required to join their respective companies with their officers in their proper places; and any act of cowardice or timidity by leaving their proper places in the ranks by skulking or retreating without orders, or refusing to march forward quickly at the command will be punished with death.

VI. The General having selected this portion of his command for arduous & honorable service, places entire confidence in officers & men & feels assured that by their soldierly conduct on all occasions they will show themselves fully to deserve it.[748]

One week later, Jenkins issued another order from Logan Courthouse, stating that it was his intention "to give his men an opportunity to see their homes & families before they return from the border; but the first thing is to strike a blow at the enemy & surely no man will act so dishonorably as to straggle off to his home until the blow is struck.

The covered bridge for which Mud Bridge was named. Thousands of troops were stationed nearby throughout the war. Credit: Family of Bernard Nicholas (courtesy of Todd Godby).

Any man so doing will be treated as a deserter." Jenkins added "his gratification at the patience & fortitude exhibited by officers & men in the tedious march they have made over mountains & water courses, & trusts that a few more days will bring us satisfactory results for all our sufferings."[749]

The Confederate cavalry attacked Hurricane Bridge on March 28 but was unsuccessful in dislodging the defenders. The mounted force then rode to Point Pleasant and skirmished fiercely with Union troops and militia on March 30. After a few hours, Jenkins and his men crossed the Kanawha River and moved quickly into Cabell County.

The Confederates set up camp briefly at Howell's Mill on Mud River where the hungry men wrapped bread dough around sticks which were held near the fire to bake for a quick breakfast. Union soldiers of the 13th (West) Virginia Infantry closed in on Howell's Mill a short time later, and Confederate pickets exchanged gunfire with their advance troops, forcing Jenkins's troopers to leave their meal behind.[750]

This regiment, commanded by Colonel William R. Brown, was part of the Federal force sent from Charleston to intercept Jenkins and his cavalry, but the Confederates "managed to cross the pike at an unguarded point – Poore's Hill, three miles East of Barboursville" and retreated down Fudges Creek. Brown and the remainder of the 13th (West) Virginia arrived half an hour later, but it was dark, and they failed to observe that the Confederates were gone. The Union troops then marched to Howell's Mill. On April 2, Brown reported, "I was at Howells Mill in pursuit of Jenkins. He had crossed and passed out about three oclock this morning, and my men were not in a condition to pursue him. He will probably pass over to the falls of Guyandotte and from thence to the Tug fork of Sandy where his wagons are."[751]

A Confederate correspondent wrote that on reaching the falls of Guyandotte,

> the command divided, and those who reside in the upper end of Wayne county, were allowed to return by way of their homes, under Col. Corns and Ferguson, who will not return, for a few days. The remainder returned, with Gen. Jenkins, keeping to the right of Guyandotte river – the route by which they entered, until they arrived at Gilbert's creek, where they sub-divided, and returned to the Virginia and Tennessee railroad, by as many different routes as possible, the better to procure subsistence...[752]

On the evening of April 3, 1863, about one hundred and forty members of the 2nd (West) Virginia Cavalry under the command of Captain David Dove left Camp Piatt in pursuit of Jenkins's force. After spending a night in Red House, the Federals resumed the march at four the next morning and arrived at about 11:00 a.m. in Chapmanville, where they captured a couple of Confederates. After a brief rest, the Union cavalry continued their expedition, following the Guyandotte River until they arrived at the mouth of Harts Creek, twelve miles from Chapmanville. The Federal soldiers learned that Jenkins had left the Guyandotte and marched toward the Big Sandy River. Dove decided not to pursue, choosing instead to continue up the Guyandotte to the mouth of Big Ugly Creek. The troops dismounted at that point and rested until 2:00 a.m. on

April 5.[753]

When the Union soldiers reached the falls of the Guyandotte, Captain Dove received information that two companies of the 36th Battalion Virginia Cavalry, commanded by Captain Peter M. Carpenter, had encamped nearby the previous night. Upon reaching the campsite, they discovered it empty and saw that the Confederates had marched in the direction of the Mud River. They followed their trail "through one of the wildest sections of country in Western Virginia."[754]

Captain Dove reported,

> About 3 o'clock I struck the Mud River road and traveled up it 1 mile to where the trail again left the road, and crossed the river and ascended a very steep and rough hill, covered by a thick woods. When the advance was about half way down the hill, on the opposite side, it came upon the enemy in a very deep ravine, into which it was almost impossible to force the horses.[755]

Captain David Dove, 2nd (West) Virginia Cavalry, led an attack on Confederates near Mud Bridge on April 5, 1863. Credit: Richard A. Wolfe.

Pickets fired on the advancing Federal cavalry, and the Confederates drew up in a line of battle to receive the Union charge. Captain Dove recorded,

> After a sharp skirmish, we drove them from their position, when a very exciting and hazardous chase ensued, the enemy scattering in every direction. During the engagement the enemy lost 1 man killed and 15 prisoners, 15 horses, and 50 stand of arms, which we destroyed. After resting an hour, I started for Hurricane Bridge...[756]

On April 13, the *Wheeling Intelligencer* noted the arrival of about seventy Confederate prisoners in Wheeling. While most of the men had been captured during the raid on Point Pleasant, some were undoubtedly taken prisoner in Cabell County. According to one description, "They were the dirtiest, scraggiest, most cadaverous looking set of vagabonds that we ever saw. Most of them are men of stout frames but they appear to have been in mud and filth and subsisting upon quarter rations for several weeks..."[757]

During Jenkins's 1863 raid into Cabell County, a squad of Confederate cavalry stopped by the home of Jacob Hinkley and forced him to join them. After a short distance, Hinkley made his escape and remained concealed in the woods until the Confederates had left the area. On October 27, 1863, Hinkley turned himself in to

Captain John Witcher and was sent to Camp Chase, where he arrived on November 15. After being confined for more than two months, Special Commissioner A. M. Galloway recommended that Hinkley be released upon taking the oath of allegiance to the United States and the new state of West Virginia.[758]

On April 11, 1863, Judge James H. Brown informed Governor Francis Pierpont, "I have just returned from Putnam Cir ct having now held the Wayne, Cabell & Putnam courts in the midst of alarms & raids. Regret exceedingly Genl Scammon did not manage to capture Jenkins & his gang."[759]

On April 17, the 5th (West) Virginia Infantry left Ceredo and set up camp in Barboursville. Companies B and C were sent to Mud Bridge and Company G to Guyandotte. Evidence of the illiteracy prevalent in the region was a plea sent by Captain E. R. Merriman for a person to attend to the business of the company "as I have not a man in the Co who can write a sentence correctly I can make no selection from my Company."[760]

Union citizens of Cabell County held a convention at the courthouse in Guyandotte on April 18 for the purpose of nominating a district judge, state senator, circuit clerk, and county officers for the first election held by the new state of West Virginia. Thomas J. Hayslip presided, while T. J. Merritt served as secretary. After B. D. McGinnis explained the object of the convention, those in attendance nominated the following candidates:

For Judge of the 8th Judicial District – Hon. Henry J. Samuels, by acclamation
State Senate – William H. Copley
House of Delegates – J. B. Baumgardner
Prosecuting Attorney – W. H. Tomlinson
Circuit Clerk – Thomas J. Merritt
Sheriff – John Alford
Recorder – Thomas J. Hayslip
Surveyor – James Felix
Commissioner Revenue – Greenville Harrison

Edward A. Smith made a motion that William H. Copley and Sidney Bowden inform Henry J. Samuels and W. H. Tomlinson of their nominations.[761]

On April 21, Z. D. Ramsdell of the 5th (West) Virginia recorded, "Today we discovered that the bridge over Mud River is in a very dangerous condition & send men & timber to cut timber to render it secure." The timbers had been removed by the militia that had gathered at Barboursville in July 1861, and repairs after the battle had provided only a temporary solution.[762]

Thomas Thornburg wrote to Henry J. Samuels from Barboursville on April 22, 1863, informing him, "Our town is full of troops the 5th Virg, all have quartered in the old houses. My family are very unpleasantly situated, a company in the church makes it very disagreeable. I wish they could be put outside town…" He added that "there are a number of southern deserters in Cabell and Wayne who are now afraid of both sides." Thornburg also informed Samuels of the death of "our old and tired friend" John

Laidley, noting that "his loss is irrep[a]rable." Congressman Kellian V. Whaley concurred with Thornburg's assessment of Laidley's death and informed Samuels that it "creates a gap in the loyal talent of this part of the state rather hard to fill, and I think adds very much to your chances of being made judge of this district."[763]

Captain Alfred F. Compston of the 5th (West) Virginia Infantry arrived from Charleston on April 23 with shocking news: Colonel John Zeigler had resigned his command of the regiment. "Deep muttering may be heard," Ramsdell observed, "as the men collect in groups about the corners of the streets." Zeigler had actually submitted his resignation on March 28, writing, "I have the honor to offer the unconditional and immediate resignation of my commission of Col. 5th Regt. Va. Vol. Infty." His offer was approved on April 4 and he was honorably discharged from the service. Documents show that Zeigler had little choice in the matter and was given the opportunity to resign despite being found incompetent by two separate boards of examination.[764]

During one of the examinations, several of Zeigler's orders were introduced as evidence. A special order issued on October 25, 1862, directed that members of his regiment "that have contracted loathsom[e] diseases" were to lose one month's pay and all cases were to be reported to him. Another, written on February 14, 1863, read:

> Commandants of Companies will go to their quarters and make dilligent cerch for a barl of cakes wich was taken from the sutlers by some of the men this evening by some of the solders and my Dear officers, you must hunt it up – it wont do – I must I will hold ech of you accoutable if you dont find it by order of John L. Zeigler.[765]

Anticipating his removal, in late March Zeigler drew up petitions seeking to procure his restoration to command and asked his officers and men to sign them. When Lieutenant Colonel Abia A. Tomlinson and several other officers refused, he called them "d___d traitors" and declared "that if he didn't keep command of the Regiment no body else should." Zeigler then "placed said officers under arrest and stationed sentinels on them, for no other reason than the fact that they had refused to sign his Petition."[766]

Colonel Rutherford B. Hayes, who commanded the First Brigade of the District of Kanawha, believed the case required immediate action. He opposed bringing formal charges against Zeigler but recommended his dismissal and requested that Tomlinson be released from arrest. A day later General E. P. Scammon forwarded the recommendation and noted that he hoped that Zeigler would be promptly dismissed. "He is evidently incompetent," Scammon wrote, "and has been so declared on two examinations. His continuance at the Head of the 5th Regt. insures its worthlessness."[767]

Major General Robert C. Schenck served as president of a board of examiners that met in Wheeling in February 1862 to consider complaints against Zeigler. The board "unanimously reported him incompetent," but according to Schenck, "owing to the sterling patriotism and bravery of the Colonel, Genl Rosecrans decided I believe, not to forward the report of the board to the President."[768]

Major General Robert C. Schenck addressed Zeigler's case on April 13 and revealed the reason he had been allowed to resign:

> Col. Zeigler is not a capable officer and never can become one, but he is a true zealous, loyal, brave man who did good service as a partisan against the rebels at the breaking out of the rebellion in Western Va and ought not to be dishonorably dismissed. For these reasons which are within my own knowledge, although he makes no statement of the cause of his resignation, as by regulation requires to do, I have determined to accept the resignation he offers.[769]

Zeigler's forced resignation angered many in the area who recalled his herculean efforts in the summer of 1861. Ralph Leete of Ironton wrote to Secretary of War Edwin Stanton, a fellow Ohioan, concerning the matter:

> We have learned with much regret that Col John L. Zeigler has been compelled to resign his command of the 5th Va Regiment of Infantry.
>
> We take the liberty to invite your attention to the subject because we in common with the people of this county are interested in the matter. More than half of the men in said Regiment are citizens of this county, which borders upon the counties of Wayne & Cabell of West Virginia.
>
> In the Spring and Summer of 1861 when North Western Virginia was overrun by Rebel Guerillas and the Union leaders had been for the most part been driven from their homes, and in the midst of the most fearful terror, and alarm of the citizens, Col Zeigler was the first man below Parkersburg to raise the Federal Standard on Virginia soil, and to organize military force to check the progress of the rebellion in that section. Our citizens on the north side of the Ohio River gathered about his Standard, and he soon had a full Regiment of true and brave men.
>
> It was this movement of his, which protected the navigation of the Ohio River and at the same time stopped the further volunteering in that part of Virginia for the Rebel army.
>
> The citizens in this part of the State of Ohio regarded the forced resignation of Col. Zeigler as a most flagrant outrage upon a brave and patriotic officer, as well as upon the Regiment, and upon this community.
>
> If protection is any recommendation to a man in these times Col Zeigler has manifested it by every act of his before and since the commencement of the present war.
>
> And further if courage and energy of character are virtuous in a military officer, then it is said, and we believe that Col Zeigler exhibited these qualities through

the long campaign which his Regiment made, and on the battle fields of Cross Keys, Cedar Mountain & Bull Run.

We are satisfied that the interest of the service demands his restoration to the command of his Regiment.[770]

United States Secretary of State Edwin M. Stanton received a letter from a number of citizens of Catlettsburg, Kentucky, on May 12 concerning Zeigler:

We have the honor to represent to you the feelings which pervade the community in regard to matters which have occurred in our neighbouring State of Va.

Being immediately upon the border & feeling that our interests and theirs are indissolubly united & that we have a right to speak when the matters come up in that department vitally interesting us – and hope we will be pardoned for presuming to make a plain unvarnished statement of the facts in regard to the case of Col. John L. Zeigler of the 5th Regt. Va Vol.

The community knows better than this the difficulties which surrounded Col Zeigler, when in the summer of 1861 'solitary and alone he sett the ball in motion' in his part of Va, and which by his indomitable energy and perseverance was crowned with such glorious success in forming & presenting to the Government a regiment, which the history of many a well fought battle bears ample testimony to their courage and endurance, as well as to the skill and prudence of their commander.

We hazzard nothing in saying that no other man in his part of Virginia could have succeeded at the time he under took it, in forming such a Regiment and much less in saying, no other could have led them to glory of renown such as he has.

In view of the foregoing statement of facts our feeling can be better imagined than expressed when we learned that an examining board called by order of Genl Scammon, and before whom Col Zeigler was ordered to appear about their labors by requesting Col Zeigler to resign a position which in our judgement he was so eminently qualified to fill, and which he had long filled not only to the complete satisfaction of a very large majority of the Regiment, but to the lasting honor and renown of the American soldier. We understand that the plea for the request was want of military qualification. To refute and disprove said plea we beg leave to refer you to Major General John C. Fremont and Major General Milroy under both of whom Col Zeigler had the honor to serve.[771]

A number of petitions were sent from members of the 5th (West) Virginia Infantry to the governor-elect of the new state offering their support for Zeigler. Most of them were identical, stating, "We are not satisfied without him and we feel confident in your ability and integrity to comply with our request in giving us back our old Colonel and then we will be contented and happy and as in duty bound will ever pray." One of the petitions read,

> We had and still have full confidence in his courage and in his devotion to the cause which has brought us into the field.
>
> We have served with him nearly two years and he has shared with us the dangers and the glories of our condition. He led us in 1861 from the Northwestern extremity of the State to 'Bull run'. He never evinced danger. He led us through some bloody battles, which thinned our ranks, and in every battle he was at the post of danger [e]ncouraging others. He always dealt with us justly...We much regret his resignation. It is unjust to him and to us and a bad thing for this Regiment. We ask his restoration to command.[772]

John L. Zeigler would not be restored to command.

On April 28, 1863, George W. Hackworth, who was imprisoned at Fort Delaware, wrote to his old friend Henry J. Samuels. Hackworth, a Cabell County resident, commanded Company F of the 1st Regiment Virginia State Line, a cavalry company. He expressed some regret over his decision to support the Confederacy, writing, "Had I considered the dictates of my own conscience, and turned a deaf ear to the facinating voice of fine eations &c. I this day would have been at home with a young wife and a good prospect to wax opulent. But now what better am I than this toad that feeds upon the vapor of a dungeon and dies dispised by all save its own family." Judge James H. Brown had presented Hackworth with the constitution of the new state and some other materials relating to West Virginia, and he had "almost concluded to abandon the Southern Army if I can honorably do so..." In closing, Hackworth noted he was leaving that day for City Point, Virginia, where he was to be exchanged.[773]

Colonel William R. Brown of the 13th (West) Virginia Infantry issued Special Order No. 1 on April 30 directing Lieutenant Colonel James R. Hall to take Companies B, E, and G and proceed to Mud Bridge. A detachment of the 5th (West) Virginia Infantry under Captain R. B. McCall was already stationed there and would report to Hall for duty upon his arrival. Hall was directed to "select a suitable site for a fortification, encamp there and fortify."[774]

Z. D. Ramsdell, quartermaster of the 5th (West) Virginia, wrote on May 2, "Today we commenced to occupy the heights near town. The weather is delightful and a better state of feeling would under our condition here as good as soldiers in time of war are rarely favored with." A week later the regiment was ordered to Charleston where they remained until the end of May. When Ramsdell learned they would return to Barboursville, he recorded, "Good for us!" On May 29, the 5th (West) Virginia left Charleston and marched to Barboursville, arriving at 4:00 p.m. Ramsdell wrote, "by dark all are comfortably located & feeling very much at home."[775]

Congressman Kellian V. Whaley attended Wayne County Court on May 5 and "had the honor of addressing a pretty large crowd of the citizens of that county." Whaley informed H. J. Samuels that he had spoken favorably of him, and he recommended Samuels print tickets to be given to potential voters to aid in his quest for a judgeship.[776]

On the following day, Company E of the 13th (West) Viginia Infantry, commanded by Captain J. D. Carter, was ordered to join the three companies at Mud Bridge, while Captain James W. Johnson was to lead a detachment from Companies A and G to the Mud River and follow it toward Hamlin. Johnson was to "obtain all the information of the enemy you can, and on your return you will destroy all the mill burrs in the grist mills between Hamlin and Mud Bridge." Two days later, Colonel Brown ordered Captain Van D. McDaniel to take part of Company C to Mud Bridge. At that point they were to follow the Mud River to Howell's Mill, where they were instructed to "take the Mill spindles or such other machinery as can easily be replaced back without injury – so as to disable the mill from corn grinding, until ordered by military authority and bring the same to this post."[777]

Captain Z. D. Ramsdell, 5th (West) Virginia Infantry. Ramsdell served as quartermaster of the regiment. Credit: Z. D. Ramsdell House (courtesy of Steven Cody Straley).

In May, General Albert G. Jenkins and his cavalry brigade were separated from his old regiment, the 8th Virginia Cavalry. On May 15, 1863, Jenkins penned an address to the men from Salem, Virginia:

Fellow Soldiers:

I cannot part from my old regiment without expressing to you the deep regret which this separation occasions me.

Unaccustomed usually to giving any demonstration to my feelings, yet I cannot forbear saying to you at this hour of parting, that next to my exile from the home of my childhood, this separation from my earliest comrades in arms, most afflicts me.

We have shared together the exposure, the hardships, and the perils of nearly the entire duration of the war: and though from not being connected with any of the large armies of the Confederacy, we have not been able to participate in the glory of battle-fields which will become of historic fame. Yet we may surely look back upon our career with some degree of pride. We have contested the occupancy of our immense frontier, and have been almost invariably successful in every encounter with the enemy. We have under the greatest difficulties and in the midst of a hostile population circumvented the entire lines of the foe. We have more than once penetrated to the Ohio River, and were the first Confederate soldiers to plant the banner of the South upon the soil of a Northern State.

In leaving you to operate with the rest of my Brigade on a new theatre, I do so with the fervent trust that we shall yet meet again: and I feel assured that under your present officers, and in your present state of efficient organization, you will add new laurels to your fame.

Soldiers – Comrades – Farewell.[778]

A correspondent from the 13th West Virginia wrote from Hurricane Bridge on June 23 and noted that part of the regiment was stationed there, and the other detachment, commanded by Lieutenant Colonel James Hall, occupied Mud Bridge. He added,

We are doing a considerable amount of scouting at present, and are snaking into camp and forwarding to headquarters a goodly number of the Butternut fraternity. A scout went out on Mud river on the 21st inst., in pursuit of some horse-thieves that were said to be prowling about in different sections of the country gathering up horses. Some of this same gang no doubt passed within a short distance of our camp, on the night of the 16th inst., and stole three horses from a Union man, who lives within some six or eight miles of this place, and went with them unmolested. It was this gang and others like them that our scout was sent out after. They succeeded in finding their camp, but the rebs had made good their escape.[779]

On June 20, 1863, the day of West Virginia's creation, First Sergeant Richard Fuller of the 5th West Virginia Infantry led a detachment of thirty soldiers on a scout into Logan County. They returned to camp at Barboursville on June 25, having captured a number of Confederate troops, including a captain and lieutenant, about "fifteen stand" of small arms, and five horses and saddles. A Union correspondent wrote,

Nobody was hurt on our side, and but two rebels, both killed. Besides this, the Sergeant sent into Camp at different times, eighteen prisoners. This is but one of a number of scouts sent out since our return to this place. Not a day passes but more or less prisoners are sent into Camp by our scouts.[780]

On July 4, Z. D. Ramsdell of the 5th West Virginia visited his family in Ceredo and had a picnic dinner. Rain moved events indoors, and Ramsdell went to the hotel to hear C. B. Webb read the Declaration of Independence and make some remarks. Ramsdell received a report on July 13 that "45 Rebels in Fortifications at Mud Bridge last night & that they stole lots of horses in that vicinity." The regiment remained in Barboursville until mid-July, when they were once again ordered to Charleston. The soldiers enjoyed their stay in the village, though "it was quite difficult to live with any degree of comfort in the hot sunshine and multitude of fleas."[781]

On July 25, a group of men from Cabell County wrote to the commandant of the United States prison at Johnson's Island concerning a fellow citizen, Roffe Adkins, confined at that place. They noted that Adkins was "a peaceful quiet citizen at home attending to his business not engaged in neighborhood fights or Bushwhacking" until Confederates occupied western Virginia in September 1862. At that time, he was conscripted into Confederate service and "taken of[f] into Southwestern Virginia." After six months, Adkins returned to Cabell County, where he was arrested by Federal troops and eventually sent to Johnson's Island. The correspondents were satisfied "that he was forced to do what he has done as above represented, and that if permitted to return home, he will be a law abiding man and loyal citizen. We therefore earnestly request his release."[782]

In response to an act passed by the legislature, J. F. Bowdens contacted West Virginia Governor Arthur Boreman on July 25 requesting permission to organize a band of minute men for the defense of Wayne County. Bowdens informed Boreman, "We are frequently annoyed with bands of guerrillas capturing horses & other property to oppose which it is decreed prudent to organize under propper authority."[783]

A number of Cabell County citizens wrote to Boreman concerning his recommendation that independent companies be organized in each county that was "over run with rebels." They declared, "It is generally known that Cabell County is the worst rebel County on the border and Loyal citi[z]ens have suffered the most." John P. Jordan was recommended as the leader for any company that would be formed in the county, even though Jordan, to whom correspondence was to be addressed, lived at Swann Creek in Gallia County, Ohio.[784]

On Sunday, July 26, a "band of some 20 horse thieves" came down Twelve Pole road all the way to the James River and Kanawha Turnpike on the Ohio River before following this road to Guyandotte. The guerrillas made their way up Beech Fork, "where there always has been a notoriously bad neighborhood." In addition to stealing two or three horses each, the Confederates also seized necessaries such as quilts, sheets, shirts, thread, and pins.[785]

John Adams, adjutant of the Wayne County militia, wrote to the adjutant general on August 3 from Ceredo to request commissions as captains for Thomas Adams, Jefferson Gilkerson, and Burwell Stephenson, "who are true & good men & who have taken hold of this work with me, with right good will." Adams was attempting to get the names of all the men in Wayne County between the ages of 18 and 45 for the purpose of putting together militia companies. He wrote, "I want the militia organized thoroughly in this Co. so that Union men can live here better than Rebels!"[786]

Bushwhackers were reported in the area above Barboursville in mid-August. It was unsafe for William Dusenberry to return home, so he stayed at the Bukey House in Guyandotte. At daybreak on August 16, Eveline Bukey rushed upstairs to Dusenberry's room and informed him that the house was surrounded by Confederates. Dusenberry slipped on his pants and crawled under the bed while his wife partially dressed. The Confederates entered the room twice but didn't spot Dusenberry. Mr. McLaughlin, a revenue officer, and Charles Dusenberry were captured but quickly liberated. Union Major Lorenzo Phelps of the 5th West Virginia was seized, and he and his abductors were spotted on the following day near Dusenberry's Mill.

On September 3, the first issue of *The Knapsack*, a paper published by the troops of the 5th (West) Virginia Infantry, contained the following:

From Guyandotte, Va., we have a private letter, stating that the rebels entered the town at two different times. The first time they took Major Phelps and Mr. McLaughlin, the Revenue officer, and the second time, Capt. Turner, whom they made to take off his shoes and walk barefooted. Mr. McLaughlin was released, however, he telling the 'rebs' that if they didn't release him, he would be darned if another morsel of provisions would find its way into the interior of that county. This took, and the rebels released him. Good for you, Mac.[788]

Dusenberry finally ran out of the house and down to the riverbank where he began waving a white handkerchief. He was spotted, and skiffs were sent from the other side of the Ohio which rescued him, along with Hayslip, Baumgardner, and a member of the 9th (West) Virginia Infantry. About ten o'clock the following morning, Dusenberry and Cynthia Ball crossed over to Guyandotte where they learned that it was too dangerous for him to stay, so he returned to Ohio. That evening he crossed back over to Guyandotte. Returning a few days later from a short trip, Dusenberry noted they were destined "for the Rebel hole called Guyandotte in West Virginia."[789]

On the evening of August 23, McLaughlin informed Dusenberry that a letter destined for Richmond written by Maggie Hamilton of Guyandotte had been intercepted. The two men consulted with former county clerk Thomas Merritt, and they decided to cross the river and get Sheriff J. B. Baumgardner to come over and arrest her. When they attempted to carry out their plan, however, "none would have anything to do with it & from information we got we thought it not safe for us to stay in Guyan tonight."[790]

Dusenberry arose early on August 24 and walked down to the riverbank intending to cross over to West Virginia, "but on looking over the River saw Guyan swarming with Rebels. There was over 150 of them under Bill Smith. They took Dave Thornburgs horses with every other b[o]th Union & Rebel they could get hold of. They also got goods from Bowden & Smith." Just before nightfall Colonel John Zeigler rode into Guyandotte with infantry and cavalry, causing a panic among some of the local citizens. Dusenberry recorded, "we saw Bro. Charles & Levi Cook running for life up the bank & called to them. A good many of us crossed over." Two young women, one of them Maggie Hamilton, were arrested.[791]

Zeigler and his troops pursued the Confederates to Barboursville but returned to Guyandotte on the morning of August 25 and soon departed on a steamboat for the Big Sandy region. Given that Zeigler had resigned five months earlier, it is unclear what troops he led and why he was present. Before his departure, Zeigler informed William and Charles Dusenberry that secessionists had again seized items from Barboursville merchant Matthew Thompson and that some of them had been at Dusenberry's Mill. On the following morning William Dusenberry learned that about ten men had been observed at the mill "tearing up everything." His wife and daughter arrived in Guyandotte later in the day and confirmed the bad news. Like many Union supporters in the town, the Dusenberrys crossed the river into Ohio.[792]

John Adams wrote to the adjutant general on August 26 from Ironton:

Since I last wrote I have had an attack of the fever & ague; my family live in Ironton, my interest, land &c is all in Wayne Co. W. V. where I am trying to do all I can, so that I can return & live there safely; but at present, as long as Rebel raiders from the South periodically visit us to arrest, shoot us & steal from us, so long I shall be obliged to be on the alert – I am willing to take my chance with armed Union men any where in the county, & if the Rebel raiders could be kept out, the Union men being organized could take care of the Secession eliment in the county.

If the Vol. Militia of Wayne Co. could be in active service all the time, I think they would soon clear out our Co. & all Cabell. They would willingly go into that service, providing they could be assured of their pay.

If there is any service you or the Gov. wish me to engage in for the State of W. V. particularly in these lower counties I am ready & willing to engage in it. I am anxious to do all I can for the new State & the State of my adoption.[793]

On August 30, Rebels accosted Mose Hatfield, stealing seven dollars from his pocket and taking various items from his home. They attempted to steal his horses but were unsuccessful for reasons unknown. The raiders did take a horse from Lou Hatfield and "plundered" Mrs. Hinchman, Levi Swann, Melville Childers and several other Union families. A group of Cabell County men including Greenville Harrison, Matthew Thompson, and Sheriff J. B. Baumgardner boarded the steamer *Victor* on the following day and departed for Charleston to request that troops be sent to Cabell County.[794]

Over the next week, alarms were raised daily that Confederate troops were in the area. On the first day of September, numerous reports reached Guyandotte of Confederate activity around Dusenberry's Mill. Several men who arrived in Guyandotte on the following afternoon reported they had heard a sizeable cavalry force passing by the falls of the river. On September 3, rumors of a Confederate raid were so convincing "that there was a general skedaddle of all the Union men over the river." Most of the refugees that remained in Guyandotte were pressed into guard duty on a cold but clear evening.[795]

William Dusenberry moved his possessions into a new residence on the following day. About 11 o'clock, "the women came screaming that the Rebels were coming up by Everetts & for us to run to Charles Cooks." Dusenberry fled for the Ohio River "double quick" and prepared to board a ferry boat tied up to the riverbank, but they "found it a false alarm & returned home again."[796]

The "infernal Rebels" did raid Dusenberry's home again on the night of September 6, stealing bacon and a number of items from his store. This occurred despite the presence of Federal troops in the area. Three companies of the 13th West Virginia Infantry had arrived in Barboursville a day earlier, and John Witcher's Union cavalry had conducted a raid up the Guyandotte River and left Barboursville on the morning of September 7 with captured prisoners and horses.[797]

Dusenberry stopped in Barboursville on September 9 and observed that "things looks pretty well used up & everything going to destruction up there..." He later ventured up the Guyandotte River and found "there was several Rebels at the mill, some of them just deserted from the Rebel Army. I felt rather unsafe to stay there all night but concluded to risk it."[798]

Two days later William Dusenberry and his brother Sam climbed the nearby ridge, cut down a paw paw tree, and carried it down to his house where it was shaped into a flagpole. On the following day, Dusenberry leaned out the window of an upstairs room and attached his flag to the pole. He wrote, "the Union men all afraid to help me for fear if the Rebels get in Here again their houses will be riddled & they say they will do mine."[799]

Circuit court opened in Guyandotte at 10:00 a.m. on September 12 with Judge Henry J. Samuels reading a speech to the grand jury. Grand jury and petit juries were called, three cases were tried in the afternoon, and court adjourned at 5:00 p.m., scheduled to meet again on the following Monday. A campaign speech was made by Captain John D. Carter of the 13th West Virginia Infantry in favor of Lieutenant Stephen Comstock, who was running for the congressional seat held by Kellian V. Whaley. No cases were held on September 14, but the grand jury heard testimony concerning Confederate activity in the county. On the following day, Zachariah Harrison was found guilty of horse stealing and sentenced to one year of incarceration.[800]

The commissioned officers of the 13th West Virginia Infantry met at their headquarters in Barboursville in September to pay tribute to one of their fallen comrades. Captain Van D. McDaniel, who headed Company C and was remembered as "one of its most worthy members," died in Point Pleasant on September 13, 1863.[801]

On September 26, Federal soldiers brought a flagpole to William Dusenberry's home on the Guyandotte River to replace his homemade staff. Four days later, having procured a line to tie the flag to the pole, Dusenberry hosted a company of Federal cavalry which watched him raise the standard.[802]

After 11:00 p.m. on October 3, Dusenberry heard gunfire in the streets of Guyandotte. He arose and quickly hid his flag, when he heard another volley "fired this side of the soldiers quarters. I thought shure the Rebels were in." Dusenberry then joined a friend on the upper porch of his home, but "hearing no more of it we returned to our beds." They later learned the gunfire had been "occasioned by a Rally got up to see how the company would turn out."[803]

On October 5, John Adams wrote again to the adjutant general, this time from Ceredo. He informed him that the general muster of the Wayne County militia would take place at Round Bottom, which he noted as being "the most central & safe position in Wayne Co." Adams believed there were enough militia to form ten companies of eighty men or more and noted that a number of Union men from the area had enlisted in Kentucky regiments. He closed by stating, "Any instructions or orders you may send us now will be obeyed. We are very indignant against the Secessionists of this county."[804]

William F. Dusenberry wrote to Colonel William Brown of the 13th West Virginia Infantry on October 16 concerning a prisoner named Perry Green Adkins. "He was the leader of the gang who plundered my house in August last for which he is now indited," Dusenberry wrote. "[H]e is a very dangerous man, and ought not to get loose again." Dusenberry requested that Adkins be turned over to civil authorities.[805]

On October 25, Robert Grey and Philip Wentz, privates in Company A of the 13th West Virginia, slipped past the guards in Guyandotte, crossed the river, and procured whiskey, which they stored in their canteens. Returning to town on the following evening, they were detained by a patrol headed by Lieutenant William Feazel of Company I. The guards found the canteens concealed under the men's clothes, but both men refused to give up their spirits and attempted to return to camp. Feazel followed the men, had them arrested, and took possession of the whiskey. Although Wentz relinquished his stash peacefully, as Feazel sought to take Grey's canteen, "he acted very inpertenantly and striped up his sleeves and spit in his hands to strike me and no doubt would have done so had I not been prepared to resist him." Lieutenant Feazel later learned that Grey "swore that he could whip all of Co. I and that the damd Co could not take his whiskey." Both men were sent under guard to Lieutenant John S. Cunningham, adjutant of the regiment.[806]

Feazel complained that he had experienced a great deal of trouble with men from Company A and respectfully requested that Cunningham inform Captain Greenbury B. Slack that "his men are continually abusing his confidence in them and that it is a serious injury to the service from him to give some of his men passes out of the lines." He added, "This I say for the good of the service and especially our regiment which is of great importance to me and all of us."[807]

P. H. McCullough wrote to Feazel from McCullough's Landing on October 26 and informed him that rumors were afloat that Confederates were around the falls of Guyandotte and on Beech Fork. McCullough believed that "part of their mission might be to carry away with them their comrade (Pine) whom they left with me." "I wish you to consult your superiors today," he informed Feazel,

> & have him taken to the hospital immediately as I am determined not to be held responsible for con[se]quences over which I could have no control were they to make a dash in at night. He can be removed in an easy ambulance is improving rapidly & will recover in a short time with proper treatment. Do what you do

quickly.[808]

McCullough was also concerned that secessionists would learn he had made the report about Pine, writing, "You need not let him know that I dictated this course as I might suffer by them hereafter." In response, Feazel wrote to Colonel William Brown of the 13th West Virginia that "I think it best with your approval for me to arrest Pine immediately and if you will send an ambulance to me I will proceed at once."[809]

In late October 1863, a company of Wayne County militia was ordered into the upper part of Wayne County in search of guerrillas under Captain "Rebel" Bill Smith. As they neared their destination, the Union force was ambushed and several of the men were captured and taken to Smith's camp. Among the prisoners was Joshua M. York, a doctor in Wayne County. York was 55 years of age when he enlisted in the militia at Cassville and had served for nineteen months when he was captured.

Sometime earlier, Union forces had killed one of Smith's men for spying, and he was determined to extract revenge. The prisoners were forced to draw lots, and Joshua M. York was the unlucky loser. On October 28, 1863, Smith ordered twenty of his men to take York aside, and he was shot and killed in cold blood. His commanding officer, Captain Thomas Damron, wrote, "He was a brave and good soldier and would obey all orders received from his officers."[810]

The November 3, 1863, issue of the *Wheeling Register* included an article about two Wayne County citizens who had been held as hostages by Union authorities:

> RELEASED. – Chas. W. and Wm. Ferguson, of Wayne county, who have been confined in the Atheneum for some time, were yesterday released, by order of Gov. Boreman. It appears that in April last a man named Brainard was carried off by the Confederates from Wayne Court House and taken to Richmond. The two Fergusons were arrested and sent here, to be held as hostages for Brainard. Information having been received by the Confederates that the two were held here for the safety of Brainard, he was released. Brainard reached his home some two weeks before the Fergusons did, and as it was feared they had not been released, Morgan Garrett was arrested in May and taken to Richmond, to be held as a hostage for the safe return of the Fergusons. The State authorities here learning that Mr. Garrett had been arrested, again seized the Fergusons, and a few weeks ago they were placed in the Atheneum. Yesterday, however, Garrett arrived from Richmond, and the two hostages were immediately set at liberty. Garrett and the Fergusons have been raised together, and have always been good friends. The happy trio sauntered around the streets in the afternoon, all well satisfied with the result, and all agreeing that it is much more agreeable to enjoy freedom than being cooped up [in] a military prison.
>
> Garrett left Richmond on Tuesday last. He has been confined in Castle Thunder since May. He states that he had plenty to eat and drink, and received the same attentions as the Confederates. There were some fifteen hundred men confined in the Castle, and all seemed to fare as well as he did. There were sutler

stands in the prison, where the men could buy something they wanted. Garrett states that the prisoners are much better cared for in Castle Thunder than in Libby Prison, and advises all his friends who may be so unfortunate as to be taken to Richmond to go to the Castle.[811]

Captain J. D. Carter of the 13th West Virginia Infantry left Barboursville on the morning of November 3, 1863, with detachments of companies C, E, F, and G totaling 105 men. Traveling south, the force arrived in Hamlin on the following evening. Two scouting parties were sent out on November 5, one up the Mud River into Boone County and the other up Middle Fork. They returned having found no armed secessionists. Over the next two days, Carter's men scouted through the lower end of Cabell County and upper part of Boone but did not see any signs of Confederates. Captain Carter noted, "The county in that part has nothing to subsist upon more than for their own necessities. There is no fat cattle, no hogs and no horses." The Union force began their return to Barboursville on November 8 and arrived in the village on the following day.[812]

Morgan Garrett was imprisoned during the war, served in the Union army, and was elected sheriff of Wayne County in 1866. Credit: Evelyn Booth Massie (courtesy of Robert Thompson).

Citizens of Cabell County wrote to West Virginia Governor Arthur Boreman on November 10 regarding one of their neighbors, Isaac Blake. Blake had been confined at Johnson's Island as a prisoner of war for six months. Although his neighbors had "nothing to say in extenuation of his past conduct," they believed he had received "sufficient punishment for past offences." The men, residents of Barboursville, urged that Blake be released and returned to his "helpless family, hoping and believing that he will in future conduct himself in a loyal and peaceful manner."[813]

Another group of citizens from Cabell wrote to the commandant of the federal prison at Johnson's Island on November 18 concerning inmate Aaron Martin, a fellow resident of the county. They described the prisoner as a "moral, steady & industrious young man" and stated he was "tired of this war & wishes to return to his home and friends."[814]

On November 16, 1863, Judge Henry J. Samuels held a term of circuit court at Guyandotte. An Ironton newspaper reported:

> The crowd of suitors, witnesses and jurors is about the same as in former years when they used to assemble at the court house at Barboursville before the rebellion. The youthful appearance of the judge, the clerk, and the members of

the bar is in remarkable contrast with the old officers and members of the bar constituting the Cabell circuit court of former times, and indicates the change made by the civil troubles. The grave and solemn visages of old Judge McComas, John Laidley and John Samuels, are not here. For more than thirty years these three men have formed the central figures of the circuit court.

The old lawyers – Fisher, Summers and Mansfield – are all gone. It will be remembered that Mansfield received a wound in the skirmish at Barboursville in July, 1861, from which he died. Fisher is somewhere in Dixie, and Summers does not come this way.

The court docket is much larger than I expected to find it, and presents a heavy show of business, both civil and criminal. Suitors in rebellion were called and their cases dismissed; the judges remarking at the time that those who were seeking the subversion of the laws and of the authority under which the court was sitting, could not use the authority of his court to aid the cause of the rebellion. Under this rule the action of his brother in the Confederate service was dismissed.

The grand jury returned a large number of presentments and indictments. I think some seventy in all. One man is indicted for refusing to list his property for taxation under the new State government, he still adhering to the seceded State of Virginia. Another is indicted for feeding armed rebels, and sundry others for taking horses and cattle, not their own, for the use of the rebels.[815]

On this same date, the state legislature passed an act requiring a test oath from all public officers:

> That I had never voluntarily borne arms against the United States; that I had voluntarily given no aid or comfort to persons engaged in armed hostilities thereto...that I had not sought, accepted, or attempted to exercise the function of any office whatever, under any authority in any way hostile to the United States...[816]

This act was later extended, requiring teachers, physicians, and all persons who were licensed by the state to take this oath. The Suitors Test Act was also enacted, giving the plaintiff or defendant the right to suggest that the opposing party was a public enemy. If they did not take an oath establishing his or her loyalty, judgment was rendered against them.

On November 18, Judge H. J. Samuels wrote Colonel William Brown of the 13th West Virginia Infantry concerning the poor in Cabell County: "It is come to my knowledge that a number of persons in the county whose male support is in the U S army are in great want and indigence and unable to procure food to sustain life. There are as yet no overseer of the poor or other officer of this county to give the public aid required and you are aware that our people have suffered so much in property that private charity will not meet the exigencies of the time." Samuels requested that Brown "afford aid in the shape of food of such persons as come within the class above named and designate Mr. John Alford sheriff of this county as the civil officer who best can inform you of worthy recipients of government bounty if you can comply with this request."[817]

Captain Milton Stewart of the 13th West Virginia Infantry, who commanded the Federal post at Barboursville, issued Special Order Number 88 on November 29, 1863. This directive instructed Sergeant Robert O. Boggess of Company B to take charge of fifteen troopers from the 3rd West Virginia Cavalry (six from Company A, five from Company B, and four from Company G) and "proceed with them to a point three miles above the falls of Guyandotte river in which vicinity he will thouroughly search the country for a gang of bushwhackers and horse thieves reputed to be consealed there." Boggess was to report to headquarters in Barboursville on Tuesday, December 1.[818]

On that same date, Captain John Jackson Solomon Paul (J.J.S.P.) Carroll of the 9th West Virginia Infantry left Guyandotte and was heading toward his home at Buffalo Shoals in Wayne County when he learned that "Rebel" Bill Smith was at the Falls of Twelve Pole with a large force and had captured Captain William Turner. Carroll rushed back to Guyandotte and informed Lieutenant William E. Feazel, Company I of the 13th West Virginia Infantry, who commanded the Union post at Guyandotte, that Smith's Confederate raiders might attack the town. Feazel immediately informed the regiment's adjutant that "I feel perfectly safe against 300 but I think it would be advisable for you to send a heavy scout toward Buffalo Shoals at once as they may find Smith and clean him out."[819]

On December 2, 1863, a member of the 13th West Virginia wrote to the Point Pleasant *Weekly Register* from Barboursville to report on activities in the area. He noted that the men did their best to obey their commanding officers although a few were "a little self-willed," which led to their incarceration in the guardhouse. The "crimes" were usually drunkenness, profanity, and theft, although the definition of the latter remained unclear. "We don't steal much," wrote the soldier, "and, indeed, I believe that it has never been decided yet, whether the appropriating of such things as chickens, ducks, geese, turkeys, pigs, sheep, and calves, to the benefit of the soldier, will properly come under the head of stealing, and especially if taken from rebels."[820]

The 13th West Virginia Infantry spent a great deal of their time scouting throughout the area and aiding local authorities in the collection of revenue, "a good amount of which has been collected since we have been here. The people think the military must be obeyed and consequently shell out, without much complaining." The correspondent also noted that Confederates were coming into camp almost daily to take the oath of allegiance.[821]

William F. Dusenberry, who was serving as deputy provost marshal, learned that Confederates and their supporters were purchasing salt in large quantities at Barboursville and shipping it up the Guyandotte River. Much of it passed through the open country above the village and on to the Beech Fork area. Dusenberry suggested putting a restriction on the sale of salt that would not allow any individual to purchase more than needed for sixty days, a plan the deputy provost marshal had implemented in Guyandotte. Dusenberry noted wryly, "I think the Rebels will keep as long as I want them without salt."822

On December 10, fifty members of the 3rd West Virginia Cavalry led by Cabell native Captain John S. Witcher returned to their camp at Charleston following a three-day scout through Wayne, Logan, and Boone counties. Witcher's men captured eighteen Confederates and thirty small arms and reported that a considerable enemy force was organizing in Abingdon, Virginia, for the purpose of launching a raid into the Kanawha Valley, an assertion that General Benjamin F. Kelley believed erroneous.823

In December, a Confederate force struck Hurricane Bridge in Putnam County. On December 13, Lieutenant Colonel James M. Comly of the 23rd Ohio Infantry reported that the "information of the approach of the enemy came from Camp Piatt, Gallipolis, and Barboursville simultaneously..." He added,

Colonel William R. Brown, 13th West Virginia Infantry. Credit: Richard A. Wolfe.

> The enemy attacked a small force at Hurricane Bridge Sunday (13th) afternoon. That night our forces escaped, with 2 missing. The enemy left, probably, at about the same time in great haste, going toward Barboursville, taking nothing with them. It is doubtful whether they discovered that our force had left. Our force was only half a company, under Captain Young, of the Eleventh Virginia Infantry. The enemy's force was about 300. The Thirteenth Virginia is at Barboursville, not under my command. They may intercept the enemy's retreat. It cannot be done from here. I have no telegraphic communication with Barboursville. Colonel Brown is in command there. Boats will commence running again to-morrow, accompanied by sufficient guards.824

Dr. Thomas H. Buffington of Guyandotte wrote to Colonel William Brown of the 13th West Virginia on December 16, believing it his duty

> to appeal to you on behalf of a widowed mother for that protection, which I as a private citizen cannot give her against the unlawful encroachments of the soldiery under the command at this point of Lieut. W. E. Feasel to whom application has been made without any success. Knowing that there is an authority, and a willingness in the government to redress the wrongs of her

private citizens, I am now taking the proper steps to obtain redress for one who has exercised forbearance till it has ceased to be a virtue."[825]

Lieutenant Colonel James R. Hall of the 13th West Virginia Infantry led an excursion into Wayne County in late 1863. He would be killed at the battle of Cedar Creek on October 19, 1864. Credit: West Virginia State Archives.

Buffington's mother owned a barn that was being used to store loose tobacco, hay, and corn. A few citizens of the town asked permission to store two wagon loads of loose tobacco in the barn and she refused, stating she did not have enough room. Buffington offered the use of a nearby building he owned, but the men returned later and began loading the tobacco in the barn owned by Buffington's mother. When he protested against their actions, they said a soldier had given them permission. When Buffington asked the soldier "what right he had to forcibly enter and occupy that building He replied that he would show his right, and walked to his gun took it up cocked it and said any interference on my part would result in my death or in other words he threatened to shoot me." Buffington complained to Lieutenant William Feazel but only received "additional insult." He informed Colonel Brown that his mother "has invariably treated soldiers kindly and this is only one of many instances in which she has been treated rudely." Her barn was still occupied "against her consent," and Buffington appealed to Brown for redress and protection. This was the same Thomas Buffington who had been in the 1856 brawl at Quaker Bottom.[826]

Colonel William R. Brown, commander of the post at Barboursville, issued Special Order Number 104 on December 23 granting John Lykins permission to run his mill "for the exclusive use of the neighborhood until further ordered but in no case will it be used to the benefit of disloyal persons unless compelled to do so." Company G of the 34th Ohio Infantry had been stationed at Lykins Mill for three weeks in January 1862.[827]

On December 28, 1863, Mary Eggars wrote to General Eliakim Parker Scammon from Barboursville concerning difficulties she was having with soldiers of the 13th West Virginia Infantry. Eggars, whose husband Joseph served in the 1st West Virginia Cavalry, lived in a large home in the village. Some officers of the 13th West Virginia Infantry had been joined by their wives, and Eggars allowed them to use two rooms in her house and "accommodated them in every way I could." Apparently, that was not enough as "they want to take the rest of my house and turn me out of doors because I wouldant give up to let them have the last room." She was harassed by the soldiers, who threw rocks through her windows after dark, and she claimed that Colonel William Brown "don't pretend to mind it for he is so bizely ingaged in spreering around with the secesh that he lets the rebels come around here and go off unharmed." Mary Eggars asked General Scammon for a bill of protection.[828]

On December 30, Lieutenant Colonel James R. Hall of the 13th West Virginia led a force of 200 Union soldiers on an expedition to determine the location of Confederates that had been reported in the vicinity of Hurricane Bridge. The Federal force left Barboursville and headed into Wayne County, where they discovered the 16th Virginia Cavalry under Colonel Milton J. Ferguson in the neighborhood of Wayne Courthouse. Hall reported, "I found it impossible to force them to fight, as they were well mounted and appeared to be only disposed to interrupt us by harassing our advance and rear guards." He informed Colonel William R. Brown that his men "would have remained out longer but for the want of rations and the sudden change in and inclemency of the weather, which rendered it impossible for the men to march."[829]

13
Depredations of the Most Shameful Character

"The best and most useful men have been forced to leave, or been killed. Our county [Wayne] has not had a fair chance. The citizens did protect themselves as long as they could do so. When the guerillas had killed several, and the U. S. troops were taken from the country, it was overrun by these robbers, and the loyal people are not strong enough. Those who would not be cowed into submission, were forced to leave, in spite of all they could do."

Charles B. Webb, Wayne County, October 12, 1864

Several citizens of Wayne County wrote Colonel William R. Brown of the 13th West Virginia Infantry on January 7, 1864, seeking protection from Confederates in the area. They noted that "last knight our neighborhood was full of rebels" and that two Union men were captured at Amacetta. The Wayne County residents informed Colonel Brown they "would be glad if you would let about 20 or 25 men come out to morrow and stay a few days. It will keep them at bay and it may be that we can ketch some of the rebs." The Wayne County citizens added the enticement that the Federal soldiers would get plenty to eat.[830]

On January 27, 1864, Captain John S. Witcher, who commanded Company G of the 3rd West Virginia Cavalry, was ordered to pursue and capture a small enemy force reported to be in the vicinity of Guyandotte. Witcher led twenty-five troopers to Guyandotte, where they crossed the suspension bridge and traveled on to the mouth of Russell Creek, about one mile from town. There Witcher learned that Confederate Captain Hurston Spurlock, who commanded Company E, 16th Virginia Cavalry, had ridden through with his men, seizing $500 and a number of prisoners. Among those captured by Spurlock were Percival S. Smith, deputy sheriff of Cabell County; John Ferguson, magistrate; Edward D. Wright, revenue commissioner of the county; and four or five veterans of the 5th and 9th West Virginia Infantry regiments. Spurlock's troops headed toward Wayne Courthouse with Witcher and his men in pursuit.

The Confederates split up about two and a half miles from Guyandotte, some

Captain Hurston Spurlock was captured a second time by Federal troops on January 27, 1864. Credit: Special Collections Department, Marshall University.

taking Twelve Pole road and others taking Beech Fork road. Witcher was informed that the largest party had taken Twelve Pole road. Believing his force too small to divide, Captain Witcher and his command followed along Twelve Pole. Many of these Union soldiers had been ambushed earlier by Spurlock and his men at the stone church on this route.[831]

About 10:00 a.m., the Union troops neared the home of Squire Barbour, approximately six miles from Wayne Courthouse. Barbour had been arrested by the Confederates only moments before. Captain Witcher reported, "I found Captain Spurlock here, strongly posted on a hill with thirty men. I immediately charged his position, firing briskly as I advanced, and after a spirited skirmish lasting about half an hour the rebels gave way and fled in all directions through the woods."

The Union cavalry followed, and two of them, recognizing Spurlock, chased after him and five of his troopers. After a pursuit of half a mile, Spurlock was captured at Falling Timber and one of his men was killed. Witcher noted that Captain Spurlock "fought bravely, firing at us at every opportunity. He shot one of my horses five times with his own hand." One of the Union soldiers, however, remarked that Spurlock and his men were "nothing but a thieveing compeny."[832]

The Federals captured five enemy soldiers and killed three of Spurlock's men, and they succeeded in recapturing two members of the 9th West Virginia Infantry and two citizens. They also seized ten Enfield rifles, five revolvers, five blankets, six pairs of "government shoes," and three horses. More than $2,000 in Confederate money was discovered in saddle bags on one of the captured horses. The released Union men informed Witcher that Smith, Wright, and Ferguson had been taken to Wayne Courthouse by the other Confederate detachment, which also retained the money and papers taken from Smith.[833]

Shortly after the fighting concluded, Lieutenant Colonel James Hall and a detachment of the 13th West Virginia Infantry arrived. After consulting with Witcher, Hall decided that their combined force was not sufficient to advance on Wayne Courthouse, so Witcher was ordered to return to Barboursville. On their return trip, the Federals were forced to swim across the Guyandotte River, and one horse drowned during the crossing. The Union cavalry, which had ridden forty miles in twelve hours without stopping to feed either horses or men, reached the village about sunset, undoubtedly exhausted from their busy day.[834]

A newspaper account of the encounter made this observation about Hurston Spurlock:

> This Captain Spurlock is one of the most desperate men in the country brave, determined and uncompromising. He has been an active and daring enemy ever since the outbreak of the rebellion. He has been in most all the fights in this part of the State and without doubt has taken the life of many a loyal soldier. Yea, he had on his head, when arrested, a hat taken from the head of one of our Lieutenants, whom his traitorous hands had taken the life of at Round Bottom, on Big Sandy river, but a short [time] before. He has robbed the loyal citizens of Wayne and adjoining counties of thousands of dollars worth of their property under the false pretense that he had the right to do so because they were disloyal to his rotten confederacy. There is no man in the country against whom the loyal people of this county have so large an account to settle because of his barbarous and inhuman treatment towards them.[835]

The writer added that "it would be a blessing to the country if he were sent to Johnson's Island, and kept in close confinement until his beloved confederacy, in which he seems to have so much confidence, be sunk into utter oblivion." Colonel William R. Brown reported that Witcher "and his brave little band deserve great credit for the gallantry with which they charged upon and scattered this band of bandits."[836]

Lieutenant William Shannon of the Wayne County militia wrote to Congressman Kellian V. Whaley from Guyandotte on February 6, 1864, requesting assistance in procuring payment for the Home Guards under his command. Shannon expressed confidence that Whaley would do his utmost since he was aware of the "servis that was don by them and the condition of the country." If they were not paid, the men "can not stay in the county all of there subsistence is exasted and to a grate degree is left in a helpless condision." Shannon feared that if the loyal citizens were forced from the area, "that will leave the Rebell theaves in posesion of the country and that's what they want..."[837]

On February 11, 1864, Companies B and E of the 13th West Virginia were ordered to Mud Bridge. On February 15, Company G received orders to report to Barboursville. Captain John S. Witcher sent out a scouting party of twenty men of the 3rd West Virginia Cavalry under Second Lieutenant Henry A. Wolfe. On February 20, twelve miles from Hurricane Bridge near the mouth of Coon Creek in present-day Lincoln County, the Union force was ambushed by Confederates under Captain Peter Carpenter. Wolfe and seven horses "were killed at the first fire." The Federal cavalry charged the Confederate position three times but were repulsed. A correspondent from Hurricane Bridge reported that Cabell and Wayne counties "are swarming with rebels" and noted "it will be impossible to dislodge them without a much larger force."[838]

Captain John S. Witcher penned a note to Adjutant General Francis P. Pierpont on February 14 from Hurricane Bridge. He notified Pierpont that Governor Boreman had commanded him to apprehend "certain disloyal citizens" from Wayne County to be used as hostages for State Senator William H. Copley, who had been seized by Confederate guerrillas. The day after receiving this directive, Witcher was ordered to Hurricane Bridge, making it impossible to arrest the secessionists, so he forwarded the order to Colonel William R. Brown.[839]

Colonel George Gallup, 14th Kentucky Infantry, led the attack on the Confederate camp in Wayne County on February 15, 1864. Credit: The Big Sandy Valley: A History of the People and Country from the Earliest Settlement to the Present Time.

Meanwhile, raids launched in Kentucky and West Virginia by members of the 16th Virginia Cavalry caught the attention of Federal authorities, who were determined to put an end to their continual threats to Union supporters. Colonel Brown ordered Lieutenant Colonel James R. Hall "to bear a flag of truce and communication" from Union General Alfred Napoleon A. Duffie to Confederate Colonel Milton J. Ferguson, who was reportedly near Wayne Courthouse. Hall, Captain Albert F. McCown, and an escort of four Federal soldiers departed on February 15. As they neared the Confederate camp, however, Hall learned that a Federal force commanded by Colonel George W. Gallup that was also in search of Ferguson's men was "between me and the rebel camp." Hall feared being mistakenly fired upon in the darkness and stopped for the night.[840]

Gallup had left camp in Louisa, Kentucky, at 8:00 p.m. on February 14 with 275 soldiers from the 14th Kentucky Infantry and 150 troops of the 39th Kentucky Infantry. After marching twenty miles in the cold night air, they reached the mouth of Laurel Creek in Wayne County at seven the next morning. Gallup divided his command, sending Captain John C. Collins and three companies of the 14th Kentucky up Laurel Creek and leading the remainder up the ridge to maneuver around the Confederate camp.

Shortly after proceeding along Laurel Creek, Collins and his men spotted the camp and stormed forward, completely surprising the Confederates. According to Gallup's report, ten of the Rebels were killed (Hall reported five), several others wounded, and forty-one, including Colonel Milton J. Ferguson, were captured. Sixteen Union prisoners were released, but four others were mistakenly killed in the attack.[841]

The Federal force also captured eighty Enfield rifles and carbines, a number of Colt army pistols, camp and garrison equipage, subsistence forage, and ammunition, and recaptured a number of horses that had been stolen from West Virginia citizens. The Kentucky units returned to camp on the following day "without the loss of a man, having marched 30 miles and back in thirty-two hours, over the hills on a bad road, and most of the time no road at all."[842]

Early on the morning of February 16, Hall and his detachment rode up the Left

Fork of Twelve Pole to the mouth of Laurel Creek. At a house about a mile up the stream, they found the body of Captain William G. Pinckard of Illinois, a mortally wounded Union soldier, and a wounded Confederate. An elderly woman and some children were the only occupants of the home, and due to the impossibility of removing Pinckard's body, Hall employed a citizen to bury him. Captain Albert McCown, sent to the scene of the attack, found the bodies of First Lieutenant Oliver W. Griswold of the 13th West Virginia Infantry, who had been captured eight days earlier by the 16th Virginia Cavalry, and Sergeant Thomas McCormick of the 9th West Virginia Infantry. Five dead Confederates were also discovered. McCown hired local citizens to bury the two Union soldiers. Lieutenant Colonel Hall reported that Confederate Major James H. Nounnan "offered every facility in his power to carry out my wishes in regard to the removal of the bodies of Lt. Griswold and Capt. Pinckard, but we could not get transportation in the

1st Lieutenant Oliver W. Griswold, 13th West Virginia Infantry, killed in the attack on the Confederate force in Wayne County on February 15, 1864. Griswold was a prisoner at the time. Credit: West Virginia State Archives.

vicinity." Hall reported that the Confederate camp "was situated between the headwaters of Laurel Creek and Lick Creek, about eighteen miles above Wayne Court-House."[843]

Company G of the 11th West Virginia Infantry moved from Coalsmouth to Barboursville in mid-February. Lieutenant Clark Elkins wrote to Lieutenant Colonel Van C. Bukey on February 19 and noted that the men were anxious to rejoin their regiment.[844]

The grueling task of scouting through Cabell and Wayne counties took a toll on the young Colonel John S. Witcher. Witcher wrote to Congressman Kellian V. Whaley from Hurricane Bridge on February 22 asking if

> you can assist me in any way getting out of the service. I have been as you are aware for the last two years scouting day and night cold and hot untill I have completely destroyed my health. In fact the last scout I have been on I gave completely out and had to stop my command until I would get better or if I could be any service to the Government in any other capacity I doe not want out tho I can not stand the kind of service I have been doeing.[845]

Noting that he had captured more prisoners than any West Virginia regiment, he complained that these accomplishments were overlooked. While other men from Ohio and Maryland were promoted, "it seems that a man from West Virginia stands no chance what ever especialy from Cabell or Wayne counties."

Witcher noted that he had clashed on several occasions during the winter with Confederates commanded by Colonel Milton J. Ferguson and that both Ferguson and a "very determined" Hurston Spurlock had been captured. "They have committed a great many depredations in here this winter," Witcher observed, "and have at this time all of our sivil officers prisners from Cabell and Wayne counties. They seem determined to put down the bogus government as they term it."[846]

In late February, Captain A. F. McCown of Company F of the 13th West Virginia Infantry wrote from headquarters at Barboursville to Lieutenant William W. Harper:

> Dear Sir: Our sutler – Mr. W. Sherwood – has a sword and belt for you, which your friends in this Regiment desire you to accept from them, as a slight token of their appreciation of your faithful services, during your connection with the Regiment.
>
> In being selected as the mouth-piece of your companions in arms, to convey to you these sentiments of their recognition of your fidelity and faithfulness in the discharge of your arduous duties, since your connection with the Regiment, I feel myself peculiarly happy, and desire to add my own congratulations, that your devotion to the cause to which we have devoted our lives, has at last been recognized in the proper quarter, and will undoubtedly meet with a just reward. Be pleased to accept from me and there whom I represent, our best wishes for your happiness and prosperity.[847]

Captain William Bartram and his company of Wayne County scouts skirmished with Confederates on March 11, 1864. Credit: Evelyn Booth Massie (courtesy of Jack L. Dickinson).

Captain William E. Feazel, who commanded the post at Guyandotte, informed Lieutenant John Cunningham that he was sending him two men arrested for desertion and two others arrested by his pickets at 3:00 a.m. on March 1. The latter soldiers belonged to the 5th West Virginia Infantry. They left that regiment to enlist in the 40th Kentucky Mounted Infantry but claimed to be seeking to rejoin the 5th West Virginia at Ceredo. Feazel believed they were Confederate soldiers but had no evidence against them.[848]

A company of Wayne County scouts under Captain William Bartram left Cassville on the evening of March 10 and marched all night scouting through the region. On the following morning, the Union men skirmished with a body of Confederates, capturing four. These men, Solomon Crabtree, Hiram Crabtree, Sr., Hiram Crabtree, Jr. of the 16th Virginia Cavalry and Nathan Frasher of the 8th Virginia Cavalry, were turned over to the provost marshal at Louisa, Kentucky.[849]

Court for the 8th judicial circuit commenced in Cabell County on Saturday, March 12, with Judge Henry Jefferson Samuels presiding in Guyandotte. There being no business to conduct, the court adjourned until March 14. On that date, sixty state cases, fifty-three chancery causes, and seventy-seven common law cases were heard, while a grand jury was in session for two days and issued about thirty indictments, primarily for robbery and selling whiskey without the proper license. Court adjourned on the following Saturday.[850]

On March 16, 1864, Major John J. Hoffman, who commanded the 2nd West Virginia Cavalry, was ordered to lead six companies into Cabell and Wayne counties "to meet and capture or destroy a rebel force under Colonel French, of the rebel army, which is reported in that region." The soldiers were provided with four days' rations and two days' forage. Colonel William Brown was ordered to cooperate with Hoffman.

Major Hoffman left that day with 220 men and marched to the mouth of Coal River, where the Union force camped for the night. He recorded,

Major John J. Hoffman, 2nd West Virginia Cavalry, led a raid into Cabell and Wayne counties March 16-18, 1864. Credit: History of the Second Regiment West Virginia Cavalry Volunteers, During the War of the Rebellion.

> The next day, 17th, I reached Barboursville about 3 p.m., and reported to Colonel Brown, Thirteenth Virginia, who ordered me to cross the river at Guyandotte and camp at the first suitable place, and I camped on the Buffington farm, 3 miles below town. Then I was ordered to proceed to Trout's Hill (Wayne Court-House), and at some point on the route would meet Colonel Brown's command, which was to cross at the falls of Guyandotte.[851]

At 3:00 a.m. on March 18, Hoffman received a message from Brown, who was in pursuit of a Confederate squad which had been spotted in the area. Hoffman and his men continued on and reached Trout's Hill at one o'clock in the afternoon. No Confederate force was found, although there were "a considerable number of the

Eighth and Sixteenth Virginia Cavalry at home on furlough, but so scattered through the hills that it is almost impossible to capture them with a mounted force, but can be effected much easier with small squads of infantry who are acquainted with the country and the residences of the men."[852]

"There is but little forage or subsistence from here to Guyandotte," Hoffman observed, "and from there to Trout Hill there is none that I saw. The roads are in very good condition and we traveled without any difficulty." Hoffman and his men returned to the Buffington farm that evening, ending the brief expedition.[853]

John Adams, one of the staunchest supporters of the Union in Wayne County, was seized by Confederate guerrillas at his home on March 17 and hauled away. Adams, who had been born in Canada in 1818 and had come to Ceredo as part of the Thayer settlement, served as the adjutant of the Wayne County militia and was extremely active in his support of the Union. Soon after, Federal authorities arrested Confederate supporters John N. Smith, William Stewart, and Erbin Walker and sent them to Wheeling, where they were confined in the Athenaeum as hostages in an effort to procure Adams's release. Four months later, however, the body of John Adams was found twelve miles from his home "perforated with twelve bullets." When this information was relayed to Governor Arthur Boreman, the secessionists were released from prison on July 28.[854]

Company F of the 13th West Virginia Infantry was ordered to Guyandotte on March 21 to relieve Company I, which moved to Barboursville. Cabell County Sheriff John Alford arrived in Point Pleasant on Friday, March 26, with six prisoners – five men and one woman – charged with robbery. A *Weekly Register* correspondent wrote, "We understand these parties are suspected guilty of much of the thieving so prevalent both in Cabell and Wayne counties, during the winter. These with all other prisoners from those counties, are sent to our jail for a greater security."[855]

General Order Number 2, issued from Federal headquarters in Charleston on February 16, apparently called for the appropriation of horses from residents of Cabell County. On March 26, 1864, Colonel William R. Brown, commanding at Barboursville, appointed Captains Williams, Harpold, and Feazel to a board of apprisers. This body, which was ordered to convene immediately, was to fix the value of each horse, provide a description of the animal, and the names of their owners.[856]

On March 27, Circuit Judge James H. Brown held court in Cabell County. The clerk recorded the continuing damage to county records:

> It appearing to the Court that so much of the Chancery order book of this Court that contained the March Term 1862 proceedings & also the proceedings of the Nov. term 1862 have been destroyed and lost It is thereupon ordered that the clerk of this court do reenter all the orders and decrees and other proceedings of said terms in the Chancery Order Book of this court. As far as we may the means by any writing to ascertain the matter that was in said Book and for which services the Clerk of this Court shall be allowed the sum of _ Dollars which is ordered to be certified to the County Court of Cabell County for Payment.[857]

On April 9, 1864, General George Crook ordered a horse returned from the regimental quartermaster of the 13th West Virginia at Barboursville to a Mrs. Black, who claimed the animal had been taken from her by Captain Milton Stewart. A few days later, an explanation was received. Apparently, the horse had been purchased by Mrs. Black from a Confederate soldier named Barker, who had used the horse in military service. Barker had been taken prisoner in May 1863 and sent to Camp Chase, and the horse, which had been seized with Barker, was not found for some time and was apparently in the possession of Captain Stewart.[858]

Captain Milton Stewart, 13th West Virginia Infantry. Credit: Richard A. Wolfe.

On this same date, Stewart and Private Isaiah McCoy traveled to regimental headquarters at Barboursville. About three miles from Mud Bridge, they were fired on by a band of bushwhackers led by Jim Mitchell of Point Pleasant concealed behind an embankment constructed for the C & O Railroad. McCoy was hit by a ball that entered the small of his back below the kidneys and exited through his groin. Captain Milton Stewart was thrown against a tree by his frightened horse, which then stomped on his chest, "rendering him insensible." One of the guerrillas insisted on shooting Stewart, but Mitchell refused. After robbing the soldiers of their horses, saddles, bridles, and revolvers, the guerrillas fled. The firing alerted the men in camp, and some of them rushed to the scene "in time to find the rebels gone, and the men badly injured." Captain James L. Botsford, assistant adjutant general for the Department of West Virginia, who had been sent from Charleston to intercept guerrillas in Logan County and happened to be in the area, led a squad in pursuit of the bushwhackers but was unsuccessful in capturing them.[859]

A meeting of the "ladies of Amacetta, Wayne county" was held on March 1, 1864, with Addie Barbour chosen as president and Ellen Hollenback secretary. The women resolved that it was their duty to present an American flag to Company G of the 3rd West Virginia Cavalry "for their unprecedented valor in defending the Government that has exalted woman to a rank in society above that of her sex, in any other portion of the world." Fannie Hollenback, Amanda Newman, Lucy Barbour, Ezzie Ray, Eliza Newman, and Evaline Ray were appointed to "a committee to make suitable inscriptions for a flag, and to procure, and present the same at the earliest convenience."[860]

The work was completed within two months, and the flag presentation was held on April 18 in Guyandotte. A large crowd "turned out en masse" to witness the pomp and circumstance.

The ceremonies were handsomely conducted by a delegation, or as some would have it, by alternates composed of six of the ladies of this place, so arranged and attired as to represent the three colors that adorn the 'Goddess of Liberty.' The delegation formed in line abreast. Miss Sack Cox, and Miss Luella Hayslip, occupied the center dressed in white; Miss Fannie Hite and Miss Amanda Smith, on the left, dressed in blue; and Miss Susie Dusenberry and Lizzie Ward, on the right dressed in red. Miss Sack Cox, bore the flag gracefully floating above the head dress of Miss Luella Hayslip, who was to deliver the presentation address. Just in the rear an elegant band of fifers and drummers from the 'Old 13th' Va. Inft. were playing the air of the 'White Cockade' completed the procession.

The company to be honored by the presentation, accompanied by companies F and G, of the 13th Va. V. I., had previously paraded just above and adjoining the town upon a nice lawn that bordered upon the Ohio River, stretching far back to the hills and just beginning to green. Here they awaited the arrival of the procession bearing the flag.

Capt. Witcher's command had formed in line occupying the center, Co. F, of the 13th Va., under command of Capt. McCown, occupied the left, and Co. G, of the 13th Va., commanded by Captain Mason occupied the right. The entire procession marched up and completed the hollow square; those bearing the flag, advancing in line abreast to the center and stood facing the Company that was to receive the honors of the day...[861]

The women halted, and the two dressed in white advanced a few steps forward leaving the remaining four in position. Sack Cox held the flag above Luella Hayslip, who addressed the soldiers "in a clear and distinct tone:"

Officers and Soldiers of Company G, 3d West Va. Cavalry: To us is confided the honor of presenting to you, in behalf of the ladies of Amacetta, the Flag of the American Union – the symbol of your nationality. To you is reserved the more arduous duty of upholding and defending it against its foes, who would wily tarnish its luster, and even wrest from you your bright escutcheon. The responsibilities entrusted to us, are this day, by this act, completed – those to you are still pending, and require no less bravery and patriotism on your part, than that which, in the hour of your country's peril, inspired you to deeds of noble daring – to forsake home, the loveliest society of kindred and friends, and bare your bosoms in the cause of freedom. Before you is martialed a formidable foe, whose purpose is to overthrow your constituted authorities and destroy that which is most dear to you – the institutions of liberty – to bring into her sacred temple the offering of tyranny with which to invoke the despotism of the world – to cast from her altars the incense of learning, of art, of social and religious refinement, and in its stead, to offer the sacrifice of human oppression.

But reflect and take courage – you are a part and parcel of the most illustrious army that graces the annals of time; whose brilliant achievements have won the respect and homage of the world that with the sympathies of the friends of freedom throughout civilization you are destined under a just and all-wise Providence to reinstate the identity of this Nation and to perpetuate the principles of her free institutions.

In presenting to you, this flag, we also extend to you, the warmest sympathies of those we represent, Fathers, 'for the support of which' in the face of the world, with a firm reliance on the protection of Divine Providence, they pledged their lives, their fortunes and their sacred honor – leaving an example your valor has proven you worthy to emulate.

To these ceremonies attaches that nationality – that love for one's country – which through the various revolutions and mutations, to which human progress is subjected, has in an eminent degree, characterized woman, and given her a position in society no less useful, no less honorable, than that which distinguishes the Statesman or the General...[862]

At the conclusion of Hayslip's address, Witcher, attended by two of his command, advanced to receive the flag, and addressed the women:

Ladies – It is with feelings of mingled pride and pleasure, that we, this day, receive at your hands the glorious Banner of our loved land of Liberty. To be presented with the Starry Emblem of our country by the loyal ladies of Wayne county, under existing circumstances, surrounded as they are, and even have been, since the commencement of this unholy rebellion, by merciless cut throats and marauders, is without a parrallel in the history of the war. It is true, that the presentation of Flags, Swords, &c., to a Regement or Company of Soldiers, is almost an every day occurrence, in some portions of the Government but as a general thing, the participants were safe from insult, violence or abuse, far inside the Federal lines...

When it became necessary to remove the Federal troops from among you, to operate in other portions of the country, and your section left exposed, and overrun by large bodies of rebel troops, and at all times infested by regular organized bands of robbers and thieves, under all these circumstances you have invariably maintained your loyal position, and at no time backward in expressing your sentiments in the presence of either friend or foe..."

We receive this Banner putting our trust in God and our revolvers, that we may never dishonor it, but jealously guard it, and with faith in our glorious cause of the Union, never leave it, until emblems of alike character shall wave over every town and village in the United States; and may we ever continue to deserve the approbations and applause of loyal friends.

Ladies in the name of Company G, I return you our sincere thanks.

According to a reporter for the Point Pleasant *Weekly Register*,

At the close of these ceremonies Capt. Witcher's company bearing their new Flag, marched in front of the hotel and awaited the return of the procession of ladies and band of fifers and drummers, when Lieut. Lesage proposed three cheers for the ladies of Amacetta, which was responded to in a manner that told more than words – after which the crowd dispersed. Those who attended the ceremony 'expressed themselves highly entertained.'[864]

On April 26, William Dusenberry prepared to board a steamer and discovered John Alford with a prisoner, Jesse Dodson, a Cabell County resident who fought for the Border Rangers. Dodson was burdened with a ball and chain, which he remonstrated with Alford to remove, to no avail. The men returned to Guyandotte and Dusenberry took Dodson to his home. About eight o'clock that evening, Alford sent him to the guard house on the suspension bridge. Dusenberry tracked down attorney James Ferguson, who visited Dodson in his temporary quarters. At noon on the following day guards brought Dodson to Dusenberry's home, where Ferguson gave him an examining trial. Dusenberry's front room was packed with complainants and interested parties. Edward Wright and his son gave testimony that Dodson had come to their home with armed men and seized a horse. Dodson was ordered to jail until court could be held. Three other prisoners were brought to Dusenberry's and fed before being turned over to Alford, Ferguson, and Captain William Feazel, who transported them to Point Pleasant.[865]

Lieutenant George Holderby, a member of the Border Rangers, was captured in Barboursville on April 28 by Union troops. Holderby was found in the home of one of his relatives by Lieutenant William Shannon of the 13th West Virginia Infantry, who had been ordered to search the residence by Colonel William R. Brown. Holderby attempted to hide by lying "crosswise at the head of a bed" but was discovered and arrested.[866]

Holderby was taken to Guyandotte and confined in the county jail on April 30. His mother, Susan Holderby, and sister, Susan Holderby Jenkins, who was married to a brother of General Albert Jenkins, arrived there on Sunday evening, May 1. As soon as the ladies entered the town, they were stopped by the commanding officer of the post, who seized Mrs. Holderby's trunk. Two Guyandotte women who were present, Miss Hite and Miss White, protested vociferously until they were finally arrested for insulting the soldiers and detained for several hours in the guardhouse.[867]

An election was held on April 28, and at Guyandotte, William Dusenberry, Silas Clark, and Isaiah Ray served as commissioners of election, a Mr. Horner and Jim Wright, clerks, and Fatty Baumgardner, crier. The polls remained open until sunset. Dusenberry was on the ballot for county school superintendent and justice of the peace and carried the precinct. He was in his office until after nine o'clock, then played euchre with James Ferguson, Henry J. Samuels, and Horner.[868]

April 28 was also the date that Captain Benjamin Haley's company of Wayne County independent scouts was organized. They were sworn into service by Abel Segur, reportedly the only justice of the peace in the county "that will attend to execute his office." Their term of service was twelve months.[869]

Dr. William Paine wrote authorities on May 5 in an effort to collect payment for himself and his daughter for providing aid and care to a wounded soldier during the previous year. One of Captain William Feazel's men was wounded in October 1863, and the officers of the company requested that Paine care for him, promising full compensation. That night the wounded soldier was taken to the home of Mrs. Russell, Dr. Paine's daughter, who expected that he would be removed the next day. On the following morning, the officers searched for a suitable place to move the soldier but were unsuccessful, so they met with Mrs. Russell and requested that she permit the wounded man to remain in her home. Despite the fact that her residence was very small, she agreed to keep him. Twice daily Mrs. Russell cleaned and dressed the soldier's wound, and since his rations were unsuitable for his condition, she purchased food and fed him.

Paine had given his bill to Feazel, who forwarded it for payment, but nothing had been received in return. Mrs. Russell had not been paid for her services and expenses, and Paine requested that she be compensated, stating, "I think she deserves it and I know she needs it."[870]

Several Union citizens wrote to Governor Arthur Boreman concerning John Hensley of Cabell County, a prisoner of war at Camp Chase. J. B. Baumgardner of Guyandotte wrote that Hensley should not have been incarcerated. "He is considered a dishonest and very mean Man," Baumgardner noted, "and I am of the opinion that private animosity sent him there." Hensley and his family, with the exception of one son, supported the Confederacy.

According to Baumgardner, Hensley's wife had recently attempted to convince Colonel William R. Brown to allow her son, a member of the regiment, to go home with her and return that same night. She failed, but her son did not appear at evening roll call. When a squad of Union soldiers went to the Hensley home, "they learned that several armed Rebels was at the house when the mother and son got home, who took him off with them. It may of been planned, or the Rebels may of just happened there, as the whole Country here is full of them outside of our Pickets. I make this statement, and leave the matter of John Hensley's release to your own judgment."[871]

Baumgardner's letter was apparently not enough to convince Boreman. Edward D. Wright informed the governor on January 17, 1865, that Hensley's family was "in a destitute condition, their [sic] being no male in the family to provide for their wants." Wright was uncertain why Hensley had been arrested and declared, "I think he has been sufficiently punished & think it best to release him." His Union neighbors shared this belief unless charges were preferred against Hensley.[872]

Flags were presented to companies F and G of the 13th West Virginia Infantry on May 9 in Guyandotte. The regiment's band showed up at noon and several of the officers arrived three hours later. The event took place in front of Thomas Hayslip's house, and the only Union women who attended were Luella Hayslip and Fannie Hite. The companies were formed before Hayslip and Hite presented the flag, and the former delivered a short address. Captains McCown and Mason made brief speeches in response. That evening, the paymaster arrived, "which made lively time in camp." A dance held that night in Guyandotte was attended by a large number of troops and finally broke up about midnight, about the same time the paymaster completed his duty.[873]

Cabell County Clerk Thomas Merritt, who died on May 15, 1864. Credit: Special Collections Department, Marshall University.

The Cabell County Circuit Court met on Monday, May 16 to pass resolutions honoring recently deceased County Clerk Thomas J. Merritt. Merritt had died at 5:00 a.m. on the previous day, and the church bell "tolled quite awhile..." Officers of the court and members of the bar requested that the Court enter resolutions in the order book "as a testimonial of their appreciation of the deceased as a man, an officer and a patriot." Merritt was described as "a reliable and afficient officer and one who possesed all the qualities for the proper discharge for duties of his office to a degree rarely found in one of his age and experience."[874]

One of the resolutions praised him "for the manly and patriotick alacrity with which he responded to the wishes of the people to serve them as a publick officer at a time of extreme peral to all officials under the loyal Goverment of Virginia." Eulogies were delivered by Judge Henry J. Samuels, William McComas, Charles Moore, Laban Moore, and others, and as a "further testimonial of respect," court was immediately adjourned until nine o'clock the following morning.[875]

Later in the week, numerous charges were filed in circuit court by the State of West Virginia, primarily for grand larceny and burglary. Two individuals were indicted for robbery, two for murder, and eleven for other felony charges. Among those indicted were noted Confederates Vincent Witcher and Hurston Spurlock.[876]

On May 16, Jerome Shelton was convicted on two counts of burglary and sentenced to fifteen years in prison. His wife Malinda was arrested for reasons unknown and confined at the home of William Dusenberry. On May 25, Mrs. Shelton gave testimony against Runnels Allen. The jury later brought in a verdict of guilty and sentenced Allen to ten years in prison. On the following day, William Dusenberry recorded that

"Mrs. Shelton was released & in the afternoon she swore out a peace warrant against Runnels Allen for some threats he had been making against her." The case was brought by Peter Holryde, and Dusenberry made Allen "give bond for $250 for his good behavior toward her." Jerome Shelton "was brought here to see his wife awhile & then he with the two Allens convicted they left of the Steamer Dumont for Point Pleasant jail. Mrs. Shelton took it very hard at parting with him..."

Just after daylight on May 30, the *Bostonia* arrived in Guyandotte. Dusenberry, Malinda Shelton, and several others boarded the boat, which was destined for Wheeling, and they arrived at Gallipolis about noon. While the *Bostonia* was unloading supplies there, the Cabell Countians went to the home of a Mr. Fitzgerald, who consented to allow Malinda Shelton to see her husband. She was taken to the jail and had a lengthy visit with him.

About seven that evening, the *Bostonia* arrived and the passengers went aboard, including the prisoners, while Malinda Shelton remained at Fitzgerald's. Adkins and the Allens were handcuffed, while a ball and chain was attached to Shelton. A few of the men, including Dusenberry, laid down on the deck about 10:00 p.m. while the rest stood watch.

One hour later the sleeping men were aroused by Alford's cries that Shelton had escaped. Alford had taken Shelton to the water closet when he suddenly jumped overboard, "Ball, chain & all." The boat was immediately halted and reversed, but the men could not find the escaped prisoner. Dusenberry observed, "He is either at the bottom of the river or had loosened the chain, dropped the ball & then swam to the shore, night very dark. Boat soon went on again, did not lay down any more." Dusenberry later found the rivet head that Shelton had cut off his shackles. Despite his dramatic escape, Shelton would be captured a short time later in Nashville, Tennessee.

Yet another flag presentation was held on the morning of May 23 in conjunction with the departure of the 13th West Virginia Infantry from Cabell County. Companies of the regiment were stationed at Guyandotte, Barboursville, and Mud Bridge. Colonel William Brown had received orders three weeks earlier "to hold himself in readiness to march upon a minutes notice," but he was still surprised when he was commanded on May 22 to move his regiment to Meadow Bluff in Greenbrier County.

One observer described the activities in Guyandotte:

The incident[s] attending the presentation were peculiarly grand and imposing. The 141st Reg. O. N. G., had arrived the previous evening to take the place of the noble 13th, which during all the night preceding had been pouring into the town preparatory to embarking on the steamers then lying at the wharf to convey them up the Kanawha to join General Crook. It was now early in the morning, just after daylight, and such a bright, clear morning as scarcely exhilarates any other section. The sun was just looming up to wake a sleeping world, the beating of drums, the clash of steel, and the rushing of trains, told the hurry and bustle of the hour, while the steamers lying at the wharf kept up a kind of commotion that gave a magnificence such as seldoms [sic] greets the eye.[877]

William Dusenberry, who had gone to bed about midnight, apparently heard the commotion. He arose and went to military headquarters where he learned that the 13th West Virginia was preparing to depart from Guyandotte at daylight. He rushed home and awakened his family at 2:00 a.m. and told Amanda Smith to begin hurried preparations for the flag presentation to Company I. The group "was surprised when they saw the Flag at its beauty. They did not expect such a fine one." Breakfast was prepared just before daylight, and a number of officers from the 13th West Virginia joined the Dusenberry family for the meal and a gift exchange.[878]

About seven o'clock that morning, Company I of the 13th West Virginia formed on the street "leading up Guyan." Eight to ten "charming belles, of which this village is proverbial, all dressed in white," started from William Dusenberry's home. A correspondent wrote,

> Silence now everywhere reigned until broken by the patriotic air of the band that accompanied the procession which moved down the river bank towards the wharf, where lay the boats with the most of the 13th Reg. already on board, near which the gallant Company I, met the procession and formed into line to receive the flag. Lieut. Hovey introduced the ladies as the chosen representatives of Union ladies of Guyandotte.[879]

Amanda Smith stepped forward and addressed Company I, informing them that "we have been moved to procure and present to you this furth gift; and, although, there is nothing extraordinary to the material of which it is composed, or the workmanship thereof, it is, nevertheless, the proud symbol of our country, now waving victoriously over every battle field..." Smith added,

> Soldiers, we only ask that it shall be received in the spirit and sentiment with which it has been gotten up, and is now presented, and that whenever you shall behold it, in whatever extremity of danger, you shall remember the sentiments of the donors. You have seen too much service to allow of exhortation from us. If we believed it possible that this noble flag could fall into dishonor in your hands, we should not commit it to your care...[880]

Following her speech, Susie Dusenberry presented the beautiful silk flag, which read "Presented by the Ladies of Guyandotte W. Va., to Co. I, 13th Reg. West Va. Volunteer Infantry," to Private Lewis Rader. Captain William Feazel offered a few remarks of thanks for the flag, assuring the women his company "would gallantly defend it until victory should crown our homes with peace." Following a brief address by Benjamin D. McGinnis, the soldiers of Company I "gave three times three cheers for the ladies of Guyandotte," and then boarded the steamboats.[881]

A short time later, the regiment began ascending the Ohio River in the steamers *Mattie Roberts* and *Le Clare* "amid cheers & Tears boath." Despite the early hour of the day, the townspeople had gathered "en mass and lined the river bank to take, I fear, to many a last farewell." The 13th West Virginia Infantry had spent months in Cabell

County and many of the soldiers had formed lasting friendships with its residents and "will live long in the memories of the people of this vicinity." William Dusenberry recorded, "a great deal of sorrow seamed to prevail all around at the 13t leaving & everything seemed gloomy all day." Dusenberry did observe that the two companies of the 141st Ohio National Guard "appear to be first rate quiet gentlemanly fellows."[882]

The 141st Regiment Ohio Volunteer Infantry was organized for one hundred days' service at Gallipolis, Ohio, from May 11-14, 1864. The regiment was composed of the 36th Battalion from Athens County; the 16th Battalion from Gallia County; a part of the 84th Battalion from Adams County; and a part of the 20th Battalion from Scioto County; all were part of the Ohio National Guard. On May 21, they were ordered to the Kanawha Valley to relieve the 13th West Virginia Infantry. Part of the 141st was sent to Cabell County a day later.[883]

Colonel Anderson D. Jaynes, who commanded the National Guard unit, established his headquarters at Barboursville. On May 25, Jaynes issued General Order Number 2, which read:

Colonel A. D. Jaynes, who commanded the 141st Ohio National Guard in Cabell County during the summer of 1864. Credit: History of Pettis County, Missouri.

> For the good and comfort of the command now located at this place, as well as to assure the Citizens of this Town and vicinity, that we come here not to tear down and destroy, but to promote and build up the Public interest, it will be necessary that the following rules be observed.
>
> The Soldiers composing this command will not be permitted to molest or destroy any person or property, or make use of profane or abusive language, but are required to obey strictly the orders of their respective officers.
>
> While we propose this, we shall expect the same rules to be observed by the Citizens of this community.
>
> The sale of spirituous liquors, except for medical purposes, will not be permitted within our lines, nor the sale of ammunition.
>
> All persons are forbidden to go out through our lines without a pass from these Head-Quarters.
>
> A strict observance of these rules will insure the good and comfort of this

community as well as of this command.[884]

Companies D and F of the 141st Ohio National Guard were stationed at Mud Bridge "in something of a fortified position on the Mud river." Private Andrew Wiseman of Company F wrote to the editor of the *Gallipolis Journal* on June 1, describing the men as "buoyant in spirits beyond what could reasonably be expected under the circumstances..." He confidently stated, "We have reason to believe there is just as good fighting material here as ever raised a rifle to the soldier." Wiseman described the tense situation in the countryside of Cabell County:

> There are some secesh prowling through the country some miles away and we have slept on our arms three nights since here. A squad of our cavalry went up the river some distance a few days since and brought back one of their number dead and two wounded by the bushwhackers who are hated even by sympathisers here.[885]

On the evening of May 29, word reached Guyandotte that a fight had occurred at Hurricane Bridge. One of the militia companies was ordered to Barboursville and several prominent Union citizens, including Judge Henry J. Samuels, crossed the river to Ohio. William Dusenberry spent most of the night waiting for the packet steamer *Bostonia No. 2*.

Captain Benjamin Haley, who commanded a company of independent scouts in Wayne County, wrote to West Virginia Governor Arthur Boreman on June 1 from their camp in Ceredo. Two Confederates had been captured and sent to the Federal post at Catlettsburg, Kentucky, while two secessionists were seized as hostages. Haley noted, "we are very much trobled with strong bands of gurillas which prevents our scouting very far in the county notwithstaning we have scouted considerable & lost no man." He described his men as "brave & hardy."[886]

On June 4, three members of Company D of the 141st Ohio National Guard took a four-horse team just outside the picket post at Mud Bridge to pick up a load of wood. Contrary to orders, the Union soldiers went without a guard and were themselves unarmed. After loading the wood into the wagon, they climbed aboard to return to camp when suddenly three armed guerrillas appeared and ordered them out. The rebels released the horses from the wagon and forced the Federals to accompany them a short distance before quickly riding away.[887]

Two days later Lieutenant Colonel Taylor W. Hampton and Adjutant Joseph M. Goodspeed started to Barboursville with a four-mule team. When the two stopped at a spring to obtain water, Goodspeed's horse kicked Hampton, fracturing his leg below the knee. Private Andrew Wiseman wrote, "I saw him a few moments after the accident and though he must have been suffering much, he bore it patiently and talked cheerfully while being conveyed to Barboursville."[888]

That evening a thunderstorm blew through the region, and lightning "struck Mud Bridge, where our pickets were stationed, shocking them severely but not dangerously." Captain Amos Mauck was now in command of this post, and Wiseman wrote, "We have plenty of ammunition, and are ready to give the rebs a warm reception, should any be so foolish as to come for us."[889]

A member of the 141st Ohio National Guard posted in Barboursville wrote to the *Highland Weekly News* in Hillsboro, Ohio, on June 6 describing affairs in Cabell County. He related that the men were armed with new Enfield rifles and were "splendidly equipped throughout." Company K was at Hurricane Bridge, two companies were stationed at Coalsmouth, two at Mud Bridge, two at Guyandotte, and four companies at Barboursville.

> This is the county seat of Cabell co. and relatively the post of greatest importance on the line. There was a sharp fight within fifteen miles south a few days ago, resulting in the loss of one man killed and four wounded on our side. We live in hourly prospect of an attack from the rebs, of whom we learn there are considerable bodies that infest the hilly region southward, made up mainly of skulkers from Lee's army, and who gain a precious livelihood by stealing, &c.

> The capture of our wagon-trains, or depots of supply, would be a god-send to these half-starved renegadoes, and they may attempt something of the kind at any moment. One of our Cos. goes out scouting at intervals, and several prisoners and some contraband property have been captured and brought into camp. Three rebel cavalrymen delivered themselves up yesterday, and will be forwarded to Camp Chase. They wish to swear allegiance and receive the benefits of the amnesty. They are only 12 days from Lee's army and they state were formerly attached to the "Stonewall Brigade."

> Yesterday being Sabbath, religious services were well attended. A Sunday School has been organized, in which I have the honor to be a teacher. A number of children and females of the village attend it, and also the ministrations of our Chaplain, who preaches in the Court House. This building and many others in this place are occupied by the military as Headquarters, Company quarters and store-houses. Although there is a large and aristocratic Secession element about here, yet our occupation is submitted to gracefully, as nothing but armed forces prevents the Union men, who are poor, from wreaking their pent-up vengeance upon the heads of their proud, rebellious neighbors.[890]

On June 8, Jaynes wrote to Major John Witcher of the 3rd West Virginia Cavalry, whose troops occupied Hurricane Bridge. It had been difficult for Jaynes to communicate with Witcher since the only horses in his camp were utilized to supply his command with daily subsistence. Colonel William Brown, whose regiment had just departed from Cabell County, had warned him it was unsafe to travel alone in Cabell County, and his infantry had been engaged in other endeavors.

Reports arrived frequently at headquarters in Barboursville that 300 to 400 Confederate troops were in the vicinity. That morning, Jaynes was informed that three or four companies under Lieutenant Colonel Vincent Witcher were assembling near

Beech Fork in preparation for an attack. Union citizens told Jaynes that the Confederates planned to raid Guyandotte in hopes of luring some of Jaynes's troops there, while the main body would strike Barboursville. Jaynes wrote, "I do not put much confidence in any of these reports, and yet, being in a neighborhood where the enemy has been troublesome, I deem it proper to keep a very close and rigid watch."[891]

Jaynes added, "I think it important that we have an understanding as to a plan of operation, and that we thoroughly scout these neighborhoods reported to be full of these murderers, who lurk around in the bushes seeking the lives of our men." He requested that Witcher call at his headquarters in Barboursville as soon as possible.[892]

Jaynes wrote to Witcher again two days later and told him that the Union men living along Twelve Pole and Beech Fork "are flocking in our lines very numerously, giving horrid accounts of the conduct of these murderers under John Chapman..." He had prepared a circular to be distributed to the leading secessionists of the area and wanted Witcher's "counsel and suggestion."[893]

Colonel Jaynes proposed to co-operate with Witcher "in some plan that will make an unhealthy state of things for these devils that seek the destruction of our men." He planned to notify secessionists who gave aid to the enemy that they would be held responsible to Union men "for all these depredations, in five times the amount by tax, and the destruction of all the property within five miles of our front when any of our commands may be bushwhacked." Jaynes hoped to meet with Witcher "as soon as may be practicable."[894]

Two civilians from Gallipolis bearing donations for Company F of the 141st Ohio National Guard boarded the steamer *Clairmont* at 9:00 a.m. on June 17. They reached Guyandotte about two o'clock that afternoon and encamped with several friends serving in the Ohio unit. On the following morning they accompanied Captain Amos Ripley and a wagon team loaded with the donations under an escort of six guards on the trip to Barboursville, which they reached about 11:00 a.m. on June 18.

They departed that afternoon for Mud Bridge and arrived just in time for dinner. One of the civilians wrote, "you may guess we were welcome visitors." When the Ohio soldiers saw the pies, cakes, butter, canned fruit, baked chickens, and other goodies, "sow belly and hard tack had to stand back." The two men remained at the Union camp until 6:30 on the evening of June 20 when they began their return to Gallipolis.[895]

Four members of the 141st Ohio National Guard volunteered to accompany the men to Barboursville. They procured an old ambulance wagon, climbed aboard, and headed down the turnpike. About three miles from the village, one of the civilians spied three "fiends of hell" atop the railroad cut about twenty yards above the road and then noted an additional group of armed men a little farther ahead. Anticipating an ambush, he yelled a warning, but a volley from above quickly followed and "leaden hail" rained down on the ambulance.

Private Anthony W. Kerns was hit, the ball passing through his cartridge box strap and entering about an inch and a half into his back. Despite the pain, Kerns discharged his Enfield and then his revolver at the guerrillas. When he attempted to fire again, his weapon temporarily jammed. As he struggled to free the cap, the moving ambulance caused the weapon to discharge a ball into the calf of his leg.

Joseph Smeltzer, who was sitting across from Kerns at the rear of the wagon, was hit three times in the initial volley, one bullet striking him in the breast, one in the right shoulder, and another in the right thigh. The coats of both civilians were pierced in several places, but the other two Ohio soldiers "did not get a scratch." The ambulance itself was hit by more than twenty bullets from the revolvers of the attackers.

One of the civilians wrote, "It is a mystery to me that they did not kill us all; the driver was as cool and calm as could be in a case of that kind; he had an old leather persuader and the moment we discovered the villains he applied it to uncle's horses as though he was determined to take us out of that critical position and he did so." The men reached Barboursville about 10:00 a.m., and the surgeon of the 141st Ohio National Guard dressed the wounds of Kerns and Smeltzer. The two civilians, accompanied by the wounded soldiers, left Barboursville later that day and reached Gallipolis on June 23.[896]

The response by Colonel Jaynes was harsh:

I am investigating the matter with the citizens along this line to-day. I have ordered every man between this and Mud Bridge, for a space of five miles north and south of the pike, to report immediately at Barboursville. All the people who live along this line, I am informed, have taken the oath and claim protection under it, claiming that they are not secesh. To men who have taken the oath, unless charges could be made and sustained, I do not feel authorized to apply General Hunter's order. I intend applying it wherever I can find a man that is a proper subject. I think I will apply it on two men to-day, unless I am or become satisfied that some reports which have been circulated about them in regard to this affair are entirely unfounded. I am going to so shape affairs that the citizens along this road shall be responsible to me for such conduct, and make them watch this road and give me information. I shall bind them in such a shape as will enable me to find out where the leading secesh are, and then deliberately destroy their property. I would not hesitate, but it is an important and serious matter, and should not be done hastily, or in the wrong place. If I knew the country and people I could apply it to much better advantage. I would rather spare two secesh than burn up one Union man's property, but a thorough overhauling will take place. I intend to know the people and be better prepared to judge the guilty party.[897]

Due to "the neglect or seeming unwillingness of the men and Officers of this command to comply with certain rules and regulations heretofore made," Jaynes issued General Order Number 8 on June 20. This directive forbade troops serving as guards for ambulances or supply trains from riding in them unless they were ill. Teamsters and ambulance drivers were to report any violations of the order, which was undoubtedly in response to the attack earlier that day near Barboursville.[898]

Special Order Number 53, issued on June 23, addressed transgressions by Privates Condee and Haning. These two soldiers had taken a "'French Furlough', as soldiers are pleased to call it, and absented themselves three days and nights from their company without leave." The general order spelled out their punishment as follows:

> They shall be put in confinement, under guard, three days and nights; drilled with their company during company drill; one hour each day drilled by a Corporal, by themselves in presence of the whole command; the balance of the day put at policing, thereby occupying the entire day; marched in front of dress-parade each day, confined in the Guard house during the night by themselves; and shall not be permitted to do any honorable duty during the time of their confinement.[899]

A group of loyal citizens from Cabell County wrote to the secretary of war on June 24 concerning William G. Egnor. Egnor, a resident of Cabell, had volunteered for service in the State Line during General Loring's 1862 occupation of the Kanawha Valley after being threatened with conscription. He remained in service until the State Line was disbanded in the spring of 1863. Egnor returned home and remained unmolested for more than a year before being captured and sent to Camp Chase. His fellow Cabell Countians requested that "you release the said W. G. Egnor and have him sent home to his family."[900]

The 7th West Virginia Cavalry was stationed in the Kanawha Valley from mid-1864 until the regiment was mustered out in August 1865. Initially the 8th (West) Virginia Infantry, the unit's designation was changed to the 7th West Virginia Cavalry on January 26, 1864. A few companies sent to Cabell County in late June to prevent Confederate incursions were stationed at Guyandotte, Barboursville, and Mud Bridge. At the latter post, soldiers guarded the covered bridge twenty-four hours a day. The Union Baptist Church was occupied as a garrison, and members of the 7th West Virginia Cavalry camped on the church grounds.[901]

George Bay, Ohio merchant shot during a robbery attempt. His brother Billy drove off the thieves. The two men would become prominent steamboat operators after the war. Credit: Special Collections Department, Marshall University.

On July 1, 1864, Cabell County commissioners met at the office of B. D. McGinnis to lay off the county into townships. The men adopted the old magisterial districts and created the five townships of Barboursville, Carroll, Guyandotte, McComas, and Union.[902]

At about 2:00 a.m. on Sunday morning, July 17, eight "desperate guerrillas" of the 34th Battalion Virginia Cavalry, commanded by Captain John L. (Jack) Keller, made an ill-fated raid into Ohio. One of the Confederates swam across the Ohio River near Guyandotte and stole a skiff belonging to L. D. Russell, docked at the mouth of Indian Guyan Creek. He rowed it to the West Virginia shore to pick up his comrades, and the party then crossed the river into Ohio.

The intent of the raiders was to rob Russell's store, which was located near where the skiff had been appropriated. Instead, they mistakenly knocked at the door of another establishment owned by George W. Bay and asked the proprietor for some cigars. As Bay opened the door to admit the men, they stormed into the building and began seizing merchandise. Bay reached for his revolver, but the Confederates began firing, striking him several times in the chest and slightly wounding his sister Sarah in the shin. Suddenly Billy Bay, George's brother, appeared at the top of the stairs with a shotgun and discharged the weapon half a dozen times. Three of the Confederates were wounded, including Captain Keller. Mill. J. Stephens was hit twice and "only went a few steps before falling." The rest of the party quickly departed from the premises and rushed toward the Ohio River. The first of the Confederates to reach the skiff pushed off without waiting for their comrades, who reportedly shot at them in an effort to convince them to return to shore.[903]

The remainder finally confiscated a "joeboat" on which they placed Captain Keller and another wounded Confederate soldier by the name of Smith. They pushed off, "some of them swimming, and calling lustily for help; and it is thought two of them were drowned." Smith was well enough to travel with his fellow cavalrymen, but Keller was left at the home of a Confederate sympathizer.[904]

Captain William Reilly, 141st Ohio National Guard. Credit: History of Scioto County, Ohio.

Captain William W. Reilly of the 141st Ohio National Guard had Keller and Stephens brought to headquarters in Guyandotte. Soon after, Keller's wife arrived and accompanied the wounded prisoners in the ambulance to Barboursville. William Dusenberry wrote, "the Doctors think they will boath die." The attempted raid caused a great deal of excitement in Guyandotte. Across the river in Ohio, a newspaper correspondent observed, "You can trace the rebs' course from the store to the river, by the blood."[905]

Just before noon on the following day, William Dusenberry and others opened the polls for an election at which he was selected as county school superintendent. Both Dusenberry and Underwood were chosen as magistrates and Holryde and Sheppard constables. Fifty-three votes were cast, and the polls closed at sunset.[906]

On July 21, Robert Holderby and

another Confederate took Mr. Baumgardner's horses and the harness from his wagon on the road just below Mrs. Shelton's and then crossed the river. William Dusenberry recorded, "Billy Baumgardner was driving & Horner was with him. They took Horner as far as Mrs. Sheltons with them."[907]

Reports of Confederates in Wayne County spread through the area on July 23. Soon after William Dusenberry retired for the night he "heard an awful yelling & thought the Rebs were making a charge in here." He dressed and quickly ascertained that the home of Mr. Cook was on fire; soldiers soon extinguished the flames.[908]

A group of Union citizens met in Guyandotte on July 28 to appoint delegates to the United States Convention, which was to take place in Grafton on August 3. B. D. McGinnis chaired the meeting and William Dusenberry was appointed secretary. The following men were selected: James H. Ferguson, Thomas J. Hayslip, William F. Dusenberry, Greenville Harrison, Thomas Thornburg, Samuel Johnston, James H. Poage, Isaiah Ray, John M. Blake, Julius Freutel, Rowland Bias, James T. Carroll, James McComas, David Harshbarger, Sidney Bowden, James H. Wright, Peter Holdrye, William L. Rodgers, and Hiram Curry. A motion that Kellian V. Whaley "be requested to become a candidate for re-election" passed, and another motion added "the President's name" to the list of delegates.[909]

On August 9, 1864, at a meeting of the Cabell County Board of Supervisors, the members pronounced:

> It appearing to the Board that the Court House of this county is in the possession of the military authorities and not in a suitable condition to enable the Board to hold their meeting therein; IT IS ORDERED That the meetings of this Board be held in the office of the recorder of Cabell County in the town of Guyandotte until otherwise ordered.[910]

Just before nightfall on August 11, some of the women in Guyandotte "got up a scare that the Rebels were coming into town." Judge H. J. Samuels and B. D. McGinnis rushed down the grade to the river, climbed aboard a store boat, and pushed out into the Ohio. William Dusenberry and Mr. Russell waded into the river and got into the boat, and the men floated slowly offshore. After a time, hearing no firing in Guyandotte, they landed the boat at the mouth of the Guyandotte and learned that the excitement was caused by the dust from a horse and buggy. That night, however, Confederate raiders did rob Cox's store boat above Guyandotte.[911]

Captain William E. Feazel wrote to Captain Julius Lesage, who commanded an independent company of State Guards from Cabell County, on August 21 from Camp White in Charleston. Feazel led Company I of the 13th West Virginia but was detached from his unit and placed in command of the provost guards in Charleston. At Lesage's request, Feazel had spoken with Major William P. Rucker, who headed the Home Guard, and was directed to provide Lesage with arms. Rucker also "says he can furnish you any number of men to fill your company at once."[912]

Rucker directed Lesage to bring his fifteen men to Camp White; there he could add the men needed to fill his company and supply them with "everything that is neccessary for fiting purposes." Feazel informed Lesage he would furnish rations and quarters for his men until the organization of his company was completed. "Dont fail to be in haste," Feazel wrote in conclusion, "for now is the time to clean out our new state establish law and order and start things to work right."[913]

A day later, Major Rucker again contacted Lesage. He had apparently written to him a week earlier and was "surprised at not hearing from you." Rucker informed Lesage that if he wanted arms and ammunition for his men, "you must come immediately to Charleston and bring your men with you." Rucker planned to lead a scouting expedition of about two hundred troops and wished for Lesage to join him.[914]

On August 25, William Dusenberry learned that the 141st Ohio National Guard had received their marching orders. On the following day, steamers arrived, and the regiment boarded to return to their homes in Ohio; "they were all the forenoon getting away." Dusenberry wrote, "not many very sorry they are gone but we do not like to be left without any protection here." He "fixed up his clothes" and just before nightfall crossed the river into Ohio. A number of other prominent Union men, including Henry J. Samuels, did the same.[915]

Dusenberry observed Union cavalry coming into Guyandotte on August 29. "I put the mare in Harmon's pasture," he wrote, "& came over home brought my flag with me & raised it." The troopers were from Company L of the 7th West Virginia Cavalry, commanded by Captain Isaac M. Rucker.[916]

Captain Benjamin Haley wrote Governor Arthur Boreman on August 30 from Ceredo and reported that ten of his Independent Scouts were sick "owing to exposure in scouting and lying out in the night time." Things had been quiet in the area for more than a month, but

> we now have Bill Smith and his gang in our midst which gives us much trouble and fatigue looking out for him also have Jim Smith the arch trator and a small gang to look after which is a great annoiance attended with considerable troubble and danger so upon the whole we have our hands full and in deed we may consider ourselves fourtuneate if we are able to compete successfully with them.[917]

Nine "disloyal citizens" had been arrested and two others were being tried at Catlettsburg, Kentucky. Haley closed by writing, "It is an expressed opinion that if this little company should be removed the the [sic] gurillas would be robing steam boats between Catlettsburg & Guyandott and it is threatened strongly as it is."[918]

On the morning of September 12, court was convened in Guyandotte, but Judge H. J. Samuels believed an attack by Confederates was imminent and discharged the jurors. Two days later, another meeting of Cabell County Union citizens was held in Guyandotte with Thomas J. Hayslip serving as chairman and William F. Dusenberry as secretary. A resolution was passed unanimously endorsing the nomination of Abraham Lincoln for president and Andrew Johnson as vice-president. The following men were nominated for local offices: Edward D. Wright, senator; James H. Ferguson, delegate; B. D. McGinnis, prosecuting attorney; Thomas J. Hayslip, recorder; Percival S. Smith, treasurer; James Felix, surveyor; and Greenville Harrison, assessor.[919]

In the early morning hours of September 15, 1864, "Rebel" Bill Smith and his guerrilla unit raided Ceredo, surprising the small detachment of State Guards which occupied the community "and sacked the place generally." Captain Benjamin Haley commanded seven men and called in nine citizens in anticipation of an attack. Haley and his men "were all gobbled up" by Smith, who took possession of seventeen weapons and accoutrements. He and his men also robbed the post office and seized all horses in the neighborhood before departing with their prisoners toward Wayne Court House. The *Wheeling Intelligencer* noted,

> The loyal citizens have been greatly annoyed for the want of necessary protection, ever since March or April last, the county being overrun by guerrillas, committing depredations of the most shameful character, such as murdering citizens, robbing houses of bed clothing and their valuables, and taking money from citizens. It would be a great relief to the loyal citizens of Wayne county if the military authorities could possibly spare soldiers sufficient to protect said county from the bands of guerrillas that are continually infesting the county, and driving the loyal citizens away from their homes.[920]

Another Union meeting was held in Guyandotte at noon on Monday, September 19. A "grand Lincoln and Johnson flag" was raised by soldiers and citizens of the town. A correspondent noted, "The first flag of the kind on the Ohio – a great change for three years, when the snake flag was raised at the same place." According to an observer, "There was only one person expressed himself for McClellan, and he was drunk on very bad whisky." James H. Ferguson and J. M. Phelps, a candidate for Congress, made speeches at the event, which, occurring on a court day, drew a large crowd.[921]

On September 30, 1864, about one hundred Confederates commanded by Major James H. Nounnan attacked the Federal post at Coalsmouth. After being repulsed, Nounnan fell back to Hurricane and was nearly captured but made his escape. On the following day, a squad from Captain Edgar B. Blundon's company of the 7th West Virginia Cavalry rode from Guyandotte toward Kanawha County, capturing about a dozen soldiers from Nounnan's detachment.[922]

The Cabell County Board of Supervisors met in Guyandotte on October 3 and ordered a levy of $1,500 to support families of soldiers who were county residents at the time of their enlistment. The soldiers stationed in Guyandotte were treated to political speeches from Benjamin McGinnis, Captain Edgar Blundon, and an attorney named Tomlinson from Point Pleasant on October 6. On the following day, votes for state officers were cast by the two companies of cavalry in Guyandotte, with Whaley receiving 110 votes for a congressional seat and Phelps receiving 11. That evening news reached town that a group of Confederates was at Sam Johnston's home. Eleven suspicious-looking armed men appeared claiming to be members of the 45th Kentucky Infantry attempting to escape from Bill Smith and Nounnan. Captain Edgar Blundon sent a detachment of the 7th West Virginia Cavalry to investigate.[923]

Congressman Kellian V. Whaley arrived in Guyandotte on the morning of October

9. A few days later Whaley met with William Dusenberry and convinced him to send a dispatch to Washington in an effort to stop the draft in Wayne County.[924]

C. B. Webb wrote from Catlettsburg, Kentucky, on October 12, expressing regret that his project to raise a company for home protection in Wayne County had failed. He detailed the two primary obstacles to completing the work:

> First. The soldiers who have returned from the army, have assurances from the Guerilla Bill Smith, that they will be permitted to stay at home if they swear not to take arms against them or the Southern Confederacy: or if they will vote for McClellan! These are men who live away from the river, three, eight and ten miles. Other soldiers, who have not been taken by the guerillas, and have had no communication with them, feel as though this is sufficient security for them, and do not wish to go into a military organization, because if they do, they do not know what will be their fate. Citizens who have been captured and released report that the rebels are particularly bitter against all who are in any way connected with the State Gov't of W. Va., militarily or other wise.
>
> The discharged soldiers will adopt the easiest and least risky policy; and that is to make no demonstration and not manifest themselves in any way. They feel that they will not be disturbed if they thus remain quiet.
>
> Another difficulty is that the citizens have been very much an[n]oyed by the company lately under Capt. Benj. Haley. It appears, from all that I can gather from the citizens, that though, a part of that company had some respect for the rights of the citizens, others had no such respect, and made abusive use of their power as armed men merely. It is said that the commander and a portion of the men were drunk a good part of the time, and threatened to kill citizens who would not approve of their drunken cabals, or, against whom they had conjured up feelings of bitterness for some imaginary wrong. They took property of citizens, loyal people; they were accustomed to shoot off their guns, often, in such a way as to endanger the lives of women and children; they at no time had pickets sufficient to guard against sudden attacks, & the whole business was so badly managed that the people considered the company no protection at all. The effect is, it prevents the hearty co-operation of citizens. They may have confidence in a few who would engage in the enterprise, but think that a sufficient number cannot be mustered in, of such men as the organisation ought to consist of.[925]

Several former members of the 5th West Virginia Infantry had found employment in Catlettsburg and were content to live there, leaving their families in Wayne County and visiting them several times a week. Despite their failure to join the endeavor, Wayne County Senator John Bowen believed the company could be raised. Webb noted, however, that the men who informed Bowen they would enlist "are most of them men who have no employment and do not wish to have, and men who would need a good deal of the strictest discipline to keep them under sufficient restraint." Webb stated he would make another attempt to form the company after the presidential election but insisted it "be composed of a majority of men whose loyalty I could not suspect."[926]

On the same day, Webb wrote to Governor Arthur Boreman and stated he

> found the 'reign of terror' in Wayne Co. complete. The guerilla, Bill Smith, rules there. His reign is absolute and undisputed. Soldiers, discharged after three years hard service are permitted to remain at home on condition that they do not take up arms against him or the Southern Confed. and especially if they will not vote for Lincoln. I voted for Lincoln four years ago, and did not then hesitate to declare myself, and my decided stand, I have reason to believe, secured eleven votes in Wayne Co. for the President. Some of them remember this against me, and I have no confidence in the assurance that I can stay in Wayne. I dare not go to what I once called my home. My wife says I have no home, when I board at a tavern two miles from my house and lots. I have risked as much as any man ought to, and can risk no more. I cannot trust the guerillas, and do not know what would be my fate if I should fall into their hands. They have sworn to exterminate the Yankees. I am one. I have been in service three years and four months, and would go in for twelve months again if that would secure safety of my family and a chance for schooling for my noble boys. But there is no good prospect for anything of the kind. My brave wife has suffered and endured all that the most heroic women are expected to, and now her husband is a refugee, forced to hide away from what he supposed was his home.[927]

Webb complained that a number of soldiers that re-enlisted in the 5th, 9th, and 13th West Virginia Infantry regiments were credited to Kanawha County but had initially joined the army from Wayne County. "There are many loyal men in the county," he wrote, "but they have not had half a chance. Circumstances have always been against us..." Webb closed by informing Boreman "that there is a feeling here that the Gov. of West Va. has been indifferent to the interests of the people of Wayne. We will try & correct the impression, because I am satisfied it is not your fault, and you have too many such cases, to be attracted to this single locality."[928]

On October 20, Captain Edgar Blundon of the 7th West Virginia Cavalry, stationed at Guyandotte, wrote Captain Julius Lesage, who commanded an independent company of West Virginia state guards, concerning illegal activity in the area:

> I am induced to believe that there is quite an extensive contraband trade being carried on between parties from the back counties and the various houses of merchandise along the river between this point and Gallipolis. Will you give the matter some attention and act at once and arrest the parties if possible which if you will report to me with the evidence I shall be greatly obliged.[929]

Colonel John Hunt Oley, commanding the Union First Separate Brigade at

Charleston, wrote Colonel W. B. Thomas at Gallipolis on October 23 concerning a rumored attack in Cabell County. Oley related that "Captain Blundon, commanding at Guyandotte, fears he will be attacked soon. If he telegraphs for assistance, please send the gun-boat and two or three companies down."[930]

On the day following Oley's dispatch, Blundon wrote to his wife and gave no indication that his command was in danger. He did inform her, "I have built a fine fort – area 360 feet – from which all the thieves in the country cannot take us." Blundon also stated that the men of his regiment "have made a record that will live in the memory of those who shall read the history of the Rebellion years hence, notwithstanding the old charge from the lips of home traitors and foreign copperheads that there was no loyalty in our new state. I think they will be compelled to yield the point now, and will be forced to feel the power of loyal hands while dealing with that chivalric, home desperadoes." He noted that at the war's outset, "Rebel sympathizers were proud and defiant. Now, humble and seemingly dependent. God bless them now, if they dare to violate any regulation..."[931]

An election was held throughout the state on October 27, 1864. William Dusenberry arrived in Guyandotte just before sundown and cast his vote. The results in Cabell County:

> President – Abraham Lincoln 191, George B. McClellan 0
> Governor – A. I. Boreman 198
> Secretary of State – Granville D. Hall 197
> Auditor of State – J. M. McWhorter 196
> Treasurer – Campbell Tarr 197
> Attorney General – Ephraim B. Hall 187
> Congress – Kellian V. Whaley 127, John M. Phelps 71
> State Senator – Edward D. Wright 195
> House of Delegates – James H. Ferguson 156, John M. Smith 47
> Recorder – Thomas J. Hayslip 203
> Treasurer – P. S. Smith 184
> Prosecuting Attorney – B. D. McGinnis 177
> Clerk Circuit Court – William Merritt 63, Benjamin F. Curry 59,
>   William McComas 57, William Wentz 18
> Surveyor – James Felix 199
> Assessor – Greenville Harrison 191[932]

The turnout for the election in Wayne County was low, attributable to the fact that "guerrillas were prowling about all the voting precincts in the county." The results at the Ceredo precinct were as follows: "For Governor 96; Secretary of State 87; Treasurer 83; Auditor 92; Attorney General 87; Congress, K. V. Whaley 94; Senator, Col. D. Wright 86; Delegate for Wayne, Abel Segur 91; Prosecuting Attorney, B. D. McGinnis of Cabell 68. All 75 votes cast in the presidential election were for Lincoln and Johnson."[933]

On the following day, Dusenberry recorded that "old Joe Dick came down. He started with a half Bbl. of pickels for me but met a lot of Rebels & they took nearly all of them." Dick also informed Dusenberry that Confederates had taken some meal and flour from Dusenberry's Mill.[934]

In early November 1864, the *Weekly Register* reported that 500 Confederates under Lieutenant Colonel Vincent Witcher raided Barboursville. They supposedly burned Union stables, robbed a store, and stole a large number of horses. Whenever they encountered citizens, they "demanded his 'greenbacks' under penalty of death." The *Register* reported, "Wayne and Cabell counties are now completely overrun with these cut-throats and robbers. Something ought to be done to protect the people of these counties."[935]

Edgar B. Blundon of the 7th West Virginia Cavalry, who had been promoted to major, wrote frequently to his wife from Guyandotte in late 1864. He informed her on November 9, "Since I came down last week, the companies have been busily engaged in constructing good, comfortable quarters for the men and horses, which work is fast approaching completion. Whether we remain here or not we are making some permanent improvements." A week later he noted, "This has been an unusually busy day. Nothing of interest occurring. The country is quiet, but will doubtless soon have the peace disturbed by another grand expedition upon some quiet farmer's property."[936]

Blundon would become a Methodist minister after the war, and he preached frequently while stationed in the Cabell County town of Guyandotte. On November 20, he wrote,

> Officially, I am progressing according to the old programme. No great change in the administration of Guyandotte. Rebels dislike me as ever but all come out when it is rumored that I am going to preach. Brother Hall, and others, told me that some Rebel ladies of the town who came out for that purpose this morning, said to him, and to them, that they were most agreeably surprised during morning service and thought I was a consistent Christian, as I did not while in prayer invoke the wrath of the Almighty upon my enemies, but, on the contrary, for His mercy to be extended to them.

He added that "General Crook comes down this week to instruct us. Hope he will be pleased."[937]

On November 24, Major Blundon informed his wife that "Dr. Rouse came today to remain with this Battallion. We are going to have our own hospital, so that we will be strictly independent in that particular."[938]

Numerous civil lawsuits would be brought against Confederates in Cabell and Wayne counties over the next few years by Union citizens who suffered damages during the war. Particularly targeted were landowners who had supported the Confederacy, such as Albert Gallatin Jenkins and his brothers. Some of the property was ordered sold, and advertisements of these land transactions were posted in local newspapers. In November, notice was given of a "Great Sale Of Lands" to be held at the Bukey House in Guyandotte in January 1865.

The lands in Green Bottom are the finest agricultural lands to be found on the Ohio River, and will be divided into lots of 100 acres each, that all may have a chance to purchase. There are several more of the finest and best improved farms in the county, in the above list, and several of them are in the best Coal and Oil regions in the country. The title to all of said lands is clear and indisputable, and under our statutes, can never be questioned by the defendants, or their heirs or grantees.[939]

Private Alfred B. Payne wrote to Governor Arthur Boreman from Guyandotte on December 1 asking him the "privalige" to raise a company of state guards in Mason County to serve in Cabell, Kanawha, or Putnam counties "for the protection of the country." Payne, a member of Company F, 7th West Virginia Cavalry, had served for three years and expected to remain in the service "as long as the war lasts if I live." He believed the formation of a new company was necessary for the public good "as I think it a very profitable business to protect our homes."[940]

Henry Jefferson Samuels of Barboursville, who had been the adjutant general for the Restored Government of Virginia and now served as a circuit judge, wrote to General George Crook from Guyandotte on December 3:

GENERAL: I most humbly beg to lay before you the condition of affairs in this portion of your command, and suggest the mode and manners by which the public interests may be subserved, in my opinion, in a few words. On my arrival here in July, 1863, I found society so far protected and the people feeling safe that I held courts in this county and Wayne during that year without interruption, but last January Colonel Ferguson, of the Sixteenth (rebel) Virginia, came into Wayne, since which time I have not been able to hold a court in Wayne County, and been restricted and crippled in holding courts here. But these matters, though important to me and the loyal people here, are nothing compared to the national interests that have suffered, and which are daily sacrificed by the present status of affairs here. The rebel guerillas have held their position in the region between the Guyandotte and Big Sandy Rivers, ready to sally out and plunder when opportunity offered, which they frequently did, on one occasion capturing General Scammon, and which to the public is their object and purpose, but concealing the true object and intent of their determination and tenacity with which they hold that region. A vast quantity of useful and indispensable articles find their way to Dixie through the medium of these guerillas. The stolen horses are laden with this contraband trade. Sympathizers land large lots of barrels and boxes from steam-boats between here and Sandy. No steam-boat has ever been captured on this section of the river, though there is scarce a night the guerillas might not capture two or three if they desired to do so. They are too astute to kill the goose that lays the golden egg, and trade restrictions are laughed to scorn as a cure for the evil. While that system was in full play in this region I myself have seen seven rebels taken with their arms whose shoes were not worn enough to erase the trademarks of neighboring Ohio merchants. The remedy consists in driving out these pests. They are here with the assent of the rebel government, and will not be called away – they must be driven out. I am satisfied Major Witcher, of the Third Virginia Cavalry, with his battalion could and would clear the country of rebels for 100 miles in the interior. They fear him. His former conduct here inspired them with caution in the field in which he operated, and he effected vastly more than ten times the number of troops who were strangers to the topography of the country and the peculiar characteristics of the people did or could have done. I will also add, that if the guerillas are expelled from the country the flattering indications for petroleum and the vast deposits of coal here would cause a large migration of capitalists to this region, and, blending their interests with that of the citizens, would throw on the side of the Government all that large class of men who are actuated by such motives, and establish a local influence that would make the return of the guerillas hazardous, the protection of life and property secure, for which I, with all the loyal men of this region, anxiously hope, and which if you will secure for us we will ever be, your obliged, humble servants.[941]

On December 19, 1864, an entry in the regimental order book of the 13th West Virginia Infantry noted: "Capt William E Feazel resigned and it caused great rejoicing among the Privates of Co I." Although Feazel had been active in military affairs in the county since prior to the raid on Guyandotte, he must not have been popular with at least some of his men.[942]

14
The War Ends?

"Whereas, A great many former residents of this township have voluntarily left their homes and taken up arms for the avowed purpose of aiding in the rebellion and fighting against, and attempting the destruction of our glorious Union, for which they are very sorry, (yes, but it is because they did not succeed,) and having committed treason in its worst form, and allied themselves to a foreign Government, the so-called Confederate States, and having renounced of their own accord and free will their homes and their citizenship, have thereby forfeited both – It is proposed that our Representatives in Congress and the Legislature, be instructed to use all the means in their power, and exert their influence to get such laws and acts passed, that such persons be considered and treated as aliens, and that they conform to the laws of the United States for naturalization."

Resolution passed at a meeting in Union Township,
Cabell County, July 14, 1865

By early 1865, the Civil War was nearing an end. In western West Virginia, however, fear and violence continued to rule the day even after the surrender of General Robert E. Lee and his army. Although the Confederacy ceased to exist, the conflict continued, and state officials found it nearly impossible to maintain control of the population in Cabell and Wayne counties.

On the first Monday of January 1865, a suit was filed in Cabell County Circuit Court by John Ferguson against Hurston Spurlock, Reece W. Elkins, John N. Buffington, Malcom McAllister, Evermont Ward, Anthony Lawson, James McCorkle, John L. Bowen, Jefferson Bowen, Jr., Henry Elkins, William Poster, James Buffington, William H. Hagan, and P. H. McCullough for false imprisonment. Damages in the amount of $30,000 were sought, and it was ordered that the non-resident defendants appear in court "and do what is necessary to protect their interests in this suit."[943]

Ceredo, founded as an abolitionist colony in 1857, was in desperate straits by 1865. The *Ironton Register* observed:

Since the breaking out of the rebellion, 'I give bread' town has been subjected to many vicissitudes. Its prospects when projected, in 1854, and later, was that of a great manufacturing city. Early in 1861, many of the yankee citizens anticipated the coming storm, and either disposed of their property or left it to the despoiler. At one time it had a regiment quartered in its midst, but of late no troops have been nearer than Guyandotte. Disloyalty has cropped out under drunkenness and personal hate, until one's life is endangered at any moment. Guerillas and rebel sympathizers occupy the principal houses vacated by the owners. Not a public building stands untouched. The window and door frames, flooring and every sleeper of the hotel have been torn out and burned up. The dismantling of the steam saw-mill, and Match and Glass Factories, have long since been accomplished. Night is made hideous by the continued debaucheries of certain desperate characters...There is not a loyal family left in Ceredo.[944]

The Ceredo House.
By the end of the war, Ceredo was devastated and most of the buildings had been stripped of anything that could be used for firewood. Credit: Ed Adkins Scrapbook, Ceredo Historical Society.

In early February, "Rebel" Bill Smith struck again, leading a detachment to Ceredo, where they surrounded the home of Jesse Middaugh (alias Jack Meadows). Middaugh had served in Company B of the 5th West Virginia Infantry until discharged in 1864, but he was apparently an undercover spy and a member of Blazer's Scouts, a Federal unit created to combat Confederate guerrillas. Middaugh served as a special agent for the Provost Department of the Union army and was known to utilize disguises and pose as a Confederate major. He was captured twice during the war but escaped on both occasions. Middaugh would not be as fortunate on this day. Grabbing a revolver, he began firing, wounding two of the guerrillas. His wife seized the weapon and threatened the attackers, who had by then entered their house, while her husband "made his motions for escape." Jim Turner, at the head of the Confederates swarming into the home, swung his gun and smashed Anna Middaugh's foot. She responded by shooting Turner through the breast, sending him to the ground. Jesse Middaugh rushed down the stairs, knocking down "all in his path" and burst out the door. He sprinted toward the woods, drawing tantalizing close to escape before he was surrounded and killed by several mounted men.[945]

Anna Middaugh and her children were driven out of the house, and she was forced to lie on the ground in a half-dressed condition. The raiders refused to allow her to get anything from the residence, which was set ablaze. The Confederates fled, leaving their dead comrade, while Middaugh and her children, now homeless, were taken to Catlettsburg, Kentucky, where "the conduct of this heroic woman is duly appreciated...and they have generously provided for her and her little ones."[946]

On February 3, 1865, slavery was abolished in West Virginia due in part to the efforts of a Cabell Countian, Delegate James H. Ferguson. Ferguson drew up the following bill, which passed both houses and became state law:

Be it enacted by the Legislature of West Virginia:

1. All persons held to service or labor as slaves in this State are hereby declared free.

2. There shall hereafter be neither slavery nor involuntary servitude in this State, except in punishment for crime, whereof the party shall have been duly convicted.[947]

During the House debate, Ferguson opposed changes to the legislation due to the possibility of delaying abolition. An observer wrote, "He wanted to strike the shackles off the slaves and make them what God intended them to be – free men, and he wanted to do it as speedily as possible."[948]

The *Wheeling Intelligencer* recorded, "This bill effectually wipes out the remnant of slavery in West Virginia at one blow. It was not offered or passed as an amendment to the Constitution. The Constitution simply prescribes a limit beyond which certain persons of certain ages shall not be held as slaves and makes no enactment at all in regard to those supposed to be left in slavery for life."[949]

At a meeting of the county's Board of Supervisors on February 9, the members sought to determine the best method for raising funds to pay bonuses for recruits from Cabell County. President Lincoln had called for 300,000 men, and Cabell County's share of the draft was seventeen. It was resolved by the board that a levy be made on the real estate of the county for $10,000. Three weeks later, it was determined to give each soldier a $400 bonus, and Julius Freutel was given authorization to borrow funds for the purpose.⁹⁵⁰

On February 13, Delegate James Ferguson of Cabell related "that a party of about two hundred rebels, formerly belonging to the commands of Gens. Jenkins and Witcher, have returned to Cabell county and have elected a clerk and organized a government under the rebel authority. They appear to come and go within our lines without hindrance."⁹⁵¹

On February 22, during a debate in the West Virginia House of Delegates on a bill "for the better organization of the State Guards," Ferguson claimed that

> every part of the county of Wayne, on the Ohio river was held by guerrillas. In the county of Cabell only one town, Guyandotte, was held by the Federal troops. The rebels have their headquarters up in Logan county, and they make forays down toward the Ohio River, stealing, murdering, and devastating the country. They enter the houses of loyal citizens and steal household furniture and bed clothing, and frequently strip women and children of wearing apparel and leave them in an actual state of nudity.⁹⁵²

Company G, 7th West Virginia Cavalry. Credit: West Virginia State Archives.

Major Edgar Blundon of the 7th West Virginia Cavalry reported from Guyandotte on March 5, 1865:

> There is but one organized band of guerillas, consisting of Bill Smith and fifteen or twenty men, in Wayne or Logan Counties, and no organization in Mason, Cabell, or Putnam. The depredations committed by them are comparatively few contrasted with the past. No boats, either steam or trading boats, have been interfered with, nor has navigation been stopped for a moment on account of guerillas. There are a few deserters from United States and rebel armies who have gone into the mountains to evade pursuit and capture who sometimes rob individuals of money and clothing without regard to political status. The men of this detachment are thoroughly acquainted with every road, stream, or path in this section, many of them having been raised in the counties named, which has rendered our efforts very successful in capturing all the notorious rebels in this country except Smith, and we are sanguine that we shall soon rid the country of him and squad.[953]

Colonel John Hunt Oley concurred with Blundon, writing, "That section of the country has not been so quiet during the war as now. There were thieves there before the war, and those there now are deserters from both armies. They are being rapidly captured or killed."[954]

On March 16, 1865, Emily Cox of Guyandotte, who would soon marry Lieutenant William Newcomb of the 7th West Virginia Cavalry, recorded in her diary, "Several Rebels came in camp and stole 4 horses Dr. Rouses included at 11 o'clock in the night." Dusenberry observed that the horses were very close to the soldiers' quarters and that the theft was not discovered until the following morning. One of the raiders must have been noted diarist and Border Ranger James D. Sedinger, as Cox noted a year later, "It has been one year tonight since Jim Se[din]ger stole Dr. Rouse horse – the dirty thief." On the following night, a group of Confederates rode into Barboursville, burned the covered bridge, and "robbed some old men."[955]

Margaret Emily Cox of Guyandotte. Cox, an ardent Union supporter, participated in several flag presentations during the Civil War. She married Lieutenant William B. Newcomb of the 7th West Virginia Cavalry in Guyandotte on June 7, 1866. Credit: West Virginia State Archives.

C. B. Webb wrote from Ceredo on March 24: "Since the murder of poor Jack Middaugh and the burning of his house by guerrillas, the people of this village are awed into a painful condition of fear and dread. Nearly all the truly loyal and best men have left, under the belief that any of them may be the next victims of Bill Smith's barbarity, as it is understood he has threatened that others must share a similar fate." Webb echoed a newspaper editorial concerning the treatment of Anna Middaugh, writing that "turning a woman half-dressed out of her house to burn it, and refusing to permit her to save even her clothing, and she wounded, is very much like the atrocities practi[c]ed by the Indians in early times, and characterized as savage cruelty."[956]

Webb observed that "oil excitement is on the increase" in Wayne County, but noted that the county's most prospective areas in the valley of Twelve Pole Creek were patrolled by "light fingered chaps who are in the habit of borrowing lone gentlemen's pocket-books, watches, or good clothes." Rumors were floating around the county that a new company of capitalists were preparing to purchase Ceredo for an unknown business venture.[957]

The March term of the Cabell County Circuit Court opened on March 24, 1865, with Judge H. J. Samuels presiding. The grand jurors met for one day and made eight indictments. Dr. William A. Jenkins, who had returned to Cabell County, sought a new trial "in the causes for which judgments were rendered at the previous courts of this county, and asked that they may be set aside." An argument ensued between attorneys for Jenkins, the brother of deceased Confederate General Albert G. Jenkins, and James H. Ferguson over interpretation of West Virginia State Code relating to test oaths required for former Confederates. Jenkins's attorneys argued that the West Virginia state legislature had "no right to pass such a law," and stated that "the people of Ohio were determined that we should restore those men to their former rights, and that we should apply no test oath to them at all; and if it was necessary, they would raise an army, march over into our State and compel us to recognize them as citizens – not as aliens."[958]

Ferguson, a member of the House of Delegates, countered that "we intended to make laws suited to our tastes…" He asserted that Jenkins "was not satisfied with the old government, and with his associates had deluged this country with blood and now when there is no hope of their 'confederacy,' they come *sneaking back* and declared every 'devil of them ought to be hung.'"[959]

Sketch of James H. Ferguson by Joseph H. Diss Debar.
Credit: *West Virginia State Archives.*

On April 4, William Dusenberry recorded: "Great excitement here all day; dispatches received that Richmond & Petersburg was taken, & that Pres Lincoln was there." Dusenberry raised his flags in celebration, and at midday the Federal troops in the town fired a salute. Some of the soldiers climbed the hill and gathered up the unexploded shells. For some reason, "they were trying to break one open when it exploded slightly hurting three of the boys."[960]

A telegraph dispatch was received in Guyandotte on the morning of April 10 bearing the news that Confederate General Robert E. Lee had surrendered his army to Union General Ulysses Grant. Instantly there was "great rejoicing among the soldiers." The men raised money to purchase material that was used by several Guyandotte women to make a large Confederate flag, which they then "draped in mourning." At 3:00 p.m. William Dusenberry raised the new flag to half mast, under the United States flag already flying at his residence. The Federal soldiers fired salutes, and speeches were made by William McComas, Henry J. Samuels, B. D. McGinnis, and others. Dusenberry recorded in his diary that nearly all the Union women in Guyandotte were in attendance and observed that "the Rebels look very gloomy."[961]

A letter written on this day by a Union soldier stationed in Guyandotte described the mood in the town and reflected on the prospect of peaceful times:

Dear Aunt: Since writing the within letter this morning, things have very materially changed here. I was then as all the rest were of a sad countenance very much distressed about the order of being ready to move. All expected that we would have to move in a few days, (and we may yet.) Just after I had finished the letter and stuck it in the envelope, had not sealed it yet. All at once I heard such another hollowing down at headquarters, as you never heard. I went down to see what was up, and they had just received the dispatch, announcing the sur[r]ender of Gen. Lee, with all his army and such another time as we have had here to day, you never saw. Some got drunk, others went to shooting, and every species of rejoicing was resorted to, and now while I am writing, this evening, they have the rebel flag floating in the breeze, from our tall pole. But, oh! how does she float, not in the glory and pride of the people as it once floated here, but it is unfurled to the breeze about three fourths from the top of the pole, and the Star Spangled Banner proudly floating above her. Ah, aunt how emblematical it is, of the humbled and dishonored Southern Confederacy, to see their flag, their boasted stars and bars, as she humbly plays in the breeze, all dressed in mourning, beneath the Stars and Stripes of America, and the friends of the latter, rejoicing under her folds making speeches, and some of their eyes filled with tears, when they express their thanks to God, for the great victories of our armies, and the bright prospect of a speedy and lasting peace. Ah, dear aunt, or sister, which ever you would rather I would call you, I hope the time is near at hand, when I can come home and enjoy the pleasant fireside of our neat little home, with my dear wife, and children, and you and yours. Feeling that my conscience is clear, of having been a good and faithful soldier, having discharged every duty enjoined upon me as a soldier of the United

States, and participated in all the hardships incident to a soldiers life. I have done my duty and have escaped thus far unharmed and I do thank God for it. Yours, Samuel.[962]

At ten o'clock on the morning of April 15, a steamer arrived in Guyandotte and left a dispatch for Major Edgar Blundon conveying the stunning news that President Abraham Lincoln had been assassinated. "All was excitement," wrote William Dusenberry, "scarcely any one believed it. I felt that it was true & could not do anything the rest of the day." He added, "The news of the death of Lincoln coming over us just as we were celebrating our glorious victories has caused the very services of all loyal men to pause. We cannot realize it to be so…" Just as the sun was setting for the day, another dispatch from Washington arrived, confirming the earlier news. "We now no longer could doubt it," Dusenberry noted, and "intense gloom pervaded all loyal citizens countenances."[963]

On the following day, gloom turned to rage in Guyandotte. Dusenberry recorded that an oil man by the name of Scott said something that caused the Union troops to beat and drive him over the suspension bridge. Jim Baumgardner was also attacked, and that afternoon "Bruser Lusher got beat & put out of town." He added, "There was a perfect reign of terror for awhile. The Rebel Sympathisers kept out of sight all day."[964]

The funeral of President Lincoln was held on April 19, 1865, in Washington, but observances were held throughout the country. In Guyandotte, "the church bell commenced tolling at sun rise & tolled every half moment during the day except during the hour there was preaching. Everything looked & was solemn. The stores all shut & business entirely suspended. On every countenance was gloom & could be read our nation's great loss."[965]

Services were held at the Methodist Church, and the chaplain of the 7th West Virginia Cavalry delivered a discourse. That evening nearly a dozen Confederates came to Guyandotte and surrendered. Dusenberry believed that some of them had previously "plundered my house."[966]

Colonel John Oley wrote to Major Edgar B. Blundon in Guyandotte on April 29 regarding policies to be implemented in the post-war period:

All rebel soldiers can be either paroled or take the oath, and then be allowed to remain at their homes, if they are not considered dangerous men by the military authorities or their loyal neighbors, but deserters from the rebel army who have banded together to rob and murder, and have not been with their proper commands can have no mercy. You will place no further restrictions upon trade except arms, ammunition, gray cloth, all articles from which ammunition is made, locomotives, cars, telegraph wires, and instruments for operating telegraphic lines, which articles are contraband.[967]

Despite the surrender of General Robert E. Lee and his army at Appomattox, civil unrest would continue in parts of West Virginia for years. James H. Ferguson, who commanded a company of the Cabell State Guards, noted on April 30, 1865, that his company had been active in combatting Confederate supporters in the county during the month. The men captured a number of horses from secessionists and were able to return five of them to their proper owners. The State Guards also seized five muskets but had no easy way of transporting them to headquarters, "and the distance being so great, they destroyed them."[968]

Others, however, were critical of the actions of Ferguson and his men and requested assistance from state authorities. Prosecuting Attorney B. D. McGinnis noted on May 21 that the commanding officer of Federal forces at Guyandotte had sent a detachment of troops to Ceredo to protect the citizens of that town from "abuses" by Ferguson's unit: "Last evening Abel Segur Esq., Delegate, and other prominent citizens of that county waited upon the commanding officer here and represented to him the condition of affairs there as truly deplorable on account of the state troops – they have collected at Ceredo a number of lewd women and are pillaging the citizens to keep them up, as well as personal abuses by them connected." McGinnis suggested that the adjutant general be sent to the area to investigate conditions.[969]

Major Edgar Blundon, 7th West Virginia Cavalry. Blundon commanded the post at Guyandotte from late 1864 through the end of the war. Credit: Richard A. Wolfe.

A mass meeting was held at the Wayne County Courthouse on Thursday, May 18, "for the purpose of devising means for the establishment of peace, civil law, and the national authority." The meeting, said to be the largest assembly there in many years, was conducted "in a quiet and orderly manner" and was compared to a "court day in civil times." A committee of five men was appointed to draft resolutions, and while their work was being completed, the crowd listened enthusiastically to a number of speakers.[970]

The resolutions, preceded by a preamble that noted the country "is just emerging from civil war, which has laid waste our fields and drenched the land in fraternal blood," included one that called on every individual to "lend his active aid and energy to the establishment of civil law, both State and National, and to its enforcement for the protection of life, liberty and property." Other resolutions reflected the crowd's approval of President Lincoln's amnesty proclamation and its appointment of Abel Segur, John B. Bowen, R. Bouton, and Isaac Bloss as delegates to represent Wayne County at a convention to be held in Charleston on June 3 "for the purpose of suppressing lawless persons, and the restoration of order throughout the State." An observer noted, "It appears to be the disposition of the people to unite their efforts to establish peace and harmony throughout the county, and it is hoped that they will, as far as possible, forget all old grudges and antagonistic or hostile feelings, and work together for good."[971]

On May 20, 1865, a similar mass meeting, described as the "largest gathering of citizens of Cabell county since the war," was held at Barboursville. William McComas delivered "a very appropriate and well timed speech," and was followed by Judge Henry J. Samuels and several other orators. All stressed "the necessity of establishing civil government, and painting the beauties of peace in contrast with the past four years of war..." Resolutions were adopted, including the following:

Judge Henry J. Samuels of Barboursville, who served as adjutant general for the Restored Government of Virginia during the Civil War. Credit: Special Collections Department, Marshall University.

> Whereas, Our country is emerging from a civil war which has disorganized society, prostrated the laws, and anarchy reigns in localities in this county and in order to restore peace, quiet, safety and harmony, we, the people of Cabell co., in Mass Meeting assembled –

> 1. Resolved, That it is the duty of every individual to lay aside all malice, hatred and ill will, and forgive all personal wrongs and injuries growing out of the war, and use every endeavor to unite and blend together in good will and affection the various elements of society, by annihilating past party lines and burying the past in oblivion.

> 2. Resolved, That it is the like duty of every individual to lend his active aid, energies and influence to the erection of Civil Government in all its branches where it is not already in force, and to the enforcement of the laws that life, liberty and property may be made safe, and confidence fully reinstated among the people.

A correspondent noted, "The best of feeling prevailed throughout, and all seemed delighted with the prospect of a speedy return to civil pursuits."[972]

In late May, a writer to the *West Virginia Journal* observed,

> The little town of Ceredo has for a long time been at the mercy of guerrillas, idle vagabonds, and soldiers of fortune. Nearly all the buildings that were not

William McComas Home, Barboursville. McComas, who was a minister, judge, and congressman, voted against secession at the Richmond Convention in 1861. He died on June 3, 1865. Credit: Special Collections Department, Marshall University.

occupied by the proprietors, are about ruined. This is the case with the buildings belonging to the company who first laid the town out in lots. Some of them were entirely demolished and burned. Two Government buildings, one hundred feet long, went that way.

Efforts continued to rebuild the town and encourage investment in Wayne County, and the writer concluded, "The prospect is very encouraging for a speedy resuscitation of the once Yankee town."[973]

On Friday evening, June 2, William McComas conversed with Judge Henry J. Samuels about obtaining the release of his son Benjamin J. McComas, a Confederate prisoner confined at Fort Delaware. Samuels "told him I thought the best plan was to write to you [President Andrew Johnson] to detail the manner in which his son went into rebellion, and his own unflinching loyalty to the government in the crises of the last four years." The elder McComas had indeed remained loyal to the Union, beginning with his vote against the Virginia Ordinance of Secession on April 17, 1861.[974]

On the following morning, William McComas had breakfast with a friend about a mile from Barboursville. After mounting his horse "in apparent health," McComas rode toward the village but was soon discovered dead by the side of the road, having fallen from his mount "in a fit of apoplexy." He was described as one of the few loyal men in Cabell, and an observer opined, "His loss will be severely felt in re-establishing law and order in South Western Virginia, where his influence always has been of great weight."[975]

On June 5, Judge Samuels informed President Andrew Johnson of McComas's death and requested the release of his son:

> He resisted secession to the last in the convention and before his people refused to take the oath of allegence to the confederacy, and as his boy was the Benjamin of his affection as in name and as I am sure no detriment can come to the country on account of it I hope you will have him discharged and sent home with the admonition that his dead father's loyalty unlocked his prison door, to go and sin no more.[976]

On June 7, Colonel John Oley, commanding the 7th West Virginia Cavalry, ordered Major Edgar B. Blundon in Guyandotte to send patrols periodically through the region between the Guyandotte and Big Sandy rivers as far as Logan Courthouse "to see that the country is kept quiet and arrest all disturbers of good order." Oley insisted the scouting parties be small in number "so as to be easy on the people in the matter of grazing, etc. Always send good men, who will commit no irregularities."[977]

On July 4, 1865, the Union citizens of Guyandotte and vicinity held a celebration in the town. A newspaper correspondent wrote, "Four years ago on that day the rattle snake flag of secession waved over the traitorous town of Guyandotte. How different now." Members of the Sabbath School, all the soldiers stationed in the community, and a large crowd of citizens "repaired to a neighboring grove" where the audience was called to order by the chairman of the event, Dr. J. H. Rouse. Following prayer and a reading of the Declaration of Independence by Major Edgar B. Blundon, B. D. McGinnis "delivered a soul-stirring and patriotic oration" that lasted nearly two hours before the crowd enjoyed a "rich and magnificent dinner." The correspondent wrote, "The day was passed pleasantly and harmoniously, and all seemed to rejoice that war and bloodshed had departed from our land forever." The writer also observed,

> The most cheering and gratifying feature was the fact that the entire audience was of the strictly loyal stripe; the rebels and their sympathizers, did not disgrace the occasion with their satanic presence, as they cannot relish a national feast. They chose to "hold up" on the occasion, and boast that the Union people of the County could not succeed with a celebration unless the traitors would condescend to cast their mite in favor of an abolition Government; but perhaps they will learn that the world will wag independent of such pusillanimous nobodies.[978]

On July 14, a number of Union citizens from Union Township in Cabell County gathered at the home of a Mrs. Goodman, reportedly used as a town hall, "to deliberate upon the ways and means for the future safety of the township." They noted that their property was still "insecure from pillage or theft, while the persons who have committed the robberies and depredations of the last four years in this township are still at large, and hold themselves secreted in close proximity to our neighborhood." One proposal was to request the governor's permission for all loyal citizens to form a Home Guard unit. Another was to prepare a petition "to obtain indemnification for the loss they may have sustained."[979]

A correspondent of the *West Virginia Journal* wrote, "Many sections of the country in the frontier counties, are still subject to lawless depredations, and those who have stood faithful to the Union are treated by the rebels as if they had been the conquerors. We are glad to see Union Township taking earnest, but *lawful* means to correct these evils."[980]

The *West Virginia Journal* reported on July 19, 1865, that a small quantity of oil with gas had been struck at the Swan Well on the Guyandotte River eight miles above Barboursville. The same issue included a story that originally appeared in the *Gallipolis Journal*: "The notorious Jeff. Jenkins concluded he would stop at Ironton the other day, and look around 'as in days of yore.' The honest, loyal men of Ironton concluded they could do without Jeff's presence, and a few hot-headed fellows 'went for him.' Jeff. made his escape in good season."[981]

On October 10, "C" wrote from Ceredo that the town was "progressing slowly but very encouragingly." Wayne County was also finding the reconstruction process challenging to implement. "The great difficulty," the writer noted, "is in the laws passed while a portion of the country was in a state of rebellion, providing test oaths which now prevents the organization of townships, because not men enough can be found in some of them who can take the oaths." While some Union men favored punishing the former Confederates, others were concerned it penalized Federal supporters as much as it did the Rebels, since the former were unable to complete county organization without the latter. "C" observed,

> We have felt the disadvantage of this for the last six months. Townships are unorganized, the free school system not in operation, roads unrepaired, and a general stagnation in all public business. The question of mod[i]fying the test oath law will be an issue in the coming election on the fourth Tuesday of this month, when we elect Delegates and Senators for the Legislature. Some of the best and most loyal men of this and adjoining counties are in favor of amending the laws so that the leading, and influential and active rebels shall be prevented from holding office; but many other good citizens, who have indirectly, and generally, through fear, aided the rebels, may have the right to vote. It will be an exciting election.[982]

As the date for the 1865 election neared, Union officials discovered "evidence that the Rebels intend to force the Inspectors to take their votes Election day." William F. Dusenberry left on October 12 for Wheeling and met with Governor Arthur Boreman, "who assured me we should have troops here on Election day." At midnight on October 25, John S. Witcher called on Dusenberry and informed him that soldiers had arrived in Barboursville. Dusenberry was one of the inspectors for the election on October 26 and noted "we rejected all Rebel votes."[983]

Voters in Cabell County cast 321 ballots for John S. Witcher, the Union candidate for House of Delegates, and 97 for James H. Ferguson, the Copperhead candidate. In the contest for state senator, Reverend Robert Hager received the same number of votes as Witcher, and Cook, the Copperhead candidate, received the same as Ferguson. A letter to the editors of the *West Virginia Journal* stated, "Cabell is all right, and a complete victory – the reward for the 'true blues.' Our young and gallant Col. Witcher was landed high and dry, by 224 majority – James H. Ferguson receiving only 97 votes! 'Well done thou good and faithful soldier, enter in to the legislative hall.'"[984]

In December 1865, Julius Lesage, supervisor of Union Township, wrote to Adjutant General Francis P. Pierpont, requesting arms and command of a "minute company." Lesage stated, "we have found it necessary at our election to go in arms to protect our selves against the threatening rebels." If given the weapons, he wrote, "I can arm over fifty men and we can here after dispense with any other troops we have in our county and the adjoining bands of individuals that still carry on the practice of horse and house stealing. The constables nor the sheriff can do any good to put down such a gang. No one but the citizens organised can do it..."[985]

The December term of the Wayne County Circuit Court began on December 15, but the cold weather caused an adjournment. The courthouse had been used by soldiers throughout the war, and it was not insulated enough for winter use and "not in good condition for holding Courts." "Rebel" Bill Smith had been at home for a week and it appeared that "he intended to brave the indignation of the people, and the indictments of the Courts, until he can do more mischief, or to bluff the whole country into permitting him to remain quietly at home." A correspondent to the *Ironton Register* complained that Confederate guerrillas defended their actions by declaring they were only following orders. Indictments for robbery, arson, murder, and other felonies were increasing, "and the *loyal* citizens are determined that the accused shall be punished or leave the country. I don't think the bravado of guerilla Smith will do him much good."[986]

West Virginians voted in favor of a constitutional amendment which disenfranchised all persons who had given voluntary aid to the Confederacy, and the amendment became part of the state constitution on February 13, 1866. The vote in Cabell County was in favor of the amendment, 295-163. County boards of registration established across the state were tasked with preventing those who had supported the Confederacy from voting. Silas Clark, Oscar W. Mather, and Percival S. Smith were appointed registrars in Cabell County.[987]

Despite these efforts to suppress former Confederates, civil unrest continued for years after the war in the border counties of Cabell and Wayne. In Cassville, Union civil authorities attempting to exercise their offices on behalf of the state of West Virginia found it nearly impossible to do so. John Holt, notary public and assessor for the 2nd District of Wayne County, informed Governor Arthur Boreman on March 22, 1866, that "it is with extreme difficulty and under great danger and hard threats that I am getting along." Holt noted that his "entire neighbourhood is Reb" with the exception of Squire Bartram and his sons. He informed Boreman that the Union men had been beaten by mobs and shot at on the streets of town and could not execute civil law unless actions were taken.[988]

Holt insisted that a militia company be raised to aid in enforcing the law, although he noted that Wayne County was mostly quiet except for the Cassville area. That community, however, required Federal troops "or else we must get out of here." Lumbermen and other former Confederates came to the town from Logan County and from across the river in Pike County, Kentucky, "with ther Bowies buckled round them hurrawing for Jeff Davis cussing the government cursing Union men." A short time prior, some of the local Home Guards were attacked about eight miles from Cassville on their way home. The Union men were beaten and abused by the former Confederates, who called them "damed abolitionist" and "swore they would not submit to our laws." The "high Sheriff" was attacked by a mob that "fell on him with clubs & weights and tried to kill him and his brother." The latter ran into Holt's home for protection, and the mob broke a window and knocked two panels from his door and "like to killed my little child." Holt asked that commissions be sent immediately. He noted they had plenty of guns but requested revolvers instead.[989]

The *West Virginia Journal* wrote,

> These defiers of law are the kind of men we are asked to confer the elective franchise upon. They are already endeavoring to organize another rebellion in our midst. Will the Union men of West Virginia suffer themselves to be hoodwinked by the conservative allies of these rebels, and give their support to those measures which will restore to power these *infernals*, who are still determined to destroy the Government and rive from the State every Union man? We hope not; but trust that every loyal man will put forth his utmost exertions, until this dangerous peril is past, through the adoption of the Constitutional Amendment, which will exclude such lawless men from participation in the Government. In the language of Andrew Johnson, 'Let traitors take a back seat,' and remain there until they show a better spirit towards those who have saved the country from their destructive influence.[990]

On April 19, 1866, Union men from Cabell County gathered at the courthouse for the purpose of ratifying the platform of the state Union party and the acts of the legislature relating to a constitutional amendment stripping citizenship rights from those that had supported the Confederacy. Hiram Curry served as chair, Captain Frank Lesage was elected secretary, and S. A. Childers, James Eaden, B. D. McGinnis, A. G. White, and William O. White were appointed to draft resolutions reflecting the sentiment of those gathered.

James H. Ferguson spoke to the crowd while the resolutions were being composed, defining his position "upon the issues of the present canvass." While admitting that some had accused him of abandoning the Union party, he assured the crowd that he still favored the proposed constitutional amendment, largely due to the "outrageous conduct of the returned rebels at the fall elections..." He noted that in "some of the border counties they elected rebel officers to the Legislature, in defiance of the laws of the State, and in others they actually knocked down and drove from the polls Union men who pretended to challenge their votes. Such men, in my opinion, are not proper subjects for the elective franchise." Ferguson observed, "I know that it is hard to punish the innocent for the acts of the guilty; but such always has been and always will be the case wherever classes of men are involved as in this case." He favored adoption of the proposed amendment "as the best thing that can be done under the circumstances," followed by another that would make "the proper distinction between those who wickedly led the people into rebellion, and those who were led in by them."[991]

Two of the resolutions expressed opposition to granting voting rights to African Americans, either in West Virginia or in former Confederate states. One resolution called for "the just punishment of traitors and rebels," and insisted "that all shall be taught that treason against a government works a forfeiture of political rights under that government..." Another endorsed the acts of the legislature in passing laws and measures designed "to secure the loyal people of the State the exclusive right to control its Government in all its departments" and commended legislative actions such as the registration law and disenfranchise amendment, "which can only withhold from traitors and rebels the rights which they have forfeited by their crimes."[992]

Isaac Bloss Jr. wrote to Governor Arthur Boreman from Ceredo on May 4, 1866. Bloss had been raising militia during the war when he was captured by Confederates in September 1862 and sent to prison in Richmond. He was released in March 1863 and returned home. After the war, he began serving as postmaster of Ceredo and was also a deputy United States marshal.

He informed Boreman that ex-Confederates "are geting very sasey in the upper part of this county." "I have to start on my bisness and I am vary much alarmd at this time," Bloss declared, "but have to go in and if the[y] see fit to murder me the[y] will have to doo it for I am bound to doo my bisness or di in the defence of my goverment." Bloss had spoken with Boreman previously about raising a company and asked his permission to do so. Claiming that he could get the unit together in five days, he told Boreman that "if there is trubel in the land I will be sure to hear it." He related that a man had been murdered in Cassville the previous week and told the governor that if he didn't get his company, "I will not doo any more bisness in this county."[993]

Elections were held in Cabell County on May 24, 1866. In addition to a referendum on the constitutional amendment, township officers and county superintendent of schools were also chosen. James Hysell was elected supervisor, E. M. Underwood, town clerk, R. Clark, constable, J. Ray, town treasurer, Mr. White and William Douthit, inspectors, Julius Freutel, overseer of the poor, and J. Plybon, school commissioner. Confederate supporters ran a ticket of their own against the constitutional amendment, but it passed by a majority of thirteen. William Dusenberry ran for one of the inspectors but was defeated by William Douthit.[994]

C. B. Webb wrote from Ceredo on May 27, 1866, in an effort to collect payment for members of Captain Calvin Fuller's company of Wayne County militia, which had been formed in early July 1863. One of the company's leaders, Lieutenant Thomas

Gilkerson, was killed on December 1, 1863, by "Rebel" Bill Smith and his men, and four weeks later, Captain Fuller and three of his men were captured in Wayne County. Also seized with Fuller were all the papers and memoranda concerning the affairs of the company. Webb noted that "the company was constantly on service, scouting and hunting the bushwhackers who had killed their Lieutenant, and there was actually no chance to make out rolls." Fuller and his sons suffered tremendously during the conflict, but "many of his company have mournful histories, and suffered much, caused by their active services in hunting rebels and protecting the country." Webb inquired if there were funds available to pay the members of the unit.[995]

In mid-June, Judge Henry J. Samuels held circuit court for a week at Wayne Courthouse. The grand jury issued nearly fifty indictments, most for misdemeanors. An observer noted that several

> horse cases, resulting from the operation of scouts, bushwhackers, and home guards during the war, were tried during this term. The people appear to be more interested in these cases than in any other, for there is hardly a landholder or even a renter in the county who has not lost a horse or in some way interested in a horse case. The cases now tried will encourage others, and at the next term we may have many more of them. Another war-related case, Hiram Bloss against John Plymale and others, was postponed because Bloss was serving on the jury. He had been captured by bushwhackers during the war and held prisoner for forty days.[996]

Union men from Carroll Township held a convention at White House on August 9 to appoint delegates to a county convention. Jeremiah Witcher chaired the gathering, and Reverend James C. Black was appointed secretary. Colonel John S. Witcher, Ephraim Griffith, William Holstein, Charles Myers, and Anderson Byess were selected as delegates, with John W. Ballard and Jacob W. May as alternates. A correspondent wrote,

> It is absolutely necessary in every County that the Union party should put out their best material in every case, for the conservatives are trying to move heaven to get into power. We must no longer remain neutral; we must be up and doing; if we do not labor they will overrun us. The past six years tells us what they do when they have the power.[997]

A Union convention was held at the Cabell County courthouse on Saturday, August 18, 1866. The meeting was called to order by James H. Ferguson, and the convention officers selected were Col. John S. Witcher, president; Dr. James H. Hysell, secretary; and Captain Frank Lesage, assistant secretary. The delegates were:

Guyandotte Township: B. D. McGinnis, Dr. James H. Hysell, E. D. Wright, William F. Dusenberry, and William O. Wright

Union Township: David Harshbarger, Philo B. Berry, Louis Diehl, Thomas Spurlock, and Richard B. Baxfield

Barboursville Township: James H. Ferguson, Roland Bias, James Baumgardner, Samuel A. Childers, William Thompson

McComas Township: R. J. Roberts, W. W. Johnson, J. S. Porter, Joshua K. Heath, George Ross

Carroll Township: Ephraim Griffith, Anderson Bias, Colonel John S. Witcher, William A. Holstein, John W. Ballard

Ferguson, McGinnis, and Harshbarger were appointed to a committee for the purpose of drafting resolutions, and they presented the following, which were read and unanimously adopted:

Resolved, That we cordially endorse the administration of Gov. Boreman, and instruct our delegates to vote for his re-nomination.

Resolved, That we also cordially endorse the course of the Senators from this District, and of Col. Witcher, our delegate in the last Legislature; and we hereby instruct our delegates to vote for the re-nomination of Edward D. Wright, our present Senator.

Resolved, That we are opposed in toto to the present policy of President Johnson, and we look upon him as having abandoned the principles upon which he was elected, and guilty of a gross betrayal of the confidence of the party who elected him.

Resolved, That we are opposed in every form to conferring the elective franchise upon persons of the African race.

Resolved, That we are opposed to the nomination of any person for any office who is opposed to the principles contained in these resolutions.

Witcher, Dusenberry, Hysell, Ferguson, McGinnis, Lesage, and Johnson were appointed delegates to represent Cabell County at the Union State Convention in Parkersburg on August 30, and the convention then adjourned until October 4.[998]

An editorial appeared in the October 24, 1866, issue of the *West Virginia Journal* that revealed political sentiments of the day:

We want every Union man in West Virginia to go to the polls and honor the memory of our brave and noble dead, by voting the true Union ticket.

Remember that gallant son of yours, whom you sent forth with your blessing, and whose bones now bleach on some of our glorious battle fields; vote next Thursday to perpetuate those glorious principles for which he sacrificed his life.

Remember your noble brother who girded on his armor and went forth at the call of his country, and laid down his life while in the bloom of youth and manhood, for the glorious principles of the Union party. Remember this, and vote the full Union ticket.

Remember such gallant spirits as Col. Thoburn, Col. Frost, Col. Hall, and thousands of others, who now sleep in the arms of death – mourned by the people of the State, their wives widowed, and their children orphaned, for the glorious principles of the Union party, and vote the whole Union ticket.

Remember that it is the murderers of those gallant spirits for whom the conservatives of our State are now enlisted and are trying to place in power. Remember this, and vote the Union ticket.[999]

On October 26, 1866, William F. Dusenberry of Guyandotte estimated that the Union Republican State ticket "has from 138 to 150 majority," and that the county slate was elected by about the same majority.[1000]

1866 Election Results
Cabell County
Governor: Arthur Boreman 305, Benjamin H. Smith 165
Secretary of State: John S. Witcher 296, J. W. Kennedy 166
Auditor: J. M. McWhorter 300, Peter Darnel 167
Treasurer: Jacob H. Bristor 302, John S. Burdett 173
Attorney General: Thayer Melvin 302, N. Richardson 173
Judge, Supreme Court: Edwin Maxwell 301, R. L Berkshire 166
Congress, 3d District: Daniel Polsley 301, John H. Oley 167
Judge, 8th Circuit: W. L. Hindman 303
State Senate, 8th: E. D. Wright 313, Mitchell Cook 164
House of Delegates: J. H. Ferguson 293, G. Harrison 179
Sheriff: John Harshbarger 292, L. J. Hoback 180
Clerk, Circuit Court: William Merritt 329, M. S. Thornburg 139
Recorder: Thomas J. Hayslip 303, E. M. Underwood 167
Prosecuting Attorney: B. D. McGinnis 308, W. H. Tomlinson 162
County Treasurer: Oscar W. Mather 290, J. W. Thornburg 178
Surveyor: James Felix 391
Assessor: Captain Francis Lesage 298, Henry C. Dunkle 168

Wayne County
Governor: Arthur Boreman 224, Benjamin H. Smith 163

Secretary of State: John S. Witcher 219, J. W. Kennedy 167
Auditor: J. M. McWhorter 219, Peter Darnel 167
Treasurer: Jacob H. Bristor 219, John S. Burdett 167
Attorney General: Thayer Melvin 219, N. Richardson 167
Judge, Supreme Court: Edwin Maxwell 216, R. L Berkshire 168
Congress, 3d District: Daniel Polsley 212, John H. Oley 166
Judge, 8th Circuit: W. L. Hindman 304
State Senate, 8th: E. D. Wright 218, Mitchell Cook 167
House of Delegates: J. S. P. Carroll 209, W. J. Dixon 173
Sheriff: M. Garrett 227, W. Queen 156
Clerk, Circuit Court: E. S. Bloss 216, G. W. Hutcherson 163
Recorder: Lewis Queen 213, William Kendrick 171
Prosecuting Attorney: William H. Enochs 230, W. H. Tomlinson 156
County Treasurer: George Adkins 220, F. Thompson 178
Surveyor: R. M. Luther 219, W. W. Brumfield 162
Assessor: A. A. Chapman 211, Lambert 166
Assessor 2: J. Marcum 218, A. Crum 167[1001]

Although those in Cabell and Wayne counties who had supported the Federal government during the tumultuous years of the Civil War retained political power in the 1866 election, their hold was tenuous, and their control of civil affairs was at times non-existent. Unrest continued to expand in the region, fueled by the opposition of ex-Confederates to the constrictions placed upon them by the new state government.

15
Federal Occupation

> *"..at no time since the surrender of Lee at Appomattox on the 9th day of April 1865 has this place [Guyandotte] stood more in need of military troops, than at the present time, for in addition to the causes set forth in the petition, it is a well known fact that the K.K.K. are organizing throughout this and the adjoining counties for no good purpose we know; and already the rebels are becoming emboldened, since they have learned that the troops are to be removed from this place…"*
>
> Thomas J. Hayslip to General George H. Thomas, June 16, 1868

Nearly two years after the end of the Civil War, civil authorities in the new state of West Virginia faced an uphill battle to enforce state and federal laws. The war had not ended for "Rebel" Bill Smith and others who continued to strike Union supporters in Wayne County. Joseph C. Wheeler wrote to elected officials concerning dire conditions and unlawful actions there, and the correspondence was published in a local newspaper. He began by observing,

> I have very reluctantly been compelled to believe that the law can no longer be administered at Wayne C. H., except upon a certain class of the citizens. A Union man who has violated the laws can be kept in prison there with perfect safety, and the sentence of the court can be executed upon him, and no one will interfere to prevent. But any one who has been active in the rebellion can not be kept there any longer than it suits the convenience of a gang of guerrillas, murderers, and horse-thieves to release him.[1002]

During the 1866 campaign, a "secret organization sprung up amongst the late rebels and their sympathizers," reportedly to support President Andrew Johnson, who was facing possible impeachment. According to Wheeler, "they openly threatened that they would rise on a given night and butcher all the Radicals in power, should his impeachment be attempted." Immediately after the election, Union men who had won county and state offices were warned not to accept their positions. Wheeler believed guerrillas had planned an attack on Colonel J. J. S. P. Carroll, a strong Union supporter from Wayne County who was elected to the House of Delegates in 1866. Several of his horses were stolen, supposedly to lure Carroll into the edge of Logan County where a large body of men was lying in wait for the purpose of killing him. He evaded the hostile force and managed to snare a prisoner who was transported to Wayne and lodged in the county jail.[1003]

Less than a month after the installation of new county officials in early 1867, "a gang of guerrillas, headed by the notorious 'Bill Smith,' dashed upon the jailor, with their revolvers pointed to his breast, and compelled him to turn the prisoner out, with whom they went shouting out of town, giving the only other Union man in town, besides the jailor, five days to leave the place or be killed, using such oaths as only demons can utter." Three days later Smith was again in the neighborhood around the courthouse "threatening to kill several Union citizens – and it is unknown where he will strike next."[1004]

Colonel J. J. S. P. Carroll of Wayne County, a target of guerrillas in 1866-1867. Carroll served in the West Virginia House of Delegates after the war. Credit: West Virginia State Archives.

Wheeler stated,

> Few Union men are afraid of 'Bill Smith' himself, but he is a cunning leader of a few desperate, brave and cruel men, and he is encouraged by leading men of the country to keep the country in an uproar and excitement, and their motive is supposed to be to intimidate Union men who are threatening to sue for damages for false imprisonment during the war, as they (the leading rebels) are telling every one what will happen to this and that one should they bring suit, &c. But whether these suits are brought or not, 'Bill Smith' or his gang, or any other rebel cannot be kept in the jail of Wayne county to be punished for any crime they may choose to commit, unless a standing army is kept there. Neither is it safe for any Union officer to stay there, unless he should 'knuckle down' to them.[1005]

The lengthy letter closed by declaring that the people of Wayne County were "compelled to choose between the stationing of troops there or the removal of the county seat." Even if soldiers were sent to the region, they would eventually be withdrawn, and Union citizens would be forced out upon their departure. Still, the "dread of being confined in a jail where they could be kept would deter many of them from committing crimes they do not now fear to commit."[1006]

In response to the public correspondence, Colonel J. J. S. P. Carroll wrote to West Virginia Governor Arthur Boreman and contacted military authorities requesting assistance. Company A of the 2nd United States Infantry, stationed in Louisville, Kentucky, departed on March 25, 1867, and reached Cincinnati on the following day. On March 27, the command, which consisted of two officers and sixty-four enlisted men, arrived at the mouth of the Big Sandy. The troops transferred to a steamer and reached the mouth of White's Creek on the following day. Eleven men and the company's baggage were left at this site, and the remaining troops marched to Trout's Hill, which they reached later in the day.

The command was headed by Major Joseph B. Collins, who wrote to Lieutenant Colonel W. F. Drum on March 31 to inform him of their arrival in Wayne County. He reported, "From what I have been able to see of the country, and from all the information I can gain from all the best citizens, I fully concur in all Col. C. says. Indeed there can be no doubt about it, and I respectfully request that I be ordered to make the disposition at once." Collins related that

Rebel Bill Smith, who continued to terrorize Union supporters for years after the end of the Civil War. Credit: Evelyn Booth Massie (courtesy of Robert Thompson).

> Lieut. Harkins informs me, that it is impossible to obtain forage or fresh beef, at this place, for the command. Up to this time he has only been able to get two small loads of his supplies from White's creek, and as it is now raining, in all probability another load cannot be hauled for a week. So soon as the plowing commences, which is now much behind the usual time, it will be impossible to have supplies hauled at any price. A citizen physician cannot be employed here. There is no ground in this vicinity that can be used for a camp, and no buildings that can be hired, for officers or men. The latter are now occupying the Court House.
>
> In view of the above facts, I respectfully suggest that a detachment of ten or fifteen men, as necessity may require, be left here; the same number be sent to Cassville, and the remainder with the Hd. Qrs. go to Ceredo. From this latter place these detachments can be regularly supplied, and all stores required at Ceredo can be sent by steamer from Louisville, Kentucky.
>
> Upon my arrival here the Court had been in session four days, and a more quiet

and well disposed class of citizens I never saw.[1007]

On April 17, Major Collins informed Drum that

so far as I have observed and can ascertain from the best portion of the inhabitants, the people of this and the adjoining counties, possibly Logan County might be excepted, are well disposed towards the General Government; the inhabitants who have lately been in rebellion, yield to it a quiet submission, more probably from compulsion than otherwise. They are by no means favorably disposed towards the State Government, and avoid or disregard their laws, whenever they can do so with impunity.

I believe a military force, of not more than one company is required in the county, for the present, and they should be stationed here, Cassville, and Ceredo. The latter place should by all means be the Head Quarters it being the most access[i]ble place.

Collins received a letter from Guyandotte on April 22 complaining of unsavory activities and disorder in the community. He spoke with United States revenue officers who had just left there and "was inclined to believe that no violence or lawlessness will be offered to the civil authorities or orderly citizens. The persons alluded to are raftsmen, who came to sell their logs and drink whiskey, both of which object the[y] will probably accomplish and return home. Some of them have already left." Major Collins pledged to go to Guyandotte and report anything "of the slightest importance."[1008]

General Order No. 5 was issued on April 24 from headquarters at Trout's Hill, directing the troops there and at the mouth of White's Creek to proceed to Ceredo and "constitute the garrison of that Post." One corporal and six privates would remain at the county seat, and a sergeant, corporal, and ten privates were ordered to Cassville. Transportation would be arranged by Lieutenant Charles Harkins, and both detachments were to be provided provisions for thirty days and the necessary camp and garrison equipage.[1009]

On the following day, Collins gave strict instructions to the small force remaining at Trout's Hill, obviously mindful of the jail incident earlier in the year that led to their presence in Wayne County:

The non-commissioned officer in charge of the detachment at this place will keep his command in good order; he will not permit any one to leave the quarters without his permission; nor will he absent himself at any time without placing one of the squad in charge; he will neither leave himself, or allow any of his men to be absent after 9 o'clock, p.m. Not more than two men will be permitted to be absent from quarters at the same time. Should there be any prisoners confined in the jail, he will, if called upon by the sheriff or jailer, see that they are safely kept, and will not permit them to be released by unauthorized persons. He will assist the civil authorities to execute the laws, at this, and in the immediate vicinity, upon their written application, reporting the facts at the earliest opportunity to his commanding officer. Ammunition will be used only for actual defence.[1010]

Collins gave similar directions to the squad at Cassville.

The *Wheeling Intelligencer* printed a letter written from Guyandotte on the evening of April 27, 1867, stating that the town

> was in a state of great excitement, occasioned by an irruption of about forty raft-men from the Tug region of Logan, who were on the rampage and swearing they intended to 'clean out' the town and drive the Union men away. The bullies were all armed, and the citizens were arming with the determination of defending themselves at all hazards.[1011]

Governor Arthur Boreman and the prosecuting attorney of Cabell County both wrote to Major Collins on May 6 concerning conditions in the area. Collins sent ten men to Guyandotte the same day and telegraphed Lieutenant Colonel W. F. Drum in Louisville requesting that another company be sent to West Virginia. The major believed this action was "absolutely indispensable, if the counties named in his Excellencies letter are to be properly protected, and they most assuredly should be, for I believe they contain a nest of lawless rebels that are spo[i]ling for a strong arm to compel them to respect the rights and lives of Union men."[1012]

West Virginia Governor Arthur I. Boreman. Credit: Library of Congress.

Drum was reluctant to send the second company. He told Collins to send "detachments of such sizes as you can spare to Cabell and Logan Counties." Collins quickly replied that he had sent troops to Cabell County but could not send any to Logan "unless you send me more troops." Drum finally directed First Lieutenant Charles Harkins with one non-commissioned officer and nine privates to "proceed by the first steamer to Guyandotte and assist the civil authorities in executing the laws and preserving the peace." Harkins was to remain there "no longer than he deems his presence necessary." The other ten soldiers would be provided with forty rounds of ammunition per man and the necessary camp and garrison equipage and would remain in Guyandotte until further orders.[1013]

Collins responded to Governor Boreman, informing him of the request for a second company. He also provided assurance that the counties noted by Boreman "shall have all the necessary assistance the civil authorities require, and all the force at my disposal will be promptly and energetically used to preserve order, and protect the rights of Union men."[1014]

At ten o'clock on the morning of May 19, Major Collins received a telegram from Lieutenant Colonel W. F. Drum informing him that an order had been issued directing a Lieutenant Naggle and twenty soldiers to report to him at Ceredo.

In May 1867, a Ceredo resident complained about the Federal troops stationed in Cabell and Wayne counties:

> The soldiers lately brought to this county for some purpose unknown to this deponent, are lying around loose, at Cassville, Ceredo, Trout's Hill, and Guyandotte, and enjoying themselves as soldiers know how to, when they have nothing particular to do. Another company of the same regiment is expected, and may be here before this letter reaches you. I understand they are coming for the benefit of their health, a good many of them having the fever and ague where they are now stationed, at Louisville, Ky.[1015]

There seems to have been very little guerrilla activity while the United States troops occupied Cabell and Wayne counties. They may have been idle at times, but their daily schedule was filled:

Head Quarters, Post of Ceredo
June 3, 1867

Memorandum
The following list of calls will be observed at this post from and after this date
Reveille: 5:00 a.m.
Breakfast: 6:00
Drill (Squad): 8:00
Surgeon Call: 8:00
Recall from Drill: 8:00
1st call for Guard Mounting: 8:45
Guard Mounting: 9:00
Fatigue Call: immediately after Guard Mounting
Recall from Fatigue: 12:00
Dinner: 12:30 p.m.
Fatigue: 2:00
Recall from Fatigue: 4:00
Drill (Company): 4:30
Recall from Drill: 5:30
1st Call for Retreat: 30 minutes before sunset
Retreat (Under Arms): 15 minutes before sunset
Tattoo: 9:00
Taps: 9:30 p.m.

On July 14, Collins notified the detachment at Guyandotte that they were relieved from duty at that point and ordered to Ceredo via the first steamer.[1016]

Judge William L. Hindman succeeded Henry J. Samuels as judge of the 8th judicial district of West Virginia when Samuels resigned on August 2, 1866. Hindman would be embroiled in constant controversy over the next year regarding his rulings allowing ex-Confederates to practice law in Cabell County without taking the test oath, and he would be impeached less than a year later. During the summer of 1867, he clashed with Major Joseph B. Collins and the United States Army, a fight he was predetermined to lose.

Second Lieutenant John C. Bateman, recruiting officer for the post at Ceredo, enlisted Alexander Smith into the service of the United States, but the recruit apparently had a change of heart. A writ of habeas corpus was filed with Judge Hindman, who scheduled a hearing on July 27. Collins claimed that "in the opinions of all the officers and majority of the citizens present the case was not decided either justly or according to the testimony." The witnesses were Smith's parents, but Collins observed that "we were aware from the commencement of the case that the trial was a farce and that the matter was already agreed upon." Judge Hindman ordered Smith discharged from the service.[1017]

Hindman met with Major Collins and informed him "that he did not want any US troops in his district – that he had eight sheriffs who he could call upon to administer the laws." Collins was frustrated by the judge's attitude and his ruling, as evidenced by his claim that to "my personal knowledge of affairs in this part of the country that there is no need of troops here, or at any of the stations furnished with detachments from this command. I therefore respectfully recommend that as our assistance is not required by the civil authorities tha[t] the troops be withdrawn."[1018]

In response to Hindman's ruling, Major Collins issued Special Order No. 19 on August 10:

> The Major General commanding the Department, having decided that the actions of the Hon. William V. Hindman, Judge of the 8th Judicial District of this State, in discharging on a writ of Habeas Corpus, Private Alexander Smith, Co. A, 2nd US Infantry from the U. S. Army, is a 'nullity' and the Bvt Brig. General commanding the District having directed that the said Smith be 'taken into custody,' 1st Lieut. Charles Harkins, 2nd US Infantry, and two non-commissioned officers will proceed immediately and arrest said Smith, wherever he may be found, and bring him to this Post.[1019]

Collins left Ceredo on the morning of September 17 and rode to Logan Courthouse, where he inspected the detachment of troops stationed there two days later. He found the men in good condition and described them as "well disciplined and fairly instructed in the ordinary drills." The commissary stores were satisfactory except for a large quantity of hard bread "which was musty, worm eaten and unfit for issue." Collins observed, "The troops are occupying tents by day, and the Court House at night. Carpenters are yet working on the Court House, and will have it completed in one month, when it will be occupied by the troops as winter quarters."[1020]

On September 21, Major Collins reviewed the posts at Cassville and Trout's Hill, "both of which were in very good order." The troops in Cassville were quartered in tents, and Collins directed the purchase of lumber to "have the tents stockaded" for winter occupation. At Trout's Hill, the soldiers occupied the courthouse and would require other quarters in the months ahead.[1021]

On September 30, Brigadier General Sidney Burbank ordered Major Joseph B. Collins to move his headquarters from Ceredo to Guyandotte. At the new post, Lieutenant Charles Harkins was ordered to purchase nails and 2,500 feet of lumber to build a laundress quarters and men's sinks. He was also directed to buy locks and hinges necessary for the hospital and a guard house. Sallie Smith, whose family was back in Guyandotte, observed, "We have Regular soldiers here, two companies quartered just across the street, from us, and drill almost front of us, every day. They are very quiet, as a general thing. Some of them get drunk, but don't disturb citizens."[1022]

The 1867 election in West Virginia was held in October. In Cabell County, Union Party candidate William Workman was a unanimous selection for state senator, James H. Ferguson was elected to the House of Delegates to represent Cabell and Lincoln counties over Lewis Hinchman, and William Algeo was elected the county superintendent of free schools.[1023]

Major Joseph B. Collins, whose command was headquartered at Guyandotte, wrote to Governor Arthur Boreman on January 14, 1868, concerning troop disposition in western West Virginia. Collins believed there was "no necessity" for the two small detachments of troops stationed at Logan and Wayne Courthouse, and he asked Boreman to recommend that both be withdrawn from those posts and moved to reinforce Cassville or Guyandotte. "From either Cassville, or here," he noted, "troops could easily be sent to either of the Court Houses, should any emergency require their services." Collins commended James H. Ferguson, who delivered the letter to Boreman: "There is no other person with whom I am acquainted that so well understands the wants of this part of the county as he does."[1024]

Lieutenant John C. Bateman issued General Order No. 1 on January 15, 1868, in response to complaints from the community "that some of the enlisted men of the command are in the frequent habit of tearing down fences and going into the plowed fields there adjoining the property of citizens..." He ordered an immediate halt to "these evils" and ordered patrols to make frequent rounds at least one mile from the post headquarters. Any soldiers discovered away from their proper posts or "in any manner interfering with the rights of property of citizens" would be arrested.[1025]

Union residents of Guyandotte wrote to Major General George H. Thomas, commanding the Department of the Cumberland, on June 16, 1868. They "most earnestly" requested that the Federal forces stationed in the town not be removed:

> In our county, and adjacent counties there is a regularly organized band of horse thieves and robbers who have been terrifying all classes of citizens to an alarming extent, and owing to the mountainous re[g]ion of this country the

civil authorities have been powerless.

But since the arrival of the U. S. forces here we have enjoyed peace and quiet, and for this reason we pray the furtherance of the protection.[1026]

The letter was signed by more than thirty citizens and was endorsed by County Recorder Thomas J. Hayslip, who identified the endorsers as "men of truth and veracity, and men who have the welfare of the county at heart." Hayslip also wrote

that at no time since the surrender of Lee at Appomattox on the 9th day of April 1865 has this place stood more in need of military troops, than at the present time, for in addition to the causes set forth in the petition, it is a well known fact that the K.K.K. are organizing throughout this and the adjoining counties for no good purpose we know; and already the rebels are becoming emboldened, since they have learned that the troops are to be removed from this place, for on yesterday 4 of them were standing on the bridge looking at a boat load of remains of Fedl Soldiers that were being removed to New Albany Indiana for re-interment when one of the party said their bones ought to be ground up to make manure to enrich the lands, the other three endorsed the sentiment; this intelligence came from a rebel himself who was nearby and perhaps thought the sentiment to[o] good to keep.[1027]

Captain F. E. Lacey issued General Order No. 12 on June 18 from Guyandotte. The detachments of Company A stationed at Logan Courthouse and Cassville were relieved and ordered to proceed to Guyandotte and report for duty to the commanding officer of that post. A non-commissioned officer and six privates from Company B were directed to Cassville to take possession of any government property left behind by the detachment moved to Guyandotte.[1028]

On June 25, General Order No. 13 was issued in compliance to a directive from the headquarters of the Military District of Kentucky. Company A of the 2nd United States Infantry was removed from the post at Guyandotte and ordered to Taylor Barracks in Louisville.[1029]

Democrats and Conservatives of Wayne County met at the county courthouse on June 27 to choose delegates to their state convention. Included among them were Charles B. Webb, W. W. Brumfield, and William Ratliff. A number of resolutions were passed, including one which declared "that all the citizens of this county who are opposed to the ruling political party in this State and its unjust and oppressive legislation, should actively engage in the coming political campaign, and each do all in his power to secure a thorough canvass of the county, so that every man who has the right to vote under the law is registered and on the day of election comes out to vote."[1030]

At 4:00 a.m. on July 3, the Federal post at Guyandotte was abandoned by Company B of the 2nd United States Infantry. The troops reached Cassville at ten o'clock on the morning of July 4 and set up their post on the east bank of the Tug Fork of the Big

Sandy River.[1031]

On July 15, 1868, Joseph C. Wheeler wrote to Governor Arthur Boreman from Ceredo. He had spoken with eight Union men from Grant Township in Wayne County, adjoining the Logan County line, who had been "scared away from their homes by the Rebels with whom they are wholly surrounded." Wheeler sought to convince the men to return to their residences, but they refused and went to Ohio instead, fearing assassination if they remained in Wayne County. A grandson of Captain Absalom Queen stopped by Ceredo and informed Wheeler that disorder in that part of Wayne County was increasing. Wheeler noted, "Union men are lying out on the watch for heavily armed men who are frequent seen in the woods near their dwellings and while it is hard to trace the threats to their true source the country is rife with threats against Union men if they do not leave the country." Queen's grandson believed "that it is a band of about 100 bad men connected with the notorious 'Bill Smith' who design to clear the country of all who would be likely to oppose them or detect their operations in stealing horses robbing &c."[1032]

Wheeler was convinced that "the whole thing is countenanced & encouraged if not instigated by the leading members of the conservative party here of whom C. B. Webb late of the 5th Va. Reg. & now U. S. Deputy Assessor is very prominent going all over the two counties of Wayne & Logan and attending the search meetings of their Lodges..." Wheeler opposed sending troops to Wayne County, but he thought a "shrewd detective" could be effective in obtaining information and would hopefully prevent "a collision of the Union & rebel citizens." He also expressed his fear that the conservative party would win the upcoming election, "which will be the beginning of great trouble here."[1033]

Wheeler, who had been involved in the formation of Union regiments in Cabell and Wayne in 1861, defended himself against various charges and asserted, "During all the war and since I suppose there is no man who has been worse hated or more misrepresented by rebels & their sympathisers than I have & it goes a little hard to be also misrepresented by those who were afraid to sho[u]lder the responsibilities I did not shrink from & which has made me so many enemies." He urged Boreman to refrain from sharing his letter "to any but true Union men."[1034]

Democrats in Cabell and Wayne counties complained that Radical Republicans were using any means necessary to maintain their grip on power. Notices for a Democratic meeting posted on the door of a storeroom in Guyandotte were torn and smeared over with lamp black. The *Mason County Journal* responded,

> It is not enough for these 'loyal scalawags' to strike true Union men and in some instances, Union soldiers from the list of registered voters; it is not enough for them to register rebels deserters who have killed Union men, (but who now promise to vote the Radical ticket,); it is not enough for them to hold their *secret* political meetings at midnight, but they must descend to these vile and even criminal means to prevent their political opponents from holding their meetings *publicly* in the light of day. Be careful Rads; your opponents may yet be compelled to 'fight the devil with fire.' You must remember that blows can

be given as well as taken.[1035]

On Saturday, September 5, "one of the largest and most enthusiastic political meetings ever assembled in this end of the State" was held in a beautiful grove about one mile from Barboursville. It was termed "a grand gala day" for the Democrats and Conservatives of Cabell County. Thousands of citizens from surrounding counties lined the roads leading into town in wagons, buggies, and carriages, on horseback and on foot, and it was noon before the crowd could reach the site. Henry J. Samuels, adjutant general of the Restored Government of Virginia during the war and a former circuit court judge, was appointed president of the meeting.[1036]

Several prominent political figures, including Johnson N. Camden, Democratic candidate for governor, delivered addresses to the crowd. Two of the orators spoke for more than two hours each. The barbecue dinner, also lengthy, was "served from two tables, each two hundred yards long, and which were crowded with people on both sides, two and three deep..." A correspondent from the *Mason County Journal* wrote, "One remarkable feature of this monster meeting, was the singular absence of drunken Radicals to create a disturbance. Not a single drunken man was seen on the ground, nor did we hear an angry word spoken."[1037]

John S. Witcher wrote to Governor Arthur Boreman from Fayette Courthouse on September 7, 1868:

> I am of the opinion from all I can find out that we will have trouble with the Rebels in Cabell Lincoln & Boone Counties. I am of the opinion they will attempt to register by force...I am sure that they will give us trouble unless we can get a few troops here and in Cabell.[1038]

John S. Witcher commanded the 3rd West Virginia Cavalry and was promoted to the rank of brevet brigadier general at the end of the war. This photo, taken in 1866, shows him as a member of the West Virginia House of Delegates. He would later serve as secretary of state and in the United States House of Representatives. Credit: West Virginia State Archives.

A Union officer had recently been driven from Peytona, where the residents "swore that no dam Grant man could speak or live in that neighbourhood." Witcher himself had been threatened: "They were about to mob me here to day. I thought at one time I should be mobed shure as they threatened my life openly."[1039]

Witcher did not think there would be serious trouble in Fayette, Jackson, Kanawha, Logan, Mason, or Putnam counties or in any part of Judge Nathaniel Harrison's judicial district due to the military presence in these areas. He believed that "with 50 or 100 men in Cabell it will keep all the adjoining counties quiet." The only concern was whether Union men would be frightened or intimidated from voting.[1040]

Another group of Guyandotte citizens, including the prosecuting attorney of Cabell County, wrote to Boreman on September 15, 1868, to inform him of the "political state of affairs as they now exist in our county at this time." On September 7, ex-Confederates had attacked voter registration boards across Cabell County, "forced themselves on the Registrars and succeeded in getting about two hundred names in the Register and swear that the Board of Registration shall not take their names off the Register, as they intend to vote in spite of all the opposition that can be brought against them."[1041]

Consequently, it was feared that the election would not be held in any Cabell County township except Guyandotte, "which we presume will be able to protect itself, unless the rebs are reinforced from the other townships." The residents implored, "We therefore as loyal citizens of the State, respectfully request that you cause troops to be sent into this county as soon as possible to stem the rebel tide that is bearing down on us." They also noted that the "same state of affairs exist in the County of Lincoln."[1042]

One of the "largest political meetings ever known in the county" was held by Democrats at Wayne Courthouse on September 19. Several speakers addressed the crowd, and "a splendid flag pole with the stars and stripes" was raised as the attendees roared with "loud huzza's" until their throats were hoarse. An observer described the events as "characterized by harmony and enthusiasm." He added,

> The flag and pole raised were the work of the disfranchised citizens at the village, and altogether a fine specimen of what love and country and accompanying enthusiasm can do in the mountains, where, it has been said, it was not safe for Union men to stay, and government officials could not safely perform their duties. Those men were just as enthusiastic over the raising the stars and stripes as any other set of men anywhere could be, and just as jealous for its safety as the loud mouthed politicians who are constantly denouncing the conservative party as rebels.[1043]

In response to threats on the electoral process, Special Order No. 2, designed to protect the county boards of registration, was issued from the post at Guyandotte on October 2. Sergeant John McConnell, along with a corporal and four privates, was to proceed to Barboursville and report to Oscar Mather, officer of registration. Sergeant Daniel B. Beard and six privates were sent to Boone Courthouse, and Sergeant John Moran and six soldiers were ordered to Lincoln Courthouse. Each detachment was to be furnished with forty rounds of ammunition per man and three days' cooked rations.[1044]

The board of registration in Wayne County requested assistance as well. On October 3, First Sergeant John Mills was ordered to take charge of a detachment of eleven members of Company B, proceed to Wayne Courthouse, and report to John Hoback, president of the registration board. Each man would be supplied with twenty rounds of ammunition and three days' cooked rations. The troops were to return to their proper stations upon being notified by Hoback that their services were no longer needed.[1045]

On October 6, Oscar Mather requested that the detachment of Federal troops sent to Barboursville a few days earlier be allowed to remain at that location. Captain Adolphus W. Kroutinger granted permission and contacted Sergeant McConnell to inform him of the decision. He also cautioned, "The detachment will be kept on hand, and no soldier allowed to leave his quarters after sunset."[1046]

Two days later Kroutinger forwarded correspondence from Mather and requested further instruction. "I have been informed by reliable authority," Kroutinger declared, "that Mr. Mather's life will be in danger should the detachment be relieved at Barboursville." He also noted that he had not heard from the troops sent to Boone and Lincoln counties, but he expected the return of the detachment sent to the latter place.[1047]

As the election neared, Republicans reminded voters it was essential that they remain in power. The October 21 issue of the *West Virginia Journal* included several large print reminders, including one that read, "The successful resistance of the rebel plot for another war may depend upon the election of a Republican Congressman from this District; then vote for the gallant Col. Witcher."[1048]

A Charleston newspaper reported the results of the 1868 election in Cabell County:

> Cabell has gone Republican by 78 on the State ticket. Ferguson's majority in the County is about the same. Wright is elected to the House of Delegates. The whole Republican County ticket is elected.

The same issue noted that "Wayne County has also gone Republican by a majority, on the State ticket. J. S. P. Carroll is elected to the House of Delegates."[1049]

Democrats, however, complained that irregular methods were used by the registration boards, which were controlled by Radical Republicans. In one township,

> the inspectors sat on each side of the table and passed the ballots *under* the table, providing a means of changing the ballots from democratic to radical before they went into the box. In Ceredo township the conservatives and democrats elected their Supervisor by one majority, but when counted by the supervisors they gave the election to the radical candidate, by some 'mysterious way' not known to honest men.
>
> The Board of registration had a squad of U. S. soldiers to 'protect' them when they sat, and soldiers were stationed at our precinct where the officers had been 'outdaciously' corrupt in registering and failing to register.[1050]

Captain Adolphus Kroutinger informed Governor Arthur Boreman on November 3 that the detachment stationed in Boone County for election protection would depart from Peytona Township on the following day and march to headquarters in

Cabell County Jail at Barboursville, guarded by Federal troops, 1868-1869. Credit: Special Collections Department, Marshall University.

Guyandotte. He added, "If, on their return, the Sergt Comd'g the detachment should report indications of any troubles, I will immediately send another detachment to the same place, which is the only recourse open for me to pursue at present..."[1051]

Two days later, Lieutenant John Waring of the 2nd United States Infantry noted that William Jordan, supervisor of elections at Mud Bridge, had deemed it unnecessary for troops to be stationed at that point. They were ordered to return to headquarters for requisitions and would then be sent to Ceredo.[1052]

On February 1, 1869, C. W. Shipe, Cabell County jailer, presented a petition to the county board of supervisors "stating that it was impossible for him to keep the jail in order while the soldiers occupied the same and as another reason, for want of sufficient coal to supply them and the county officer...It is, therefore, ordained, that the said soldiers do give up possession of said Court House to the Sheriff of the county."[1053]

Captain Kroutinger informed headquarters of the request on February 5 and stated he had investigated the matter and learned both parties were to blame. The detachment at Barboursville had assisted civil authorities for more than two months by furnishing two men each night to guard and protect the prisoners in the jail. Kroutinger "ordered the detachment into a vacant room opposite the Court House with strict orders not to go near the Court House or jail except called in by the Sheriff or the Hon. Judge Ferguson." He also observed, "By my own information and reliable reports the jailor Mr. C Shipe is a regular Secesh and a man of but low character."[1054]

On March 9, the Federal troops stationed in the county received orders for their return to Louisville on March 12. The soldiers began packing up equipment and material and had an auction sale on the following day. That Friday night, the soldiers loaded and boarded the *Fleetwood*, but the mail arrived with instructions to remain in Guyandotte until further notice. The men unloaded the boat and returned to their quarters. On March 15, Kroutinger and his company finally left Cabell County for Louisville. Their departure led to "a noisy time at the wharf boat. Jim Wright, Jim Sedinger, Irving Smith, Chubb Scott and several others were about half tight & Billy Rogers and Sam Johnston raised the mischief until near night."[1055]

The struggle over political control in the county and the state continued. In a July 30, 1869, letter from Cabell Courthouse, a resident noted that West Virginia State Code required each county board of registration to appoint a registrar in each township "on or before the first Monday in July in each year." These registrars were to "sit at some convenient place in his Township or Ward" on the first Monday in August "in order to make a correct register of all the qualified voters therein." Those persons not registered but claiming the right to vote were to apply to the registrar.[1056]

The writer to the *Cabell County Press* complained that no registrars had been appointed and the members of the Board of Registration had not been qualified.

> What does it mean? Are the rights of the people to be trampled upon in this way and whole communities to be disfranchised on account of the neglect of the Governor to appoint officers who will accept the positions? I call attention to this matter that the Governor may act promptly and appoint men who will accept. If the Radical party by the acts of their Boards of Registration have rendered this office so detestable to public opinion that no radical can be found in the county who will serve as one of such, let the Governor appoint three honest Conservatives in the county who will lift the office from disgrace and at the same time so act as to give quiet and content to our people.[1057]

A letter to the editor of the *Cabell County Press* complained about the manner in which voters were stricken from the rolls by the registration boards:

> Several of the parties named were notified to appear before the Board; they were not granted a trial, their names were stricken out without one tittle of evidence having been heard. They registered again, and the petty tyrants struck them from the dash, as follows.

Cabell C. H.
September 2, 1869

To John Kirby, Robert Wiley, A. D. Simmons, Geo. W. Summers, D. P. Smith, George W. Sheff, Wm. Black, H. V. and John G. Chapman. Take notice, that the registrar for Grant township has returned his books to this office, and that your names are on the books contrary to law, and the orders of the board; you will take notice that your names will be erased without notice or trial, as you have once been rejected by the Board of Registration.

The writer was particularly vexed by the fact that the names of the members of the Board of Registration were not included, nor the time and place where they met.[1058]

A Liberal Republican candidate for the state senate, W. O. Wright, recorded his opinions on measures likely to be considered by the next legislature, including voting rights. According to Wright,

> a liberal policy toward those who are disfranchised should be adopted. And if elected, it will be my purpose to carry out that policy and use all the means in my power to effect such legislation as will remove all political disabilities and restore the franchise at the earliest period possible, believing that to be the surest means of effecting that harmony which is so essential to the material development of our new State, and the encouragement of the moral and industrial interests of society. The day for the Restriction policy has passed away – it is to be hoped forever – a brighter day dawns with the bow of promise spanning the future of our State and national politics.[1059]

Surprisingly, Wright's position was echoed by Congressman John S. Witcher. In a letter to the Point Pleasant *Weekly Register*, Witcher wrote, "I am free to say, that in my opinion, the time has arrived when we can with perfect safety repeal every proscriptive law upon our statute books. I therefore, favor the election of such Republicans to represent us in the next Legislature as will vote for the immediate repeal of what are known as the Lawyers, Suitors and Teachers Test Oaths, and to so amend, by joint Resolution, the State Constitution, so as to restore the elective franchise and the right to hold office, to those of our citizens who participated in the rebellion or gave aid and comfort to the same." As Witcher noted,

> These laws were passed as war measures, or at least until the issues growing out of the war were settled. In fact, a majority of those whom the law was intended to reach for the time being, were fresh from the battle field where they had taken an oath to support the Southern Confederacy; many of whom were yet parrolled [sic] prisoners of war. The State had been organized in their absence, and contrary to their wishes, and while many were saying at the time the restrictive laws were passed, that the State was a 'bogus State' and would again be reunited to the old Commonwealth of Virginia. They were pass[ed] before Congress had agreed upon any general plan of reconstruction of the South and before it was known what disposition would be made of the late rebels in our midst. Under all these circumstances I think the laws were right and just, they were in fact, indispensable. If some such laws had not been enacted for the protection of the State and those who so nobly stood by the government in her hour of need, the rebel element could have combined and elected to office men of their own views, and could have dictated the terms upon which they should be admitted to their former positions in the Union, thus setting a precedent

unknown in the history of nations.

But, these reasons cannot longer be with propriety urged. For four year[s] the war has been over, the passions and prejudices of the people have had time to cool. The Confederate and Federal soldier have returned to their homes each and all living under the same flag, as friends and neighbors, each and all jointly interested in the future prosperity and happiness of our State and nation. And so far as I know, the former has lived up strictly to his parole. He is paying his portion of the taxes to support the government cheerfully. To this it will be said by some, that the property of the rebels that got up the war should be confiscated and made to pay the entire war debt which was contracted in putting down the rebellion, and that the law has been set at defiance repeatedly in our own State. To those I would say that the Government in its magnanimity has said that it would not confiscate their property, and has extended to them a free and full pardon for all past offenses, from which there is no appeal. And that when you come to examine into and ferret out the leaders and getters up of the disturbances that have taken place in our State, you will not find the rebel soldier engaged in them, but the politician, that is contending for place and power, who now, that the clash of arms has ceased, ventures out from his boom-proof, where he was protected during the war by Federal bayonets, and attempts to make cheap political capital by fighting the battles of the country over again. I do not believe that to-day there is in the State of West Virginia one rebel soldier in a hundred, that would go into the same war under the same circumstances. They, so far as I have been able to discover, accept the situation in good faith. I have always contended, that when they did that, every restriction that has been placed on them by the State and Federal Government should be removed as speedily as possible. Besides this, they have been pardoned by the Government including the leaders and getters up of the rebellion. The reconstruction of the South we may say is a fixed fact. Seven of the ten States are admitted back into the Union, and I have no doubt but that the other three will be knocking for re-admission this fall, when Congress assembles, and that too, upon terms submitted to them by a Republican Congress.

The State of West Virginia, as I before remarked, whose status had been questioned, has been recognized by every branch of the Government, up to the Supreme Court of the United States; and I do not believe that should the opposition get into power, that they would ever make a moove [sic] looking to the restoration of West Virginia to East Virginia.

We have just emerged as it were, from a great national contest where all the issues growing out of the war were met and discussed and settled forever, let us hope, by the election of Gen. Grant as President. Then with our trusted and tried friend as President, and every office in the gift of the people in the hands of its friends, with the country at peace with all foreign nations, I ask then, what have we to fear from a conquered, law abiding and industrious people. I appeal to every brave soldier and true Union man that has the love of his country at heart, if they think it is right to longer oppress those who went into the rebellion, from honest convictions which had been instilled into many of them from childhood up, that their first allegiance was due their State. Then let us say to these men, you have erred, but we can and will forgive you, and my word for it, we will never have cause to rejoice that we had the courage and magnanimity to do it. It should be the aim of all to forget the late terrible war, with all its sufferings, privations and hardships. Although some things may appear to us as if they were written in letters of living fire, let us banish them forever in order that we may once more enter upon that peace and prosperity that God in His wisdom, intended we should do as a nation.[1060]

A Barboursville resident wrote to the *Cabell County Press* on October 23, 1869, concerning the upcoming election. "On next Thursday," the writer noted, "the people of this county will be called upon to perform the highest duties of citizens known to our laws – that of choosing officers to represent them in the halls of Legislation and in the various County and Township offices. Let no man be derelict in his duty on that day." Although a Republican, he urged the election of Democratic candidates for the Senate and House of Delegates. One believed "the time has come when the bitter feelings engendered by the war should be buried and the people should forget the past and all come together as a band of patriots and work for the common good." Another stated unequivocally that he would "use all his influence to remove from our statute books all laws making distinctions between the people for acts growing out of the rebellion" and would favor a constitutional amendment removing the test oath clause.[1061]

A correspondent to the *Cabell County Press* reported that the election

passed off very quietly in this place; but very little interest being manifested by either party. Quite a number of Democrats staid away from the polls, refusing to vote on the ground that 'it was no use, the Republicans would carry the county.' Returns show to the contrary...Returns from Wayne county show a majority for the Democracy of 200.[1062]

According to the papers, the results were as follows:

Guyandotte Township, William Workman (Republican) over Mitchell Cook (Democrat) 30-21 for Senate, House of Delegates, William A. Holstein (R) over J. S. Wilkinson (D) 28-26, for School Superintendent, J. W. Church, Assessor, H. Bumgardner over S. A. Childers 28-16, for Supervisor William Wintz, Clerk Charles O. Dusenberry over D. J. Smith 31-1, Overseer of the Poor T. M. Eves; School Commission, George F. Miller 50, L J. Hoback 44, E. Edens 21, W. Eggers 23, for constable William Douthit over Nathan Collins 48-26, for Treasurer Joseph T. Hysell over John Plybon 29-21, for Road Surveyor L. P.

Carter over E. M. Clark 29-1

Barboursville Township, Cook 52-22, Wilkinson 52-22, Church 60-6, Childers 44-29, Assessor – S. A. Childers 44, H. J. Bumgardner 29, Supervisor – T. Thornburg 51, Jos. Eggers 26, Clerk – C. J. Burnett 52, V. Mathers 1, Overseer Poor, Jas. McDermitt 72, Treasurer – J. H. Salmon 49, D. Harshbarger 25, Constable – A. J. Dick 56, Surveyor – John Mills 50, Charles Waugh 23.

McComas Township – Workman 41-7, Holstein 40-8, Church 28, S. A. Childers 6, R. J. Roberts, Republican elected Supervisor.

Union Township – The Democrats have a majority in this township of 40. The vote stood 13 to 53.

Grant Township – Holstein received a majority of 3 in this township.[1063]

In 1870 several communities, including Ceredo, Guyandotte, and Maple Grove (site of Marshall College), vied to be the terminus of the Chesapeake & Ohio Railroad. In response to an earlier letter criticizing Guyandotte, a resident of the community replied on February 25, 1870, revealing the condition of the town five years after the war:

But to remind us of our misfortunes, over which we had no control, was 'the most unkindest cut of all.' It would have been more truthful if Native had written desolated instead of 'dilapidated village.' It is too true that we were visited during the late terrible war with tyranny and blood by an infamous Clarkson, followed with torch and whiskey, by, if possible, a more infamous Z[ei]gler, who sought to complete the hell-begun work.

And it is true that around the black and mouldering ruins of houses and gardens there is a luxuriant crop of 'dog-fennel'...

I find three good church buildings, and many other houses of equal capacity to any in the vicinity of Maple Grove. Seven stores, three or four groceries, shops, saloons, and a good place for empty pint bottles; and another small item or two, i.e., three steam saw mills and one wire suspension bridge in this 'dilapidated village.' The 'unseemly sheds,' I presume, has reference to the frame and roofing of a large stable on Bridge Street, which in the better days of this place, were kept a stud of from twenty to thirty-five horses for the accommodation of natives and visitors, but now only serves as a shelter from wind and rain, for the studs of the good country people.[1064]

A letter to the *Cabell County Press* from the Cabell Court House dated June 1 echoed a complaint voiced a year prior concerning the failure of the governor to appoint a board of registration in the county. The writer noted,

The month of May has passed and yet no Board has qualified. Have any, or will any be appointed by the Governor? Last year we had no Board. Two were appointed and both refused to qualify, until it was too late to register any one. The attention of the Governor was called to it in vain. Is the same infamous trick to be played over again. We appeal to Governor Stevenson to act fairly in this matter. Will he do it? We shall see.[1065]

The Republican County Committee of Cabell County held a convention in Barboursville on June 15, 1870. The following nominations were made for delegates from each township to represent Cabell in the upcoming state congressional and senatorial conventions:

Union Township: George M. Rouse, Julius Lesage and Anthony Bicker. Guyandotte Township: Benjamin D. McGinniss, Julius Freutel and W. O. Wright. Barboursville Township: Joseph Eggers, David Harshbarger and V. W. Mather. Grant Township: A. L. Beckett, J. N. Rousey and T. Hawkins. McComas Township: A. Hinchman, S. J. Swann and R. J. Roberts.

The single resolution offered and adopted was a pledge to strengthen the Republican party in preparation for the fall election to "present a bold, solid and united front to the mixed, mongrel, so-called Democracy."[1066]

On Thursday, October 20, a meeting of the "Southerners of Barboursville" was held at the courthouse. The purpose of the gathering was to pay tribute to General Robert E. Lee, who had died eight days earlier. In addition to "eloquent and feeling tributes" by Lucien C. Ricketts and Dr. C. D. Moss, those gathered passed resolutions which were unanimously adopted:

Resolved, That in the death of Gen. Robert E. Lee, earth has yielded her brightest jewel to the casket of Heaven. He stood alone, in solitary preeminence, a towering monument, a land mark upon the utmost verge of human greatness, beneath whose shadow the struggling great perish, but around whose summit the light of eternity must play. That peerless above the giants in head, and heroes in heart of the nineteenth century stands the matchless name of Robert E. Lee.

Resolved, 2nd, That, although he has grown grey in the service of his God, his country and truth, yet we most grievously feel the weight of the stroke that cut him from us.

Resolved, 3rd, That in his death the country has lost an exemplary citizen, the church a zealous member, learning and justice a firm friend, and tyranny [sic] an inexorable foe.

Resolved 4th, That tho no marble monument may rear its lofty form to commemmorate his distinguished public and private virtues, yet the greatness and glory of his manhood and character will be as enduring as the stars, and the transcendenth grandeur of his example will be, like the unwithering cedars of Lebanon, unfading in our remembrance.

Resolved 5th, That we offer our sincere condolence to the unhappy remnant of his family in the dark and bitter days of its humiliation and suffering; and earnestly commend them to an humble acquiescence in the will of that Providence, which is all wise, and whose exalted attributes are incomprehensible to fallen, finite mortality.[1067]

On October 27, 1870, voters went to the polls throughout the state. Although many ex-Confederates were still disenfranchised, African American voters had been afforded the right to vote due to the passage of the 15th Amendment to the United States Constitution. William Dusenberry recorded that six black citizens voted in Guyandotte, which caused "[m]uch excitement."[1068]

> Cabell County results:
> Jacob and the whole State ticket, 146 majority.
> Hereford, for Congress, 129 majority.
> Kline, Democrat, for State Senate, 156 majority.
> Ferguson, Democrat, for House of Delegates, 170 majority.
> Miller, Democrat, for Clerk of Circuit Court, 201 majority.
> Smith, Democrat, for Sheriff, 214 majority.
>
> Wayne County results:
> 350 Democrat majority.
> Lamack Adkins, Independent Democrat for Sheriff, 105 majority over Brumfield, regular Democrat and Capt. Waymer, Republican. Wm. Shannon, Independent Democrat, elected over Marcum, regular Democrat, for House of Delegates, by 104 majority.[1069]

Democrats swept the election of 1870, marking the end of Republican rule in West Virginia for a quarter century. Many of the Union leaders who had helped form the new state were voted from office. One of those ousted from political power was General John S. Witcher, who was defeated in his bid for re-election to Congress. The *Cabell County Press* wrote, "This gentleman though defeated deserves the mead of praise from his party having made the most active and vigorous campaign of any of his compeers."[1070]

Epilogue

"We thought we never had seen a more poetic realization in Nature of the turning the sword into the reaping-hook sentiment, than that in the great gilt ball which surmounts the courthouse dome. The Union soldiers had found it an attractive mark for their rifle-bullets, until it was pierced many times with large, ragged holes through which the purple martins now creep in and out, to and from the nests they have built in its hollow space."

Description of the Cabell County Courthouse at Barboursville,
Appleton's Journal, June 15, 1872

The new city of Huntington, selected by Collis P. Huntington as the terminus of the Chesapeake and Ohio Railroad, was created in 1871 and quickly eclipsed the historic community of Guyandotte. Peter Cline Buffington, the first mayor of Huntington, made a considerable amount of money during the Civil War selling horses to the Confederate government, auctioning government property, serving as a clerk in the commissary offices in Pearisburg and Peterstown, and leasing slaves to work in the quartermaster department. Buffington also served in the Virginia General Assembly in Richmond. His son, Edward Stanard Buffington, who fought for the Confederacy as a young soldier, was mayor of Huntington from 1879 to 1880. Democrats, many of them ex-Confederates, were in political control of both Cabell and Wayne counties.[1071]

The Ohio River port of Guyandotte, which had been devastated by the war, began rebuilding, as indicated by an 1872 article:

Among the business men and business houses now in Guyandotte, there are the following: Twenty-two mercantile and grocery houses; two of furniture; one drug store; two hardware stores; one clothing store, three millinery stores; two boot and shoe manufactories; one jewelry store, one photograph gallery, two blacksmith shops, three lumber yards; four hotels; one tin shop; three saw mills; one planing mill; two paint shops; two plastering firms; three stone and brick masons, three carpenter firms, one cabinet maker, one woolen factory, five saloons; one harness shop, one tailor shop, two real estate firms, six legal firms,

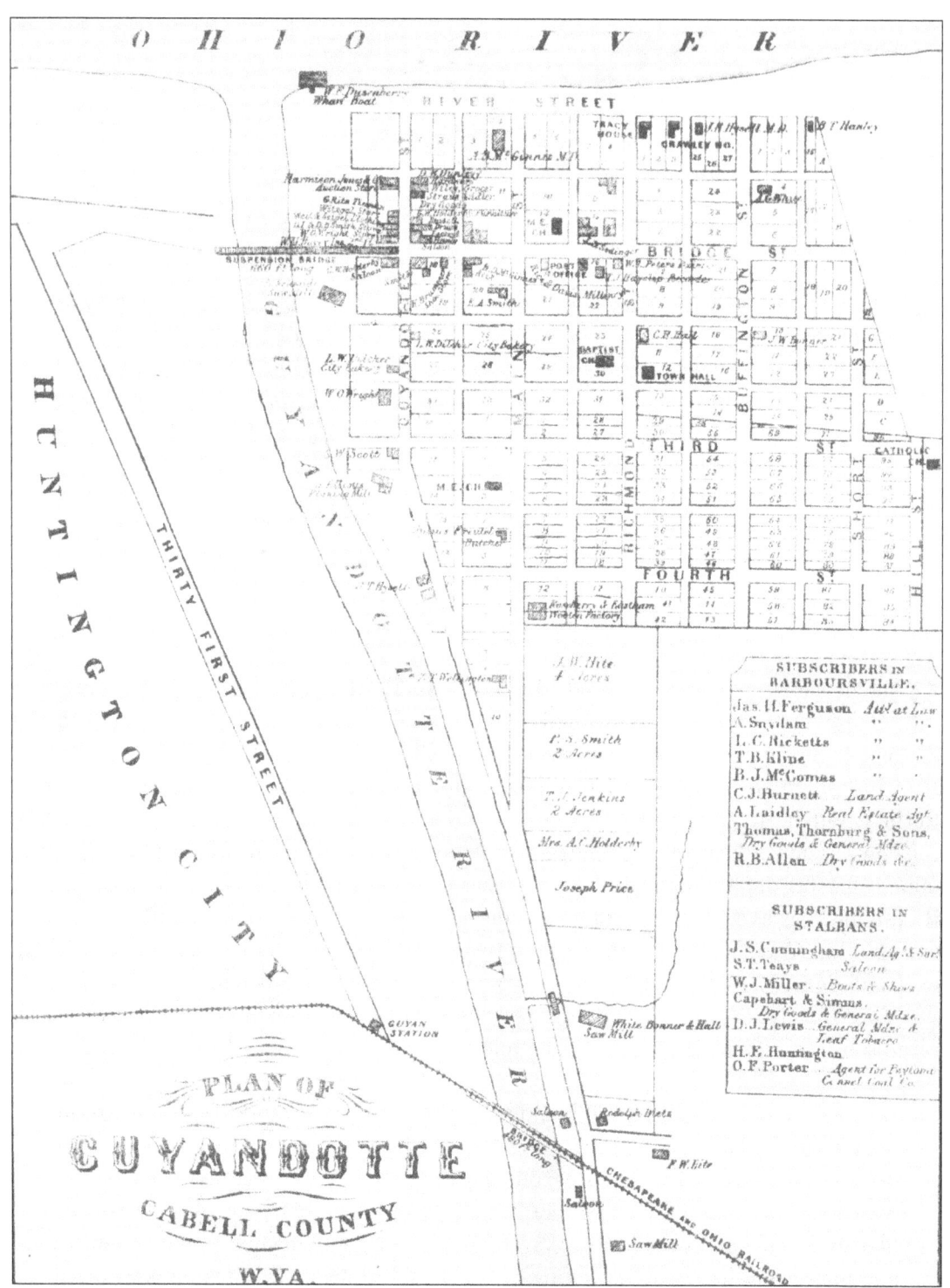

Guyandotte, from White's Topographical, County & District Atlas of West Virginia, 1873.

one livery stable, one book and stationary store, one bakery, two barber shops, two billiard saloons, and sundry other establishments, all of which are well supported…The population of Guyandotte is supposed to be about 1,000 at the present time, and increasing daily.[1072]

In April 1874, former Border Ranger James D. Sedinger was elected mayor of Guyandotte.

Democrats also gained political control of the new state of West Virginia enabling ex-Confederates to regain their citizenship rights. The state capitol was moved from Wheeling to Charleston and a new constitution was adopted in 1872, reflecting the change in political power and the determination to obliterate the constitution created by wartime supporters of the Federal government and replace it with one more reflective of their affinity for their mother state. Some of the lawsuits brought against Albert G. Jenkins and other prominent Confederates by Union residents of Cabell County were eventually overturned due to the change in political power in the state.

The completion of the C&O Railroad stimulated growth in Wayne County. The railroad was extended west past Ceredo to Catlettsburg, and a spur line opened from Ceredo to Trout's Hill. The timber industry flourished as a result, and the population of the county nearly doubled between 1870 and 1880. Eli Thayer was forced to sell his interest in Ceredo, however, and Charles B. Hoard took over the property. He moved to the community in 1870, but development was limited.[1073]

Eli Thayer and Charles B. Hoard, architects of Ceredo.
Credit: Special Collections Department, Marshall University.

Soldiers from both sides sought to start their lives anew in the years following the war. Some remained in Cabell and Wayne counties, while others moved away to pursue new opportunities. Following his capture in Wayne County in February 1864, Milton J. Ferguson was imprisoned at Camp Chase, Fort Delaware, and Hilton Head Island before being exchanged in late 1864. Following the war, Ferguson returned to Wayne County but was unable to resume his law practice due to the required test oath. He moved to Kentucky, where he was elected judge, but returned to Wayne County after the restrictions against ex-Confederates were lifted. Milton Jameson Ferguson died on April 22, 1881, and was buried in Fairview Cemetery in Wayne County. His brother, Joseph M. Ferguson, served in the West Virginia House of Delegates in 1872 and 1873. Another Confederate officer from Wayne County, Hurston Spurlock, was elected to the West Virginia House of Delegates and served from 1877 to 1878.

Lucian Cincinnatus "Cooney" Ricketts had ridden with the Border Rangers during the war until August 22, 1863, his sixteenth birthday, when he was enrolled at Virginia Military Institute by Albert Gallatin Jenkins. There he was joined by his friend Edward Stanard Buffington. On May 15, 1864, Cooney and his classmates fought in the battle of New Market. Cooney recalled:

Painting of Milton J. Ferguson, Wayne County Courthouse. Credit: Robert Thompson.

> On that occasion (at the battle of New Market) I was detached from the company to serve personally with Gen. Scott Shipp, then commandant of the battalion...Gen. 'Jno.' C. Breckinridge, commanding, gave orders for all mounted officers to go into the charge dismounted and not deeming that the order applied to me, and being mounted, rode into the battle on horseback, being the only person on horseback on the firing line of the cadets or elsewhere along the line until Gen. Breckinridge and his staff later appeared.[1074]

Ricketts earned special praise from his peers. Francis Lee Smith later wrote, "I would like to see some mention of 'Cooney' Ricketts for I thought he acted with great gallantry, mounted on Shaw's horse, riding ahead and in front of the corps when we became engaged with the enemy. I was put on that horse (after being wounded of course) and rode him into New Market."[1075]

On the day following the battle, Ricketts carried a report back to General Francis H. Smith, superintendent of VMI, in Lexington. After the military school was burned, Ricketts rejoined his old company and was with them when they rode away from Appomattox to avoid surrender. After the war, he studied law and was admitted to the bar in 1869. Ricketts married Fannie Lenora Miller of Barboursville on May 16, 1871, and had five children. He twice served as Cabell County's prosecuting attorney and was a federal land examiner under President Grover Cleveland. Lucian Cincinnatus "Cooney" Ricketts died on September 18, 1906, and was buried in Spring Hill Cemetery.

Some of the citizens of Cabell and Wayne County settled elsewhere after the war because of political restrictions or in hopes of a fresh start. Confederate Captain Henry Clay Everett, who had commanded the Border Rangers during the war, moved to Alleyton, Texas, along with Guyandotte friends Victor and Lawrence LeTulle. In 1867, Henry Clay Everett's wife Kate and three of their children died during a yellow fever epidemic. Everett established the Everett Farm a year later, raising cotton and selling post oak timber to the Buffalo Bayou, Brazos and Colorado Railway.[1076]

When he died on March 5, 1885, the *Colorado Citizen* observed, "A sadness and gloom has resided on our neighborhood for sometime in consequence of the long-continued and severe illness of our neighbor and fellow-citizen, Capt. H. C. Everett, which was deepened by the announcement of his death on the 5th inst. A good man and citizen has been taken from us, whose place it will be hard to fill, we shall miss him more than we can now anticipate." The article also noted that before Captain Everett's death, a telegram had been sent to one of his brothers in West Virginia:

> He came just in time to see the last expiring breath. The Captain was conscious and aroused up enough to recognize him. He was so grief stricken and being aged and not stout he was fearful if he did not hurry, he would not reach home; so he hurried off before his brother was buried, to be buried, as he said, at home.[1077]

Captain Henry Clay Everett of Guyandotte, who commanded the Border Rangers. Everett moved to Alleyton, Texas, after the war and became a prominent farmer and businessman.
Credit: Marilyn Brasher Wade.

John H. Oley, one of the founders and most prominent citizens of the new city of Huntington. Credit: Special Collections Department, Marshall University.

One of the most important leaders in the new city of Huntington was John Hunt Oley, who had served as a Union officer in Cabell and Wayne counties from 1861 to 1865 and had risen in rank from captain to brevet brigadier general during the war. He became a business associate of Collis P. Huntington after the war and returned to Cabell County in 1871 to sell land parcels in the new city. He served as the recorder of Huntington from 1871 until his death and was a leader in the field of education. General John Hunt Oley died on March 11, 1888, at the home of D. W. Emmons and is buried in Spring Hill Cemetery. On the day of his funeral, all business in the city of Huntington was suspended.

Between 1861 and 1870, John S. Witcher had been instrumental in the defense of western Virginia and the establishment and

General John S. Witcher. Following his defeat in the 1870 congressional election, Witcher was appointed collector of revenue and pension agent and then served in the United States Army until his retirement in 1899. He is interred in Arlington National Cemetery. Credit: Massachusetts Commandery Military Order of the Loyal Legion and the US Army Military History Institute.

administration of a new state. He served as circuit clerk of Cabell County before joining the Union army in late 1862. He quickly rose through the ranks and was promoted to brevet brigadier general at the end of the war. Witcher was elected to the House of Delegates in 1865, and a year later he became West Virginia's secretary of state. Elected to Congress in 1868, he was defeated for re-election in 1870 at the age of thirty-one. Witcher was appointed a collector of internal revenue in West Virginia and served as a pension agent in Washington before becoming major and paymaster in the United States Army on June 30, 1880. He served in this capacity until his retirement in 1899. John S. Witcher died in Salt Lake City, Utah, on July 8, 1906, and was buried in Arlington Cemetery.

Alfred S. Proctor, whose abolitionist sentiments sparked the brawl in Quaker Bottom, Ohio, on March 14, 1856, was married a few months after that event, sold his business interests, and moved to Illinois. Proctor served the Union with distinction during the Civil War and was wounded twice while a sergeant for the 86th Illinois Infantry. In August 1864, he was appointed first lieutenant in the 57th Regiment, United States Colored Troops by President Abraham Lincoln and promoted to captain in early 1865. When he submitted his resignation from Fort Smith, Arkansas, on April 20, 1866, Proctor asked to be mustered out of the service instead of being discharged and stated the justification for his request:

> The insurrection heretofore existing is now at an end. Peace is restored throughout the land. My own expectations in entering the service, and those of the Government in accepting me are fully accomplished. My obligations, therefore, and its just claims upon me are at an end. I am, by limitation of service – 'the end of the war' – entitled to muster-out, with whatever of credit and pecuniary advantage may attach to that mode of closing up my military record.

> I beg leave to state in addition, that I entered the service in the summer of 1862, as a volunteer, in the dark days of our country, and have served faithfully and patiently, in whatever position assigned me, until this grand consummation of my hopes, covering a period of nearly four years, and that during that time I have spent but four days at my home.

I have a family and property that I have long neglected, that are suffering for want of my personal attention and to which I feel that duty now calls me.

His commanding officer, Colonel Paul Harwood, wrote, "Capt. Proctor is one of the most efficient and faithful officers in the 57th U. S. Col. Infantry and I would earnestly recommend that if the exigencies of the service will permit that his request may be granted for a 'muster out' instead that of a discharge as it will be no more than justice to an officer of his merit." Alfred S. Proctor died on December 10, 1896, in Rome, Illinois.[1078]

Veterans organizations played an important role in shaping public sentiment and memory regarding the Civil War. Camp Garnett, United Confederate Veterans, was chartered in Huntington on April 25, 1890. Camp Garnett was named for Brigadier General Robert S. Garnett, who was the first general officer killed in the Civil War. On June 1, 1895, this chapter had 252 members listed on its roster. These former soldiers spent much of their time raising money to purchase a Confederate burial plot in Spring Hill Cemetery and worked to bring home their comrades who had fallen far from home. Through their efforts, the remains of General Albert Gallatin Jenkins, who died in 1864 from wounds received in the battle of Cloyd's Mountain, were moved from Green Bottom to the Confederate plot in Spring Hill. Committees were formed to "look after any confederates in destitute circumstances" and to raise money for a soldiers' home. In 1898 they resolved to notify the governor of the state "that all able-bodied members of this camp are ready in the event of war between the United States and Spain to respond to the call of their country."[1079]

The Huntington Chapter of the United Daughters of the Confederacy and Camp Garnett, UCV, dedicated a Confederate monument on June 23, 1900, at the Confederate plot in Spring Hill. Hundreds of veterans came from surrounding counties and joined the huge procession which traveled from the courthouse to the cemetery to witness the unveiling. The bugle call was sounded by Sylvester Summers, a bugler for the 8th Virginia Cavalry during the war. A band played "Carry Me Back to Old Virginia" as the veil was pulled away, revealing a bronze Confederate soldier. Speeches were made by Mrs. L. G. Buffington, President of the Huntington Chapter of the United Daughters of the Confederacy, Colonel C. L. Thompson, Commandant of Camp Garnett, and Colonel Arnett of Wheeling. A tree limb fell and destroyed the soldier in the 1960s, leaving only the base of the monument.[1080]

The Border Rangers had their own veterans' organization in Huntington after the war. By 1901, these old soldiers met annually on the anniversary of the company's formation. The *Huntington Advertiser* commented, "It is a good thing to watch a meeting of the survivors of the Border Rangers and see them shake hands and talk over their old experiences."[1081]

The Wayne County chapter of the United Confederate Veterans was named Camp Spurlock for Hurston and Burwell Spurlock. On September 14-15, 1906, the largest Civil War veterans' reunion in Wayne County history was held at the county seat. All trains running to Wayne offered reduced fares to veterans and their families, and more than two thousand persons attended the historic event. Citizens of Wayne County

Survivors of the Border Rangers, Co. E, 8th Virginia Cavalry, C.S.A. Lucien C. "Cooney" Ricketts is in the front row, third from the right. Diarist James D. Sedinger is in the back row, second from the left. Credit: Jack L. Dickinson.

provided "basket dinners," the Wayne Cornet Band furnished the music, and the crowd was entertained by a number of lengthy speeches. Tents were set up to provide lodging for the veterans. One of the featured speakers was Lucien C. Ricketts, whose address traced the life of General Albert Gallatin Jenkins. Ricketts died just a few days later.[1082]

The Grand Army of the Republic (GAR), a fraternal organization comprised of soldiers and sailors who served the Union during the war, had a chapter in Huntington named Bailey Post No. 4. The group held Decoration Day observances and erected a monument on the grounds of the Cabell County Courthouse. In his thesis, "'Let Us Bury And Forget:' Civil War Memory and Identity In Cabell County, West Virginia, 1865-1915," Seth Adam Nichols observed, "The monument's placement on the courthouse grounds demonstrates the symbolic effort of G.A.R. members to reinforce the Northern identity of Huntington." The Grand Army of the Republic also had members in Wayne County and held a reunion at Dickson about 1900. During the first week of June 1912, Camp Garnett and GAR members placed flowers on the graves of both Union and Confederate soldiers buried in Spring Hill Cemetery.[1083]

An iron statue of a Union soldier was erected at the corner of Ninth Street and Fifth Avenue in Huntington in 1880. Thirty-five years later, it was removed. The initial

GAR reunion at Dickson, Wayne County.
Credit: Special Collections Department, Marshall University.

plan was to relocate the monument in Ritter Park, but it was instead taken to the city dump. This decision may have been influenced by United Confederate Veterans' plans to create a new monument dedicated to the "Women of the South" which was to be erected in Ritter Park and would have dwarfed the worn Union statue. According to Nichols, "The destruction of the Union statue is one of the many clues revealing the complicated issues and feelings regarding memory of the Civil War within Cabell County."[1084]

Several of the church buildings in Cabell County filed claims with the federal government for damages incurred during the Civil War. George E. Thornburg, G. W. Ayers, and J. E. Cyrus, trustees of the Barboursville Methodist Episcopal Church South, petitioned the Court of Claims in 1906. They noted that in the fall of 1861 Federal troops took possession of the building and used it at various times through the war years. The trustees specifically listed Company G of the 5th West Virginia Infantry, part of the 13th West Virginia Infantry, and parts of the 34th and 40th Ohio Infantry regiments as units that occupied the structure. Although they asked for "reasonable rental value," including repairs required to return the building to its pre-war condition, of $1,500, the Court of Claims in 1907 only awarded the church $500.[1085]

The trustees of the Guyandotte Methodist Episcopal Church South filed a petition with the Court of Claims in 1904 for the destruction of their church during the war. The brick building was 36 by 50 feet and "contained the usual and necessary church furniture." Federal forces took possession of the building in 1861, using it as a commissary storehouse and for other military purposes before tearing it down and appropriating the contents for the use of the United States Army. A new church had been constructed, but the trustees were awarded $2,000 later that year for the destruction of its predecessor.[1086]

In 1904, the trustees of the Guyandotte Baptist Church also filed a petition with the Court of Claims. The building was described as "48 by 32 feet, 16 feet in height, constructed of brick and at that time reasonably worth the sum of $2,000." Following the burning of the church on November 11, 1861, "the brick from the said building was used by the military forces of the United States in building quarters and for other purposes." The request of the trustees was fully granted.[1087]

Other churches in Cabell County were damaged during the war. The Union Baptist Church was practically gutted, with the lumber burned for firewood by Federal troops who had occupied the building throughout much of the war. The soldiers had left the church building without floors, seats, gallery, door, or windows, but the basic structure remained standing. Services were held in the home of Reverend John Calvin Rece until the congregation was reorganized in 1867. Between 1867 and 1875, repairs were undertaken. The gallery was rebuilt, and seats and a pulpit were installed. Bayonet scars are visible on the door lintels of the structure, and shell and Minie-ball marks can be seen in the brickwork of the old church. The Bloomingdale Church was torn down during the war by Union troops who took the lumber to Barboursville for use in their camp as firewood.

In 1907, workers grading one of Guyandotte's main streets for the streetcar line dug up 241 lead bullets of varying sizes and makes. Also uncovered were a number of silver mounted army revolvers, "revealing the fact that they had lain in the earth for almost half a century."[1088]

An undated article regarding the site of the first battle in Cabell County noted, "The old fortification hill is being plowed up, and this old landmark, which has so long been a vestige of our civil war, where the battle of Barboursville was fought, will soon pass into oblivion."[1089]

In 1929, Morris Harvey College announced that a memorial was to be erected at the site of the battle of Barboursville. According to a newspaper article,

> The site of the battle, one of the first of that war in this state, has been college property for some years, but marking of the spot has not been feasible until recently on account of construction of new buildings taking place near it. Until the ground was graded for construction of Rosa Harvey and McDonald Halls, remains of Confederate earth works might be seen. The spot lies directly between these two great dormitory buildings, and is now being put into grass by the campus force.
>
> It is planned to make a small park of the area, placing in its center a Civil War

cannon, which the War Department has agreed to furnish. Other war material may be placed about this, and two flag poles are to be erected on either side of it. From one the national emblem will be flown daily, and from the other will float the flag of Morris Harvey College. A bronze tablet will tell the story of the battle.[1090]

More than one hundred and fifty years after the war concluded, citizens of Cabell and Wayne counties still have an abiding interest in the conflict fought here so long ago. Annual reenactments and Civil War events, such as Guyandotte Civil War Days, have been celebrated for years, continuing the effort to observe this most important period in our nation's history. Although the war concluded more than a century and a half ago, we still remember.

Notes

Chapter One

1. *Acts Passed at a General Assembly of the Commonwealth of Virginia* (Richmond, VA: Samuel Pleasants, Junior, Printer for the Commonwealth, 1809), 45.
2. *Ibid*.
3. George S. Wallace, *Cabell County Annals and Families* (Richmond, VA: Garrett and Massie, 1935), 10.
4. "Interview with H. C. Everett," F. B. Lambert Collection, Special Collections Department, Marshall University (MUSCD), 9; Henry Howe, *Historical Collections of Virginia* (Charleston, SC: Babcock & Co., 1845), 209.
5. Frances B. Gunter, *Barboursville* (1986), 8; Howe, *Historical Collections of Virginia*, 209; J. W. Miller, "History of Barboursville Community" (Morgantown, WV: Agricultural Extension Division, 1925), 1.
6. William A. Birt, "A Historical Sketch of Milton, Cabell County, West Virginia," *West Virginia History*, Volume 23, Number 1 (October 1961), 50.
7. Jack L. Dickinson and Kay Stamper Dickinson, *Gentleman Soldier of Greenbottom: The Life of Brig. Gen. Albert Gallatin Jenkins, CSA*, (The Authors: 2011); Karen N. Cartwright Nance, "Green Bottom." e-WV: The West Virginia Encyclopedia. 05 August 2016. Web. 26 December 2018.
8. Howe, *Historical Collections of Virginia*, 209.
9. *Post Office Directory; or Business Man's Guide to the Post Offices in the United States*, compiled by D. D. T. Leech (New York, NY: J. H. Colton and Company, 1857), 180-81. Cabell County postmasters were: Barboursville, William C. Miller; Bloomingdale, William F. Dusenberry; Falls Mill, Enoch D. Blankenship; Greenbottom, Thomas E. Hannan; Guyandotte, Lewis Sedinger; Hamlin, James C. Black; Mud, Thomas Roberts; Mud Bridge, John M. Rece; Paw Paw Bottom, James McComas; Ten Mile, James M. Drake; and Thorndike, Edmund B. Malcolm.
10. *Acts Passed at a General Assembly of the Commonwealth of Virginia*, (Richmond, VA: Samuel Shepherd, Printer for the Commonwealth, 1842) 36-38; Howe, *Historical Collections of Virginia*, 506; *Post Office Directory*, 190. Postmasters in Wayne County were: Adkinsville, Milton J. Ferguson; Amacetta, William Kindrick; Falls of 12 Pole, Francis A. Spurlock; Falls of Tug, William Ratcliffe; Fort Gay, William Ferguson; Hubbardstown, Casper Custner; Round Bottom, John Gilkison, Jr.; Savage Grant,

Urban Walker; and Wayne Court House, Burwell Ferguson.

11. *Ceredo Crescent*, July 9, 1859.

12. According to Karen Nance, Peter Clarke resided in Guyandotte in what is now known as the Madie Carroll House. *Guyandotte Herald*, February 2, 1855.

13. Wallace, *Cabell County Annals*, 125.

14. *Acts of the General Assembly of Virginia*, 1857-1858 (Richmond, VA: William F. Ritchie, Public Printer, 1858), 122.

15. "West Virginia Census by County and Race, 1790-2010," West Virginia Archives and History website, http://www.wvculture.org/history/teacherresources/censuspopulationrace.html.

Chapter Two

16. "Early Records of Cabell and Mason Counties, W. Va., Presented by Buford Chapter, of Huntington, and Colonel Charles Lewis Chapter, of Point Pleasant, West Va.," Daughters of the American Revolution, 14.

17. Lewis and Jack [Fullerton] (Free Negroes), Cabell County, December 28, 1836, Legislative Petitions Digital Collection, Library of Virginia. At the time of the petition, Lewis was forty-three years of age and Jack was thirty-nine. Lewis had four children; they and his wife were owned by Abia Rece. Jack also had children. They and his wife were owned by Adam Black. Lewis Fullerton and wife Ann appear on the 1850 census in Cabell County. Lewis is listed alone in 1860, noted as being sixty-five years of age.

18. *See* Carrie Eldridge, *Cabell County's Empire For Freedom: The Manumission of Sampson Sanders' Slaves* (Huntington, WV: John Deaver Drinko Academy for American Political Institution and Civic Culture, Marshall University, 1999).

19. For a detailed study of the case, see James L. Hale, *The Long Road to Freedom: The Story of the Enslaved Polley Children* (Lulu Publishing Services, 2014). *See also* "Polley vs. Ratcliff: A New Way To Address An Original Sin?" by Atiba R. Ellis, West Virginia University College of Law, Legal Studies Research Paper No. 2012-19, 777-806, 2012; Peyton Polly Collection, Ohio Historical Center Archives Library (OHCAL); Robert Michael Thompson, *Few Among the Mountains: Slavery in Wayne County, West Virginia* (Genoa, WV: The Author, 2015).

20. John Laidley to Salmon P. Chase, March 26, 1856, Polly Collection, OHCAL; Harrison Polly and Nelson Polly vs. William Ratliff and Jarrett Ratliff, Cabell County, 1854, Virginia Court of Appeals Records, Lewisburg, West Virginia State Archives (WVSA).

21. Ralph Leete to Salmon P. Chase, March 31, 1856 and July 25, 1856, Polly Collection, OHCAL.

22. S. S. Rice to John Laidley, April 3, 1857 and John Laidley to Salmon P. Chase, September 15, 1857, Polly Collection, OHCAL.

23. S. S. Rice to Salmon P. Chase, February 16, 1859, Polly Collection, OHCAL.

24. A. M. Gangewer to Ralph Leete, November 12, 1859, Polly Collection,

OHCAL.

25. Ralph Leete to A. M. Gangewer, November 25, 1859, Polly Collection, OHCAL.

26. *Ironton Register*, April 10, 1856. Karen Nance discovered and shared the articles relating to this event, for which the author is deeply indebted.

27. *Ironton Register*, June 26, 1856. Alfred S. Proctor, the son of Jacob Proctor, one of the early pioneers of Ohio, was born on May 16, 1820. When Alfred was fourteen, he was kicked in the forehead by a horse, fracturing his skull and nearly killing him. After his father's death, Alfred moved in with his brother Jacob, a merchant in Burlington, Ohio, and the two men later became partners. See Find A Grave entry for Alfred S. Proctor by Baxter B. Fite III.

28. *Ibid.*

29. *Ironton Register*, March 20, 1856; *Ironton Register*, February 28, 1856.

30. *Ironton Register*, June 26, 1856.

31. *Ibid.*

32. *Ibid.*

33. *Star of the Kanawha Valley*, April 16, 1856; *Ironton Register*, March 20, 1856; *Ironton Register*, April 3, 1856.

34. *Ironton Register*, April 10, 1856.

35. *Ironton Register*, June 26, 1856; *Star of the Kanawha Valley*, April 16, 1856.

36. *Ironton Register*, April 10, 1856.

37. *Ironton Register*, June 26, 1856.

38. *Ironton Register*, April 10, 1856.

39. *Ironton Register*, April 3, 1856; *Ironton Register*, March 20, 1856.

40. *Ironton Register*, April 10, 1856.

41. *Ironton Register*, March 20, 1856.

42. *Star of the Kanawha Valley*, April 16, 1856.

43. *Ironton Register*, April 10, 1856.

44. *Ironton Register*, April 17, 1856; *Ironton Register*, April 10, 1856.

45. *Ironton Register*, April 17, 1856.

46. *Ironton Register*, April 3, 1856.

47. William P. Smith to Sallie P. Smith, January 20, 1857, Smith Family Correspondence, Accession No. 1997/11.0662, MUSCD.

48. McClintic, "Ceredo: An Experiment in Colonization," 1, WVSA.

49. *Ibid.*, 21.

50. *Kanawha Valley Star*, August 11, 1857.

51. *Kanawha Valley Star*, October 13, 1857.

52. *Ibid.*; *Kanawha Valley Star*, September 1, 1857.

53. McClintic, "Ceredo: An Experiment...," 22-23, WVSA; *Kanawha Valley Star*, September 8, 1857.

54. *Kanawha Valley Star*, October 13, 1857.

55. *Ironton Register*, October 22, 1857. According to author Robert Michael Thompson, the church was located near the current Spring Valley Bridge.

56. *Ibid.*

57. *Ibid.*
58. *Ibid.*
59. *Ironton Register*, January 28, 1858.
60. *Ceredo Crescent*, July 10, 1858.

Chapter Three

61. Granville Parker, *The Formation of the State of West Virginia* (Wellsburg, WV: Glass and Son, 1875), 1-3.
62. *Ibid.*, 2.
63. *Ironton Register*, December 15, 1859.
64. Parker, *The Formation of the State of West Virginia*, 24.
65. Dickinson and Dickinson, *Gentleman Soldier of Greenbottom*, 45.
66. *Ironton Register*, April 19, 1860.
67. In November of 1864, the *Ironton Register* listed four men who voted for Abraham Lincoln in the 1860 election: K. Hesseltine, James Elzea, Abner Cook, and John Schenberg; *Ironton Register*, November 22, 1864.
68. Parker, *The Formation of the State of West Virginia*, 34-35.
69. *Wheeling Intelligencer*, January 28, 1861. Granville Davisson Hall, in *The Rending of Virginia*, expressed his belief that the writer was Z. D. Ramsdell, although he lived in Ceredo, not Amacetta.
70. Wallace, *Cabell County Annals*, 492-495. William's brother, David McComas, was also an attorney and prominent politician. He served as a judge of the Circuit Superior Court and was a member of the General Court. He also served in the Virginia State Senate from 1830 to 1836 and the Virginia House of Delegates, 1843-1844. On March 28, 1831, David McComas gave a fiery speech from the Senate floor upholding the right of secession from the Union. The speech was given much publicity immediately preceding secession and the Civil War. Burwell Spurlock would be arrested during the Union seizure of Wayne Courthouse in 1861. According to W. L. Mansfield, Spurlock remained in eastern Virginia during the war and was a defendant with other Wayne County secessionists in lawsuits filed after the close of the conflict.
71. Huntington *Sunday Advertiser*, October 8, 1922.
72. *Cabell County Press*, December 20, 1869.
73. *Kanawha Valley Star*, April 30, 1861. According to one member of the Border Rangers, the name was given to the company at Camp Davis by Private (later Sergeant) James Wellington, who would later accidentally drown in the Guyandotte River at Logan Courthouse.
74. *Cabell County Press*, December 20, 1869; Wallace, *Cabell County Annals*, 332.
75. *Kanawha Valley Star*, April 30, 1861.
76. *Ibid.*
77. Wallace, *Cabell County Annals*, 332.
78. *Cabell County Press*, December 20, 1869.

79. James D. Sedinger, "Diary of a Border Ranger," Boyd B. Stutler Collection, WVSA. For information on the Border Rangers, see Jack L. Dickinson's publications, *Jenkins of Greenbottom: A Civil War Saga* and *8th Virginia Cavalry*.

80. *Kanawha Valley Star*, April 30, 1861.

81. *Kanawha Valley Star*, May 1861.

82. Sallie P. Smith to Julia Sprague, April 22, 1861, Smith Family Correspondence, MUSCD.

83. *Ironton Register*, May 2, 1861.

84. Diary of Victoria Hansford Hays, Stutler Collection, WVSA.

85. William D. Wintz, editor, *Civil War Memoirs of Two Rebel Sisters* (Charleston, WV: Pictorial Histories Publishing Company, 1989), 23.

86. Sedinger, "Diary of a Border Ranger," Stutler Collection, WVSA.

87. William Dusenberry Papers, 1843-1903, Accession No. 1992/08.0551, MUSCD.

88. Wallace, *Cabell County Annals*, 34.

89. Joe Griffith, *History of Company G, 11th West Virginia Volunteer Infantry From Coalsmouth to Richmond, 1862-1865* (Roswell, GA: The Author, 1995), 27.

90. Undated article, "Condition of Eli Thayer's Colony in Virginia"; Parker, *The Formation of the State of West Virginia*, 36.

91. *Wheeling Intelligencer*; Parker, *The Formation of the State of West Virginia*, 36; *Ironton Register*, May 30, 1861.

92. *Richmond Dispatch*, June 1, 1861.

93. *Wheeling Intelligencer*, June 4, 1861.

94. *Ibid*.

95. *Ibid*.

96. *Ironton Register*, May 30, 1861.

97. *Wheeling Intelligencer*, June 13, 1861.

98. *Ironton Register*, June 13, 1861.

99. *Ironton Register*, June 6, 1861.

100. *Ironton Register*, June 13, 1861.

101. *Ibid*.

102. Wallace, *Cabell County Annals*, 35.

103. George T. Walton to John S. Carlile, June 21, 1861, Pierpont Papers, Library of Virginia (LVA).

104. *Ibid*.

105. The request came from J. C. Plybun, Isaiah Ray, J. Graham, H. N. Stevenson, and S. Nation. Cabell County Citizens to the Central Committee, June 24, 1861, Pierpont Papers, LVA.

106. Undated article, "Condition of Eli Thayer's Colony in Virginia."

107. Petition from Wayne County citizens to Francis H. Pierpont, June 26, 1861, Pierpont Papers, LVA.

108. *Wheeling Intelligencer*, July 8, 1861.

109. *Wheeling Intelligencer*, July 9, 1861.

110. Kellian V. Whaley to Francis H. Pierpont, June 29, 1861, Pierpont Papers,

LVA.

111. *Ibid.*

112. B. D. McGinnis to John S. Carlile and the Central Committee, June 29, 1861, Pierpont Papers, LVA.

113. *Ibid.*

114. B. D. McGinnis to Francis H. Pierpont, July 1, 1861, Pierpont Papers, LVA.

115. Hiram Welch to Francis H. Pierpont, July 1, 1861, Pierpont Papers, LVA. The Order of the Star Spangled Banner was an anti-immigrant society that would form the nucleus of the Know Nothing movement.

116. Z. D. Ramsdell to Francis H. Pierpont, July 2, 1861, Pierpont Papers, LVA.

117. John Adams to Francis H. Pierpont, July 2, 1861, Pierpont Papers, LVA.

118. *Ibid.*

119. Parker, *The Formation of the State of West Virginia*, 36-37.

120. Francis H. Pierpont to B. D. McGinnis, July 4, 1861, Pierpont Papers, LVA.

121. B. D. McGinnis to Francis H. Pierpont, July 9, 1861, Pierpont Papers, LVA.

122. Sedinger, "Diary of a Border Ranger," Stutler Collection, WVSA.

123. *Ironton Register*, July 18, 1861.

124. Sedinger, "Diary of a Border Ranger," Stutler Collection, WVSA.

125. *Wheeling Intelligencer*, July 13, 1861.

126. John H. Dickerson to J. D. Cox, July 12, 1861, Department of Kanawha, National Archives (NA).

127. *Ironton Register*, July 18, 1861.

Chapter Four

128. Jacob Dolson Cox, *Military Reminiscences of the Civil War* (New York, NY: Charles Scribner and Sons, 1900), Volume One, 62-63. In his July 2 correspondence to Cox, McClellan wrote, "Repress any outbreaks that may occur at Guyandotte or Barboursville." George B. McClellan to J. D. Cox, July 2, 1861, *Official Records*, Series I, Volume II, 197.

129. Melburn C. Spaulding, "Records of Official Correspondence of the Federal and Confederate Armies in the Kanawha River Valley, 1861-1864," 1976, WVSA.

130. *Louisville Journal*, July 11, 1861.

131. *Toledo Blade*, July 13, 1861; *Ironton Register*, July 18, 1861.

132. *Toledo Blade*, July 13, 1861.

133. *Cincinnati Commercial*, July 13, 1861.

134. *Toledo Blade*, July 13, 1861; *Cincinnati Commercial*, July 13, 1861.

135. *Cincinnati Commercial*, July 17, 1861.

136. *Ironton Register*, July 18, 1861.

137. Frank Ball and J. W. Miller, "Now and Then-Mostly Then," *West Virginia Review*, January 1935; Frank Ball, "'Uncle Billy' Miller, 90 Years Old, Recalls Battle of Mud River," courtesy of Terry Lowry; "William L. Mansfield's Civil War History of (Wayne) County," Lambert Collection, MUSCD; "The Fight At Barboursville," John

W. Barbour's Report, Lambert Collection, MUSCD.

138. This event occurred on the morning of July 12, 1861. Union Citizens Files, F. D. B[e]uhring, NA. Beuhring, a "prominent Secessionist," was arrested by Colonel John L. Zeigler in August 1861.

139. *Wheeling Intelligencer*, July 18, 1861.

140. Regimental record book of General Jacob D. Cox, May-November 1861, Mudd Library, Oberlin College (MLOC).

141. *Wheeling Intelligencer*, July 18, 1861.

142. *Louisville Journal*, July 25, 1861.

143. Dispatch sent by Lieutenant Colonel George W. Neff, July 13, 1861, regimental record book of General Jacob D. Cox, May-November 1861, MLOC; *Louisville Journal*, July 25, 1861.

144. "The Fight at Barboursville," William L. Johnson Report, Lambert Collection, MUSCD. According to a newspaper account, "When the cry was given that the enemy was coming, some confusion among our men took place, but for which the loss of the enemy would have been much larger. The mishap was that, in seizing the guns and shot pouches, some of our men took others instead of their own, which they did not discover until after the first fire." See *Richmond Dispatch*, July 29, 1861. Grandma Blake's farm was on the site of the Orchard Hills Golf Course.

145. "'Uncle Billy' Miller..."

146. *Wheeling Intelligencer*, July 18, 1861.

147. Roy Bird Cook Collection, Box 8, Volume 25, West Virginia and Regional History Center (WVRHC).

148. B. F. McCune to H. J. Samuels, December 11, 1861, Adjutant General's Papers, Union Regiments, Miscellaneous Correspondence, WVSA.

149. William Clark Reynolds Diary, WVSA; Jack L. Dickinson, 8*th Virginia Cavalry* (Lynchburg, VA: H. E. Howard, Inc., 1986), 13; "The Fight at Barboursville," William L. Johnson Report, Lambert Collection, MUSCD.

150. *Wheeling Intelligencer*, July 18, 1861.

151. *Louisville Journal*, July 25, 1861; Dispatch sent by Lieutenant Colonel George W. Neff, July 13, 1861, regimental record book of General Jacob D. Cox, May-November 1861, MLOC.

152. *Louisville Journal*, July 25, 1861.

153. Terry Lowry, *The Battle of Scary Creek* (Charleston, WV: Pictorial Histories Publishing Company, 1982), 95.

154. *Wheeling Intelligencer*, July 18, 1861; Dispatch sent by Lieutenant Colonel George W. Neff, July 13, 1861, regimental record book of General Jacob D. Cox, May-November 1861, MLOC.

155. *Wheeling Intelligencer*, July 18, 1861. One Union soldier said they "ran across the joists like squirrels and charged up the hill, driving the rebels at the point of the bayonet from their stronghold. They fled in every direction, leaving their dead and wounded on the field." See *Louisville Journal*, July 25, 1861.

156. "The Fight At Barboursville," "Lucky" Savage's Report, Lambert Collection, MUSCD; *Wheeling Intelligencer*, July 18, 1861.

157. *Wheeling Intelligencer*, July 18, 1861; Lambert Collection, MUSCD.

158. Ball, "'Uncle Billy' Miller..."

159. *Cincinnati Gazette*, July 1861; "The Fight At Barboursville," Mary Barbour's Report, Lambert Collection, MUSCD.

160. Ball and Miller, "Now and Then..."

161. Ball, "'Uncle Billy' Miller..."

162. Sedinger, "Diary of a Border Ranger," Stutler Collection, WVSA; *Ironton Register*, July 18, 1861.

163. *Confederate Veteran*, Volume XXV, November 1917, 504; Sedinger, "Diary of a Border Ranger," Stutler Collection, WVSA.

164. *Cincinnati Commercial*, July 17, 1861.

165. *Ibid*.

166. W. L. Mansfield's History of the Civil War in Wayne County, Lambert Collection, MUSCD; "Colonel Joseph J. Mansfield," by Byron T. Morris, *Wayne County News*, March 2, 1978. Courtesty of Judge Stephen Lewis. In November 1865, his widow, Amanda Frances Mansfield, married Dr. Harrison Walker, a Wayne County native who served as assistant surgeon of the 16th Virginia Cavalry. Colonel Joseph J. Mansfield is buried on the hill in Elmwood Cemetery, just south of Wayne on West Virginia State Route 37.

167. Dispatch sent by Lieutenant Colonel George W. Neff, July 13, 1861, regimental record book of General Jacob D. Cox, May-November 1861, MLOC; *Wheeling Intelligencer*, July 18, 1861.

168. Dispatch sent by Lieutenant Colonel George W. Neff, July 13, 1861, regimental record book of General Jacob D. Cox, May-November 1861, MLOC.

169. *Cincinnati Commercial*, July 17, 1861; *Annual Report of the Adjutant General of the State of Kentucky* (Frankfort, KY: Kentucky Yeoman Office, John H. Harney, Public Printer, 1866). Company A: H. B. Martin, slightly; William Fitz, slightly; James Milligan, slightly; John Smith, slightly; Frank McLaughlin, dangerously. Company B: John Reynolds, slightly; William Reid, slightly; John Burns, slightly; William Scanlin, slightly; Ferdinand Heiskell, slightly; James Patterson, seriously. Company F: Elihu Harper, slightly. Company K: John Hempfling, slightly.

170. "The Fight At Barboursville," Interview with Ben Swann, Lambert Collection, MUSCD.

171. Harold Faller, "Barboursville Saw First Civil Strife," *Herald-Advertiser*, August 4, 1929.

172. "The Fight At Barboursville," "Lucky" Savage's Report, Lambert Collection, MUSCD.

173. George B. McClellan to E. D. Townsend, July 19, 1861, *Official Records*, Series I, Volume II, 288.

174. *Cincinnati Commercial*, July 17, 1861; *Louisville Journal*, July 25, 1861.

175. *Ironton Register*, July 18, 1861.

176. *Cincinnati Commercial*, July 17, 1861.

177. Cox, *Military Reminiscences*, 68; *Cincinnati Commercial*, July 17, 1861; *Louisville Journal*, July 25, 1861.

178. *Ironton Register*, July 18, 1861.
179. *Ibid*.
180. *Ironton Register*, July 25, 1861.

Chapter Five

181. Granville Parker to Francis H. Pierpont, July 15, 1861, Pierpont Papers, LVA.
182. L. W. Wolcott to Francis Pierpont, 1861, Adjutant General's Papers, Union Regiments, Miscellaneous Correspondence, WVSA.
183. Jeremiah Hare to Francis Pierpont, November 11, 1861, Adjutant General's Papers, Union Militia, WVSA; Sallie P. Smith to Julia Sprague, October 4, 1862, Smith Family Correspondence, MUSCD
184. L. J. Hampton and John D. Mims to Francis H. Pierpont, July 17, 1861, Pierpont Papers, LVA.
185. Civil War Governors of Kentucky: Digital Documentary Edition, biography of John L. Zeigler; *Adventures, Struggles, Trials and Services of the 5th Regiment, Virginia Volunteer Infantry*, edited by Marlitta H. Perkins (Staffordsville, KY: Eastern Kentucky Research & Publishing, 2015).
186. L. J. Hampton to William Ratliff, July 17, 1861, Pierpont Papers, LVA.
187. John Adams to Francis H. Pierpont, July 17, 1861, Pierpont Papers, LVA.
188. *Ironton Register*, December 22, 1864; Perkins, *Adventures, Struggles, Trials and Services of the 5th Regiment*.
189. C. Hall to C. D. Burk, July 29, 1861, Pierpont Papers, LVA.
190. William Ratliff to Francis H. Pierpont, July 28, 1861, Pierpont Papers, LVA.
191. L. J. Hampton to Francis H. Pierpont, July 28, 1861, Pierpont Papers, LVA.
192. Robert Hager to Haley Smith, July 31, 1861 and Robert Hager to Francis H. Pierpont, July 30, 1861, Pierpont Papers, LVA.
193. Mrs. E. T. Sanders Correspondence, July 31, 1861, Pierpont Papers, LVA. Peter C. Buffington later become the first mayor of Huntington. See Epilogue.
194. John B. Bowen and L. J. Hampton to Francis H. Pierpont, August 2, 1861, Pierpont Papers, LVA.
195. Kellian V. Whaley to Francis H. Pierpont, August 7, 1861, Pierpont Papers, LVA.
196. Unknown to Francis H. Pierpont, August 7, 1861, Pierpont Papers, LVA.
197. John L. Zeigler to Francis H. Pierpont, n.d., Pierpont Papers, LVA.
198. Unknown to Francis H. Pierpont, August 7, 1861, Pierpont Papers, LVA.
199. John L. Zeigler to Francis H. Pierpont, August 22, 1861, Pierpont Papers, LVA.
200. William Reany to W. S. Rosecrans, August 20, 1861, RG 393, Department of Western Virginia, NA.
201. William Reany to W. S. Rosecrans, August 25, 1861, RG 393, Department of Western Virginia, NA.

202. *Ibid.*

203. *The Rebellion Record*, Volume 3, 1862, Document 14; Ralph Leete to Francis H. Pierpont, August 26, 1861, Pierpont Papers, LVA; T. N. Davey to Francis Pierpont, August 28, 1861, Governor Francis Pierpont Telegram Collection, WVRHC.

204. Kellian V. Whaley to Francis H. Pierpont, September 20, 1861, Pierpont Papers, LVA; Jesse and Hurston Spurlock were cousins, and Jesse was Hurston's father-in-law.

205. A. M. McGinnis to Francis Pierpont, October 22, 1861, Pierpont-Samuels Papers, WVSA; P. S. Smith to H. J. Samuels, October 25, 1861, Pierpont-Samuels Papers, WVSA.

206. J. C. Wheeler to H. J. Samuels, November 6, 1861; L. J. Hampton to H. J. Samuels, December 6, 1861; James Campbell to H. J. Samuels, December 6, 1861, Pierpont-Samuels Papers, WVSA.

207. *Catlettsburg Advocate*, August 28, 1861.

208. Jesse Spurlock to Henry J. Samuels, November 7, 1861, Adjutant General's Papers, Union Regiments, Miscellaneous Correspondence, WVSA.

209. Ralph Leete to Francis H. Pierpont, August 26, 1861, Pierpont Papers, LVA.

210. Samuel Almond to J. D. Cox, August 31, 1861, Pierpont Papers, LVA.

211. *Ironton Register*, September 26, 1861. Alex H. Samuels was captured at Point Pleasant on March 30, 1863, and was confined in several different prisons. He apparently obtained his release and re-enlisted on April 30. Samuels was killed in action on January 3, 1864, near Jonesville, Virginia, while leading a charge on a Union artillery battery. Due to the efforts of the United Confederate Veterans, Camp Garnett Chapter, Samuels's remains were returned to the county and buried in the Confederate plot in Spring Hill Cemetery in 1895.

212. John S. Carlile to Francis H. Pierpont, September 2, 1861, Pierpont Papers, LVA.

213. John Zeigler to Francis H. Pierpont, September 3, 1861, Pierpont Papers, LVA.

214. Kellian V. Whaley to Francis H. Pierpont, September 10, 1861, Pierpont Papers, LVA. Tomlinson was commissioned a major in the 5th (West) Virginia Infantry on October 11, 1861.

215. Kellian V. Whaley to Francis H. Pierpont, September 11, 1861, Pierpont Papers, LVA.

216. Kellian V. Whaley to Francis H. Pierpont, September 12, 1861, Pierpont Papers, LVA.

217. *Ironton Register*, May 3, 1888.

218. *Ibid.*

219. F. L. Burdette, "History of Ona and Surrounding Country, Past and Present," 1925.

220. Union Citizens Files, NA (fold3.com).

221. *Ibid.*

222. Calendar of Virginia State Papers and Other Manuscripts, Volume 11, 359;

J. C. Wheeler to Francis H. Pierpont, September 13, 1861, Pierpont Papers, LVA.

223. H. J. Samuels to Francis H. Pierpont, September 13, 1861, Pierpont Papers, LVA; John L. Zeigler to Francis H. Pierpont, September 20, 1861, Pierpont Papers, LVA.

224. H. J. Samuels to Francis H. Pierpont, September 13, 1861, Pierpont Papers, LVA.

225. John H. Oley to Francis H. Pierpont, September 14, 1861, Pierpont Papers, LVA.

226. John Zeigler to Francis H. Pierpont, October 2, 1861, Pierpont Papers, LVA.

227. James A. Groom to George L. Hartsuff, September 15, 1861, RG 393, Department of Western Virginia, Correspondence Received, NA.

228. *Ibid*.

229. John H. Oley to George L. Hartsuff, September 16, 1861, RG 393, Department of Western Virginia, Correspondence Received, NA.

230. John Zeigler to H. J. Samuels, October 8, 1861, Adjutant General's Papers, Union Regiments, 5th West Virginia Infantry, WVSA.

231. *Wheeling Intelligencer*, October 12, 1861.

232. John L. Zeigler to Francis H. Pierpont, October 1, 1861, Pierpont Papers, LVA.

233. *Ironton Register*, October 31, 1861.

234. Sallie P. Smith to Julia Sprague, October 8, 1861, Smith Family Correspondence, MUSCD. The letter also included the names of "Rack Wood, Res Moore…and one other man I don't know what his name is."

235. Kellian V. Whaley to H. J. Samuels, October 11, 1861, Adjutant General's Papers, Union Regiments, 9th West Virginia Infantry, WVSA.

236. Kellian V. Whaley to Francis H. Pierpont, October 11, 1861, Pierpont Papers, LVA.

237. W. S. Rosecrans to Francis H. Pierpont, October 18, 1861, Francis H. Pierpont Civil War Telegram Series, WVRHC.

238. T. N. Davey to Francis Pierpont, October 22, 1861, Francis H. Pierpont Civil War Telegram Series, WVRHC; *Wheeling Intelligencer*, October 23, 1861.

239. John Zeigler to H. J. Samuels, October 31, 1861, Adjutant General's Papers, Union Regiments, 5th West Virginia Infantry, WVSA.

240. "History and Life of John A. Bowen," As Written by Himself on Thanksgiving Day, November 29, 1928, At his Home in Proctorville, Ohio, at the Ripe Old Age of 84, Toney C. Bowen, great-great-grandson. Typed by Linda Cunningham Fluharty and accessed at http://www.lindapages.com/jabowen.txt.

241. A. Sanders Piatt to William Rosecrans, October 24, 1861, RG 393, Department of Western Virginia, NA.

242. T. N. Davey to H. J. Samuels, October 26, 1861, Adjutant General's Papers, Union Regiments, 5th West Virginia Infantry, WVSA; *Ironton Register*, October 31, 1861.

243. J. C. Wheeler to H. J. Samuels, October 28, 1861, Pierpont-Samuels Papers, WVSA.

244. Kellian V. Whaley to Francis H. Pierpont, October 28, 1861, Pierpont Papers, LVA.

245. Jesse Spurlock to H. J. Samuels, October 28, 1861, Pierpont-Samuels Papers, WVSA.

246. B. D. McGinnis to H. J. Samuels, October 29, 1861, Adjutant General's Papers, Union Regiments, Miscellaneous Correspondence, WVSA.

247. Diary of Francis G. Hale, Albert and Shirley Small Special Collections Library, University of Virginia Libraries (UVL).

248. *Ibid.*

249. *Ibid.*

250. T. N. Davey to Francis Pierpont, November 2, 1861, Adjutant General's Papers, Union Regiments, 5th West Virginia Infantry, WVSA.

251. Hale Diary, UVL.

252. War Claims, United States Senate, 43rd Congress, 1st Session, Report No. 272, April 15, 1874. Holden later filed a claim for $5,139 for his home and furniture. Despite support from Kellian V. Whaley, Eli Thayer, John Zeigler, and others, the committee refused to compensate Holden for his loss, stating "Would this testimony, if the originals were before us, be sufficient to fix liability for the loss by this fire upon the United States? We think not. No testimony is taken of any officer in charge of the hospital, nor of any inmate of it, to establish the manner in which the accident occurred; whether it was by negligence of those who occupied it, by unavoidable accident, or otherwise. The petitioner does not state whether he was paid rent; whether his tenant, who it seems was occupying in his absence, was paid; whether any contract was made with the officers for its occupation; whether it was insured; indeed, no particulars are given beyond the statement that the house was occupied as a hospital, and was burned. In the absence of more explicit testimony we cannot report that this claim ought to be allowed, and ask to be discharged from its further consideration."

253. Joseph C. Wheeler to Henry J. Samuels, November 3, 1861, Pierpont-Samuels Papers, WVSA.

254. William Ludwig to George Ludwig, November 3, 1861, William E. Brooks Papers, WVRHC.

255. T. N. Davey to H. J. Samuels, November 5, 1861, Adjutant General's Papers, Union Regiments, 5th West Virginia Infantry, WVSA.

256. Jeremiah Hare to Francis Pierpont, November 11, 1861, Adjutant General's Papers, Union Militia, WVSA.

257. Telegram, John L. Zeigler to Francis Pierpont, November 5, 1861, Francis H. Pierpont Civil War Telegram Series, WVRHC.

258. Hale Diary, UVL.

259. *Ibid.*

260. Joseph C. Wheeler to Henry J. Samuels, November 6, 1861, Pierpont-Samuels Papers, WVSA.

261. Archibald Reynolds to H. J. Samuels, November 19, 1861, Pierpont-Samuels Papers, WVSA. Initially held captive in Winfield, Reynolds was moved to Camp

Chase after the raid on Guyandotte. There he saw the Guyandotte citizens who had been arrested by Federal authorities on November 11 and sent to prison.

262. Jesse Spurlock to H. J. Samuels, November 7, 1861, Adjutant General's Papers, Union Regiments, Miscellaneous Correspondence, WVSA.

263. Jesse Spurlock to H. J. Samuels, October 28, 1861 and November 7, 1861, Adjutant General's Papers, Union Regiments, Miscellaneous Correspondence, WVSA.

264. T. N. Davey to H. J. Samuels, November 8, 1861, Adjutant General's Papers, Union Regiments, 5th West Virginia Infantry, WVSA.

265. T. N. Davey to H. J. Samuels, November 9, 1861, Pierpont Papers, LVA.

266. A. Sanders Piatt to W. S. Rosecrans, November 9, 1861, RG 393, Department of Western Virginia, Correspondence Received, NA.

267. William Ludwig to George Ludwig, November 10, 1861, Brooks Papers, WVRHC.

268. Hale Diary, UVL.

269. *Ironton Register*, April 10, 1862; William Feazel to H. J. Samuels, November 10, 1861, Adjutant General's Papers, Union Regiments, 9th West Virginia Infantry, WVSA.

Chapter Six

270. John B. Floyd to J. P. Benjamin, November 19, 1861, *Official Records*, Series I, Volume V, 288; John Clarkson to John B. Floyd, *Official Records*, Series I, Volume V, 377; *Richmond Dispatch*, December 2, 1861.

271. J. T. R. Martin to Ma, November 24, 1861, J. T. R. Martin Collection, Filson Historical Society (FHS).

272. *Richmond Dispatch*, December 2, 1861.

273. *Cabell County Press*, December 6, 1869.

274. *Richmond Dispatch*, December 2, 1861; B. F. McCune to H. J. Samuels, December 11, 1861, Adjutant General's Papers, Union Regiments, Miscellaneous Correspondence, WVSA.

275. Sedinger, "Diary of a Border Ranger," Stutler Collection, WVSA. Sedinger had a younger brother who died from drowning in the Guyandotte River on March 20, 1859. *Richmond Dispatch*, April 7, 1859.

276. *Richmond Dispatch*, December 2, 1861.

277. "Interview with Henry Clay Everett," Lambert Collection, MUSCD.

278. *Ironton Register*, March 27, 1862; John W. Barbour, "The Fight At Guyandotte," Lambert Collection, MUSCD.

279. J. H. Rouse, *Horrible Massacre at Guyandotte* (n. p., 1862), 6; *Ironton Register*, March 27, 1862; *Gallipolis Journal*, November 21, 1861. Dr. J. H. Rouse wrote that the attack commenced at seven o'clock.

280. Statement of J. H. Shoemaker, November 23, 1861, Union Citizens Files, NA (fold3.com).

281. Rebecca Baumgardner, Union Citizens Files, NA (fold3.com). They would remain there until the conclusion of the battle. After the firing ceased, Henry Baumgardner climbed the stairs and after a short while hollered, "come up boys there is no danger, it is all over."

282. Sedinger, "Diary of a Border Ranger," Stutler Collection, WVSA.

283. *Richmond Dispatch*, December 2, 1861.

284. *Ironton Register*, March 27, 1862.

285. Rouse, *Horrible Massacre at Guyandotte*, 7.

286. *Ironton Register*, January 23, 1862.

287. K. V. Whaley to Governor Francis H. Pierpont, Official Report of the Battle of Guyandotte, *Calendar of Virginia State Papers and Other Manuscripts*, Volume 11, 365; *Ironton Register*, January 23, 1862; *Richmond Dispatch*, December 2, 1861.

288. *Ironton Register*, January 23, 1862.

289. J. C. Wheeler to Francis H. Pierpont, December 11, 1861, Pierpont Papers, LVA.

290. Sedinger, "Diary of a Border Ranger," Stutler Collection, WVSA.

291. *Richmond Dispatch*, December 2, 1861.

292. Barbour, "Fight At Guyandotte," Lambert Collection, MUSCD; Rouse, *Horrible Massacre at Guyandotte*, 11. Barbour identified the victim as James Lawhorn. Wilson B. Moore would be killed in Cabell County in a brutal encounter with members of the West family on December 13, 1868. See *Gallipolis Journal*, December 24, 1868; Dusenberry Papers, MUSCD.

293. *Ironton Register*, November 21, 1861. In a letter published in the *McArthur Democrat* on January 30, 1862, Alzira J. Scott of Guyandotte claimed that Captain William Turner, "who thought he (Mr. Everett) was guilty of killing three of Colonel Whaley's men is now satisfied that he was mistaken and is willing to do all in his power to satisfy the community, that he is innocent."

294. *Ironton Register*, March 27, 1862.

295. *Ibid*.

296. *Ibid*.

297. K. V. Whaley to Governor Francis H. Pierpont, Official Report of the Battle of Guyandotte, *Calendar of Virginia State Papers and Other Manuscripts*, Volume 11, 365. Captain Henry Clay Pate, who commanded the Petersburg Rangers, had been defeated and captured by John Brown and his men at the battle of Black Jack in Kansas on June 2, 1856.

298. *Wheeling Intelligencer*, December 5, 1861; *Ironton Register*, April 10, 1862.

299. Sedinger, "Diary of a Border Ranger," Stutler Collection, WVSA; *Richmond Dispatch*, December 2, 1861; Rouse, *Horrible Massacre at Guyandotte*, 11. *Richmond Dispatch*, November 25, 1861; Sallie P. Smith to Julia Sprague, October 4, 1862, Smith Family Correspondence, MUSCD.

300. *Richmond Enquirer*, November 26, 1861; J. T. R. Martin to Ma, November 24, 1861, J. T. R. Martin Collection, FHS; *Richmond Dispatch*, December 2, 1861.

301. Percival Smith, Union Citizens Files, NA (fold3.com).

302. Hugo Deitz, Union Citizens Files, NA (fold3.com).

303. *Ironton Register*, January 23, 1862. In the spring of 1862, William Wilson sought to serve as first lieutenant of Company C of the 9th (West) Virginia Infantry. J. C. Wheeler noted that "I brought him over with me and put him in command of the company to drill them &c and after spending two days ascertained that his leg was too weak on account of his wound to stand the service & voluntarily declined the position." J. C. Wheeler to H. J. Samuels, April 6, 1862, Adjutant General's Papers, Union Regiments, 9th West Virginia Infantry, WVSA.

304. Statement of J. C. Wheeler, November 14, 1861, Adjutant General's Papers, WVSA.

305. *Gallipolis Journal*, November 21, 1861.

306. *Ibid*.

307. *Gallipolis Journal*, November 14, 1861.

308. *Ibid.*; Rouse, *Horrible Massacre at Guyandotte*, 7-8.

309. Rouse, *Horrible Massacre at Guyandotte*, 7-12.

310. *Ironton Register*, March 27, 1862.

311. *Ibid*.

312. *Ibid*.

313. *Ibid*.

314. *Richmond Dispatch*, November 25, 1861.

315. Rouse, *Horrible Massacre at Guyandotte*, 9.

316. For accounts of the Shelton-Fuller feud see *Ironton Register*, November 21, 1861; "Achilles Fuller," Lambert Collection, MUSCD; *Wheeling Intelligencer*, November 15, 1861; "Civil War Days Were Dark Days In Cabell County," Huntington *Herald-Advertiser*, June 17, 1934; "The Fuller/Shelton Feud, Cabell County, West Virginia," by Kelly Winifred Shivel, April 13, 1992.

317. *Wheeling Intelligencer*, November 15, 1861; *Richmond Enquirer*, November 26, 1861.

318. A. M. McGinnis to H. J. Samuels, n.d., Adjutant General's Papers, WVSA; *Official Records*, Series II, Volume II, 1437. The report on Albert Fuller: "Albert Fuller – Native of Cabell County, Va.; aged eighteen; an unruly boy. His father and brothers Unionists. Albert Fuller was passing the house of Henry Shelton, a secessionist, armed with a musket and bayonet going in the direction of the Federal forces at Barboursville in company with another youth. W. Ward is the other youth. Shelton took the gun from him. Fuller went on to Barboursville, and a company of Ziegler's U. S. cavalry were sent to arrest Shelton. The boy who was with him went back to Fuller's father. Fuller's father and brother came on to Shelton's and killed him before Ziegler's cavalry arrived. Fuller's brother went to Ziegler's camp and thence to Ohio. His father was killed by a son of Shelton. I think Fuller ought not to be discharged but from the imperfection of the testimony I cannot advise where he should be sent for trial. I think he was the cause of Shelton's death and ought in some way to be brought to justice either by the State or Confederate authorities; but the seat of justice of the Confederate States for this district (Charleston, Kanawha County) and the committing of the offense are both in the possession of the enemy. I would suggest the propriety of an act of the Legislature of Virginia authorizing the

trial in some other county. Witnesses examined, Peters, Poteet, Beekman, Wilson."

319. *Ironton Register*, March 27, 1862.

320. "Army Paper of 1861 Tells of Attack on Guyandotte," Huntington *Herald-Advertiser*, December 16, 1968.

321. *Ironton Register*, November 14, 1861; *McArthur Democrat*, January 30, 1862.

322. Ralph Leete to William Dennison Jr., November 11, 1861, Letters Received by the Office of the Adjutant General, NA (https://www.fold3.com/image/299554383). Leete's letter was forwarded by Governor Dennison to General George B. McClellan, commander of the Army of the Potomac.

323. *Gallipolis Journal*, November 21, 1861.

324. *Richmond Dispatch*, December 2, 1861; John B. Floyd to J. P. Benjamin, *Official Records*, Series I, Volume V, 288; *Ironton Register*, November 14, 1861.

325. *Richmond Dispatch*, December 2, 1861; *Richmond Enquirer*, November 26, 1861.

Chapter Seven

326. John W. Barbour, "Fight at Guyandotte," Lambert Collection, MUSCD.

327. John W. Hite, Union Citizens Files, NA (fold3.com). When citizens of Guyandotte raised a Virginia state flag on the Ohio River bank on April 20, John W. Hite, a "peaceable quiet citizen," was "strongly opposed." He was listed as a broker in the 1860 census. When civil war erupted, Hite, like many Cabell Countians, found it difficult to decide which side was in the right but he "was determined to take no active part on either side." He was among those described by Union prisoner Dr. J. H. Rouse, however, as being "treacherous beings who participated in the fiendish work of betraying their neighbors and townsmen" of Guyandotte.

328. *Ironton Register*, April 10, 1862; History of 9th West Virginia Infantry, Adjutant General's Papers, Union Regiments, 9th West Virginia Infantry, WVSA. According to the regimental history and the November 21 issue of the *Gallipolis Journal*, a one-inch sea grass line was used to bind the column.

329. *Ironton Register*, March 27, 1862; *Gallipolis Journal*, November 21, 1861; Rouse, *Horrible Massacre at Guyandotte*, 15.

330. Rouse, *Horrible Massacre at Guyandotte*, 14.

331. William Ludwig to George Ludwig, November 14, 1861, Brooks Papers, WVRHC.

332. *Tiffin Weekly Tribune*, March 3, 1862.

333. B. F. McCune to H. J. Samuels, December 11, 1861, Adjutant General's Papers, Union Regiments, Miscellaneous Correspondence, WVSA.

334. Rouse, *Horrible Massacre at Guyandotte*, 15-16. In testimony at Richmond, Thomas Kyle declared that he was 72 years old and was willing to take the oath of allegiance. However, he had voted in several elections held by the Restored Government of Virginia and "it is proved that Kyle said Yankee bullets were the best pills for secessionists; that he took a musket to guard the court-house from

secessionists," a task Kyle claimed he was compelled to do. An official wrote, "I am at a loss what to recommend here. The vote to sustain the western revolutionary government I consider treason against Virginia, and the State authorities ought to decide whether they will prosecute him for this act."

335. *Wheeling Intelligencer*, December 5, 1861.

336. *Richmond Dispatch*, November 23, 1861; *Richmond Enquirer*, November 26, 1861. According to this article, the prisoners did not arrive until November 25, under the charge of Captain Henry Clay Pate and a guard of twenty Confederate soldiers.

337. Report of J. C. Wheeler, November 13, 1861, *Official Records*, Series I, Volume V, 411-12.

338. Robert Stewart to H. J. Samuels, December 28, 1861, Adjutant General's Papers, Union Regiments, Miscellaneous Correspondence, WVSA.

339. *Ironton Register*, November 14, 1861.

340. Interview with H. C. Everett, 4, Lambert Collection, MUSCD; John W. Barbour, "Fight At Guyandotte," Lambert Collection, MUSCD. A cooper makes or repairs casks and barrels.

341. *Guyandotte Centennial 1810-1910*, edited by Wiatt Smith (The Guyandotte Centennial and Cabell Homecoming Association, 1910), 79-80.

342. "History of the First Guyandotte Baptist Church," courtesy of Samuel Everett Pierce.

343. Report of J. C. Wheeler, November 13, 1861, *Official Records*, Series I, Volume V, 412; *Guyandotte Centennial*, 67-68.

344. *Marietta Republican*, November 22, 1861; *Jackson Standard*, November 21, 1861; *Jackson Standard*, December 19, 1861.

345. Ralph Leete to William Dennison, November 11, 1861, Pierpont Papers, LVA.

346. *Ibid*.

347. Albert D. Richardson, *A Personal History of Ulysses S. Grant* (Hartford, CT: Bliss and Company, 1868), 73-75.

348. *Portsmouth Times*, November 23, 1861.

349. *Ibid*.

350. *Ibid*.; Alexandria *Local News*, November 18, 1861.

351. Margaret J. Bailey to Francis Pierpont, 1861, Adjutant General's Papers, Union Regiments, Miscellaneous Correspondence, WVSA.

352. John Glidden to Francis H. Pierpont, January 12, 1862, Pierpont Papers, LVA.

353. *Report of the Committees of the House of Representatives, 1861-1862* (Washington, DC: Government Printing Office, 1862), Report No. 130, Margaret J. Bailey. Margaret Bailey wrote to President Ulysses S. Grant on March 12, 1874, asking for his assistance: "Having made application for Increase Pension under Act of March 3rd 1873, for my children, my claim was *rejected*, because I was allowed a pension under Special Act of Congress. My husband was an old school mate of yours & was also at West Point. His name Dr George Bartlett Bailey Jr. son of Dr George B Bailey of Georgetown Ohio. He was killed at Guyandotte Va in 1861 while acting as

Lieut. Col. of the 9th Regt. West Va Vols., leaving me with very little means and five children. Hon. Chilton White and others succeeded in getting me a pension. The Act of March 1873 gives $2.00 per month to each child under sixteen years from July 25 1866, and, as I draw only the same as other widows do who were not on the Pension Rolls by Special Act. I am now almost helpless with Paralysis and find it very hard to get along and this increase would be a great help..." *The Papers of Ulysses S. Grant*, Volume 25, edited by John Y. Simon, (Carbondale, IL: Southern Illinois University Press, 1874), 358. The Ohio History Center preserves a silk United States flag made by the women of Aberdeen in Brown County, Ohio, and presented to Captain George B. Bailey of Company G, 1st Ohio Volunteers in 1861.

354. Wallace, *Cabell County Annals*, 81.
355. *Gallipolis Journal*, November 14, 1861.
356. *Wheeling Intelligencer*, November 13, 1861.
357. *Ironton Register*, November 14, 1861.
358. *Wheeling Intelligencer*, n.d.; Z. D. Ramsdell, quartermaster for the 5th (West) Virginia, justification for payment of bill, Z. D. Ramsdell Collection, Z. D. Ramsdell House, Ceredo. Ramsdell wrote, "The enemy remained in the neighborhood several days, and it was during this time that commanders of squads of militia and citizens, important scouts, spies, witnesses and assistants in planning the fortifications, were subsisted by Adam Browne, to the amount of $33."
359. *Ibid.*
360. *Gallipolis Journal*, November 21, 1861.
361. *Ironton Register*, November 14, 1861.
362. *Wheeling Intelligencer*, November 15, 1861.
363. George Sprecher to Wife, November 15, 1861, George Sprecher's Civil War Letters, http://genealogysurnames.net/SprecherWarLetters.html; Telegram, Joseph J. Lightburn to Francis Pierpont, November 13, 1861, Pierpont Civil War Telegram Series, WVRHC.
364. *Wheeling Intelligencer*, November 13, 1861; *Ironton Register*, December 5, 1861.
365. *Marietta Republican*, November 22, 1861.
366. *Ironton Register*, November 14, 1861.
367. *Wheeling Intelligencer*, November 21, 1861.
368. *Ibid.*
369. *Cincinnati Commercial*, November 19, 1861. Hooper B. Stevens and his family lived on the Jenkins plantation, where Stevens served as a caretaker. During the war, he fell prey to Home Guards from Mason County and from across the river in Crown City, Ohio. Butcher knives, animals, and everything else of value were taken from the Stevens family without reimbursement. On one occasion, Home Guards from Crown City followed Stevens across the Ohio River. His son ran into the house, grabbed a rifle, and began to fire on the Union men but his father knocked the barrel upwards as the trigger was pulled. The incensed Ohio men attacked father and son, and Hooper B. Stevens was arrested for treason. He was taken to Guyandotte for trial, but the judge dismissed the case for lack of evidence. The Home Guards attempted to ambush

Stevens on his return trip to Green Bottom, but he made his way through fields and woods to safety. See Denver Yoho, "Civil War...Life On The Jenkins' Farm with the Home Guard," *Cabell Record*, July 11, 1996.

370. *Ibid.*

371. *Ironton Register*, November 21, 1861.

372. Telegram, Abia A. Tomlinson to Francis Pierpont, November 16, 1861, Pierpont Civil War Telegram Series, WVRHC.

373. *Gallipolis Journal*, November 21, 1861; *Gallipolis Dispatch*, November 21, 1861.

374. *Wheeling Intelligencer*, November 23, 1861.

375. *Gallipolis Journal*, November 28, 1861.

376. *Ironton Register*, December 5, 1861.

377. *Gallipolis Journal*, December 19, 1861.

378. James E. Wood to H. J. Samuels, December 4, 1861, Adjutant General's Papers, Union Regiments, Miscellaneous Correspondence, WVSA. One of the cavalrymen captured at Guyandotte was James Franklin Adams, who was born near Barboursville on August 26, 1844. Adams was paroled in a prisoner exchange on February 19, 1863, re-enlisted, and earned the Medal of Honor at Nineveh, Virginia, on November 12, 1864. He died on March 12, 1922, and is buried in Oaklawn Cemetery near Barboursville.

379. J. C. Wheeler to Francis Pierpont, November 29, 1861, Adjutant General's Papers, Union Regiments, 9th West Virginia Infantry, WVSA.

380. Eliza Morey to H. J. Samuels, November 24, 1861, Samuels-Pierpont Papers, WVSA.

381. B. F. McCune to H. J. Samuels, December 11, 1861, Adjutant General's Papers, Union Regiments, Miscellaneous Correspondence, WVSA; Elizabeth Thompson to H. J. Samuels, December 15, 1861, Adjutant General's Papers, Union Regiments, Miscellaneous Correspondence, WVSA.

382. Emily Morris to H. J. Samuels, December 27, 1861, Adjutant General's Papers, Union Regiments, Miscellaneous Correspondence, WVSA.

383. Emily Morris to H. J. Samuels, January 8, 1862, Pierpont-Samuels Papers, WVSA.

384. *Ironton Register*, May 1, 1862.

385. John C. Paxton to H. J. Samuels, December 20, 1861, Adjutant General's Papers, Union Regiments, 2nd West Virginia Cavalry, WVSA.

386. J. C. Wheeler to H. J. Samuels, December 29, 1861, Adjutant General's Papers, Union Regiments, 9th West Virginia Infantry, WVSA.

387. P. J. Smith to H. J. Samuels, December 30, 1861, Adjutant General's Papers, Union Regiments, Miscellaneous Correspondence, WVSA.

388. *Official Records*, Series II, Volume II, 1437.

389. Thomas H. Monroe to Francis H. Pierpont, January 4, 1862, Pierpont Papers, LVA.

390. Charles Roffe to Jacob D. Cox, January 5, 1863, Union Citizens Files, NA (fold3.com).

391. J. C. Wheeler to H. J. Samuels, December 31, 1861, Adjutant General's Papers, Union Regiments, 9th West Virginia Infantry, WVSA.

392. A. M. McGinnis to H. J. Samuels, n.d., Adjutant General's Papers, Union Regiments, Miscellaneous Correspondence, WVSA.

393. *Ibid.*

394. *Ibid.*

395. Robert Stewart to H. J. Samuels, November 14, 1861, Adjutant General's Papers, Union Regiments, Miscellaneous Correspondence, WVSA.

396. Robert Stewart to H. J. Samuels, December 28, 1861, Adjutant General's Papers, Union Regiments, Miscellaneous Correspondence, WVSA.

397. John Laidley et al to William S. Rosecrans, n.d., Adjutant General's Papers, WVSA.

398. S. M. E. Russell to Henry J. Samuels, December 27, 1861, Adjutant General's Papers, Union Regiments, Miscellaneous Correspondence, WVSA; Petition of Cabell County citizens, Adjutant General's Papers, Union Regiments, Miscellaneous Correspondence, WVSA. The petition was signed by P. S. Smith, Hugo Deitz, O. Moore, D. W. Thornburg, W. L. Cloud, N. Wellington, J. W. Everett, E. Wellington, R. P. Smith, and P. S. Smith, Jr.

399. David Frampton, Robert Reynolds, Peter R. Everett, P. M. Russell, and others to Francis H. Pierpont, December 30, 1861, Pierpont Papers, LVA. The word "over" appears at the bottom of the document, indicating more information, probably additional names, on a subsequent page, but it was not found.

400. J. C. Wheeler to H. J. Samuels, January 24, 1865, Adjutant General's Papers, Union Regiments, 9th West Virginia Infantry, WVSA; Thomas J. Poteet to H. J. Samuels, January 20, 1862, Pierpont-Samuels Papers, WVSA.

401. J. C. Wheeler to H. J. Samuels, January 25, 1865, Adjutant General's Papers, Union Regiments, 9th West Virginia Infantry, WVSA.

402. Dusenberry Papers, MUSCD.

403. J. C. Wheeler to H. J. Samuels, January 26, 1862, Pierpont-Samuels Papers, WVSA.

404. *Ibid.*

405. H. J. Samuels to Joseph Darr, n.d., Edward Smith, Union Citizens Files, NA (fold3.com).

406. Charles Everett correspondence, Charles Everett, Union Citizens Files, NA (fold3.com).

407. Testimony of T. J. Smith, Charles Everett, Union Citizens Files, NA (fold3.com).

408. Testimony of David Earls, Charles Everett, Union Citizens Files, NA (fold3.com).

409. Jacob Bumgardner to Francis Pierpont, January 6, 1862; St. Mark Russell to Francis H. Pierpont, January 5, 1862; David Frampton to Francis H. Pierpont, January 4, 1862; Unknown to Francis H. Pierpont, January 7, 1862, all from Pierpont Papers, LVA.

410. Testimony of William C. Rogers. William C. Rogers (Rodgers), Union

Citizens Files, NA (fold3.com).

411. Civil War Soldiers, Confederate, Miscellaneous, Frank Bing, NA (fold3.com).

412. Francis Bing to Joseph Darr, April 22, 1862, and July 16, 1862, Francis Bing, Union Citizens Files, NA (fold3.com).

413. Jonathan Morris to Francis H. Pierpont, March 11, 1862, Pierpont Papers, LVA.

414. Hillary McVickers to H. J. Samuels, June 19, 1862, Pierpont-Samuels Papers, WVSA; Point Pleasant *Weekly Register*, June 12, 1862.

415. Thomas Ross to H. J. Samuels, June 30, 1862, Adjutant General's Papers, Union Regiments, Miscellaneous Correspondence, WVSA.

416. *Ironton Register*, February 19, 1863.

417. R. L. Stewart to H. J. Samuels, July 5, 1864, Adjutant General's Papers, Union Regiments, 9th West Virginia Infantry, WVSA.

418. Kellian V. Whaley to unidentified, Adjutant General's Papers, Union Regiments, 9th West Virginia Infantry, WVSA.

Chapter Eight

419. P. H. McCullough to H. J. Samuels, November 15, 1861, Pierpont-Samuels Papers, WVSA.

420. William Bolles to H. J. Samuels, November 16, 1861, Adjutant General's Papers, Union Regiments, 2nd West Virginia Cavalry, WVSA.

421. Charles Wilgus to H. J. Samuels, November 20, 1861, Adjutant General's Papers, Union Regiments, Miscellaneous Correspondence, WVSA.

422. Thomas Thornburg to H. J. Samuels, November 23, 1861, Adjutant General's Papers, Union Regiments, Miscellaneous Correspondence, WVSA.

423. *Ibid.*

424. Eliza Morey to H. J. Samuels, November 24, 1861, Adjutant General's Papers, Union Regiments, Miscellaneous Correspondence, WVSA.

425. M. A. Cruikshank to H. J. Samuels, November 30, 1861, Adjutant General's Papers, Union Regiments, Miscellaneous Correspondence, WVSA.

426. J. C. Wheeler to Francis H. Pierpont, December 11, 1861, Pierpont Papers, Library of Virginia.

427. *Ibid.*

428. *Ibid.*

429. J. C. Wheeler to H. J. Samuels, December 16, 1861, Adjutant General's Papers, Union Regiments, Miscellaneous Correspondence, WVSA.

430. *Ironton Register*, September 19, 1861; *Ironton Register*, September 26, 1861.

431. *Wheeling Intelligencer*, November 18, 1861.

432. George D. Pyle to Uncle, January 9, 1862, Terry Lowry Collection; Junius Jones Diary, WVSA.

433. J. C. Wheeler to H. J. Samuels, December 17, 1861, Adjutant General's Papers, Union Regiments, 9th West Virginia Infantry, WVSA.

434. J. L. Wallar to J. A. J. Lightburn, December 21, 1861, Adjutant General's Papers, Union Regiments, 2nd West Virginia Cavalry, WVSA.

435. J. L. Wallar to J. A. J. Lightburn, December 28, 1861, Adjutant General's Papers, Union Regiments, 2nd West Virginia Cavalry, WVSA.

436. *Ironton Register*, December 1861.

437. John C. Paxton to Francis H. Pierpont, December 24, 1861, Pierpont Papers, LVA.

438. Junius Jones Diary, WVSA.

439. James C. Black to H. J. Samuels, December 25, 1861, Union Citizens Files, NA (fold3.com).

440. *Ibid.*

441. William H. Copley to Francis H. Pierpont, January 4, 1862, Pierpont Papers, LVA; Abel Segur and William Kendrick were elected for District One; William Bartram, Benjamin Davis, David Wilson, and David Bartram for District Three; and Jackson Spaulding, James Roman, and Joseph D. York for District Four; Certification of Election, G. Harrison and R. Bukey, December 31, 1861, Pierpont Papers, LVA.

442. *Ironton Register*, January 9, 1862.

443. E. M. Norton to Joseph Darr, December 31, 1861, Union Citizens Files, NA (fold3.com).

444. Nathan Clay, Union Citizens Files, NA (fold3.com). Testimony of J. L. Wallar, November 18, 1862, *United States vs. Nathan H. Clay*, Confederate, Miscellaneous, NA (fold3.com).

445. *Ibid.*

446. *Ibid.*

447. Confederate, Miscellaneous, NA (fold3.com). Clay would be imprisoned again in November 1862 and claimed that he was impressed by Jenkins's cavalry during their 1862 incursion into Cabell County.

448. Milton J. Ferguson to H. J. Samuels, January 3, 1862, Adjutant General's Papers, Union Regiments, Miscellaneous Correspondence, WVSA; List of Prisoners from Cabell County Confined in the Athen[a]eum in Wheeling, January 20, 1862, Pierpont-Samuels Papers, WVSA. This latter list also included the names of W. H. Cynes, with being in arms at Barboursville, and Presley Stowers and Thomas Scales, charges unknown. Ferguson would be exchanged later in the year.

449. Hurston Spurlock to H. J. Samuels, November 11, 1861, Pierpont-Samuels Papers, WVSA.

450. Sallie P. Smith to Irving Smith, January 2, 1862, Smith Family Correspondence, MUSCD.

451. *Ibid.*

452. *Ibid.*

453. Thomas Thornburg to H. J. Samuels, January 6, 1862, Adjutant General's Papers, Union Regiments, Miscellaneous Correspondence, WVSA.

454. *Ibid.*

455. John Laidley to H. J. Samuels, January 6, 1862, Pierpont-Samuels Papers, WVSA.

456. *Ibid*.

457. Sallie P. Smith to Julia Sprague, January 10, 1862, Smith Family Correspondence, MUSCD. One of the sons of Dudley Smith, Dudley Irving Smith, would be elected sheriff of Cabell County in 1870.

458. *Ibid*.

459. W. H. Langley to Francis H. Pierpont, January 15, 1862, RG 393, Department of Western Virginia, NA.

460. Junius Jones Diary, WVSA.

461. G. B. McClellan to W. S. Rosecrans, February 6, 1862, *Official Records*, Series I, Volume LI, Part I, 525.

462. William Bolles to Francis H. Pierpont, February 7, 1862, Pierpont Papers, LVA.

463. Junius Jones to Parents, February 7, 1862, Junius Marion Jones Collection, WVSA.

464. *Ibid*.

465. T. W. Everett to H. J. Samuels, February 7, 1862, Pierpont-Samuels Papers, WVSA.

466. *Ibid*.

467. *Ibid*.

468. W. C. Starr to H. J. Samuels, February 14, 1862, Pierpont-Samuels Papers, WVSA.

469. Francis H. Pierpont to William S. Rosecrans, November 12, 1861, Union Citizens Files, NA (fold3.com).

470. Socrates Glaze to O. B. Evans, 1861, Union Citizens Files, NA (fold3.com).

471. Socrates Glaze to William S. Rosecrans, December 14, 1861, Union Citizens Files, NA (fold3.com).

472. Socrates Glaze to Joseph Darr, January 11, 1862, Union Citizens Files, NA (fold3.com). In March 1862, Albert Jenkins leased the Green Bottom farm to his father-in-law James Bowlin for ten years. See Dickinson and Dickinson, *Gentleman Soldier of Greenbottom*, 73.

473. Socrates Glaze to Williams S. Rosecrans, February 1, 1862, Union Citizens Files, NA (fold3.com).

474. William Bolles to C. Goddard, February 14, 1862; Socrates Glaze to William S. Rosecrans, Union Citizens Files, NA (fold3.com).

475. *Ibid*.

476. Socrates Glaze to William S. Rosecrans, February 1, 1862, Union Citizens Files, NA (fold3.com).

477. *Ibid*.

478. Abraham Smith to Cousin, February 16, 1862, Smith Family Correspondence, MUSCD.

479. *Ibid*.

480. William Turner to H. J. Samuels, February 20, 1862, Pierpont-Samuels Papers, WVSA.

481. *Ibid*. This reference is to Confederate Lieutenant Colonel Vincent Witcher,

who commanded the 34th Virginia Cavalry Battalion.

482. *Ibid.*

483. J. C. Wheeler to H. J. Samuels, November 29, 1861, Adjutant General's Papers, Union Regiments, Miscellaneous Correspondence, WVSA.

484. *Ibid.*

485. Stephen Spurlock to H. J. Samuels, January 16, 1862, Pierpont-Samuels Papers, WVSA.

486. Jesse Spurlock to H. J. Samuels, November 11, 1861, Adjutant General's Papers, Union Regiments, Miscellaneous Correspondence, WVSA.

487. *Ibid.*

488. *Ibid.*

489. *Ibid.*

490. Sallie P. Smith to Julia Sprague, February 23, 1862, Smith Family Correspondence, MUSCD.

491. Granville Parker to Francis H. Pierpont, March 7, 1862, Pierpont Papers, LVA.

492. Joseph Gaston to Francis Pierpont, March 14, 1862, Pierpont-Samuels Papers, WVSA.

493. F. H. Pierpont to George L. Hartsuff, March 20, 1862, RG 393, Department of Western Virginia, NA.

494. *Ironton Register*, March 20, 1862.

495. Point Pleasant *Weekly Register*, April 10, 1862.

496. *Ironton Register*, March 27, 1862.

497. Leonard Skinner to Francis H. Pierpont, March 26, 1862, Pierpont Papers, LVA.

498. Dusenberry Papers, MUSCD.

499. Kellian V. Whaley to Francis H. Pierpont, March 31, 1862, Pierpont Papers, LVA.

500. Dusenberry Papers, MUSCD.

501. *Ibid.*

502. *Wheeling Intelligencer*, April 11, 1862.

503. Point Pleasant *Weekly Register*, April 10, 1862.

504. J. D. Cox to John C. Fremont, *Official Records*, Series I, Volume XII, Part II, 46.

505. A. M. McGinnis to H. J. Samuels, April 1862, Pierpont-Samuels Papers, WVSA.

506. J. B. Baumgardner to H. J. Samuels, April 6, 1862, Pierpont-Samuels Papers, WVSA.

507. Junius Jones Diary, Junius Marion Jones Collection, WVSA.

508. Junius Jones to Parents, Junius Marion Jones Collection, WVSA.

509. Junius Jones Diary, Junius Marion Jones Collection, WVSA.

510. John Laidley to H. J. Samuels, April 10, 1862, Pierpont-Samuels Papers, WVSA.

511. Point Pleasant *Weekly Register*, April 24, 1862.

512. *Ironton Register*, April 24, 1862.
513. *Ironton Register*, May 1, 1862.
514. Point Pleasant *Weekly Register*, May 1862.
515. *Ironton Register*, January 23, 1862; *Ironton Register*, April 17, 1862.
516. *Ironton Register*, May 15, 1862; Final Statement of John Hardee, Adjutant General's Papers, Union Regiments, 9th West Virginia Infantry, WVSA.
517. *Pomeroy Weekly Telegraph*, June 6, 1862.
518. Dusenberry Papers, MUSCD.

Chapter Nine

519. William Ludwig to George Ludwig, November 14, 1861, Brooks Papers, WVRHC.
520. *Cincinnati Commercial*, November 13, 1861.
521. Hale Diary, UVL.
522. *Cincinnati Commercial*, November 13, 1861.
523. William Ludwig to George Ludwig, November 18, 1861, Brooks Papers, WVRHC.
524. Hale Diary, UVL.
525. *Ibid.*
526. William Ludwig to George Ludwig, November 27, 1861, Brooks Papers, WVRHC.
527. George Sprecher to Wife, December 5, 1861, Sprecher's Civil War Letters, scanned by Susan Isaac, from http://genealogysurnames.net/SprecherWarLetters.html.
528. Hale Diary, UVL.
529. Interview with Sampson Sanders Simmons, Lambert Collection, MUSCD.
530. George Sprecher to Wife, December 8, 1861, Sprecher's Civil War Letters.
531. *New York Illustrated News*, December 28, 1861.
532. Hale Diary, UVL.
533. George Sprecher to Wife, December 15, 1861, Sprecher's Civil War Letters.
534. *Ibid.*
535. *Ibid.*
536. *Tiffin Weekly Tribune*, January 3, 1862.
537. George Sprecher to Wife, December 11, 1861, Sprecher's Civil War Letters.
538. Pension Papers, William Collins, NA, courtesy of Terry Lowry. According to these records, Collins was "killed while on duty as messenger." *Tiffin Weekly Tribune*, January 10, 1862.
539. *Harpers Weekly*, February 7, 1863; *Tiffin Weekly Review*, January 10, 1862. Oral tradition claimed that the execution of the Zouaves was due to their "abuse" of a local woman. See Jack L. Dickinson, *Wayne County, West Virginia in the Civil War* (Salem, MA: Higginson Book Company, 2003). A more recent interview with descendant Rayburn Adkins related the oral tradition that the Union soldiers had

captured Rayfield (Rafe) Lenting Blankenship, a nephew of Helena Gilkerson, and were escorting him to camp at Barboursville. Blankenship convinced the Zouaves to stop at his aunt's house, where the Federal soldiers were captured. See Dr. Michael Jessee Adkins, "The Zouave Caves: An Investigation of Murder, Mystery, and Rebellion in Appalachia," *International Journal of Arts and Humanities*, October 2018. It seems more likely that the Zouaves were simply taken captive while passing through the area on their way to Wayne Courthouse.

540. *Ibid.*

541. *Ibid.*

542. Interview with William L. Johnson, Lambert Collection, MUSCD. Two of the men who allegedly participated in the murders, L. A. Pritchett and William D. Pritchett, took the oath of allegiance on November 3, 1864. Union Citizens Files, NA (fold3.com).

543. Hale Diary, UVL.

544. John L. Toland to H. J. Samuels, December 23, 1861, Adjutant General's Papers, Union Regiments, Non-West Virginia, 34th Ohio Infantry, WVSA.

545. *United States vs. Jerome Shelton*, Confederate, Miscellaneous, NA (fold3.com).

546. *Ibid.*

547. *Ibid.*

548. J. C. Wheeler to H. J. Samuels, December 27, 1861, Adjutant General's Papers, Union Regiments, 9th West Virginia Infantry, WVSA.

549. *Cincinnati Press*, January 4, 1862.

550. Hale Diary, UVL.

551. Hale Diary, UVL.

552. *Ibid*; Interview with William L. Johnson, Lambert Collection, MUSCD; *Harpers Weekly*, February 7, 1863; *Bucyrus Journal*, January 24, 1862; Dusenberry Papers, MUSCD. According to Francis Hale, the name of the Union sympathizer was Spencer "Dock" Bontecew.

553. *Ibid.*

554. Hale Diary, UVL.

555. *Ibid.*

556. *Ibid.*

557. *Ibid.*

558. *Ibid.*

559. *Ibid.*

560. *Ibid.*

561. William Ludwig to George Ludwig, January 1, 1862, Brooks Papers, WVRHC.

562. Hale Diary, UVL.

563. Dusenberry Papers, MUSCD.

564. Dusenberry Papers, MUSCD.

565. Hale Diary, UVL.

566. *Humorous, Pathetic, and Descriptive Incidents of the War*, by Alf Burnett (Cincinnati, OH: R. W. Carroll & Co., Publishers, 1864), 220-21.

567. *Wheeling Intelligencer*, January 4, 1862.
568. Regimental Order Book of the 34th Ohio Infantry, NA.
569. Union Citizens Files, John Lykin[s], NA (fold3.com).
570. *Ibid.*
571. *Ibid.*
572. *Ibid.*
573. *Harpers Weekly*, February 7, 1863; Hale Diary, UVL; Dusenberry Papers, MUSCD.
574. Regimental Order Book of the 34th Ohio Infantry, NA.
575. *Bucyrus Journal*, January 24, 1862. Peitzel would die of wounds received in the battle of Fayetteville in September 1862.
576. Dusenberry Papers, MUSCD.
577. *Bucyrus Journal*, February 7, 1862.
578. *Ibid.*
579. Dusenberry Papers, MUSCD.
580. A. Sanders Piatt to David Tod, January 31, 1862, Adjutant General's Papers, Correspondence to the Governor and Adjutant General, WVSA.
581. Dusenberry Papers, MUSCD.
582. James Wallar to J. A. J. Lightburn, February 4, 1862, Calvin Adkins, Union Citizens Files, NA (fold3.com).
583. William Ratliff to Joseph Darr, n.d. Calvin Adkins, Union Citizens Files, NA (fold3.com).
584. *Bucyrus Journal*, February 21, 1862.
585. George Sprecher to Wife, February 6, 1862, Sprecher's Civil War Letters.
586. A. Sanders Piatt to Edwin Stanton, February 6, 1862, *Official Records*, Series I, Volume LI, Part I, 524-525.
587. George B. McClellan to William S. Rosecrans, February 6, 1862, *Official Records*, Series I, Volume LI, Part I, 525.
588. William S. Rosecrans to George B. McClellan, February 7, 1862, *Official Records*, Series I, Volume LI, Part I, 527; William S. Rosecrans to George B. McClellan, February 7, 1862, *Official Records*, Series I, Volume LI, Part I, 527.
589. *Ibid.*
590. *Wheeling Intelligencer*, February 19, 1862. No Linn Creek could be found in West Virginia. There is a tributary of Twelve Pole Creek named Lynn Creek at Lavalette and a Big Lynn Creek at East Lynn. Both are in Wayne County.
591. *Wheeling Intelligencer*, February 19, 1862. Three separate accounts note that Stephens/Stevens was one of the men who shot the Union soldiers on Beech Fork, but none of them give his first name. In the 1860 census, a Benjamin Stephens, aged 50, lived in the household next to Ira Gilkerson, and only six households from his brother Leander Gilkerson, who owned the mill. However, it appears that Benjamin Stephens survived the war and married in 1868. Perhaps the newspaper account was incorrect or exaggerated, and Stephens was captured rather than killed.
592. George Sprecher to Wife, February 15, 1862, Sprecher's Civil War Letters.
593. *Bucyrus Journal*, March 14, 1862; Dusenberry Papers, MUSCD.

594. Susan Holderby to William Rosecrans, March 8, 1862, Susan Holderby, Union Citizens Files, NA (fold3.com). Susan Holderby was the largest slaveholder in the Guyandotte District of Cabell County. *See* Cicero M. Fain, III, *Black Huntington: An Appalachian Story* (Urbana, IL: University of Illinois Press), 2019.

595. *Ibid.*; Deposition of Susan A. Holderby, February 21, 1862, Susan Holderby, Union Citizens Files, NA (fold3.com).

596. George Hartstuff to J. D. Cox, February 28, 1862, Susan Holderby, Union Citizens Files, NA (fold3.com).

597. J. D. Cox to F. E. Franklin, March 4, 1862, Susan Holderby, Union Citizens Files, NA (fold3.com).

598. *Ibid.*

599. Susan Holderby to William Rosecrans, March 8, 1862, Susan Holderby, Union Citizens Files, NA (fold3.com).

600. Susan Holderby to William Rosecrans, April 8, 1862, Susan Holderby, Union Citizens Files, NA (fold3.com).

601. *Ibid.*

602. *Bucyrus Journal*, March 14, 1862.

603. *Ibid.*

604. Dusenberry Papers, MUSCD.

605. *Ibid*; Junius Jones to Parents, March 20, 1862, Junius Jones Collection, WVSA.

606. H. J. Samuels to William S. Rosecrans, March 19, 1862, Pierpont-Samuels Papers, WVSA.

607. Thomas Thornburg to H. J. Samuels, April 4, 1862, Pierpont-Samuels Papers, WVSA.

608. Dusenberry Papers, MUSCD.

609. Thomas Thornburg to H. J. Samuels, April 4, 1862, Pierpont-Samuels Papers, WVSA.

610. *Ibid.*

611. In addition to the Zouaves murdered at Beech Fork, the following members of the 34th Ohio died during their service in Cabell County: George Gibbs, G, died March 13, 1862, Barboursville; Sgt. Samuel Balser, H, died January 24, 1862, Barboursville; Henry Minshall, G, died March 9, 1862, Barboursville; Ferdinand Roads, B, died January 4, 1862, Camp Toland; James Cutler, I, died February 6, 1862, Camp Toland; Thomas Young, I, died January 5, 1862, Camp Toland Hospital; James T. Swisher, K, died December 25, 1862, Camp Toland.

612. Adkins, "The Zouave Caves," 550.

Chapter Ten

613. James C. Black to Francis Pierpont, n.d., Pierpont-Samuels Papers, WVSA.

614. Albert Tracy to J. A. J. Lightburn, May 10, 1862, *Official Records*, Series I, Volume XII, Part III, 164-65.

615. John B. Baumgardner to H. J. Samuels, May 14, 1862, Pierpont-Samuels Papers, WVSA.

616. "Memorialists" to H. J. Samuels, May 14, 1862, Pierpont-Samuels Papers, WVSA; John Laidley Correspondence, May 15, 1862, Pierpont-Samuels Papers, WVSA.

617. Dusenberry Papers, MUSCD.

618. *Ibid.*

619. John V. Young to H. J. Samuels, May 24, 1862, Adjutant General's Papers, Union Regiments, 11th West Virginia Infantry, WVSA. Information regarding Young's command provided by Phil Hatfield.

620. William Shannon to H. J. Samuels, June 24, 1862, Pierpont-Samuels Papers, WVSA.

621. Dusenberry Papers, MUSCD.

622. *Ibid.*

623. *Ibid.*

624. John S. Laidley to Henry J. Samuels, July 25, 1862, Adjutant General's Papers, Union Regiments, Miscellaneous Correspondence, WVSA.

625. *Ibid.*

626. Dudley I. Smith to Aunt, July 20, 1862, Smith Family Correspondence, MUSCD.

627. *Ibid.*

628. J. D. Cox to George D. Ruggles, July 25, 1862, *Official Records*, Series I, Volume XII, Part III, 508; J. A. J. Lightburn to Jacob D. Cox, July 27, 1862, *Official Records*, Series I, Volume XII, Part III, 513.

629. Jacob D. Cox to J. A. J. Lightburn, July 27, 1862, *Official Records*, Series I, Volume XII, Part III, 513-14.

630. *Ibid.*

631. Dusenberry Papers, MUSCD.

632. Rudolphus Bukey to H. J. Samuels, July 30, 1862, Pierpont-Samuels Papers, WVSA.

633. Dusenberry Papers, MUSCD.

634. *Ibid.*; Sallie P. Smith to Julia Sprague, August 12, 1862, Smith Family Correspondence, MUSCD.

635. *Ironton Register*, August 14, 1862.

636. Sallie P. Smith to Julia Sprague, August 12, 1862, Smith Family Correspondence, MUSCD.

637. *Ibid.*

638. *Ibid.*

639. *Ibid.*

640. "The Retreat of the Union Forces from the Kanawha Valley in 1862," by John L. Vance, *Sketches of War History*, 1861-1865, Military Order of the Loyal Legion of the United States, Ohio, Volume IV, 118.

641. Dusenberry Papers, MUSCD.

642. *Ibid.*

643. *Ibid.*

644. Jack L. Dickinson, *Jenkins of Greenbottom: A Civil War Saga* (Charleston, WV: Pictorial Histories Publishing Company, 1988), 50.

645. *Ironton Register*, September 18, 1862. Organization of the 91st Ohio Infantry began in July 1862 and the regiment was filled in one month. After drilling for a short time, the men received their arms, and five companies were ordered to Ironton in August to defend the community against an anticipated Confederate raid. They were joined by the remainder of the regiment on September 3. On the following day, the 91st Ohio was ordered to Guyandotte, where they remained twenty-four hours and returned to Ironton. They were mustered into the service of the United States "for three years unless sooner discharged" on September 7, 1862. *See Ironton Register*, August 3, 1865.

646. *Ibid.*

647. J. J. Sutton, *History of the 2nd Regiment West Virginia Volunteer Cavalry* (Portsmouth, OH: 1892), 60. Sutton lists the location as the farm of Warren Rece, who was Abia's son and was listed in his household in the 1860 census.

648. *Ibid.*

649. *Ibid.* A few months later, Major William Powell would be awarded the Medal of Honor for his actions on November 26, 1862, at Sinking Creek, (West) Virginia, in Greenbrier County. He led about twenty men on a raid and captured more than one hundred Confederates without the loss of a man. Soon after this expedition, Powell was wounded in battle and taken captive. He was imprisoned in Richmond and forced to survive on bread and water. Powell wrote to General Albert Jenkins, pleading his case for better treatment. He eventually received a special thirty-day parole and was exchanged for Confederate Colonel Richard H. Lee. After his release, Powell returned to the army and was promoted to major general on March 13, 1865. After resigning his command, Powell built a home overlooking the Ohio River in Clifton (Mason County) which still stands today. See Whitelaw Reid, *Ohio in the War: Her Statesmen, Her Generals, and Soldiers*, Volume I (Cincinnati, OH: Moore, Wilstach and Baldwin, 1868), 109.

650. Lawrence County, Ohio Veterans' Grave Registration, Briggs Lawrence County Public Library; Jack L. Dickinson, *8th Virginia Cavalry* (Lynchburg, VA: H. E. Howard, Inc., 1986).

651. Sedinger, "Diary of a Border Ranger," Stutler Collection, WVSA.

652. *Ironton Register*, September 18, 1862.

653. *Ibid.*

654. *Ibid.*

655. *Ibid.*; *Wheeling Intelligencer*, September 1862.

656. Dickinson and Dickinson, *Gentleman Soldier of Greenbottom*, 141. The Confederates were able to add a substantial number of recruits during their September 1862 offensive. Nearly sixty men enlisted in the 36th Battalion Virginia Cavalry on September 17 in Cabell County.

657. James A. Bartram to H. J. Samuels, September 13, 1862, Pierpont-Samuels Papers, WVSA.

658. *Ironton Register*, September 18, 1862.

659. *Gallipolis Dispatch*, October 1, 1862; *Philadelphia Inquirer*, November 27, 1862. See Terry Lowry, *The Battle of Charleston and the 1862 Kanawha Valley Campaign* (Charleston, WV: 35th Star Publishing, 2016), 265. One of the accounts recorded that another attack occurred at Foster's Landing at 3:30 p.m. on the following day. According to this soldier, "a company of rebels, about one hundred in number were drawn up in line, and as the boat passed poured a perfect hail of bullets through and through the cabin, fore and aft. About fifty Minnie balls passed through the boat." In 1850, Wayne County Delegate Jeremiah Wellman introduced a petition from the citizens of Cabell and Wayne counties for the construction of a turnpike from Martin Hull's landing on the Ohio River in Cabell County to the Wayne County community of Amacetta. *Journal of the House of Delegates of Virginia for the Session of 1850-51* (Richmond, VA: William F. Ritchie, 1850), 345-46.

660. Peter Harshbarger to John Harshbarger, September 17,1862, Peter Harshbarger Letters, Courtesy of Mrs. Catherine Ball.

661. Peter Harshbarger to David Harshbarger, n.d., Harshbarger Letters.

662. *Wheeling Intelligencer*, October 1, 1862.

663. *Ibid*.

664. *Ironton Register*, September 25, 1862.

665. J. A. J. Lightburn to H. G. Wright, September 23, 1862, *Official Records*, Series I, Volume XVI, Part II, 542; H. G. Wright to David Tod, September 24, 1862, *Official Records*, Series I, Volume XVI, Part II, 542.

666. *Ironton Register*, October 2, 1862. Sheriff Nixon turned to the new state of West Virginia for relief, and on October 3, 1863, an act passed the legislature instructing the auditor to credit Nixon for the full amount. *Acts of the Legislature of West Virginia*, October 3, 1863.

667. *Wheeling Intelligencer*, October 1, 1862.

668. A. M. McGinnis to H. J. Samuels, October 8, 1862, Pierpont-Samuels Papers, WVSA.

669. *Ironton Register*, October 9, 1862.

670. Sallie P. Smith to Julia Sprague, October 4, 1862, Smith Family Correspondence, MUSCD.

671. *Ibid*.

672. *Ibid*.

673. *Ibid*.

Chapter Eleven

674. John W. Taylor to Catharine Hawk, October 17, 1861, accessed at http://www.rootsweb.ancestry.com/~inhenry/letters1862.htm.

675. *Indiana True Republican*, October 30, 1862; Civil War Diary of George W. Miller, Purdue University (PU).

676. George Woodbury to Brother, October 19, 1862, Terry Lowry Collection.

677. Isaac Little to James Coats, October 18, 1862, Isaac Little Letters, FHS; Order Book of the 84th Indiana Infantry, NA; Civil War Diary of B. F. Morris, transcribed by David E. Zehner, WVSA; Isaac Little to Sally Little, October 23, 1862, Little Letters, FHS.

678. James Clover to Sister, October 18, 1862, *Clovers of Franklin County, Ohio: A Study of Henry Clover, His Ancestors and Descendants*, created, edited and maintained by June Clover Byrne for the Clover Family Historical Society, Civil War Letters from James Clover 1862-63, accessed at http://freepages.genealogy.rootsweb.ancestry.com/~clover/oh/henrypeter/peterelkjamesletters.html; Isaac Little to James Coats, October 18, 1862, Little Letters, FHS.

679. *Indiana True Republican*, October 30, 1862.

680. Isaac Little to Sally Little, October 17, 1862, Little Letters, FHS.

681. Isaac Little to James Coats, October 18, 1862, Little Letters, FHS.

682. Isaac Little to James Coats, October 18, 1862, Little Letters, FHS.

683. Isaac Little to Sally Little, October 17, 1862, Little Letters, FHS.

684. Isaac Little to Sally Little, October 17, 1862, Little Letters, FHS; John W. Turner to John Hawk, October 17, 1862, accessed at http://www.rootsweb.ancestry.com/~inhenry/letters1862.htm.

685. Isaac Little to James Coats, October 18, 1862, Little Letters, FHS.

686. *Ibid*.

687. Civil War Diary of B. F. Morris, WVSA; Civil War Diary of George W. Miller, PU; Charles Wilgus to H. J. Samuels, October 18, 1862, Pierpont-Samuels Papers, WVSA. Miller refers to the scouting party as "our caverly squadron."

688. Isaac Little to James Coats, October 18, 1862, Little Letters, FHS.

689. Isaac Little to Sally Little, undated, Little Letters, FHS.

690. Isaac Little to James Coats, October 18, 1862, Little Letters, FHS.

691. Civil War Diary of George W. Miller, PU; Zophar D. Ramsdell Diary, 1862, Ceredo Historical Museum and Ramsdell House, Town of Ceredo (CHM).

692. William T. Caldwell to H. J. Samuels, November 28, 1862, Adjutant General's Papers, Union Militia Collection, WVSA. Caldwell noted that in addition to this skirmish, the company was also fired on by bushwhackers, wounding one of the Union militia. He lists James Haley and Nelson Wyley as the wounded men, but does not note which was wounded in the skirmish with Witcher's men.

693. Special Order No. 13, October 19, 1862; General Order No. 4, October 22, 1862; General Order Number 3, October 27, 1862; all from Order Book of the 84th Indiana Infantry, NA.

694. Isaac Little to James Coats, October 23, 1862, Little Letters, FHS.

695. Isaac Little Letter, Undated, Little Letters, FHS; Isaac Little to Sally Little, October 18, 1862, Little Letters, FHS.

696. Isaac Little to Sally Little, October 17, 1862, Little Letters, FHS.

697. Isaac Little Letter, Undated, Little Letters, FHS; *Indiana True Republican*, November 4, 1862.

698. Isaac Little to Sally Little, October 17, 1862, Little Letters, FHS.

699. Isaac Little to James Coats, October 18, 1862, Little Letters, FHS.

700. Isaac Little to George Coats, undated, Little Letters, FHS.

701. Isaac Little to Sally Little, October 23, 1862, Little Letters, FHS.

702. *Ibid.*

703. *Ibid.*

704. *Ibid.*

705. G. M. Bascom to Jonathan Cranor, October 20, 1862, *Official Records*, Series I, Volume XIX, Part II, 458; J. D. Cox to N. H. McClean, October 20, 1862, *Official Records*, Series I, Volume XIX, Part II, 458-59.

706. Isaac Little to Sally Little, October 22, 1862, Little Letters, FHS; Civil War Diary of George W. Miller, PU.

707. Isaac Little to Sally Little, October 23, 1862, Little Letters, FHS.

708. *Indiana True Republican*, November 6, 1862.

709. J. D. Cox to Jonathan Cranor, October 24, 1862, *Official Records*, Series I, Volume XIX, Part II, 481.

710. Isaac Little to Sally Little, October 25, 1862, Little Letters, FHS.

711. Civil War Diary of George W. Miller, PU; History of the 84th Indiana Infantry, Order Book of the 84th Indiana Infantry, NA; History of the 40th Ohio Infantry; Order Book of the 40th Ohio Infantry, NA; "A Civil War History of the Eighty-Fourth Indiana Regiment," as recorded by Samuel Huddleston, transcribed by Sharon Ogzewalla, accessed at http://www.hcgs.net/84thindiana.html; Morris Diary, WVSA.

712. *Ohio State Journal*, November 3, 1862.

713. *Indiana True Republican*, November 20, 1862.

714. Isaac Little to Sally Little, October 25, 1862, Little Letters, FHS.

715. Civil War Diary of B. F. Morris, WVSA; J. D. Cox to N. H. McClean, October 15, 1862, *Official Records*, Series I, Volume XIX, Part II, 432-33.

716. *Indiana True Republican*, November 6, 1862.

717. Order book of the 84th Indiana Infantry, NA.

718. Huddleston, "A Civil War History of the Eighty-Fourth Indiana Regiment."

719. *Ibid.*

720. *Indiana True Republican*, November 6, 1862.

721. *Indiana True Republican*, November 13, 1862; Civil War Diary of George W. Miller, PU.

722. *Ibid.*

723. *Indiana True Republican*, November 27, 1862; *Indiana True Republican*, November 13, 1862.

724. *Ibid.*; Isaac Little to Sally Little, October 23, 1862, Little Letters, FHS.

725. J. D. Cox to Jonathan Cranor, November 2, 1862, *Official Records*, Series I, Volume XIX, Part II, 534-35.

726. Thomas J. Merritt to H. J. Samuels, November 6, 1862, Pierpont-Samuels Papers, WVSA.

727. Special Order Number 3, November 11, 1862, Order Book of the 84th Indiana Infantry, NA.

728. John Laidley to H. J. Samuels, November 13, 1862, Pierpont-Samuels

Papers, WVSA.

729. Isaac Little to Sally Little, November 15, 1862, Little Letters, FHS.

730. *Randolph County Journal*, November 28, 1862.

731. John B. Floyd to John Letcher, December 16, 1862, *Official Records*, Series I, Volume XXI, 1065-1066; *Marietta Register*, December 19, 1862; Point Pleasant *Weekly Register*, December 18, 1862.

732. Loose Letters – Muster Rolls, 13th West Virginia Infantry, NA.

733. *Ironton Register*, November 27, 1862.

734. *Ibid.*; Witchers Cavalry Co to Francis H. Pierpont, March 8, Adjutant General's Papers, Union Regiments, 3rd West Virginia Cavalry, WVSA.

735. Order Book of 13th West Virginia Infantry, NA; Point Pleasant *Weekly Register*, December 18, 1862.

736. C. H. Mullen to H. J. Samuels, December 17, 1862, Pierpont-Samuels Papers, WVSA. Mullen's appeal was apparently forwarded to Major Joseph Darr, who noted on the same date, "I send today to Ceredo for evidence against Mullen."

737. Unidentified to Fritz Walker, December 29, 1862, Union Citizens Files, NA (fold3.com).

738. Fritz Walker to Joseph Darr, January 6, 1863, Union Citizens Files, NA (fold3.com).

739. *Ibid.*

Chapter Twelve

740. *Wheeling Intelligencer*, January 8, 1863.

741. Wallace, *Cabell County Annals*, 11-13.

742. John Laidley to Francis Pierpont, January 23, 1863, Pierpont-Samuels Papers, WVSA.

743. Point Pleasant *Weekly Register*, February 26, 1863.

744. Accounts of the murder of Calvary Gibson can be found in the *Gallipolis Journal*, February 26, 1863; *Ironton Register*, March 26, 1863; *Wheeling Intelligencer*, February 24, 1863; *Wheeling Intelligencer*, March 25, 1863.

745. *Wheeling Intelligencer*, April 7, 1863.

746. *Wheeling Intelligencer*, April 10, 1863.

747. *Ironton Register*, May 1, 1863.

748. General Order Book, Jenkins's Cavalry Brigade, 1863, WVSA (courtesy Maryann Hannis).

749. *Ibid.*

750. Mrs. Walter Mitchell, "History of Cabell Creek Community" (Morgantown, WV: Agricultural Extension Division, 1925).

751. *Richmond Enquirer*, April 24, 1863; Mitchell, "History of Cabell Creek Community"; William R. Brown to John V. Young, April 2, 1863, Cook Collection, WVRHC.

752. *Richmond Enquirer*, April 24, 1863.

753. David Dove to J. C. Paxton, April 7, 1863, *Official Records*, Series I, Volume XXV, Part I, 79.

754. *Ibid*.

755. *Ibid*.

756. *Ibid*, 80. Among those captured by Dove's force were the following members of the 8th Virginia Cavalry: James H. Porter of Company C; Charles A. Smith, James T. Turner (D2), and Isaac Blake (D2) of Company D; James Canterbury, William A. Carpenter, Andy J. Lucas, and William Owens of Company G. See Dickinson, *8th Virginia Cavalry*.

757. *Wheeling Intelligencer*, April 13, 1861.

758. These men were part of the 36th Battalion Virginia Cavalry. A. M. Galloway to L. C. Turner, February 4, 1864, Arthur I. Boreman Papers, WVSA.

759. J. H. Brown to Francis H. Pierpont, April 11, 1863, Adjutant General's Papers, Union Regiments, Miscellaneous Correspondence, WVSA.

760. E. R. Merriman to H. J. Samuels, March 28, 1863, Adjutant General's Papers, Union Regiments, 5th West Virginia Infantry, WVSA.

761. *Wheeling Intelligencer*, May 8, 1863.

762. Ramsdell Diary, 1863, CHM.

763. Thomas Thornburg to H. J. Samuels, April 22, 1863, Adjutant General's Papers, Union Regiments, Miscellaneous Correspondence, WVSA; K. V. Whaley to H. J. Samuels, May 14, 1863, Adjutant General's Papers, Union Regiments, 9th West Virginia Infantry, WVSA.

764. Ramsdell Diary, 1863, CHM; Civil War Compiled Services Records, 5th West Virginia Infantry, John L. Zeigler, WVSA.

765. Civil War Compiled Services Records, 5th West Virginia Infantry, John L. Zeigler, WVSA.

766. *Ibid*.

767. *Ibid*.

768. *Ibid*.

769. *Ibid*.

770. Ralph Leete et al to Edwin Stanton, June 22, 1863, Boreman Papers, WVSA. The letter contained a number of signatures including those of the mayor of Ironton and the prosecuting attorney of Lawrence County.

771. Citizens from Catlettsburg, Kentucky, to Edwin M. Stanton, May 12, 1863, Petitions, Boreman Papers, WVSA.

772. Petitions from Members of the 5th (West) Virginia Infantry to the Governor of West Virginia, June 11, 1863, Petitions, Boreman Papers, WVSA. Two of the petitions were addressed to the "Governor of Western Virginia." John L. Zeigler moved to Catlettsburg, where he ran two hotels. He died on January 15, 1890, and is buried in Catlettsburg Cemetery.

773. George W. Hackworth to Henry J. Samuels, April 28, 1863, Adjutant General's Papers, Union Regiments, Miscellaneous Correspondence, WVSA. Hackworth would serve in the West Virginia House of Delegates after the war.

774. Special Orders No. 10, Record Group (RG) 94, Records of the Adjutant

General's Office, Book Records of Volunteer Union Organization, 13th West Virginia Infantry; Order Book, Companies B, C, H, & K, NA (courtesy of Phil Hatfield).

775. Ramsdell Diary, 1863, CHM.

776. K. V. Whaley to H. J. Samuels, May 14, 1863, Adjutant General's Papers, Union Regiments, 9th West Virginia Infantry, WVSA.

777. Special Orders No. 11, 12, and 13, RG 94, Records of the Adjutant General's Office, Book Records of Volunteer Union Organization, 13th West Virginia Infantry, NA; Order Book, Companies B, C, H, & K, NA (courtesy of Phil Hatfield).

778. General Order Book, Jenkins's Cavalry Brigade, 1863, WVSA (courtesy Maryann Grannis).

779. Point Pleasant *Weekly Register*, July 2, 1863.

780. *Gallipolis Journal*, July 9, 1863.

781. Ramsdell Diary, 1863, CHM; *Ironton Register*, January 19, 1865.

782. Cabell County Citizens to Commandant of the U. S. Prison at Johnson Island, July 25, 1863, Petitions, Boreman Papers, WVSA. The letter was signed by Henderson Drake, A. McComas, James M. McComas, Jefferson McComas, Isaac McComas, and Stephen Paine.

783. J. F. Bowdens to Arthur Boreman, July 25, 1863, Adjutant General's Papers, WVSA.

784. Loyal Citizens of Cabell County to Arthur I. Boreman, n.d., Boreman Papers, WVSA. The letter was signed by John P. Jordan, Isaac Arthur, John Arthur, William A. Sims, Lewis Neal, Richard Bexfield, Washington Arthur, Theodore Henry, Julius Lesage, Valentine Blake, John V. Arthur, Harvey Spurlock, Samuel H Davis, Joseph L Davis, Thomas P. Arthur, William T. Arthur, William Polley, James L. Jordan, Jeremiah B. Jordan, Alexander Cremeans, Joseph Cremeans, John Denison, Benjamin Jewel, and John M. Blake, Esquire.

785. John Adams to the Adjutant General of West Virginia, August 6, 1863, Adjutant General's Papers, Union Militia Collection, WVSA.

786. John Adams to the Adjutant General of West Virginia, August 3, 1863, Adjutant General's Papers, Union Militia Collection, WVSA.

787. Dusenberry Papers, MUSCD; *The Knapsack*, Organ of the Fifth Va Vol Infantry, U. S. A., September 3, 1863.

788. *The Knapsack*, Issue 1, September 3, 1863.

789. Dusenberry Papers, MUSCD.

790. *Ibid.*

791. *Ibid.*

792. *Ibid.*

793. John Adams to the Adjutant General of West Virginia, August 26, 1863, Adjutant General's Papers, Union Militia Collection, WVSA.

794. Dusenberry Papers, MUSCD.

795. *Ibid.*

796. *Ibid.*

797. *Ibid.*

798. *Ibid.*

799. *Ibid.*

800. *Ibid.*

801. Point Pleasant *Weekly Register*, September 24, 1863.

802. Dusenberry Papers, MUSCD.

803. *Ibid.*

804. John Adams to the Adjutant General of West Virginia, October 5, 1863, Adjutant General's Papers, Union Militia Collection, WVSA.

805. William F. Dusenberry to William R. Brown, October 16, 1863, Loose Letters – Muster Rolls, 13th West Virginia Infantry, NA.

806. William Feazel to John S. Cunningham, October 26, 1863, Loose Letters – Muster Rolls, 13th West Virginia Infantry, NA.

807. *Ibid.*

808. P. H. McCullough to William E. Feazel, October 26, 1863, Loose Letters – Muster Rolls, 13th West Virginia Infantry, NA.

809. *Ibid.*

810. Pension Files of Joshua York (photocopies), Civil War Artificial Collection, WVSA. Several letters were sent to Governor Arthur Boreman requesting a pension for York's widow, Jane York.

811. *Wheeling Register*, November 3, 1863.

812. Loose Letters – Muster Rolls, 13th West Virginia Infantry, NA.

813. Cabell County Citizens to Arthur I. Boreman, November 10, 1863, Petitions, Boreman Papers, WVSA. The correspondence was signed by Thomas Thornburg, J. B. Baumgardner, and Matthew Thompson.

814. Cabell County Citizens (B. F. Curry, B. B. Wilkinson, William H. H. Pine, Perry Johnson, William Johnson, Harvey Johnson, Anderson Byess, Andrew Johnson) to Commander of the Prison of Johnson Island and Governor of West Virginia, November 18, 1863, Petitions, Boreman Papers, WVSA.

815. Wallace, *Cabell County Annals*, 13-15.

816. *Ibid.*, 38.

817. Henry J. Samuels to William R. Brown, November 18, 1863, Loose Letters – Muster Rolls, 13th West Virginia Infantry, NA.

818. Special Order Number 88, Loose Letters – Muster Rolls, 13th West Virginia Infantry, NA.

819. William E. Feazel correspondence, Loose Letters – Muster Rolls, 13th West Virginia Infantry, NA. According to a letter written from Guyandotte, Confederates entered the town a second time that month. Captain William Turner was captured and was forced to remove his shoes and walk barefooted. See *The Knapsack*, Organ of the Fifth Va Vol Infantry, U. S. A., September 3, 1863.

820. *Wheeling Intelligencer*, December 17, 1863.

821. Point Pleasant *Weekly Register*, December 17, 1863.

822. William F. Dusenberry to William Brown, December 4, 1863, Loose Letters – Muster Rolls, 13th West Virginia Infantry, NA.

823. B. F. Kelley to G. W. Cullum, December 11, 1863, *Official Records*, Series I, Volume XXIX, Part II, 556.

824. James M. Comly to George W. Cullum, December 15, 1863, *Official Records*, Series I, Volume XXIX, Part I, 977-78.

825. Thomas H. Buffington to William Brown, December 16, 1863, Adjutant General's Papers, Union Regiments, 13th West Virginia Infantry, WVSA.

826. *Ibid*.

827. Special Order Number 104, December 23, 1863, Loose Letters – Muster Rolls, 13th West Virginia Infantry, NA.

828. Mary Eggars to Elijah Parker Scammon, December 28, 1863, Adjutant General's Papers, Union Regiments, 13th West Virginia Infantry, WVSA.

829. James R. Hall to William R. Brown, January 10, 1864, Adjutant General's Papers, Union Regiments, 13th West Virginia Infantry, WVSA.

Chapter Thirteen

830. Wayne County Citizens to William R. Brown, January 7, 1864, Loose Letters – Muster Rolls, 13th West Virginia Infantry, NA.

831. Report of John S. Witcher, January 29, 1864, *Official Records*, Series I, Volume LI, Part I, 211-12; Robert Cobbs to Mother, February 2, 1864, William Robert Cobbs Collection, WVSA.

832. *Ibid*. Confederate, Miscellaneous, Hurston Spurlock, NA (fold3.com).

833. Report of John S. Witcher, January 29, 1864, *Official Records*, Series I, Volume LI, Part I, 211-212; Robert Cobbs to Brother, January 30, 1864, Cobbs Collection, WVSA.

834. Report of John S. Witcher, January 29, 1864, *Official Records*, Series I, Volume LI, Part I, 212.

835. *Wheeling Intelligencer*, January 30, 1864.

836. *Ibid*; William R. Brown to M. P. Avery, January 30, 1864, *Official Records*, Series I, Volume LI, Part I, 1140.

837. William Shannon to Kellian V. Whaley, February 6, 1864, Kellian Van Rensalear Whaley Collection, WVSA.

838. *Wheeling Intelligencer*, March 2, 1864; *Official Records*, Series I, Volume XXXIII, 158. Lieutenant Henry A. Wolfe's body was returned to Portsmouth, Ohio. He was "buried from the Swan Hotel," with his remains interred in Greenlawn Cemetery. See Nelson W. Evans, *A History of Scioto County, Ohio* (Portsmouth, OH: The Author, 1903), 244.

839. John S. Witcher to Francis P. Pierpont, February 14, 1864, Adjutant General's Papers, Union Militia, WVSA; Field History of the 13th Regiment West Virginia Volunteer Infantry for the Year 1864, WVSA.

840. *Wheeling Intelligencer*, February 25, 1864.

841. Report of George W. Gallup, February 19, 1864, *Official Records*, Series I, Volume XXXII, Part I, 394-95.

842. *Ibid*.

843. *Wheeling Intelligencer*, February 25, 1864; *Wheeling Intelligencer*, March 4,

1864.

844. Clark Elkins to Van H. Bukey, February 19, 1864, Loose Letters – Muster Rolls, 13th West Virginia Infantry, NA.

845. John S. Witcher to Kellian V. Whaley, February 22, 1864, Whaley Collection, WVSA.

846. *Ibid.*

847. Point Pleasant *Weekly Register*, March 24, 1864.

848. William E. Feazel to John Cunningham, Loose Letters – Muster Rolls, 13th West Virginia Infantry, NA.

849. William Bartram Correspondence, March 10, 1864, Adjutant General's Papers, Union Militia, WVSA.

850. Point Pleasant *Weekly Register*, March 24, 1864. According to the article, "The Bar was composed of the following named gentlemen: Hon. Judge Bolle, Wm. McComas, Esq., Colonel G. Parker, Hon. L. T. Moore, Catlettsburg, Ky.; Ralph Leete, Esq., Ironton, Ohio; Edgar I. Leete, Esq., New York City; W. H. Horner, Esq. and B. D. McGinnis, Esq., Guyandotte; C. P. T. Moore, Esq., Point Pleasant and E. M. Fitzgerald, Esq., Prosecuting Attorney."

851. Report of John J. Hoffman, March 21, 1864, *Official Records*, Series I, Volume XXXIII, Part I, 250-51.

852. *Ibid.*

853. *Ibid.*

854. *Wheeling Intelligencer*, July 29, 1864.

855. Field History of the 13th Regiment West Virginia Volunteer Infantry for the year 1864, WVSA; Point Pleasant *Weekly Register*, March 31, 1864.

856. Correspondence, March 26, 1864, Loose Letters – Muster Rolls, 13th West Virginia Infantry, NA.

857. Cabell County Chancery Order Book 1.

858. Correspondence, April 9, 1864, Loose Letters – Muster Rolls, 13th West Virginia Infantry, NA.

859. Point Pleasant *Weekly Register*, April 26, 1864; *Gallipolis Journal*, April 21, 1864.

860. Point Pleasant *Weekly Register*, May 5, 1864.

861. *Ibid.*

862. *Ibid.*

863. *Ibid.*

864. *Ibid.*

865. Dusenberry Papers, MUSCD.

866. Point Pleasant *Weekly Register*, May 12, 1864.

867. Point Pleasant *Weekly Register*, May 5, 1864; Dusenberry Papers, MUSCD.

868. Dusenberry Papers, MUSCD.

869. Benjamin Haley to G. W. Brown, Adjutant General's Papers, Union Militia, WVSA.

870. Correspondence, Loose Letters – Muster Rolls, 13th West Virginia Infantry, NA.

871. J. B. Baumgardner to Arthur I. Boreman, May 6, 1864, Petitions for Pardon, Boreman Papers, WVSA.

872. E. D. Wright to Arthur I. Boreman, January 17, 1865, Petitions for Pardon, Miscellaneous, Prisoners of War, Boreman Papers, WVSA.

873. Dusenberry Papers, MUSCD.

874. *Ibid.*

875. Cabell County Chancery Order Book 1.

876. *Ibid.*

877. Point Pleasant *Weekly Register*, June 2, 1864; Point Pleasant *Weekly Register*, June 30, 1864.

878. Dusenberry Papers, MUSCD.

879. Point Pleasant *Weekly Register*, June 30, 1864; Dusenberry Papers, MUSCD.

880. Point Pleasant *Weekly Register*, June 30, 1864.

881. Point Pleasant *Weekly Register*, June 30, 1864; Dusenberry Papers, MUSCD.

882. Point Pleasant *Weekly Register*, June 30, 1864; Dusenberry Papers, MUSCD; Point Pleasant *Weekly Register*, June 2, 1864.

883. *Official Roster of the Soldiers of the State of Ohio in the War of the Rebellion, 1861-1866*, Volume IX (Cincinnati, OH: The Ohio Valley Press, 1889), 2. The 141st Regiment Ohio National Guard remained on guard duty in the area until August 25, when they returned to Gallipolis. The unit was mustered out on September 3, 1864, on expiration of their term of service.

884. General Order Number 2, May 25, 1864, Thomas Angell Military Papers (MS115), Ohio University Libraries, Mahn Center for Archives and Special Collections (OUL).

885. *Gallipolis Journal*, June 9, 1864.

886. Benjamin R. Haley to Arthur Boreman, June 1, 1864, Adjutant General's Papers, Union Militia, WVSA.

887. *Gallipolis Journal*, June 23, 1864.

888. *Ibid.*

889. *Ibid.*

890. *Highland Weekly News*, June 23, 1864.

891. A. D. Jaynes to John S. Witcher, June 8, 1864, *Official Records*, Series I, Volume XXXVII, Part I, 609-10.

892. *Ibid.*

893. A. D. Jaynes to John S. Witcher, June 10, 1864, *Official Records*, Series I, Volume XXXVII, Part I, 623-24.

894. *Ibid.*

895. *Gallipolis Journal*, July 7, 1864.

896. *Ibid.*

897. A. D. Jaynes to John S. Witcher, June 21, 1864, *Official Records*, Series I, Volume XXXVII, Part I, 659-60.

898. General Order Number 8, June 20, 1864, Angell Military Papers, OUL.

899. Special Order Number 53, June 23, Angell Military Papers, OUL.

900. Cabell County Citizens to Secretary of War, June 24, 1864, Petitions and

Requests for Pardon, Boreman Papers, WVSA.

901. William A. Birt, "A Historical Sketch of Milton, Cabell County, West Virginia," *West Virginia History*, Volume 23, Number 1 (October 1961), 51; Ronald R. Turner, *7th West Virginia Cavalry*, 1989. A cemetery northwest of the church contains the remains of Civil War soldiers. Most of the deaths were caused by smallpox and typhoid, but both Union and Confederate soldiers are said to be buried here. The only marked headstone of a Civil War soldier is that of Andrew William Adkins, who served in Company K of the 7th West Virginia Cavalry. Adkins was born about 1845, the son of Andrew and Susan Adkins. He enlisted on November 30, 1862, in Coalsmouth (now St. Albans). Adkins was 5'7", with light complexion, blue eyes, and red hair. He died on April 13, 1864, and was buried on a hillside overlooking the Mud River.

902. Dusenberry Papers, MUSCD.

903. *Ironton Register*, July 21, 1864. Bay would later recall that he refused admittance to the men but they "battered in the door with their gunstocks." Bay and his brother William survived the encounter and became noted rivermen in the postwar period, building, owning and operating forty steamboats on the Ohio. George W. Bay later resided in Huntington at 610 Fifth Avenue, where he died on February 6, 1916. See *Ironton Daily Republican*, February 8, 1916.

904. *Ibid.*

905. Dusenberry Papers, MUSCD.

906. *Ibid.*

907. *Ibid.*

908. *Ibid.*

909. Point Pleasant *Weekly Register*, August 11, 1864.

910. Wallace, *Cabell County Annals*, 15.

911. Dusenberry Papers, MUSCD.

912. William E. Feazel to Julius Lesage, August 21, 1864, James H. Ferguson Collection, WVSA.

913. *Ibid.*

914. William P. Rucker to Julius Lesage, August 22, 1864, Ferguson Collection, WVSA.

915. Dusenberry Papers, MUSCD.

916. *Ibid.*

917. Benjamin Haley to Arthur Boreman, August 30, 1864, Adjutant General's Papers, Union Militia, WVSA.

918. *Ibid.*

919. Dusenberry Papers, MUSCD; Point Pleasant *Weekly Register*, September 22, 1864.

920. Benjamin Haley to Arthur Boreman, March 20, 1865, Adjutant General's Papers, Union Militia, WVSA; Dusenberry Papers, MUSCD; *Wheeling Intelligencer*, September 24, 1864.

921. *Ironton Register*, September 22, 1864.

922. Point Pleasant *Weekly Register*, October 6, 1864.

923. Dusenberry Papers, MUSCD.

924. *Ibid.*

925. C. B. Webb to Unidentified, October 12, 1864, Adjutant General's Papers, Union Militia, WVSA.

926. *Ibid.*

927. C. B. Webb to Arthur Boreman, October 12, 1864, Adjutant General's Papers, Union Militia, WVSA.

928. *Ibid.*

929. Edgar Blundon to Julius Lesage, October 20, 1864, Ferguson Collection, WVSA.

930. John H. Oley to W. B. Thomas, October 23, 1864, *Official Records*, Series I, Volume XLIII, Part II, 455.

931. Edgar B. Blundon to Sallie Blundon, October 23, 1864, Major Edgar Blundon Letters, Stutler Collection, WVSA.

932. *Ironton Register*, November 1864; Dusenberry Papers, MUSCD.

933. Point Pleasant *Weekly Register*, November 24, 1864.

934. Dusenberry Papers, MUSCD.

935. Point Pleasant *Weekly Register*, November 1864.

936. Edgar B. Blundon to Sallie Blundon, November 9 and November 15, 1864, Blundon Letters, WVSA.

937. Edgar B. Blundon to Sallie Blundon, November 20, 1864, Blundon Letters, WVSA.

938. Edgar B. Blundon to Sallie Blundon, November 24, 1864, Blundon Letters, WVSA.

939. Point Pleasant *Weekly Register*, December 15, 1864. For a detailed look at the court cases against the Jenkins brothers, see Dickinson and Dickinson, *Gentleman Soldier of Greenbottom*.

940. Alfred B. Payne to Arthur Boreman, December 1, 1864, Adjutant General's Papers, Union Militia, WVSA.

941. H. J. Samuels to George Crook, December 3, 1864, *Official Records*, Series I, Volume XLIII, Part II, 737-38.

942. Regimental Order Book of the 13th West Virginia Infantry, WVSA.

Chapter Fourteen

943. Point Pleasant *Weekly Register*, February 2, 1865.

944. *Ironton Register*, February 9, 1865.

945. Dickinson, *Wayne County, West Virginia in the Civil War*, 113-17.

946. *Wheeling Intelligencer*, February 21, 1865; Point Pleasant *Weekly Register*, March 2, 1865; Point Pleasant *Weekly Register*, March 9, 1865. See also Robert Michael Thompson, *Twelve Pole Terror: The Legend of Rebel Bill Smith* (Wayne, WV: The Author, 2015), 86-89.

947. *Acts of the Legislature of West Virginia* (Wheeling, WV: John F. M'Dermot,

Public Printer, 1865), 6.

948. *Wheeling Intelligencer*, January 31, 1865.

949. *Wheeling Intelligencer*, February 1865.

950. Wallace, *Cabell County Annals*, 43. The conclusion of the war ended the need for this draft.

951. *Wheeling Intelligencer*, February 14, 1865.

952. Point Pleasant *Weekly Register*, March 2, 1865.

953. Edgar Blundon Correspondence, March 5, 1865, *Official Records*, Series I, Volume XLIII, Part II, 738-39.

954. John Hunt Oley Correspondence, March 10, 1865, *Official Records*, Series I, Volume XLIII, Part II, 739.

955. Emily Cox Diary, Newcomb Family Collection, WVSA.

956. *West Virginia Journal*, March 24, 1865.

957. *Ibid.*

958. *West Virginia Journal*, April 5, 1865. General Albert Gallatin Jenkins died on May 21, 1864, from wounds received in the battle of Cloyd's Mountain.

959. *Ibid.*

960. Dusenberry Papers, MUSCD.

961. *Ibid.*

962. *Gallipolis Journal*, April 20, 1865.

963. *Ibid.*

964. *Ibid.*

965. *Ibid.*

966. *Ibid.*

967. John H. Oley to Edgar B. Blundon, April 29, 1865, *Official Records*, Series I, Volume LXVI, Part III, 1014-15.

968. James H. Ferguson to Quartermaster General of the State of West Virginia, April 30, 1865, Adjutant General's Papers, Union Militia, WVSA.

969. B. D. McGinnis to Arthur I. Boreman, May 21, 1865, Adjutant General's Papers, Union Militia, WVSA.

970. *West Virginia Journal*, May 31, 1865.

971. *Ibid.*

972. *Ibid.*

973. *Ibid.*

974. H. J. Samuels to Andrew Johnson, June 5, 1865, Confederate Amnesty Papers, NA (fold3.com).

975. *West Virginia Journal*, June 14, 1865. J. H. R. was the writer of the death notice.

976. H. J. Samuels to Andrew Johnson, June 5, 1865, Confederate Amnesty Papers, NA (fold3.com). The sons of William McComas divided over the war, as had their father and his brother before them. William Wirt McComas and Benjamin Jefferson McComas were Southern supporters, while Hamilton C. McComas and Elisha W. McComas were loyal to the Union. William W., a doctor who practiced medicine in Guyandotte, commanded a Confederate artillery company (Company B,

Wise Legion Artillery.) He was killed at the battle of South Mills, North Carolina, on April 19, 1862. Benjamin Jefferson was a lawyer and farmer who served as a captain, Company B, 30th Battalion Virginia Sharpshooters under General Jubal Early. Hamilton C. was an attorney and a colonel in the Union army. He moved to New Mexico after the war and was killed by Chiricahua Apaches on March 28, 1883. Elisha W. was also an attorney who was sympathetic to the Union. He had previously served two terms in the Virginia legislature and in 1855 was elected lieutenant governor of Virginia, a post he resigned in 1857. Irene McComas, the daughter of William McComas, was hired as a teacher in Barboursville on June 3, 1867, at a salary of $40 per month but lost her position when she failed to take the test oath on June 25, 1867.

977. John H. Oley to Edgar B. Blundon, June 7, 1865, *Official Records*, Series I, Volume XLVI, Part III, 1263.

978. *Ironton Register*, July 27, 1865.

979. *West Virginia Journal*, August 2, 1865. John P. Jordan served as president of the meeting and Henry Bicker as secretary.

980. *Ibid*.

981. *West Virginia Journal*, July 19, 1865.

982. *Ironton Register*, October 12, 1865.

983. Dusenberry Papers, MUSCD.

984. *West Virginia Journal*, November 1, 1865.

985. Julius Lesage to Francis M. Pierpont, December 5, 1865, Adjutant General's Papers, Union Militia, WVSA.

986. *Ironton Register*, December 28, 1865.

987. Wallace, *Cabell County Annals*, 38.

988. John Holt to Arthur Boreman, March 22, 1866, Boreman Papers, WVSA.

989. *Ibid*.

990. *West Virginia Journal*, May 9, 1866.

991. *West Virginia Journal*, May 2, 1866.

992. *Ibid*.

993. Isaac Bloss to Arthur Boreman, May 4, 1866, Boreman Papers, WVSA.

994. Dusenberry Papers, MUSCD.

995. C. B. Webb to James E. Hana, May 27, 1866, Adjutant General's Papers, Union Militia, WVSA.

996. *West Virginia Journal*, June 20, 1866.

997. *West Virginia Journal*, August 15, 1866.

998. *West Virginia Journal*, August 29, 1866.

999. *West Virginia Journal*, October 24, 1866.

1000. *West Virginia Journal*, October 31, 1866.

1001. *West Virginia Journal*, November 14, 1866.

Chapter Fifteen

1002. *West Virginia Journal*, February 27, 1867.

1003. *Ibid.*

1004. *Ibid.*

1005. *Ibid.*

1006. *Ibid.*

1007. Joseph B. Collins to W. F. Drum, March 31, 1867, RG 393, Military District of Kentucky, Post of Guyandotte, 1867-1869, NA.

1008. Joseph B. Collins to W. F. Drum, April 22, 1867, RG 393, Military District of Kentucky, NA.

1009. General Order No. 5, April 24, 1867, RG 393, Military District of Kentucky, NA.

1010. Order by Major Joseph B. Collins, April 25, 1867, RG 393, Military District of Kentucky, NA.

1011. *West Virginia Journal*, May 8, 1867.

1012. Joseph B. Collins to W. F. Drum, May 6, 1867, RG 393, Military District of Kentucky, NA.

1013. Special Order No. 2, May 6, 1867, RG 393, Military District of Kentucky, NA.

1014. Joseph B. Collins to Arthur Boreman, May 6, 1867, RG 393, Military District of Kentucky, NA.

1015. *West Virginia Journal*, May 22, 1867.

1016. Special Order No. 14, July 14, 1867, RG 393, Military District of Kentucky, NA.

1017. Joseph B. Collins to W. F. Drum, July 26, 1867, RG 393, Military District of Kentucky, NA.

1018. *Ibid.*

1019. Special Order No. 19, August 10, 1867, RG 393, Military District of Kentucky, NA.

1020. Joseph B. Collins to W. F. Drum, September 23, 1867, RG 393, Military District of Kentucky, NA.

1021. *Ibid.*

1022. Special Order No. 105, September 30, 1867, RG 393, Military District of Kentucky, NA; Special Order No. 39, October 24, 1867, RG 393, Military District of Kentucky, NA; Sallie P. Smith to Julia Sprague, Smith Family Correspondence, MUSCD.

1023. *West Virginia Journal*, October 30, 1867.

1024. Joseph Collins to Arthur Boreman, January 14, 1868, Boreman Papers, WVSA.

1025. General Order No. 1, January 15, 1868, RG 393, Military District of Kentucky, NA.

1026. Cabell County Citizens to George H. Thomas, June 16, 1868, Adjutant General's Papers, Union Regiments, Miscellaneous Correspondence, WVSA. The letter was signed by Charles Ryan, Jacob Hiltbruner, Hon. J. F. Hayslip, J. H. Wright, John C. Brannon, J. B. Shultz, William Shultz, Rev. Spencer King, Charles Fisher, W. H. Newcomb, J. Harshbarger, SCC, J. H. Hysell, J. W. Rider, B. D. McGinnis, Pros Atty., Julius Freutel, R. H. L. Hayslip, Asst PA, John L. Douthit, William H. Douthit, H. C. Lecky, H. Hayslip, J. D. Chewning, R. Bukey, William Lecky, Charles O. Dusenberry, Fisher D. Bowen, Spencer Lecky, Henry Maupin, Joseph Gibson, Jerry Engle, Joseph T. Hysell, and V. S. Dobbins.

1027. Thomas J. Hayslip to George H. Thomas, June 16, 1868, Adjutant General's Papers, Union Regiments, Miscellaneous Correspondence, WVSA.

1028. General Order No. 12, June 18, 1868, RG 393, Military District of Kentucky, NA.

1029. General Order No. 13, June 25, 1868, RG 393, Military District of Kentucky, NA.

1030. *Mason County Journal*, July 8, 1868.

1031. F. E. Lacey to W. F. Drum, July 4, 1868, RG 393, Military District of Kentucky, NA.

1032. J. C. Wheeler to Arthur Boreman, July 15, 1868, Boreman Papers, WVSA.

1033. *Ibid*.

1034. *Ibid*.

1035. *Mason County Journal*, August 26, 1868.

1036. *Mason County Journal*, September 9, 1868.

1037. *Ibid*.

1038. John S. Witcher to Arthur Boreman, September 7, 1868, Boreman Papers, WVSA. Judge Harrison's circuit was composed of Greenbrier, McDowell, Mercer, Monroe, and Pocahontas counties. The judge was forced to resign his seat in 1870. See "The Notorious Nathaniel Harrison," by Kenneth R. Bailey, *West Virginia Historical Society Journal*, Spring 2013.

1039. *Ibid*.

1040. *Ibid*.

1041. Cabell County Citizens to Arthur I. Boreman, September 15, 1868, Petitions, Miscellaneous, Boreman Papers, WVSA. The letter was signed by T. J. Hayslip, Recorder, C. C., B. D. McGinnis, Prosecuting Attorney, O. W. Mather, County Registrar, John Alford, J. H. Ferguson, James Baumgardner, J. H. Hysell, and Julius Freutel.

1042. *Ibid*.

1043. *Mason County Journal*, September 30, 1868.

1044. Special Order No. 2, October 2, 1868, RG 393, Military District of Kentucky, NA.

1045. Special Order No. 48, October 3, 1868, RG 393, Military District of Kentucky, NA.

1046. Adolphus W. Kroutinger to Officer of Registration, Barboursville, October 6, 1868; Adolphus W. Kroutinger to John McConnell, October 6, 1868, RG 393, Military District of Kentucky, NA.

1047. Adolphus W. Kroutinger Correspondence, October 8, 1868, RG 393,

Military District of Kentucky, NA.

1048. *West Virginia Journal*, October 21, 1868.

1049. *West Virginia Journal*, October 28, 1868.

1050. *Mason County Journal*, November 20, 1868.

1051. Adolphus W. Kroutinger to Arthur Boreman, November 3, 1868, RG 393, Military District of Kentucky, NA.

1052. John Waring to Corporal John, November 5, 1868; John Waring to Sidney Burbank, November 6, 1868, RG 393, Military District of Kentucky, NA.

1053. Correspondence to Arthur I. Boreman, November 2, 1868, Boreman Papers, WVSA; Cabell County Board of Supervisors, Book 1.

1054. Adolphus Kroutinger to Military District of Kentucky, February 5, 1869, RG 393, Military District of Kentucky, NA. Charles Shipe of Barboursville served in the 3rd West Virginia Cavalry during the war.

1055. Dusenberry Papers, MUSCD.

1056. *Cabell County Press*, July 31, 1869.

1057. *Ibid*.

1058. *Cabell County Press*, September 6, 1869.

1059. *Cabell County Press*, October 11, 1869.

1060. *Cabell County Press*, October 9, 1869.

1061. *Cabell County Press*, October 25, 1869.

1062. *Cabell County Press*, November 1, 1869.

1063. *Ibid*.

1064. *Cabell County Press*, February 28, 1870. Collis P. Huntington selected the Maple Grove location for the site of the railroad's terminus. The city of Huntington, named for the railroad magnate, was incorporated in 1871.

1065. *Cabell County Press*, June 6, 1870.

1066. *Cabell County Press*, June 20, 1870.

1067. *Cabell County Press*, October 24, 1870.

1068. Dusenberry Papers, MUSCD. On March 3, 1869, West Virginia became the second state to ratify this amendment.

1069. *Cabell County Press*, October 31, 1870.

Epilogue

1070. *Cabell County Press*, October 31, 1870; *Cabell County Press*, November 7, 1870.

1071. *Democratic Banner*, April 9, 1874. Only thirty-six of the 1,500 Guyandotte citizens voted. In addition to Sedinger, J. L. Caldwell, C. K. Bramer, W. Eastham, and J. H. Wright were elected councilmen, T. J. Hayslip was selected as recorder, and J. H. Hysell, treasurer. The article concluded, "The ticket is a good one. Now look out for improvements."

1072. *Cabell County Press*, August 1, 1872.

1073. Dickinson, *Wayne County, West Virginia in the Civil War*, 128.

1074. William Couper, *The VMI New Market Cadets* (Charlottesville, VA: The Michie Company, 1933), 170.

1075. *Ibid*.

1076. "A Candlestick From My Great-Great-Grandfather," by Marilyn Brasher Wade, 2014, accessed at https://www.thestoryoftexas.com/discover/texas-story-project/a-candlestick-from-my-great-great-grandfather.

1077. *Colorado Citizen*, March 12, 1885. Courtesy of Marilyn Brasher Wade.

1078. Find A Grave entry, Captain Alfred Stephen Proctor, by Baxter B. Fite III, Jim Thornton, and Sandy Harrison.

1079. Minutes of Camp Garnett, "A History of Camp Garnett, United Confederate Veterans, Camp #902 Huntington, West Virginia," Jack L. Dickinson and Mark Meadows, October 1987.

1080. "Monument At Huntington, W. Va.," *Confederate Veteran*, Volume 8 (1900), 403.

1081. *Huntington Advertiser*, February 23, 1901.

1082. *Ibid*.

1083. Seth Adam Nichols, "'Let Us Bury And Forget:' Civil War Memory and Identity In Cabell County, West Virginia, 1865-1915," Master's Thesis, Marshall University, 2016, 111.

1084. *Ibid.*, 1.

1085. Findings of Court of Claims in case of Methodist Episcopal Church South, Barboursville, West Virginia, Senate Documents, Serial Set ID 5267, S. doc. 39, December 3, 1907.

1086. Findings of Court of Claims in case of Methodist Episcopal Church South, Guyandotte, West Virginia, Senate Documents, Serial Set ID 4764, S. doc. 22, December 7, 1904.

1087. Findings of Court of Claims in case of Baptist Church, Guyandotte, West Virginia, Senate Documents, Serial Set ID 4764, S. doc. 55, December 14, 1904.

1088. *Raleigh Register*, December 12, 1907.

1089. Unidentified article, courtesy of Brandon Ray Kirk.

1090. Undated article, *Cabell Record*.

Bibliography

Manuscripts

Adjutant General's Papers, Union Militia, West Virginia State Archives
Adjutant General's Papers, Union Regiments, West Virginia State Archives
Ed Adkins Scrapbook, Ceredo Historical Society Museum
Thomas Angell Military Papers (MS115), Mahn Center for Archives and Special Collections, Ohio University Libraries
Major Edgar Blundon Papers, Boyd Blynn Stutler Collection, West Virginia State Archives
Arthur I. Boreman Papers, West Virginia State Archives
William E. Brooks Papers, West Virginia and Regional History Center
Cabell County Court Records, Book 1, 1814-1866
Cabell County Records, Chancery Order Book 1
Cabell County Records, Will Book 1
Cabell County Records, Will Book 2
Civil War Artificial Collection, West Virginia State Archives
Civil War Compiled Service Records, West Virginia State Archives
James Clover Letters, *Clovers of Franklin County, Ohio: A Study of Henry Clover, His Ancestors and Descendants*. Created, edited and maintained by June Clover Byrne for the Clover Family Historical Society, accessed at http://freepages.rootsweb.com/~clover/genealogy/oh/henrypeter/peterelkjamesletters.html
William Robert Cobbs Collection, West Virginia State Archives
Roy Bird Cook Collection, West Virginia and Regional History Center
Jacob Dolson Cox Papers, Mudd Library, Oberlin College
William Dusenberry Papers, 1843-1903, Accession No. 1992/08.0551, Special Collections Department, Marshall University
James H. Ferguson Collection, West Virginia State Archives
Diary of Francis G. Hale, Albert and Shirley Small Special Collections Library, University of Virginia
Letters of Peter E. Harshbarger, courtesy of Mrs. Catherine Ball
Diary of Victoria Hansford Hays, Boyd Blynn Stutler Collection, West Virginia State Archives
Junius Jones Diary, West Virginia State Archives

Junius Marion Jones Collection, West Virginia State Archives
F. B. Lambert Collection, Special Collections Department, Marshall University
Lawrence County, Ohio Veterans' Grave Registration, Briggs Lawrence County Public Library
Legislative Petitions Digital Collection, Library of Virginia
Letters Received by the Office of the Adjutant General, National Archives (fold3.com)
Isaac Little Letters, Filson Historical Society
Loose Letters – Muster Rolls, 13th West Virginia Infantry, National Archives
J. T. R. Martin Collection, Filson Historical Society
Civil War Diary of George W. Miller, Purdue University
B. F. Morris Diary, David E. Zehner Collection, West Virginia State Archives
Newcomb Family Collection, West Virginia State Archives
Francis H. Pierpont Papers, Library of Virginia
Pierpont-Samuels Papers, West Virginia State Archives
Governor Francis Pierpont Telegram Collection, West Virginia and Regional History Center
Peyton Polly Collection, Ohio Historical Center Archives Library
George D. Pyle Letter, Terry Lowry Collection
Zophar D. Ramsdell Diaries, Ceredo Historical Museum and Ramsdell House, Town of Ceredo
Record Group 94, Records of the Adjutant General's Office, National Archives
Record Group 393, Military District of Kentucky, National Archives
Record Group 393, Department of Western Virginia (Mountain Department), National Archives
Regimental Order Book of the 40th Indiana Infantry, National Archives
Regimental Order Book of the 84th Indiana Infantry, National Archives
Regimental Order Book of the 34th Ohio Infantry, National Archives
Regimental Order Book of the 13th West Virginia Infantry, National Archives
William Clark Reynolds Diary, West Virginia State Archives
James D. Sedinger, "Diary of a Border Ranger," Boyd Blynn Stutler Collection, West Virginia State Archives
Smith Family Letters, Accession No. 1997/11.0662, Special Collections Department, Marshall University
George Sprecher's Civil War Letters, http://genealogysurnames.net/SprecherWarLetters.html.
Union Citizens Files, National Archives (fold3.com)
Virginia Court of Appeals Records, Lewisburg, West Virginia State Archives
"West Virginia Census by County and Race, 1790-2010," West Virginia Archives and History website, http://www.wvculture.org/history/teacherresources/censuspopulationrace.html
Kellian Van Rensalear Whaley Collection, West Virginia State Archives
George Woodbury Letter, Terry Lowry Collection

Publications

1860 Cabell County (W) VA Census Annotated. Compiled by Ernestine Hippert. Huntington, WV: KYOVA Genealogical Society, 1993.

Acts of the General Assembly of Virginia. Richmond, VA: William F. Ritchie, Public Printer, 1858.

Acts of the Legislature of West Virginia. Wheeling, WV: John F. M'Dermot, Public Printer, 1865.

Acts Passed at a General Assembly of the Commonwealth of Virginia. Richmond, VA: Samuel Pleasants, Junior, Printer for the Commonwealth, 1809.

Acts Passed at a General Assembly of the Commonwealth of Virginia. Richmond, VA: Samuel Shepherd, Printer for the Commonwealth, 1842.

Adkins, Dr. Michael Jessee. "The Zouave Caves: An Investigation of Murder, Mystery, and Rebellion in Appalachia." *International Journal of Arts and Humanities*, October 2018.

Annual Report of the Adjutant General of the State of Kentucky. Frankfort, KY: Kentucky Yeoman Office, John H. Harney, Public Printer, 1866.

Annual Report of the Adjutant General of the State of West Virginia. Wheeling, WV: John F. McDermot, Public Printer, 1864.

Bailey, Kenneth R. *Alleged Evil Genius: The Life and Times of Judge James H. Ferguson*. Charleston, WV: Quarrier Press, 2006.

Ball, Frank. "'Uncle Billy' Miller, 90 Years Old, Recalls Battle of Mud River." Courtesy of Terry Lowry.

Ball, Frank and J. W. Miller. "Now and Then – Mostly Then." *West Virginia Review*, January 1935.

Beach, John N. *History of the Fortieth Ohio Volunteer Infantry*. London, OH: Shepherd & Craig, Printers, 1884.

A Biographical History of Eminent and Self Made Men of the State of Indiana. Cincinnati, OH: Western Biographical Publishing Company, 1880.

Birt, William A. "A Historical Sketch of Milton, Cabell County, West Virginia," *West Virginia History*, Volume 23, Number 1 (October 1961).

Bowen, John A. "History and Life of John A. Bowen," As Written by Himself on Thanksgiving Day, November 29, 1928, At his Home in Proctorville, Ohio, at the Ripe Old Age of 84, Toney C. Bowen, great-great-grandson. Typed by Linda Cunningham Fluharty and accessed at http://www.lindapages.com/jabowen.txt.

Burdette, F. L. "History of Ona Community." Morgantown, WV: Agricultural Extension Division, 1925.

Burnett, Alf. *Humorous, Pathetic, and Descriptive Incidents of the War*. Cincinnati, OH: R. W. Carroll & Co., Publishers, 1864.

Casto, James E. *Huntington: An Illustrated History*. Northridge, CA: Windsor Publications, 1985.

Civil War Governors of Kentucky: Digital Documentary Edition, Biography of John

L. Zeigler.

Cohen, Stan. *West Virginia Civil War Sites*. Charleston, WV: Pictorial Histories Publishing Company, 1990.

Cole, Scott. *34th Battalion Virginia Cavalry*. Lynchburg, VA: H. E. Howard, Inc., 1993.

Confederate Veteran. Nashville, TN: 1893-1932.

Couper, William. *The VMI New Market Cadets*. Charlottesville, VA: The Michie Company, 1933.

Cox, Jacob D. *Military Reminiscences of the Civil War*. New York, NY: Charles Scribner and Sons, 1900.

Dickinson, Jack L. *8th Virginia Cavalry*. Lynchburg, VA: H. E. Howard, Inc., 1986.

Dickinson, Jack L. *16th Virginia Cavalry*. Lynchburg, VA: H. E. Howard, Inc., 1989.

Dickinson, Jack L. *Cooney Ricketts: Child of the Regiment*. Charleston, WV: Pictorial Histories Publishing Company, 2001.

Dickinson, Jack L. *Jenkins of Greenbottom: A Civil War Saga*. Charleston, WV: Pictorial Histories Publishing Company, 1988.

Dickinson, Jack L. *Records of the 16th Regiment Virginia Cavalry*. Huntington, WV, 1984.

Dickinson, Jack L. *Wayne County, West Virginia in the Civil War*. Salem, MA: Higginson Book Company, 2003.

Dickinson, Jack L. and Kay Stamper Dickinson. *Gentleman Soldier of Greenbottom: The Life of Brig. Gen. Albert Gallatin Jenkins, CSA*. The Authors, 2011.

Dickinson, Jack L. and Mark Meadows. Minutes of Camp Garnett, "A History of Camp Garnett, United Confederate Veterans, Camp #902 Huntington, West Virginia," October 1987.

Dyer, Frederick H. *A Compendium of the War of the Rebellion*, Volume II, Part III, Regimental Histories, 1908.

Earl, J. A. "Methodism in Huntington." *Christian Education Bulletin*, July 1950.

Early Records of Cabell and Mason Counties, W. Va., Presented by Buford Chapter, of Huntington, and Colonel Charles Lewis Chapter, of Point Pleasant, West Va.

Eldridge, Carrie. *Cabell County's Empire for Freedom: The Manumission of Sampson Sanders' Slaves*. Heritage Books, 2004.

Ellis, Atiba R. "Polley vs. Ratcliff: A New Way To Address An Original Sin?" West Virginia University College of Law, Legal Studies Research Paper No. 2012-19, 2012.

Ely, William. *The Big Sandy Valley: A History of the People and Country from the Earliest Settlement to the Present Time*. Catlettsburg, KY: Central Methodist, 1887.

Evans, Nelson W. *A History of Scioto County, Ohio*. Portsmouth, OH: The Author, 1903.

Fain, Cicero M. III. "The African American Experience in Antebellum Cabell County, Virginia/West Virginia, 1810-1865." *Ohio Valley History*, Volume 11, Number 3 (Fall 2011).

Fain, Cicero M. III. *Black Huntington: An Appalachian Story*. Urbana, IL: University of Illinois Press, 2019.

Fain, Cicero M. III. *Race, River, and the Railroad: Black Huntington, West Virginia, 1871-1929*. Dissertation, Ohio State University, 2009.
Findings of Court of Claims in case of Methodist Episcopal Church South, Barboursville, West Virginia. Senate Documents, Serial Set ID 5267, S. doc. 39, December 3, 1907.
Findings of Court of Claims in case of Methodist Episcopal Church South, Guyandotte, West Virginia. Senate Documents, Serial Set ID 4764, S. doc. 22, December 7, 1904.
Findings of Court of Claims in case of Baptist Church, Guyandotte, West Virginia. Senate Documents, Serial Set ID 4764, S. doc. 55, December 14, 1904.
Fite, Baxter B. III. Biography of Alfred S. Proctor. Find A Grave (findagrave.com/memorial/30173998/alfred-stephen-proctor).
Flournoy, H. W., editor. *Calendar of Virginia State Papers and Other Manuscripts*, Volume 11. Richmond, VA: 1893.
Griffith, Joe. *History of Company G, 11th West Virginia Volunteer Infantry From Coalsmouth to Richmond, 1862-1865*. Roswell, GA: The Author, 1995.
Griffith, Rev. Bryce W. and Everett Samuel Pierce. "History of the First Guyandotte Baptist Church."
Gunter, Frances B. *Barboursville*. 1986.
Hale, James L. *The Long Road to Freedom: The Story of the Enslaved Polley Children*. Lulu Publishing Services, 2014.
Hall, Granville Davisson. *The Rending of Virginia: A History*. Chicago, IL: Mayer & Miller, 1902.
"History of the Guyandotte United Methodist Church 1804-1986." Gathered from notes by Mary Poindexter Hennen during conversation with "Aunt Becky" Wellington.
"History of the Union Baptist Church 1810-1871."
Howe, Henry. *Historical Collections of Virginia*. Charleston, SC: Babcock & Company, 1845.
Huddleston, Samuel. "A Civil War History of the Eighty-Fourth Indiana Regiment," as recorded by Samuel Huddleston. Transcribed by Sharon Ogzewalla, accessed at http://www.hcgs.net/84thindiana.html.
Johnson, Patricia Givens. *The United States Army Invades the New River Valley May 1864*. Christiansburg, VA: Walpa Publishing, 1986.
Journal of the House of Delegates of Virginia for the Session of 1850-51. Richmond, VA: William F. Ritchie, 1850.
Knauss, William H. *The Story of Camp Chase*. Nashville, TN: Publishing House of the ME Church South, 1906.
Lang, Theodore F. *Loyal West Virginia from 1861 to 1865*. Baltimore, MD: Deutsch Publishing Company, 1895.
Livingston, John. *Portraits of Eminent Americans Now Living: With Biographical and Historical Memoirs of Their Lives and Actions*. New York, NY: Cornish, Lamport & Company, 1853.
Love, Charles. "History of Martha Community." Morgantown, WV: Agricultural

Extension Division, 1925.

Lowry, Terry. *The Battle of Charleston and the 1862 Kanawha Valley Campaign*. Charleston, WV: 35th Star Publishing, 2016.

Lowry, Terry. *The Battle of Scary Creek*. Charleston, WV: Pictorial Histories Publishing Company, 1982.

McClintic, Elizabeth Knight. "Ceredo: An Experiment in Colonization." Thesis, Wellesley College, 1937.

McKernon, Mary L. *The Church at Blue Sulphur Springs, Mud River Baptist, 1807-.* Huntington, WV: OIC, 1987.

Miller, J. W. "History of Barboursville Community." Morgantown, WV: Agricultural Extension Division, 1925.

Mitchell, Mrs. Walter. "History of Cabell Creek Community." Morgantown, WV: Agricultural Extension Division, 1925.

Moore, Frank, editor. *The Rebellion Record: A Diary of American Events, With Documents, Narratives, Illustrative Incidents, Poetry, Etc*. New York, NY: G. P. Putnam, 1864-1868.

Nance, Karen. "Green Bottom," e-WV: The West Virginia Encyclopedia. 05 August 2016. Web. 26 December 2018.

Nichols, Seth Adam. "Let Us Bury and Forget:" Civil War Memory and Identity in Cabell County, West Virginia, 1865-1915." Master's Thesis, Marshall University, 2016.

Official Roster of the Soldiers of the State of Ohio in the War of the Rebellion, 1861-1866, Volume IX. Cincinnati, OH: The Ohio Valley Press, 1889.

Parker, Granville. *The Formation of the State of West Virginia*. Wellsburg, WV: Glass and Son, 1875.

Perkins, Marlitta H., editor. *Adventures, Struggles, Trials and Services of the 5th Regiment, Virginia Volunteer Infantry*. Staffordsville, KY: Eastern Kentucky Research & Publishing, 2015.

Post Office Directory; or Business Man's Guide to the Post Offices in the United States. Compiled by D. D. T. Leech. New York, NY: J. H. Colton and Company, 1857.

Quackenbush, Eugene. *Map of the State of Virginia: Showing the Advantages of the Harbor of West Point as an Entrepot for Emmigration and the Shipment of the Products of the Southern and Western States*. New York, NY: Ed. W. Welcke & Brother, 1875.

Reid, Whitelaw. *Ohio in the War: Her Statesmen, Her Generals, and Soldiers*, Volume I. Cincinnati, OH: Moore, Wilstach, and Baldwin, 1868.

Report of the Committees of the House of Representatives, 1861-1862. Washington, DC: Government Printing Office, 1862, Report No. 130, Margaret J. Bailey.

Richardson Albert D. *A Personal History of Ulysses S. Grant*. Hartford, CT: Bliss and Company, 1868.

Rouse, J. H. *Horrible Massacre at Guyandotte, Va., and a Journey to the Rebel Capital: With a Description of Prison Life in a Tobacco Warehouse at Richmond*. The Author, 1862.

Rowsey, Jeanettte M. *The Lost Village of Barboursville*. Huntington, WV: JRC

Publishing, 2013.
Ruffner, Rev. H. "Notes of a Tour from Virginia to Tennessee, in the Months of July and August, 1839." *Southern Literary Messenger*, Volume 5. Richmond, VA: Thomas W. White, 1839.
Scott, John L. *36th and 37th Battalions Virginia Cavalry*. Lynchburg, VA: H. E. Howard, Inc., 1986.
Shivel, Kelly Winifred. "The Fuller/Shelton Feud, Cabell County, West Virginia." April 13, 1992.
Sifakis, Stewart. *Who Was Who In The Confederacy*. New York, NY: Facts on File, 1988.
Simon, John Y. (editor). *The Papers of Ulysses S. Grant*, Volume 25. Carbondale, IL: Southern Illinois University Press, 1874.
Smith, Jo Ann. "Cabell County, Lincoln County, Wayne County, West Virginia Cemeteries."
Smith, Wiatt (editor). *Guyandotte Centennial, 1810-1910*. The Guyandotte Centennial and Cabell County Homecoming Association, 1910.
Spaulding, Melburn C. "Record of Official Correspondence of the Federal and Confederate Armies in the Kanawha River Valley, 1861-1864." 1976.
Stutler, Boyd. *The Civil War in West Virginia*. Charleston, WV: Education Foundation, 1963.
Sutton, J. J. *History of the 2nd Regiment West Virginia Volunteer Cavalry*. Portsmouth, OH: 1882.
Thomas, Emory. *Bold Dragoon: The Life of J. E. B. Stuart*. New York, NY: Vintage Books, 1986.
Thompson, Robert Michael. *Fear No Man: The Life of Colonel Milton Jameson Ferguson*. Genoa, WV: The Author, 2011.
Thompson, Robert Michael. *Few Among the Mountains: Slavery in Wayne County, West Virginia*. Genoa, WV: The Author, 2015.
Thompson, Robert Michael. *Ramsdell: A Southern Yankee*. Wayne, WV: The Author, 2018.
Thompson, Robert Michael. *Twelve Pole Terror: The Legend of Rebel Bill Smith*. Wayne, WV: The Author, 2015.
Turner, Ronald R. *7th West Virginia Cavalry*. 1989.
United States War Department. *War of the Rebellion: A Compilation of the Official Records of the Union and Confederate Armies*. 128 Volumes. Washington, DC: Government Printing Office, 1880-1901.
"Up the Guyandotte." *Appleton's Journal*, June 15, 1872.
Vance, John L. "The Retreat of the Union Forces from the Kanawha Valley in 1862," *Sketches of War History, 1861-1865*, Military Order of the Loyal Legion of the United States, Volume IV. Cincinnati, OH: R. Clarke & Company, 1896.
Wade, Marilyn Brasher. "A Candlestick From My Great-Great-Grandfather," 2014, accessed at https://www.thestoryoftexas.com/discover/texas-story-project/a-candlestick-from-my-great-great-grandfather.
Wallace, George S. *Cabell County Annals and Families*. Richmond, VA: Garrett-

Massie, 1935.

Wallace, Lee A., Jr. *A Guide to Virginia Military Organizations 1861-65*. Revised 2nd Edition. Lynchburg, VA: H. E. Howard, 1986.

"West Virginia Census by County and Race, 1790-2010," West Virginia Archives and History, accessed at http://www.wvculture.org/history/teacherresources/censuspopulationrace.html.

White, Colonel Robert. *Confederate Military History: West Virginia*. Secaucus, NJ: Blue and Grey Press, 1988.

White, M. Wood. *White's Topographical, County & District Atlas of West Virginia. Counties of Cabell, Wayne, Lincoln, Logan*. 1873.

Wintz, William, editor. *Civil War Memoirs of Two Rebel Sisters*. Charleston, WV: Pictorial Histories Publishing Company, 1989.

Newspapers

Alexandria Local News
Bucyrus Journal
Cabell County Press
Cabell Record
Catlettsburg Advocate
Ceredo Crescent
Cincinnati Commercial
Cincinnati Gazette
Cincinnati Press
Colorado Citizen
Democratic Banner
Gallipolis Dispatch
Gallipolis Journal
Guyandotte Herald
Harpers Weekly
Highland Weekly News
Huntington Herald-Advertiser
Huntington Sunday Advertiser
Indiana True Republican
Ironton Daily Republican
Ironton Register
Jackson Standard
Kanawha Valley Star
The Knapsack
Louisville Journal
Marietta Register
Marietta Republican
Mason County Journal
McArthur Democrat
New York Illustrated News
Ohio State Journal
Philadelphia Inquirer
Point Pleasant Weekly Register
Pomeroy Weekly Telegraph
Portsmouth Times

Randolph County Journal (Indiana)
Richmond Dispatch
Richmond Enquirer
Star of the Kanawha Valley
Tiffin Weekly Review
Tiffin Weekly Tribune
Toledo Blade
West Virginia Journal
Wheeling Intelligencer

Index

Abbs Valley, Virginia 252
Aberdeen, Ohio 378
Abingdon, Virginia 272
Adams, James Franklin 379
Adams, John 50, 75, 263, 265, 267, 282
Adams, Rev. 21-22
Adams, Thomas 248, 263
Adams County, Ohio 291
Adkins, Andrew 401
Adkins, Andrew William 401
Adkins, Boyd 66
Adkins, Calvin 197
Adkins, Elijah 196
Adkins, George 326
Adkins, James 166
Adkins, Lamack 347
Adkins, Perry Green 267
Adkins, Roffe 263
Adkins, Susan 401
Adkins, Ten 213
Adkins, Thomas T. 85, 157
Adkins, Wash 18, 75, 81
Adkinsville 9, 361
Alford, George 243
Alford, John 94, 141, 158, 205, 209, 256, 271, 282, 286, 289, 406
Algeo, William 334
Allen, Robert 91, 98
Allen, Runnels 288-89
Alleyton, Texas 352-53
Almond, Samuel 82
Amacetta 9, 35, 47, 50, 275, 283-86, 361, 364, 391
Appomattox, surrender at 314, 327, 335, 352
Arlington National Cemetery 65, 354
Arthur, Isaac 396

Arthur, John 396
Arthur, John V. 396
Arthur, Thomas P. 396
Arthur, Washington 396
Arthur, William T. 396
Ashland 245
Ashland, Kentucky 28, 30
Ashworth, G. H. 86, 157
Athenaeum Prison 156-57, 180, 194, 197, 213, 245, 268, 282
Athens County, Ohio 291
Austin, George 66
Ayers, George W. 357

Bailey, George B. 106, 108, 127-28, 377-78
Bailey, Margaret J. 128, 377-78
Bailey Post No. 4, Grand Army of the Republic 356
Baisden, James 89-90
Ball, Cynthia 264
Ball, Flamen 67, 70
Ballangee, Absalom 64-65
Ballard, John W. 323-24
Balser, Samuel 195, 388
Barbour, Addie 283
Barbour, John 105, 248
Barbour, Joseph 157
Barbour, Lucy 283
Barbour, Squire 276
Barboursville 4-5, 7, 10, 16, 19, 36, 42, 45, 55, 58-70, 73, 75, 77-78, 81-85, 88, 98, 101, 104, 114-15, 120-21, 135, 141, 143, 147-50, 153, 156-58, 160-61, 167, 171-74, 177, 179, 181-86, 188, 190-93, 195-200, 202-5, 208-10, 216-20, 222, 225,

230-32, 236, 238-39, 241-42, 245, 247, 251, 254, 256, 262-66, 269-74, 276-77, 279-83, 289, 291-97, 304-5, 311, 316-20, 337-40, 344, 349, 352, 358, 361, 366, 375, 379, 382, 388, 404, 407
Barboursville Cemetery 67
Barboursville Methodist Episcopal Church, South 220, 357
Bartram, David 153, 382
Bartram, James 223
Bartram, Squire 321
Bartram, William 153, 280, 382
Bateman, John C. 333-34
Bates, A. J. 157
Baumgardner, Billy 298
Baumgardner, Henry 106, 374
Baumgardner, J. B. 173, 209, 217, 256, 264-65, 286-87, 324, 397, 406
Baumgardner, Jacob 142
Baumgardner, Jim 314
Baumgardner, John 166
Baumgardner, Rebecca 106
Baumgardner's Hotel 106, 111
Baxfield/Bexfield, Richard B. 324, 396
Bay, George W. 296-97, 401
Bay, Sarah 297
Bay, William 296-97, 401
Bazell, James 244
Beall, Samuel 214
Beard, Daniel B. 338
Beckett, A. L. 346
Beech Fork 58-59, 75, 94, 186-88, 190, 195, 205, 263, 267, 271, 276, 294, 387-88
Beekman, Lewis 116, 136, 376
Beekman and Enshimer Clothing Store 123
Bell, John 34-35
Bellamy, Matthew 98
Ben Franklin 45, 193
Benjamin, Judah P. 141
Bennett, Jesse 3
Berkshire, R. L. 325-26

Berridge, Thomas 112, 133
Berry, Philo B. 324
Beuhring, Fredrick D. 58-60, 367
Bias, Anderson 323-24, 397
Bias, James C. 188, 190
Bias, Roland 247, 298, 324
Bicker, Anthony 346
Bicker, Henry 404
Big Sandy River 7, 9-10, 24, 29, 80, 90, 93, 99, 122, 148, 160, 181, 198, 231, 236-37, 240, 242, 254, 265, 277, 305, 318, 329, 335-36
Big Ugly Creek 254
Bing, Francis 142-43, 157
Black, Adam 14, 362
Black, James C. 147, 153, 194, 323, 361
Black, William 341
Black Jack, battle of 374
Blackwood, Bob 91
Blagg, Captain 52
Blagg, John 112
Blake, Grandma 61, 64-65, 367
Blake, Isaac 269, 395
Blake, John M. 154, 247, 298, 396
Blake, Valentine 396
Blankenship, Enoch 91, 361
Blankenship, Rayfield Lenting 386
Blazer's Scouts 308
Bledsoe, Peter 157
Bloomingdale 7, 361
Bloomingdale Church 358
Bloss, E. S. 326
Bloss, Hiram 323
Bloss, Isaac 315, 322
Blundon, Edgar B. 300, 302-4, 311, 314-15, 318
Boggess, Robert O. 271
Bolles, William M. 125-26, 139, 147-48, 162-65, 169, 173, 177
Bontecew, Spencer "Dock" 386
Boone County 7, 42, 46, 49, 77, 209, 269, 272, 337, 339
Boone Courthouse 77, 338
Booton, Asa 7

Border Rangers 37-42, 51-52, 56, 61, 65, 74, 104, 106, 108, 110, 112, 182, 210, 214, 286, 352-53, 355-56, 364
Boreman, Arthur 263, 268-69, 277, 282, 287, 292, 299, 302-3, 305, 319-20, 322, 325, 329, 331, 334-38, 341, 397
Boston 122
Bostonia 289
Bostonia No. 2 292
Botetourt County, Virginia 6
Botsford, James L. 283
Bowden, Sidney 225, 256, 298
Bowdens, J. F. 263
Bowen, Fisher 58, 406
Bowen, Hugh 58
Bowen, Jefferson Jr. 307
Bowen, John 93
Bowen, John B. 248-49, 301, 315
Bowen, John L. 141, 157, 307
Bowlin, James B. 132, 164-65, 383
Bowlin, Margaret 82
Boyd, Samuel S. 229-30, 238, 240
Bragg, Joe 106, 127
Bragg, Samuel 194
Bramer, C. K. 407
Bramlett, William 140-41
Brannon, John C. 406
Brattin, A. T. 112
Breckinridge, John 34-35, 352
Bristor, Jacob H. 325-26
Broadwell Tigers, 198
Brown, A. J. M. 66
Brown, Charles 240
Brown, Ethan A. 180-81
Brown, George P. 157
Brown, James H. 170, 172, 241, 251, 256, 260, 282
Brown, John 33, 374
Brown, William R. 254, 260-61, 267-68, 270, 272-75, 277-78, 281-82, 286-87, 289, 293
Brown County, Ohio 127, 378

Browne, Adam 378
Brumfield, Bill 217
Brumfield, W. W. 46, 249, 326, 335
Buckhannon 217
"Buena Vista" 200-201
Buffalo 45, 212, 218, 220
Buffalo Bayou, Brazos and Colorado Railway 353
Buffalo Shoals 75, 271
Buffington, Edward Stanard 349, 352
Buffington, James 20-21, 23, 307
Buffington, John N. 307
Buffington, Mrs. L. G. 355
Buffington, Peter C. 39, 77, 158-59, 349, 369
Buffington, Thomas 21-23, 272-73
Buffington, William 13
Buffington, William 21-23, 38
Buffington Mill 5, 123
Bukey, Eveline 264
Bukey, Rodolphus 214, 382, 406
Bukey, Van C. 279
Bukey House 264, 304
Bull Run, First 128
Bull Run, Second 259-60
Bumgardner, H. J. 344-45
Burbank, Sidney 334
Burdett, John S. 325-26
Burks, Thomas 106, 127
Burlington, Ohio 15, 45, 221, 225, 363
Burnett, C. J. 345
Burns, John 368
Burres, William 242

Cabell, William H. 3, 7
Cabell County Board of Supervisors 298, 300
Cabell County Circuit Court 266, 288, 307, 312
Cabell Courthouse 5, 10, 16, 45, 59, 61, 161, 198-99, 204-5, 248, 293, 298, 340-41, 345, 349
Cabell County Militia (120th Virginia) 58

Cabell County Press 341, 344-45, 347
Caldwell, J. L. 407
Caldwell, William T. 233, 392
Camden, Gideon 34
Camden, Johnson N. 337
Camp Broadwell 193
Camp Chase 48, 76, 128-29, 140-43, 157-58, 166, 169, 180, 196, 213-14, 245, 256, 283, 287, 293, 296, 351, 372-73
Camp Clay 56
Camp Crittenden 56, 59, 67
Camp Davis 364
Camp Dennison 67, 179
Camp Dickerson 103
Camp Franklin 193
Camp Garnett, United Confederate Veterans 355-56, 370
Camp Lucas 179
Camp McFall 229
Camp Paxton 94, 96, 138, 141, 150, 154, 162, 193
Camp Piatt 177, 254, 272
Camp Pierpont 80, 82, 84, 86, 88-90, 93, 96-97, 99
Camp Ratliff 76
Camp Red House 96
Camp Spurlock, United Confederate Veterans 355
Camp Toland 186, 190, 193, 196, 198, 204, 388
Camp Tompkins 41, 47, 62, 65, 74
Camp White 298
Campbell, David 15
Campbell, John 70
Canterbury, James 395
Carlile, John 43, 46, 83
Carnifex Ferry, battle of 142
Carpenter, Peter M. 243, 255, 277
Carpenter, William A. 395
Carroll, J. J. S. P. 271, 326-29, 339
Carroll, James T. 298
Carroll, Mary 124
Carroll, Thomas 124

Carter, G. M. 236
Carter, George 13
Carter, John D. 261, 266, 269
Carter, L. P. 344-45
Cassville 9, 89, 92-93, 98, 268, 280, 320-22, 329-32, 334-35
Castelow, John 186-88
Castle Thunder Prison 268-69
Catlettsburg, Kentucky 28, 76, 78, 82, 89, 91, 140, 149, 151, 211, 237, 259, 292, 299, 301, 309, 351, 395, 399
Cedar Mountain, battle of 259
Cerbe, John L. 186-88
Ceredo 24-31, 35, 40, 47, 50, 75-76, 78-80, 83-84, 86-89, 93-94, 96, 99, 104, 108, 122, 125-27, 129-30, 132, 142, 148, 151-52, 158, 161, 170, 172, 197, 209, 211, 225-26, 233, 235, 242, 244-45, 248, 250-51, 256, 263, 267, 280, 282, 292, 300, 307-9, 312, 315-17, 319, 322, 329-30, 332-34, 336, 339, 345, 351, 364, 378, 394
Chapman, A. A. 326
Chapman, Absolom 106
Chapman, Emerson/Emmerson 157, 249
Chapman, H. V. 341
Chapman, John G. 294, 341
Chapmanville 121, 212, 214-15, 242, 254
Charles Adkins Cemetery (Mars Cemetery) 205
Charleston 46, 81, 83, 91, 208-9, 212-13, 218, 236, 239, 254, 260, 263, 272, 282-83, 298, 303, 315, 339, 351
Charleston, South Carolina 37
Chase, Salmon P. 16-17
Chesapeake and Ohio Railroad 10, 25, 29, 61, 283, 345, 351
Chewning, J. D. 406
Chickamauga, battle of 68

Childers, Greenville A. 141, 157
Childers, Lewis 141
Childers, Melville 265
Childers, Samuel A. 172, 247-48, 321, 324, 344-45
Childers, William T. 157
Church, J. W. 344-45
Cincinnati, Ohio 5, 40, 44, 52, 56-57, 65, 96, 129, 157, 179-80, 223, 329
Cincinnati Commercial 57, 77, 130-33
Cincinnati Gazette 29
City Point, Virginia 260
Clairmont 294
Clark, E. M. 345
Clark, Roland 111-12, 322
Clark, Silas 286, 320
Clark, W. R. S. 196
Clarke, Peter 362
Clarksburg Convention 42
Clarkson, John 103-4, 109-11, 118, 139, 147, 149, 208, 214, 242-43, 345
Clay, Nathan 156
Clendenin, William 3
Clermont County, Ohio 179
Cleveland, Grover 352
Cleveland Morning Leader 131-32
Clifton 390
Cloud, W. L. 380
Clover, James 230
Cloyd's Mountain, battle of 355, 403
Coal Mountain 65
Coal River 3, 41, 236, 281
Coalsmouth 61, 65, 279, 293, 300, 401
Coalter, John 4
Coffman, John 122
Cole, George W. 197
Collier 52
Collins, James 197
Collins, John C. 278
Collins, Joseph B. 329-34
Collins, Nathan 344
Collins, William 186-88, 385
Colorado Citizen 353

Columbus, Ohio 48, 76, 94, 101, 128, 139-40, 142
Comly, James M. 272
Compston, Alfred F. 257
Comstock, Stephen 266
Conine, James W. 91-92
Connor, Charles 6
Cook, Abner 364
Cook, Charles 266
Cook, Levi 264
Cook, Mitchell 325-26, 344-45
Coon Creek 277
Copley, William H. 46, 84, 153, 251, 256, 278
Corinth, battle of 68
Corns, James 62, 104, 108, 254
Covington, Kentucky 77
Covington, Virginia 10
Cox, Emily 284, 311
Cox, Jacob D. 52, 55-56, 82, 137, 144, 173, 178, 200-201, 211-12, 230, 233, 235-36, 240-41, 366
Cox, Nelson 46
Crabtree, Hiram 281
Crabtree, Hiram Jr. 281
Crabtree, Solomon 281
Cranor, Jonathan 229-31, 233-38, 240
Cremeans, Alexander 396
Cremeans, Joseph 396
Cricket No. 2 52
Crittenden, John J. 35
Crook, George 283, 289, 304-5
Cross Keys, battle of 259
Crown City, Ohio 378
Cruikshank, M. A. 149
Cunningham, John S. 267, 280
Cunningham, William P. 243
Curry, Benjamin F. 303, 397
Curry, Hiram 298, 321
Curry, William 157
Curtis, Rollin L. 151
Custner, Casper 361
Cutler, James 388
Cynes, W. H. 382

Cyrus, J. E. 357

Damron, Thomas 100, 268
Damron, Wilson 100
Darnel, Peter 325-26
Darr, Joseph 142, 155-56, 164, 194, 202, 213-14, 245, 394
Davey, Thomas N. 81, 93, 96-97, 100
Davis, Benjamin 153, 382
Davis, Jefferson 37, 110-11, 321
Davis, Joseph I. 396
Davis, Samuel H. 396
Deal, Elisha 174
Decker, James A. 43
Deitz, Hugo 111, 119-20, 380
Denison, John 396
Dennison, William Jr. 19, 48, 52, 117, 126, 376
Devil's Elbow 183-84
Dick, A. J. 345
Dick, Andy 225
Dick, Dave 64
Dick, Joseph 188, 303-4
Dickerson, John H. 52
Dickson, 9, 357
Diehl, Louis 324
Dixon, W. J. 326
Dobbins, V. S. 406
Dock's Creek 75
Dodson, Jesse 286
Dolen, George 171, 205
Donnovan, John 67
Douglas, Stephen 34-35
Douthit, Charlotte Temple 124
Douthit, John 124, 139, 406
Douthit, William 121, 124, 160, 322, 344, 406
Dove, David 254-55, 395
Drake, Henderson 122, 396
Drake, James M. 361
Drum, W. F. 329-32
Dry Creek 61
Duffie, Alfred Napoleon 278
Dumont 289

Dundas, James 158
Dunkle, Harvey 75
Dunkle, Henry C. 325
Dusenberry, Charles 196, 264-65, 344, 406
Dusenberry, Cynthia 217
Dusenberry, Sam 266
Dusenberry, Susie 284, 290
Dusenberry, T. C. 114
Dusenberry, William 141, 171, 177, 192, 196, 199, 203, 209-10, 212-13, 216-17, 264-67, 271-72, 286, 288-92, 297-99, 301, 303-4, 311, 313-14, 319-20, 322-25, 347, 361
Dusenberry's Mill 65, 137-38, 157, 182, 190, 192, 195-96, 238, 265

Eaden, James 321
Earls, David 141
Early, Jubal 404
Edwards, Herman C. 195
Edwards, James B. 249
Eggars, Joseph 273-74, 344-46
Eggars, Mary 273-74
Egnor, William G. 296
18th Independent Battery, Ohio Light Artillery (Portsmouth Artillery) 223
8th Virginia Cavalry 40, 82-83, 103, 105, 108, 140, 217, 252, 261-62, 282, 355, 395
84th Indiana Infantry 229-32, 234-242
86th Illinois Infantry 354
11th West Virginia Infantry 209-10, 272, 279
Elkins, Clark 279
Elkins, Henry 307
Elkins, Lewis 157
Elkins, Reece W. 307
Elmwood Cemetery 368
Elzea, James 364
"Emigrant Aid Society" 24
Emmons, D. W. 353
Engle, Jerry 406
Enochs, William H. 326

Ephison, George 166
Evans, Oliver P. 164-65, 198
Everett, Charles 141-42
Everett, H. C. 104-5
Everett, Henry Clay 37, 211, 352-53
Everett, J. W. 380
Everett, Jenny 120
Everett, John 26
Everett, John S. 109, 221, 374
Everett, Kate 110, 114, 352
Everett, Peter 142
Everett, Tarleton W. 104-5, 128-29, 162
Eves, Frank 59
Eves, T. M. 344
Ewing, Thomas 37

Fairmont 46
Fairview Cemetery 351
Fairview Riflemen 65
Faller, Harold 67
Falls Mill 7, 361
Falls of Guyandotte 188, 191, 254-55, 265, 267, 271, 281
Falls of Tug 9, 361
Fall of Twelve Pole 9, 94, 271, 361
Falling Timber 276
Fannie McBurnie 52, 55
Fayette County 103, 337
Fayette Courthouse 337
Fayette Township, Ohio 45
Fayetteville 144
Fayetteville, battle of 181, 205, 387
Feazel, William 99, 101, 213-14, 267, 271-73, 280, 282, 286-87, 290, 298-99, 306
Felix, James 256, 300, 303, 325
Ferguson, Burwell 362
Ferguson, Charles W. 268
Ferguson, D. P. 225
Ferguson, James H. 166, 286-87, 298-300, 303, 309-10, 312, 314-15, 320-25, 334, 339-40, 347, 406
Ferguson, John 154, 247, 275-76, 307

Ferguson, Joseph M. 351-52
Ferguson, Milton J. 40, 58, 62, 74-76, 97, 156-57, 254, 274, 278, 280, 305, 351-52, 361
Ferguson, William 268, 361
Ferrill, F. M. 85
Fielder, William 154
5th Virginia Cavalry 103
5th West Virginia Infantry 75, 78, 80-81, 83-84, 87-97, 99-100, 104, 122, 125, 132-33, 148, 156, 158, 166, 199, 232-33, 235, 242, 245, 256-64, 280, 301-2, 308, 336, 357, 370
57th United States Colored Infantry 354-55
1st Kentucky Infantry 59-60
1st Ohio Volunteers 378
1st Regiment Virginia State Line 260
1st West Virginia Cavalry 135, 273
Fisher, Charles 406
Fitz, William 368
Fitzgerald, E. M. 399
Fitzhugh, Henry 104
Flat Top Mountain 211-12
Fleetwood 341
Flesher, Andrew 46
Floyd, John B. 103, 118, 148, 243
Focht, William H. 236
Forbes, Hannibal 200
Forest Hotel 110
Fort Delaware 247, 260, 317, 351
Fort Gay 9, 361
Fort Henry 198-99
Fort Smith, Arkansas 354
Fort Sumter 37, 127
40th Kentucky Mounted Infantry 280
40th Ohio Infantry 229, 233, 237, 239, 242, 357
45th Kentucky Infantry 300
41st Ohio Infantry 132-33
Foster's Landing 391
Four Pole Creek 7, 58
Fourteen Mile Creek 166
14th Kentucky Infantry 278

4th West Virginia Infantry 74, 129-30, 170, 172, 209, 214-16, 218, 226
Frampton, David 142
France, Benjamin 157
Franklin, Freeman 93, 121, 186, 198, 200, 202
Franklin County, Pennsylvania 75
Frasher, Nathan 281
Fraze, Sam 234
Frazier, Mart 98
Fremont, John C. 173, 202, 208, 259
Freutel, Julius 149, 298, 309, 322, 346, 406
Frost, Daniel 99, 325
Fry, Joshua 6
Fudges Creek 254
Fuller, Achilles 114-16, 138, 173, 375
Fuller, Albert 114-17, 138, 375-76
Fuller, Calvin 323
Fuller, Eb 85
Fuller, John 115, 375
Fuller, S. F. 93
Fuller, Richard 252
Fullerton, Ann 362
Fullerton, Jack 13-15, 362
Fullerton, Lewis 13-15, 362
Fullerton, William 13

Gallia County, Ohio 46, 263, 291
Gallipolis, Ohio 47-48, 55, 66, 121, 129-30, 133-34, 208, 223, 229, 272, 289, 294-95, 303, 400
Gallipolis Journal 134, 292
Galloway, A. M. 256
Gallup, George W. 278
Gangewer, A. M. 19
Gardner, Joseph 21, 67
Garfield, James 198
Garnett, Robert S. 355
Garrett, Morgan 268-69, 326
Gaston, Joseph 169
Georgetown, Ohio 377
German Home Guard Company 68-70
Getaway, Ohio 45

Gibbs, George 388
Gibson, Calvary 249-50
Gibson, Joseph 406
Gilbert's Creek 254
Giles County, Virginia 3, 7
Gilkerson, Helena 179, 186, 191, 386
Gilkerson, Ira 387
Gilkerson, Jefferson 263
Gilkerson, Leander 387
Gilkerson, Thomas 322-23
Gilkerson's Mill 179, 186-87, 191, 195, 387
Gilkinson, Wash 61
Gilkison, John Jr. 361
Gillen, E. F. 76
Glaze, Socrates 164-65
Glenville 217
Glenwood 223, 225
Glidden, John 128
Goodspeed, Joseph M. 292
Grand Army of the Republic 356-57
Grant, Ulysses 127, 313, 343, 377
Grant, William L. 171
Grayson, Kentucky 237
Green Bottom 6-7, 47, 52, 129, 132, 165, 169, 218, 220, 229, 305, 355, 361, 379, 383
Green Bottom Baptist Church 40
Greenbrier County 81, 289, 390
Greenlawn Cemetery 398
Greenup County, Kentucky 75
Grey, Robert 267
Griffith, Ephraim 323-24
Griswold, Oliver 279
Groom, James A. 88-89
Guthrie, J. V. 59
Guyandotte 4, 7, 10, 13, 20-28, 33-35, 37-38, 41, 43-47, 49-53, 55-61, 67-70, 73-74, 77, 83, 91-95, 98, 101, 103-42, 144-45, 147-55, 157-65, 167-77, 181, 186, 190, 193, 198-99, 203, 207, 209-23, 225-27, 229-42, 245, 247-48, 251, 256, 263-67, 269-73, 275, 277, 280-94, 296-300,

302-6, 308, 310-11, 313-15, 317-18, 330-32, 334-35, 337-38, 345, 349-51, 358, 361, 366, 373, 376-77, 379, 390, 397, 399, 407
Guyandotte Baptist Church 124, 358
Guyandotte Civil War Days 359
Guyandotte Herald 10
Guyandotte Methodist Episcopal Church, South 158, 239-40, 314, 357-58
Guyandotte Mountain 122
Guyandotte Navigation Company 10
Guyandotte River 4-5, 7, 60-61, 64-65, 84, 101, 105-6, 109, 111-12, 114, 121-22, 127, 151, 161, 174-76, 182, 190, 192, 195, 208, 211, 216, 219-20, 225, 230, 236-37, 242, 254, 266, 271, 276, 298, 305, 319, 364, 373
Guyandotte River Railroad Company 10
Guyandotte suspension bridge 107-8, 115, 225, 237, 275
Guyandotte Unionist 25-26, 48

Hackworth, George 247, 260, 395
Hagan, William H. 307
Hager, Robert 42-43, 77, 320
Hale, Francis 95-97, 179-82, 184, 190-92, 386
Haley, Benjamin 287, 292, 299-301
Haley, James 392
Hall, Charles 21
Hall, Ephraim B. 303
Hall, Granville D. 364
Hall, James R. 260, 262, 273-74, 276, 278-79
Hall, John 172
Hall, Nathaniel 22
Hall, William 217
Hambleton, Charles 218, 220
Hamilton, Maggie 264
Hamlin 7, 147, 153, 207-8, 261, 269, 361
Hampton, L. J. 74-77
Hampton, Taylor W. 292
Hanley, Patrick 86
Hanley, William 85-86, 157
Hannan, Thomas 6
Hannan, Thomas E. 361
Hansford, Victoria 41
Hardee, John 177
Hare, Jeremiah 74, 97
Harkins, Charles 329-31, 334
Harler, Charles 213-14
Harper, Elihu 368
Harper, William W. 280
Harpers Ferry 33
Harris, Henry 166
Harrison, Greenville 137, 172, 216, 247, 256, 265, 298, 300, 303, 325
Harrison, Nathaniel 337, 406
Harrison, Zachariah 266
Harrison County 42
Harshbarger, David 224, 298, 324, 345-46
Harshbarger, John 224, 325, 406
Harshbarger, Peter 224-25
Harts Ceek 254
Hartsuff, George L. 88-89, 153, 156, 169, 200
Harwood, Paul 355
Haskellville, Ohio 45
Hatfield, Lewis 209
Hatfield, Mose 265
Hatfield Hotel 196, 203, 220
Hatton, Alvin 94
Hatton, George A. 157
Hawley, C. G. 52
Hayes, Rutherford B. 257
Hayslip, Carey 108, 150
Hayslip, J. F. 406
Hayslip, Louella 283-84, 288
Hayslip, R. H. L. 406
Hayslip, Thomas J. 113-14, 256, 264, 288, 298-99, 303, 325, 327, 335, 406-7
Hazard, Thomas R. 95
Heath, Joshua K. 324

Heiskell, Ferdinand 368
Hempfling, John 368
Hendrick, William 153
Henry, Theodore 396
Hensley, John 85, 287
Hensley, Sol 157
Hensley, William 86
Hereford, Frank 347
Herndon's Battalion 249-50
Highland Weekly News 293
Hillsboro, Ohio 293
Hiltbruner, Jacob 138, 406
Hiltbruner, Mary 120
Hiltbruner, Stephen 120, 138, 140-41
Hiltbruner's Store 123
Hilton Head Island Prison 351
Hinchman, Adam 244, 346
Hinchman, Lewis 334
Hinchman, William 121, 136-38, 141, 174, 205, 244
Hindman, William L. 325-26, 333
Hinkley, Jacob 255-56
Hite, Fannie 284, 288
Hite, John 106, 111, 114, 119-20, 141, 157-58, 376
Hoard, Charles B. 351
Hoback, John 338-39
Hoback, L. J. 325, 344
Hoffman, John J. 281-82
Holden, Frederik 96, 372
Holderby, George W. 37, 123, 200
Holderby, Robert 138, 140, 155-56, 200, 286, 297
Holderby, Susan 156, 200-202, 286, 388
Holderby, William 4
Hollenbeck, Ellen 283
Hollenback, Fannie 283
Holryde, Peter 289, 297-98
Holstein, William 324, 344-45
Holt, David 152
Holt, John 320-21
Holton, George A. 194-95
Horner, W. H. 286-87, 399

Howe, Henry 5-6, 8
Howell's Mill 243-44, 252, 254
Hubbardstown 9, 361
Huddleston, Tom 110-11
Hudson, C. H. 152
Huff's Creek 10, 122
Hull's Landing (Martin) 223, 391
Huntington 6, 77, 88, 349, 353, 355-56, 369, 401, 407
Huntington, Collis P. 349, 353, 407
Huntington *Herald Advertiser* 67, 355
Hurricane Bridge 65, 95, 220, 239-40, 254-55, 262, 272, 274, 277, 279, 292-93, 300
Hurricane Creek 240
Hutcherson, G. W. 326
Hysell, James H. 171, 322-24, 406-7
Hysell, Joseph T. 344, 406

Indian Guyan Creek 297
Ironton, Ohio 16, 29, 48, 52, 56, 68-70, 76-77, 80, 82, 90, 111-12, 117, 125-26, 129, 133, 143-44, 208, 221-23, 265, 318, 390, 395, 399
Ironton Register 19, 23-24, 33, 43, 45, 52, 67, 69, 93, 117, 123, 129-30, 150, 152, 154-55, 175, 216, 223, 226, 307, 320

Jackson County 337
Jackson County, Ohio 150
Jackson Standard 126
James River and Kanawha Turnpike 10, 27, 114-15, 263
Jarrell, John 59, 92-93
Jaynes, Anderson D. 291-95
Jenkins, Albert Gallatin 7, 26, 29, 34-35, 39-42, 45, 47, 52, 56-57, 60-62, 65, 77, 80, 82, 103-4, 117, 125, 129, 132-36, 141-42, 148-50, 164-65, 169, 186, 200, 208, 211-12, 217-24, 230, 241, 245, 252-56, 261-62, 304, 310, 312, 351-52, 355-56, 378, 383, 390, 403

Jenkins, Janetta 7
Jenkins, Susan Holderby 200, 286
Jenkins, Thomas 7, 133, 164, 200, 304
Jenkins, Virginia 60, 65, 132
Jenkins, William 7
Jenkins, William Alexander 7, 133, 164, 304, 312, 319
Jewell, Benjamin 396
Jewell, Mott 141, 157
Johnson, Alexander 140-41
Johnson, Andrew 397
Johnson, Andrew (President) 299-300, 318, 327
Johnson, David Alexander 140
Johnson, Harvey 397
Johnson, James W. 245, 261
Johnson, John C. 82
Johnson, Perry 397
Johnson, Samuel 225
Johnson, W. W. 324
Johnson, William 397
Johnson, William L. 187-88
Johnson's Island Prison 263, 269
Johnston, Samuel 298, 341
Jones, Junius 151, 153, 161-62, 173-74
Jonesville, Virginia 370
Jordan, James L. 396
Jordan, Jeremiah B. 396
Jordan, John P. 263, 396, 404
Jordan, Thomas 24
Jordan, William 339
Jordons, John 63, 67
Joy, Thomas 154
Justice, David 15

Kanawha, District of the 257
Kanawha County 3, 7, 19, 77-78, 300, 302, 305, 337
Kanawha River 45-46, 82, 90, 99, 148, 216, 240, 254, 289
Kanawha Salines 245
Kanawha Valley 40-41, 43, 47, 49, 55-56, 68, 74, 76, 97, 103, 177, 179, 203, 207, 209, 217, 220, 222, 224, 229, 243, 272, 291, 296
Kanawha Valley, Department of the 42
Kanawha Valley Star 25, 39-40
Kansas 20, 374
Keaton, William 249-50
Keenan, A. J. 26, 113, 205
Keller, John L. 296-97
Kelley, Benjamin F. 272
Kendrick/Kindrick, William 326, 361, 382
Kennedy, J. W. 325-26
Kentucky, Military District of 335
Kentucky Court of Appeals 19
Kerns, Anthony W. 294-95
Keyser, James 157
Keyser's Store 58
King, Spencer 406
Kingsolver, Louis 213-14
Kirby, John 341
The Knapsack 264
Krout's Creek 27
Kroutinger, Adolphus W. 338-40
Kyle, Thomas 121, 149, 205, 376-77

Lacey, F. E. 335
Laidley, Albert 46, 136, 158-59, 172
Laidley, John 16-18, 78, 158-59, 172, 174, 209-11, 214, 241, 245, 248, 251, 256-57, 270
Laidley, Mary Hite 18
Laidley, W. S. 38-39
Lamartine 159
Langley, Andrew 112
Langley, William H. 112, 160-61
Laurel Creek 279
Lavalette 9
Lawhorn, James 374
Lawrence, William H. 85-86, 195
Lawrence County, Ohio 15, 17, 20, 44, 46, 49, 90, 122, 129, 135, 143, 150, 215, 221, 395
Lawrence County Courthouse 69, 218
Lawrence County Home Guard 122-23
Lawson, Anthony 307

Lawson, John 86, 112, 118, 133-34
Le Clare 290
Lecky, H. C. 406
Lecky, Spencer 406
Lecky, William 406
Lee, Richard H. 390
Lee, Robert E. 307, 313-14, 346-47
Leete, Edgar I. 399
Leete, Ralph 16-17, 19, 82, 117, 258-59, 376, 399
Lesage, Francis 244, 286, 321, 323-25
Lesage, Julius 244, 298-99, 302, 320, 346, 396
Letcher, John 35, 50, 77
LeTulle, Lawrence 352
LeTulle, Victor 124, 352
Libby Prison 144
Liberty 129, 134
Lick Creek 279
Lightburn, Joseph A. J. 130, 142, 151, 156, 172, 197, 208, 212, 216, 218, 220, 222, 225
Lincoln, Abraham 17, 34-35, 37, 46, 58, 299-300, 302-3, 309, 313-15, 354, 364
Lincoln County 7-8, 122, 147, 207-8, 277, 338-39
Lincoln Courthouse 338
Little, Isaac 231-32, 234-38, 241
Little, Joseph 80
Little Guyandotte River 3
Lloyd, Jack 183
Logan County 7, 46, 77, 103, 148, 199, 215, 221, 232-33, 235, 243, 252, 262, 272, 283, 310-11, 321, 328, 337
Logan Courthouse 37, 104, 122, 135, 138, 158, 186-87, 192, 198, 205, 253, 318, 333-35, 364
Long, Al 106
Long Branch 7
Loring, William Wing 217, 225, 229, 243, 296
Louisa, Kentucky 81, 137, 142, 151, 153, 186, 211, 278, 281, 335
Louisville, Kentucky 56, 60-61, 329, 340
Love, Leonidas 158, 218
Lucas, Andy J. 395
Ludwig, William 96, 101, 179-80
Lunceford, Reuben 225
Lunsford, Calvary 67
Lunsford, Mary 64
Lunsford, Richard 58
Lunsford, Wheeler 67
Lusher, Bruser 314
Lusher, Charles 213
Lusher, Irwin (Irving) 213
Lusher, James 204
Lusher, John 213-14
Lusher, Johnson 172
Lusher, Lewis 84, 213-14
Lusher, Robert M. 213-14
Luther, R. D. 47
Luther, R. M. 326
Lykins, John 193-94, 273
Lykins Mill 153, 193-94, 273
Lynn Creek 152, 199, 387

Madison County, Virginia 15
Madison Creek 186
Mahone, William 195
Malcolm, Edmund B. 361
Mansfield, Amanda Frances 368
Mansfield, Joseph J. 31-32, 40, 58, 64-66, 270, 368
Mansfield, W. L. 65, 364
Maple Grove 345, 407
Marietta, Ohio 129
Marrowbone Creek 7
Marshall Academy/Marshall College 6, 37, 345
Martin, Aaron 269
Martin, H. B. 368
Mason City 99
Mason County 3, 6-7, 48, 251, 311, 337, 378, 390
Mason County Journal 336

Massie, William 144
Mather, Oscar 220, 320, 325, 338-39, 406
Mather, V. W. 345-46
Mattie Roberts 290
Mauck, Amos 292
Maupin, Henry 91, 98, 135, 406
Maxwell, Edwin 325-26
May, Jacob W. 323
Maynard, James 233
Mays, John D. 157, 183
Mays, Robert 187-88
McAllister, Malcom 307
McCall, R. B. 260
McCausland, John 42
McChesney, William R. 66
McClellan, George B. 55, 67, 161, 198, 210, 300-301, 303, 366, 376
McComas, Benjamin J. 316-17, 403-4
McComas, David 364, 403
McComas, Elisha 36
McComas, Elisha W. 213-14, 403-4
McComas, Hamilton C. 403-4
McComas, Irene 404
McComas, Isaac 396
McComas, James 10, 298, 396
McComas, Jefferson 396
McComas, Samuel 16, 270
McComas, William 16, 36-37, 288, 303, 313, 316-18, 364, 399, 403
McComas, William Wirt 403-4
McConnell, John 338
McConnelsville, Ohio 169
McCorkle, James 81, 307
McCormick, Thomas 279
McCown, Albert F. 278-80, 284, 288
McCoy, Blackburn 157
McCoy, Isaiah 283
McCullough, P. H. 147, 267-68, 307
McCullough's Landing 267
McCune, B. F. 135
McDaniel, Van D. 261, 266
McDermitt, James 345
McDowell, R. M. P. 112

McElroy, Barney 67
McGinnis, A. B. 38, 58, 124
McGinnis, A. M. 138-39, 173, 226
McGinnis, Allen 116, 138-39, 149, 173
McGinnis, Benjamin D. 47, 49, 51-52, 94-95, 248, 251, 256, 290, 296, 298-300, 303, 313, 315, 318, 321, 323-25, 346, 399, 406
McGinnis, Ira J. 37-38
McGinnis, John 116, 138-39, 173
McGinnis, L. H. 38
McLaughlin, Frank 264, 368
McLean, N. H. 230
McMahon, Wayne 106
McMillian, James 188, 190
McVickers, Hillary 143
McWhorter, J. M. 303, 325-26
Meadow Bluff 289
Meigs County, Ohio 150
Melvin, Thayer 325-26
Merrill, J. M. 221
Merriman, E. R. 89, 94, 256
Merritt, Thomas 158, 241, 256, 264, 288
Merritt, William 4
Merritt, William 303, 325
Middaugh, Anna 309, 312
Middaugh, Jesse 308-9, 312
Miller, A. J. 81
Miller, Fannie Lenora 352
Miller, George F. 344
Miller, George W. 236, 392
Miller, H. H. 38-39
Miller, Henry 111, 123, 157
Miller, Isaac 21
Miller, Isom 187-88
Miller, John G. 10, 245-46
Miller, John W. 64
Miller, William C. 5, 10, 61, 64, 219, 361
Millersport, Ohio 114
Milligan, James 368
Mills, John 137, 345
Mills, John 338

Milroy, Robert H. 230, 235, 259
Milstead, Henry 21
Milton 220
Mims, John D. 74
Minshall, Henry 192-93, 388
Mitchell, Jim 283
Mitchell's Battery 229
Monroe, Thomas 137
Monroe County 217
Moore, C. P. T. 399
Moore, Charles 288
Moore, Laban 211, 288, 399
Moore, Lafe 151
Moore, Owen 26
Moore, Res 371
Moore, Wilson B. 109, 141, 204, 241, 374
Moran, John 338
Morey, Cynthia 174
Morey, Eliza 135, 149, 174
Morey, Frances 174
Morey, Frank 135, 149, 174
Morris, Charles 157, 171, 182
Morris, Emily 135-36
Morris, Jonathan 92, 105, 107, 109, 113-14, 117, 135-36, 143, 171
Morris, Putnam Deputy Sheriff 249
Morris, William 194
Morris Harvey College 358-59
Moss, C. D. 346
Moss, Virginius R. 141, 204
Moundsville 130
Mount Union meeting house 59
Mud 7, 361
Mud Bridge 6-7, 61, 93, 95-99, 101, 120, 148, 156, 179-82, 190, 193, 197-98, 203, 208, 218-20, 224, 245, 253, 255-56, 260-63, 277, 283, 289, 292-96, 339, 361
Mud River 6, 61, 98, 104, 148, 156, 188, 197, 240, 254-56, 261-62, 269, 292, 401
Mullen, C. H. 245, 394
Muskingum County, Ohio 150

Myers, Charles 323

Naomi 221
Naret, Edward 212
Nashville, Tennessee 289
Nashville, battle of 68
Neal, H. S. 52
Neal, Lewis 396
Neal, Thomas 171
Neff, Andrew J. 242
Neff, George W. 60-63, 65-66
Nesbitt, Albert 95
New Market, battle of 42, 352
New River 122
New Virginia 43
New York 144, 399
New York Arsenal 82
New York Illustrated News 183-84
Newbern, Virginia 122
Newcomb, William 311, 406
Newman, Amanda 283
Newman, Eliza 283
Newman, Joseph 188, 190
Nicely, Zachariah 86, 194
Nicholas, Wilson Cary 6
Nichols, Seth Adam 356-57
Nigley, Joseph 8
91st Ohio Infantry 218, 222, 390
Nineveh, Virginia 379
9th West Virginia Infantry 78, 84, 90, 92-94, 96, 98-99, 101, 108, 120, 123, 128, 135, 143-44, 149-51, 161-62, 166, 171, 173-77, 190, 210, 214, 264, 276, 279, 302, 375
Nixon, William 152, 156, 225, 391
Noble, Matt 60
Noel, Rodrick 58-59
Noel, Winston 188
Norton, Edward M. 155
Norton, Jesse S. 47-48
Nounnan, James H. 279, 30

Oak Hill, Ohio 49
Oaklawn Cemetery 379

Ohio, Department of the 55-56
Ohio, Medical Board of 92
Ohio River 3-5, 7-8, 10, 15, 22-24, 29-30, 33, 37-38, 43-46, 52, 55-56, 75, 103-4, 112, 122-23, 125, 129-30, 132, 196, 208, 215, 221, 226, 229-30, 235, 243, 262-63, 266, 284, 297-98, 300, 305, 310, 349, 376, 378, 390-91, 401
Ohio State Journal 238
Oley, John Hunt 87-89, 302-3, 311, 314, 318, 325-26, 353
Ona 84
141st Ohio Infantry 289, 291-97, 299, 400
Ong, Isaac 21, 26, 114
Ong, John W. 38, 114
Ordinance of Secession, Virginia 36-39, 43-44, 46, 81, 197, 243, 317-18
Ormstead, Ralph 89-90
Orr, Samuel 242
Owens, William 395

Paine, Stephen 213, 396
Paine, William 287
Paintsville, Kentucky 177
Parker, Granville 34, 43, 51, 73-74, 168, 172, 399
Parkersburg 29, 33, 150, 251, 258, 324
Pate, Henry Clay 110, 374, 377
Patterson, James 368
Paw Paw Bottom 7, 361
Paxton, John 136, 152, 173, 205, 218-19, 222
Paxton, Sayres G. 165
Payne, Alfred B. 305
Payne, Uriah 106-7, 113-14
Pearisburg, Virginia 122, 349
Peck, William V. 20
Peitzel, Alonzo 195, 387
Peters, Lewis 21, 38, 111, 136, 140
Petersburg, Virginia 313
Petersburg Rangers 374
Peterstown 349

Petit, Hugh 136
Peyton, Perry 141, 157
Peyton, William 85
Peytona 337, 339
Phelps, John M. 300, 303
Phelps, Lorenzo 251, 264
Phelps, Vincent 165
Philippi, battle of 194
Piatt, Abram Sanders 93, 100-101, 160-61, 179, 184, 196-98, 200
Piatt's Zouaves (see 34th Ohio Infantry)
Pierpont, Francis H. 46-52, 73-84, 86-90, 92-94, 96-97, 100, 128, 130, 133, 135, 137, 140, 143, 148-49, 152-53, 160-62, 164, 167-69, 171, 207-12, 244, 246, 248, 256, 277
Pierpont, Francis P. 320
Pigeon Creek 243
Pike County, Kentucky 15, 321
Pinckard, William G. 279
Pine, William H. H. 267-68, 397
Pittsburgh, Pennsylvania 5
Planter's Hotel 37
Plybon, John 344
Plybun, J. C. 365
Plymale, John 166, 322
Poague, George 113
Poague, James H. 153, 298
Point Pleasant 33-34, 47-49, 51, 82, 126, 130, 144, 208, 217-18, 232, 252, 254-55, 266, 282-83, 286, 289, 300, 370, 399
Point Pleasant *Weekly Register* 172, 174, 271, 282, 286, 304, 342
Polley, Peyton 15
Polley, William 396
Pollock, Granville 134
Polsley, Daniel 325-26
Pomeroy, Ohio 78
Pomeroy Telegraph 223
Poore's Hill 58, 84-86, 157, 182, 188, 190, 194, 214, 250, 254
Porter, J. S. 324
Porter, James H. 395

Portland, Ohio 240
Portsmouth, Ohio 48, 78, 99, 127-29, 224, 398
Portsmouth Artillery 223
Poster, William 307
Poteet, Clem 138-39
Poteet, James 140, 218
Poteet, Skelton 140, 173
Poteet, Thomas 140
Powell, William H. 68-71, 175-77, 218-19, 390
Prague, J. H. 251
Preston, W. R. 217
Prestonsburg, Kentucky 96
Prichett, Lewis A. 187-88, 386
Prichett, William D. 187-88, 386
Princeton, battle of 205
Pritchard 9
Proctor, Alfred S. 20-23, 123, 354-55, 363
Proctor, Jacob 363
Proctorville, Ohio 20, 44-45, 57, 70, 74, 122, 125, 166, 211, 215, 217, 221, 232
Putnam County 6-7, 65, 74, 92, 148, 174, 249-50, 256, 272, 305, 311, 337
Pyle, George D. 151

Quaker Bottom, Ohio 20-21, 24, 44, 46, 159, 168, 226, 273, 354
Queen, Absalom 121, 151, 336
Queen, Lewis 326

Raccoon Creek 7, 191
Racine, Ohio 217
Rader, Lewis 290
Radford, Henry 21-22
Raleigh County 103, 198, 211
Ramsdell, Zophar D. 35, 49, 50, 88, 233, 248, 256, 260-61, 263, 364, 378
Ratliff, William 15-17, 19, 37, 46, 75-76, 78, 100, 197, 335, 361

Ravenswood 217
Ray, Evaline 283
Ray, Ezzie 283
Ray, Isaiah 286, 298, 365
Reany, William 80-81
Rece, Abia 188, 218-19, 361, 390
Rece, John Calvin 111, 358
Rece, John M. 361
Rece, Margaret Ann 110-11
Rece, Warren 390
Reckard, Salmon 22-23
Red House 93, 193, 254
Reeves, Braxton P. 219
Regnier, Henry A. 223
Reid, William 368
Reilly, William W. 297
Reorganized/Restored Government of Virginia 15, 46, 49, 76-77, 80, 82-83, 86, 135, 158, 168, 171, 197, 207, 305, 316, 376
Reynolds, Archibald 99, 372-73
Reynolds, James 61, 66
Reynolds, John 368
Reynolds, Robert 140-41
Rice, S. S. 17
Richmond, Indiana 240
Richmond, Virginia 35, 122, 134-38, 140-41, 144, 148, 150, 158, 160, 165, 168, 186, 209-10, 268-69, 313, 376
Richmond Convention 36-37, 39, 43, 76, 79, 317
Richmond Dispatch 43
Richmond Enquirer 116, 118
Richmond Examiner 25
Ricketts, Albert Gallatin 42
Ricketts, Elijah 38, 114, 136, 142, 163-64
Ricketts, Girard D. 26
Ricketts, Jennie 114
Ricketts, Lucian Cincinnatus "Cooney" 41-42, 105, 123, 346, 352, 356
Ricketts, Virginia 123, 162-64
Rider, J. W. 406

Ripley 212, 217
Ripley, Amos 294
Ritter Park 356-57
Roads, Ferdinand 388
Roanoke Island 199
Roberts, R. J. 324, 345-46
Roberts, Thomas 361
Robinson, Elihu 151
Rodgers, William L. 298
Roffe, Charles 137-38, 204, 214
Rogers, William C. 106, 142, 340-41
Roman, James 153, 382
Rome, Illinois 355
Rome, Ohio 20
Rome Chapel 41
Roseberry and Eastman mill 123
Rosecrans, William S. 80, 87, 91-93, 101, 140, 160-61, 164-65, 190, 198, 200, 202-4, 257
Ross, George 324
Ross, John 122
Ross, Thomas 114, 134, 144
Round Bottom 9, 79, 267, 277, 361
Rouse, George M. 346
Rouse, James 98, 106-7, 112-13, 129, 171, 304, 311, 318, 373, 376
Rousey, J. N. 346
Rucker, Isaac M. 299
Rucker, William P. 298-99
Ruffner, David 3
Ruffner, Henry 3
Ruggles, George D. 211
Russell, Dollie 110
Russell, George 140
Russell, John 124
Russell, L. D. 297
Russell, Mark 13
Russell, P. M. 380
Russell, St. Mark 38, 120, 142
Russell, St. Mark Jr. 123, 140
Russell, W. H. H. 214-16
Russell Creek 115-16, 275
Rutland, Ohio 143
Ryan, Charles 406

Ryan, Isaac M. 45

Saint Albans 41, 401
Saint Louis, Missouri 132
Salem, Virginia 261
Salisbury, North Carolina 138, 143-44
Salmon, J. H. 345
Salt Lake City, Utah 354
Salt Sulphur Springs 217
Samuels, Alexander H. 39, 82, 135, 370
Samuels, George W. 16
Samuels, Henry Jefferson 10, 16-17, 78, 82, 86, 91-92, 94, 96-99, 101, 134-41, 147-51, 153, 157-58, 162-64, 166, 173, 188, 190, 194, 199, 204-5, 209-11, 213-14, 223, 226, 232, 241, 245-46, 256-57, 260, 266, 269-70, 281, 287-88, 292, 298-99, 305-6, 313, 316-18, 323, 333
Samuels, John 270
Sanders, Mrs. E. T. 77
Sanders, Oscar 153
Sanders, Sampson 15, 192
Sandusky, Ohio 140
Sandy Rangers 62
Sandy Valley Advocate 9, 223
Sanford, Marine 86
Savage, George "Lucky" 63, 67, 141, 157
Savage Grant 9, 361
Scales, Thomas 141, 382
Scammon, Eliakim P. 256-57, 259, 273-74, 305
Scanlin, William 368
Scary Creek, battle of 65, 81, 142, 181
Schelling, William 69
Schenberg, John 364
Schenck, Robert G. 257-58
Scioto County, Ohio 291
Scott, Alzira J. 117, 126, 374
Scott, Chubb 340
Scott, Sanaford 205
Seamonds, Robert 142
2nd Kentucky Infantry 55-68, 73-75,

166-67, 182
2nd United States Infantry 329-35, 338-40
2nd West Virginia Cavalry 125, 136, 147, 150-56, 161-62, 169-71, 173-77, 186, 190, 197, 203-4, 218-22, 226, 254-55, 281
Second Wheeling Convention 15
Sedinger, James D. 21, 42, 52, 65, 104, 106, 108, 158, 220-21, 311, 341, 351, 373, 407
Sedinger, Lewis 26, 361
Segur, Abel 153, 248, 287, 303, 315
Seven Mile Creek 112
7th West Virginia Cavalry 296, 299-300, 302, 304-5, 310-11, 314, 317
Shannon, William 210, 277, 286, 347
Shaw, John W. 196, 203
Sheff, George W. 341
Shelton, George 115, 375
Shelton, Henry 114-15, 173, 375
Shelton, Jerome 10, 157, 188, 190, 208, 288-89
Shelton, Malinda 288-89
Shiloh, battle of 68
Shipe, C. W. 340
Shipe, Charles 244, 407
Shipp, Scott 352
Shoemaker, Charles 171, 205
Shoemaker, George 152
Shoemaker, J. H. 106
Shoemaker, James 119
Showans, Presley 86
Shrewsbury, John 3
Shultz, J. B. 406
Shultz, William 406
Simmons, A. D. 341
Simmons, Conwelsey 171, 205, 210
Simmons, Sampson Sanders 182
Sims, William A. 396
Sinking Creek, raid on 390
16th Virginia Cavalry 143, 252, 274-75, 278-79, 282, 305
Skinner, Leonard 163, 166, 171

Slack, Greenbury 78, 267
Smeltzer, Joseph 295
Smith, Abraham 165-66, 227
Smith, Alexander 333
Smith, Amanda 284, 290
Smith, Benjamin 152, 325
Smith, Bill 84, 264, 267, 271, 299-302, 308-9, 311-12, 320, 323, 327-29
Smith, Charles A. 395
Smith, Chubb 341
Smith, Dudley 159-60, 166, 383
Smith, Dudley Irving 157, 211, 340-41, 344, 383
Smith, Edward 40, 74, 106, 110-11, 117, 120, 141, 157-58, 165-66, 227
Smith, Francis H. 352
Smith, Francis Lee 352
Smith, Hamilton 144
Smith, Jacob Hurd 65
Smith, James 95, 299
Smith, James E. 81, 166, 199
Smith, John 368
Smith, John M. 303
Smith, John N. 282
Smith, Josephine 111, 227
Smith, Mary Ann 119
Smith, "Mexico" 58, 62
Smith, Nate 234
Smith, Percival S. 21, 40, 110-11, 119, 124, 137, 163, 275-76, 299, 303, 320, 380
Smith, Percival S. Jr. 380
Smith, R. P. 380
Smith, Sallie P. 40-41, 91, 110, 157-60, 165, 168, 207, 215-16, 226-27, 334
Smith, Samuel 157
Smith, T. J. 141
Smith, William G. 210
South Mills, battle of 404
South Point, Ohio 129
Spaulding, Jackson 382
Spencer 217
Spencer, Warner 66
Sprague, Julia 91

Sprecher, George 130, 184-85, 197, 199
Spring Hill Cemetery 352-53, 355, 370
Spurlock, Burwell 8, 36-37, 75, 79, 81, 355, 364
Spurlock, Francis A. 361
Spurlock, George 13
Spurlock, Harvey 396
Spurlock, Hurston 73, 76, 79-81, 94, 100, 168, 275-77, 280, 288, 352, 355, 370
Spurlock, Jamison 58, 166
Spurlock, Jesse 13, 81-82, 94, 99-100, 167-68, 370
Spurlock, Stephen 58-59, 167
Spurlock, Thomas 324
Stanton, Edwin 198, 258-59
Starr, Benjamin 84
Starr, William C. 162-64
Steel, Lafe 234
Stephens/Stevens, Benjamin 187-88, 199, 387
Stephens, Mill. J. 297
Stephenson, Burwell 263
Stevens, Hooper B. 378
Stevenson, H. N. 365
Stevenson, William E. 345
Stewart, James 139, 142
Stewart, Milton 271, 283
Stewart, R. L. 144
Stewart, Robert 123, 139
Stewart, William 282
Stones River, battle of 68
Stout, Silas F. 242
Stowers, Presley 382
Strother, Stephen 81-82
Suiter, Joshua 124-25
Summers, George W. 19, 270, 341
Summers, Sylvester 355
Supreme Order of the Star Spangled Banner 49
Swan 218, 221-22
Swan Hotel 398
Swan Well 319

Swann, Ben 67, 217
Swann, C. M. 205
Swann, Calvary 171
Swann, Levi 265
Swann, S. J. 346
Sweetland, Charles 196
Swisher, James T. 388
Symmes Creek, Ohio 225

Tarr, Campbell 303
Tassen, John 85
Taylor Barracks 335
Tazewell County, Virginia 3, 7
Telegraph No. 3 129, 133-34
Ten Mile 7, 122, 361
10th Ohio Volunteer Infantry 88
Thackston, B. H. 38
Thayer, Eli 13, 24-29, 35, 50, 282, 351, 372
3rd West Virginia Cavalry 242-44, 271-72, 275, 277, 284-85, 293, 306, 407
Thirteen Mile Creek 47
13th West Virginia Infantry 209, 213, 217, 242-43, 245, 254, 260-62, 266-74, 275-77, 279-80, 282-91, 298, 302, 306, 357
30th Battalion Virginia Sharpshooters 404
34th Battalion Virginia Cavalry 197, 296-97, 384
34th Ohio Infantry 93, 95-101, 120-21, 130, 148, 151, 160-61, 179-205, 208, 357, 386
39th Kentucky Infantry 278
36th Ohio Infantry 205
36th Virginia Cavalry Battalion 255, 390, 395
Thomas, George H. 327, 334-35
Thomas, Landford 114
Thomas, W. B. 303
Thompson, Boston 213
Thompson, C. L. 355
Thompson, Elizabeth 135
Thompson, George 225

Thompson, Matthew 61, 104, 121, 135, 140, 149, 265, 397
Thompson, Thomas 58-59
Thompson, William 324
Thornburg, D. W. 380
Thornburg, David 264
Thornburg, George 61, 357
Thornburg, J. W. 325
Thornburg, M. S. 325
Thornburg, Thomas 10, 137, 148-49, 158, 204-5, 256, 298, 345, 397
Thorndike 7, 361
Tiffin Weekly Tribune 186
Tod, David 196, 225
Toland, John 101, 188, 192-93
Tom's Creek 58, 64
Tomlinson, Abia Allen 83-84, 90, 133, 257, 370
Tomlinson, W. H. 251, 256, 325
Townsend, E. D. 67
Tracy, Albert 208-9
Trough Fork Company 233
Trout, Abraham 8
Trout's Hill 9, 43, 50, 58, 75, 81, 99, 136, 151-52, 156-57, 170, 197, 281-82, 329-30, 332-34, 351
Trusler, Nelson 241
Tug Fork militia 81
Tug Fork River 3, 7, 99, 133, 254, 335
Turley, John A. 218
Turner, James T. 395
Turner, Jim 309
Turner, John 231
Turner, William 95, 105, 109, 128, 152, 158-59, 167-68, 205, 211, 213-14, 264, 271, 374, 397
Twelve Pole Creek 7, 9, 15, 24, 29-30, 50, 75, 93, 152, 156, 166, 192, 211, 221, 263, 276, 279, 294, 312, 387
23rd Ohio Infantry 272
Twyman, James 15

Underwood, E. M. 297, 322, 325
Union, Ohio 20

Union Baptist Church 296, 358, 401
United Confederate Veterans 356-57, 370
United Daughters of the Confederacy, Huntington Chapter 355
United States Military Academy 127, 377

Valley Rangers 113
Vance, John L. 216
Vertigans, Edward G. 113
Victor 78, 265
Victor No. 2 67, 69-70
Victor No. 3 221
Vienna, battle of 128
Vinton County, Ohio 150
Virginia Board of Public Works 10
Virginia Central Railroad 28-29
Virginia Court of Appeals 16
Virginia General Assembly 6-7, 10, 35, 349
Virginia Military Institute 42, 352
Virginia State Line 260
Virginia and Tennessee Railroad 254

Walker, Fritz 245-46
Walker, Harrison 368
Walker, Urban 282, 362
Wallar, J. L. 151-52, 156, 197
Walnut Grove circuit 74
Walton, Eli 157-58
Walton George 46
Ward, Evermont 307
Ward, Lizzie 284
Ward, Thomas 4, 13
Ward, William 114-15, 375
Waring, John 339
Warren, G. D. 38
Washington, D.C. 29, 35, 48, 92, 144, 171, 173, 217, 224, 301, 314, 354
Washington Baptist Church 13, 27-28
Waugh, Charles 345
Wayne, Anthony 8
Wayne Cornet Band 356

Wayne County Circuit Court 17, 261, 320
Wayne County Militia 31, 58, 61, 79, 156, 210, 222, 233, 263, 267-68, 280, 282, 287, 322
Wayne Courthouse 9, 31, 40, 44, 48, 58, 80-82, 94, 133, 157, 186, 268, 274, 276, 278-79, 281, 300, 315, 323, 327, 334, 338, 362, 364, 386
Webb, Charles B. 248-49, 263, 275, 301-2, 312, 322-23, 335
Webb, James 86, 194-95
Welch, Hiram 49
Wellington, James 364
Wellman, Jeremiah 391
Wellman, John 8
Wentz, Philip 267
Wentz, William 303
West, Isaac 65
West, Samuel 190
West Virginia Journal 316, 319-20, 321, 339
West Virginia State Code 312
Western Virginia, Department of 88-89, 200, 202, 204
Western Virginia, District of 229
Weston 217
Whaley, Kellian V. 48-49, 78, 81, 83-84, 86, 90-94, 96, 98, 101, 105, 108-10, 114, 117-18, 120-22, 128, 142, 144-45, 148, 151, 171, 217, 233, 257, 261, 266, 277, 279, 298, 300, 303, 372, 374
Wheeler, J. H. 59
Wheeler, Joseph C. 18, 48, 86, 94, 96, 98-99, 105, 112, 117, 124, 135-36, 138, 140-41, 149-51, 166, 190, 327-28, 335-36, 375
Wheeling 5, 43, 46, 48, 80, 82, 86, 94, 99, 137, 139-41, 155, 157, 161, 165-66, 180, 188, 193, 199, 212-13, 245, 250, 282, 289, 319, 351
Wheeling Convention, First 42-43
Wheeling Convention, Second 44, 46, 49
Wheeling Intelligencer 33, 35, 43, 48, 52, 116, 130-31, 134, 150, 172, 193, 197, 225, 255, 300, 309
Wheeling Register 268
White, A. G. 113, 172, 321
White, Caroline 57
White, Chilton 378
White, John 111
White, William O. 321
White's Creek 329-30
Wiley, Robert 341
Wilgus, Charles 148, 221, 232
Wilkinson, B. B. 397
Wilkinson, J. S. 344-45
Willard, George 52
Willis, Captain 45
Willis, Hugh 85
Willis, William 92
Wilson, Asa 136
Wilson, David 382
Wilson, James 246
Wilson, Joel 15
Wilson, William 108, 111-12, 375
Winfield 179, 240, 245, 372
Wintz, William 344
Wise, Henry A. 29, 33, 55, 67, 75-76, 79
Wiseman, Andrew 292-93
Wiseman, John J. 132
Witcher, Jeremiah 194, 324
Witcher, John S. 51, 158, 177, 216-17, 242-44, 250-52, 256, 266, 272, 275-77, 279-80, 284-85, 293-94, 306, 320, 323-26, 337, 339, 342-44, 347, 353-54
Witcher, Vincent 93-94, 121, 173, 190, 210, 225, 232-33, 245, 288, 293, 304, 310, 383, 392
Wolcott, L. W. 74
Wolcott, Lucien M. 162-63
Wolfe, Henry A. 277, 398
Wood, James E. 112, 134-35
Wood, Rack 371

Woodbury, George 230
Woodruff, William E. 55-57, 59-61, 67, 73, 95, 180, 213, 227
Woods, James 188
Woodward Guards 57, 65-66
Workman, William 334, 344-45
Worrell, Henry 213
Wright, Edward D. 42, 46, 49, 153, 226, 251, 275-76, 286-87, 299, 303, 323-26, 339
Wright, H. G. 225
Wright, J. H. 406
Wright, James H. 286, 298, 340, 407
Wright, William O. 323, 341-42, 346
Wyley, Nelson 392
Wyoming County 46, 103
Wyoming Courthouse 122
Wyson, Eden 157
Wytheville, battle of 193

York, Jane 397
York, Joseph D. 153, 382
York, Joshua M. 268, 397
Young, John 209-10, 272
Young, Thomas 388

Zeigler, John 43, 73-84, 86, 88-93, 95-100, 122, 126-27, 129, 132, 139-40, 142, 230, 233, 244-45, 257-60, 264-65, 367, 372, 375, 395
Zeigler, Susan 75
Zouave Cave 188, 205
Zouave Gazette 117

About the Author

Joe Geiger, Jr. has worked at West Virginia Archives and History since 1998 and is West Virginia's state historian and state archivist. A graduate of Marshall University, he formerly served as an adjunct instructor in the history departments at Marshall University and West Virginia State University. He is the author of *Civil War in Cabell County, West Virginia 1861-1865* and *Holding the Line: The Battle of Allegheny Mountain*.

35th Star Publishing
Charleston, West Virginia
www.35thstar.com

www.ingramcontent.com/pod-product-compliance
Lightning Source LLC
Chambersburg PA
CBHW050635150426
42811CB00052B/821